THE LANAHAN READINGS

in the

American Polity

SIXTH EDITION

THE LANAHAN READINGS

in the

American Polity

SIXTH EDITION

———

Ann G. Serow
Everett C. Ladd

LANAHAN PUBLISHERS, INC.

Baltimore

The text of this book was composed
in Bembo with display type set in Garamond.
Composition by BYTHEWAY PUBLISHING SERVICES.
Manufacturing by THE P.A. HUTCHISON COMPANY.

ISBN-10 1-930398-19-0
ISBN-13 978-1-930398-19-1

LANAHAN PUBLISHERS, INC.
324 Hawthorne Road
Baltimore, MD 21210-2303
410 366 2434
LANAHAN@AOL.COM
WWW.LANAHANPUBLISHERS.COM

6 7 8 9 0

To Our Students

CONTENTS

PART TWO

The Constitution, Democracy, and Separation of Powers

PART THREE

Federalism

PART FOUR

Congress

PART FIVE

The Presidency

PART SIX

The Executive Branch

PART SEVEN

The Judiciary

No Longer Just "Nine Old Men" [FDR]

PART EIGHT

Civil Liberties and Civil Rights

PART NINE

Public Opinion and the Media

PART TEN

Interest Groups

After Your Time in Congress—
Now What?

PART ELEVEN

Voting and Elections

Running the Campaign

PART TWELVE

Political Parties

PART THIRTEEN

Political Economy and Public Welfare

It's About Real People

PART FOURTEEN

America in a Changed World

PREFACE

The first edition of THE LANAHAN READINGS IN THE AMERI-
CAN POLITY began a happy new collaboration of the editors with LANAH-
AN PUBLISHERS, INC., and Don Fusting, who founded this new publishing
company in 1995. During the previous decade, we had worked closely
and confidently with Don on two earlier versions of this book, *The American Polity Reader*, and we were pleased that the association would continue—in fact, quite pleased as it turned out: the fifth edition of THE LA-
NAHAN READINGS was assigned in well over four hundred classrooms.

Launching another new edition of an established volume is still a big
step. What matters to students using the volume, however, is what's between the covers. Here, readers of the new sixth edition will find in large
measure both fundamental continuity in basic design and big changes in
specific readings.

There's good reason for continuity. This book is designed to help undergraduates who are taking the basic American government course better understand their country's political system by providing essential readings on American ideas, constitutional system, core political institutions,
public opinion, political competition, and policy debates. All of these
readings have in fact shown exceptional continuity over time because
they reflect the views and values of a society that is strikingly similar now
in this twenty-first century to what it was when the United States was
founded in the late eighteenth century.

At first glance, this proposition might seem surprising. After all, in
some regards the America we now inhabit differs greatly from that of
George Washington, James Madison, and Thomas Jefferson. They traveled
either on foot or, quite literally, by horsepower; we travel faster and more
comfortably in automobiles and jet planes. They could communicate only
face to face or through the written word; we have now gone beyond the
telephone to the Internet. The average life expectancy in their day was
thirty-three years; in ours, seventy-five—and so on is the process of change
across so many of the physical dimensions of life.

But in social and political values, Americans in 1776 and now, in the twenty-first century, are strikingly similar people. That's true because America's founding brought the nation to modernity so abruptly and completely. It was a profound break from the aristocratic past that dominated European life—and indeed life in countries all around the world. The great French social commentator, Alexis de Tocqueville, grasped this fact more fully perhaps than anyone else and wrote what is still the most insightful book on American society, *Democracy in America* (Volume I, 1835 and Volume II, 1839). "The emigrants who colonized America at the beginning of the seventeenth century," Tocqueville wrote, "in some way separated the principle of democracy from all those other principles against which they contended when living in the heart of the old European societies, and transplanted that principle only on the shores of the New World." He did not study America, Tocqueville went on, "just to satisfy curiosity, however legitimate; I sought there lessons from which we might profit. . . . I accept that [democratic] revolution as an accomplished fact, or a fact that soon will be accomplished, and I selected of all the peoples experiencing it that nation in which it has come to the fullest and most peaceful completion. . . . I admit that I saw in America more than America; it was the shape of democracy itself which I sought, its inclinations, character, prejudices, and passions."

Now, over 175 years after Tocqueville wrote, America remains a democratic nation and an intensely individualist society—the latter encompassing much of what he understood when he used the term "democracy." This broad continuity in social values and social structure goes far to explain the institutional continuities we find in THE LANAHAN READINGS.

The world of American politics and the demographics of the American people keep changing, nonetheless. Students need readings on the country's political institutions and its political competition that present the American polity in a fresh, contemporary form. So for the sixth edition of THE LANAHAN READINGS IN THE AMERICAN POLITY, we have replaced over a third of the selections.

New readings in this edition include topics on executive privilege (see #14); climate change and the "tug of war" between the national government and the states (#17); "local activism" of some "renegade" cities when the federal government cannot get things done (#18); the current state of the Senate filibuster (#21); women in the Senate (#22); presidential power and the fight against terrorism (#31); the executive order (#32); Chief Justice Roberts, a divided Court, and the Affordable Care Act (#42); the *Obergefell v. Hodges* ruling on same-sex marriage and a John Roberts' dissent (#47); *Citizens United* and the opening of campaign money floodgates (#57); the increasing influence of Latino voters (#58); the use of microtargeting and algorithms in campaigns (#64); and more money than ever to finance them (#65); electoral realignment (#67); diversity and political parties (#70); religion and politics (#71); inequality (#74); and maybe the U.S. should fix up the mess at home before further adventures abroad (#84).

For the sixth edition, we have also added a new section which you will see throughout the table of contents variously entitled "Tweets and Dog Whistles—How Washington Talks" (see Part Four), "Winning the Office" (Part Five), "Where's My Office?" (Part Six), "After Your Time in Congress—Now What" (Part Ten), and others. We have made no effort to distribute these consistently within each Part, but we think we are consistent in including under these sections articles that will bring your students, at times, in an amusing way, at others, in a poignant way, into the reality of political life within and beyond the "beltway."

To guide readers through these and all other selections, a brief description of each article appears in brackets below its listing in the table of contents. To help orient students, we continue to provide brief introductions to each article. In doing so, we can offer some political, and occasionally, historical and cultural background to the selections. To help students further, we again continue the process of writing footnotes not to dredge up obscure and unnecessary information, but to make clear those words, phrases, and allusions that students need defined or explained in order to understand the particular reading.

As with each new edition, Ann Serow has written the *Instructor's Guide and Quiz Book*. This ancillary gives instructors an ample amount of questions with which to test their students on each of the readings, and also, some further ideas on how the selections can be used. For example, there are a number of readings that can be set up in a point-counterpoint arrangement for instructors who might want to include this approach in their classroom.

Returning to our opening comments, we have been engaged in this project for over twenty years. We believe that the continuity of having the same team, author/editor and publishing editor, has helped keep the goals of the book in focus: This is a book for students of American government and the list of selections was made, and revised, for them. They, too, have contributed heavily to the reader-making process by their in-class comments. The selections can truly be said to have been class-tested. For this, the book is again dedicated to these willing and observant participants, our students.

NOTE OF ACKNOWLEDGMENT   Much appreciation goes to our young political scientist-proofreaders for their many hours of assistance: Lily Wu, Emily Kirton, Alexandra Banasiewicz, Kendall Allerton, Melani Norsigian, Richard Ferris, Ahmad Chughtai, Benjamin Waldman, Alexis De-Lucia, Koby Quansah, Evan Kelmar, and special thanks to Constantino Portal.

AGS

PART ONE

American Political Ideas

1

ALEXIS DE TOCQUEVILLE

From *Democracy in America*

In May of 1831, a fancily-dressed, young French aristocrat arrived in the United States to begin his "scientific" study of a new social and political phenomenon, American democracy. After nine months of traveling across the new nation, interviewing numerous Americans from all walks of life, Alexis de Tocqueville returned to France to write Democracy in America, *the single best source with which to begin our exploration of American government and politics. Tocqueville saw the United States as a unique nation. From the start, Americans were all equal. Some were richer and others were poorer, but all who were not indentured or enslaved had an equal opportunity from the start. This clearly was not the case in any other nineteenth-century nation. To the young visitor, this idea of equality was America's identifying mark, a most cherished, if elusive, national virtue.*

AFTER THE BIRTH of a human being his early years are obscurely spent in the toils or pleasures of childhood. As he grows up the world receives him, when his manhood begins, and he enters into contact with his fellows. He is then studied for the first time, and it is imagined that the germ of the vices and the virtues of his maturer years is then formed.

This, if I am not mistaken, is a great error. We must begin higher up; we must watch the infant in his mother's arms; we must see the first images which the external world casts upon the dark mirror of his mind; the first occurrences which he witnesses; we must hear the first words which awaken the sleeping powers of thought, and stand by his earliest efforts, if we would understand the prejudices, the habits, and the passions which will rule his life. The entire man is, so to speak, to be seen in the cradle of the child.

The growth of nations presents something analogous to this: they all bear some marks of their origin; and the circumstances which accompanied their birth and contributed to their rise affect the whole term of their being.

If we were able to go back to the elements of states, and to examine the oldest monuments of their history, I doubt not that we should discover in them the primal cause of the prejudices, the habits, the ruling passions, and, in short, of all that constitutes what is called the national character: we should there find the explanation of certain customs which now seem at variance with the prevailing manners; of such laws as conflict with established principles; and of such incoherent opinions as are here and there to be met with in society, like those fragments of broken chains which we sometimes see hanging from the vault of an edifice, and supporting nothing. This might explain the destinies of certain nations which seem borne on by an unknown force to ends of which they themselves are ignorant. But hitherto facts have been wanting to researches of this kind: the spirit of inquiry has only come upon communities in their latter days; and when they at length contemplated their origin, time had already obscured it, or ignorance and pride adorned it with truth-concealing fables.

America is the only country in which it has been possible to witness the natural and tranquil growth of society, and where the influence exercised on the future condition of states by their origin is clearly distinguishable. . . .

America, consequently, exhibits in the broad light of day the phenomena which the ignorance or rudeness of earlier ages conceals from our researches. Near enough to the time when the states of America were founded, to be accurately acquainted with their elements, and sufficiently removed from that period to judge of some of their results, the men of our own day seem destined to see further than their predecessors into the series of human events. Providence has given us a torch which our forefathers did not possess, and has allowed us to discern fundamental causes in the history of the world which the obscurity of the past concealed from them.

If we carefully examine the social and political state of America, after having studied its history, we shall remain perfectly convinced that not an opinion, not a custom, not a law, I may even say not an event, is upon record which the origin of that people will not explain. The readers of this book will find the germ of all that is to follow in the present chapter, and the key to almost the whole work.

The emigrants who came at different periods to occupy the territory now covered by the American Union, differed from each other in many respects; their aim was not the same, and they governed themselves on different principles.

These men had, however, certain features in common, and they were all placed in an analogous situation. The tie of language is perhaps the strongest and the most durable that can unite mankind. All the emigrants spoke the same tongue; they were all offsets from the same people. Born in a country which had been agitated for centuries by the struggles of faction, and in which all parties had been obliged in their turn to place themselves under the protection of the laws, their political education had been perfected in this rude school, and they were more conversant with the notions of right, and the principles of true freedom, than the greater part of their European contemporaries. At the period of the first emigrations, the parish system, that fruitful germ of free institutions, was deeply rooted in the habits of the English; and with it the doctrine of the sovereignty of the people. . . .

Another remark, to which we shall hereafter have occasion to recur, is applicable not only to the English, but to . . . all the Europeans who successively established themselves in the New World. All these European colonies contained the elements, if not the development, of a complete democracy. Two causes led to this result. It may safely be advanced that on leaving the mother country the emigrants had in general no notion of superiority one over another. The happy and the powerful do not go into exile, and there are no surer guaranties of equality among men than poverty and misfortune. It happened, however, on several occasions, that persons of rank were driven to America by political and religious quarrels. Laws were made to establish a gradation of ranks; but it was soon found that the soil of America was opposed to a territorial aristocracy. To bring that refractory land into cultivation, the constant and interested exertions of the owner himself were necessary; and when the ground was prepared, its produce was found to be insufficient to enrich a master and a farmer at the same time. The land was then naturally broken up into small portions, which the proprietor cultivated for himself. Land is the basis of an aristocracy, which clings to the soil that supports it; for it is not by privileges alone, nor by birth, but by landed property handed down from generation to generation, that an aristocracy is constituted. A nation may present immense fortunes and extreme wretchedness; but unless those fortunes are territorial there is no true aristocracy, but simply the class of the rich and that of the poor. . . .

In virtue of the law of partible inheritance, the death of every proprietor brings about a kind of revolution in the property; not only do his possessions change hands, but their very nature is altered; since they are parcelled into shares, which become smaller and smaller at each division. This is the direct and, as it were, the physical effect of the law. It follows, then, that in countries where equality of inheritance is established by law, property, and especially landed property, must have a tendency to perpetual diminuation. . . .

. . . But the law of equal division exercises its influence not merely upon the property itself, but it affects the minds of the heirs, and brings their passions into play. These indirect consequences tend powerfully to the destruction of large fortunes, and especially of large domains. . . .

Great landed estates which have once been divided never come together again; for the small proprietor draws from his land a better revenue, in proportion, than the large owner does from his; and of course he sells it at a higher rate. The calculations of gain, therefore, which decide the rich man to sell his domain, will still more powerfully influence him against buying small estates to unite them into a large one.

What is called family-pride is often founded upon an illusion of self-love. A man wishes to perpetuate and immortalize himself, as it were, in his great-grandchildren. Where the *esprit de famille* ceases to act, individual selfishness comes into play. When the idea of family becomes vague, indeterminate, and uncertain, a man thinks of his present convenience; he provides for the establishment of his succeeding generation, and no more.

Either a man gives up the idea of perpetuating his family, or at any rate, he seeks to accomplish it by other means than that of a landed estate. . . .

I do not mean that there is any deficiency of wealthy individuals in the United States; I know of no country, indeed, where the love of money has taken stronger hold on the affections of men, and where a profounder contempt is expressed for the theory of the permanent equality of property. But wealth circulates with inconceivable rapidity, and experience shows that it is rare to find two succeeding generations in the full enjoyment of it. . . .

. . .The social condition of the Americans is eminently democratic; this was its character at the foundation of the Colonies, and it is still more strongly marked at the present day. . . .

America, then, exhibits in her social state an extraordinary phenomenon. Men are there seen on a greater equality in point of fortune and intellect, or, in other words, more equal in their strength, than in any other country of the world, or in any age of which history has preserved the remembrance.

The political consequences of such a social condition as this are easily deducible.

It is impossible to believe that equality will not eventually find its way into the political world as it does everywhere else. To conceive of men remaining for ever unequal upon a single point, yet equal on all others, is impossible; they must come in the end to be equal upon all. . . .

2

CYNTHIA FARRAR

Dinner with Democracy

Professor Cynthia Farrar invited twenty residents of New Haven, CT, for dinner at Yale University once a week for several months to talk about what democracy means. They were of varied backgrounds and interests, from all walks of life. They found that both individual freedom and the community's well-being were important to true democracy. Also, democracy was not only about politics. Renowned Yale (and University of Chicago) professor Harold Lasswell wrote long ago that politics is "who gets what, when, how." But, Professor Farrar's diners concluded that often, the need to represent group interests and deliver on "who gets what" interfered with real democracy. Exchanging views over dinner in New Haven every week for several months yielded no decisions, no public policy, no budgetary outcomes. It wasn't ancient Athens, just twenty-one people having dinner, sharing their ideas, and that was all; maybe, that was more than enough.

ON A THURSDAY EVENING in January, twenty-one people stood in line in an undergraduate cafeteria, collected their food on trays, and slowly gathered in an adjacent room. A few were affiliated with the university; most were not. Lawyers, political activists, a judge; neighborhood leaders, community organizers, a former mayor; business and religious leaders, a journalist, Yale undergraduates; men and women, of various ages, races, ethnicities, and backgrounds—all stood uncertainly around the room. They had been invited to participate in an extended discussion of democracy. Each week, they would join Yale students and other members of the public at lectures in a special course called Democratic Vistas, taught by fifteen Yale professors from different disciplines. Each week, they would read assigned texts. And each week, they would meet for dinner, with me, and talk.

The first conversation was stilted. I talked too much. Their eyes flicked around the room. They wondered what they had gotten themselves into. To get the discussion going, I asked the group to analyze itself in democratic terms. If this group were to make decisions on behalf of the larger community, how would we assess whether they could legitimately do so? By way of answer, individuals offered guesses as to why they had been invited, why someone (me) had thought they had something to contribute to the discussion: certain kinds of experience or understanding? representing or resembling a particular group in society? commitment to the process itself or to the common good? ability to enlarge the perspectives of others? I posed a further question: if we were to consider ourselves a democratic entity, what would that mean? Would we have to operate in a particular way, such as take turns running the class? What would each person be entitled to expect and be required to contribute? What if some people talked all the time, others not at all? In response, some said that each person brought his or her own agenda. Others questioned the premise that we could act like a democracy: there wasn't enough time; not everyone who needed to be present was there; we weren't trying to produce anything, not even decisions. At the end of the hour and a half, amid the clattering of trays and scraping of chairs, I wondered if anyone would return the following week.

I also wondered what I had gotten them into. I had started from an intuition: that this discussion group would not just talk about democracy, but enrich it. What this might mean became clearer to me over the course of the term. Certainly the initial session was a blind alley. Whatever I may have thought they might accomplish as a group, it would definitely not be defined by adherence to standard democratic procedures and the traditional framework of democratic legitimacy: for example, being chosen by a larger constituency through a fair and open process, making decisions on behalf of that constituency through mechanisms such as majority rule, being accountable for the consequences of those decisions, and the like. Indeed, their contribution might well reside, I thought, in a region not often explored by democratic theorists or reflected in attempts to reform democratic practice. This region was charted by the ancient Athenians and has begun to be mapped more systematically in recent years. Call it participatory democracy, or deliberative democracy. Its defining features are, roughly, these: active participation by a broad range of citizens, a deliberative and at times contentious process of problem solving and decision making, a process that is seen as transforming the individual citizens' civic capacity but preserving their individuality. My own study of the origins of democratic theory in Athens, and my attempts to expand the scope of public participation in local governance, had led me into this territory.

Thirteen weeks after our initial meeting, eighteen people reflected on what we had been through. Their remarks suggest that they too had glimpsed hitherto unfamiliar but appealing democratic terrain:

• "I think it's rare to find oneself in a setting with people who live their lives in a different place in this culture. I don't normally find myself in settings where people have views and experiences that are so totally different from my own. And people who are in the world of business or academia or the judiciary. I think that one of the things that is peculiar, in a way, about this democracy is the extent to which we all do tend to hang out with people who are like ourselves."

- "There's a certain awe and wonder you get when you sit in a large group of people and discuss in an academic context intensely personal ideas and approaches. Because it really forces you to bring more out than you might otherwise."
- "Before the class started, if you had asked me my thoughts about democracy, I probably would have answered in exclusively political terms. And because of the nature of the class, I would hardly exclude the political, but I now think of it as a much more complex mosaic and I can appreciate the fact that democracy has a lot to do with the way that we think and the way that we live, apart from the way that we vote."
- "A lot of my experience with people who disagreed with me politically, or with whom I disagreed politically, was of a nasty contention. And to see that you could do this and if you did it right, you would still be civil to each other and reach some sort of mutual understanding while perhaps not agreeing, but nonetheless, some sort of civility. It was encouraging. And it has made me think very seriously about running for office."
- "I, who am thirteenth generation in the U.S., have always considered myself a persecuted underdog as a woman. And it seems really odd to other people. But I now see people who feel like underdogs in different kinds of ways, and I think that's what I will take forward."
- "The effect of severing these ties that we have with constituencies we normally represent is that we were able to create a little political community in which we were all created equal. While outside of this room, we are really unequal in social status and wealth and ability, age, other variables. So this was sort of an ideal of citizenship, in which people come together and leave aside their constituencies or the social position they represent and are able to interact with each other as equals."
- "I think one of the other things that made this group successful is that it's not only that there's a defined amount of time and structure and an ending point and sort of an abstractness, but also that we all made a commitment to be here. Even when we disagreed, we got to know who the personalities were and how the discussion went and how people interact with each other and how to talk and not talk and listen, and feel part of this group. And knowing that the same faces would be there each time."

The democratic meaning of what we came to think of as Dinner with Democracy rests not primarily in what people said about each week's topic—though what they said was shrewd, thoughtful, and enlightening—but in what they did together and what the experience did to them. This structured, extended, and challenging discourse among a diverse group of individuals offers a glimpse of an aspect of democratic citizenship not comprehended—indeed, sidelined—by most theories, and many practices, of democracy. Some forms of political theory are concerned with abstract questions of legitimacy (and some political theorists of this kind do invoke ideals of collective civic deliberation to make their case). Another kind of political theory considers the actual activity of political communities—which is my concern here—but tends to ignore the as-yet-unrealized potential for different forms of political engagement.

Interpreters of democracy often frame their analysis in terms of contrasting extremes. Discussions of democratic governance offer two alternatives: (1) reliance on the modern structures of the bureaucratic state, overseen to some degree by a system of representative government said to reflect the will of the people; (2) partly in response to the detachment of the administrative model from popular influence, direct involvement by the people in decision making, through a system of initiatives and referendums. Left off the spectrum is the possibility of regular, ongoing, and direct participation of the people in a governance system that requires collective deliberation and a process of mutual political education, not just the casting of individual votes for either a candidate or a proposal.

Discussions of the relationship between individual and society in a democratic context also offer two alternatives: (1) extreme individualism (libertarianism or assimilation of political processes to the workings of the market); (2) partly in response to the perceived excesses of democratic capitalism, an appeal to community solidarity, to the shaping of individual preferences and values through identification with a group. The invocation of community carries the risk of repressing individuality. Left off the spectrum in this second contrast is the possibility of substantive political engagement with others who are not part of a "natural" group, but who are fellow citizens different in other respects from oneself. From this perspective, citizens are neither members of a tribe nor consumers; what they have in common is citizenship, and they engage in constant renegotiation of the inevitable tensions between public goods and private interests, community and individual.

In both cases, what is missing is recognition of the power of structured engagement among political equals, which not only permits them to express and aggregate existing preferences, but also transforms their understanding of and capacity to contribute to civic decision making. The participants in Dinner with Democracy did not in any meaningful sense "choose" what occurred. They agreed to join a process and to be open to the possibility of being transformed by it. The structure of the discussions worked on them. They attended, perhaps, because each in his or her own way had an intuition that however rich their lives, however active their involvement in civic affairs (and they were unusual in their civic commitments, from coaching youth baseball to running a program for ex-cons to serving on every significant nonprofit board in New Haven), some important elements were missing: exposure to people different from themselves, the opportunity to argue and articulate their views under challenge, a chance to reflect on the truths they held to be self-evident. They entered, and sustained, a genuinely "political" space of a kind that modern democracy tends to spurn or, at the very least, to corrode. . . .

Indeed, the conversation continually returned to fundamental questions of power: Is choice freedom? Is equality of opportunity really equality? Or are appeals to "choice" and "equality of opportunity"—at least at times—masks for the exercise of power and freedom by those with resources, and the disempowerment of those without? They wished not to challenge the basic commitment of American democracy to freedom and to equal opportunity, but rather to ask what those commitments yield in practice. The participants recognized that the market simultaneously promotes the general welfare and greater inequality, and that other practices considered essential to our democratic society have a comparable effect. Public education, they acknowledged, both diffuses knowledge among the general population and accelerates the advancement of the talented. What seemed important to many of the diners-with-democracy was the resulting increase in fragmentation and polarization. With respect to both wealth and knowledge, they argued that the greatest risk of investing in freedom of choice at the expense of commonness was isolating those left behind both economically, by technological advances, and physically, in concentrated pockets of rooted poverty and despair created by the choices made by others. . . .

The diners-with-democracy identified two characteristics of their own dinner discussions as the key to dealing with the tensions between liberty and equality inherent in democracy: exposure to difference; and a sense of commonness, initially contrived, and then forged. Their experience offers a distinctively political perspective on citizenship. That is, what the citizen-diners said and what they did suggested that it is essential to create a space within which the claims of the individual and society, of money and power and justice, can be explicitly addressed by those affected, treated as equal members. They intimated that a threshold level of resources and education is required for this. Yet they were skeptical that the operation of the existing political system could accomplish any of these ends. These citizens of New Haven and surrounding towns talked in detail about the ways in which politics, perhaps especially at the local level, had been corrupted:

- "[If you're running for office], you focus only on those people who are for you or leaning for you. Some of those people, after the first phone call, never hear again from a political person. And that's the way the system works today. And it's become more and more sanitized to the point where there isn't really an election anymore. It's who's got the most friends to come out to the polls."

- "How do decisions get made and who makes them? . . . It seems to me that the aspirations associated with the founding of this country had to do with the idea of no taxation without representation. And the idea that people should be able to have some degree of power over things that they care about, things connected to their own self-realizing activities. How many of us think that we have any power to affect things that matter to us?"

- "In my neighborhood, it was a policy of people to state that they had no intention of running for office. And they say that in order to develop a trust to get things done."

- "Periodically, in my twelve years in New Haven, people have asked me about whether or not I would run for mayor. And my response is, 'I am queen of my own bedroom, I am captain of my own tub, I am head of my own organization.' And the reason why I say that is because it's very, very hard not to be corrupted in the current political process. And you have to know that the pressure's going to be there and that's going to work against the very reason why you decided to run for political office or the very reason why you decided to participate in community activities anyway."

- "Last night I had to go in front of the Board of Aldermen to ask the mayor to put us in for $35,000 in the Community Development Block Grant allocation. . . . One of them says, 'Well, why should we give you this money?' By the end of five minutes, it dawned on me, they were talking about our money as if it was their money. It's not your money. I'm a representative of a community coming to the representatives of the people for a piece of the people's money to do people's work. Can you stop it? But this is the kind of thing that turns people off."

... Participants in Dinner with Democracy recognized that they were able to engage with each other as equals in part because they left their constituencies and pet projects at the door to the dining hall—and perhaps also precisely *because* they were not being asked to make decisions that would affect others. Members of the group dealt with each other openly and flexibly, as individuals rather than as "representatives" of any particular group or initiative. In a comment quoted earlier, another participant noted that "the effect of severing these ties that we have with constituencies we normally represent is that we were able to create a little political community in which we were all created equal." If they were to make decisions, they would have to take particular groups into account— to act as if they had been selected to represent some group or other, and to be accountable to them for the outcome. This would increase partisanship, inflexibility, a focus on particularist interests, perhaps. As one remarked, "It's a real luxury not to come to any conclusion." But he went on to draw an inference about reforming the way in which existing political structures function: "It's an argument for the point that there ought to be more times when we're not sitting down in a crisis, trying to come out with a conclusion because, then, maybe we'd be more prepared to listen to each other when it was important." ...

... Democracy—alone among political systems—relies on the virtue but also the stubborn individuality of all of its citizens. Disorder is a risk; so is conformity. The challenge is to keep alive both quirkiness and solidarity, both equality and realization of man's individual potential. No system can deliver this result—though some make it easier, while others prevent it entirely. What is required, ... is continual engagement, imagination, persuasion, openness. This can be accomplished only through the process of interaction between self and other, which is often too ragged and contingent, too much influenced by status and power, and too narrowly bounded, to serve democratic purposes. A more varied and rich and demanding fare—dinner with democracy as the table setting, perhaps—may be needed to sustain the democratic experiment.

3

JAMES DAVISON HUNTER

The Enduring Culture War

Professor James Davison Hunter finds deeply held, contrasting views within the United States about the moral and religious principles that underlie our politics. The author compares the "traditionalist or orthodox" view with the "progressivist" view: hold to values that have characterized the nation's past or change culture to be more accepting of new norms. True, only a small number of citizens feel very strongly and are "white-hot" about their position. But many other average citizens feel strongly too, Hunter contends. The author then goes on to explain how the power of language and symbols can affect the views of the citizenry in general by controlling the way "to frame the terms of public discussion." He then provides an interesting example of "framing": the debate that occurred during the 1990s in North Carolina over the issue of outcomes-based education. Influential opposing national interest groups became involved and a "culture war" was underway. Hunter concludes that the middle ground exists, but it is not easily heard.

IN THE LAST HALF OF THE TWENTIETH CENTURY, it was widely presumed that distinctions of faith and religious community had been largely settled and were thus no longer politically important. The Catholicism of John F. Kennedy in the 1960 election was the exception that proved the rule, and in this sense, it was the last gasp of a dying fear. In the main, the sense prevailed that every religious faith had been domesticated through its relegation to the private sphere. The diversity that mattered now was a diversity of race, ethnicity, class, gender, and sexual orientation. These have occupied an enormous amount of time and attention over the last forty to fifty years and, . . . to great effect.

But something unexpected is suggested by the idea of a "culture war," especially as it was first articulated. It suggests that the contours of difference have changed yet again in ways that raise a troubling possibility: though configured in ways that are unfamiliar and possibly unprecedented, perhaps religious and moral differences remain politically consequential in late modern America after all. Perhaps, long after it was thought settled, the normative differences rooted in sacred cosmologies (and the communities in which they are embedded) have come to challenge the project of liberal democracy again. . . .

The heart of the culture war argument was that American public culture was undergoing a realignment that, in turn, was generating significant tension and conflict. These antagonisms were playing out not just on the surface of social life (that is, in its cultural politics) but at the deepest and most profound levels, and not just at the level of ideology but in its public symbols, its myths, its discourse, and through the institutional structures that generate and sustain public culture.

Thus underneath the myriad political controversies over so-called cultural issues, there were yet deeper crises over the very meaning and purpose of the core institutions of American civilization. Behind the politics of abortion was a controversy over a momentous debate over the meaning of motherhood, of individual liberty, and of our obligations to one another. Within the politics of government patronage, including the dispute over the National Endowment for the Arts and its funding of controversial art, one could find a more consequential dispute over what constitutes art in the first place and the social ideals it symbolically communicates. Beyond the politics of educational curriculum, the quarrels over textbooks in public schools constituted a more serious disagreement over the national ideals Americans pass on to the next generation. Behind the contentious argument about the legal rights of gays and lesbians was a more serious debate over the fundamental nature of the family and appropriate sexuality. Within the politics of church and state, the various (and seemingly trivial) altercations over Ten Commandment presentations on public property overlaid a more significant debate about the role of religious institutions and religious authority in an increasingly secular society. And so it goes. Cumulatively, these debates concerning the wide range of social institutions amounted to a struggle over the meaning of America.

This, however, was not the end of the matter. Underneath the push and pull of these institutional conflicts were competing moral ideals as to how public life ought to be ordered and maintained. These were not mere political ideologies, reducible to party platforms or political scorecards, but rather moral visions from which the policy discussions and political disputes derived their passion. Embedded within institutions, these ideals were articulated in innumerable ways with every conceivable nuance and shade of variation. *As they were translated into the signs and symbols of public discourse,* however, they lost their complexity and nuance and thus divided into sharply antagonistic tendencies.

One moral vision—the traditionalist or orthodox—is predicated upon the achievements and traditions of the past as the foundation and guide to the challenges of the present. Though this vision is often tinged with nostalgia and is at times resistant to change, it is not simply reactionary, backward looking, or static. Rather, the order of life sustained by this vision is, at its best, one that seeks deliberate continuity with the ordering principles inherited from the past. The social end is the reinvigoration and realization of what are considered to be the very noblest ideals and achievements of civilization.

Against this is a progressivist moral vision that is ambivalent to the legacy of the past, regarding it partly as a useful point of reference and partly as a source of oppression. Instead, the order of life embraced by this vision is one that idealizes experimentation and thus adaptation to and innovation with the changing circumstances of our time. Although sometimes marked by traces of utopian idealism, it is not merely an uncritical embrace of all things new. The aim of the progressivists' vision is the further emancipation of the human spirit and the creation of an inclusive and tolerant world. . . .

Another way to say this is that against the old axis of tension and conflict that was rooted in political economy, a "new" axis of tension and conflict has emerged that is fundamentally cultural in nature. The historical significance of this new axis has been evident in the ways in which it cuts across age-old divisions among Protestants, Catholics, and Jews. The orthodox traditions in these faiths now have much more in common with each other than they do with progressives in their own faith tradition, and vice versa. The polarity of *this* axis seems to better account for the variation in positions on a wide range of popular domestic disputes. In turn, it is the polarities of *these* controversies through which a far-reaching struggle for national identity is carried on. . . .

It is clear that within themselves, traditionalists and permissivists do not have political positions that align perfectly with their moral dispositions. Yet the alignment is fairly close, and for this reason these groups represent a natural and broader constituency receptive to political and social mobilization.

The point is this: no matter how one approaches the question, social dissensus is very much present in public opinion. Forming the grassroots support for competing visions are factions that constitute the white-hot core of difference and dissensus. Disproportionately motivated and active in these issues, they are the most likely to write letters, send checks to the special interest groups and parties that represent them, and volunteer on behalf of their cause. Although these highly partisan citizens may only make up 5 percent of the American population on one side of the cultural divide or the other, in actual numbers they account for 10 to 12 million people on each side. Extending out to less committed constituencies, the numbers who align themselves on one side of the cultural divide or the other can range up to 60 million each.

But this still leaves open the question, are these factions and the larger constituencies of which they are a part politically significant? In his review of [the book titled] *Culture Wars* for *Contemporary Sociology,* Steven Brint posed the question this way: "Can one have a proper war when two-thirds of the army are noncombatants?" The answer brings us back to one of the central contentions of the original argument about the culture war: it has everything to do with the institutions and elites that provide leadership to these factions. . . .

To take the structural and institutional approach in cultural analysis is, in part, to think of culture as objects produced. Culture takes the form of ideas, information, news—indeed, knowledge of all kinds—and these in turn are expressed in pronouncements, speeches, edicts, tracts, essays, books, film, works of art, laws, and the like. At the heart of the production and distribution of cultural output is language. It is, of course, at the root of culture for it provides a medium through which people experience reality. Through both its structure and its meaning, language provides the categories through which people understand themselves, others, and the larger world around them. The power of language resides in its ability to objectify, to make identifiable and "objectively" real the various and ever changing aspects of our experience. When objects are named, when relationships are described, when standards of evaluation are articulated, and when situations are defined, they can acquire a sense of facticity. For this reason formal education, the media of mass communications (including television, radio, newspapers, magazines, and the like), art and music, and religious pronouncements (such as sermons, edicts, policy statements, moral instruction, liturgies and rituals, and the like) all become important conduits for communication and socialization—mechanisms through which a particular vision of reality is defined and maintained. It stands to reason that influence over language, the cultural output through which public language is mediated, and the institutions that produce and manage it all are extraordinarily powerful.

The development and articulation of the more elaborate systems of meaning and the vocabularies that make them coherent are more or less exclusively the realm of elites. They are the ones who provide the concepts, supply the grammar, and explicate the logic of public discussion. They are the ones who define and redefine the meaning of public symbols and provide the legitimating or delegitimating narratives of public figures or events. In all of these ways and for all of these reasons, it is they and the strategically placed institutions they serve that come to frame the terms of public discussion.

In sum, there are elites who are enormously influential for the sway they have over the content and direction of cultural production within specific institutions. These are supported by 5 to 8 percent of the population who are the grassroots activists, the "cultural warriors" who generate and organize resources on behalf of their respective associations and factions. There are yet larger parts of the population whose fundamental orientation leans one way or another but who also tend to be more moderate and less motivated. Yet they can and are mobilized for action in public affairs (even if only by voting) under certain circumstances. . . .

Consider briefly a case concerning school reform in Gaston County, North Carolina, in the early 1990s. The school district there was ranked among the bottom 17 school districts in the state (out of 120) in terms of students' academic performance, high dropout rates, and so on. To rectify this matter, the Board of Education put together the Odyssey Project that incorporated five elements of reform, including a change in pedagogy called "outcomes-based education." The school district won a $2 million grant as the beginning of a $20 million grant in a national competition to implement this reform. Through the work of a local Baptist pastor who drew on the support and materials of Citizens for Excellence in Education (CEE)—a religiously based, special interest organization concerned about secular reforms in the public schools—an opposition was mobilized. The CEE was dead set against outcomes-based education, saying it manipulated and indoctrinated children with secular humanism, New Age thinking, and hostility to Christianity. As its director put it, outcomes-based education marked "the end of academic education in America." It was not long before parents and other citizens "packed school board meetings where they monopolized the use of the microphone, harassed school board members, wrote letters to local newspapers, distributed fliers urging parents to act swiftly in order to save their children from the dire effects of this 'radical' school program, circulated warnings [through e-mail] and gathered signatures on petitions."

Soon enough, another national special interest organization, People for the American Way, became involved in direct ways. People for the American Way claimed that the CEE and other organizations of the religious right posed a dire threat to freedom and tolerance in the United States. Each organization was able to use this local dispute to promote its own larger interests far beyond Gaston County. Neither organization conceded rhetorical space or was willing to consider any compromise. A substantive debate about the merits of the reform proposal never occurred, and in the end, all reform efforts were scuttled, the remaining grant funds were forfeited, the school superintendent was forced to resign, and a community was divided. And still, in the end, it was the children of Gaston County who paid the highest price. . . .

The culture war does not manifest itself at all times in all places in the same way. It is episodic and, very often, local in its expressions. Examples abound: the dispute over the fate of Terri Schiavo in Pinellas Park, Florida; the conflict over teaching "intelligent design" in Kansas City; the controversy over a teacher in the Bronx who was suspended for bringing bibles to P.S. 5; a clash over a Civil War statue in Richmond, Virginia; the tempest over a priest in St. Paul who refused to serve communion to gays at Mass; the fury of parents in Mustang, Oklahoma, after the superintendent excised a nativity scene at the end of the annual Christmas play; the dispute over speech codes at the University of Pennsylvania; the row over release time for religious instruction in the public schools in Staunton, Virginia; and on it goes.

Yet because what is under dispute and what is at stake is culture at its deepest levels, carried by organizations relating to larger movements, these local, often disparate conflicts are played out repeatedly in predictable ways. The nation was not divided by the Odyssey Program, but the community of Gaston County, North Carolina, was for a time and profoundly, with serious consequences. So have been and are communities and regions all over the nation whenever an event fraught with moral meaning and cultural significance occurs that compels communities to take positions and make decisions.

Are local and national elites and the organizations they represent politically significant? They certainly were in this instance, and as it has become clear over the years, they are in virtually every other instance of cultural conflict as well. It is in their interest to frame issues in stark terms, to take uncompromising positions, and to delegitimate their opponents. Clearly, entire populations are not divided at anywhere near the level of intensity of the activists and the rhetoric, but because issues are often framed in such stark terms, public choices are forced. In such circumstances even communities and populations that would prefer other options, and much greater reason and harmony in the process, find themselves divided. . . .

To be sure, elites, activists, the institutions they lead and grassroots support they mobilize, and the larger publics that form their natural constituencies are enormously consequential. Yet their importance is not just measured by the power to frame issues. It is also inversely measured by the lack of influence of the majority of Americans, who are in the middle, to contradict this framing and offer an alternative. If the culture war is a myth and the real story is about the consensus that exists in "the middle," then why is it that the middle cannot put forward, much less elect, a moderate who represents that consensus, with all of its complexity and ambivalence on so many issues? If the center is so vital, then why is it that the extremes are overrepresented in the structures of power—not least, political power? In the case of the dispute over educational reform in Gaston County, where was that contented middle—that consensus that critics suggest is so broad and dynamic? In this dispute and in others like it, the middle was there, but as the outcome showed, it was also, sadly, inconsequential.

4

C. WRIGHT MILLS

From *The Power Elite*

C. Wright Mills's book The Power Elite *stands as a classic in political science. In it he offers one of several possible answers to the question "Who rules America?" A three-part elite rules, he believes, composed of corporate, political, and military leaders. These sectors of American life are connected, creating an "interlocking" power structure with highly centralized decision-making. Mills considers a conspiracy theory to account for the power elite's control, but rejects it for something much more frightening. Average Americans are like "trusting children" who rely on the power elite to run things smoothly and well. Today, a half-century after Mills wrote, his ideas seem a bit ultra-dramatic and overstated. However, recent political events recall Mills's view: the 2008 recession bailout of big banks and companies such as AIG; the Supreme Court's 2010 decision in* Citizens United v. Federal Election Commission, *allowing corporations and labor unions to contribute large sums of money to campaigns; and the creation of Super PACS as a way for wealthy individuals and groups to circumvent previous campaign contribution limits. And all of this has occurred at a time when the gap in wealth between the richest and the poorest Americans has grown wider. Mills offers a warning about power in America that is timeless, one that many people believe is truer now than ever before.*

———

THE POWERS OF ORDINARY men are circumscribed by the everyday worlds in which they live, yet even in these rounds of job, family, and neighborhood they often seem driven by forces they can neither understand nor govern. "Great changes" are beyond their control, but affect their conduct and outlook none the less. The very framework of modern society confines them to projects not their own, but from every side, such changes now press upon the men and women of the mass society, who accordingly feel that they are without purpose in an epoch in which they are without power.

But not all men are in this sense ordinary. As the means of information and of power are centralized, some men come to occupy positions in American society from which they can look down upon, so to speak, and by their decisions mightily affect, the everyday worlds of ordinary men and women. They are not made by their jobs; they set up and break down jobs for thousands of others; they are not confined by simple family responsibilities; they can escape. They may live in many hotels and houses, but they are bound by no one community. They need not merely "meet the demands of the day and hour"; in some part, they create these demands, and cause others to meet them. Whether or not they profess their power, their technical and political experience of it far transcends that of the underlying population. What Jacob Burckhardt said of "great men," most Americans might well say of their elite: "They are all that we are not."

The power elite is composed of men whose positions enable them to transcend the ordinary environments of ordinary men and women; they are in positions to make decisions having major consequences. Whether they do or do not make such decisions is less important than the fact that they do occupy such pivotal positions: their failure to act, their failure to make decisions, is itself an act that is often of greater consequence than the decisions they do make. For they are in command of the major hierarchies and organizations of modern society. They rule the big corporations. They run the machinery of the state and claim its prerogatives. They direct the military establishment. They occupy the strategic command posts of the social structure, in which are now centered the effective means of the power and the wealth and the celebrity which they enjoy.

The power elite are not solitary rulers. Advisers and consultants, spokesmen and opinion-makers are often the captains of their higher thought and decision. Immediately below the elite are the professional politicians of the middle levels of power, in the Congress and in the pressure groups, as well as among the new and old upper classes of town and city and region. Mingling with them, in curious ways which we shall explore, are those professional celebrities who live by being continually displayed but are never, so long as they remain celebrities, displayed enough. If such celebrities are not at the head of any dominating hierarchy, they do often have the power to distract the attention of the public or afford sensations to the masses, or, more directly, to gain the ear of those who do occupy positions of direct power. More or less unattached, as critics of morality and technicians of power, as spokesmen of God and creators of mass sensibility, such celebrities and consultants are part of the immediate scene in which the drama of the elite is enacted. But that drama itself is centered in the command posts of the major institutional hierarchies.

The truth about the nature and the power of the elite is not some secret which men of affairs know but will not tell. Such men hold quite various theories about their own roles in the sequence of event and decision. Often they are uncertain about their roles, and even more often they allow their fears and their hopes to affect their assessment of their own power. No matter how great their actual power, they tend to be less acutely aware of it than of the resistances of others to its use. Moreover, most American men of affairs have learned well the rhetoric of public relations, in some cases even to the point of using it when they are alone, and thus coming to believe it. The personal awareness of the actors is only one of the several sources one must examine in order to understand the higher circles. Yet many who believe that there is no elite, or at any rate none of any consequence, rest their argument upon what men of affairs believe about themselves, or at least assert in public.

There is, however, another view: those who feel, even if vaguely, that a compact and powerful elite of great importance does now prevail in America often base that feeling upon the historical trend of our time. They have felt, for example, the domination of the military event, and from this they infer that generals and admirals, as well as other men of decision influenced by them, must be enormously powerful. They hear that the Congress has again abdicated to a handful of men decisions clearly related to the issue of war or peace. They know that the bomb was dropped over Japan in the name of the United States of America, although they were at no time consulted about the matter. They feel that they live in a time of big decisions; they know that they are not making any. Accordingly, as they consider the present as history, they infer that at its center, making decisions or failing to make them, there must be an elite of power.

On the one hand, those who share this feeling about big historical events assume that there is an elite and that its power is great. On the other hand, those who listen carefully to the reports of men apparently involved in the great decisions often do not believe that there is an elite whose powers are of decisive consequence.

Both views must be taken into account, but neither is adequate. The way to understand the power of the American elite lies neither solely in recognizing the historic scale of events nor in accepting the personal awareness reported by men of apparent decision. Behind such men and behind the events of history, linking the two, are the major institutions of modern society. These hierarchies of state and corporation and army constitute the means of power; as such they are now of a consequence not before equaled in human history—and at their summits, there are now those command posts of modern society which offer us the sociological key to an understanding of the role of the higher circles in America.

Within American society, major national power now resides in the economic, the political, and the military domains. Other institutions seem off to the side of modern history, and, on occasion, duly subordinated to these. No family is as directly powerful in national affairs as any major corporation; no church is as directly powerful in the external biographies of young men in America today as the military establishment; no college is as powerful in the shaping of momentous events as the National Security Council. Religious, educational, and family institutions are not autonomous centers of national power; on the contrary, these decentralized areas are increasingly shaped by the big three, in which developments of decisive and immediate consequence now occur.

Families and churches and schools adapt to modern life; governments and armies and corporations shape it; and, as they do so, they turn these lesser institutions into means for their ends. Religious institutions provide chaplains to the armed forces where they are used as a means of increasing the effectiveness of its morale to kill. Schools select and train men for their jobs in corporations and their specialized tasks in the armed forces. The extended family has, of course, long been broken up by the industrial revolution, and now the son and the father are removed from the family, by compulsion if need be, whenever the army of the state sends out the call. And the symbols of all these lesser institutions are used to legitimate the power and the decisions of the big three.

The life-fate of the modern individual depends not only upon the family into which he was born or which he enters by marriage, but increasingly upon the corporation in which he spends the most alert hours of his best years; not only upon the school where he is educated as a child and adolescent, but also upon the state which touches him throughout his life; not only upon the church in which on occasion he hears the word of God, but also upon the army in which he is disciplined.

If the centralized state could not rely upon the inculcation of nationalist loyalties in public and private schools, its leaders would promptly seek to modify the decentralized educational system. If the bankruptcy rate among the top five hundred corporations were as high as the general divorce rate among the thirty-seven million married couples, there would be economic catastrophe on an international scale. If members of armies gave to them no more of their lives than do believers to the churches to which they belong, there would be a military crisis.

Within each of the big three, the typical institutional unit has become enlarged, has become administrative, and, in the power of its decisions, has become centralized. Behind these developments there is a fabulous technology, for as institutions, they have incorporated this technology and guide it, even as it shapes and paces their developments.

The economy—once a great scatter of small productive units in autonomous balance—has become dominated by two or three hundred giant corporations, administratively and politically interrelated, which together hold the keys to economic decisions.

The political order, once a decentralized set of several dozen states with a weak spinal cord, has become a centralized, executive establishment which has taken up into itself many powers previously scattered, and now enters into each and every cranny of the social structure.

The military order, once a slim establishment in a context of distrust fed by state militia, has become the largest and most expensive feature of government, and, although well versed in smiling public relations, now has all the grim and clumsy efficiency of a sprawling bureaucratic domain.

In each of these institutional areas, the means of power at the disposal of decision makers have increased enormously; their central executive powers have been enhanced; within each of them modern administrative routines have been elaborated and tightened up.

As each of these domains becomes enlarged and centralized, the consequences of its activities become greater, and its traffic with the others increases. The decisions of a handful of corporations bear upon military and political as well as upon economic developments around the world. The decisions of the military establishment rest upon and grievously affect political life as well as the very level of economic activity. The decisions made within the political domain determine economic activities and military programs. There is no longer, on the one hand, an economy, and, on the other hand, a political order containing a military establishment unimportant to politics and to money-making. There is a political economy linked, in a thousand ways, with military institutions and decisions. On each side of the world-split running through central Europe and around the Asiatic rimlands, there is an ever-increasing interlocking of economic, military, and political structures. If there is government intervention in the corporate economy, so is there corporate intervention in the governmental process. In the structural sense, this triangle of power is the source of the interlocking directorate that is most important for the historical structure of the present.

The fact of the interlocking is clearly revealed at each of the points of crisis of modern capitalist society—slump, war, and boom. In each, men of decision are led to an awareness of the interdependence of the major institutional orders. In the nineteenth century, when the scale of all institutions was smaller, their liberal integration was achieved in the automatic economy, by an autonomous play of market forces, and in the automatic political domain, by the bargain and the vote. It was then assumed that out of the imbalance and friction that followed the limited decisions then possible a new equilibrium would in due course emerge. That can no longer be assumed, and it is not assumed by the men at the top of each of the three dominant hierarchies.

For given the scope of their consequences, decisions—and indecisions—in any one of these ramify into the others, and hence top decisions tend either to become co-ordinated or to lead to a commanding indecision. It has not always been like this. When numerous small entrepreneurs made up the economy, for example, many of them could fail and the consequences still remain local; political and military authorities did not intervene. But now, given political expectations and military commitments, can they afford to allow key units of the private corporate economy to break down in slump? Increasingly, they do intervene in economic affairs, and as they do so, the controlling decisions in each order are inspected by agents of the other two, and economic, military, and political structures are interlocked.

At the pinnacle of each of the three enlarged and centralized domains, there have arisen those higher circles which make up the economic, the political, and the military elites. At the top of the economy, among the corporate rich, there are the chief executives; at the top of the political order, the members of the political directorate; at the top of the military establishment, the elite of soldier-statesmen clustered in and around the Joint Chiefs of Staff and the upper echelon. As each of these domains has coincided with the others, as decisions tend to become total in their consequence, the leading men in each of the three domains of power—the warlords, the corporation chieftains, the political directorate—tend to come together, to form the power elite of America. . . .

The conception of the power elite and of its unity rests upon the corresponding developments and the coincidence of interests among economic, political, and military organizations. It also rests upon the similarity of origin and outlook, and the social and personal intermingling of the top circles from each of these dominant hierarchies. This conjunction of institutional and psychological forces, in turn, is revealed by the heavy personnel traffic within and between the big three institutional orders, as well as by the rise of go-betweens as in the high-level lobbying. The conception of the power elite, accordingly, does *not* rest upon the assumption that American history since the origins of World War II must be understood as a secret plot, or as a great and co-ordinated conspiracy of the members of this elite. The conception rests upon quite impersonal grounds.

There is, however, little doubt that the American power elite—which contains, we are told, some of "the greatest organizers in the world"—has also planned and has plotted. The rise of the elite, as we have already made clear, was not and could not have been caused by a plot; and the tenability of the conception does not rest upon the existence of any secret or any publicly known organization. But, once the conjunction of structural trend and of the personal will to utilize it gave rise to the power elite, then plans and programs did occur to its members and indeed it is not possible to interpret many events and official policies of the fifth epoch without reference to the power elite. "There is a great difference," Richard Hofstadter has remarked, "between locating conspiracies *in* history and saying that history *is*, in effect, a conspiracy . . . "

The structural trends of institutions become defined as opportunities by those who occupy their command posts. Once such opportunities are recognized, men may avail themselves of them. Certain types of men from each of the dominant institutional areas, more far-sighted than others, have actively promoted the liaison before it took its truly modern shape. They have often done so for reasons not shared by their partners, although not objected to by them either; and often the outcome of their liaison has had consequences which none of them foresaw, much less shaped, and which only later in the course of development came under explicit control. Only after it was well under way did most of its members find themselves part of it and become gladdened, although sometimes also worried, by this fact. But once the co-ordination is a going concern, new men come readily into it and assume its existence without question.

So far as explicit organization—conspiratorial or not—is concerned, the power elite, by its very nature, is more likely to use existing organizations, working within and between them, than to set up explicit organizations whose membership is strictly limited to its own members. But if there is no machinery in existence to ensure, for example, that military and political factors will be balanced in decisions made, they will invent such machinery and use it, as with the National Security Council. Moreover, in a formally democratic polity, the aims and the powers of the various elements of this elite are further supported by an aspect of the permanent war economy: the assumption that the security of the nation supposedly rests upon great secrecy of plan and intent. Many higher events that would reveal the working of the power elite can be withheld from public knowledge under the guise of secrecy. With the wide secrecy covering their operations and decisions, the power elite can mask their intentions, operations, and further consolidation. Any secrecy that is imposed upon those in positions to observe high decision-makers clearly works for and not against the operations of the power elite.

There is accordingly reason to suspect—but by the nature of the case, no proof—that the power elite is not altogether "surfaced." There is nothing hidden about it, although its activities are not publicized. As an elite, it is not organized, although its members often know one another, seem quite naturally to work together, and share many organizations in common. There is nothing conspiratorial about it, although its decisions are often publicly unknown and its mode of operation manipulative rather than explicit.

It is not that the elite "believe in" a compact elite behind the scenes and a mass down below. It is not put in that language. It is just that the people are of necessity confused and must, like trusting children, place all the new world of foreign policy and strategy and executive action in the hands of experts. It is just that everyone knows somebody has got to run the show, and that somebody usually does. Others do not really care anyway, and besides, they do not know how. So the gap between the two types gets wider.

5

RICHARD ZWEIGENHAFT
G. WILLIAM DOMHOFF

From *Diversity in the Power Elite*

In the previous excerpt, C. Wright Mills presented his interpretation of who holds power in America: a small elite. Mills wrote his classic book decades ago. Richard Zweigenhaft and G. William Domhoff revisit Mills's thesis by examining the composition of today's power elite—assuming, of course, that there is such an elite. The authors offer a fascinating account of Jews, women, blacks, Latinos, Asian Americans, and gay men and lesbians in the elite, including many personal stories of interesting and powerful individuals. The excerpt here looks at corporate women and their discovery that golf is key to success. Zweigenhaft and Domhoff then explore several prominent African Americans and the relevance of skin color in acceptance into the elite. Among their brief biographies is that of then-senator Barack Obama. Their conclusion? Yes, the elite look different today, but no, they are not really so different than when Mills wrote.

INJUSTICES BASED ON RACE, gender, ethnicity, and sexual orientation have been the most emotionally charged and contested issues in American society since the end of the 1960s, far exceeding concerns about social class and rivaled only by conflicts over abortion. These issues are now subsumed under the umbrella term *diversity*, which has been discussed extensively from the perspectives of both the aggrieved and those at the middle levels of the social ladder who resist any changes.

... [W]e look at diversity from a new angle: we examine its impact on the small group at the top of American society that we call the *power elite*, those who own and manage large banks and corporations, finance the political campaigns of conservative Democrats and virtually all Republicans at the state and national levels, and serve in government as appointed officials and military leaders. We ask whether the decades of civil disobedience, protest, and litigation by civil rights groups, feminists, and gay and lesbian rights activists have resulted in a more diverse power elite. If they have, what effects has this new diversity had on the functioning of the power elite and on its relation to the rest of society? ...

According to many popular commentators, the composition of the higher circles in the United States had indeed changed by the late 1980s and early 1990s. Some went even further, saying that the old power elite had been pushed aside entirely. Enthusiastic articles in mainstream magazines, such as one in the late 1980s in *U.S. News & World Report* entitled "The New American Establishment," have also appeared, celebrating a new diversity at the top and claiming that "new kinds of men and women" have "taken control of institutions that influence important aspects of American life." School and club ties are no longer important, the article announced, highlighting the new role of women with a picture of some of the "wise women" who had joined the "wise men" who dominated the old establishment.

Then, in July 1995, *Newsweek* ran a cover story titled "The Rise of the Overclass," featuring a gallery of one hundred high-tech, media, and Wall Street stars, including women as well as men and previously excluded racial and ethnic groups as well as whites with Western European backgrounds, all of whom supposedly came from all rungs of the social ladder. The term *overclass* was relatively new, but the argument—that the power elite was dead and had been superseded by a diverse meritocratic elite—was not.

More recently, David Brooks, a conservative columnist for the *New York Times*, has made the same kind of claims in two books about the upper-middle class. In the second, *On Paradise Drive: How We Live Now (and Always Have) in the Future Tense,* he refers to a time, presumably in the distant past, "back when the old WASP elite dominated," and contrasts those bad old days with the current era of a "new educated elite." He goes on to reassure the reader, "There is no single elite in America. Hence, there is no definable establishment to be oppressed by and to rebel against."

We are wary about these claims announcing the demise of the old elites and the arrival of new elites because they never have been documented systematically. Moreover, they are suspect because similar claims have been made repeatedly in American history and have been proved wrong each time. In popular books and magazines from the 1830s, 1920s, and 1950s, for example, leading commentators of the day asserted that there used to be a tightly knit and cohesive governing group in the United States, but no longer. A closer look several decades later at each of these supposedly new eras invariably showed that the new power group was primarily the old one after all, with a few additions and alterations here and there. . . .

But is any of the talk about . . . upward mobility true? Can anecdotes, dime novels, and self-serving autobiographical accounts about diversity, meritocracy, and upward social mobility survive a more systematic analysis? Have very many women or members of other previously excluded groups made it to the top? Has class lost its importance in shaping life chances?

. . . [W]e address these and related questions within the framework provided by the iconoclastic sociologist C. Wright Mills in his classic *The Power Elite*, published half a century ago in 1956 when the media were in the midst of what Mills called the "Great American Celebration," and still accurate today in terms of many of the issues he addressed. In spite of the Great Depression of the 1930s, Americans had pulled together to win World War II, and the country was both prosperous at home and influential abroad. Most of all, according to enthusiasts, the United States had become a relatively classless and pluralistic society, where power belonged to the people through their political parties and public opinion. Some groups certainly had more power than others, but no group or class had too much. The New Deal and World War II had forever transformed the corporate-based power structure of earlier decades.

Mills challenged this celebration of pluralism by studying the social backgrounds and career paths of the people who occupied the highest positions in what he saw as the three major institutional hierarchies in postwar America, the corporations, the executive branch of the federal government, and the military. He found that almost all members of this leadership group, which he called the power elite, were white, Christian males who came from "at most, the upper third of the income and occupational pyramids," despite the many Horatio Algeresque claims to the contrary. A majority came from an even narrower stratum, the 11 percent of U.S. families headed by businesspeople or highly educated professionals like physicians and lawyers. Mills concluded that power in the United States in the 1950s was just about as concentrated as it had been since the rise of the large corporations, although he stressed that the New Deal and World War II had given political appointees and military chieftains more authority than they had exercised previously.

It is our purpose, therefore, to take a detailed look at the social, educational, and occupational backgrounds of the leaders of these three institutional hierarchies to see whether they have become more diverse in terms of gender, race, ethnicity, and sexual orientation, and also in terms of socioeconomic origins. Unlike Mills, however, we think the power elite is more than a set of institutional leaders; it is also the leadership group for the small upper class of owners and managers of large, income-producing properties, the 1 percent of American households that owned 44.1 percent of all privately held stock, 58.0 percent of financial securities, and 57.3

percent of business equity in 2001, the last year for which systematic figures are available. (By way of comparison, the bottom 90 percent, those who work for hourly wages or monthly salaries, have a mere 15.5 percent of the stock, 11.3 percent of financial securities, and 10.4 percent of business equity.) Not surprisingly, we think the primary concern of the power elite is to support the kind of policies, regulations, and political leaders that maintain this structure of privilege for the very rich. . . .

The power elite depicted by C. Wright Mills was, without doubt, an exclusively male preserve. On the opening page of *The Power Elite*, Mills stated clearly that "the power elite is composed of men whose positions enable them to transcend the ordinary environments of ordinary men and women." Although there were some women in the corporate, political, and military worlds, very few were in or near the higher circles that constituted the power elite. Are they there now? If so, how substantial and how visible is their presence? When did they arrive, and how did they get there? What are their future prospects? . . .

In 1990, Elizabeth Dole, then secretary of labor (and, since January 2003, a member of the Senate), initiated a department-level investigation into the question of whether or not there was a "glass ceiling" blocking women and minorities from the highest ranks of U.S. corporations. When the report was issued by the Federal Glass Ceiling Commission in 1995, comments by the white male managers who had been interviewed and surveyed supported the earlier claims that upper management was willing to accept women and minorities only if they were not too different. As one manager explained, "What's important is comfort, chemistry, relationships, and collaborations. That's what makes a shop work. When we find minorities and women who think like we do, we snatch them up."

One *Fortune* 500 labor relations executive used the phrase "comfort zone" to make the same point about "chemistry" and reducing "uncertainty": "You need to build relationships," she said, "and you need to be pretty savvy. And for a woman or a person of color at this company, you have to put in more effort to get into this comfort zone."

Much has been made of the fact that men have traditionally been socialized to play competitive team sports and women have not. In *The Managerial Woman*, Margaret Hennig and Anne Jardim argue that the experience of having participated in competitive team sports provides men with many advantages in the corporate world. Playing on sports teams teaches boys such things as how to develop their individual skills in the context of helping the team to win, how to develop cooperative, goal-oriented relationships with teammates, how to focus on winning, and how to deal with losing. "The experience of most little girls," they wrote in the mid-1970s, "has no parallel." Although the opportunities for young women to participate in competitive sports, including team sports like basketball and soccer, have increased dramatically in recent years, far fewer opportunities were available when many of the women now in higher management in U.S. corporations were young.

Just as football is often identified as the classic competitive and aggressive team sport that prepares men for the rough-and-tumble (and hierarchical) world of the corporation, an individual sport, golf, is the more convivial, but still competitive, game that allows boys to play together, shoot the breeze, and do business. As Marcia Chambers shows in *The Unplayable Lie*, the golf course, and especially the country club, can be as segregated by sex as the football field. Few clubs bar women, but some clubs do not allow women to vote, sit on their governing boards, or play golf on weekend mornings.

Many women managers are convinced that their careers suffer because of discrimination against them by golf clubs. In a study of executives who manage "corporate-government affairs," Denise Benoit Scott found that the women in such positions "share meals with staff members and other government relations officials but never play golf." In contrast, men in such positions "play golf with a broad range of people in business and government, including legislators and top corporate executives." As one of the women she interviewed put it, "I wish I played golf. I think golf is the key. If you want to make it, you have to play golf."

Similarly, when the editors of *Executive Female* magazine surveyed the top fifty women in line-management positions (in sales, marketing, production, and general management with a direct impact on the company's bottom line), they asked them why more women had not made it to the "upper reaches of corporate America." The most frequently identified problem was the "comfort factor"—the men atop their corporations wanted others around them with whom they were comfortable, and that generally meant other men similar to themselves. One of the other most frequently identified problems, not unrelated to the comfort factor, was the exclusion from "the social networks—the clubs, the golf course—where the informal networking that is so important to moving up the ladder often takes place."

Based on the interviews they conducted for *Members of the Club*, Dawn-Marie Driscoll and Carol Goldberg also conclude that there is an important connection between golf and business. Both Driscoll and Goldberg have held directorships on major corporate boards. They establish their insider status at the beginning of their book: "We are both insiders. We always have been and probably always will be." In a section entitled

"The Link That Counts," they explain how they came to realize the importance of golf: "We heard so many stories about golf that we began to pay more attention to the interaction between golf and business. We realized the importance of golf had been right in front of our eyes all the time, but because neither of us played golf, we had missed it as an issue for executive women. But golf is central to many business circles."

A few months before Bill Clinton was elected president, his future secretary of energy had some pertinent comments about the importance of fitting into corporate culture and the relevance of playing golf. "Without losing your own personality," said Hazel O'Leary, then an executive vice president at Northern States Power in Minnesota, "it's important to be part of the prevailing corporate culture. At this company, it's golf. I've resisted learning to play golf all my life, but I finally had to admit I was missing something that way." She took up golf.

There is evidence that the golf anxiety expressed by women executives has its counterpart in the attitudes held by male executives: in its 1995 report, the Federal Glass Ceiling Commission found that many white male executives "fretted" that minorities and women did not know how to play golf.

Whether or not playing golf is necessary to fit in, it is clear that women who make it into the corporate elite must assimilate sufficiently into the predominantly male culture to make it into the comfort zone. As Kathleen Jamieson points out, however, this can place them in a double bind. On the one hand, women in the corporate world are expected to be competitive and tough-minded, but not too competitive or tough-minded, or they risk being called ballbusters. On the other hand, women in the corporate world are expected to be feminine enough to be seen as attractive and caring, but not too feminine, lest their appearance and behavior be seen as inappropriate or as an indication that they are tender-minded. . . .

Throughout the century, scholars have demonstrated that a disproportionate number of black professionals have been light skinned, and that blacks with darker skin are more likely to be discriminated against. Horace Mann Bond found, for example, that many "early Negro scholars" were "light-complexioned" individuals from families that had been part of the antebellum "free colored population" or born to "favored slaves." He explained their success in the following way: "The phenomenon was not due, as many believed, to the 'superiority' of the white blood; it was a social and economic, rather than a natural selection. Concubinage remained an openly sustained relationship between white men and Negro women in the South for fifty years after the Civil War; the children of such unions were more likely to have parents with the money, and the tradition, to send a child to school, than the former field hand slaves who were now sharecroppers and day laborers."

The authors of the Glass Ceiling Commission's report argue that "gradations in skin color" have continued to affect the career chances of men and women of color. They write,

Color-based differences are inescapable but nobody likes to talk about them. These are complicated differences because they are not exclusively racial and not exclusively ethnic. The unstated but ever-present question is, "*Do they look like us?*"

Though it is mostly covert, our society has developed an extremely sophisticated, and often denied, acceptability index based on gradations in skin color. It is not as simple a system as the black/white/colored classifications that were used in South Africa. It is not legally permissible, but it persists just beneath the surface, and it can be and is used as a basis for decision making, sometimes consciously and sometimes unconsciously. It is applied to African Americans, to American Indians, to Asian and Pacific Islander Americans, and to Hispanic Americans, who are described in a color shorthand of black, brown, yellow, and red. . . .

Colin Powell captured the essence of skin color's role in the broader context of not being too different from, and thus threatening to, whites. In a lengthy *New Yorker* profile, Henry Louis Gates Jr. asked Powell to explain polls that showed him having greater appeal among whites than among blacks. Powell, described by Gates as "light-skinned and blunt-featured," cut through sociological jargon and the need for statistical analyses:

One, I don't shove it in their face, you know? I don't bring any stereotypes or threatening visage to their presence. Some black people do. Two, I can overcome any stereotypes or reservations they have, because I perform well. Third thing is, *I ain't that black.* . . . I speak reasonably well, like a white person. I am very comfortable in a white social situation, and I don't go off in a corner. My features are clearly black, and I've never denied what I am. It fits into their general social setting, so they do not find me threatening. I think there's more to it than that, but I don't know what it is." . . .

The three blacks who have served in the U.S. Senate in modern times represent three eras. Indeed, if Edward Brooke, born in 1919, was a product of the old black middle class of the mid-twentieth century, and Carol Moseley-Braun, born in 1947, was a product of the race-conscious 1960s, Barack Obama, born in 1961, is a product of the increasingly biracial and bicultural world of the 1980s and 1990s. . . .

Barack Obama's mother, a white woman born in Kansas, met his father, a Kenyan, in 1959 when they were students at the University of

Hawaii. When Obama was a toddler, his father left Hawaii to do graduate work in economics at Harvard (the scholarship he won was not big enough to enable him to take his wife and son with him), and upon completing his doctoral degree, he returned to Africa.

His parents divorced, and a few years later, Obama's mother met and married an Indonesian. She and six-year-old Barack moved to Jakarta, where Barack lived for four years before returning to Hawaii to live with his maternal grandparents (his grandfather sold insurance and his grandmother worked in a bank).

Despite his family's middle-class background, he was accepted at Punahou Academy, Hawaii's most exclusive prep school. He began college at Occidental before transferring to Columbia, from which he graduated in 1983. After three years working in Chicago as a community organizer, he went to the Harvard Law School, where he became the first black editor of the *Harvard Law Review*. After graduating from law school in 1991, and before returning to Chicago, he spent a year working on the book that was to become *Dreams from My Father*, a memoir that describes his growing up in Hawaii and Indonesia and his search as a young adult to learn more about his father, his family in Kenya, and his own racial identity. He returned to Chicago, practiced civil rights law, and taught at the University of Chicago Law School. When the opportunity arose, he ran for and was elected to the state senate representing a district that included both Hyde Park (home of the university) and some of the most impoverished ghettos on the South Side.

Seven years after his election to the state senate, Obama burst upon the national scene in March 2004 when he beat six others to win the Democratic primary for Senate (he won 53 percent of the vote). The polls indicated that he was well ahead of Jack Ryan, his wealthy, white, Republican opponent, when a sex scandal led Ryan to withdraw from the race. The Illinois Republicans had a hard time finding someone to run against him, and, thus, with no opponent back in Illinois, in July 2004 Obama traveled to Boston to deliver an electrifying keynote address at the Democratic National Convention.

Finally, after various possible candidates turned them down, including former football coach Mike Ditka, the Illinois Republicans came up with Alan Keyes, a hard-core, right-wing, conservative African American who had been an unsuccessful candidate in many previous political races, even though he was a resident of Maryland and a few years earlier had railed against Hillary Clinton for running for the Senate in New York when she was not a resident of that state. When November rolled around, Barack Obama won a landslide victory, with 70 percent of the vote.

Obama is immensely popular with whites, in part, because he is so comfortable among them. As he said about the white voters from rural areas and small towns in Illinois, "I know those people. Those are my grandparents. The food they serve is the food my grandparents served when I was growing up. Their manners, their sensibility, their sense of right and wrong—it's all totally familiar to me."

Whites are also comfortable with him, in part for the same reasons they are comfortable with Colin Powell. His biracial and multicultural background (and his light skin) insulate him from the stereotypes they hold of African Americans, and, as a result, like Powell, he is perceived as nonthreatening. . . .

. . . [The] power elite and Congress are more diverse than they were before the civil rights movement and the social movements that followed in its train brought pressure to bear on corporations, politicians, and government. Although the power elite is still composed primarily of Christian, white men, there are now Jews, women, blacks, Latinos, and Asian Americans on the boards of the country's largest corporations; presidential cabinets are far more diverse than was the case fifty years ago; and the highest ranks of the military are no longer filled solely by white men. In the case of elected officials in Congress, the trend toward diversity is even greater for women and the other previously excluded groups that we have studied. At the same time, we have shown that the incorporation of members of the different groups has been uneven.

. . . [W]e look at the patterns that emerge from our specific findings to see if they help explain the gradual inclusion of some groups and the continuing exclusion of others. We also discuss the impact of diversity on the power elite and the rest of American society. We argue that most of the effects were unexpected and are ironic. The most important of these ironies relates to the ongoing tension between the American dream of individual advancement and fulfillment ("liberal individualism") and the class structure: we conclude that the racial, ethnic, and gender diversity celebrated by the power elite and the media actually reinforces the unchanging nature of the class structure and increases the tendency to ignore class inequalities. . . .

In what may be the greatest and most important irony of them all, the diversity forced upon the power elite may have helped to strengthen it. Diversity has given the power elite buffers, ambassadors, tokens, and legitimacy. This is an unintended consequence that few insurgents or social scientists foresaw. . . .

The black and white liberals and progressives who challenged Christian, white, male homogeneity in the power structure starting in the 1950s

and 1960s sought to do more than create civil rights and new job opportunities for men and women who had previously been mistreated and
excluded, important though these goals were. They also hoped that new
perspectives in the boardrooms and the halls of government would spread
greater openness throughout the society. The idea was both to diversify
the power elite and to shift some of its power to underrepresented groups
and social classes. The social movements of the 1960s were strikingly successful in increasing the individual rights and freedoms available to all
Americans, especially African Americans. As we have shown, they also
created pressures that led to openings at the top for individuals from
groups that had previously been ignored.

But as some individuals made it, and as the concerns of social movements, political leaders, and the courts gradually came to focus more and
more on individual rights and individual advancement, the focus on "dis-
tributive justice," general racial exclusion, and social class was lost. The
age-old American commitment to individualism, reinforced by tokenism
and reassurances from members of the power elite, won out over the
commitment to greater equality of income and wealth that had been one
strand of New Deal liberalism and a major emphasis of left-wing activism
in the 1960s.

We therefore conclude that the increased diversity in the power elite
has not generated any changes in an underlying class system in which the
top 1 percent of households (the upper class) own 33.4 percent of all mar-
ketable wealth, and the next 19 percent (the managerial, professional, and
small business stratum) have 51 percent, which means that just 20 percent
of the people own a remarkable 84 percent of the privately owned wealth
in the United States, leaving a mere 16 percent of the wealth for the bottom 80 percent (wage and salary workers)....

...These intertwined dilemmas of class and race lead to a nation that
celebrates individualism, equal opportunity, and diversity but is, in reality,
a bastion of class privilege, African American exclusion, and conservatism.

6

ROBERT DAHL

From *Who Governs?* and from
A Preface to Democratic Theory

In any city in the United States—like New Haven, Connecticut—as in the entire nation, political power is no longer in the hands of a few people as it once was early in American history. Nor is power spread evenly among all citizens. Influential political theorist Robert Dahl presents here the classic statement of pluralism: the dispersion of power among many groups of people. Dahl differentiates the "political stratum," made up of interested and involved citizens, from the "apolitical stratum," those who do not take an active part in government. These two segments of society are vastly different in their degree of involvement, yet they are closely tied together in many ways in a pluralist system. At least in theory, anyone can enter the political stratum where numerous interest groups compete and bargain for their goals. Public policy is made by "the steady appeasement of relatively small groups." Because of this "strange hybrid," Dahl contends, pluralism is the best way to describe how power is distributed in America.

IN A POLITICAL SYSTEM where nearly every adult may vote but where knowledge, wealth, social position, access to officials, and other resources are unequally distributed, who actually governs?

The question has been asked, I imagine, wherever popular government has developed and intelligent citizens have reached the stage of critical self-consciousness concerning their society. It must have been put many times in Athens even before it was posed by Plato and Aristotle.

The question is peculiarly relevant to the United States and to Americans. In the first place, Americans espouse democratic beliefs with a fervency and a unanimity that have been a regular source of astonishment to foreign observers . . . [such as] Tocqueville and Bryce. . . .

In the course of the past two centuries, New Haven has gradually changed from oligarchy to pluralism. Accompanying and probably causing this change—one might properly call it a revolution—appears to be a profound alteration in the way political resources are distributed among the citizens of New Haven. This silent socioeconomic revolution has not substituted equality for inequality so much as it has involved a shift from cumulative inequalities in political resources—to use an expression introduced a moment ago—to noncumulative or dispersed inequalities. This point will grow clearer as we proceed. . . .

In the political system of the patrician oligarchy, political resources were marked by a cumulative inequality: when one individual was much better off than another in one resource, such as wealth, he was usually better off in almost every other resource—social standing, legitimacy, control over religious and educational institutions, knowledge, office. In the political system of today, inequalities in political resources remain, but they tend to be *noncumulative.* The political system of New Haven, then, is one of *dispersed inequalities.* . . .

Within a century a political system dominated by one cohesive set of leaders had given way to a system dominated by many different sets of leaders, each having access to a different combination of political resources. It was, in short, a pluralist system. If the pluralist system was very far from being an oligarchy, it was also a long way from achieving the goal of political equality advocated by the philosophers of democracy and incorporated into the creed of democracy and equality practically every American professes to uphold.

An elite no longer rules New Haven. But in the strict democratic sense, the disappearance of elite rule has not led to the emergence of rule by the people. Who, then, rules in a pluralist democracy? . . .

One of the difficulties that confronts anyone who attempts to answer the question, "Who rules in a pluralist democracy?" is the ambiguous relationship of leaders to citizens.

Viewed from one position, leaders are enormously influential—so influential that if they are seen only in this perspective they might well be considered a kind of ruling elite. Viewed from another position, however, many influential leaders seem to be captives of their constituents. Like the blind men with the elephant, different analysts have meticulously examined different aspects of the body politic and arrived at radically different conclusions. To some, a pluralistic democracy with dispersed inequalities is all head and no body; to others it is all body and no head. . . .

Two additional factors help to account for this obscurity. First, among all the persons who influence a decision, some do so more directly than others in the sense that they are closer to the stage where concrete alternatives are initiated or vetoed in an explicit and immediate way. Indirect influence might be very great but comparatively difficult to observe and weigh. Yet to ignore indirect influence in analysis of the distribution of influence would be to exclude what might well prove to be a highly significant process of control in a pluralistic democracy.

Second, the relationship between leaders and citizens in a pluralistic democracy is frequently reciprocal: leaders influence the decisions of constituents, but the decisions of leaders are also determined in part by what they think are, will be, or have been the preferences of their constituents. Ordinarily it is much easier to observe and describe the distribution of influence in a political system where the flow of influence is strongly in one direction (an asymmetrical or unilateral system, as it is sometimes called) than in a system marked by strong reciprocal relations. In a political system with competitive elections, such as New Haven's, it is not unreasonable to expect that relationships between leaders and constituents would normally be reciprocal. . . .

In New Haven, as in other political systems, a small stratum of individuals is much more highly involved in political thought, discussion, and action than the rest of the population. These citizens constitute the political stratum.

Members of this stratum live in a political subculture that is partly but not wholly shared by the great majority of citizens. Just as artists and intellectuals are the principal bearers of the artistic, literary, and scientific skills of a society, so the members of the political stratum are the main bearers of political skills. If intellectuals were to vanish overnight, a society would be reduced to artistic, literary, and scientific poverty. If the political stratum were destroyed, the previous political institutions of the society would temporarily stop functioning. In both cases, the speed with which the loss could be overcome would depend on the extent to which the elementary knowledge and basic attitudes of the elite had been diffused. In an open society with widespread education and training in civic attitudes, many citizens hitherto in the apolitical strata could doubtless step into roles that had been filled by members of the political stratum. However, sharp discontinuities and important changes in the operation of the political system almost certainly would occur.

In New Haven, as in the United States, and indeed perhaps in all pluralistic democracies, differences in the subcultures of the political and the apolitical strata are marked, particularly at the extremes. In the political stratum, politics is highly salient; among the apolitical strata, it is remote. In the political stratum, individuals tend to be rather calculating in their choice of strategies; members of the political stratum are, in a sense, relatively rational political beings. In the apolitical strata, people are notably less calculating; their political choices are more strongly influenced by inertia, habit, unexamined loyalties, personal attachments, emotions, transient impulses. In the political stratum, an individual's political beliefs tend to fall into patterns that have a relatively high degree of coherence and internal consistency; in the apolitical strata, political orientations are disorganized, disconnected, and unideological. In the political stratum, information about politics and the issues of the day is extensive; the apolitical strata are poorly informed. Individuals in the political stratum tend to participate rather actively in politics; in the apolitical strata citizens rarely go beyond voting and many do not even vote. Individuals in the political stratum exert a good deal of steady, direct, and active influence on government policy; in fact some individuals have a quite extraordinary amount of influence. Individuals in the apolitical strata, on the other hand, have much less direct or active influence on policies.

Communication within the political stratum tends to be rapid and extensive. Members of the stratum read many of the same newspapers and magazines; in New Haven, for example, they are likely to read the *New York Times* or the *Herald Tribune*, and *Time* or *Newsweek*. Much information also passes by word of mouth. The political strata of different communities and regions are linked in a national network of communications. Even in small towns, one or two members of the local political stratum usually are in touch with members of a state organization, and certain members of the political stratum of a state or any large city maintain relations with members of organizations in other states and cities, or with national figures. Moreover, many channels of communication not designed specifically for political purposes—trade associations, professional associations, and labor organizations, for example—serve as a part of the network of the political stratum.

In many pluralistic systems, however, the political stratum is far from being a closed or static group. In the United States the political stratum does not constitute a homogeneous class with well-defined class interests. In New Haven, in fact, the political stratum is easily penetrated by anyone whose interests and concerns attract him to the distinctive political culture of the stratum. It is easily penetrated because (among other reasons) elections and competitive parties give politicians a powerful motive for expanding their coalitions and increasing their electoral followings.

In an open pluralistic system, where movement into the political stratum is easy, the stratum embodies many of the most widely shared values and goals in the society. If popular values are strongly pragmatic, then the political stratum is likely to be pragmatic; if popular values prescribe reverence toward the past, then the political stratum probably shares that reverence; if popular values are oriented toward material gain and personal advancement, then the political stratum probably reflects these values; if popular values are particularly favorable to political, social, or economic equality, then the political stratum is likely to emphasize equality. The apolitical strata can be said to "govern" as much through the sharing of common values and goals with members of the political stratum as by other means. However, if it were not for elections and competitive parties, this sharing would—other things remaining the same—rapidly decline.

Not only is the political stratum in New Haven not a closed group, but its "members" are far from united in their orientations and strategies. There are many lines of cleavage. . . .

Because of the ease with which the political stratum can be penetrated, whenever dissatisfaction builds up in some segment of the electorate party politicians will probably learn of the discontent and calculate whether it might be converted into a political issue with an electoral payoff. If a party politician sees no payoff, his interest is likely to be small; if he foresees an adverse effect, he will avoid the issue if he can. As a result, there is usually some conflict in the political stratum between intellectuals, experts, and others who formulate issues, and the party politicians themselves, for the first group often demands attention to issues in which the politicians see no profit and possibly even electoral damage.

The independence, penetrability, and heterogeneity of the various segments of the political stratum all but guarantee that any dissatisfied group will find spokesmen in the political stratum, but to have a spokesman does not insure that the group's problems will be solved by political action. Politicians may not see how they can gain by taking a position on an issue; action by government may seem to be wholly inappropriate; policies intended to cope with dissatisfaction may be blocked; solutions may be improperly designed; indeed, politicians may even find it politically profitable to maintain a shaky coalition by keeping tension and discontent alive and deflecting attention to irrelevant "solutions" or alternative issues. . . .

. . . In devising strategies for building coalitions and allocating rewards, one must take into account a large number of different categories of citizens. It would be dangerous to formulate strategies on the assumption that most or all citizens can be divided into two or three categories, for a successful political coalition necessarily rests upon a multiplicity of groups and categories. . . .*

. . . I defined the "normal" American political process as one in which there is a high probability that an active and legitimate group in the population can make itself heard effectively at some crucial stage in the process of decision. To be "heard" covers a wide range of activities, and I do

---

*At this point, the excerpt from *Who Governs?* ends, and the excerpt from *A Preface to Democratic Theory* begins.—EDS.

not intend to define the word rigorously. Clearly, it does not mean that every group has equal control over the outcome.

In American politics, as in all other societies, control over decisions is unevenly distributed; neither individuals nor groups are political equals. When I say that a group is heard "effectively" I mean more than the simple fact that it makes a noise; I mean that one or more officials are not only ready to listen to the noise, but expect to suffer in some significant way if they do not placate the group, its leaders, or its most vociferous members. To satisfy the group may require one or more of a great variety of actions by the responsive leader: pressure for substantive policies, appointments, graft, respect, expression of the appropriate emotions, or the right combination of reciprocal noises.

Thus the making of governmental decisions is not a majestic march of great majorities united upon certain matters of basic policy. It is the steady appeasement of relatively small groups. . . .

To be sure, reformers with a tidy sense of order dislike it. Foreign observers, even sympathetic ones, are often astonished and confounded by it. Many Americans are frequently dismayed by its paradoxes; indeed, few Americans who look upon our political process attentively can fail, at times, to feel deep frustration and angry resentment with a system that on the surface has so little order and so much chaos.

For it is a markedly decentralized system. Decisions are made by endless bargaining; perhaps in no other national political system in the world is bargaining so basic a component of the political process. In an age when the efficiencies of hierarchy have been re-emphasized on every continent, no doubt the normal American political system is something of an anomaly, if not, indeed, at times an anachronism. For as a means to highly integrated, consistent decisions in some important areas—foreign policy, for example—it often appears to operate in a creaking fashion verging on total collapse.

Yet we should not be too quick in our appraisal, for where its vices stand out, its virtues are concealed to the hasty eye. Luckily the normal system has the virtues of its vices. With all its defects, it does nonetheless provide a high probability that any active and legitimate group will make itself heard effectively at some stage in the process of decision. This is no mean thing in a political system.

It is not a static system. The normal American system has evolved, and by evolving it has survived. It has evolved and survived from aristocracy to mass democracy, through slavery, civil war, the tentative uneasy reconciliation of North and South, the repression of Negroes and their halting liberation; through two great wars of worldwide scope, mobilization, far-flung military enterprise, and return to hazardous peace; through numerous periods of economic instability and one prolonged depression with mass unemployment, farm "holidays," veterans' marches, tear gas, and even bullets; through two periods of postwar cynicism, demagogic excesses, invasions of traditional liberties, and the groping, awkward, often savage, attempt to cope with problems of subversion, fear, and civil tension.

Probably this strange hybrid, the normal American political system, is not for export to others. But so long as the social prerequisites of democracy are substantially intact in this country, it appears to be a relatively efficient system for reinforcing agreement, encouraging moderation, and maintaining social peace in a restless and immoderate people operating a gigantic, powerful, diversified, and incredibly complex society.

This is no negligible contribution, then, that Americans have made to the arts of government—and to that branch, which of all the arts of politics is the most difficult, the art of democratic government.

7

CORNEL WEST

From *Race Matters*

The opening pages of Professor Cornel West's book tell an unforgettable story of the pervasiveness of racism in the United States. Think about it the next time you wait for a taxi. Keep his words in mind when you recall the plight of many of the residents of New Orleans in the aftermath of Hurricane Katrina in 2005. Remember West's experience as you reflect on the 2014 and 2015 deaths of young African American men during encounters with the local police in Ferguson, Missouri, Staten Island, New York, Madison, Wisconsin, and Baltimore, Maryland. In an America that promises a chance for life, liberty, and the pursuit of happiness to all its citizens, "race matters," West contends. He challenges all Americans to change their thinking about race: the problems of African Americans are not their problems but American problems. West identifies the issues that threaten to disrupt the fabric of the nation—economic, social, political, spiritual—and he suggests a broad outline for solutions.

THIS PAST SEPTEMBER my wife, Elleni, and I made our biweekly trek to New York City from Princeton. I was in good spirits. My morning lecture on the first half of Plato's *Republic* in my European Cultural Studies course had gone well. And my afternoon lecture on W. E. B. Du Bois's *The Souls of Black Folk* in my Afro-American Cultural Studies course had left me exhausted yet exhilarated. Plato's powerful symbolism of Socrates' descent to the great port of Piraeus—the multicultural center of Greek trade and commerce and the stronghold of Athenian democracy—still rang in my ears. And Du Bois's prescient pronouncement—"The problem of the twentieth century is the problem of the color line"—haunted me. In a mysterious way, this classic twosome posed the most fundamental challenges to my basic aim in life: to speak the truth to power with love so that the quality of everyday life for ordinary people is enhanced and white supremacy is stripped of its authority and legitimacy. Plato's profound—yet unpersuasive—critique of Athenian democracy as inevitably corrupted by the ignorance and passions of the masses posed one challenge, and Du Bois's deep analysis of the intransigence of white supremacy in the American democratic experiment posed another.

As we approached Manhattan, my temperature rose, as it always does when I'm in a hurry near the Lincoln Tunnel. How rare it is that I miss the grinding gridlock—no matter the day or hour. But this time I drove right through and attributed my good luck to Elleni. As we entered the city, we pondered whether we would have enough time to stop at Sweetwater's (our favorite place to relax) after our appointments. I dropped my wife off for an appointment on 60th Street between Lexington and Park avenues. I left my car—a rather elegant one—in a safe parking lot and stood on the corner of 60th Street and Park Avenue to catch a taxi. I felt quite relaxed since I had an hour until my next engagement. At 5:00 P.M. I had to meet a photographer who would take the picture for the cover of this book on the roof of an apartment building in East Harlem on 115th Street and 1st Avenue. I waited and waited and waited. After the ninth taxi refused me, my blood began to boil. The tenth taxi refused me and stopped for a kind, well-dressed, smiling female fellow citizen of European descent. As she stepped in the cab, she said, "This is really ridiculous, is it not?"

Ugly racial memories of the past flashed through my mind. Years ago, while driving from New York to teach at Williams College, I was stopped on fake charges of trafficking cocaine. When I told the police officer I was a professor of religion, he replied "Yeh, and I'm the Flying Nun. Let's go, nigger!" I was stopped three times in my first ten days in Princeton for driving too slowly on a residential street with a speed limit of twenty-five miles per hour. (And my son, Clifton, already has similar memories at the tender age of fifteen.) Needless to say, these incidents are dwarfed by those like Rodney King's beating* or the abuse of black targets of the FBI's COINTELPRO† efforts in the 1960s and 1970s. Yet the memories cut like a merciless knife at my soul as I waited on that godforsaken corner. Finally I decided to take the subway. I walked three long avenues, arrived late, and had to catch my moral breath as I approached the white male photographer and white female cover designer. I chose not to dwell on this everyday experience of black New Yorkers. And we had a good time talking, posing, and taking pictures.

When I picked up Elleni, I told her of my hour spent on the corner,

*In 1992, four Los Angeles policemen were charged in criminal court with using unnecessary force in the arrest of Rodney King, a black man whom they had stopped while he was driving.—EDS.
†COINTELPRO was the FBI's "counterintelligence program," conducted over decades but most active in the 1960s. FBI Director J. Edgar Hoover used COINTELPRO to investigate and harass Americans whose activities were considered by the bureau to be subversive: socialist and communist sympathizers; anti-Vietnam War protestors; and especially, black citizens active in the civil rights movement. The press was instrumental in uncovering COINTELPRO's secret machinations in the mid-1970s.—EDS.

my tardy arrival, and the expertise and enthusiasm of the photographer and designer. We talked about our fantasy of moving to Addis Ababa, Ethiopia—her home and the site of the most pleasant event of my life. I toyed with the idea of attending the last day of the revival led by the Rev. Jeremiah Wright of Chicago at Rev. Wyatt T. Walker's Canaan Baptist Church of Christ in Harlem. But we settled for Sweetwater's. And the ugly memories faded in the face of soulful music, soulful food, and soulful folk.

As we rode back to Princeton, above the soothing black music of Van Harper's Quiet Storm on WBLS, 107.5 on the radio dial, we talked about what *race* matters have meant to the American past and of how much race *matters* in the American present. And I vowed to be more vigilant and virtuous in my efforts to meet the formidable challenges posed by Plato and Du Bois. For me, it is an urgent question of power and morality; for others, it is an everyday matter of life and death. . . .

What happened in Los Angeles in April of 1992 was neither a race riot nor a class rebellion.* Rather, this monumental upheaval was a multiracial, trans-class, and largely male display of justified social rage. For all its ugly, xenophobic resentment, its air of adolescent carnival, and its downright barbaric behavior, it signified the sense of powerlessness in American society. Glib attempts to reduce its meaning to the pathologies of the black underclass, the criminal actions of hoodlums, or the political revolt of the oppressed urban masses miss the mark. Of those arrested, only 36 percent were black, more than a third had full-time jobs, and most claimed to shun political affiliation. What we witnessed in Los Angeles was the consequence of a lethal linkage of economic decline, cultural decay, and political lethargy in American life. Race was the visible catalyst, not the underlying cause.

The meaning of the earthshaking events in Los Angeles is difficult to grasp because most of us remain trapped in the narrow framework of the dominant liberal and conservative views of race in America, which with its worn-out vocabulary leaves us intellectually debilitated, morally disempowered, and personally depressed. The astonishing disappearance of the event from public dialogue is testimony to just how painful and distressing a serious engagement with race is. Our truncated public discussions of race suppress the best of who and what we are as a people because they fail to confront the complexity of the issue in a candid and critical manner. The predictable pitting of liberals against conservatives, Great So-

---

*Rioting occurred in Los Angeles after a jury, made up of white citizens, acquitted the policemen who had been accused in the beating of Rodney King.—Eds.

ciety Democrats against self-help Republicans, reinforces intellectual parochialism and political paralysis.

The liberal notion that more government programs can solve racial problems is simplistic—precisely because it focuses *solely* on the economic dimension. And the conservative idea that what is needed is a change in the moral behavior of poor black urban dwellers (especially poor black men, who, they say, should stay married, support their children, and stop committing so much crime) highlights immoral actions while ignoring public responsibility for the immoral circumstances that haunt our fellow citizens.

The common denominator of these views of race is that each still sees black people as a "problem people," in the words of Dorothy I. Height, president of the National Council of Negro Women, rather than as fellow American citizens with problems. Her words echo the poignant "unasked question" of W. E. B. Du Bois, who, in *The Souls of Black Folk* (1903), wrote:

They approach me in a half-hesitant sort of way, eye me curiously or compassionately, and then instead of saying directly, How does it feel to be a problem? they say, I know an excellent colored man in my town. . . . Do not these Southern outrages make your blood boil? At these I smile, or am interested, or reduce the boiling to a simmer, as the occasion may require. To the real question, How does it feel to be a problem? I answer seldom a word.

Nearly a century later, we confine discussions about race in America to the "problems" black people pose for whites rather than consider what this way of viewing black people reveals about us as a nation.

This paralyzing framework encourages liberals to relieve their guilty consciences by supporting public funds directed at "the problems"; but at the same time, reluctant to exercise principled criticism of black people, liberals deny them the freedom to err. Similarly, conservatives blame the "problems" on black people themselves—and thereby render black social misery invisible or unworthy of public attention.

Hence, for liberals, black people are to be "included" and "integrated" into "our" society and culture, while for conservatives they are to be "well behaved" and "worthy of acceptance" by "our" way of life. Both fail to see that the presence and predicaments of black people are neither additions to nor defections from American life, but rather *constitutive elements of that life*.

To engage in a serious discussion of race in America, we must begin not with the problems of black people but with the flaws of American society—flaws rooted in historic inequalities and longstanding cultural stereotypes. How we set up the terms for discussing racial issues shapes our perception and response to these issues. As long as black people are viewed as a "them," the burden falls on blacks to do all the "cultural" and "moral" work necessary for healthy race relations. The implication is that only certain Americans can define what it means to be American—and the rest must simply "fit in."

The emergence of strong black-nationalist sentiments among blacks, especially among young people, is a revolt against this sense of having to "fit in." The variety of black-nationalist ideologies, from the moderate views of Supreme Court Justice Clarence Thomas in his youth to those of Louis Farrakhan today, rest upon a fundamental truth: white America has been historically weak-willed in ensuring racial justice and has continued to resist fully accepting the humanity of blacks. As long as double standards and differential treatment abound—as long as the rap performer Ice-T is harshly condemned while former Los Angeles Police Chief Daryl F. Gates's antiblack comments are received in polite silence, as long as Dr. Leonard Jeffries's anti-Semitic statements are met with vitriolic outrage while presidential candidate Patrick J. Buchanan's anti-Semitism receives a genteel response—black nationalisms will thrive.

Afrocentrism, a contemporary species of black nationalism, is a gallant yet misguided attempt to define an African identity in a white society perceived to be hostile. It is gallant because it puts black doings and sufferings, not white anxieties and fears, at the center of discussion. It is misguided because—out of fear of cultural hybridization and through silence on the issue of class, retrograde views on black women, gay men, and lesbians, and a reluctance to link race to the common good—it reinforces the narrow discussions about race.

To establish a new framework, we need to begin with a frank acknowledgment of the basic humanness and Americanness of each of us. And we must acknowledge that as a people—*E Pluribus Unum*—we are on a slippery slope toward economic strife, social turmoil, and cultural chaos. If we go down, we go down together. The Los Angeles upheaval forced us to see not only that we are not connected in ways we would like to be but also, in a more profound sense, that this failure to connect binds us even more tightly together. The paradox of race in America is that our common destiny is more pronounced and imperiled precisely when our divisions are deeper. The Civil War and its legacy speak loudly here. And our divisions are growing deeper. Today, eighty-six percent of white suburban Americans live in neighborhoods that are less than 1 percent black, meaning that the prospects for the country depend largely on how its cities fare in the hands of a suburban electorate. There is no escape from our interracial interdependence, yet enforced racial hierarchy dooms us as a nation to collective paranoia and hysteria—the unmaking of any democratic order.

The verdict in the Rodney King case which sparked the incidents in Los Angeles was perceived to be wrong by the vast majority of Americans. But whites have often failed to acknowledge the widespread mistreatment of black people, especially black men, by law enforcement agencies, which helped ignite the spark. The verdict was merely the occasion for deep-seated rage to come to the surface. This rage is fed by the "silent" depression ravaging the country—in which real weekly wages of all American workers since 1973 have declined nearly 20 percent, while at the same time wealth has been upwardly distributed.

The exodus of stable industrial jobs from urban centers to cheaper labor markets here and abroad, housing policies that have created "chocolate cities and vanilla suburbs" (to use the popular musical artist George Clinton's memorable phrase), white fear of black crime, and the urban influx of poor Spanish-speaking and Asian immigrants—all have helped erode the tax base of American cities just as the federal government has cut its supports and programs. The result is unemployment, hunger, homelessness, and sickness for millions.

And a pervasive spiritual impoverishment grows. The collapse of meaning in life—the eclipse of hope and absence of love of self and others, the breakdown of family and neighborhood bonds—leads to the social deracination and cultural denudement of urban dwellers, especially children. We have created rootless, dangling people with little link to the supportive networks—family, friends, school—that sustain some sense of purpose in life. We have witnessed the collapse of the spiritual communities that in the past helped Americans face despair, disease, and death and that transmit through the generations dignity and decency, excellence and elegance.

The result is lives of what we might call "random nows," of fortuitous and feeling moments preoccupied with "getting over"—with acquiring pleasure, property, and power by any means necessary. (This is not what Malcolm X meant by this famous phrase.) Post-modern culture is more and more a market culture dominated by gangster mentalities and self-destructive wantonness. This culture engulfs all of us—yet its impact on the disadvantaged is devastating, resulting in extreme violence in everyday life. Sexual violence against women and homicidal assaults by young black men on one another are only the most obvious signs of this empty quest for pleasure, property, and power.

Last, this rage is fueled by a political atmosphere in which images, not ideas, dominate, where politicians spend more time raising money than debating issues. The functions of parties have been displaced by public polls, and politicians behave less as thermostats that determine the climate of opinion than as thermometers registering the public mood. American politics has been rocked by an unleashing of greed among opportunistic public officials—who have followed the lead of their counterparts in the private sphere, where, as of 1989, 1 percent of the population owned 37 percent of the wealth and 10 percent of the population owned 86 percent of the wealth—leading to a profound cynicism and pessimism among the citizenry.

And given the way in which the Republican Party since 1968 has appealed to popular xenophobic images—playing the black, female, and homophobic cards to realign the electorate along race, sex, and sexual-orientation lines—it is no surprise that the notion that we are all part of one garment of destiny is discredited. Appeals to special interests rather than to public interests reinforce this polarization. The Los Angeles upheaval was an expression of utter fragmentation by a powerless citizenry that includes not just the poor but all of us.

What is to be done? How do we capture a new spirit and vision to meet the challenges of the post-industrial city, post-modern culture, and post-party politics?

First, we must admit that the most valuable sources for help, hope, and power consist of ourselves and our common history. As in the ages of Lincoln, Roosevelt, and King, we must look to new frameworks and languages to understand our multilayered crisis and overcome our deep malaise.

Second, we must focus our attention on the public square—the common good that undergirds our national and global destinies. The vitality of any public square ultimately depends on how much we *care* about the quality of our lives together. The neglect of our public infrastructure, for example—our water and sewage systems, bridges, tunnels, highways, subways, and streets—reflects not only our myopic economic policies, which impede productivity, but also the low priority we place on our common life.

The tragic plight of our children clearly reveals our deep disregard for public well-being. About one out of every five children in this country lives in poverty, including one out of every two black children and two out of every five Hispanic children. Most of our children—neglected by overburdened parents and bombarded by the market values of profit-hungry corporations—are ill-equipped to live lives of spiritual and cultural quality. Faced with these facts, how do we expect ever to constitute a vibrant society?

One essential step is some form of large-scale public intervention to ensure access to basic social goods—housing, food, health care, education, child care, and jobs. We must invigorate the common good with a mixture of government, business, and labor that does not follow any existing blueprint. After a period in which the private sphere has been sacralized and the public square gutted, the temptation is to make a fetish of the public square. We need to resist such dogmatic swings.

Last, the major challenge is to meet the need to generate new leadership. The paucity of courageous leaders—so apparent in the response to the events in Los Angeles—requires that we look beyond the same elites and voices that recycle the older frameworks. We need leaders—neither saints nor sparkling television personalities—who can situate themselves within a larger historical narrative of this country and our world, who can grasp the complex dynamics of our peoplehood and imagine a future grounded in the best of our past, yet who are attuned to the frightening obstacles that now perplex us. Our ideals of freedom, democracy, and equality must be invoked to invigorate all of us, especially the landless, propertyless, and luckless. Only a visionary leadership that can motivate "the better angels of our nature," as Lincoln said, and activate possibilities for a freer, more efficient, and stable America—only that leadership deserves cultivation and support.

This new leadership must be grounded in grass-roots organizing that highlights democratic accountability. Whoever *our* leaders will be as we approach the twenty-first century, their challenge will be to help Americans determine whether a genuine multiracial democracy can be created and sustained in an era of global economy and a moment of xenophobic frenzy.

Let us hope and pray that the vast intelligence, imagination, humor, and courage of Americans will not fail us. Either we learn a new language of empathy and compassion, or the fire this time will consume us all.*

---

*In *The Fire Next Time* (1963), African-American writer James Baldwin quotes a black slave's prophecy, found in a song recreated from the Bible, "God gave Noah the rainbow sign, no more water, the fire next time!"—Eds.

8

MICHAEL KAMMEN

From *People of Paradox*

Thinking about the United States, its history, culture, and politics, as a paradox is one of the most useful ways to tie together all the themes and facts in American government. Historian Michael Kammen offers a some-times-fanciful, sometimes-profound analysis of the many paradoxes that riddle American life. Citizens expect their leaders to be "Everyman and Superman," he perceptively observes. Kammen takes on the difficult issue of the American melting pot; he substitutes the metaphor of a "super-highway" to explain nicely the country and its people. He points out paradoxes in all aspects of American life, ending with a poetic vision of the super-highway, along the side of the road, at Thanksgiving. Many scholars and thinkers are quoted in Kammen's piece, but his top source opens the selection: "We have met the enemy and he is us," cartoon character Pogo recognizes.

———

We have met the enemy and he is us.

—Pogo

. . . OUR INHERITANCE has indeed been bitter-sweet, and our difficulty in assessing it just now arises from the fact that American institutions have had too many uncritical lovers and too many unloving critics. We have managed to graft pride onto guilt—guilt over social injustice and abuses of power—and find that pride and guilt do not neutralize each other, but make many decisions seem questionable, motives suspect, and consciences troubled.

Perhaps so many American shibboleths seem to generate their very opposites because they are often half-truths rather than the wholesome verities we believe them to be. Perhaps we ought to recall Alice in Wonderland playing croquet against herself, "for this curious child was very fond of pretending to be two people. 'But it's no use now,' thought poor Alice, 'to pretend to be two people! Why, there's hardly enough of me left to make one respectable person!'" . . .

This dualistic state of mind may be found also in the domestic political values subscribed to by most Americans. We are comfortable believing in both majority rule and minority rights, in both consensus and freedom, federalism and centralization. It may be perfectly reasonable to support majority rule with reservations, or minority rights with certain other reservations. But this has not been our method. Rather, we have tended to hold contradictory ideas in suspension and ignore the intellectual and behavioral consequences of such "doublethink." . . .

Americans have managed to be both puritanical and hedonistic, idealistic and materialistic, peace-loving and war-mongering, isolationist and interventionist, conformist and individualist, consensus-minded and conflict-prone. "We recognize the American," wrote Gunnar Myrdal in 1944, "wherever we meet him, as a practical idealist." . . .

Americans expect their heroes to be Everyman and Superman simultaneously. I once overheard on an airplane the following fragment of conversation: "He has none of the virtues I respect, and none of the vices I admire." We cherish the humanity of our past leaders: George Washington's false teeth and whimsical orthography, Benjamin Franklin's lechery and cunning. The quintessential American hero wears both a halo *and* horns.

Because our society is so pluralistic, the American politician must be all things to all people. Dwight Eisenhower represented the most advanced industrial nation, but his chief appeal rested in a naive simplicity which recalled our pre-industrial past. Robert Frost once advised President Kennedy to be as much an Irishman as a Harvard man: "You have to have both the pragmatism and the idealism." The ambivalent American is ambitious and ambidextrous; but the appearance of ambidexterity—to some, at least—suggests the danger of double-dealing and deceit. The story is told of a U.S. senator meeting the press one Sunday afternoon. "How do you stand on conservation, Senator?" asked one panelist. The senator squirmed. "Well, I'll tell you," he said. "Some of my constituents are for conservation, and some of my constituents are against conservation, and I stand foresquare behind my constituents." . . .

Raymond Aron, the French sociologist, has remarked that a "dialectic of plurality and conformism lies at the core of American life, making for the originality of the social structure, and raising the most contradictory evaluations." Americans have repeatedly reaffirmed the social philosophy of individualism, even making it the basis of their political thought. Yet they have been a nation of joiners and have developed the largest associations and corporations the world has ever known. Nor has American respect for the abstract "individual" always guaranteed respect for particular persons.

There is a persistent tension between authoritarianism and individualism in American history. The genius of American institutions at their

best has been to find a place and a use for both innovators and consolida-
tors, rebellious dreamers and realistic adjudicators. "America has been
built on a mixture of discipline and rebellion," writes Christopher Jencks,
"but the balance between them has constantly shifted over the years." Our
individualism, therefore, has been of a particular sort, a collective individualism. Individuality is not synonymous in the United States with singu-
larity. When Americans develop an oddity they make a fad of it so that
they may be comfortable among familiar oddities. Their unity, as Emerson
wrote in his essay on the New England Reformers, "is only perfect when
all the uniters are isolated."

How then can we adequately summarize the buried historical roots of
our paradoxes, tensions, and biformities? The incongruities in American
life are not merely fortuitous, and their stimuli appear from the very beginning. "America was always promises," as Archibald MacLeish has put it.
"From the first voyage and the first ship there were promises." Many of
these have gone unfulfilled—an endless source of ambiguity and equivo-
cation. . . .

Above all other factors, however, the greatest source of dualisms in
American life has been unstable pluralism in all its manifold forms: cultural, social, sequential, and political. *E pluribus unum* is a misbegotten
motto because we have *not* become one out of many. The myth of the
melting pot is precisely that: a myth. Moreover, our constitutional system
seems to foster fragmentation of power while our economic-technologi-
cal system seems to encourage consolidation of power. Thus the imperatives of pluralism under conditions of large-scale technology commonly
conflict with principles and practices of constitutional democracy. . . .

It has been the impulse of our egalitarianism to make all men American and alike, but the thrust of our social order and intolerance to accen-
tuate differences among groups. We have achieved expertise at both xeno-
phobia and self-hate! At several stages of our history, population growth
has outstripped institutional change. The result in many cases has been
violence, vigilante movements, or economic unrest, all with the special
coloration of unstable pluralism. Because there are significant variations in
state laws regulating economic enterprise, taxation, and welfare payments,
people and corporations move to tax-sheltered states and to those with
the most generous welfare provisions. In this way mobility becomes a
function of pluralism.

I do not argue that pluralism is a peculiarly American phenomenon.
But I do believe that unstable pluralism on a scale of unprecedented proportion is especially American. . . .

There is a sense in which the super-highway is the most appropriate

American metaphor. We have vast and anonymous numbers of people rushing individually (but simultaneously) in opposite directions. In between lies a no-man's-land, usually landscaped with a barrier of shrubs and trees, so that we cannot see the road to Elsewhere, but cannot easily turn back either. Indeed, the American experience in some spheres has moved from unity to diversity (e.g., denominationalism), while in other areas it has flowed in the opposite direction, from diversity to unity (e.g., political institutions). Along both roads we have paused from time to time in order to pay substantially for the privilege of traveling these thoroughfares.

There have always been Americans aware of unresolved contradictions between creed and reality, disturbed by the performance of their system and culture. Told how much liberty they enjoy, they feel less free; told how much equality they enjoy, they feel less equal; told how much progress they enjoy, their environment seems even more out of control. Most of all, told that they should be happy, they sense a steady growth in American unhappiness. Conflicts *between* Americans have been visible for a very long time, but most of us are just beginning to perceive the conflicts *within* us individually.

It is a consequence of some concern that our ambiguities often appear to the wider world as malicious hypocrisies. As when we vacillate, for example, between our missionary impulse and our isolationist instinct. From time to time we recognize that the needs of national security and the furtherance of national ideals may both be served by our vigorous but restrained participation in world affairs. At other times these two desiderata tug in opposite directions. However much we desperately want to be understood, we are too often misunderstood. . . .

Because of our ambivalent ambiance, we are frequently indecisive. "I cannot be a crusader," remarked Ralph McGill, "because I have been cursed all my life with the ability to see both sides." Our experience with polarities provides us with the potential for flexibility and diversity; yet too often it chills us into sheer inaction, or into contradictory appraisals of our own designs and historical development. Often we are willing to split the difference and seek consensus. "It is this intolerable paradox," James Reston writes, "of being caught between the unimaginable achievements of men when they cooperate for common goals, and their spectacular failures when they divide on how to achieve the simple decencies of life, that creates the present atmosphere of division and confusion." . . .

We have reached a moment in time when the national condition seems neither lifeless nor deathless. It's like the barren but sensuous serenity of the natural world in late autumn, before Thanksgiving, containing the promise of rebirth and the potential for resurrection. On bare branches whose leaves have fallen, buds bulge visibly in preparation for spring. Along the roadside, goldenrod stands sere and grizzled, and the leafless milkweed with its goosehead pods strews fluff and floss to every breeze, thereby seeding the countryside with frail fertility. The litter of autumn becomes the mulch, and then the humus, for roots and tender seeds. So it was, so it has been, and so it will be with the growth of American Civilization.

9

ROBERT BELLAH/OTHERS

From *Habits of the Heart*

American ideology touches more than just government and politics. It also guides the nation's social, economic, religious, and cultural life. It is fitting, therefore, that an important comment on American ideology comes from the discipline of sociology. Robert Bellah and his colleagues borrow Alexis de Tocqueville's phrase "habits of the heart" to explore the place of individualism in American life. The authors concede that individualism is the single most important ingredient in the nation's values, illustrating it with the symbol of cowboy-heroes Shane and the Lone Ranger. But, they contend, individualism cannot exist without being balanced by a sense of community.

INDIVIDUALISM LIES AT THE VERY CORE of American culture. Every one of the four traditions we have singled out is in a profound sense individualistic. There is a biblical individualism and a civic individualism as well as a utilitarian and an expressive individualism. Whatever the differences among the traditions and the consequent differences in their understandings of individualism, there are some things they all share, things that are basic to American identity. We believe in the dignity, indeed the sacredness, of the individual. Anything that would violate our right to think for ourselves, judge for ourselves, make our own decisions, live our lives as we see fit, is not only morally wrong, it is sacrilegious. Our highest and noblest aspirations, not only for ourselves, but for those we care about, for our society and for the world, are closely linked to our individualism. Yet, as we have been suggesting repeatedly in this book, some of our deepest problems both as individuals and as a society are also closely linked to our individualism. We do not argue that Americans should abandon individualism—that would mean for us to abandon our deepest identity. But individualism has come to mean so many things and to contain such contradictions and paradoxes that even to defend it requires that we analyze it critically, that we consider especially those tendencies that would destroy it from within. . . .

The question is whether an individualism in which the self has become the main form of reality can really be sustained. What is at issue is not simply whether self-contained individuals might withdraw from the public sphere to pursue purely private ends, but whether such individuals are capable of sustaining either a public *or* a private life. If this is the danger, perhaps only the civic and biblical forms of individualism—forms that see the individual in relation to a larger whole, a community and a tradition—are capable of sustaining genuine individuality and nurturing both public and private life. . . .

America is also the inventor of that most mythic individual hero, the cowboy, who again and again saves a society he can never completely fit into. The cowboy has a special talent—he can shoot straighter and faster than other men—and a special sense of justice. But these characteristics make him so unique that he can never fully belong to society. His destiny is to defend society without ever really joining it. He rides off alone into the sunset like Shane,* or like the Lone Ranger moves on accompanied only by his Indian companion. But the cowboy's importance is not that he is isolated or antisocial. Rather, his significance lies in his unique, individual virtue and special skill and it is because of those qualities that society needs and welcomes him. Shane, after all, starts as a real outsider, but ends up with the gratitude of the community and the love of a woman and a boy. And while the Lone Ranger never settles down and marries the local schoolteacher, he always leaves with the affection and gratitude of the people he has helped. It is as if the myth says you can be a truly good person, worthy of admiration and love, only if you resist fully joining the group. But sometimes the tension leads to an irreparable break. Will Kane, the hero of *High Noon*, abandoned by the cowardly townspeople, saves them from an unrestrained killer, but then throws his sheriff's badge in the dust and goes off into the desert with his bride. One is left wondering where they will go, for there is no longer any link with any town. . . .

[T]he cowboy . . . tell[s] us something important about American individualism. The cowboy . . . can be valuable to society only because he is a completely autonomous individual who stands outside it. To serve society, one must be able to stand alone, not needing others, not depending on their judgment, and not submitting to their wishes. Yet this individualism is not selfishness. Indeed, it is a kind of heroic selflessness. One accepts the necessity of remaining alone in order to serve the values of the group. And this obligation to aloneness is an important key to the American moral imagination. Yet it is part of the profound ambiguity of the mythology of American individualism that its moral heroism is always just a step away from despair. . . .

. . . The inner tensions of American individualism add up to a classic case of ambivalence. We strongly assert the value of our self-reliance and

---

*Shane is the gunfighter-hero of the 1953 western film *Shane*.—Eds.

autonomy. We deeply feel the emptiness of a life without sustaining social commitments. Yet we are hesitant to articulate our sense that we need one another as much as we need to stand alone, for fear that if we did we would lose our independence altogether. The tensions of our lives would be even greater if we did not, in fact, engage in practices that constantly limit the effects of an isolating individualism, even though we cannot articulate those practices nearly as well as we can the quest for autonomy. . . .

. . . It is now time to consider what a self that is not empty would be like—one that is constituted rather than unencumbered, one that has, let us admit it, encumbrances, but whose encumbrances make connection to others easier and more natural. Just as the empty self makes sense in a particular institutional context—that of the upward mobility of the middle-class individual who must leave home and church in order to succeed in an impersonal world of rationality and competition—so a constituted self makes sense in terms of another institutional context, what we would call, in the full sense of the world, community.

Communities, in the sense in which we are using the term, have a history—in an important sense they are constituted by their past—and for this reason we can speak of a real community as a "community of memory," one that does not forget its past. In order not to forget that past, a community is involved in retelling its story, its constitutive narrative, and in so doing, it offers examples of the men and women who have embodied and exemplified the meaning of the community. These stories of collective history and exemplary individuals are an important part of the tradition that is so central to a community of memory. . . .

Examples of such genuine communities are not hard to find in the United States. There are ethnic and racial communities, each with its own story and its own heroes and heroines. There are religious communities that recall and reenact their stories in the weekly and annual cycles of their ritual year, remembering the scriptural stories that tell them who they are and the saints and martyrs who define their identity. There is the national community, defined by its history and by the character of its representative leaders from [early colonist] John Winthrop to [civil rights leader] Martin Luther King, Jr. Americans identify with their national community partly because there is little else that we all share in common but also partly because America's history exemplifies aspirations widely shared throughout the world: the ideal of a free society, respecting all its citizens, however diverse, and allowing them all to fulfill themselves. Yet some Americans also remember the history of suffering inflicted and the gap between promise and realization, which has always been very great. At some times, neighborhoods, localities, and regions have been communities in America, but that has been hard to sustain in our restless and mobile society. Families can be communities, remembering their past, telling the children the stories of parents' and grandparents' lives, and sustaining hope for the future—though without the context of a larger community that sense of family is hard to maintain. Where history and hope are forgotten and community means only the gathering of the similar, community degenerates into lifestyle enclave. The temptation toward that transformation is endemic in America, though the transition is seldom complete.

People growing up in communities of memory not only hear the stories that tell how the community came to be, what its hopes and fears are, and how its ideals are exemplified in outstanding men and women; they also participate in the practices—ritual, aesthetic, ethical—that define the community as a way of life. We call these "practices of commitment" for they define the patterns of loyalty and obligation that keep the community alive. And if the language of the self-reliant individual is the first language of American moral life, the languages of tradition and commitment in communities of memory are "second languages" that most Americans know as well, and which they use when the language of the radically separate self does not seem adequate. . . . Sometimes Americans make a rather sharp dichotomy between private and public life. Viewing one's primary task as "finding oneself" in autonomous self-reliance, separating oneself not only from one's parents but also from those larger communities and traditions that constitute one's past, leads to the notion that it is in oneself, perhaps in relation to a few intimate others, that fulfillment is to be found. Individualism of this sort often implies a negative view of public life. The impersonal forces of the economic and political worlds are what the individual needs protection against. In this perspective, even occupation, which has been so central to the identity of Americans in the past, becomes instrumental—not a good in itself, but only a means to the attainment of a rich and satisfying private life. But on the basis of what we have seen in our observation of middle-class American life, it would seem that this quest for purely private fulfillment is illusory: it often ends in emptiness instead. On the other hand, we found many people . . . for whom private fulfillment and public involvement are not antithetical. These people evince an individualism that is not empty but is full of content drawn from an active identification with communities and traditions. Perhaps the notion that private life and public life are at odds is incorrect. Perhaps they are so deeply involved with each other that the impoverishment of one entails the impoverishment of the other. Parker Palmer is probably right when he says that "in a healthy society the private and the public are not mutually exclusive, not in competition with each other. They are, instead, two halves of a whole, two poles of a paradox. They work together dialectically, helping to create and nurture one another."

Certainly this dialectical relationship is clear where public life degenerates into violence and fear. One cannot live a rich private life in a state of siege, mistrusting all strangers and turning one's home into an armed camp. A minimum of public decency and civility is a precondition for a fulfilling private life. On the other hand, public involvement is often difficult and demanding. To engage successfully in the public world, one needs personal strength and the support of family and friends. A rewarding private life is one of the preconditions for a healthy public life.

For all their doubts about the public sphere, Americans are more engaged in voluntary associations and civic organizations than the citizens of most other industrial nations. In spite of all the difficulties, many Americans feel they must "get involved." In public life as in private, we can discern the habits of the heart that sustain individualism and commitment, as well as what makes them problematic. . . .

The communities of memory of which we have spoken are concerned in a variety of ways to give a qualitative meaning to the living of life, to time and space, to persons and groups. Religious communities, for example, do not experience time in the way the mass media present it—as a continuous flow of qualitatively meaningless sensations. The day, the week, the season, the year are punctuated by an alternation of the sacred and the profane. Prayer breaks into our daily life at the beginning of a meal, at the end of the day, at common worship, reminding us that our utilitarian pursuits are not the whole of life, that a fulfilled life is one in which God and neighbor are remembered first. Many of our religious traditions recognize the significance of silence as a way of breaking the incessant flow of sensations and opening our hearts to the wholeness of being. And our republican tradition, too, has ways of giving form to time, reminding us on particular dates of the great events of our past or of the heroes who helped to teach us what we are as a free people. Even our private family life takes on a shared rhythm with a Thanksgiving dinner or a Fourth of July picnic.

In short, we have never been, and still are not, a collection of private individuals who, except for a conscious contract to create a minimal government, have nothing in common. Our lives make sense in a thousand ways, most of which we are unaware of, because of traditions that are centuries, if not millennia, old. It is these traditions that help us to know that it does make a difference who we are and how we treat one another.

PART TWO

The Constitution, Democracy, and Separation of Powers

10

JAMES MADISON

From *The Federalist 10* and *51*

This is the most important reading in an American government class. Federalist 10 and 51 are the first and last word on U.S. government and politics. In Federalist 10, *James Madison first takes up the idea of "faction," by which he means any single group (especially the mob-like majority, but perhaps even a tiny minority) that tries to dominate the political process. Can faction be removed from politics? No, he admits, for a variety of reasons that deeply illuminate his assessment of the American people. But faction can be controlled by a republican (representative) system. Madison favored a large and diverse nation; if there were many groups, no one faction would ever be able to dominate. In* Federalist 51, *he continues, citing the structural features that characterize American government. Power will be separated among different departments, or branches, of government, independent from one another. Power will be divided between the national and state levels, a system called federalism.*

Signing these papers "Publius," Madison, along with Alexander Hamilton and John Jay, wrote eighty-five essays collectively known as The Federalist Papers, *which were published in several New York newspapers on behalf of the ratification of the new Constitution in 1787. Madison's genius is revealed not only in the workable system of government he helped create for America, but also in his vision of the United States in the future, very much as it is today. His overall philosophy of government is here too, surprising as it might be upon an initial reading: "Ambition must be made to counteract ambition." Don't miss that paragraph, since it contains warnings that resonate across the centuries.*

No. 10: Madison

AMONG THE NUMEROUS ADVANTAGES promised by a well-constructed Union, none deserves to be more accurately developed than its tendency to break and control the violence of faction. The friend of popular governments never finds himself so much alarmed for their character and fate as when he contemplates their propensity to this dangerous vice. He will not fail, therefore, to set a due value on any plan which, without violating the principles to which he is attached, provides a proper cure for it. The instability, injustice, and confusion introduced into the public councils have, in truth, been the mortal diseases under which popular governments have everywhere perished, as they continue to be the favorite and fruitful topics from which the adversaries to liberty derive their most specious declamations. The valuable improvements made by the American constitutions on the popular models, both ancient and modern, cannot certainly be too much admired; but it would be an unwarrantable partiality to contend that they have as effectually obviated the danger on this side, as was wished and expected. Complaints are everywhere heard from our most considerate and virtuous citizens, equally the friends of public and private faith and of public and personal liberty, that our governments are too unstable, that the public good is disregarded in the conflicts of rival parties, and that measures are too often decided, not according to the rules of justice and the rights of the minor party, but by the superior force of an interested and overbearing majority. However anxiously we may wish that these complaints had no foundation, the evidence of known facts will not permit us to deny that they are in some degree true. It will be found, indeed, on a candid review of our situation, that some of the distresses under which we labor have been erroneously charged on the operation of our governments; but it will be found, at the same time, that other causes will not alone account for many of our heaviest misfortunes; and, particularly, for that prevailing and increasing distrust of public engagements and alarm for private rights which are echoed from one end of the continent to the other. These must be chiefly, if not wholly, effects of the unsteadiness and injustice with which a factious spirit has tainted our public administration.

By a faction I understand a number of citizens, whether amounting to a majority or minority of the whole, who are united and actuated by some common impulse of passion, or of interest, adverse to the rights of other citizens, or to the permanent and aggregate interests of the community.

There are two methods of curing the mischiefs of faction: the one, by removing its causes; the other, by controlling its effects.

There are again two methods of removing the causes of faction: the one, by destroying the liberty which is essential to its existence; the other, by giving to every citizen the same opinions, the same passions, and the same interests.

It could never be more truly said than of the first remedy that it was worse than the disease. Liberty is to faction what air is to fire, an aliment without which it instantly expires. But it could not be a less folly to abolish liberty, which is essential to political life, because it nourishes faction than it would be to wish the annihilation of air, which is essential to animal life, because it imparts to fire its destructive agency. The second expedient is as impracticable as the first would be unwise. As long as the reason of man continues fallible, and he is at liberty to exercise it, different opinions will be formed. As long as the connection subsists between his reason and his self-love, his opinions and his passions will have a reciprocal influence on each other; and the former will be objects to which the latter will attach themselves. The diversity in the faculties of men, from which the rights of property originate, is not less an insuperable obstacle to a uniformity of interests. The protection of these faculties is the first object of government. From the protection of different and unequal faculties of acquiring property, the possession of different degrees and kinds of property immediately results; and from the influence of these on the sentiments and views of the respective proprietors ensues a division of the society into different interests and parties.

The latent causes of faction are thus sown in the nature of man; and we see them everywhere brought into different degrees of activity, according to the different circumstances of civil society. A zeal for different opinions concerning religion, concerning government, and many other points, as well of speculation as of practice; an attachment to different leaders ambitiously contending for pre-eminence and power; or to persons of other descriptions whose fortunes have been interesting to the human passions, have, in turn, divided mankind into parties, inflamed them with mutual animosity, and rendered them much more disposed to vex and oppress each other than to co-operate for their common good. So strong is this propensity of mankind to fall into mutual animosities that where no substantial occasion presents itself the most frivolous and fanciful distinctions have been sufficient to kindle their unfriendly passions and excite their most violent conflicts. But the most common and durable source of factions has been the various and unequal distribution of property. Those who hold and those who are without property have ever formed distinct interests in society. Those who are creditors, and those who are debtors, fall under a like discrimination. A landed interest, a manufacturing interest, a mercantile interest, a moneyed interest, with many lesser interests, grow up of necessity in civilized nations, and divide them into different classes, actuated by different sentiments and views. The regulation of these various and interfering interests forms the principal task of modern legislation and involves the spirit of party and faction in the necessary and ordinary operations of government.

No man is allowed to be a judge in his own cause, because his interest would certainly bias his judgment, and, not improbably, corrupt his integrity. With equal, nay with greater reason, a body of men are unfit to be both judges and parties at the same time; yet what are many of the most important acts of legislation but so many judicial determinations, not indeed concerning the rights of single persons, but concerning the rights of large bodies of citizens? And what are the different classes of legislators but advocates and parties to the causes which they determine? Is a law proposed concerning private debts? It is a question to which the creditors are parties on one side and the debtors on the other. Justice ought to hold the balance between them. Yet the parties are, and must be, themselves the judges; and the most numerous party, or in other words, the most powerful faction must be expected to prevail. Shall domestic manufacturers be encouraged, and in what degree, by restrictions on foreign manufacturers? are questions which would be differently decided by the landed and the manufacturing classes, and probably by neither with a sole regard to justice and the public good. The apportionment of taxes on the various descriptions of property is an act which seems to require the most exact impartiality; yet there is, perhaps, no legislative act in which greater opportunity and temptation are given to a predominant party to trample on the rules of justice. Every shilling with which they overburden the inferior number is a shilling saved to their own pockets.

It is in vain to say that enlightened statesmen will be able to adjust these clashing interests and render them all subservient to the public good. Enlightened statesmen will not always be at the helm. Nor, in many cases, can such an adjustment be made at all without taking into view indirect and remote considerations, which will rarely prevail over the immediate interest which one party may find in disregarding the rights of another or the good of the whole.

The inference to which we are brought is that the *causes* of faction cannot be removed and that relief is only to be sought in the means of controlling its *effects*.

If a faction consists of less than a majority, relief is supplied by the republican principle, which enables the majority to defeat its sinister views by regular vote. It may clog the administration, it may convulse the society; but it will be unable to execute and mask its violence under the forms of the Constitution. When a majority is included in a faction, the form of popular government, on the other hand, enables it to sacrifice to its ruling passion or interest both the public good and the rights of other citizens. To secure the public good and private rights against the danger of such a faction, and at the same time to preserve the spirit and the form of popular government, is then the great object to which our inquiries are directed. Let me add that it is the great desideratum by which alone this form of government can be rescued from the opprobrium under which it has so long labored and be recommended to the esteem and adoption of mankind.

By what means is this object attainable? Evidently by one of two only. Either the existence of the same passion or interest in a majority at the same time must be prevented, or the majority, having such coexistent passion or interest, must be rendered, by their number and local situation, unable to concert and carry into effect schemes of oppression. If the impulse and the opportunity be suffered to coincide, we well know that neither moral nor religious motives can be relied on as an adequate control. They are not found to be such on the injustice and violence of individuals, and lose their efficacy in proportion to the number combined together, that is, in proportion as their efficacy becomes needful.

From this view of the subject it may be concluded that a pure democracy, by which I mean a society consisting of a small number of citizens, who assemble and administer the government in person, can admit of no cure for the mischiefs of faction. A common passion or interest will, in almost every case, be felt by a majority of the whole; a communication and concert results from the form of government itself; and there is nothing to check the inducements to sacrifice the weaker party or an obnoxious individual. Hence it is that such democracies have ever been spectacles of turbulence and contention; have ever been found incompatible with personal security or the rights of property; and have in general been as short in their lives as they have been violent in their deaths. Theoretic politicians, who have patronized this species of government, have erroneously supposed that by reducing mankind to a perfect equality in their political rights, they would at the same time be perfectly equalized and assimilated in their possessions, their opinions, and their passions.

A republic, by which I mean a government in which the scheme of representation takes place, opens a different prospect and promises the cure for which we are seeking. Let us examine the points in which it varies from pure democracy, and we shall comprehend both the nature of the cure and the efficacy which it must derive from the Union.

The two great points of difference between a democracy and a republic are: first, the delegation of the government, in the latter, to a small number of citizens elected by the rest; secondly, the greater number of citizens and greater sphere of country over which the latter may be extended.

The effect of the first difference is, on the one hand, to refine and enlarge the public views by passing them through the medium of a chosen body of citizens, whose wisdom may best discern the true interest of their country and whose patriotism and love of justice will be least likely to sacrifice it to temporary or partial considerations. Under such a regulation it may well happen that the public voice, pronounced by the representatives of the people, will be more consonant to the public good than if pronounced by the people themselves, convened for the purpose. On the other hand, the effect may be inverted. Men of factious tempers, of local prejudices, or of sinister designs, may, by intrigue, by corruption, or by other means, first obtain the suffrages, and then betray the interests of the people. The question resulting is, whether small or extensive republics are most favorable to the election of proper guardians of the public weal; and it is clearly decided in favor of the latter by two obvious considerations.

In the first place it is to be remarked that however small the republic may be the representatives must be raised to a certain number in order to guard against the cabals of a few; and that however large it may be they must be limited to a certain number in order to guard against the confusion of a multitude. Hence, the number of representatives in the two cases not being in proportion to that of the constituents, and being proportionally greatest in the small republic, it follows that if the proportion of fit characters be not less in the large than in the small republic, the former will present a greater option, and consequently a greater probability of a fit choice.

In the next place, as each representative will be chosen by a greater number of citizens in the large than in the small republic, it will be more difficult for unworthy candidates to practise with success the vicious arts by which elections are too often carried; and the suffrages of the people being more free, will be more likely to center on men who possess the most attractive merit and the most diffusive and established characters.

It must be confessed that in this, as in most other cases, there is a mean, on both sides of which inconveniencies will be found to lie. By enlarging too much the number of electors, you render the representative too little acquainted with all their local circumstances and lesser interests; as by reducing it too much, you render him unduly attached to these, and too little fit to comprehend and pursue great and national objects. The federal Constitution forms a happy combination in this respect; the great and aggregate interests being referred to the national, the local and particular to the State legislatures.

The other point of difference is the greater number of citizens and extent of territory which may be brought within the compass of republican than of democratic government; and it is this circumstance principally which renders factious combinations less to be dreaded in the former than in the latter. The smaller the society, the fewer probably will be the distinct parties and interests composing it; the fewer the distinct parties and interests, the more frequently will a majority be found of the same party; and the smaller the number of individuals composing a majority, and the smaller the compass within which they are placed, the more easily will they concert and execute their plans of oppression. Extend the sphere and you take in a greater variety of parties and interests; you make it less probable that a majority of the whole will have a common motive to invade the rights of other citizens; or if such a common motive exists, it will be more difficult for all who feel it to discover their own strength and to act in unison with each other. Besides other impediments, it may be remarked that, where there is a consciousness of unjust or dishonorable purposes, communication is always checked by distrust in proportion to the number whose concurrence is necessary.

Hence, it clearly appears that the same advantage which a republic has over a democracy in controlling the effects of faction is enjoyed by a large over a small republic—is enjoyed by the Union over the States composing it. Does this advantage consist in the substitution of representatives whose enlightened views and virtuous sentiments render them superior to local prejudices and to schemes of injustice? It will not be denied that the representation of the Union will be most likely to possess these requisite endowments. Does it consist in the greater security afforded by a greater variety of parties, against the event of any one party being able to outnumber and oppress the rest? In an equal degree does the increased variety of parties comprised within the Union increase this security? Does it, in fine, consist in the greater obstacles opposed to the concert and accomplishment of the secret wishes of an unjust and interested majority? Here again the extent of the Union gives it the most palpable advantage.

The influence of factious leaders may kindle a flame within their particular States but will be unable to spread a general conflagration through the other States. A religious sect may degenerate into a political faction in a part of the Confederacy; but the variety of sects dispersed over the entire face of it must secure the national councils against any danger from that source. A rage for paper money, for an abolition of debts, for an equal division of property, or for any other improper or wicked project, will be less apt to pervade the whole body of the Union than a particular member of it, in the same proportion as such a malady is more likely to taint a particular county or district than an entire State.

In the extent and proper structure of the Union, therefore, we behold a republican remedy for the diseases most incident to republican government. And according to the degree of pleasure and pride we feel in being republicans ought to be our zeal in cherishing the spirit and supporting the character of federalists.   *Publius*

No. 51: Madison

To WHAT EXPEDIENT, then, shall we finally resort, for maintaining in practice the necessary partition of power among the several departments as laid down in the Constitution? The only answer that can be given is that as all these exterior provisions are found to be inadequate the defect must be supplied, by so contriving the interior structure of the government as that its several constituent parts may, by their mutual relations, be the means of keeping each other in their proper places. Without presuming to undertake a full development of this important idea I will hazard a few general observations which may perhaps place it in a clearer light, and enable us to form a more correct judgment of the principles and structure of the government planned by the convention.

In order to lay a due foundation for that separate and distinct exercise of the different powers of government, which to a certain extent is admitted on all hands to be essential to the preservation of liberty, it is evident that each department should have a will of its own; and consequently should be so constituted that the members of each should have as little agency as possible in the appointment of the members of the others. Were this principle rigorously adhered to, it would require that all the appointments for the supreme executive, legislative, and judiciary magistracies should be drawn from the same fountain of authority, the people, through channels having no communication whatever with one another. Perhaps such a plan of constructing the several departments would be less difficult in practice than it may in contemplation appear. Some difficulties, however, and some additional expense would attend the execution of it. Some deviations, therefore, from the principle must be admitted. In the constitution of the judiciary department in particular, it might be inexpedient to insist rigorously on the principle: first, because peculiar qualifications being essential in the members, the primary consideration ought to be to select that mode of choice which best secures these qualifications; second, because the permanent tenure by which the appointments are held in that department must soon destroy all sense of dependence on the authority conferring them.

It is equally evident that the members of each department should be as little dependent as possible on those of the others for the emoluments annexed to their offices. Were the executive magistrate, or the judges, not independent of the legislature in this particular, their independence in every other would be merely nominal.

But the great security against a gradual concentration of the several powers in the same department consists in giving to those who administer each department the necessary constitutional means and personal motives to resist encroachments of the others. The provision for defense must in this, as in all other cases, be made commensurate to the danger of attack. Ambition must be made to counteract ambition. The interest of the man must be connected with the constitutional rights of the place. It may be a reflection on human nature that such devices should be necessary to control the abuses of government. But what is government itself but the greatest of all reflections on human nature? If men were angels, no government would be necessary. If angels were to govern men, neither external nor internal controls on government would be necessary. In framing a government which is to be administered by men over men, the great difficulty lies in this: you must first enable the government to control the governed; and in the next place oblige it to control itself. A dependence on the people is, no doubt, the primary control on the government; but experience has taught mankind the necessity of auxiliary precautions.

This policy of supplying, by opposite and rival interests, the defect of better motives, might be traced through the whole system of human affairs, private as well as public. We see it particularly displayed in all the subordinate distributions of power, where the constant aim is to divide and arrange the several offices in such a manner as that each may be a check on the other—that the private interest of every individual may be a sentinel over the public rights. These inventions of prudence cannot be less requisite in the distribution of the supreme powers of the State.

But it is not possible to give to each department an equal power of self-defense. In republican government, the legislative authority necessarily predominates. The remedy for this inconveniency is to divide the legislature into different branches; and to render them, by different modes of election and different principles of action, as little connected with each other as the nature of their common functions and their common dependence on the society will admit. It may even be necessary to guard against dangerous encroachments by still further precautions. As the weight of the legislative authority requires that it should be thus divided, the weakness of the executive may require, on the other hand, that it should be fortified. An absolute negative on the legislature appears, at first view, to be the natural defense with which the executive magistrate should be armed.

But perhaps it would be neither altogether safe nor alone sufficient. On ordinary occasions it might not be exerted with the requisite firmness, and on extraordinary occasions it might be perfidiously abused. May not this defect of an absolute negative be supplied by some qualified connection between this weaker department and the weaker branch of the stronger department, by which the latter may be led to support the constitutional rights of the former, without being too much detached from the rights of its own department?

If the principles on which these observations are founded be just, as I persuade myself they are, and they be applied as a criterion to the several State constitutions, and to the federal Constitution, it will be found that if the latter does not perfectly correspond with them, the former are infinitely less able to bear such a test.

There are, moreover, two considerations particularly applicable to the federal system of America, which place that system in a very interesting point of view.

First. In a single republic, all the power surrendered by the people is submitted to the administration of a single government; and the usurpations are guarded against by a division of the government into distinct and separate departments. In the compound republic of America, the power surrendered by the people is first divided between two distinct governments, and then the portion allotted to each subdivided among distinct and separate departments. Hence a double security arises to the rights of the people. The different governments will control each other, at the same time that each will be controlled by itself.

Second. It is of great importance in a republic not only to guard the society against the oppression of its rulers, but to guard one part of the society against the injustice of the other part. Different interests necessarily exist in different classes of citizens. If a majority be united by a common interest, the rights of the minority will be insecure. There are but two methods of providing against this evil: the one by creating a will in the community independent of the majority—that is, of the society itself; the other, by comprehending in the society so many separate descriptions of citizens as will render an unjust combination of a majority of the whole very improbable, if not impracticable. The first method prevails in all governments possessing an hereditary or self-appointed authority. This, at best, is but a precarious security; because a power independent of the society may as well espouse the unjust views of the major as the rightful interests of the minor party, and may possibly be turned against both parties. The second method will be exemplified in the federal republic of the United States. Whilst all authority in it will be derived from and dependent on the society, the society itself will be broken into so many parts, interests and classes of citizens, that the rights of individuals, or of the minority, will be in little danger from interested combinations of the majority. In a free government the security for civil rights must be the same as that for religious rights. It consists in the one case in the multiplicity of interests, and in the other in the multiplicity of sects. The degree of security in both cases will depend on the number of interests and sects; and this may be presumed to depend on the extent of country and number of people comprehended under the same government. This view of the subject must particularly recommend a proper federal system to all the sincere and considerate friends of republican government, since it shows that in exact proportion as the territory of the Union may be formed into more circumscribed Confederacies, or States, oppressive combinations of a majority will be facilitated; the best security, under the republican forms, for the rights of every class of citizen, will be diminished; and consequently the stability and independence of some member of the government, the only other security, must be proportionally increased. Justice is the end of government. It is the end of civil society. It ever has been and ever will be pursued until it be obtained, or until liberty be lost in the pursuit. In a society under the forms of which the stronger faction can readily unite and oppress the weaker, anarchy may as truly be said to reign as in a state of nature, where the weaker individual is not secured against the violence of the stronger; and as, in the latter state, even the stronger individuals are prompted, by the uncertainty of their condition, to submit to a government which may protect the weak as well as themselves; so, in the former state, will the more powerful factions or parties be gradually induced, by a like motive, to wish for a government which will protect all parties, the weaker as well as the more powerful. It can be little doubted that if the State of Rhode Island was separated from the Confederacy and left to itself, the insecurity of rights under the popular form of government within such narrow limits would be displayed by such reiterated oppressions of factious majorities that some power altogether independent of the people would soon be called for by the voice of the very factions whose misrule had proved the necessity of it. In the extended republic of the United States, and among the great variety of interests, parties, and sects which it embraces, a coalition of a majority of the whole society could seldom take place on any other principles than those of justice and the general good; whilst there being thus less danger to a minor from the will of a major party, there must be less pretext, also, to provide for the security of the former, by introducing into the government a will not dependent on the latter, or, in other words, a will independent of

the society itself. It is no less certain than it is important, notwithstanding
the contrary opinions which have been entertained, that the larger the
society, provided it lie within a practicable sphere, the more duly capable
it will be of self-government. And happily for the *republican cause*, the
practicable sphere may be carried to a very great extent by a judicious
modification and mixture of the *federal principle*.   *Publius*

RICHARD HOFSTADTER

From *The American Political Tradition*

Richard Hofstadter, one of the nation's leading historians, explores the real thoughts and motivations behind the men whom all schoolchildren have been taught to revere as Founding Fathers. Hofstadter's classic work points out the ambivalence of those who wrote the Constitution: they viewed human beings as selfish and untrustworthy, yet they strongly believed in the importance of self-government. The founders' ambivalence toward democracy led them to design the political system the United States still lives with today, one in which each interest (or branch or layer of government or economic class or region . . .) would be checked and balanced by competing interests. Hofstadter goes on to interpret what the near-sacred idea of liberty meant to the founders. Liberty was not really related to democracy, he contends, but rather ensured the freedom to attain and enjoy private property. To make this idea clearer, test the author's thesis against current political debates.

. . . THE MEN WHO DREW UP the Constitution in Philadelphia during the summer of 1787 had a vivid Calvinistic sense of human evil and damnation and believed with Hobbes that men are selfish and contentious. They were men of affairs, merchants, lawyers, planter-businessmen, speculators, investors. Having seen human nature on display in the marketplace, the courtroom, the legislative chamber, and in every secret path and alleyway where wealth and power are courted, they felt they knew it in all its frailty. To them a human being was an atom of self-interest. They did not believe in man, but they did believe in the power of a good political constitution to control him.

This may be an abstract notion to ascribe to practical men, but it follows the language that the Fathers themselves used. General Knox, for example, wrote in disgust to Washington after the Shays Rebellion that Americans were, after all, "men—actual men possessing all the turbulent passions belonging to that animal." Throughout the secret discussions at the Constitutional Convention it was clear that this distrust of man was first and foremost a distrust of the common man and democratic rule. . . .

And yet there was another side to the picture. The Fathers were intellectual heirs of seventeenth-century English republicanism with its opposition to arbitrary rule and faith in popular sovereignty. If they feared the advance of democracy, they also had misgivings about turning to the extreme right. Having recently experienced a bitter revolutionary struggle with an external power beyond their control, they were in no mood to follow Hobbes to his conclusion that any kind of government must be accepted in order to avert the anarchy and terror of a state of nature. . . .

Unwilling to turn their backs on republicanism, the Fathers also wished to avoid violating the prejudices of the people. "Notwithstanding the oppression and injustice experienced among us from democracy," said George Mason, "the genius of the people is in favor of it, and the genius of the people must be consulted." Mason admitted "that we had been too democratic," but feared that "we should incautiously run into the opposite extreme." James Madison, who has quite rightfully been called the philosopher of the Constitution, told the delegates: "It seems indispensable that the mass of citizens should not be without a voice in making the laws which they are to obey, and in choosing the magistrates who are to administer them." James Wilson, the outstanding jurist of the age, later appointed to the Supreme Court by Washington, said again and again that the ultimate power of government must of necessity reside in the people. This the Fathers commonly accepted, for if government did not proceed from the people, from what other source could it legitimately come? To adopt any other premise not only would be inconsistent with everything they had said against British rule in the past but would open the gates to an extreme concentration of power in the future. . . .

If the masses were turbulent and unregenerate, and yet if government must be founded upon their suffrage and consent, what could a Constitution-maker do? One thing that the Fathers did not propose to do, because they thought it impossible, was to change the nature of man to conform with a more ideal system. They were inordinately confident that they knew what man always had been and what he always would be. The eighteenth-century mind had great faith in universals. . . .

. . . It was too much to expect that vice could be checked by virtue; the Fathers relied instead upon checking vice with vice. Madison once objected during the Convention that Gouverneur Morris was "forever inculcating the utter political depravity of men and the necessity of opposing one vice and interest to another vice and interest." And yet Madison himself in the *Federalist* number 51 later set forth an excellent statement of the same thesis:

> Ambition must be made to counteract ambition. . . . It may be a reflection on human nature that such devices should be necessary to control the abuses of government. But what is government itself, but the greatest of all reflections on human nature? If men were angels, no government would be necessary. . . . In fram-

ing a government which is to be administered by men over men, the great difficulty lies in this: you must first enable the government to control the governed; and in the next place oblige it to control itself.

... If, in a state that lacked constitutional balance, one class or one interest gained control, they believed, it would surely plunder all other interests. The Fathers, of course, were especially fearful that the poor would plunder the rich, but most of them would probably have admitted that the rich, unrestrained, would also plunder the poor. ...

In practical form, therefore, the quest of the Fathers reduced primarily to a search for constitutional devices that would force various interests to check and control one another. Among those who favored the federal Constitution three such devices were distinguished.

The first of these was the advantage of a federated government in maintaining order against popular uprisings or majority rule. In a single state a faction might arise and take complete control by force; but if the states were bound in a federation, the central government could step in and prevent it. ...

The second advantage of good constitutional government resided in the mechanism of representation itself. In a small direct democracy the unstable passions of the people would dominate lawmaking; but a representative government, as Madison said, would "refine and enlarge the public views by passing them through the medium of a chosen body of citizens." ...

The third advantage of the government ... [was that] each element should be given its own house of the legislature, and over both houses there should be set a capable, strong, and impartial executive armed with the veto power. This split assembly would contain within itself an organic check and would be capable of self-control under the governance of the executive. The whole system was to be capped by an independent judiciary. The inevitable tendency of the rich and the poor to plunder each other would be kept in hand. ...

It is ironical that the Constitution, which Americans venerate so deeply, is based upon a political theory that at one crucial point stands in direct antithesis to the mainstream of American democratic faith. Modern American folklore assumes that democracy and liberty are all but identical, and when democratic writers take the trouble to make the distinction, they usually assume that democracy is necessary to liberty. But the Founding Fathers thought that the liberty with which they were most concerned was menaced by democracy. In their minds liberty was linked not to democracy but to property.

What did the Fathers mean by liberty? What did Jay mean when he spoke of "the charms of liberty"? Or Madison when he declared that to destroy liberty in order to destroy factions would be a remedy worse than the disease? Certainly the men who met at Philadelphia were not interested in extending liberty to those classes in America, the Negro slaves and the indentured servants, who were most in need of it, for slavery was recognized in the organic structure of the Constitution and indentured servitude was no concern of the Convention. Nor was the regard of the delegates for civil liberties any too tender. It was the opponents of the Constitution who were most active in demanding such vital liberties as freedom of religion, freedom of speech and press, jury trial, due process, and protection from "unreasonable searches and seizures." These guarantees had to be incorporated in the first ten amendments because the Convention neglected to put them in the original document. Turning to economic issues, it was not freedom of trade in the modern sense that the Fathers were striving for. Although they did not believe in impeding trade unnecessarily, they felt that failure to regulate it was one of the central weaknesses of the Articles of Confederation, and they stood closer to the mercantilists than to Adam Smith. Again, liberty to them did not mean free access to the nation's unappropriated wealth. At least fourteen of them were land speculators. They did not believe in the right of the squatter to occupy unused land, but rather in the right of the absentee owner or speculator to preempt it.

The liberties that the constitutionalists hoped to gain were chiefly negative. They wanted freedom from fiscal uncertainty and irregularities in the currency, from trade wars among the states, from economic discrimination by more powerful foreign governments, from attacks on the creditor class or on property, from popular insurrection. They aimed to create a government that would act as an honest broker among a variety of propertied interests, giving them all protection from their common enemies and preventing any one of them from becoming too powerful. The Convention was a fraternity of types of absentee ownership. All property should be permitted to have its proportionate voice in government. Individual property interests might have to be sacrificed at times, but only for the community of propertied interests. Freedom for property would result in liberty for men—perhaps not for all men, but at least for all worthy men. Because men have different faculties and abilities, the Fathers believed, they acquire different amounts of property. To protect property is only to protect men in the exercise of their natural faculties. Among the many liberties, therefore, freedom to hold and dispose [of] property is paramount. Democracy, unchecked rule by the masses, is sure to bring arbitrary redistribution of property, destroying the very essence of liberty. . . .

A cardinal tenet in the faith of the men who made the Constitution was the belief that democracy can never be more than a transitional stage in government, that it always evolves into either a tyranny (the rule of the rich demagogue who has patronized the mob) or an aristocracy (the original leaders of the democratic elements). . . .

What encouraged the Fathers about their own era, however, was the broad dispersion of landed property. The small land-owning farmers had been troublesome in recent years, but there was a general conviction that under a properly made Constitution a *modus vivendi* could be worked out with them. The possession of moderate plots of property presumably gave them a sufficient stake in society to be safe and responsible citizens under the restraints of balanced government. Influence in government would be proportionate to property: merchants and great landholders would be dominant, but small property-owners would have an independent and far from negligible voice. It was "politic as well as just," said Madison, "that the interests and rights of every class should be duly represented and understood in the public councils," and John Adams declared that there could be "no free government without a democratical branch in the constitution." . . .

. . . At the very beginning contemporary opponents of the Constitution foresaw an apocalyptic destruction of local government and popular institutions, while conservative Europeans of the old regime thought the young American Republic was a dangerous leftist experiment. Modern critical scholarship, which reached a high point in Charles A. Beard's *An Economic Interpretation of the Constitution of the United States*, started a new turn in the debate. The antagonism, long latent, between the philosophy of the Constitution and the philosophy of American democracy again came into the open. Professor Beard's work appeared in 1913 at the peak of the Progressive era, when the muckraking fever was still high; some readers tended to conclude from his findings that the Fathers were selfish reactionaries who do not deserve their high place in American esteem. Still more recently, other writers, inverting this logic, have used Beard's facts to praise the Fathers for their opposition to "democracy" and as an argument for returning again to the idea of a "republic."

In fact, the Fathers' image of themselves as moderate republicans standing between political extremes was quite accurate. They were impelled by class motives more than pietistic writers like to admit, but they were also controlled, as Professor Beard himself has recently emphasized, by a statesmanlike sense of moderation and a scrupulously republican philosophy. Any attempt, however, to tear their ideas out of the eighteenth-century context is sure to make them seem starkly reactionary. Consider, for example, the favorite maxim of John Jay: "The people who own the country ought to govern it." To the Fathers this was simply a swift axiomatic statement of the stake-in-society theory of political rights, a moderate conservative position under eighteenth-century conditions of property distribution in America. Under modern property relations this maxim demands a drastic restriction of the base of political power. A large portion of the modern middle class—and it is the strength of this class upon which balanced government depends—is propertyless; and the urban proletariat, which the Fathers so greatly feared, is almost one half the population. Further, the separation of ownership from control that has come with the corporation deprives Jay's maxim of twentieth-century meaning even for many propertied people. The six hundred thousand stockholders of the American Telephone & Telegraph Company not only do not acquire political power by virtue of their stock-ownership, but they do not even acquire economic power: they cannot control their own company.

From a humanistic standpoint there is a serious dilemma in the philosophy of the Fathers, which derives from their conception of man. They thought man was a creature of rapacious self-interest, and yet they wanted him to be free—free, in essence, to contend, to engage in an umpired strife, to use property to get property. They accepted the mercantile image of life as an eternal battleground, and assumed the Hobbesian war of each against all; they did not propose to put an end to this war, but merely to stabilize it and make it less murderous. They had no hope and they offered none for any ultimate organic change in the way men conduct themselves. The result was that while they thought self-interest the most dangerous and unbrookable quality of man, they necessarily underwrote it in trying to control it. . . .

12

ALEXIS DE TOCQUEVILLE

From *Democracy in America*

In 1831, the young French aristocrat observed America's ever-growing equality, an equality that produces reverence for the majority's viewpoint. If all citizens are basically equal, the camp with the most number of people wins fair and square. Tocqueville's assessment? "Dangerous," he believes. The Frenchman explains the way a monarch or a dictator oppresses his people, contrasting that overt kind of oppression with the more covert form that exists in a democracy. His accusation is shocking and unexpected: "I know no country in which there is so little true independence of mind and freedom of discussion as in America." But before you get angry, follow Tocqueville's argument carefully. He explains how a system based on majority rule can be just as—or more—oppressive than a monarchy. Tocqueville discusses the plight of the minority in America and he warns us about the possible consequences of pushing the minority aside. Consider, readers, whether the nation heeded Tocqueville's warning. Consider also whether the nation heeded the warning too well: maybe tyranny of the majority is the least of our problems today.

THE VERY ESSENCE of democratic government consists in the absolute sovereignty of the majority; for there is nothing in democratic states which is capable of resisting it....

...The moral authority of the majority is partly based upon the notion, that there is more intelligence and more wisdom in a great number of men collected together than in a single individual, and that the quantity of legislators is more important than their quality. The theory of equality is in fact applied to the intellect of man; and human pride is thus assailed in its last retreat, by a doctrine which the minority hesitate to admit, and in which they very slowly concur....

The moral power of the majority is founded upon yet another principle, which is, that the interests of the many are to be preferred to those of the few. It will readily be perceived that the respect here professed for the rights of the majority must naturally increase or diminish according to the state of parties. When a nation is divided into several irreconcilable factions, the privilege of the majority is often overlooked, because it is intolerable to comply with its demands.

If there existed in America a class of citizens whom the legislating majority sought to deprive of exclusive privileges, which they had possessed for ages, and to bring down from an elevated station to the level of the ranks of the multitude, it is probable that the minority would be less ready to comply with its laws. But as the United States were colonized by men holding equal rank amongst themselves, there is as yet no natural or permanent source of dissension between the interests of its different inhabitants.

There are certain communities in which the persons who constitute the minority can never hope to draw over the majority to their side, because they must then give up the very point which is at issue between them. Thus, an aristocracy can never become a majority whilst it retains its exclusive privileges, and it cannot cede its privileges without ceasing to be an aristocracy.

In the United States, political questions cannot be taken up in so general and absolute a manner; and all parties are willing to recognize the rights of the majority, because they all hope to turn those rights to their own advantage at some future time. The majority therefore in that country exercises a prodigious actual authority, and a moral influence which is scarcely less preponderant; no obstacles exist which can impede, or so much as retard its progress, or which can induce it to heed the complaints of those whom it crushes upon its path. This state of things is fatal in itself and dangerous for the future. . . .

A majority taken collectively may be regarded as a being whose opinions, and most frequently whose interests, are opposed to those of another being, which is styled a minority. If it be admitted that a man, possessing absolute power, may misuse that power by wronging his adversaries, why should a majority not be liable to the same reproach? . . .

Unlimited power is in itself a bad and dangerous thing; human beings are not competent to exercise it with discretion; and God alone can be omnipotent, because his wisdom and his justice are always equal to his power. But no power upon earth is so worthy of honour for itself, or of reverential obedience to the rights which it represents, that I would consent to admit its uncontrolled and all-predominant authority. When I see that the right and the means of absolute command are conferred on a people or upon a king, upon an aristocracy or a democracy, a monarchy or a republic, I recognize the germ of tyranny, and I journey onwards to a land of more hopeful institutions.

In my opinion the main evil of the present democratic institutions of the United States does not arise, as is often asserted in Europe, from their weakness, but from their overpowering strength; and I am not so much alarmed at the excessive liberty which reigns in that country, as at the very inadequate securities which exist against tyranny.

When an individual or a party is wronged in the United States, to whom can he apply for redress? If to public opinion, public opinion constitutes the majority; if to the legislature, it represents the majority, and implicitly obeys its injunctions; if to the executive power, it is appointed by the majority and remains a passive tool in its hands; the public troops consist of the majority under arms; the jury is the majority invested with the right of hearing judicial cases; and in certain States even the judges are elected by the majority. However iniquitous or absurd the evil of which you complain may be, you must submit to it as well as you can.

If, on the other hand, a legislative power could be so constituted as to represent the majority without necessarily being the slave of its passions; an executive, so as to retain a certain degree of uncontrolled authority; and a judiciary, so as to remain independent of the two other powers; a government would be formed which would still be democratic without incurring any risk of tyrannical abuse.

I do not say that tyrannical abuses frequently occur in America at the present day; but I maintain that no sure barrier is established against them, and that the causes which mitigate the government are to be found in the circumstances and the manners of the country more than in its laws. . . .

It is in the examination of the display of public opinion in the United States, that we clearly perceive how far the power of the majority surpasses all the powers with which we are acquainted in Europe. Intellectual principles exercise an influence which is so invisible and often so inappreciable, that they baffle the toils of oppression. At the present time the most absolute monarchs in Europe are unable to prevent certain notions, which are opposed to their authority, from circulating in secret throughout their dominions, and even in their courts. Such is not the case in America; as long as the majority is still undecided, discussion is carried on; but as soon as its decision is irrevocably pronounced, a submissive silence is observed; and the friends, as well as the opponents, of the measure, unite in assenting to its propriety. The reason of this is perfectly clear: no monarch is so absolute as to combine all the powers of society in his own hands, and to conquer all opposition, with the energy of a majority, which is invested with the right of making and of executing the laws.

The authority of a king is purely physical, and it controls the actions of the subject without subduing his private will; but the majority possesses a power which is physical and moral at the same time; it acts upon the will as well as upon the actions of men, and it represses not only all contest, but all controversy.

I know no country in which there is so little true independence of mind and freedom of discussion as in America. In any constitutional state in Europe every sort of religious and political theory may be advocated and propagated abroad; for there is no country in Europe so subdued by any single authority, as not to contain citizens who are ready to protect the man who raises his voice in the cause of truth, from the consequences of his hardihood. If he is unfortunate enough to live under an absolute government, the people is upon his side; if he inhabits a free country, he may find a shelter behind the authority of the throne, if he require one. The aristocratic part of society supports him in some countries, and the democracy in others. But in a nation where democratic institutions exist, organized like those of the United States, there is but one sole authority, one single element of strength and of success, with nothing beyond it.

In America, the majority raises very formidable barriers to the liberty of opinion: within these barriers an author may write whatever he pleases, but he will repent it if he ever step beyond them. Not that he is exposed to the terrors of an auto-da-fé, but he is tormented by the slights and persecutions of daily obloquy. His political career is closed for ever, since he has offended the only authority which is able to promote his success. Every sort of compensation, even that of celebrity, is refused to him. Before he published his opinions, he imagined that he held them in common with many others; but no sooner has he declared them openly, than he is loudly censured by his overbearing opponents, whilst those who think, without having the courage to speak, like him, abandon him in silence. He yields at length, oppressed by the daily efforts he has been making, and he subsides into silence, as if he was tormented by remorse for having spoken the truth.

Fetters and headsmen were the coarse instruments which tyranny formerly employed; but the civilization of our age has refined the arts of despotism, which seemed however to have been sufficiently perfected before. The excesses of monarchical power had devised a variety of physical means of oppression: the democratic republics of the present day have rendered it as entirely an affair of the mind, as that will which it is intended to coerce. Under the absolute sway of an individual despot, the body was attacked in order to subdue the soul; and the soul escaped the blows which were directed against it, and rose superior to the attempt; but such is not the course adopted by tyranny in democratic republics; there the body is left free, and the soul is enslaved. The sovereign can no longer say, "You shall think as I do on pain of death;" but he says, "You are free to think differently from me, and to retain your life, your property, and all that you possess; but if such be your determination, you are henceforth an alien among your people. You may retain your civil rights, but they will be useless to you, for you will never be chosen by your fellow-citizens if you solicit their suffrages; and they will affect to scorn you, if you solicit their esteem. You will remain among men, but you will be deprived of the rights of mankind. Your fellow-creatures will shun you like an impure being; and those who are most persuaded of your innocence will abandon you too, lest they should be shunned in their turn. Go in peace! I have given you your life, but it is an existence incomparably worse than death."

Monarchical institutions have thrown an odium upon despotism; let us beware lest democratic republics should restore oppression, and should render it less odious and less degrading in the eyes of the many, by making it still more onerous to the few. . . .

The tendencies which I have just alluded to are as yet very slightly perceptible in political society; but they already begin to exercise an unfavourable influence upon the national character of the Americans. I am inclined to attribute the singular paucity of distinguished political characters to the ever-increasing activity of the despotism of the majority in the United States. . . .

In free countries, where every one is more or less called upon to give his opinion in the affairs of state; in democratic republics, where public life is incessantly commingled with domestic affairs, where the sovereign authority is accessible on every side, and where its attention can almost always be attracted by vociferation, more persons are to be met with who speculate upon its foibles, and live at the cost of its passions, than in absolute monarchies. Not because men are naturally worse in these States than elsewhere, but the temptation is stronger, and of easier access at the same time. The result is a far more extensive debasement of the characters of citizens.

Democratic republics extend the practice of currying favour with the many, and they introduce it into a greater number of classes at once: this is one of the most serious reproaches that can be addressed to them. In democratic States organized on the principles of the American republics, this is more especially the case, where the authority of the majority is so absolute and so irresistible, that a man must give up his rights as a citizen, and almost abjure his quality as a human being, if he intends to stray from the track which it lays down. . . .

If ever the free institutions of America are destroyed, that event may be attributed to the unlimited authority of the majority, which may at some future time urge the minorities to desperation, and oblige them to have recourse to physical force. Anarchy will then be the result, but it will have been brought about by despotism. . . .

13

DAVID BRIAN ROBERTSON

From *The Constitution and America's Destiny*

*"Politicians, not philosophers, political scientists, or plundering speculators":
that is how Professor David Brian Robertson describes the framers of the
Constitution. They understood how compromises were made. Robertson
takes us into the minds of the framers—or at least into what we think they
were thinking. We learn about James Madison, in particular, and the pragmatic approach he took toward creating a document that all delegates could
accept. In explaining Madison's strategy, Robertson mentions some of the
key features of the Constitution that are basic to an understanding of American government. National and state governmental power, the roles of the
House and the Senate, the power of the executive, the authority of the courts
are all delicately balanced. The result, observes Robertson, is a system that is
"hard to use." That was the plan. Only through the skillful use of the Constitution's many impediments and ambiguities can results be achieved. Many
different groups must be brought together and kept together for any action to
take place. Throughout American history, and today, smart politicians have
known how to do this. That was the plan.*

[T]here can be no doubt but that the result [of the Constitutional Convention]
will in some way or other have a powerful effect on our destiny.
—JAMES MADISON to Thomas Jefferson, June 6, 1787

WHAT PROBLEMS WERE THE U.S. CONSTITUTION'S authors trying
to solve? How did they imagine their Constitution would answer these
problems? We know the framers intended to change America's destiny,
and we know they succeeded. But how did they intend to transform the
way American government uses its power and the way Americans use
their government? What kinds of politics were the delegates to the Constitutional Convention trying to make—and what kinds of politics *did*
their design make? For all that has been written about the Constitution,
we do not have satisfactory answers to these questions.

Practicing politicians wrote the Constitution, and they expected politicians to use it. To understand the enduring effects of the Constitution on
America's destiny, we need to know what its designers thought they were
doing. We need to understand the circumstances that convinced these

politicians that they could and should reconstitute the nation's government. We need to understand precisely how these circumstances shaped their strategies for building a new government. We need to reconstruct how these politicians used such strategies to design their Constitution, provision by provision. Better answers to these questions can help us better understand how Americans have used the government they have inherited. . . .

The delegates who made the Constitution were first and foremost politicians, not philosophers, political scientists, or plundering speculators. These politicians had helped nurture a dozen infant state republics through a devastating war and the turbulence of economic depression. Circumstances forced them to learn the art of sustaining political support while conducting any government's most unpopular activities, such as collecting taxes. These republican politicians had mastered the skills of using policy to balance conflicting demands placed on government. A given set of economic policies could accommodate voters, pacify them, divide them, and selectively mobilize them. At the same time, economic policies could stabilize and grow state economies and secure the support of economic elites. These politicians fully understood that public policy makes politics, and the two are inseparable. Those who seek public office must promise to use government in some beneficial way and deliver on these promises, while those who seek public policy depend on those who win and hold government office.

These politicians set out to change the path of American politics, to alter the nation's destiny. They ultimately succeeded by changing the process for selecting national policy makers, by expanding national government authority, and by building a new process for using that authority. They succeeded, first, because pressing political and economic problems made it an opportune moment to reconstitute the national government. The convention met in a political climate that provided some intense but vague and unfocused support for change. Second, they succeeded because the convention's leaders drew on their own diagnosis of the national situation to propose remedies for these problems. These remedies provided a malleable starting point for deliberating constitutional design. Third, they succeeded because most were willing to come to acceptable political compromises about that design, even though none anticipated the final Constitution or found it fully satisfactory.

At the convention, these delegates behaved like republican legislators because most of them *were* legislators. Even though the convention lacked the features of an established legislature today, the delegates employed familiar legislative scripts to develop the Constitution as they would a major change of law: they agreed to rules for debate and voting, used a Committee of the Whole to facilitate the initial consideration of the agenda, took hundreds of votes on substance and procedure, created special committees to deal with difficult issues, and relied on a Committee of Detail to develop a provisional draft. Although they understood that a constitution had to be different from ordinary legislation, they conducted the *process* for crafting the Constitution much the way they had made public policy in Congress or in state legislatures. The Constitutional Convention, then, can be studied with the analytical tools used to analyze other pathbreaking American policy developments, such as Reconstruction, the Sherman Anti-Trust Act of 1890, the Clayton Act of 1914, the National Industrial Recovery Act of 1933, the Social Security Act of 1935, the Civil Rights Act of 1964, the Clean Air Act of 1970, or other "superstatutes." Like legislators today, some delegates attempted to manipulate the terms of the debates and the scope of conflict, and adjusted provisions to enlarge their political support. Through persuasion, bargaining, threats, and evasion, the delegates built coalitions, undermined others, and produced a series of interdependent, politically satisfactory decisions. The Constitutional Convention, of course, was no ordinary legislative process. The stakes were higher. The Constitution affected a virtually unlimited range of politically significant issues, and the final product necessarily would be more general than a statute law.

The Constitution's design resulted from a series of compromises about substantive issues, policy making procedures, and the control of policy makers. The goals of the Constitution are the collective goals of the thirty-nine individuals willing to sign the final product. The central analytical problem for this book is to describe that zone of acceptable compromise and to explain how the Constitution's provisions together satisfied the framers' goals. . . .

The delegates' strategies matter so much because the framers did not and could not write into the Constitution "directly and unerringly" the interests of the nation's propertied elites. The most influential delegates—particularly James Madison—were rebuilding the American state to make it stable and powerful enough to pursue the nation's long-term interests. Their government had to nurture the nation's prosperity long into the future. These state builders took it for granted that private property, free markets, and commercial expansion were essential for future prosperity, and they appreciated that propertied elites were key agents for expanding markets and driving economic development. But many framers viewed the interests of these elites as too narrow, short-term, uninformed, and conflicted to provide much reliable guidance for redesigning the nation's basic political structure and recasting long-term policy. The framers were trying to balance the government's basic needs (especially for revenue), their own ambitions for the nation's destiny, the clashing claims of different economic interests, and the demands of the more numerous citizens of modest means. Even when they were inclined to implement propertied elites' preferences, policy makers had to balance economic development against the demands of the nation's emerging democracy. Legislators needed a broader constituency to win elections to office. They had to show some responsiveness to the grievances of those with modest means. At the very least, elected policy makers had to make any program of market-driven economic development acceptable and legitimate for a majority of the constituents to whom their political fates were tethered.

In any case, it is impossible to enter the mind of an individual delegate to determine how he balanced principles and interests when he took a position on an issue of constitutional design. Jack Rakove observed that "[w]hat is elusive is the interplay between ideas and interests" in the Constitution's design. A delegate's idealistic argument for strong national powers may have concealed a driving ambition to elevate his state or to seek the personal prestige and power of national office. Another delegate's defense of state prerogatives may have reflected sincere dedication to the principle of constituent representation and a deeply held belief in the superiority of the social, economic, and political order of his state. We can never know for certain. What is certain is that the delegates used ideas as rhetorical weapons to defend positions that closely matched their political interests. Political calculations shaped delegates' views of the stakes in most of the choices about the Constitution's design. Political calculations and negotiations, not just abstract ideas, settled the disputes these choices engendered. By expanding the concept of interest beyond personal pecuniary gain and selfish parochialism to include political interests, it is much easier to see how closely the delegates' ideas and interests aligned with one another in their policy strategies.

James Madison's policy strategy requires an especially careful analysis because Madison's ideas set the convention's agenda and shaped its politics. Madison's Virginia Plan sought to establish a national policy-making system independent of the state governments and armed with most of the authority to govern the national economy. The national government would assume full authority to manage economic development for the interest of the republic as a whole. Even after the defeat of provisions crucial to his agenda, Madison and his allies fought to inject this strategy into national government powers and institutions such as the presidency. Understanding the politics of the Constitution requires a careful understanding of the way Madison defined the nation's problems and the way his plan would mitigate them. . . .

James Madison was in a superb position to shape the convention's initial agenda. Already an experienced politician though barely thirty-six years old, Madison was a knowledgeable and respected authority on American politics and public policy. He had helped write Virginia's Constitution of 1776, served in the state's House of Delegates, and represented Virginia in the Continental Congress. In Congress, he served on many key committees and worked behind the scenes to broker coalitions supportive of extending Congress's powers. He played a major role in initiating the Annapolis Convention of 1786.

Madison, a natural political strategist, had mastered the arts of republican politics and policy making. He was proficient at manipulating agendas, locating points of policy compromise, and building coalitions. He understood how procedural motions could be used tactically to gain leverage in the legislative process. He instinctively appreciated that he could advance his agenda by breaking apart legislative proposals (or by combining them). He creatively coupled problems and solutions to win allies for policy measures he favored. Just three months before the convention, for example, he used national security concerns to justify Confederation aid to Massachusetts for suppressing Shays's Rebellion.* Madison conceded that although "there might be no particular evidence" of British interference, "there was sufficient ground for a general suspicion of readiness in [Great Britain] to take advantage of events in this Country, to warrant precautions ag[ain]st her." He worked behind the scenes to cultivate allies in state legislatures and other political bodies where he had no direct influence. Madison was patient and tenacious in policy combat, displaying a doggedness that may have worn even on his allies. And when his efforts produced results that fell short of his goals, he repeatedly accepted half a loaf rather than none, "much disposed to concur in any expedient not inconsistent with fundamental principles."

Madison was not chiefly a political philosopher but rather a policy strategist, adept at using broad theoretical ideas to advance his goals. It is difficult to read Madison's writings without appreciating his gift for ab-

---

*In the western part of Massachusetts in 1786, Daniel Shays, a Revolutionary War veteran, organized a group of poor farmers whose farms were being foreclosed due to their inability to pay the debts they owed. The mob was angry at judges and bankers who represented the propertied elite. Shays and his followers showed up in Springfield where they tried to attack the armory to seize weapons. Massachusetts was not able to control the mob effectively, causing American political leaders to question the ability of the Articles of Confederation to maintain property rights and leading them to call a convention in 1787 to form a new constitution with a stronger national government.—EDS.

straction and generalization, his tendency to develop theory and then apply its logic to sort through facts, his propensity to use lists of general
reasons to justify his claims, and his willingness to use global abstractions
to combat adversaries. An opponent at the convention, William Paterson,
may well have had Madison's style in mind when he noted that "A little
practicable Virtue [is] preferable to Theory." ...

The Constitutional Convention used no predetermined blueprint to
lay out the national policy process. Republican principles demanded only
that the powers to legislate, to execute the law, and to judge legal disputes
be separated in some way. Practical experience encouraged a bicameral
legislature, an executive with veto power, and courts divorced from the
play of politics. The delegates assumed that skilled republican politicians
would use the process to advantage themselves and their constituents. Beyond these indefinite guidelines, the convention built the policy process
piece by piece. Decisions about the policy process were pushed along by
an evolving web of agreements about whom each branch would represent, what powers the national government would have, and what role
each institution would play in using this process.

As the delegates grew less certain about the consequences of their
choices, political logic dictated that they should arm their favored agents
with the will and ability to stop policies threatening to their vital interests.
They could not agree on the exact boundaries of national authority, but
they could agree that by building separate defenses for their favored institutions, they could reduce the danger that the national government would
use its authority to take advantage of their constituents. Their choices in
turn forced them to adjust the powers and independence of these institutions to one another. The Senate gained extraordinary powers to ratify
treaties, confirm presidential appointees, and try impeachments. The House
gained nominal authority to initiate revenue measures. The president
gained influence over the policy agenda, major appointments, and foreign
affairs. Courts gained more autonomy to interpret state and national laws.
The convention rejected efforts to build institutional collaboration into
national policy making, including proposals to require the joint exercise
of veto power by the president and the Supreme Court, the creation of a
privy council, and the eligibility of sitting members of Congress to serve
in executive offices.

When their work was done, the delegates found that they had created
a policy-making process with more complexity and rivalry of purpose
than any of them originally anticipated. They had infused each institution
with a different perspective on the nation's interests. They had given each
institution the power to block the use of government. By doing so, they

made it difficult and costly to make effective national public policy, that is, to use the government for any purpose. Public policy would succeed only if it survived a gauntlet of institutions, each deliberately anchored by different constituencies, calendars, and powers.

Members of Congress would be tied to distinct geographical constituencies, and the interests of these constituents would shape their perception of national interests. Most U.S. representatives would concern themselves primarily with the welfare of regions smaller than a state. U.S. senators would act on behalf of the state governments and statewide constituencies. Representatives and senators could pursue reelection. Each Congress would have a two-year frame of reference, because the political dynamics in each house could change after every national election. Veto points would abound: the Senate and House effectively could veto each other, and the president could veto any bill on which they could agree. It would be relatively easy for one institution to exercise its independent power to stop legislation, but it would be relatively difficult to engineer the institutional cooperation required to enact laws. On the other hand, it would be difficult, costly, and time-consuming for representatives of existing regional interests to construct the political majorities necessary for lawmaking. Only an extraordinarily large geographical majority could win concurrent House and Senate approval for any public policy measure. For example, no law could be passed in the first Congress without, at a bare minimum, the consent of representatives of 55 percent of the American population. No treaty or major appointment could be made without the assent of senators representing nine of the thirteen states.

Compared with Congress, the president and his appointees to the national courts would serve much larger constituencies, and their constituencies would greatly broaden their perception of national interests. The president would represent at least a large number of voters in many parts of the nation. Given a four-year term, the president would serve during two Congresses. The possibility of reelection to additional terms further lengthened his time horizon. The president's agenda-setting, administrative, and foreign-policy powers armed the office with the power to change the path of public policy. Presidents could frame policy agendas aimed at directing policy outcomes and building political support well into the future, and so would define the national interest in terms of prospective achievements that cultivate a chosen national constituency. Presidents could be expected to build new national political orders or to articulate existing ones. The president would tend to pursue national interests more proactively than Congress, more coherently, and for longer time horizons. While the Senate embodied [Roger] Sherman's aspiration to protect the interests of the states, the office of the president embodied Madison's ambition to instill in national policy makers the means and motive to pursue national interests, independent of the states.

No institution would view public policy in a longer time horizon than the national judiciary, whose judges would not have to cultivate voters to stay in office. Compared with Congress, and like the president, the national judiciary would have more latitude to define national interests broadly. But judges would lack the policy tools necessary for fine-tuning a future policy agenda. Judges' tools were reactive. They could only respond to disputes about actions already authorized by other institutions. Judges could settle disputes about existing national law and strike down laws inconsistent with the Constitution. Together, these powers would allow judges to defend existing political arrangements rather than to fashion new ones. Judges would have incentives to interpret national interest in the context of the political order in which they had been appointed. The national judiciary would tend to frame national interests more coherently than Congress but more reactively than the president.

The delegates' compromises, in short, produced a policy-making system that would be hard to use. Different institutions with different perspectives on national interest would share responsibility for major steps in the policy process, from setting the policy agenda to implementing law. . . .

The Constitution gave American politicians extraordinary responsibilities, while at the same time made it extraordinarily hard for them to fulfill these responsibilities. It gave the Congress the duty to make laws for the entire nation, but has encouraged its members to view public policy primarily through the lens of the short-term, parochial interests of their local constituents. It gave the president a duty to formulate plans for achieving future national interests, but limited his capacity to pursue these interests. It gave the courts the duty to ensure the supremacy of federal law, but insulated courts so they can only react to individual conflicts about public policy long after the policy's initiation. Founded on the principle of rule by the people, the Constitution tacitly gave unelected judges the duty of rising above politics to protect established national interests. Founded on the principle of majority rule, the Constitution has obstructed and complicated the construction of majorities.

While Americans revere their Constitution, its paradoxes have fostered frustration and cynicism about their government. These frustrations are rooted in the way the framers answered the agonizing questions they confronted: how can a popularly controlled government promote national well-being without also being a threat? James Madison, Roger Sherman, and the other delegates who wrote the Constitution understood this question just as well—and even better—than we do now. These politicians crafted an answer that suited both their ideals and their vital political interests. Politicians designed the United States Constitution. Ingenious politicians use it. Altering the U.S. Constitution therefore can offer no panacea for curing America's political frustrations. Changing the Constitution is hard, and the results are unpredictable. There are no guarantees that any politically feasible change in the Constitution today would do more good than harm. No one who reflects on presidents' struggle for power in the past forty years, for example, can be confident that making it easier for presidents to get their way would unambiguously benefit the nation.

Instead of changing their Constitution, Americans must learn to use it better. To repeat: making this national policy process work requires very broad-based political coalitions and sustained, concerted effort. To use this government, Americans must engage in politics. They must build and sustain the large political coalitions necessary to align the House, the Senate, the presidency, the courts, and a large number of states. Building coalitions requires understanding the interests of many different kinds of people, forging an understanding of the common interests of these people, locating a common set of objectives that can motivate their continuing cooperation, and working constantly to anticipate and remedy the endless, inevitable conflicts that threaten their cooperative effort. American history abounds with ingenious, tough-minded leaders who have constructed politics in this way. These leaders have spotted opportunities in the Constitution's structural constraints, and they have learned to mold the ambiguities of American politics into new possibilities for political cooperation.

14

MARK ROZELL

From *Executive Privilege*

When a president does not want to give information to Congress or to the public, the reason cited is executive privilege. Mark Rozell examines what, exactly, that means, although there's no real answer to the question. While the excerpt occasionally refers to issues during Richard Nixon's administration, especially the Watergate scandal and President Nixon's claim of executive privilege, the tension between the executive branch and the legislative branch in terms of the Congress investigating actions of the president's administration continue into recent times. Presidents don't want to reveal certain information, whether because of national security concerns or political motives. Congress or the media want to know. It's a balance, writes Rozell. In order to find that balance, Rozell ultimately sends us to some weighty sources: John Locke, Baron de Montesquieu, and the Framers of the Constitution. The system of separation of powers concedes that the president has a right to keep some information secret, out of reach of the public or the legislature. Separation of powers likewise recognizes that there is a legitimate need to know what goes on inside the executive branch. The balance is fluid and changing and will always be so.

EXECUTIVE PRIVILEGE POSES a complex dilemma: a presidential administration sometimes needs to conduct the duties of government in secret, yet the coordinate branches and the public need information about the executive branch so that they can fulfill their democratic responsibilities. This study proposes that the resolution to the dilemma of executive branch secrecy and democratic accountability is in the founders' theory of the separation of powers. That theory allows for a carefully exercised and properly constrained presidential power of executive privilege.

Not all will agree. In a political system predicated on democratic accountability, many analysts believe that there can be no legitimate basis at all for executive privilege. Raoul Berger certainly is not alone in the view that executive branch secrecy is indefensible. In his 1885 book *Congressional Government,* political scientist and future president of the United States Woodrow Wilson argued that representative government must be predicated on openness. He explained that Congress had the high responsibility of investigating administration activities. "It is the proper duty of a representative body to look diligently into every affair of government and to talk much about what it sees." The Wilsonian view is echoed by David Wise, who maintains that executive privilege is a "dubious doctrine." Wise believes that executive privilege cannot be legitimate under a separation of powers system, in which the legislative branch has extensive investigating powers. Among the justifications given for withholding information, none is more prominent than national security concerns. Although most would agree that some limits on access to national security information are reasonable, Wise argues that because "*all* information is of possible value to an adversary," adopting a standard is not possible. "Moreover, 'national security' is a term of political art, which can be defined by a given administration to coincide with its political interests. The men in power tend, sometimes unconsciously, to equate their own personal and partisan interests with the national interest, no matter how noble their motives."

Wise is particularly concerned about freedom of the press issues. Democratic accountability cannot exist, he believes, in a society in which the press is limited in what it can investigate and report. Consequently, executive privilege cannot coexist with the Bill of Rights and accountable government. "Freedom to publish about government is either absolute, or it does not exist," Wise says. "Once qualified, it may be described as something else, but not as freedom of the press."

Morton H. Halperin and Daniel N. Hoffman also argue that executive branch leaders use national security as a reason to withhold vital information from Congress, the bureaucracy, and the public and thus destroy democratic accountability. In their view, secrecy often originates from "a domestic political need." Furthermore, they maintain that secrecy threatens the basic liberties guaranteed by the Bill of Rights. "The Framers sought to design a structure for effective leadership that would not threaten liberty." Halperin and Hoffman argue that the Framers—concerned with individual liberties—purposefully did not grant a presidential power of privilege in Article II of the Constitution. According to them, secrecy fosters official "lying," and consequently, public policy must be based on complete openness in governmental deliberations. They believe that openness is "constitutionally necessary" and that it protects citizens against those leaders who scheme to "prevent the American public from learning the truth."

Halperin and Hoffman also admit that they are concerned with more than just protecting liberty and democratic accountability. They believe that open government will also ensure a number of policy changes that they desire, such as decreased defense budgets and less U.S. intervention in international affairs.

For our purposes, the major concerns about executive privilege are the rights of citizens and governmental accountability. Nearly five decades ago, James Wiggins wrote that "each added measure of secrecy measurably diminishes our freedom." During the Watergate period,* investigative reporter Clark Mollenhoff testified before Congress that executive privilege "would eventually destroy all of our freedom. . . . It is unfortunate that shortsighted editorial writers and superficial politically motivated legal scholars have occasionally given a degree of support to this so-called time honored doctrine and this phony well-established precedent of executive privilege."

A classic slippery-slope argument characterizes many of the critiques of executive privilege: allow any measure of withholding of information, and ultimately all our liberties will be undermined and democratic accountability destroyed. This argument is countered by the views of other analysts who believe that current limitations on secrecy policies are not in the public interest. . . .

Clearly, no one has discovered exactly how to balance the competing and valid claims of freedom of information and governmental secrecy. As the former director of the Central Intelligence Agency, Stansfield Turner, has asked, "how much does a congressional committee need to know to be sure nothing illegal or immoral is being done? Can it know that much without exposing sensitive and necessary operations?" Turner correctly answers that there is no easy way to balance such competing needs to ensure both accountability and the capability of people who maintain secrets to do their jobs.

The dilemma of executive privilege is made even more complex by a number of other factors explored in this study. First, in popular culture, journalism, and even scholarship, there is a long-standing glorification of the strong presidency. Presidents are encouraged from all these venues to achieve "greatness" through activist policy agendas and bold leadership gestures. Less admiration is reserved for presidents who act cautiously in

---

*Watergate began with the 1972 break-in at the Democratic National headquarters by several men associated with President Nixon's re-election committee. Watergate ended two years later with the resignation of President Nixon. Nixon and his closest aides were implicated in the cover-up of the Watergate burglary. Tapes made by President Nixon of his Oval Office conversations revealed lying and obstruction of justice at the highest levels of government. Before the Supreme Court ordered the president to turn over the tapes to Congress, the president resisted, claiming executive privilege.—EDS.

the exercise of their powers. Nonetheless, presidents also are expected to conform to the letter of the law in exercising their powers. Presidents who attempt to achieve their goals through the use of prerogative powers often find that they are in conflict with legislators who wish to share in the exercise of such powers themselves or who have enacted legal restrictions on presidential authority. History is replete with examples of presidents who, out of some real or perceived necessity, acted beyond the strict letter of the law. Some got away with it and are honored by scholars as "great" presidents (e.g., Jefferson, Lincoln, the two Roosevelts); others did not and are scorned by scholars (e.g., Nixon, Reagan).

Second, even among those who agree that presidents possess independent prerogative powers, there is little agreement regarding the circumstances under which such powers can be exercised legitimately. As Daniel P. Franklin has written, "prerogative powers are difficult to discuss, let alone define, in a society that cannot agree about how much liberty should be sacrificed for the sake of security."

Third, the Constitution is silent on the question of executive branch secrecy. Does this mean that the Framers intended to exclude the exercise of that power forever? Or does it mean that secrecy in the executive branch is such an obvious necessity that no one thought of putting it in the Constitution?

Fourth, the Supreme Court has never recognized an absolute "right to know" or "right to receive information." At most, the First Amendment may recognize a right to receive ideas.

Fifth, the issue of executive privilege concerns questions of both foreign and domestic policy. Nonetheless, the presumption in favor of executive privilege has always been strongest in areas of national security and foreign policy. Yet, if there is a necessity to hold leaders accountable for their actions, how can Congress's and the public's need for information be less valid in some policy areas than in others?

Sixth, often there are demands that withheld information be released without delay. From the perspective of those who claim a need to know, the issue of timeliness of information may be of utmost concern. Those who withhold information often make the case that the cause of democratic accountability is not necessarily better served by immediate disclosure of information as opposed to later disclosure, when the need for secrecy is not so compelling.

Seventh, different views on executive privilege generally reflect different institutional perspectives. Presidents see themselves as imbued with worldwide responsibilities and as the representatives of the national interest. They may perceive members of Congress who demand to play an active role in setting foreign policy or in scrutinizing executive branch foreign policy actions as meddling in areas where legislators do not belong. Members of Congress believe that they have the duty not only to play an active role in the policy process but also to investigate all areas of executive branch activity. Louis Henkin has observed that "if the Framers provided no guidance as to where to find the powers of the federal government in international matters, of course they provided no guidance as to how such unenumerated federal authority is allocated between Congress and the president."

Different institutional perspectives may also be reinforced by different partisan ones. Certainly that has often been the case during periods of divided government. During the Reagan-Bush years, Republicans most often defended presidential powers and prerogatives, while Democrats vigorously challenged presidential authority. During the first two years of the Clinton presidency, the Democratic Party majority did not seriously investigate executive branch activities, despite much evidence of potential wrongdoing. Once the Republican Party achieved majority status in Congress in 1995, a cycle of continuous investigations of the Clinton White House and even of prepresidential activities began.* During the early months of the George W. Bush presidency, a GOP-led House committee continued its investigation of Clinton-era scandals, despite opposition from the Justice Department and Attorney General John Ashcroft. Additionally, there was some serious congressional pushback against some of Bush's executive privilege claims by a GOP-led Congress in the first two years of his first term. But not surprisingly, legislative investigations and executive privilege clashes with Bush became much more pronounced after the Democrats became the majority party in 2007. . . .

The opponents of executive privilege persuasively argue that government secrecy is undemocratic and leads to abuses of power, but they often overstate their case. For example, it is true that the Framers wanted to preserve liberty by restricting power, but they certainly never set out to

---

*The White House years of Bill Clinton were marked by intense congressional scrutiny of many political and personal details of the former Arkansas governor's life as well as those of his wife, Hillary Rodham Clinton. Among the events investigated were Whitewater (a land deal) and the alleged sexual harassment of a state employee, Paula Jones. Once Clinton was elected president in 1992, the Clinton family became embroiled in the so-called Travelgate controversy involving the firing of White House employees. The most dramatic charge made against President Clinton involved his sexual involvement with White House intern Monica Lewinsky that resulted in Clinton's 1998 impeachment by the House of Representatives for lying to a federal grand jury, thereby obstructing justice. President Clinton was tried in the Senate and not convicted on either charge.—Eds.

cripple executive power. Any power can be used to do right or to do wrong. The Framers sought to devise institutional mechanisms to counterbalance the abuse of power, but they never intended to destroy power altogether as a means of protecting our liberties.

When exercised under the appropriate circumstances, executive privilege has clear constitutional, political, and historical underpinnings. The American separation of powers system provides for executive privilege, but not without limitations. The exercise of that power is always open to challenge by those with compulsory power. Many claims of executive privilege fail the balancing test because, in a democratic system, the presumption generally should be in favor of openness. Unfortunately, one defense of executive privilege is based on the false claim that this power is an absolute, unlimited prerogative. This claim clearly is as misguided as the belief that the Framers rejected for all times and under all circumstances any such exercise of presidential power. Rather, the Framers provided the president with a general grant of power that would enable him to take the actions he deemed necessary, primarily to protect the national security. . . .

Although executive privilege is a legitimate power with constitutional underpinnings, it is not an unlimited, unfettered presidential power. Traditionally, presidents who have exercised executive privilege have done so without rejecting in principle the prerogative either of Congress to conduct inquiries or the judiciary to question presidential authority. For the most part, presidents have recognized the necessity of a balancing test to weigh the importance of competing institutional claims. Presidents have weighed in favor of executive privilege to protect the nation's security, the public interest, and the candidness of internal White House deliberations.

President Richard M. Nixon went beyond the traditional defenses of executive privilege. Although he claimed, like his predecessors, to have used executive privilege for the public good, his actions did not evidence public-interest motivations. He invoked executive privilege for purposes of political expediency and used that power as a vehicle to withhold embarrassing and incriminating information.

The Nixon era brought about a fundamental change in the way that executive privilege is perceived and exercised. Prior to Nixon, many presidents confidently asserted this authority, and the coordinate branches of government generally accepted the legitimacy of executive privilege. In the post-Watergate era, most presidents have been reluctant to assert executive privilege, and many members of Congress have characterized all exercises of executive branch secrecy as Nixonian attempts to conceal and deceive. Nixon's exercise of executive privilege has had a profound and lasting impact on the status of that constitutional power. . . .

The dilemma of executive privilege is one of permitting governmental secrecy in a political system predicated on leadership accountability. On the surface, the dilemma is a complex one to resolve: how can democratically elected leaders be held accountable by the public when they are able to deliberate in secret or make secretive decisions?

Under certain circumstances, presidential exercise of executive privilege is compatible with our constitutional system. But in recent years executive privilege has fallen into disrepute because of various misuses and abuses of that power. The modern pattern is one of executive branch recriminations toward legislators and independent counsels for meddling where they do not belong and counteraccusations that executive branch failure to divulge all information constitutes either criminal activity or an attempt to conceal embarrassing information. Currently, there appears to be a lack of recognition by the political branches of each other's legitimate powers and interests in the area of governmental secrecy. To restore some sense of balance to the modern debate over executive privilege, the following must be recognized.

First, when used under appropriate circumstances, executive privilege is a legitimate constitutional power. The weight of the evidence refutes the assertion that executive privilege is a "constitutional myth." Consequently, presidential administrations should not be devising schemes to achieve the ends of executive privilege while avoiding any mention of this constitutional principle. Furthermore, Congress must recognize that the executive branch—like the legislative and judicial branches—has a legitimate need to deliberate in secret and that not every assertion of executive privilege is automatically a devious attempt to conceal wrongdoing.

Second, executive privilege is not an unlimited, unfettered presidential power. Executive privilege should be exercised only rarely and for the most compelling reasons. Congress has the right—and often the duty—to challenge presidential assertions of executive privilege when such assertions clearly are not related to such legitimate needs as protecting national security or the candor of internal deliberations. Merely proclaiming that certain materials have a bearing on national security or internal deliberations does not automatically end the debate in the executive's favor. Presidents need to demonstrate more than just some vague interest in security or secrecy for an executive privilege claim to stand.

Third, there are no clear, precise constitutional boundaries that determine, a priori, whether any particular claim of executive privilege is legitimate. The resolution to the dilemma of executive privilege is found in the political ebb and flow of our separation of powers system. There is no need for any precise definition of the constitutional boundaries surrounding executive privilege. Such a power cannot be subject to precise definition, because it is impossible to determine in advance all the circumstances under which presidents may have to exercise that power. The separation of powers system provides the appropriate resolution to the dilemma of executive privilege and democratic accountability. . . .

The Framers' theory of the separation of powers can resolve the dilemma of executive privilege and the right to know. Such an understanding begins with the writings of the most influential thinkers of modern constitutionalism: Locke and Montesquieu [the European political thinkers who most directly influenced the framers of the U.S. Constitution]. Locke articulated a system of separated powers to limit the potential for governmental tyranny. As Louis W. Koenig has written, "John Locke would have been flabbergasted" by the Nixon assertion that any action undertaken by the president is legal. Yet limited governmental power can never bow to the "fundamental law of nature," which counsels self-preservation. Therefore, Locke advocated a strong executive capable of acting with unity and "despatch," one with the "power to act with discretion, for the public good, without the prescription of the law, and sometimes against it." Montesquieu similarly advocated a governmental system in which power checks power but that allows the executive to act independent of the direct popular will when necessary.

A proper understanding of the separation of powers is rooted in the founding period and the early years of the Republic. The founders recognized an implied constitutional prerogative of presidential secrecy—a power that they believed was necessary and proper. The leading founders either exercised or acknowledged the right of executive branch secrecy in the early years of the Republic. In devising our constitutional system, they sought to limit governmental powers to reduce the threat of tyranny. But this perceived need to limit power never implied either weak government or a subordinate executive branch. As political scientist L. Peter Schultz has written, "the separation of powers constitutes an attempt to solve one of the major problems of government, that of providing for both reasonable government and forceful government without sacrificing either."

It is well recognized that the leading founders exercised considerable foresight in establishing a constitutional system capable of adapting to the needs of changing times. That foresight has been especially useful in the areas of national security and foreign policy, where claims of executive privilege are especially compelling. In writing Article II of the Constitution, the Framers did not constrain presidential power with constitutional exactitude.

Finally, a proper understanding of the separation of powers is founded on the notion that there are inherent limitations on the prerogative powers of the presidency. Both Congress and the judiciary, when given good reason to believe that a claim of privilege is being abused, have institutional mechanisms to compel the president to divulge information. The separation of powers system provides the vital mechanisms by which the other branches of government can challenge executive claims of privilege. The answer to the question of how executive privilege can properly be exercised and constrained is found in an examination of the roles of the other branches of government in ensuring that the executive branch does not abuse the right to withhold information.

PART THREE

Federalism

15

JAMES MADISON

From *The Federalist 39* and *46*

Ratification of the Constitution in 1787 required delicate and persuasive diplomacy. The Articles of Confederation, flawed as they were in allowing virtually no centralized governmental power, did give each state the near-total independence valued after their experiences as English colonies. The proponents of the new Constitution had to convince the states to adopt a new structure of government that would strengthen national power. In Nos. 39 and 46, Madison first discusses the importance of representative government. Then he turns to the "bold and radical innovation" that both divided and shared power between the national government and the state governments—what we today call federalism. The approval of the Constitution was to be by the people of the states, and once in operation, the government would be both national and federal. But, Madison explained, the American people would be the ultimate repository of power. State governments would always claim the citizenry's top loyalty, unless the people chose otherwise. Publius argued successfully in the great American tradition of compromise; there was something for everyone in the Constitution.

No. 39: Madison

. . . THE FIRST QUESTION that offers itself is whether the general form and aspect of the government be strictly republican. It is evident that no other form would be reconcilable with the genius of the people of America; with the fundamental principles of the Revolution; or with that honorable determination which animates every votary of freedom to rest all our political experiments on the capacity of mankind for self-government. If the plan of the convention, therefore, be found to depart from the republican character, its advocates must abandon it as no longer defensible.

What, then, are the distinctive characters of the republican form? . . .

If we resort for a criterion to the different principles on which different forms of government are established, we may define a republic to be, or at least may bestow that name on, a government which derives all its powers directly or indirectly from the great body of the people, and is administered by persons holding their offices during pleasure for a limited period, or during good behavior. It is *essential* to such a government that it be derived from the great body of the society, not from an inconsiderable proportion or a favored class of it; otherwise a handful of tyrannical nobles, exercising their oppressions by a delegation of their powers, might aspire to the rank of republicans and claim for their government the honorable title of republic. It is *sufficient* for such a government that the persons administering it be appointed, either directly or indirectly, by the people; and that they hold their appointments by either of the tenures just specified; otherwise every government in the United States, as well as every other popular government that has been or can be well organized or well executed, would be degraded from the republican character. According to the constitution of every State in the Union, some or other of the officers of government are appointed indirectly only by the people. According to most of them, the chief magistrate himself is so appointed. And according to one, this mode of appointment is extended to one of the co-ordinate branches of the legislature. According to all the constitutions, also, the tenure of the highest offices is extended to a definite period, and in many instances, both within the legislative and executive departments, to a period of years. According to the provisions of most of the constitutions, again, as well as according to the most respectable and received opinions on the subject, the members of the judiciary department are to retain their offices by the firm tenure of good behavior. . . .

"But it was not sufficient," say the adversaries of the proposed Constitution, "for the convention to adhere to the republican form. They ought with equal care to have preserved the *federal* form, which regards the Union as a *Confederacy* of sovereign states; instead of which they have framed a *national* government, which regards the Union as a *consolidation* of the States." And it is asked by what authority this bold and radical innovation was undertaken? . . .

First.—In order to ascertain the real character of the government, it may be considered in relation to the foundation on which it is to be established; to the sources from which its ordinary powers are to be drawn; to the operation of those powers; to the extent of them; and to the authority by which future changes in the government are to be introduced.

On examining the first relation, it appears, on one hand, that the Constitution is to be founded on the assent and ratification of the people of America, given by deputies elected for the special purpose; but, on the other, that this assent and ratification is to be given by the people, not as individuals composing one entire nation, but as composing the distinct and independent States to which they respectively belong. It is to be the assent and ratification of the several States, derived from the supreme authority in each State—the authority of the people themselves. The act, therefore, establishing the Constitution will not be a *national* but a *federal* act.

That it will be a federal and not a national act, as these terms are understood by the objectors—the act of the people, as forming so many independent States, not as forming one aggregate nation—is obvious from this single consideration: that it is to result neither from the decision of a *majority* of the people of the Union, nor from that of a *majority* of the States. It must result from the *unanimous* assent of the several States that are parties to it, differing not otherwise from their ordinary dissent than in its being expressed, not by the legislative authority, but by that of the people themselves. . . . Each State, in ratifying the Constitution, is considered as a sovereign body independent of all others, and only to be bound by its own voluntary act. In this relation, then, the new Constitution will, if established, be a *federal* and not a *national* constitution.

The next relation is to the sources from which the ordinary powers of government are to be derived. The House of Representatives will derive its powers from the people of America; and the people will be represented in the same proportion and on the same principle as they are in the legislature of a particular State. So far the government is *national*, not *federal*. The Senate, on the other hand, will derive its powers from the States as political and coequal societies; and these will be represented on the principle of equality in the Senate, as they now are in the existing Congress. So far the government is *federal*, not *national*. The executive power will be derived from a very compound source. The immediate election of the President is to be made by the States in their political characters. The votes allotted to them are in a compound ratio, which considers them partly as distinct and coequal societies, partly as unequal members of the same society. . . . From this aspect of the government it appears to be of a mixed character, presenting at least as many *federal* as *national* features. . . . The idea of a national government involves in it not only an authority over the individual citizens, but an indefinite supremacy over all persons and things, so far as they are objects of lawful government. Among a people consolidated into one nation, this supremacy is completely vested in the national legislature. Among communities united for particular purposes, it is vested partly in the general and partly in the municipal legislatures. In the former case, all local authorities are subordinate to the supreme; and may be controlled, directed, or abolished by it at pleasure. In the latter, the local or municipal authorities form distinct and independent portions of the supremacy, no more subject, within their respective spheres, to the general authority than the general authority is subject to them, within its own sphere. In this relation, then, the proposed government cannot be deemed a *national* one; since its jurisdiction extends to certain enumerated objects only, and leaves to the several States a residuary and inviolable sovereignty over all other objects. . . .

If we try the Constitution by its last relation to the authority by which amendments are to be made, we find it neither wholly *national* nor wholly *federal*. Were it wholly national, the supreme and ultimate authority would reside in the *majority* of the people of the Union; and this authority would be competent at all times, like that of a majority of every national society to alter or abolish its established government. Were it wholly federal, on the other hand, the concurrence of each State in the Union would be essential to every alteration that would be binding on all. The mode provided by the plan of the convention is not founded on either of these principles. In requiring more than a majority, and particularly in computing the proportion by *States*, not by *citizens*, it departs from the national and advances towards the *federal* character; in rendering the concurrence of less than the whole number of States sufficient, it loses again the *federal* and partakes of the *national* character.

The proposed Constitution, therefore, even when tested by the rules laid down by its antagonists, is, in strictness, neither a national nor a federal Constitution, but a composition of both. In its foundation it is federal, not national; in the sources from which the ordinary powers of the government are drawn, it is partly federal and partly national; in the operation of these powers, it is national, not federal; in the extent of them, again, it is federal, not national; and, finally in the authoritative mode of introducing amendments, it is neither wholly federal nor wholly national.   *Publius*

No. 46: Madison

. . . I proceed to inquire whether the federal government or the State governments will have the advantage with regard to the predilection and support of the people. Notwithstanding the different modes in which they are appointed, we must consider both of them as substantially dependent on the great body of the citizens of the United States. I assume this position here as it respects the first, reserving the proofs for another place. The federal and State governments are in fact but different agents and trustees of the people, constituted with different powers and designed for different purposes. The adversaries of the Constitution seem to have lost sight of the people altogether in their reasonings on this subject; and to have viewed these different establishments not only as mutual rivals and enemies, but as uncontrolled by any common superior in their efforts to usurp the authorities of each other. These gentlemen must here be reminded of their error. They must be told that the ultimate authority, wherever the derivative may be found, resides in the people alone, and that it will not depend merely on the comparative ambition or address of the different governments whether either, or which of them, will be able to enlarge its sphere of jurisdiction at the expense of the other. Truth, no less than decency, requires that the event in every case should be supposed to depend on the sentiments and sanction of their common constituents. . . .

Many considerations, besides those suggested on a former occasion, seem to place it beyond doubt that the first and most natural attachment of the people will be to the governments of their respective States. . . .

If . . . the people should in future become more partial to the federal than to the State governments, the change can only result from such manifest and irresistible proofs of a better administration as will overcome all their antecedent propensities. And in that case, the people ought not surely to be precluded from giving most of their confidence where they may discover it to be most due; but even in that case the State governments could have little to apprehend, because it is only within a certain sphere that the federal power can, in the nature of things, be advantageously administered.   *Publius*

16

ANDREW KARCH

From *Democratic Laboratories*

The title of Andrew Karch's book is taken from Supreme Court Justice Louis Brandeis's use of the phrase in a 1932 dissent. The state governments provide a place to try out new policy ideas that may later be used in other states or in the whole country; the states are "laboratories of democracy." Ideas that come from one state, Karch explains, can become policy in another state through the process of diffusion. The author discusses the importance of state governments, especially since the 1994 Republican congressional victory. "Devolution," as it has been termed, allowed the states a more prominent role in shaping policy and fitting it to the needs of each state. Karch mentions welfare reform as a prime example of devolution. Currently, state experiments with charter schools and with health care reform have provided critical information on the workability of these new programs. The author stresses the significance of the Internet in allowing states to share information efficiently. It's not clear whether the "devolution revolution" that Karch describes will continue in a time of economic problems, increased federal spending, and reliance on the national government for solutions to what ails the nation, but we can be quite sure that ideas developed in Washington, D.C., will have had their start in the states.

HOW DO NEW IDEAS SPREAD? What turns a little-known product or behavior into something with widespread popularity? These straightforward questions have captured the popular imagination. Malcolm Gladwell recently wrote a national best seller devoted to the notion that "ideas and products and messages and behaviors spread just like viruses do." He argued that the best way to understand the emergence of such phenomena as fashion trends and crime waves was to think of them as epidemics. Like an epidemic, modern change tends to occur in one dramatic moment. Rather than building slowly and steadily, change happens in a hurry, with small causes having large effects.

Gladwell's observations resonate with a long-standing scholarly literature on the emergence and diffusion of innovations. In fields ranging from anthropology and rural sociology to marketing and public health, analysts have examined the processes through which new ideas, practices, and objects spread. These innovations need not be new in an objective sense. Instead, they need only be perceived as new by an individual or another unit of adoption. If the idea, practice, or object seems new to a potential adopter, it is an innovation. Diffusion is the process "through which an innovation is communicated through certain channels over time among the members of a social system." Spread is a critical component of this definition. Diffusion is not merely the fact of increasing usage or incidence. It implies movement from the source of an innovation to an adopter. . . .

In a political setting, diffusion implies a process of learning or emulation during which decision makers look to other cities, states, or countries as models to be followed or avoided. Diffusion occurs, in other words, when the likelihood that an innovation will be adopted in jurisdiction A is significantly affected by the existence of that innovation in jurisdiction B. Diffusion does not occur when officials in multiple jurisdictions adopt the same innovation completely independently, nor does it occur when later adopters are unaware of the existence of the innovation elsewhere. In contrast, diffusion implies that extant versions of an innovation affect officials' decisions to create the same political form or to enact the same policy. Diffusion occurs, in sum, when decision makers draw on others' experiences to evaluate the effectiveness of a new political form or idea. . . .

One of the most famous metaphors in American jurisprudential history speaks implicitly to the concept of policy diffusion. In a 1932 dissent, Supreme Court justice Louis Brandeis wrote, "It is one of the happy incidents of the federal system that a state may, if its citizens choose, serve as a laboratory; and try novel social and economic experiments without risk to the rest of the country." Since this landmark dissent, the fifty states have with great regularity been referred to as "laboratories of democracy." Actors from across the political spectrum have invoked this metaphor to describe the states' innovative potential. Liberal and conservative judges have cited Brandeis's metaphor more than three dozen times, and it clearly appeals to a nation of "compulsive tinkerers."

The metaphor of laboratories of democracy implies an almost scientific process, in which the enactment of a policy innovation prompts its evaluation, then other lawmakers use this information to determine whether they, too, will put the program in place. Each new policy is assessed along a set of objective dimensions. If the evaluators agree that the policy achieves its stated goals, other states will enact an identical program once they are made aware of its achievements. For example, if Oklahoma policymakers enact a program to contain health care costs and if this policy innovation succeeds, officials in other states will endorse similar programs. If the innovation is unsuccessful, it will not be adopted elsewhere. Thus, the laboratories metaphor describes a systematic and rational process of trial and error. . . .

Recent developments have catapulted the fifty states to a more prominent place in the American political system. For the past two decades, the states have served as a main locus of policy-making. As a result, now is a timely occasion to examine diffusion in this setting. From abortion and capital punishment to education and the environment, several important policy decisions are being made in state houses across the country, in addition to in the nation's capital. Two main factors contributed to this state resurgence. National political developments, especially the emergence of a Republican congressional majority [from the 1994 elections until the 2006 elections], were one important factor. The second factor was a set of reforms at the state level that strengthened state political institutions.

National developments shifted significant policy-making prerogatives from the national government to the fifty states, with changes in party politics playing a critical role. Republican politicians long considered intergovernmental reform to be a central element of their domestic political agenda. In the early 1970s, President Richard Nixon advanced a proposal called the New Federalism, which emphasized an administrative rationale for devolving policy-making authority to the states. Nixon wanted to restructure the roles and responsibilities of government at all levels in an effort to make the system function more efficiently. Ronald Reagan and Newt Gingrich married these administrative concerns to a larger debate over the legitimate scope and definition of the public sector. For Reagan, Gingrich, and other Republicans, devolution was a way to solve administrative problems and to cut back the reach of government programs.

When the 1994 midterm elections produced a Republican majority in both houses of Congress for the first time in decades, this shift sparked a fundamental rethinking of the relationship between the states and the national government. While many Republican initiatives stalled, others devolved additional policy-making prerogatives to state officials. Perhaps the most prominent example occurred in 1996, when national lawmakers endorsed landmark welfare reform legislation. The Personal Responsibility and Work Opportunity Reconciliation Act placed a time limit on welfare receipt and incorporated stringent work requirements on beneficiaries. It also granted state policymakers unprecedented discretion over the provisions of their welfare programs. Since 1996, state lawmakers have used this discretion to create diverse approaches to welfare policy. Welfare reform is one of many instances in which the states have taken the lead in the making of public policy in response to national legislation.

The partisan shift in Congress was crucial, but other national developments also facilitated the resurgence of the states. Sometimes congressional stalemates, caused by divided government or party polarization, prompted state lawmakers to act in the absence of a national mandate. When national lawmakers could not agree on legislation or did not address specific topics, state officials sometimes developed innovative policy solutions on their own. This dynamic was fairly common in health care policy. During the late 1980s and early 1990s, many states implemented innovative health care programs, such as MinnesotaCare (Minnesota), MassCare (Massachusetts), and the State Health Insurance Program (Hawaii). When legislation for comprehensive national health care reform failed in 1994, state officials attempted to address this vacuum by proposing their own solutions. Over the past two decades, in health care and in other policy arenas, state officials have regularly taken independent action.

In part, state officials' ability to take action grew out of institutional changes that better equipped the states to serve as laboratories of democracy. Reforms of legislatures and executive branches are the second factor that contributed to the resurgence of the states. In institutional terms, the fifty states are stronger than they were a generation ago. In the 1960s, state governments were not professional operations, and many reformers believed that state governments lacked the resources they needed to be effective. Today this is a less pressing concern. James Morone explains: "Once upon a time, good old boys ran the states with winks and backslaps. No more." The institutional capabilities of state governments increased dramatically between the 1960s and the 1980s, thanks to a series of constitutional and institutional reforms. These reforms made state legislatures more professional and enhanced the administrative capacities of the executive branch. As a result, state officials can make a credible claim that they are well equipped to design innovative public policies. . . .

If the fifty states serve as laboratories, they currently are better equipped to take on this task. Institutional changes transformed them from weak backwaters into a strong counterpart to the national government. Around the same time that these state-level changes occurred, developments at the national level granted the states a more prominent place in the American political system. This combination of institutional reforms and national developments contributed to the resurgence of the states and encouraged state officials to design and enact many policy innovations. These laboratories of democracy have been particularly busy in recent years, and the range of recent state activity is quite impressive. In education policy, dozens of states followed suit after the Minnesota state legislature became the first to approve charter school legislation. In health care policy, at least thirty-eight states adopted each of the following policies: small business insurance reforms, high-risk insurance pools, preexisting condition legislation, certificate of need, health care commissions, guaranteed renewal legislation, portability, and guaranteed issue. These and other recent innovations illustrate why the American states are a good setting in which to examine the phenomenon of policy diffusion. . . .

State officials typically have access to libraries and other reference centers whose main job is to collect and distribute information that will be useful during the formulation of public policy. In Virginia, for example, the Legislative Reference Center in Richmond serves the information needs of the Virginia General Assembly. Its collection includes state legislation, legal publications, and topical information to support the research needs of representatives and legislative staff. A shelf near the entrance of the reference center provides introductory materials that describe the information available in the collection. These materials include a bookmark that describes the functions of the center. It states: "We compile state comparative data on a variety of issues. One of our most frequently asked questions is: 'What are other states doing in the area of . . . ?'" The notion of policy diffusion presumes that lawmakers have access to and are sometimes influenced by this type of comparative information. One could reasonably argue that an awareness of and interest in developments elsewhere is the essence of policy diffusion, and this bookmark suggests that such a dynamic is at least a semiregular occurrence. . . .

Public officials currently operate in an information-rich environment. Compared to their predecessors, they generally have more resources at their disposal. These varied resources provide access to a wider range of policy-relevant information. Several recent institutional, technological, and organizational changes facilitate the generation and the collection of policy-relevant information. . . .

In recent decades, institutional changes augmented state officials' ability to gather policy-relevant information. These changes . . . made an especially profound impact on the legislative branch. As late as the mid-1960s, reformers argued that these bodies were ill equipped to process information and to study emerging policy problems. One response to the reformers' complaints was a dramatic increase in the number and the quality of legislative staff. Today, a larger and more qualified staff can gather information for state legislators, although there remain important disparities across states. Legislative staffers are now such an important part of state government, in fact, that a common complaint about the recent imposition of term limits in some states has been that term limits increase the power of unelected legislative staffers. Larger and more professional staffs also serve the executive branch of many state governments.

Technological advancements seem to make more information resources available for state officials. The emergence of new information technologies, such as the Internet, increased the ease and speed with which many organizations can provide policy-relevant information. The representative of one professional association explains: "The advances are enormous. Compared with what is going on now, we were asleep fifteen years ago." Technological shifts also increased the ease and speed with which state officials can consult policy-relevant information. State officials can examine model legislation and statutory language online without contacting an organization directly. In addition, they can mark up legislation and send it to a professional association for comment. This electronic exchange is significantly easier than relying on a telephone, a fax machine, or snail mail. In the past, finding information sometimes involved phone calls and waiting for the mail. Today, similar information is often only a click of the mouse away.

Additional technological changes also make it easier for officials to consult their colleagues in other states. Travel is less onerous than it was in the past, facilitating attendance at regional and national meetings of professional organizations that bring together lawmakers and staff from across the country. Alan Rosenthal argues that "legislation tends to spread like wildfire" because of these conferences. Public officials frequently discuss new programs with one another at these meetings, learning about the substantive impact and political feasibility of policy innovations. When state lawmakers and their staff travel to these out-of-state meetings, they often look for bills to introduce when they return to their own states. Attendees also forge long-lasting bonds at these meetings, and they can use these connections to develop legislation once they return to their own states. A legislative staffer in Massachusetts explains the significance of such connections: "If someone called me and asked me to send information on our laws on managed care or HMOs I would know exactly what chapter to go to whereas someone from another state wouldn't. People do the same thing for me when I know exactly what I'm looking for." Communications technologies, such as e-mail and relatively inexpensive long-distance phone calls, facilitate quick correspondence. It is not much of a stretch to imagine that these connections facilitate the dissemination of policy-relevant information. In sum, technological changes suggest that state officials are more closely connected than they were in the past and are therefore better able to exchange ideas and information. . . .

In the foreword to a book on state-level economic policy during the

1980s, Bill Clinton, then governor of Arkansas, used the "laboratories of democracy" metaphor to describe how officials in the states "learn from one another, borrowing, adapting, and improving on each other's best efforts." This quotation alludes to one of the complexities of policy diffusion, because it implies that lawmakers amend the policy templates that they import. Although officials sometimes copy programs that exist elsewhere, it is more common for them to "adapt" and "improve" these examples. In other words, they customize a policy innovation to "fit" their state in the same way that an individual tailors a suit after buying it off the rack. Policy innovations, as a result, take on various forms in the jurisdictions in which they are enacted. Programs that purport to be the same sometimes vary quite significantly across states. . . .

. . . The political forces that affect state lawmaking and the spread of innovative policy ideas are topics of great contemporary significance. The states recently emerged from their worst financial crisis since the Second World War. Constrained by balanced budget requirements that prevented them from running large deficits, state officials responded to this situation in several different ways. Extensive service cuts were one common strategy. Ironically, the scope and magnitude of the cuts testify to the expansive role of state governments. They affected everything from nursing home care and community colleges to homeland security and health care for the poor. It is no exaggeration to claim that state governments reach into almost every corner of American citizens' lives.

In recent years, many officials at the national level have proposed to grant state lawmakers additional policy-making discretion in several areas where the national and state governments currently share responsibility. For example, some of these proposals would provide state governments with lump sum payments to run social programs, such as Head Start and Medicaid. Currently national regulations affect the operation of these programs, but some individuals want state officials to have the power to structure these policies as they see fit. Rather than attaching strings to national grants, they want state policymakers to operate free of any regulations. Proponents of this "devolution revolution" argue that removing these strictures will allow state lawmakers to develop innovative policy ideas and to adapt existing programs to specific conditions within their states. The debate over devolution resonates . . . with the notion that the fifty states can serve as laboratories of democracy. . . .

17

ERIN RYAN

From *Federalism and the Tug of War Within*

"Who gets to decide?" *asks author Erin Ryan, referring to the competition between the national government and state governments. That competition is built into the U.S. Constitution, the author explains. A multitude of issues illustrate the tension inherent in American federalism, as the national government and state governments simultaneously conflict and cooperate to carry out public policy. The example selected in this excerpt involves the environment: climate change. Don't be too concerned about mastering the details of the state and regional environmental programs that Ryan explains, although it is interesting to read about the intricacies involved in the policies and their regulations. The "tug of war within" federalism determines the quality of the water we drink, the air we breathe, and ultimately, the health of the planet.*

THROUGH FEDERALISM DIRECTIVES both express and implied, the Constitution mandates a federal system of dual sovereignty, establishing new authority in a national government while preserving distinct authority within the more local state governments. Nevertheless, federalism has taken different forms in countless nations worldwide and over the course of history. What exactly does the Constitution require in allocating unique authority to the separate state and federal governments? Are these allocations meant to be mutually exclusive? If not, what should happen in areas of legitimate overlap?

In practical terms, the question really comes down to *who gets to decide*—the state or federal government? In allocating authority this way, the Constitution essentially tells us who should determine what regulatory policy looks like in various public spheres. To be sure, some realms of governance are uncontroversially committed to one side or the other—for example, the powers to coin money, wage war, and regulate interstate commerce are delegated to the national government, while the states administer elections, local zoning, and police services. But between the easy extremes are realms in which it is much harder to know what the Constitution says about who calls the shots. Locally regulated land uses become entangled with the protection of navigable waterways that implicate in-

terstate commerce. State and local police remain bound by federal pro-
scriptions against unreasonable search and self-incrimination. And to what
extent should national regulations apply to the integral operations of state
government?

In fact, American governance is so characterized by overlapping state
and federal jurisdiction that it has been compared not only to a layer cake
but to a marble cake, with entangled swirls of interlocking local and national law. Even so, when policy-making conflicts erupt within these contexts of jurisdictional overlap, the "who gets to decide" question looms
large. Is this a realm in which federal power legitimately preempts contrary state law under the Supremacy Clause, or a policy-making realm
beyond the federally enumerated powers that has been purposefully reserved to the states? And even if federal law *could* legally trump local initiative, does that necessarily mean that it should? How should we decide?

For that matter, when the looming question is "who gets to decide—
the state or federal government," then the critical corollary becomes "who
gets to decide *that?*" When either the regulatory context or the federalism
directive itself is unclear, which branch of government should determine
what the Constitution is actually trying to say about who decides regulatory policy? Are these decisions appropriately committed to the discretion of Congress, where federalism concerns will be safeguarded by the
political process in which state-elected representatives make national
laws? Or should the Supreme Court be the final arbiter of these issues, by
creating judicially enforceable federalism constraints? We generally entrust
the Supreme Court to interpret the constitutional meaning of antimajoritarian individual rights, but is structural federalism different? What
is the proper role of the executive branch, especially in an age of increasing executive agency power? Is there a role for state governmental actors
in interpreting these questions?

In other words, interpreting federalism not only requires that we figure out what the Constitution tells us about *who gets to decide*—who calls
the shots in which regulatory context—but also what it says about *who
decides whether* it will be the state or federal government. The Constitution
allocates authority not only vertically between local and national actors,
but horizontally among the three separate branches of government. The
legislative, executive, and judicial branches each bring different interpretive resources to the constitutional project based on their distinct features
of institutional design. How should each branch participate in the interpretation and implementation of American federalism? At times, political
and judicial federalism rhetoric draws heavily on a model of "zero-sum"
federalism, suggesting winner-takes-all jurisdictional competition between

state and federal policy makers and either/or oversight by legislative or judicial arbiters. But how well does this model reflect what actually happens in practice, deep within the intertwining folds of federalism-sensitive governance? How well should it?

The constitutional ambiguity that makes answering these questions so difficult leads to the next question, often overlooked in the federalism discourse: *which federalism?*—or, which theoretical model of federalism should we use in interpreting this textual ambiguity? The Constitution mandates but incompletely describes American dual sovereignty, leaving certain matters open for interpretation by unspecified decision makers who must employ some kind of theory—a philosophy about how federalism should operate—in order to fill in these gaps. Yet constitutional interpreters can choose from more than one theoretical model of federalism in doing so, just as the Supreme Court has done over the centuries in which its jurisprudence has swung back and forth in answering similar questions differently at various times. The "dual federalism" model, dividing state and federal jurisdiction largely along lines of subject matter, has predominated federalism theory at various points in American history, especially during the nineteenth century. A model of tolerating greater jurisdictional overlap, often referred to as "cooperative federalism," has predominated federalism practice since at least the New Deal. And there are other alternatives. Are these different approaches to understanding federalism—each sharing basic contours but diverging on the details—all valid? If more than one are valid, how should we choose among them?

The "which federalism" dilemma leads back to the ultimate issue, the most important of all: *why federalism?* Why did the architects of the Constitution choose a federal system? What is our federal system of government meant to accomplish? If we can understand what American federalism is for, then we are in a better position to choose which model of federalism to follow in answering the perennial questions about who decides what in which context. However, this last question proves more difficult than at first it may seem, because American federalism is really *for* a number of different things—a collection of goals that are not always themselves in agreement. Here is where federalism theory gets especially interesting, and where this book makes its most important contribution.

As the Court regularly reaffirms, structural federalism is not an end in itself; it is crafted in service of the Constitution's more substantive commitments. Exploring the *why* of federalism yields a number of good governance values that undergird it, each representing an ideal in governance that federalism helps accomplish: checks and balances between opposing centers of power that protect individuals, governmental accountability and transparency that enhance democratic participation, local autonomy that enables interjurisdictional innovation and competition, and the regulatory synergy that federalism enables between the unique capacities of local and national government for coping with interjurisdictional problems that neither could resolve alone. Each of these principles advances the ideal system of government that the framers of the Constitution sought to build, and they have since gone on to take root in international good governance norms. Nevertheless—and as demonstrated by the Supreme Court's vacillating federalism jurisprudence—these values exist in tension with one another, setting federalism interpretation up as a site of contest between honorable but occasionally competing principles.

The tug of war between competing federalism principles is built into American dual sovereignty by design. For example, the strong checks and balances enabled by parallel state and federal governments compromise the value of governmental transparency to some extent, making it necessarily harder for average Americans to understand which elected representatives are responsible for which policies simply by virtue of there being two choices. Similarly, if local autonomy and innovation were all that mattered, there would be no need for a national government at all; its existence reflects a purposeful choice to prioritize the individual-rights' protective features of a system of checks and balances and the pragmatic problem-solving value of a national federation for coping with shared interests and border-crossing problems. Meanwhile, powerful tension can exist between the goal of preserving offsetting centers of state and federal power while also harnessing problem-solving synergy between them in collaborative contexts. Some regulatory contexts exacerbate these tensions more than others, but they are implicated in all federalism controversies to varying degrees.

As noted, the fields of environmental law, land use law, and public health and safety regulation especially showcase federalism's internal tug of war. Sometimes, these fields involve regulatory attempts to grapple with relatively newly identified problems—that is, problems without a historically settled answer to the question of who should decide, such as climate change. Other times, evidence increasingly reveals that a previously presumed "local" problem—such as water pollution, disease control, marriage legitimacy, waste disposal, disaster response, or even land use planning—also has important national implications. Meanwhile, such presumably national problems as telecommunications, counterterrorism, and even international relations are increasingly bound up with exercises of state and local authority. The "proper" level of regulatory authority in these areas is often contested, underscoring conflicts between federalism values that have resulted in judicial and political controversy. . . .

Of course, the most ominous interjurisdictional problem of them all is that of climate change, both domestically and internationally. In the United States, regulators venturing into this arena confront substantial risks of litigation under conditions of jurisprudential instability and uncertain federalism theory. They also risk that financial and intellectual capital invested in regulatory innovation will be squandered if their efforts are overturned or preempted by later governance at a higher level. For a long time, these daunting risks led to abdication on both sides. However, many have finally decided that the risk of taking no action to confront the problem is an even worse alternative.

The explosion of climate governance in the last decade—especially at the state and local level—demonstrates a chief benefit of jurisdictional overlap as a source of regulatory backstop. This is the view of checks and balances that departs from the separationist model, emphasizing how overlapping local and national authority protects individual rights and regulatory obligations against neglect by the other side. This section describes climate governance as an interjurisdictional problem, reviews the risks of abdication and liability, and then explores the promising efforts of local and state governments to act in the face of these risks during a period of federal regulatory gridlock.

Scientific consensus about the looming changes in global climate suggest the need for interjurisdictional governance of a sort the world has not yet seen, involving both mitigation and adaptation measures domestically and internationally. Decades of study by the Intergovernmental Panel on Climate Change (IPCC), a joint effort by the United Nations Environment Program and the World Meteorological Organization, show "high confidence" in human contributions to climate change through the emission of carbon dioxide and other gases that trap heat in the atmosphere. The atmospheric collection of these "greenhouse gases" is expected to create profound changes in world weather patterns. If current trends continue, the IPCC predicts arctic warming and polar ice reduction, sea level rise leading to coastal flooding and land loss, changes in ocean salinity and wind patterns, widespread changes in global precipitation patterns, and increases in extreme weather, including droughts, drenching rains, heat waves, and more intense hurricanes. Indeed, these changes are already upon us, suggested not only by the force of storms like Katrina, but by the catastrophic flooding that displaced tens of millions in Pakistan, the mudslides that killed thousands in China, and the Russian heat wave that set the countryside ablaze—all in just the summer of 2010.

Regulatory responses are needed to mitigate the anthropogenic causes of further climate change and to adapt to the harms that are already inevitable. Mitigation efforts focus on reducing greenhouse gas emissions and increasing carbon sinks (to capture carbon dioxide and other greenhouse gases underground, in the ocean, or within expanses of protected forests.) Adaptation efforts range from proposals to build protective levees around low-lying coastal areas like New York City to global geoengineering efforts that would introduce stratospheric aerosols into the atmosphere to reflect sunlight. Even "climate skeptics" who contest the scientific consensus on the anthropogenic role in climate change must concede the need for regulatory adaptation to the changes that are already observable. Nevertheless, both mitigation and adaptation are likely to raise the same hurdles that have complicated responses to other interjurisdictional environmental problems (such as wetlands loss and radioactive waste) and natural disasters (such as pandemic flu and hurricanes).

Climate is the overarching public commons, and coping with forecasted changes will require regulatory response from every point along the spectrum of political scale. After all, climate change connects the most local of all happenings—the decisions each of us makes about where we decide to live, how we get to work, and what we eat—with the most global of all happenings: shifts in planetary weather patterns that will decide, in larger terms, where whole populations can live, what they can grow for food, and what policies nation states will follow in pursuit of their changing interests. With the high costs of avoiding it and even higher costs of avoidance, climate change is the mother of all collective action problems.

Because greenhouse gases are produced locally but mix evenly in the atmosphere regardless of origin, climate mitigation necessarily requires the exercise of authority from the local to the national to the international level (hopefully in meaningful coordination). Local efforts are necessary to cope, for example, with the impacts of countless personal commuting decisions through climate-sensitive land use planning and transportation initiatives. But national and international efforts are needed to cope with the interstate commerce and collective action features of the problem. Otherwise, action taken in one locale can be effectively negated by free riders in another, and regulated industries in one jurisdiction may relocate (or "leak") to less stringently regulated alternatives. Climate adaptation governance will involve similar jurisdictional overlap, triggering local authority to cope with rapid changes in land use and public safety issues and the various national responsibilities implicated during the Katrina emergency.

As with so many other interjurisdictional quandaries, then, the challenge of climate governance is to locate the ideal equipoise between two competing goods: (1) a strong centralized program that can achieve the needed cumulative results, and (2) continued room for the kind of vibrant local innovation and interjurisdictional competition that can provide new ideas and regulatory backstops in case of failed national policy. The same dilemma exists both internationally and domestically, although this discussion is limited to climate governance in the United States. And in U.S. climate policy, the potential for serious federalism conflict is everywhere. The ghost of classical dualism haunts climate governance both through the heightened risk of litigation associated with regulatory crossover and by encouraging regulatory abdication in the face of that uncertainty.

During a long period of federal abdication, state and local actors overcame the fears of liability and lost investment to enter the regulatory field in force. After a decade of federal inaction on climate governance, states have taken the lead in developing a broad variety of initiatives using their police powers to regulate for the health and welfare of their citizens. Most climate regulatory efforts fall into two main categories: those that take aim at the supply and demand of electricity generation, and those that focus on the transportation sector. Initiatives targeting electricity supply and demand include state and regional carbon cap-and-trade markets; renewable portfolio standards; electric power plant carbon emission standards; public benefit funds, tax credits, and other public subsidy programs; net metering and green pricing; energy efficiency resource and products standards; building energy codes; and local government initiatives such as installing energy-efficient lighting.

The regional carbon caps are the most ambitious state-based programs (though perhaps more poetic than potent, given the dilemma of regional restraint in the global greenhouse gas arena). In creating and regulating new interstate markets, they are the most vulnerable to federal preemption. But as federalism innovators in the absence of national action, three regional groups and one state have instituted their own carbon cap-and-trade systems. In the Northeast and Mid-Atlantic regions, ten states have joined the Regional Greenhouse Gas Initiative (RGGI) and pledged to reduce carbon dioxide emissions from their power sectors by 10 percent by 2018. RGGI states held their ninth carbon auction in September of 2010. In the West, seven states joined four Canadian provinces to form the Western Climate Initiative, with plans to begin carbon trading by 2012. In the Midwest, six states and one Canadian province formed the Midwest

Greenhouse Gas Reduction Accord, pledging to establish a multisector cap-and-trade system to meet regional greenhouse gas reduction targets. The State of California is creating its own state-wide program, with plans to adopt cap-and-trade regulations by 2011 and begin trading in 2012.

Twenty-eight states and the District of Columbia are also reducing greenhouse gas emissions by regulating the electricity supply sector directly, including the establishment of renewable portfolio standards that require electric utility companies to generate a certain portion of their electricity from renewable sources. For example, thanks to its vast wind resources, Texas was able to meet its initial renewable supply targets and then double them in a second round of legislation. Other states directly limit the amount of greenhouse gasses their power plants emit. For example, the California Public Utility Commission established a greenhouse gas emission cap, then forbade in-state power plants from entering into long-term supply contracts that would violate the cap. This controversial move has required careful navigation of the federalism and preemption concerns raised by the fact that California retailers often obtain power from out-of-state suppliers in interstate commerce.

States also use monetary incentives to promote emissions reductions, some through tax credits and direct subsidies to promote renewable energy and increased energy efficiency. Approximately twenty-five states have established Public Benefit Funds for this purpose, funded by surcharges on consumer utility bills. Some have also created programs to subsidize particular renewable technologies or encourage their use by consumers. For example, California has established a fund of $3.3 billion to subsidize installation of solar power systems in homes and businesses. Eighteen states have enacted "net metering" programs, which allow consumers generating electricity through home-based solar or wind collectors to sell excess back to the grid. Forty-one states allow "green pricing," which enable consumers to choose electricity generation from renewable sources by adding small premiums to their electric bills.

States also regulate electricity on the demand side. Nineteen states are grappling with growing energy demand by establishing energy efficiency resource and product standards, encouraging more efficient production methods among generators by setting minimum energy-savings targets for electricity generation and heating fuels. Eight states have established similar efficiency standards for consumer appliances as of 2008, generating further federalism controversy. Electrical appliance standards are normally subject to federal preemption, but the Department of Energy has proposed waiving preemption so that states can exceed federal minimum standards. California estimates that it can save consumers $3 billion and eliminate the need for three new power plants just by improving product efficiency.

States are also regulating the energy efficiency of buildings, in recognition of the fact that residential and commercial buildings use over 70 percent of electricity consumed in the United States. Most states have building energy codes, though they generally set modest energy savings goals. Thirty-one state and local governments also require or encourage compliance with voluntary green building rating systems, such as LEED (Leadership in Energy and Environmental Design) and Green Globe standards. Colorado requires that any new or renovated building whose total project cost includes at least 25 percent in state funds must comply with "standards of an independent third-party green building certification system, such as LEED." Boston was the first major U.S. city to require all buildings over fifty thousand square feet to be certifiable under LEED standards. Local governments are also seeking to promote energy efficiency, implementing municipal solid waste management programs that use less energy and recover landfill gasses, installing energy-efficient lighting, and adopting efficiency building codes. Boulder, Colorado went even farther and adopted the nation's first energy tax in 2006.

On the transportation side, some states are now regulating greenhouse gas emissions from motor vehicles. In another move that sparked substantial federalism controversy, California became the first state to directly target greenhouse gas emissions from passenger cars and light trucks, ultimately winning a contested waiver from EPA to exceed the national standard under the Clean Air Act. Because other states are permitted to choose the alternative motor vehicle standards under the California waiver rule, fourteen states have now adopted California's new greenhouse gas emissions standards, and approximately eleven others have indicated an interest. California is now considering implementing a low-carbon fuel standard, perhaps launching a new national model. Municipalities are also incorporating climate concerns into their land use planning decisions, revising transportation plans and investing in mass transit to reduce vehicle miles traveled, and encouraging carpooling and bicycle commuting.

Finally, states have approached climate governance through more holistic measures. Thirty-eight states either already have or are creating statewide nonbinding climate action plans varying in specificity, baselines, and targets. Seventeen states have statewide emission-reduction targets. States also participate in several greenhouse gas emission registries, which develop uniform protocols for measuring, reporting, and verifying greenhouse gas emissions in several industrial sectors. The largest is the Climate Registry, a not-for-profit organization representing forty states, eleven

Canadian provinces, six Mexican states, and three tribal nations. The California Climate Action Registry, formed by the state at the request of energy investors, provides a greenhouse gas registry for organizations to report their emissions and offsets. The Climate Action Reserve is another program that sets standards for measuring carbon offsets for the purpose of credits, pricing, and trade.

Nevertheless, this wealth of state activity may not be enough to cope with the problem, given substantial concerns about leakage and regulatory inefficiencies. Most advocates for climate governance argue that federal leadership is critical. Even state climate governance proponents tend to see regional efforts as a "next-best strategy in the absence of serious national leadership." At the same time, successful state and local initiatives are exceedingly vulnerable to preemption against a constitutional backdrop in which most of these initiatives overlap with potential exercises of the federal commerce, property, and foreign affairs powers. . . .

The challenge for climate governance will be how best to continue reaping the benefits of interjurisdictional innovation and regulatory backstop that local initiatives have thus far provided without undermining the national forces that may ultimately be necessary to produce satisfactory results. It will require implementing a strong centralized program without crippling the laboratories of ideas that have given us our most promising tools to date. The profound breadth of overlap implied by meaningful climate governance suggests that the ramifications of climate federalism will redound in both directions. Federalism will certainly influence the development of American climate policy. And by role modeling the reality and necessity of jurisdictional overlap, climate policy will—in turn—influence the development of American federalism.

18

LORI RIVERSTONE-NEWELL

From *Renegade Cities, Public Policy, and the Dilemmas of Federalism*

Intergovernmental relations usually refers to the relationship between the national government in Washington, D.C. and the fifty state governments across the country. But Professor Lori Riverstone-Newell extends the meaning of federalism to include the cities that are incorporated by the states. Some of these cities have struck out on their own, employing "local activism" to institute policies that they wish to pursue apart from the states or national government. Maybe these cities disagree with a national policy (homemade church pies or same-sex marriage). Maybe they perceive the highly polarized politics at the national level as stalling effective government action: so the cities decide to act on their own. States, too, have rebelled against national foot-dragging, Riverstone-Newell mentions. Many cities have elevated their profiles in recent decades, with innovative economic, educational and demographic outreach. Now they want "a seat at the table," even if they're just a city within a state that's within a vast country.

—

IN MARCH 2011, the town of Sedgwick, Maine, population 1,196, became the first in the nation to declare itself to be "food sovereign"—fully capable and within its rights to grow and sell food without state or federal inspections, among other regulations. "The primary goal of the ordinance is to exempt local farm products from [state and federal] licensure and inspection if the products are only going to be sold by the producer directly to a willing consumer." The ordinance, voted into law at a town meeting, proclaims the town to be "duty bound under the Constitution of the State of Maine to protect and promote unimpeded access to local foods" and that it is "unlawful for any law or regulation adopted by the state or federal government to interfere with the rights recognized by this Ordinance." Notably, since 2011, at least thirteen towns in nine states, from Maine to California, have since passed similar ordinances. Bills like that passed in Sedgwick have been unsuccessfully introduced in several states.

Congress's Food Safety Modernization Act of 2010, known among some local food sovereignty supporters as "the Patriot Act for food" generated this activism. Many small farmers believe that the Act, meant to "enhance the safety of food produced in America and imported from overseas, and to prevent food-borne illness" threatens their livelihood by potentially subjecting them to expensive regulations. They are particularly worried about sections that may prevent the sale or gifting of locally grown foods and meat and dairy products. Says Deborah Evans, one of the crafters of Sedgwick's ordinance,

> There's a possibility that the homemade church pies and baked beans brought and shared to church outings and firemen's picnics could be banned by the federal government's rules. They say such items would be "grandfathered" but could we really take them seriously? Or is it an effort to ensure that such items would need to be purchased at Walmart or wherever to be brought to such events? By fighting to preserve the right to purchase and consume the local food we've enjoyed for 200 years, we can begin to take back our other rights as well!

Local autonomy and power within the American intergovernmental system has evolved over the past three hundred years. Localities have shifted from autonomous, relatively isolated governments to subordinate units, subject to state and federal demands and interference. At the same time, they are "mini-sovereigns," semi-autonomous units that are legally and politically responsible to their local constituents for an array of services and functions. This "contradictory status" of localities—administrative unit and mini-sovereign—looms large, affecting local capacity, decision-making, and implementation plans. Nevertheless, they are not powerless. Local leaders, like other governments within the intergovernmental system, strategize and act politically in order to protect their interests and influence other governments, even higher governments, to their liking. When diplomatic strategies—bargaining, negotiating, and so forth—fail to generate the desired response, local leaders sometimes engage in activism by using their positions of authority to purposefully—pointedly—challenge the authority of higher governments.

Local activism has the potential to stimulate policy change by engaging the public and the media. In this book, we define local activism as *official* acts of defiance that can reasonably be understood as deliberate attempts to spotlight unfavorable higher laws and policies in order to engage the media and "expand the scope of conflict" to the public. With sufficient exposure, higher government leaders are pressured to reconsider, or at least defend, their policy positions.

Activism has been used to influence a variety of foreign and domestic policies since the early 1980s. Several high-profile cases of local activism have captured national attention; indeed, some of these cases have successfully generated a favorable response from higher governments or the courts. Recall, for example, San Francisco's licensing of same-sex marriage in 2004. Gavin Newsom, the city and county's former mayor, issued an executive order permitting same-sex couples to legally marry. This order defied state law, which defined marriage as a union between one man and one woman. As a result, the constitutionality of same-sex marriage bans was presented to federal courts. With a recent decision in favor of same-sex marriage recognition by the Ninth Circuit Court of Appeals, the issue is currently before the United States Supreme Court.

While the San Francisco gay marriage case is unusual in its impact and visibility, it is not an isolated event. Across the nation, localities large and small have attempted to signal their preferences and provoke policy movement by enacting thousands of ordinances, resolutions, and executive orders in policy areas reserved to state and/or federal purview.

The range of issues targeted for activism is wide. Some of the earliest cases involve national foreign policy: The nuclear-free zone movement, divestment of local funds from firms conducting business with or in South Africa, and the sanctuary city movement of the 1980s—a response to the Reagan administration's support of Central American authoritarian regimes and the Contra rebels in Nicaragua—involved more than 1,000 localities across the nation. More recently, local governments have generated over 400 resolutions opposing the USA PATRIOT Act (Patriot Act); several localities have enacted ordinances criminalizing participation with the Act's enforcement. In addition, at the close of 2007, over 270 localities had passed resolutions protesting the war in Iraq.

Controversial social matters have been targeted for local activism as well. For example, local gun control efforts produced more than 50 ordinances leading up to the U.S. Supreme Court decision *District of Columbia v. Heller.** Also, in contrast to the estimated 100 local policies meant to deter undocumented immigrants that were active in 2010, 120 policies in other communities restrained city employees—including police—from ascertaining and/or reporting an individual's immigration status to the federal government. An estimated 100 resolutions, executive orders, and ordinances—both supportive and unsupportive—have addressed same-sex couples' rights since 1980. Examples of other policy areas targeted by local activists include medical marijuana, living wages, the placement of

*In *District of Columbia v. Heller* (2008), the U.S. Supreme Court decided that the Second Amendment protects the right of citizens of D.C. to own a legal firearm. Two years later, in *McDonald v. Chicago*, the Court extended that right to citizens of all states, based on the Fourteenth Amendment's due process clause.—EDS.

cellular towers, Kyoto environmental protocols, and corporate person-hood. Food sovereignty is the most recent effort.

What compels local leaders to activism? Why choose activism to stim-ulate policy change rather than a less confrontational, more diplomatic, approach? The limited legal status of localities in the United States sets the stage: As Iowa Judge John F. Dillon put it in 1868, localities are "mere ten-ants at the will of the legislature," unable to exercise any powers not spe-cifically granted by their states. As "creatures of the states," localities are devoid of the sovereignty and protections that state and national govern-ments enjoy. They are, according to David Berman, legally "no better off than conquered provinces."

Because of their legal subordination, localities are highly disadvan-taged in the intergovernmental arena. They are on the "asking side," un-able to impose their will upon state or national governments. This subor-dination is "an invisible force operating in the background," a force that compels local governments to maintain vigilance and to strategically de-fend and promote their interests against the actions of other governments. As a consequence of this political weakness, dissenting localities have only a few means with which to attempt to promote policy changes at the national and state level. Local activism is one. . . .

Although branded "arrogant," "lawless," "silly," and even "charlatans" by their critics, local officials often defend their activism as civil disobedi-ence—acts of conscience made necessary by the persistent policy failures of state and federal legislatures. Others claim that they are forced to act due to degrading local conditions caused by state or federal actions or inaction, or a perceived "distant" condition that is incompatible with local values. The many political, economic, and social developments that have likely played a part include policy conservatism and centralization at the national level; a changed, more aggressive leadership style at the local lev-el; increased interest group activity in localities, and all levels of govern-ment; economic recession(s); heightened party polarization and legislative gridlock; and rising popular discontent with higher, especially national, government.

Local governments are not alone in their activism. A growing body of literature has documented the recent growth of state activism against fed-eral policy. Dale Krane writes that there has been a centralizing "trend toward coercive federalism . . . since the 1980s." The states, particularly during the Bush administration, responded to federal interference with: "(i) resistance to many of the Bush policy positions and (ii) heightened independent policy activity." Some states have simply refused to cooperate with certain aspects of federal policy. For example, the "Food and Drug Administration's (FDA) ban on the importation of prescription drugs was defied by several states." Others passed resolutions opposing, for instance, the REAL ID Act and the Patriot Act. We see similar behavior today as states respond to the Patient Protection and Affordable Care Act.*

State frustration with federal inaction has contributed to this aggression. The ongoing inability of federal legislators to work together burdens the states by preventing policy remedies in matters reserved to federal control: "the difficulty of enacting federal legislation, the frequent existence of partisan polarization at the federal level, and the multiplicity of veto points that can impede policy action" prevents timely and sufficient federal policy responses, leaving the states with little choice but to act, despite their lack of authority to do so.

Localities have also suffered from legislative gridlock and higher government inaction. Further, the absence of gridlock does not guarantee issue resolution; policies adopted by higher governments may be mismatched to local conditions or desires, failing to satisfactorily resolve, or even reflect, local issues. Some localities have confronted state and federal inertia by becoming innovative policy laboratories, taking it upon themselves to, for example, enforce living wages, mandate local healthcare, require same-sex benefits for city employees, and pass "labor-friendly ordinances." According to legal scholar Richard Schragger, these and other progressive policy innovations are a "function of a growing dissatisfaction with national responses to . . . problems and a renewed energy and aggressiveness at the local level."

Local activism is a symbolic expression of disapproval, a "performance" designed to "expand the scope of conflict" and force open the public debate. With sufficient media attention and public support, local activism has the capacity to compel state and/or national leaders to defend, and potentially reconsider, their unfavorable policies or behaviors. . . .

. . . The rising status and visibility of cities, especially central cities, has made resistance to higher authority less risky. Cities are not the less-than-desirable places that they used to be and, as a result, many have enjoyed an urban resurgence. After decades of population loss and decline, many cities, beginning in the late 1970s, began to focus on revitalization and resto-

---

*An example of some states' unwillingness to follow parts of the Affordable Care Act is the rejection by more than a dozen states of the extension of Medicaid benefits to cover low income residents. The Supreme Court's decision in *National Federation of Independent Business v. Sebelius* (2012), the case that declared the ACA constitutional under the national government's power to tax, did find that states could legitimately refuse Medicaid expansion.—EDS.

ration of their infrastructure, built environment, and economic base. This coincided with new economic opportunities brought by the globalizing economy, as well as the nation's associated shift away from manufacturing to knowledge- and service-based jobs. The new interrelated employment sectors have found revitalized and revitalizing localities eager to accommodate the unique needs of today's agglomerating industries and the people who work within them.

Richard Schragger points to new economic stability, local policy experimentation, the educational level of city residents (compared to other areas), and urban diversity as reasons for urban resurgence—a condition in which cities are no longer losing population even as they have renewed economic clout. Today's localities enjoy higher levels of professionalism, economic vitality, self-sufficiency, and even national and international visibility and prestige than ever before. Entrepreneurial, strong, charismatic mayors, reinforced by a general sense among the population that state and federal leaders are no longer "tuned in" to the people, have created conditions in which cities sense greater autonomy and independence than was once the case.

Although formally weak, intergovernmental interdependence, public distrust for higher governments, and improved self-sufficiency permits today's frustrated localities—whether invited or uninvited—to participate in the "dialog" that is federalism, with its exchanges that span the "polite conversations and collaborative discussions that cooperative federalism champions. . . . to restrained disagreement to fighting words." Localities interject all along the continuum, sometimes winning a seat at the table, particularly when state or federal officials believe that there is more to be gained than lost by including them. Local leaders have also found that when their accommodation cannot be negotiated, other means of pressure exist. . . .

PART FOUR

Congress

19

DAVID MAYHEW

From *Congress: The Electoral Connection*

*Congressional scholar David Mayhew admits from the start that his expla-
nation for the motivation of members of Congress is one-dimensional: they
are "single-minded seekers of reelection." While Mayhew's thesis is intentionally narrow and his examples a bit out-of-date (none of the members
cited in the excerpt is still in the House), reelection remains a primary mo-
tivator for congressional behavior. To attain reelection, representatives use
three strategies. They advertise, so that their names are well-known. They
claim credit for goodies that flow to their districts. And they take positions on
political issues. Mayhew's theme, illustrated with amusing examples, may
seem cynical, but it is doubtlessly realistic. Perhaps his analysis should have
been fair warning to members of Congress about the public's growing disillusionment with the national legislature.*

———

. . . I SHALL CONJURE UP a vision of United States congressmen
as single-minded seekers of reelection, see what kinds of activity that goal
implies, and then speculate about how congressmen so motivated are likely to go about building and sustaining legislative institutions and making
policy. . . .

I find an emphasis on the reelection goal attractive for a number of
reasons. First, I think it fits political reality rather well. Second, it puts the
spotlight directly on men rather than on parties and pressure groups,
which in the past have often entered discussions of American politics as
analytic phantoms. Third, I think politics is best studied as a struggle among
men to gain and maintain power and the consequences of that struggle.
Fourth—and perhaps most important—the reelection quest establishes an
accountability relationship with an electorate, and any serious thinking
about democratic theory has to give a central place to the question of accountability. . . .

Whether they are safe or marginal, cautious or audacious, congressmen must constantly engage in activities related to reelection. There will
be differences in emphasis, but all members share the root need to do
things—indeed, to do things day in and day out during their terms. The
next step here is to present a typology, a short list of the *kinds* of activities
congressmen find it electorally useful to engage in. . . .

One activity is *advertising*, defined here as any effort to disseminate one's name among constituents in such a fashion as to create a favorable image but in messages having little or no issue content. A successful congressman builds what amounts to a brand name, which may have a generalized electoral value for other politicians in the same family. The personal qualities to emphasize are experience, knowledge, responsiveness, concern, sincerity, independence, and the like. Just getting one's name across is difficult enough; only about half the electorate, if asked, can supply their House members' names. It helps a congressman to be known. "In the main, recognition carries a positive valence; to be perceived at all is to be perceived favorably." A vital advantage enjoyed by House incumbents is that they are much better known among voters than their November challengers. They are better known because they spend a great deal of time, energy, and money trying to make themselves better known. There are standard routines—frequent visits to the constituency, nonpolitical speeches to home audiences, the sending out of infant care booklets and letters of condolence and congratulation. . . .

Some routines are less standard. Congressman George E. Shipley (D., Ill.) claims to have met personally about half his constituents (i.e. some 200,000 people). For over twenty years Congressman Charles C. Diggs, Jr. (D., Mich.) has run a radio program featuring himself as a "combination disc jockey-commentator and minister." Congressman Daniel J. Flood (D., Pa.) is "famous for appearing unannounced and often uninvited at wedding anniversaries and other events." Anniversaries and other events aside, congressional advertising is done largely at public expense. Use of the franking privilege has mushroomed in recent years; in early 1973 one estimate predicted that House and Senate members would send out about 476 million pieces of mail in the year 1974, at a public cost of $38.1 million—or about 900,000 pieces per member with a subsidy of $70,000 per member. By far the heaviest mailroom traffic comes in Octobers of even-numbered years. There are some differences between House and Senate members in the ways they go about getting their names across. House members are free to blanket their constituencies with mailings for all boxholders; senators are not. But senators find it easier to appear on national television—for example, in short reaction statements on the nightly news shows. Advertising is a staple congressional activity, and there is no end to it. For each member there are always new voters to be apprised of his worthiness and old voters to be reminded of it.

A second activity may be called *credit claiming*, defined here as acting so as to generate a belief in a relevant political actor (or actors) that one is personally responsible for causing the government, or some unit thereof, to do something that the actor (or actors) considers desirable. The political logic of this, from the congressman's point of view, is that an actor who believes that a member can make pleasing things happen will no doubt wish to keep him in office so that he can make pleasing things happen in the future. The emphasis here is on individual accomplishment (rather than, say, party or governmental accomplishment) and on the congressman as doer (rather than as, say, expounder of constituency views). Credit claiming is highly important to congressmen, with the consequence that much of congressional life is a relentless search for opportunities to engage in it.

Where can credit be found? . . . For the average congressman the staple way of doing this is to traffic in what may be called "particularized benefits." . . .

In sheer volume the bulk of particularized benefits come under the heading of "casework"—the thousands of favors congressional offices perform for supplicants in ways that normally do not require legislative action. High school students ask for essay materials, soldiers for emergency leaves, pensioners for location of missing checks, local governments for grant information, and on and on. Each office has skilled professionals who can play the bureaucracy like an organ—pushing the right pedals to produce the desired effects. But many benefits require new legislation, or at least they require important allocative decisions on matters covered by existent legislation. Here the congressman fills the traditional role of supplier of goods to the home district. It is a believable role; when a member claims credit for a benefit on the order of a dam, he may well receive it. Shiny construction projects seem especially useful. . . .

The third activity congressmen engage in may be called *position taking*, defined here as the public enunciation of a judgmental statement on anything likely to be of interest to political actors. The statement may take the form of a roll call vote. The most important classes of judgmental statements are those prescribing American governmental ends (a vote cast against the war; a statement that "the war should be ended immediately") or governmental means (a statement that "the way to end the war is to take it to the United Nations"). . . .

The ways in which positions can be registered are numerous and often imaginative. There are floor addresses ranging from weighty orations to mass-produced "nationality day statements." There are speeches before home groups, television appearances, letters, newsletters, press releases, ghostwritten books, *Playboy* articles, even interviews with political scientists. . . . Outside the roll call process the congressman is usually able to tailor his positions to suit his audiences. . . .

... On a controversial issue a Capitol Hill office normally prepares two form letters to send out to constituent letter writers—one for the pros and one (not directly contradictory) for the antis. Handling discrete audiences in person requires simple agility, a talent well demonstrated in this selection from a Nader profile*:

"You may find this difficult to understand," said Democrat Edward R. Roybal, the Mexican-American representative from California's thirtieth district, "but sometimes I wind up making a patriotic speech one afternoon and later on that same day an anti-war speech. In the patriotic speech I speak of past wars but I also speak of the need to prevent more wars. My positions are not inconsistent; I just approach different people differently." Roybal went on to depict the diversity of crowds he speaks to: one afternoon he is surrounded by balding men wearing Veterans' caps and holding American flags; a few hours later he speaks to a crowd of Chicano youths, angry over American involvement in Vietnam. Such a diverse constituency, Roybal believes, calls for different methods of expressing one's convictions.

Indeed it does.

---

*Ralph Nader is a public-interest activist who has dedicated himself to protecting the American people against both governmental and private industry wrong-doing. One of Nader's best known campaigns came in the 1960s against General Motors, whose Chevrolet Corvair, Nader claimed, was "unsafe at any speed." In the 1996, 2000, 2004, and 2008 presidential elections, he ran as a third-party candidate.—EDS

20

RICHARD FENNO

From *Home Style*

Stated simply, political scientist Richard Fenno had a wonderful idea for a book. Instead of studying members of Congress at work in Washington, D.C., on the House floor, legislating, he researched them in what has always seemed their most obscure, out-of-the-spotlight moments. At home, in their districts, very little was known about legislators until Fenno's work. He opens with the psychological concept of "presentation of self," a technique designed to "win trust" from constituents. Fenno makes mention of the important "delegate" and "trustee" models of representation. Legislators do not explain every detail of their policy positions to the voters, rather, they want voters to trust them enough to allow them "voting leeway" back in Washington.

MOST HOUSE MEMBERS spend a substantial proportion of their working lives "at home." Even those in our low frequency category return to their districts more often than we would have guessed. Over half of that group go home more than once a month. What, then, do representatives do there? Much of what they do is captured by Erving Goffman's idea of *the presentation of self.* That is, they place themselves in "the immediate physical presence" of others and then "make a presentation of themselves to others." Goffman writes about the ordinary encounters between people "in everyday life." But, the dramaturgical analogues he uses fit the political world, too. Politicians, like actors, speak to and act before audiences from whom they must draw both support and legitimacy. Without support and legitimacy, there is no political relationship.

In all his encounters, says Goffman, the performer will seek to control the response of others to him by expressing himself in ways that leave the correct impressions of himself with others. His expressions will be of two sorts—"the expressions that he gives and the expression that he gives off." The first are mostly verbal; the second are mostly nonverbal. Goffman is particularly interested in the second kind of expression—"the more theatrical and contextual kind"—because he believes that the performer is more likely to be judged by others according to the nonverbal than the verbal elements of his presentation of self. Those who must do the judging, Goffman says, will think that the verbal expressions are more controllable and manipulable by the performer. And they will, therefore, read his nonverbal "signs" as a check on the reliability of his verbal "signs." Basic to this reasoning is the idea that, of necessity, every presentation has a largely "promissory character" to it. Those who listen to and watch the presentation cannot be sure what the relationship between themselves and the performer really is. So the relationship must be sustained, on the part of those watching, by inference. They "must accept the individual on faith." In this process of acceptance, they will rely heavily on the inferences they draw from his nonverbal expressions—the expressions "given off."

Goffman does not talk about politicians; but politicians know what Goffman is talking about. The response they seek from others is political support. And the impressions they try to foster are those that will engender political support. House member politicians believe that a great deal of their support is won by the kind of individual self they present to others, i.e., to their constituents. More than most other people, they consciously try to manipulate it. Certainly, they believe that what they say, their verbal expression, is an integral part of their "self." But, with Goffman, they place special emphasis on the nonverbal, "contextual" aspects of their presentation. At the least, the nonverbal elements must be consistent with the verbal ones. At the most, the expressions "given off" will become the basis for constituent judgment. Like Goffman, members of Congress are willing to emphasize the latter because, with him, they believe that their constituents will apply a heavier discount to what they say than to how they say it or to how they act in the context in which they say it. In the members' own language, constituents want to judge you "as a person." The comment I have heard most often during my travels is: "he's a good man" or "she's a good woman," unembossed by qualifiers of any sort. Constituents, say House members, want to "size you up" or "get the feel of you" "as a person," or "as a human being." And the largest part of what House members mean when they say "as a person" is what Goffman means by expressions "given off." Largely from expressions given off comes the judgment: "he's a good man," "she's a good woman."

So members of Congress go home to present themselves as a person and to win the accolade: "he's a good man," "she's a good woman." With Goffman, they know there is a "promissory character" to their presentation. And their object is to present themselves as a person in such a way that the inferences drawn by those watching will be supportive. The representatives' word for these supportive inferences is *trust*. It is a word they use a great deal. When a constituent trusts a House member, the constituent is saying something like this: "I am willing to put myself in your hands temporarily; I know you will have opportunities to hurt me, although I may not know when those opportunities occur; I assume—and I will continue to assume until it is proven otherwise—that you will not hurt me; for the time being, then, I'm not going to worry about your behavior." The ultimate response House members seek is political support. But the instrumental response they seek is trust. The presentation of self—that which is given in words and given off as a person—will be calculated to win trust. "If people like you and trust you as individual," members often say, "they will vote for you." So trust becomes central to the representative-constituent relationship. For their part, constituents must rely on trust. They must "accept on faith" that the congressman is what he says he is and will do what he says he will do. House members, for their part, are quite happy to emphasize trust. It helps to allay the uncertainties they feel about their relationship with their supportive constituencies. If members are uncertain as to how to work for support directly, they can always work indirectly to win a degree of personal trust that will increase the likelihood of support or decrease the likelihood of opposition.

Trust is, however, a fragile relationship. It is not an overnight or a one-time thing. It is hard to win; and it must be constantly renewed and re-won. "Trust," said one member, "is a cumulative thing, a totality thing. . . . You do a little here and a little there." So it takes an enormous amount of time to build and to maintain constituent trust. That is what House members believe. And that is why they spend so much of their working time at home. Much of what I have observed in my travels can be explained as a continuous and continuing effort to win (for new members) and to hold (for old members) the trust of supportive constituencies. Most of the communication I have heard and seen is not overtly political at all. It is, rather, part of a ceaseless effort to reenforce the underpinnings of trust in the congressman or the congresswoman as a person. Viewed from this perspective, the archetypical constituent question is not "What have you done for me lately?" but "How have you looked to me lately?" In sum, House members make a strategic calculation that helps us understand why they go home so much. *Presentation of self enhances trust; enhancing trust takes time; therefore, presentation of self takes time. . . .*

Explaining Washington activity, as said at the outset, includes justifying that activity to one's constituents. The pursuit of power, for example, is sometimes justified with the argument that the representative accumulates power not for himself but for his constituents. In justifying their policy decisions, representatives sometimes claim that their policy decisions follow not what they want but what their constituents want. Recall the member who justified his decision not to support his own highway bill with the comment, "I'm not here to vote my own convictions. I'm

here to represent my people." Similarly, the member who decided to yield
to his constituent's wishes on gun control said, "I rationalize it by saying
that I owe it to my constituents if they feel that strongly about it." But this
is not a justification all members use. The independent, issue-oriented
Judiciary Committee member mentioned earlier commented (privately)
with heavy sarcasm,

All some House members are interested in is "the folks." They think "the folks"
are the second coming. They would no longer do anything to displease "the
folks" than they would fly. They spend all their time trying to find out what "the
folks" want. I imagine if they get five letters on one side and five letters on
the other side, they die.

An alternative justification, of course, is that the representative's policy
decisions are based on what he thinks is good public policy, regardless of
what his constituents want. As the Judiciary Committee member told his
constituents often, "If I were sitting where you are, I think what I would
want is to elect a man to Congress who will exercise his best judgment on
the facts when he has them all." At a large community college gathering
in the heart of his district, a member who was supporting President Nixon's Vietnam policy was asked, "If a majority of your constituents signed a
petition asking you to vote for a date to end the war, would you vote for
it?" He answered,

It's hard for me to imagine a majority of my constituents agreeing on anything.
But if it did happen, then no, I would not vote for it. I would still have to use my
own judgment—especially where the security of the country is involved. You can
express opinions. I have to make the decision. If you disagree with my decisions,
you have the power every two years to vote me out of office. I listen to you, believe me. But, in the end, I have to use my judgment as to what is in your best
interests.

He then proceeded to describe his views on the substantive question.
   To political scientists, these two kinds of policy justification are very
familiar. One is a "delegate" justification, the other a "trustee" justification. The two persist side by side because the set of constituent attitudes
on which each depends also exist side by side. Voters, that is, believe that
members of Congress should follow constituents' wishes; and voters also
believe that members of Congress should use their own best judgment.
They want their representatives, it has been said, to be "common people
of uncommon judgment." Most probably, though we do not know, voters
want delegate behavior on matters most precious to them and trustee
behavior on all others. Nonetheless, both kinds of justification are acceptable as a general proposition. Both are legitimate, and in explaining their

Washington activity members are seeking to legitimate that activity. They use delegate and trustee justifications because both are legitimating concepts.

If, when they are deciding how to vote, House members think in terms of delegates and trustees, it is because they are thinking about the terms in which they will explain (i.e., justify or legitimate) that vote back home if the need to do so arises. If members never had to legitimate any of their policy decisions back home, they would stop altogether talking in delegate or trustee language. . . .

Members elaborate the linkage between presentation and explanation this way: There are at most only a very few policy issues on which representatives are constrained in their voting by the views of their reelection constituencies. They may not *feel* constrained, if they agree with those views. But that is beside the point; they are constrained nevertheless. On the vast majority of votes, however, representatives can do as they wish—provided only that they can, when they need to, explain their votes to the satisfaction of interested constituents. The ability to get explanations accepted at home is, then, the essential underpinning of a member's voting leeway in Washington.

So the question arises: How can representatives increase the likelihood that their explanations will be accepted at home? And the answer House members give is: They can win and hold constituent trust. The more your various constituencies trust you, members reason, the less likely they are to require an explanation of your votes and the more likely they are to accept your explanation when they do ask for it. The winning of trust, we have said earlier, depends largely on the presentation of self. Presentation of self, then, not only helps win votes at election time. It also makes voting in Washington easier. So members of Congress make a strategic calculation: *Presentation of self enhances trust; trust enhances the acceptability of explanations; the acceptability of explanations enhances voting leeway; therefore, presentation of self-enhances voting leeway.* . . .

The traditional focus of political scientists on the policy aspects of representation is probably related to the traditional focus on activity in the legislature. So long as concentration is on what happens in Washington, it is natural that policymaking will be thought of as the main activity of the legislature and representation will be evaluated in policy terms. To paraphrase Woodrow Wilson, it has been our view that Congress in Washington is Congress at work, while Congress at home is Congress on exhibition. The extrapolicy aspects of representational relationships have tended to be dismissed as symbolic—as somehow less substantial than the relationship embodied in a roll call vote in Washington—because what goes on at home has not been observed. For lack of observation, political scientists have tended to downgrade home activity as mere errand running or fence mending, as activity that takes the representative away from the important things—that is, making public policy in Washington. As one small example, the "Tuesday to Thursday Club" of House members who go home for long weekends—have always been criticized out of hand, on the assumption, presumably, that going home and doing things there was, ipso facto, bad. But no serious inquiry was ever undertaken into what they did there or what consequences—other than their obvious dereliction of duty—their home activity might have had. Home activity has been overlooked and denigrated and so, therefore, have those extra policy aspects of representation which can only be studied at home.

Predictably, the home activities described in this book will be regarded by some readers as further evidence that members of Congress spend too little of their time "on the job"—that is, in Washington, making policy. However, I hope readers will take from the book a different view—a view that values both Washington and home activity. Further, I hope readers will entertain the view that Washington and home activities may even be mutually supportive. Time spent at home can be time spent in developing leeway for activity undertaken in Washington. And that leeway in Washington should be more valued than the sheer number of contact hours spent there. If that should happen, we might then ask House members not to justify their time spent at home, but rather to justify their use of the leeway they have gained therefrom—during the legislative process in Washington. It may well be that a congressman's behavior in Washington is crucially influenced by the pattern of support he has developed at home, and by the allocational, presentational, and explanatory styles he displays there. To put the point most strongly, perhaps we can never understand his Washington activity without also understanding his perception of his various constituencies and the home style he uses to cultivate their support. . . .

21

STEVEN SMITH

From *The Senate Syndrome*

When students of American government first learn about the U.S. Congress, one of the most important pieces of information gleaned concerns the Senate and its custom of allowing unlimited debate—the filibuster. The reality is that dramatic filibusters in which a handful of senators take the Senate floor, talking uninterrupted for many hours or many days about proposed legislation that they deeply oppose is a view that is largely the stuff of movies or of history. The Senate filibuster still exists today, albeit significantly altered in 2013, but it's less dramatic than in political lore. Steven Smith discusses the 2013 rule change that disallowed filibusters to delay the vote for presidential nominees to executive branch positions and for lower federal court judgeships. Then-Majority Leader Harry Reid's strategy and tactics in bringing about this change make for interesting insider reading. Still, the need for sixty votes for cloture to end a filibuster on legislation (and in theory, on a Supreme Court nomination) can result in a Senate marked by obstruction and delay. The ability of senators to filibuster provides a protection for the minority, especially a minority that feels very strongly about a proposal. Although James Madison and the Framers of the Constitution might agree with the importance of minority rights, the Senate filibuster is not a formal part of the Constitution. It's a rule of the Senate, decided upon by the Senate. Whether the 2013 rule change will prove permanent is not yet clear. Nor are Senate-watchers clear on the cure for "the Senate syndrome."

ON NOVEMBER 21, 2013, the United States Senate changed. Using a procedure called the "nuclear option," Democratic majority leader Harry Reid (D-NV) made a point of order that the Senate can close debate on the consideration of a presidential nomination, other than to the Supreme Court, by a simple majority vote. Because Reid's point of order was inconsistent with Senate Rule XXII, the cloture rule that requires a three-fifths majority of all senators to close debate, the presiding officer ruled against Reid's point of order. Then, by a 48–52 vote, the Senate failed to sustain the ruling, thereby adopting the precedent that Reid requested. In a few minutes, the Senate had overturned a practice, over two hundred years old, that allowed a minority of senators to prevent a vote on nominations.

Republicans, and one prominent Democrat, Carl Levin (D-MI), protested that the Senate had changed in fundamental ways. An important minority right, the ability to block or delay action on presidential nominations, had been swept away. Moreover, the reform-by-ruling procedure used to establish the new precedent improperly circumvented the standing rule of the Senate that requires a two-thirds majority to close debate on a measure to change the rules. The Democratic leader, they argued, had turned the Senate into a second House of Representatives; in the House a majority can freely alter the rules governing debate to suit its convenience. The procedure would surely be used again and again. The Senate would never be the same.

Reid and most Democrats insisted that they were responding to unrelenting and unprecedented obstruction of presidential nominations by the minority Republicans. They pointed to Republicans' repeated violation of promises to reduce partisan obstructionism, which, they contended, had already altered the character of Senate decision making. Forcing a change in Senate procedure through a majority-backed precedent, they argued, would restore normalcy to Senate action on nominations. It would send a message that there was a limit to the majority's tolerance of the all-out minority obstructionism that the Democrats had endured for years.

My purpose in this book is to explain how the Senate arrived at this point and what it means for the Senate as a policy-making body. Senators of both parties believe that the Senate is broken and dysfunctional; many outsiders do as well. What they mean is that senators' use of inherited parliamentary rules and practices has undermined their role as senators and harmed the role of the Senate as a national policy-making institution. This is an important story—about how an important institution has evolved in recent decades and about how America is governed.

The U.S. Senate has a special place in American policy making. Its members embody the federal character of American governance by representing states, have a role in the appointment of judges and executive branch officials and in ratifying treaties, serve terms longer than those of representatives and presidents, and enjoy visibility in the nation and their home states that is unmatched by most representatives and judges. Along with the Senate's relatively small size and the continuity associated with its staggered terms of office, these features facilitate creativity, collaboration, and risk-taking. During much of its history, the Senate has achieved distinction for promoting new policy ideas, striking key compromises among competing interests, and generating presidential candidates.

The Senate of the last quarter century does not look much like that. The institution's characteristic individualism, long enabled by its informal, accommodative, civil, and flexible procedural environment, has given way to ill-mannered outbursts, policy stalemate, and procedural warfare motivated by deep partisan divisions. Senators recognize that their institution has changed and complain about it with some frequency. Many of them blame the other party's policy extremism and procedural abuses for the institution's problems. While the partisanship originates outside the Senate and is brought into the institution by elected senators, the Senate's procedural heritage makes that partisanship debilitating.

The procedural warfare of the modern Senate has taken the form of minority obstructionism and a majority response to control floor proceedings. Obstruction comes in the form of filibusters, threatened filibusters, or simple objections to the common unanimous consent requests to move legislation and nominations to a vote. A filibuster is a refusal to allow a matter to come to a vote, often by demonstrating a willingness to endlessly debate the issue. Obstruction, once uncommon and newsworthy, has become a standard feature of minority party parliamentary strategy and is so routine that it seldom warrants journalistic attention. The majority party has responded by looking for procedural shortcuts, limiting minority amendments, and more carefully managing time, all of which has changed the way the Senate does business.

The combination of minority-motivated obstruction and majority-imposed restrictions has created a pattern of behavior that I call the Senate syndrome. This syndrome has blossomed in the last two decades, but it has origins deeper in Senate history. Explaining its emergence and consequences is my challenge in this book. . . .

Constitutions, laws, institutional rules, and informal norms create sources of positive and negative power for political actors. Sources of positive power involve the assignment of authority to act and resources that make someone or a group capable of acting. Sources of negative power involve the ability to block action that others want to pursue. To political scientists, an actor who can block action is known as a veto player. American national government, with three branches and a bicameral legislature, is notable for the way positive power is shared and for the large number of veto players. Positive power is shared among several institutions. To enact legislation, a simple majority of the House and Senate, along with the president, must approve the legislation, unless, in the event of a presidential veto, a two-thirds majority can be mustered in both houses of Congress. The House and Senate can effectively veto legislation by withholding majority support. And the Supreme Court can veto legislation on constitutional or other grounds as it deems necessary. Every student of American government knows that much.

The Senate has added a potentially important complication. Due to the absence in its rules of a limit on debate for most legislation, the Senate allows a senator to speak without a time limit on most matters. By taking turns, a team of senators can hold the floor indefinitely. Typically, the Senate manages to deal with the uncertainties of unlimited debate through unanimous consent agreements that lend some order to floor proceedings. In fact, a central function of the majority leader, working with bill managers, is to negotiate such agreements. An individual senator may refuse consent to a request to limit debate. Ending debate without unanimous consent requires the adoption of a cloture motion. Under the Senate's Rule XXII, a three-fifths majority of all elected senators is required to pass a cloture motion, except on a measure to amend the rules, which requires a two-thirds majority of voting senators. The effect of these cloture thresholds is to make it more difficult for a majority to exercise positive power and easier for the minority to exercise negative power. In fact, with a few exceptions, a minority of at least 41 senators can withhold permission for the Senate to conclude debate and vote on a matter.

A long debate conducted for the purpose of preventing a vote is called a "filibuster" in Senate parlance. The term was first used in Congress in the mid-nineteenth century to describe protracted debate intended to prevent voting on a motion or measure. The term was used at the time to describe military adventurers and pirates operating in the Caribbean and other places. It came to be used more generally to describe efforts to obstruct legislative action on legislation, nominations, and treaties, although the term is most commonly associated with marathon speeches by a minority of senators that are intended to delay or prevent a vote that they would likely lose.

The Framers of the Constitution did not create the filibuster. The Constitution requires a two-thirds majority for taking a few specified actions (the override of a presidential veto, ratification of treaties, impeachment, expulsion of a senator, or approval of a constitutional amendment or convention), which gives a sizable minority the ability to prevent the Senate (and, in some cases, the House) from acting. On other matters, including the passage of legislation and confirmation of presidential nominations to executive and judicial positions, the Constitution is silent on the number of votes required and is taken to imply that decisions are made by simple-majority vote. How the House and Senate structure the decision-making process to get a measure to a vote is subject to the rules adopted by each house. The ability of a Senate minority to block action on legislation or nomination with a filibuster and the "supermajority" threshold for cloture are products of rules adopted by the Senate. Effectively, through its own rulemaking power, the Senate has made it possible for a large minority to block a majority by preventing a vote, in essence granting a veto power to the minority.

A central theme of this book is the large and unanticipated increase in the Senate minority's use of extraconstitutional veto power in recent decades. The minority party leadership even refers to the institution as the "60-vote Senate," which reflects the new behavior and expectations that have emerged in the last quarter century. The majority party has been deeply frustrated by these developments and has made countermoves of its own, setting off cycles of procedural maneuvers that have escalated the use and abuse of the Senate's parliamentary rules.

Grappling with the Senate Syndrome

I am writing this introduction in late 2013, just after the majority party Democrats acted to limit filibusters on presidential nominations. . . .

The new precedent of 2013 was one of the most important procedural developments in Senate history. The new threshold reshaped the strategic calculations of presidents and senators involved in the nomination and confirmation process. The reform-by-ruling approach to establishing a new procedure had been used before, but the approach had never been used to directly and explicitly undermine Rule XXII.

The Senate changed itself in a significant way. At this writing, senators and outsiders are still speculating about the implications of the 2013 precedent. Would the minority be tamed by the experience, or would it retaliate with more obstructionism on other matters? Would future Senate majorities use the reform-by-ruling technique to circumvent Rule XXII and acquire other changes in the rules that sizable minorities oppose? . . .

The nuclear option—reform by ruling—was used for a direct attack on Rule XXII in November 2013. Appeals to senators of both parties to collaborate had produced little change in the Senate in 2013. A budget and appropriations bills were left unpassed by the start of the fiscal year on October 1, several major bills passed by one house or the other were ignored when sent to the other house, and important presidential nominations to executive and judicial posts were blocked by the Senate minority. The division between the parties was as deep as ever.

In November 2013, after years of frustration, Majority Leader Harry Reid acquired enough support from fellow Democrats to support his point of order that a simple majority may invoke cloture on a presidential nomination to executive and judicial branch positions, with the exception of the Supreme Court. After decades of parliamentary warfare, as the Senate syndrome seemed to have a vice grip on the institution, Democrats moved to change the rules by extraordinary means. The successful move surprised most senators and outside observers.

Reid's move rocked the Senate. For the first time, simple-majority cloture became the effective rule of the Senate for an important class of business. The Senate had limited debate for certain classes of legislation before, but it had never combined the cloture process with a simple-majority threshold until it accepted Reid's point of order. Moreover, for the first time, the reform-by-ruling approach was used to modify or qualify the provisions of Rule XXII in a major way. The self-perpetuating nature of the filibuster was undercut, at least for the moment. . . .

Reid's strategy was simple and direct and, perhaps most important, was implemented quickly once he had the votes. Among the decisions Reid made was to exclude nominations to the Supreme Court from the point of order. Over the years, even reform-oriented Democrats had expressed some doubt about the wisdom of reducing the threshold for cloture for judicial nominations, because federal judges serve life terms. Setting aside Supreme Court nominations surely made it easier to attract the support of some party colleagues who held this view.

Reid also chose a "brute force" approach in offering a point of order concerning the threshold for cloture on nominations rather than introducing a reform resolution. A reform resolution could have been filibustered, but the Democrats could have made the argument, practiced for many years by reformers, that the Constitution implies that, contrary to the text of Rule XXII, a simple majority may invoke cloture on a measure related to the rules. Reid also paid no attention to the argument that a simple majority should be allowed to consider changes in the rules at the start of a Congress. Reid ignored the constitutional arguments, made the simple argument about making the Senate work, and took the quickest and most direct procedural path to establishing a new precedent. . . .

As expected, critics of Reid's move warned that the Senate had taken a big step in transforming the institution into another House of Representatives. They meant that the ability of the simple majority to freely change the rules would eventually lead majorities to change the rules in ways that limit minority and individual rights and empower a majority to gain action on legislation at will. It might take decades to happen, but, step-by-step, interparty conflict would lead majority parties to seek greater control over Senate proceedings. Reformers do not fear this outcome, but there were at least a few senators, including Reid, who were sitting on the fence on filibuster reform and found this argument persuasive.

Even if the Senate moved to simple-majority cloture for all matters, the chamber would remain a distinctive body. Six-year, staggered terms, state-based representation of two senators per state, the vice president designated as the presiding officer, and the Senate's much smaller size make it highly likely that the Senate will continue to be very different from the House. The mix of policy preferences in the Senate will not be identical to those of the House, and the Senate will continue to operate more informally and tolerate more debate than the House. Perhaps most important, the Senate's presiding officer is not a majority party leader granted strong parliamentary powers, as in the House.

The long-term effects of Reid's move are uncertain, though there was no shortage of speculation in the immediate aftermath of Reid's move. On the one hand, reformers may be emboldened, and majorities may be less strongly handicapped by arguments about Senate tradition. There may be effort to codify the new precedent in Rule XXII, which now hangs limply with the burden of a precedent that undercuts its explicit provisions for an important class of Senate business. A codification may produce additional change. On the other hand, minorities may be more selective in their efforts to block or delay majority action. If so, the Senate syndrome will become less acute and the incentive for further reform will be diminished. . . .

The Reid move is among the three or four most important events in the procedural history of the Senate. Ignoring the plain text of a standing rule, a majority of senators changed the effective rule by merely declaring it to be something else. The move was radical by Senate standards, but it was not precipitous. It followed years of minority obstruction and only modestly effective majority party responses—years of the intensifying Senate syndrome.

22

MICHELE SWERS

From *Women in the Club*

Michele Swers subtitles her book "Gender and Policy Making in the Senate," a topic she has written about frequently in previous works. The excerpt from this book begins with a mention of the controversial "war on women," a campaign theme that dramatically divides the political parties and the American electorate. Female voters comprise a critical, growing voting bloc and winning their support is essential. Within the U.S. Senate, female senators are center stage with both Democrats and Republicans eager to spotlight their party's star women. Swers examines some of the norms and customs of the modern U.S. Senate. Then she turns to the Senate's women. Female senators have been and continue to be influential on issues of social policy, including health, education, reproductive rights, and workplace pay. In addition, Swers finds, Senate women are deeply involved in military and defense issues. In part, this focus on military matters is a way for female senators to break out of stereotypical roles. Swers cites some interesting examples, including former New York Senator Hillary Clinton. "They want to seem strong on defense," Swers writes. Still, female senators continue to have their credibility on military issues challenged. As one Senate staffer remarked to Swers, "Armed Services and defense as a whole is a boys club." Still.

IN THE MONTHS LEADING UP to the 2012 presidential election, the Republican and Democratic parties were locked in a battle for women's votes. Democrats and President Barack Obama's campaign accused Republicans of waging a "war on women." Republicans and Republican presidential candidate Mitt Romney countered that Democrats were instigating a false gender war and President Obama's policies undermined the interests of women. The women of the Senate played key roles in this quest for the hearts and minds of female voters. Female Democratic senators took to the Senate floor, called press conferences, and appeared on political news shows to shine a spotlight on Republican policies that hurt women including Republican efforts to defund Planned Parenthood and Republican opposition to coverage of contraception in Obama's health reform bill. The Democratic women also lamented Republican obstruction of the Violence Against Women Act and the Paycheck Fairness Act, a bill to strengthen equal pay legislation. Patty Murray (D-WA), the head of the Democratic Senate Campaign Committee, launched an advertisement denouncing the Republican war on women and urging voters to elect more women to the Senate (http://www.youtube.com/watch?v =MohCoT_fH1U).

In response, Republicans deployed their own female surrogates to push back on the Democratic message of a war on women. Republican senator Kelly Ayotte (R-NH) became a prominent spokesperson for the Republican Party and the Romney campaign. Utilizing her moral authority as a woman, Ayotte countered that Republican opposition to forcing employers, including Catholic universities and hospitals, to cover contraception was a matter of religious freedom and not women's health. Republicans frequently noted that the economy was the top concern of women voters and that more than 92% of the jobs lost on Obama's watch were women's jobs.

Clearly, both Republican and Democratic women utilize the power of their position as senators to influence the public debate over the representation of women's interests and to shape policy that addresses the needs of women and their families. The emergence of women as a significant force in the Senate is a recent phenomenon. Indeed, the United States Senate is among the most powerful legislative institutions in western democracies. At the same time it is in many ways the least representative. In both its demographic makeup and its institutional rules the Senate defies ideals of equal representation. For most of its history the Senate has been a white male bastion, and the number of women and minorities in the Senate continues to lag far behind their share of the U.S. population. The institutional structure and rules of the Senate are antimajoritarian. The filibuster gives individuals and small groups of senators the ability to obstruct legislation and the allocation of two seats for each state gives outsized influence to senators representing small state populations. In contrast to the House of Representatives, the Founders intended for the Senate to be the less responsive body, cooling the passions of the masses in an effort to reach decisions that reflect the national character and interest. As a result of this design, the Senate has often been described as both the world's greatest deliberative body and an insular old boys club where powerful white men meet behind closed doors to shape public policy.

The modern Senate club is a study in contradictions. Senators are freewheeling policy entrepreneurs whose large staffs, ready media access, and institutional prerogatives, including the ability to offer nongermane amendments, place holds, and threaten filibusters, allow them to become important players on any issue they choose. At the same time, ideological polarization and tight electoral competition between the parties has created a Senate divided into partisan teams. Senators work together to create a party message and policy agenda. They are expected to be loyal to the team or risk a loss of standing and influence with their colleagues.

The evolution of the Senate into an institution that is both partisan and individualistic coincided with the opening up of the Senate to new groups, particularly women. As late as 1991, women constituted only 2% of the Senate membership. By 2001, 13% of senators were women and the number of women in the Senate was equivalent to the proportion of women serving in the House. In the 112th Congress (2011–12), women make up 17% of the Senate's membership. While the number of women in the Senate remains relatively small, the power wielded by individuals and the procedural rules protecting participation rights give senators out-sized influence and an ability to engage any and all policy areas regardless of committee assignment or majority/minority party status.

By focusing on the Senate, I can examine how gender influences legislative behavior on a wider range of issues from social welfare policy to national security. Moreover, if senators feel strongly about championing gender-related causes, the organization of the Senate gives them the resources and tools to force consideration of these interests, thus magnifying senators' influence beyond their numbers. In this book, I utilize the fact that senators are policy generalists who are involved in a wide variety of issues and wield extensive individual prerogatives to analyze the ways in which gender influences the legislative behavior of senators. I demonstrate that gender is a fundamental identity that affects the way senators look at policy questions, the issues they prioritize, and the perspective they bring to develop solutions. The importance of gender also transcends individual identity, creating opportunities and imposing obstacles in the electoral and governing arena that senators must confront when they design their political strategies and build their legislative reputations.

My research shows that, as they develop their legislative portfolio, female senators take into account long-standing public assumptions and voter stereotypes about women's policy expertise. The strong link between gender and women's interests on various social welfare and women's rights issues enhances the credibility of women in these policy areas. Thus, women are able to leverage their gender to influence policy debates on a range of issues from health care and education to abortion rights and pay equity. These "women's issues" routinely constitute at least one-third of the Senate agenda. By contrast, deeply held voter perceptions that men are more capable of handling defense policy hinder women's efforts to become leaders on defense issues. To counteract voter stereotypes that portray women as soft on defense, female senators construct policy records to demonstrate toughness and seek out opportunities for position taking through cosponsorship to highlight their support for the military. . . .

Contrary to voter stereotypes about defense policy expertise and trends in public opinion demonstrating that women are less supportive of war, there were no gender differences in support for the Iraq War resolution or the amendments offered to modify the resolution. Moreover, women and men were equally likely to offer amendments to the defense authorization bills. Focusing on the substantive content of senators' amendments, all senators were more active proponents of "soft defense initiatives" that expand benefits for military personnel and veterans rather than the "hard defense proposals" concerning weapons and war.

Yet senators are cognizant of gender stereotypes and party reputations on national security, and they utilize their policy activity strategically to counter these stereotypes. For example, both Republican and Democratic women were more active cosponsors of amendments to the defense authorization bill than were their male colleagues. Thus, these female senators engaged in position taking through cosponsorship to advertise their defense policy activism and expertise to constituents. Furthermore, Democratic women were more likely than their male partisan colleagues to cosponsor soft defense policies that provide benefits for the troops and veterans. This activism reflects the association of social welfare policies with women and the Democratic Party and allows senators to demonstrate support for our troops. Moreover, Senate staffers maintain that Democratic women must overcome the double bind of gender stereotypes and the Democratic Party's reputation for weakness on national security. Therefore, Democratic women look for opportunities to highlight their defense credentials in their legislative activity and to promote their support for the troops by appearing at military and veterans' events in their states, particularly when they are up for re-election. . . .

Establishing their defense credentials with voters, and more broadly, constituents, is a primary concern according to staffers for Republican and Democratic women senators. A Republican staffer stated simply, "[W]omen definitely have a higher mountain to get over with voters on military issues and with the constituent groups [military veterans, defense contractors] that pay attention in their state." To establish their expertise, women work to develop a legislative profile on defense issues and promote their policy expertise through outreach to constituents and voters. For example, one staffer pointed to the value of committee seats on defense-related committees for women senators trying to earn their bona fides with voters. "Women want to get on defense and foreign policy committees to establish their credibility on the issue. Voters don't question a man's ability on defense issues. Senior male senators with no defense experience, no one will say they are not tough. Women need these committees to show they are tough and fit to lead in that area because the women are not likely to have served in the military." Similarly, the decision of Hillary Clinton (D-NY) to seek a seat on Armed Services was often brought up as evidence of her desire to show voters she has the capability to become commander-in-chief.

The need to demonstrate toughness is even more imperative for Democratic women who face the double bind of gender and being associated with the Democratic Party's reputation as soft on defense. Thus, a Democratic staffer said, "On defense women have a hurdle and Democratic women have an extra hurdle. They have to work harder to prove themselves to voters on defense and foreign policy issues. They will offer amendments and more bills to support the troops." Another Democratic staffer maintained, "Republican women get more credibility on defense because they are men with different body parts, but they carry the Republican tide, which is stronger on defense. Hutchison (R-TX), Murray (D-WA), and Mikulski (D-MD) are all on Defense Appropriations, but Hutchison is more associated with the subject." Similarly, a Democratic staffer complained, "The Democratic Party is not good at giving cover to their members on defense issues the way the Republicans are, so the Republican women can always rely on the view of their party as good on defense to protect them with voters."

To inoculate themselves with voters, women senators also utilize their constituent events to raise their profile on defense policy. Thus, the chief of staff for a Democratic woman noted that constituent events related to defense or veterans take on heightened importance for female senators. "If a politician will normally do 10% of their public events on foreign policy then they will do more public events, 25%, to get themselves in front of those audiences more." Similarly, another Democratic chief of staff noted, "[T]hey visit the bases and all the commanders, the families of those overseas. They want to seem strong on defense. All the senators do the Memorial and Veterans Day events, but the women are concerned about it to a more extraordinary degree, it is never just another event for them. They also look for opportunities to be a leader for the active military, guard, reservists, and veterans and of course protecting their bases in the BRAC process."

Female senators, particularly Democratic women, also design their

campaign strategies to demonstrate strength on national security and re-
fute the criticism that they are weak on defense. Several staffers referred to
Mary Landrieu's (D-LA) reputation as "Military Mary" on the hill. "Landrieu is very vocal on defense. She never met a shipbuilding program she
did not like, which is because of the Louisiana shipbuilding industry. She
has a conservative electorate and is not helped by being a woman. She
needs to be more pro-military and guns than the military in that electorate.
In her 2002 campaign she had camouflage 'Military Mary' bumper stick-
ers." Conversely, staff reported that Landrieu's Democratic counterpart,
John Breaux (D-LA), who retired in 2004, did not feel compelled to trumpet his national security credentials and utilized his reputation as a centrist
dealmaker to move his reputation from a House member who protected
home industries to a national player on health and tax issues. . . .

While there is strong evidence that women, particularly Democratic
women, are more concerned about shoring up their reputation on national security with voters and constituent groups, within the Senate,
staffers generally agreed that women who choose to engage national security do not face any additional hurdles with Senate colleagues. For example, a Democratic defense staffer said, "[C]redibility is not an issue
among senators. Senators see individuals and abilities, what you intend to
do in the club." Similarly, another longtime Democratic defense staffer
said,

> It is harder to distinguish gender issues today. Credibility problems for women
> have diminished over time. Senatorial courtesy still exists, so there will be no overt
> or detectable credibility problems, but over time a senator gets a reputation as be-
> ing serious on an issue and knowledgeable or someone who just gets the defer-
> ence due a senator and this is it. There was a woman who was on the [Armed
> Services] Committee who would be a voice for her state but was not interested in
> broader issues, and she got the deference on state issues but was not looked at as a
> heavyweight. Hillary Clinton [D-NY] was respected, disciplined, hardworking,
> and knowledgeable in national security issues. If you are good and demonstrate it,
> you get respect. Constituents see your voting record and if they are getting their
> share of the pie, but colleagues will see if you are engaged or not engaged.

Other staffers felt that a female senator may have to work harder to
establish herself as an expert on defense policy, but once that reputation
is built, gender has no impact. Thus, a Republican defense staffer said,
"[I]nside the Senate it is not a big problem to be a woman. Women can
undo the stereotypes by boning up on technical issues." Similarly, a Democratic defense staffer maintained, "[T]here is an original assumption that
the military will deal with male members and staff first because there is

the outside possibility they have military service. Up until you have a chance to act on an issue there is more automatic credibility to men, but things sort themselves out quickly when there is action. There are impediments for women getting into the conversation but what matters is the outcome. Gender is never the deciding factor."

Describing the process by which Kay Bailey Hutchison (R-TX) and Hillary Clinton (D-NY) developed their reputations on national security, staffers believed that these senators were cognizant of gender stereotypes as they worked to establish themselves as experts on defense policy issues. Therefore, they carefully planned their engagement on these issues and worked very hard to build their reputations. The evolution of Kay Bailey Hutchison's (R-TX) reputation as a player on defense issues was described as follows:

It took time to develop her credentials on the military. She traveled wherever Texans were stationed. She had differences with the Clinton administration on the Balkans and wrote editorials in the *Washington Post* and *New York Times*. She hired a first-rate foreign policy chief of staff and hired a full bird colonel for her defense LA [Legislative Assistant]. She came to the table with the interest and the ideas, and her staff helped insert her in the debates. Today she has leverage at the Pentagon and the State Department.

Similarly, Hillary Clinton was described as having successfully gained entry into the defense policy world by studying the issues and nurturing the right relationships with colleagues and important leaders at the Pentagon. Laying the groundwork for a presidential run, Clinton gave up her seat on the Budget Committee in the 108th Congress to become the first Senator from New York on Armed Services in the panel's more than fifty-year history. One committee staffer noted,

Clinton has gone out of her way to engage on hard and soft defense issues and in defense planning at the closed-door level. She has been proactive on veterans' issues, but most of the issues she engages are hard defense. When she joined Armed Services she literally brought the other senators on both sides of the aisle coffee, and she did not say much, but if a Republican wanted a bill to be bipartisan they would go to her. Only recently has she emerged as a partisan Democrat, but Republicans on Armed Services love her because she knows what she is talking about. She makes a point of getting her photo taken with generals and name dropping the generals' names, "I am happy to see a particular general is here today." It is important for a senator to be comfortable with the flag officers and be able to talk about hard-edge issues. Hillary has the double problem of being a woman and running for president, and her husband's relationship with the military was disastrous so she has to repair that and find a new way of dealing with them.

Thus, staffers viewed gender as an additional constraint that Clinton and Hutchison had to consider as they sought to establish a reputation on military issues. However, they were able to navigate this additional barrier to emerge as experts in the eyes of colleagues and the defense establishment.

In addition to doing one's homework to master the substance of defense policy, senators who want to develop a reputation on national security must also attract media attention for their activities. Some staffers felt that the media is less likely to consider women as national security experts. Thus, in a 2005 article on women in the Senate, Debbie Stabenow (D-MI) complained, "[A]fter 9/11, it really pained me that Mary Landrieu, who, at the time, chaired the Armed Services Subcommittee on Emerging Threats, was not interviewed on television. . . . Look at the Sunday-morning talk shows—very rarely are women acknowledged as authorities on a topic. . . ." In a study of the Sunday morning shows, I found that women senators had to achieve higher levels of seniority and committee leadership than male senators before they were invited to speak as defense policy experts. Beyond lamenting the lack of women utilized as experts on defense, other staff felt the media was more likely to question the defense policy expertise of women senators in comparison with men. For example, one Republican staffer was disturbed by the initial reporting when Susan Collins (R-ME) was given responsibility for the Intelligence Overhaul bill created in response to the report of the 9/11 Commission. "In the beginning of the bill, the press coverage continually asked why she was qualified to take the lead on this bill, despite the fact that she had served on the Armed Services Committee for seven years. I suspect that a man would not have received as much scrutiny."

While their position as senators minimizes or eliminates the barriers for female senators as they seek to influence defense policy within Congress, staffers universally assert that the military and therefore defense politics are dominated by a male culture in which there are few female Senate staffers working on defense policy and few women in key positions in the military leadership or among defense lobbyists. This male-oriented culture creates barriers for those women who do work on defense politics as they seek to gain the respect of policy stakeholders in the Pentagon and defense lobbying community. One male Democratic staffer asserted that there is a hierarchy of who has credibility in the defense policy arena. "On and off the hill women have a harder time getting into defense issues regardless of recent advances in gender norms. The hierarchy is a man with military service doing defense policy, a man doing national security without serving in the military, a woman who served in the military (note a woman with military service is below a man without any), and a woman who never served in the military." Similarly, a female Democratic defense staffer recounted,

Armed Services and defense as a whole is a boys club. There are not many women staff in the defense world. The high-ranking professional staff are always men. There are not many uniformed women who can then serve as Senate liaisons [from the Pentagon]. The lobbyists are mostly men. If you are a woman lobbyist in that industry you are expected to act like one of the guys. There is a big stag fest, dinner in the winter in a big hotel in D.C. Anyone who is anyone in defense is there drinking whiskey, smoking cigars. It is a very masculine event. The few women who are there just have to suck it up and roll up their sleeves.

Female defense staffers felt that gender stereotypes were most likely to create problems in their relations with the stakeholder groups outside the Senate, particularly among older generation constituent groups and lobbyists. Thus, a female Democratic defense staffer said, "[I]t is the outside perception, Pentagon, industry, administration lobbyists. Among lobbyists it is a generational thing, Veterans of Foreign Wars is more sexist than the Reserves Association because those guys are younger. I get used to being called honey. Stereotypes can change with hard work and longevity and a willingness to learn. The military is about respect, and you gain respect with the military if you know how to deal with your [senator's] power."

23

PAUL STAROBIN

Pork: A Time-Honored Tradition Lives On

Journalist Paul Starobin's look at congressional "pork" updates a classic subject. Pork, a project that a representative can secure for her or his district, has been a central part of congressional politics from the start. In times past, pork was easier to notice—edifices like canals, highways, bridges—as well as less controversial. The United States needed these infrastructure improvements, and the money was available for a generous pork barrel. Today, pork carries a different connotation. Starobin lists the new forms that pork takes in the "post-industrial" era. Modern pork projects don't look like those of the past. And the pork barrel, while as popular as always, isn't nearly as deep as it once was. Legislators are under pressure to cut, not spend, and pork—often called "earmarks" today—is a perfect target. But what is pork anyway? Some other district's waste-treatment plant.

POLITICAL PORK. Since the first Congress convened two centuries ago, lawmakers have ladled it out to home constituencies in the form of cash for roads, bridges and sundry other civic projects. It is a safe bet that the distribution of such largess will continue for at least as long into the future.*

Pork-barrel politics, in fact, is as much a part of the congressional scene as the two parties or the rules of courtesy for floor debate. . . .

And yet pork-barrel politics always has stirred controversy. Critics dislike seeing raw politics guiding decisions on the distribution of federal money for parochial needs. They say disinterested experts, if possible, should guide that money flow.

And fiscal conservatives wonder how Congress will ever get a handle on the federal budget with so many lawmakers grabbing so forcefully for pork-barrel funds. "Let's change the system so we don't have so much porking," says James C. Miller III, director of the White House Office of Management and Budget (OMB). Miller says he gets complaints on the order of one a day from congressional members taking issue with OMB suggestions that particular "pork" items in the budget are wasteful.

*The interesting, little-known, and ignominious origin of the term "pork barrel" comes from early in American history, when a barrel of salt pork was given to slaves as a reward for their work. The slaves had to compete among themselves to get their piece of the handout.—EDS.

But pork has its unabashed defenders. How, these people ask, can law-makers ignore the legitimate demands of their constituents? When a highway needs to be built or a waterway constructed, the home folks quite naturally look to their congressional representative for help. Failure to respond amounts to political suicide.

"I've really always been a defender of pork-barreling because that's what I think people elect us for," says Rep. Douglas H. Bosco, D-Calif.

Moreover, many accept pork as a staple of the legislative process, lu-bricating the squeaky wheels of Congress by giving members a personal stake in major bills. . . .

Not only does the flow of pork continue pretty much unabated, it seems to be spreading to areas that traditionally haven't been subject to pork-barrel competition. Pork traditionally was identified with public-works projects such as roads, bridges, dams and harbors. But, as the econ-omy and country have changed, lawmakers have shifted their appetites to what might be called "post-industrial" pork. Some examples:

• *Green Pork.* During the 1960s and 1970s, when dam-builders fought epic struggles with environmentalists, "pork-barrel" projects stereotypi-cally meant bulldozers and concrete. But many of today's projects are more likely to draw praise than blame from environmentalists. The list includes sewer projects, waste-site cleanups, solar energy laboratories, pollution-control research, parks and park improvements and fish hatch-eries, to name a few. . . .

• *Academic Pork.* Almost no federal funds for construction of university research facilities are being appropriated these days, except for special projects sponsored by lawmakers for campuses back home. Many of the sponsors sit on the Appropriations committees, from which they are well positioned to channel such funds. . . .

• *Defense Pork.* While the distribution of pork in the form of defense contracts and location of military installations certainly isn't new, there's no question that Reagan's military buildup has expanded opportunities for lawmakers to practice pork-barrel politics. . . .

This spread of the pork-barrel system to new areas raises a question: What exactly is pork? Reaching a definition isn't easy. Many people con-sider it wasteful spending that flows to a particular state or district and is sought to please the folks back home.

But what is wasteful? One man's boondoggle is another man's civic pride. Perhaps the most sensible definition is that which a member seeks for his own state or district but would not seek for anyone else's constitu-ency.

Thus, pork goes to the heart of the age-old tension between a lawmaker's twin roles as representative of a particular area and member of a national legislative body. In the former capacity, the task is to promote the local interest; in the latter it is to weigh the national interest. . . .

Like other fraternities, the system has a code of behavior and a pecking order. It commands loyalty and serves the purpose of dividing up federal money that presumably has to go somewhere, of helping re-elect incumbents and of keeping the wheels of legislation turning. . . .

When applied with skill, pork can act as a lubricant to smooth passage of complex legislation. At the same time, when local benefits are distributed for merely "strategic" purposes, it can lead to waste. . . .

Just about everyone agrees that the budget crunch has made the competition to get pet projects in spending legislation more intense. Demand for such items has not shrunk nearly as much as the pool of available funds.

24

JOHN ELLWOOD
ERIC PATASHNIK

In Praise of Pork

Pork-barrel spending is high on Americans' list of gripes against Congress. "Asparagus research and mink reproduction" typify the wasteful spending that seems to enrich congressional districts and states while bankrupting the nation. Recently, "earmarks" have been criticized as the newest technique for putting pork into bills. John Ellwood and Eric Patashnik take a different view. Pork is not the real cause of the nation's budget crisis, they believe. In fact, pork projects may be just what members of the House and Senate need to be able to satisfy constituents in order to summon the courage to vote for real, significant, painful budget cuts.

IN A WHITE HOUSE address ... [in] March [1992], President [George H.W.] Bush challenged Congress to cut $5.7 billion of pork barrel projects to help reduce the deficit.* Among the projects Bush proposed eliminating were such congressional favorites as funding for asparagus research, mink reproduction, and local parking garages. The examples he cited would be funny, said the President, "if the effect weren't so serious." ...

Such episodes are a regular occurrence in Washington. Indeed, since the first Congress convened in 1789 and debated whether to build a lighthouse to protect the Chesapeake Bay, legislators of both parties have attempted to deliver federal funds back home for capital improvements and other projects, while presidents have tried to excise pork from the congressional diet. ...

In recent years, public outrage over government waste has run high. Many observers see pork barrel spending not only as a symbol of an out-of-control Congress but as a leading cause of the nation's worsening bud-

*The "pork-barrel" refers to congressional spending on projects that bring money and jobs to particular districts throughout America, thereby aiding legislators in their reelection bids. The interesting, little-known, and ignominious origin of the term "pork barrel" comes from early in American history, when a barrel of salt pork was given to slaves as a reward for their work. The slaves had to compete among themselves to get their piece of the handout.—EDS.

get deficit. To cite one prominent example, *Washington Post* editor Brian Kelly claims in his recent book, *Adventures in Porkland: Why Washington Can't Stop Spending Your Money*, that the 1992 federal budget alone contains $97 billion of pork projects so entirely without merit that they could be "lopped out" without affecting the "welfare of the nation."

Kelly's claims are surely overblown. For example, he includes the lower prices that consumers would pay if certain price supports were withdrawn, even though these savings (while certainly desirable) would for the most part not show up in the government's ledgers. Yet reductions in pork barrel spending have also been advocated by those who acknowledge that pork, properly measured, comprises only a tiny fraction of total federal outlays. For example, Kansas Democrat Jim Slattery, who led the battle in the House in 1991 against using $500,000 in federal funds to turn Lawrence Welk's birthplace into a shrine, told *Common Cause Magazine*, "it's important from the standpoint of restoring public confidence in Congress to show we are prepared to stop wasteful spending," even if the cuts are only symbolic. In a similar vein, a recent *Newsweek* cover story, while conceding that "cutting out the most extreme forms of pork wouldn't eliminate the federal deficit," emphasizes that doing so "would demonstrate that Washington has the political will to reform its profligate ways."

The premise of these statements is that the first thing anyone— whether an individual consumer or the United States government—trying to save money should cut out is the fluff. As *Time* magazine rhetorically asks: "when Congress is struggling without much success to reduce the federal budget deficit, the question naturally arises: is pork *really* necessary?"

Our answer is yes. We believe in pork not because every new dam or overpass deserves to be funded, nor because we consider pork an appropriate instrument of fiscal policy (there are more efficient ways of stimulating a $5 trillion economy). Rather, we think that pork, doled out strategically, can help to sweeten an otherwise unpalatable piece of legislation.

No bill tastes so bitter to the average member of Congress as one that raises taxes or cuts popular programs. Any credible deficit-reduction package will almost certainly have to do both. In exchange for an increase in pork barrel spending, however, members of Congress just might be willing to bite the bullet and make the politically difficult decisions that will be required if the federal deficit is ever to be brought under control.

In a perfect world it would not be necessary to bribe elected officials to perform their jobs well. But, as James Madison pointed out two centuries ago in *Federalist* 51, men are not angels and we do not live in a perfect world. The object of government is therefore not to suppress the imperfections of human nature, which would be futile, but rather to harness the pursuit of self-interest to public ends.

Unfortunately, in the debate over how to reduce the deficit, Madison's advice has all too often gone ignored. Indeed, if there is anything the major budget-reform proposals of the last decade (Gramm-Rudman, the balanced-budget amendment, an entitlement cap*) have in common, it is that in seeking to impose artificial limits on government spending without offering anything in return, they work against the electoral interests of congressmen instead of with them—which is why these reforms have been so vigorously resisted.

No reasonable observer would argue that pork barrel spending has always been employed as a force for good or that there are no pork projects what would have been better left unbuilt. But singling out pork as the culprit for our fiscal troubles directs attention away from the largest sources of budgetary growth and contributes to the illusion that the budget can be balanced simply by eliminating waste and abuse. While proposals to achieve a pork-free budget are not without superficial appeal, they risk depriving leaders trying to enact real deficit-reduction measures of one of the most effective coalition-building tools at their disposal.

In order to appreciate why congressmen are so enamored of pork it is helpful to understand exactly what pork is. But defining pork is not as easy as it sounds. According to *Congressional Quarterly*, pork is usually considered to be "wasteful" spending that flows to a particular state or district in order to please voters back home. Like beauty, however, waste is in the eye of the beholder. As University of Michigan budget expert Edward M. Gramlich puts it, "one guy's pork is another guy's red meat." To a district plagued by double-digit unemployment, a new highway project is a sound investment, regardless of local transportation needs.

Some scholars simply define pork as any program that is economically inefficient—that is, any program whose total costs exceed its total benefits. But this definition tars with the same brush both real pork and programs that, while inefficient, can be justified on grounds of distributional equity or in which geographic legislative influence is small or nonexistent.

*Many attempts have been made in past years to lower the deficit. In 1985, the Gramm-Rudman-Hollings law set dollar-limit goals for deficit reduction, to be followed by automatic percentage cuts; however, many programs were exempted. A 1995 balanced-budget amendment passed the House, but failed to get two-thirds of the Senate's approval. Entitlement caps would seek to limit the total amount the federal government could pay out in programs such as Medicare, Medicaid, Social Security, and food stamps.—EDS.

A more promising approach is suggested by political scientist David Mayhew in his 1974 book, *Congress:The Electoral Connection.* According to Mayhew, congressional life consists largely of "a relentless search" for ways of claiming credit for making good things happen back home and thereby increasing the likelihood of remaining in office. Because there are 535 congressmen and not one, each individual congressman must try to "peel off pieces of governmental accomplishment for which he can believably generate a sense of responsibility." For most congressmen, the easiest way of doing this is to supply goods to their home districts.

From this perspective, the ideal pork barrel project has three key properties. First, benefits are conferred on a specific geographical constituency small enough to allow a single congressman to be recognized as the benefactor. Second, benefits are given out in such a fashion as to lead constituents to believe that the congressman had a hand in the allocation. Third, costs resulting from the project are widely diffused or otherwise obscured from taxpayer notice.

Political pork, then, offers a congressman's constituents an array of benefits at little apparent cost. Because pork projects are easily distinguished by voters from the ordinary outputs of government, they provide an incumbent with the opportunity to portray himself as a "prime mover" who deserves to be reelected. When a congressman attends a ribbon-cutting ceremony for a shiny new building in his district, every voter can *see* that he is accomplishing something in Washington. . . .

"It's outrageous that you've got to have such political payoffs to get Congress to do the nation's business," says James Miller, OMB director under Ronald Reagan. Miller's outrage is understandable but ultimately unproductive. Human nature and the electoral imperative being what they are, the pork barrel is here to stay.

But if pork is a permanent part of the political landscape, it is incumbent upon leaders to ensure that taxpayers get something for their money. Our most effective presidents have been those who have linked the distribution of pork to the achievement of critical national objectives. When Franklin Roosevelt discovered he could not develop an atomic bomb without the support of Tennessee Senator Kenneth McKellar, chairman of the Appropriations Committee, he readily agreed to locate the bomb facility in Oak Ridge. By contrast, our least effective presidents—Jimmy Carter comes to mind—have either given away plum projects for nothing or waged hopeless battles against pork, squandering scarce political capital and weakening their ability to govern in the process.

The real value of pork projects ultimately lies in their ability to induce rational legislators into taking electorally risky actions for the sake of the public good. Over the last ten years, as the discretionary part of the budget has shrunk, congressmen have had fewer and fewer opportunities to claim credit for directly aiding their constituents. As Brookings scholar R. Kent Weaver has argued, in an era of scarcity and difficult political choices, many legislators gave up on trying to accomplish anything positive, focusing their energies instead on blame avoidance. The result has been the creation of a political climate in which elected officials now believe the only way they can bring the nation back to fiscal health is to injure their own electoral chances. This cannot be good for the future of the republic.

Politics got us into the deficit mess, however, and only politics can get us out. According to both government and private estimates, annual deficits will soar after the mid-1990s, and could exceed $600 billion in 2002 if the economy performs poorly. Virtually every prominent mainstream economist agrees that reducing the deficit significantly will require Congress to do what it has been strenuously trying to avoid for more than a decade—rein in spending for Social Security, Medicare, and other popular, middle-class entitlement programs. Tax increases may also be necessary. From the vantage point of the average legislator, the risk of electoral retribution seems enormous.

If reductions in popular programs and increases in taxes are required to put our national economic house back in order, the strategic use of pork to obtain the support of key legislators for these measures will be crucial. . . .

. . . [T]he president should ignore the advice of fiscal puritans who would completely exorcise pork from the body politic. Favoring legislators with small gifts for their districts in order to achieve great things for the nation is an act not of sin but of statesmanship. To be sure, determining how much pork is needed and to which members it should be distributed is difficult. Rather than asking elected officials to become selfless angels, however, we would ask of them only that they be smart politicians. We suspect Madison would agree that the latter request has a far better chance of being favorably received.

25

SENATOR JOHN McCAIN

Hey There! SenJohnMcCain Is Using Twitter

Tweeting on Feb. 25, 26, 27 and March 2, 3, 4, 5, 6, 2009, Senator John McCain takes a jab—actually a lot of jabs—at Congress's Omnibus Budget Bill and the amusing earmarks contained in it. In truth, President Barack Obama himself acknowledged that the bill was loaded with pork, much of it decided by Congress before the 2008 election. President Obama stated that he would resist such pork projects in future budget bills. Still, Senator McCain could not resist pointing out such items like Mormon cricket control in Utah ($1 million), genetic improvements to switchgrass ($1.4 million), and pig odor research in Iowa ($1.7 million). Sprinkled among the pork entries are tweets about McCain's daily activities, from voting to speeches to TV appearances. One of his tweets reveals that the senator has had a little help from one of his young aides on how to use Twitter.

February 25–February 27, 2009

1. #6. $1 million for mormon cricket control in Utah—is that the species of cricket or a game played by the brits?   *8:30 AM Feb 27th from web*

2. #7. $300,000 for the Montana World Trade Center—enough said   *8:21 AM Feb 27th from web*

3. #8. $200,000 "tattoo removal violence outreach program to help gang members or others shed visible signs of their past" REALLY?   *7:50 AM Feb 27th from web*

4. going to the floor   *6:40 AM Feb 27th from web*

5. #9. $475,000 to build a parking garage in Provo City, Utah   *6:33 AM Feb 27th from web*

6. #10. $1.7M "for a honey bee factory" in Weslaco, TX   *6:06 AM Feb 27th, from web*

7. top 10 projects on the way . . .   *5:34 AM Feb 27th from web*

8. Tmr I am gonna tweet the TOP TEN PORKIEST PROJECTS in the Omnibus Spending bill the Congress is about to pass   *10:08 AM Feb 26th from web*

9. Mary Hood actually did the interview for CBS on my new found love of twittering.   *8:43 AM Feb 26th from txt*

10. I'm doing an interview with cbs in a few minutes   *8:09 AM Feb 26th from txt*

11. YEs!! I am twittering on my blackberry but not without a little help!   *6:07 AM Feb 26th from txt*

12. house votes 398-24 to freeze auto pay raise! great! who were the 24?   *2:39 PM Feb 25th from web*

13. steve nash hurt? amare too! what now for the suns!   *2:30 PM Feb 25th from web*

14. votes at 5:45   *2:21 PM Feb 25th from web*

15. on my way to an interview with KTVK, channel 3 in PHX . . . tune in tonight   *12:06 PM Feb 25th from web*

16. I appreciate Senator Byrd speaking in favor of my Constitutional point of order   *10:54 AM Feb 25th from web*

17. vote on my Constitutional Point of Order at 2.   *10:45 AM Feb 25th from web*

18. now on my way to AEI to give a speech on Winning the War in Afghanistan   *8:24 AM Feb 25th from web*

19. ICYMI: I filed a constitutional point of order on the DC Representative bill   *8:23 AM Feb 25th from web*

20. on my way to the floor.   *7:11 AM Feb 25th from web*

February 27–March 2, 2009

1. #1. $951,500 for Sustainable Las Vegas   *1:03 PM Mar 2nd from web*

2. and the number 1 porkiest project for today . . .   *1:00 PM Mar 2nd from web*

3. #2. $250,000 to enhance research on Ice Seal populations   *7:58 AM Mar 2nd from web*

4. #3. $150,000 for a rodeo museum in South Dakota   *12:58 PM Mar 2nd from web*

5. #4. $143,000 for Nevada Humanities to develop and expand an online encyclopedia - Anyone heard of Wikipedia?   *12:57 PM Mar 2nd from web*

6. #5. cont: why shouldn't we "float" a Hawaiian voyage for others?   *12:57 PM Mar 2nd from web*

7. #5. $238,000 for the Polynesian Voyaging Society in Hawaii - During these tough economic times with Americans out of work . . .   *12:56 PM Mar 2nd from web*

8. #6. $100,000 for the regional robotics training center in Union, SC - Does R2D2 or CP30 know about this?   *12:48 PM Mar 2nd from web*

9. #7. $1,427,250 for genetic improvements of switchgrass - I thought switchgrass genes were pretty good already, guess I was wrong. *12:38 PM Mar 2nd from web*

10. Hopefully for a Back in the Saddle Again exhibit, Autry's most popular song for those of you too young to remember America's Favorite Cowboy   *9:18 AM Mar 2nd from web*

11. #8. $167,000 for the Autry National Center for the American West in Los Angeles, CA   *9:14 AM Mar 2nd from web*

12. #9. $143,000 to teach art energy - Art can produce energy? If so, then investing in the arts may lead to energy independence.   *8:50 AM Mar 2nd from web*

13. #10. $100,000 for the Central Nebraska World Trade Center   *8:36 AM Mar 2nd from web*

14. Back by popular demand, another Top 10 . . .   *8:36 AM Mar 2nd from web*

15. #1. $1.7 million for pig odor research in Iowa   *2:37 PM Feb 27th from web*

16. and the #1 project is . . .   *2:26 PM Feb 27th from web*

17. #2. $2 million "for the promotion of astronomy" in Hawaii - because nothing says new jobs for average Americans like investing in astronomy   *1:56 PM Feb 27th from web*

18. #3. $332,000 for the design and construction of a school sidewalk in Franklin, Texas - not enough $ for schools in the stimulus?   *12:19 PM Feb 27th from web*

19. #4. $2.1 million for the Center for Grape Genetics in New York - quick peel me a grape.   *10:55 AM Feb 27th from web*

20. #5. $650,000 for beaver management in North Carolina and Mississippi   *10:52 AM Feb 27th from web*

March 3–March 4, 2009

1. today's top 10 to come shortly   *6:50 AM Mar 4th from web*

2. on my way to the wh to meet with the President on contract reform with sen Levin   *6:50 AM Mar 4th from web*

3. introduced line item veto with Feingold and congressman ryan   *6:45 AM Mar 4th from web*

4. #1. $951,500 for the Oregon Solar Highway   *1:48 PM Mar 3rd from web*

5. and the #1 project   *1:48 PM Mar 3rd from web*

6. meeting with Henry McMaster - "tell it all. . ."   *1:15 PM Mar 3rd from web*

7. #2. $900,000 for fish management – how does one manage a fish ... *12:57 PM Mar 3rd from web*

8. #3. $380,000 to revitalize downtown Aliceville, AL   *11:32 AM Mar 3rd from web*

9. 4. $380,000 for lighthouses in Maine   *11:23 AM Mar 3rd from web*

10. meeting with the French Defense Minister, Herve Morin   *11:00 AM Mar 3rd from web*

11. taking a break for policy lunch   *10:11 AM Mar 3rd from web*

12. #5. $819, 000 for catfish genetics research in Alabama   *9:34 AM Mar 3rd from web*

13. #6. $190,000 for the Buffalo Bill Historical Center in Cody, WY   *9:23 AM Mar 3rd from web*

14. #7. $400,000 for copper wire theft prevention efforts   *8:50 AM Mar 3rd from web*

15. #8. $47,500 to remodel and expand a playground in Ottawa, IL   *8:29 AM Mar 3rd from web*

16. #9. $209,000 to improve blueberry production and efficiency in GA   *8:20 AM Mar 3rd from web*

17. #10. $285,000 for the Discovery Center of Idaho in Boise, ID   *8:06 AM Mar 3rd from web*

18. and coming up, Tuesday's Top 10   *8:04 AM Mar 3rd from web*

19. SASC hearing   *8:04 AM Mar 3rd from web*

20. meeting with PM Tony Blair   *5:24 AM Mar 3rd from web*

March 4–March 5, 2009

1. #4. $95,000 for Hawaii Public Radio   *11:04 AM Mar 5th from web*

2. #5. $59,000 for Dismal Swamp and Dismal Swamp Canal in Virginia.   *10:52 AM Mar 5th from web*

3. #6. $632,000 for the Hungry Horse Project⁻   *10:47 AM Mar 5th from web*

4. off to lunch with Senator Michael Bennett   *10:16 AM Mar 5th from web*

5. #7. $95,000 for the state of New Mexico to find a dental school location   *10:15 AM Mar 5th from web*

6. #8. $143,000 for the Historic Jazz Foundation in Kansas City, MO   *8:37 AM Mar 5th from web*

7. @ hearing to ensure in the rush to get "out the door" the $787 billion in stimulus funds, there isn't waste, fraud and abuse.   *8:02 AM Mar 5th from web*

8. on my way to the homeland hearing   *7:46 AM Mar 5th from web*
9. #9. $190,000 for the Guam Public Library in Hagatna, Guam *7:27 AM Mar 5th from web*
10. #10. $3,806,000 for a Sun Grant Initiative in SD   *6:41 AM Mar 5th from web*
11. Thursday's top 10 porkiest projects coming soon   *5:45 AM Mar 5th from web*
12. if you wanna know more go to my website: http://mccain.senate .gov   *12:10 PM Mar 4th from web*
13. #4. All 13 earmarks for PMA group, which has been raided by the FBI for corruption, totaling over $10 million - THE BEST GOVERNMENT $ CAN BUY   *11:50 AM Mar 4th from web*
14. #5. 150,000 for lobster research - similar to lobster management? *11:02 AM Mar 4th from web*
15. #6. $950,000 for a Convention Center in Myrtle Beach, SC *9:53 AM Mar 4th from web*
16. see the sea turtles on your $238,000 Polynesian Voyage   *9:48 AM Mar 4th from web*
17. #7. $7,100,000 for the conservation and recovery of endangered Hawaiian sea turtle populations   *9:46 AM Mar 4th from web*
18. #8. $118,750 for a building to house an aircraft display in Rantoul, IL   *8:38 AM Mar 4th from web*
19. #9. $380,000 for a recreation and fairground area in Kotzebue, AK   *8:37 AM Mar 4th from web*
20. 10. $190,000 to build a Living Science Museum in New Orleans, LA   *8:09 AM Mar 4th from web*

March 5–March 6, 2009

1. on with John C. Scott - KVOI-AM (Tucson)   *37 minutes ago from web*
2. Just finished fox and now watching Lindsey on MTP   *about 16 hours ago from txt*
3. #1. $75,000 for the "Totally Teen Zone" in Albany, GA   *11:58 AM Mar 6th from web*
4. and the number one project of the day . . .   *11:54 AM Mar 6th from web*
5. #2. $1,284,525 for Rolls Royce - does that include a car?   *11:51 AM Mar 6th from web*
6. #3. $122,821 for the Greater Toledo Arts Commission   *11:39 AM Mar 6th from web*

7. #4. $190,000 for the Berkshire Theatre in Stockbridge, MA
   11:35 AM Mar 6th from web
8. #5. $2,128,000 for a Ferry Boat, San Juan, PR   *11:22 AM Mar 6th
   from web*
9. #6. $385,000 for the Utah World Trade Center - Utah too?
   10:35 AM Mar 6th from web
10. #7. $228,000 for "streetscaping" in Bridgeville, PA   *10:18 AM Mar
    6th from web*
11. #8. $380,000 for a recreation and fairground area in Kotzebue,
    AK   *9:11 AM Mar 6th from web*
12. #9. $237,500 for a new museum in San Jose, CA   *8:49 AM Mar
    6th from web*
13. on my way to the floor to continue to talk pork   *8:04 AM Mar 6th
    from web*
14. Back by popular demand . . . #10 $190,000 to rebuild a dock in Gold
    Beach, OR   *6:28 AM Mar 6th from txt*
15. Having breakfast with secretary gates @ the pentagon.   *6:11 AM
    Mar 6th from txt*
16. on hannity now!   *1:35 PM Mar 5th from web*
17. #1. $1.9 million for the Pleasure Beach Water Taxi Service Project,
    CT   *1:35 PM Mar 5th from web*
18. #2. $143,000 for the Dayton Society of Natural History in Dayton,
    OH   *12:11 PM Mar 5th from web*
19. attending subcommittee on federal financial management   *11:40
    AM Mar 5th from web*
20. #3. $143,000 for the Historic Jazz Foundation in Kansas City, MO
    11:22 AM Mar 5th from web

26

CHUCK McCUTCHEON
DAVID MARK

From *Dog Whistles, Walk-Backs, and Washington Handshakes*

*Chuck McCutcheon and David Mark subtitle their dictionary-like book
"Decoding the Jargon, Slang, and Bluster of American Political Speech." If
you're planning a visit to the nation's capital, applying for an internship
there, or just watching C-SPAN in the middle of the night, here's some
terminology to be familiar with. This excerpt contains only a few of the authors' amusing and much-used picks. It's an unusual selection for this collection, and I hope not to have to "walk back" from it.*

No matter what your political beliefs, you probably long
ago reached one conclusion about our nation's public servants: They can
be confusing as hell.

They've acquired that reputation in part because Washington, D.C.,
has become spectacularly, even proudly, indecipherable to most outsiders.
It has its own political culture, including a specific language. It is a lexicon,
a jargon—a code, if you will—that can be alien to those not in the know.
(By our estimate, and from our experience, it takes roughly a year of
working there to *start* to get in the know.) Insider-y sounding political
jargon often makes it into the news media, but seldom with any explanation or in any meaningful context. This helps sow confusion, which in
turn is one of the factors that have fueled the searing and seemingly unending contempt for all things Beltway. . . .

In recent years there's been an increasing realization that all of government needs to be far better explained—witness the emergences of
fact-checking sites like the *Tampa Bay Times'* Pulitzer Prize–winning
PolitiFact, the popularity of blogs that delve far more deeply into the details of politics than most conventional media, and by-now common observations in media about how the infusion of massive sums of money has
irrevocably changed the mechanics of legislating. We'd also like to think
that the flood of politics-related TV shows and movies—*Scandal, Veep,
Alpha House, House of Cards,* and so on—indicates at least a partial desire

among the public to understand what really goes on at the White House, on Capitol Hill, and elsewhere.

We hope—and this hope may be "quixotic," to use a political-journalism cliché we explore—that this book can augment those much-needed services for those of you who are sincerely confused and who aren't obsessive readers of *Politico* or *Real Clear Politics*. . . .

Attack dog: A politico who's obviously willing to utter scathingly partisan things—a spokesman, insult comic, and source of blogosphere cacophony rolled into one. This figure can be a bit more mainstream than a *bomb thrower*, whose verbal volleys generally are more indiscriminate. *Surrogates*, for example, are more likely to serve as attack dogs.

The attack dog that relished the role more than anyone in recent memory was Sarah Palin. Even after her 2008 turn as John McCain's running mate, she still delivers attack lines such as "How's that 'hopey-changey' stuff working out for you?" with glee. But *all* vice presidential nominees, and vice presidents, play this role. (Witness Joe Biden's campaign-trail sound-bite eruptions in both 2008 and 2012; one of the most heated moments of the latter was when he told a predominantly African American audience that Mitt Romney's plan was to "put y'all back in chains.") So do the chairmen of the Republican and Democratic national committees. And during the 2012 presidential campaign, the dogs often were governors with a potential interest in running someday for the White House, including Maryland Democrat Martin O'Malley and New Jersey Republican Chris Christie.

That kind of negativity turns off voters who don't agree with their views. But people who can serve *red meat* to the base get noticed within party circles.

These days, one of the most prominent attackers is Republican representative Marsha Blackburn of Tennessee, who regularly appears on cable television to blast Obamacare and other topics. She called the administration's response to the 2012 terrorist attack in Benghazi, Libya, "probably more serious than Watergate."

On the Democratic side is Alan Grayson of Florida, who sent a fund-raising e-mail in 2013 likening the tea party to the Ku Klux Klan and who made this infamous comment on health care: "If you get sick, America, the Republican health care plan is this: Die quickly." Grayson was beaten in 2010, but won back a seat in a redrawn district two years later. . . .

"Mr. Chairman": In the high-school-like atmosphere that prevails in Congress, only a small group of lawmakers have significant power. Along with the elected leadership in the House and Senate, committee chairmen can wield real clout.

It's customary to give these powerful barons due deference. Colleagues refer to committee heads as "Mr. Chairman" or, more commonly these days, "Madame Chairwoman." The aforementioned former Ohio representative Jim Traficant was known for calling virtually everyone he encountered "Mr. Chairman," from his colleagues to lowly aides. It was because, as Hill staffer-turned-lobbyist John Feehery remembers, "There were a lot of chairmen around, and it was better to be safe than sorry." . . .

Workhorse/show horse: Age-old expressions describing, in the first case, politicians who dutifully introduce bills and show up to hearings—in other words, the substantive stuff of governing—and, in the second, those who hold incessant news conferences, churn out press releases, and indulge in grandstanding.

Hillary Rodham Clinton is among the many who embraces the term: "I believe I am a workhorse," she told NBC News during her 2008 presidential bid. Another Democrat, California representative Brad Sherman, also was quick to describe himself that way even after being asked in 2012 why he had been the original sponsor of just three pieces of legislation. "Well, I'm a workhorse, not a show horse," he told MSNBC. "I never go into a meeting saying my name has to be first on the list [of introduced bills] . . . I cosponsored and worked to pass 140 bills that are now law."

Washingtonian magazine helpfully identifies the top members of Congress in each category with its annual anonymous survey of hundreds of congressional staffers. The "workhorse" winners usually change from year to year, though they often are part of their party leadership, such as Democratic whip Dick Durbin of Illinois, or intellectual leaders of their party, such as GOP House Budget Committee chairman Paul Ryan.

The *Washingtonian*-chosen show horses have been remarkably consistent. In the Senate the winner invariably has been Chuck Schumer (D-NY), who is widely known for his unquenchable thirst for the media spotlight (though in 2012, he also tied with three other senators for "biggest workhorse"). In the House, the crown has belonged almost exclusively for a decade to Sheila Jackson Lee (D-TX), who is infamous for her long-winded speeches (including one at singer Michael Jackson's funeral) and for once saying: "I am a queen, and I demand to be treated like a queen." Jackson Lee has been unapologetic about her activities, saying she tries to work hard on behalf of her constituents. And those constituents appear not to mind; since 1994, she has never gotten less than 70 percent of the vote in any election. . . .

Shocked: A favorite ironic and sarcastic way to make a point about official hypocrisy by quoting Captain Renault from the movie *Casablanca.* "I'm shocked, shocked to find that gambling is going on in here!" says Renault, who happens to be a regular at the casino.

Senate Judiciary Committee chairman Patrick Leahy invoked the line in a November 2013 interview with C-SPAN's *Newsmakers.* Asked about reports of National Security Agency spying on foreign leaders, the Vermont Democrat said even U.S. allies shouldn't be surprised about such espionage activities. "Hearing these complaints from some of these other countries, it's like the old *Casablanca* movie, 'I'm shocked to find gambling going on here.'"

Leahy was hardly the first to compare NSA activities to the classic 1940s flick. At a congressional hearing weeks earlier, Director of National Intelligence James Clapper used the "shocked" line in dismissing the outcry over the tapping of German chancellor Angela Merkel's cell phone. "Some of this reminds me a lot of the classic movie *Casablanca:* 'My God, there's gambling going on here!'" Clapper said during a public hearing of the House Intelligence Committee. . . .

Straw man: The tendency of politicians to argue against positions that nobody actually holds—in other words, an imaginary opponent. By extension, this mischaracterizes opponents' views, making them easier to argue against. This approach assumes voters are stupid and incapable of critical thinking.

The Online Etymology Dictionary dates its figurative use to 1896. Though politicians of all kinds employ it, presidents, naturally, have the loudest megaphone to put forward such fallacies.

Conservatives regularly inveigh against President Barack Obama for constructing too many straw men. In particular they cite his second inaugural speech, in January 2013, for containing a series of straw-man arguments. "We reject the belief that America must choose between caring for the generation that built this country and investing in the generation that will build its future," Obama said. "For we remember the lessons of our past, when twilight years were spent in poverty and parents of a child with a disability had nowhere to turn."

But that was a false verbal construct. Nobody was proposing pushing Granny off a cliff. What *was* at issue in D.C. budget battles was some sort of balance in spending and tax priorities, not a total abolition of programs to help the elderly and disabled, as Obama seemed to be implying. That led Representative Paul Ryan of Wisconsin, the 2012 Republican vice-presidential nominee, to blast Obama's "straw man" attack on the Republican Party over entitlement programs. Ryan told *The Laura Ingra-*

ham Show the next day the speech demonstrated the president did not understand the Republican position on entitlements such as Medicare and Social Security.

Obama's immediate predecessor, George W. Bush, was himself a master of straw-man phony issues. A March 2006 Associated Press article detailed numerous examples of Bush's use of the "straw man argument." The AP noticed that Bush frequently began sentences with "some say" or "some in Washington believe," referring to "Democrats or other White House opponents." By not naming them, Bush was more free to omit "an important nuance or [substitute] an extreme stance that bears little resemblance to their actual position." Bush could then knock "down a straw man of his own making" that nobody would actually defend. . . .

Throw under the bus: The opposite of loyalty; an all-too-frequent occurrence in which someone ditches or trashes a friend, employee, or associate.

Examples of throwing someone under the bus in politics date back to the 1990s and are legion. The *Washington Post*'s David Segal branded it "*the* cliché of the 2008 campaign" and observed it doesn't make logical sense: It ostensibly refers to a campaign bus, and by extension a politician and his or her cause. Because the person being cut loose presumably is aboard the bus, how can they be tossed beneath a vehicle in which they're riding?

It was often used in the run-up to and during the October 2013 government shutdown. Congressional Republicans decided one way to frustrate Senate Democrats—and, by extension, President Barack Obama— was to make lawmakers vote to keep their subsidies for health insurance, as provided by the Affordable Care Act (aka Obamacare). But a Republican bill to kill the subsidies also affected congressional staff. "I understand it politically, and as a talking point," one Republican staffer told *Mother Jones*. "But Congress literally threw staff under the bus on this. . . . You're hurting staff assistants who are sorting your mail." . . .

"We need to have a conversation about . . .": A favorite that politicians use, closely related to *pivot,* to try to steer a potentially messy debate in an advantageous direction. It's code for, "Let's not jump to conclusions about this; just shut up and listen to *my* view of things."

Thus, when mass shootings such as the one in Newtown, Connecticut, have occurred, President Barack Obama talked about the need for a conversation about gun control. Or about federal drug policy, after Colorado and Washington state legalized marijuana use in 2012. Or race, after any number of incidents in which it was a factor. Or about balancing privacy and national security after Edward Snowden revealed the extent of the National Security Agency's domestic snooping.

Not to single out Obama. Former Florida governor Jeb Bush has talked about his party's need to have a conversation with Hispanics. And as the Republican Party's image took a shellacking during the 2013 government shutdown, House Speaker John Boehner proclaimed on the House floor: "We need to sit down and have a conversation about the big challenges that face our country." . . .

Judicial activism: A legal decision or pattern of decisions that you don't like.

Claims of judicial activism for decades found a home on the right. Conservatives likened the 1973 *Roe v. Wade* decision, which decriminalized abortion, to "judicial activism" by unelected judges. In later years critics of the landmark abortion decision, including President George W. Bush, would characterize it as "legislating from the bench."

After years of Republican presidents shifting the federal judiciary to the right, liberals later began using judicial activism when politically convenient. The Supreme Court's December 2000 *Bush v. Gore* case proved a tipping point. The justices voted to halt the recount of ballots in Florida and, in effect, make George W. Bush president. Particularly galling to Democrats was the justices' declaration that the *Bush v. Gore* ruling applied only to the presidential election case before them, with no precedential value.

The notion of judicial activism literally came to a head during President Barack Obama's 2010 State of the Union speech. Obama, a one-time *Harvard Law Review* editor and later University of Chicago constitutional law lecturer, took issue with the Supreme Court's recent *Citizens United* decision, which said that corporations could spend as much as they wanted to sway voters in federal elections. "Last week, the Supreme Court reversed a century of law that I believe will open the floodgates for special interests—including foreign corporations—to spend without limit in our elections." Justice Samuel Alito was seen frowning and mouthing the words "not true." . . .

Washington handshake: Greeting somebody while looking over his or her shoulder to see if there could be a more important person in the room.

During his rise to prominence, and during his heady days as House Speaker, Newt Gingrich was said to be a master of the Washington handshake. Relationships for the Republican bomb thrower were transactional and discardable when a new shiny object appeared that could aid his upward trajectory.

The Washington handshake is only the most visible manifestation of insincerity by many D.C. actors. People who previously held prestigious job titles—members of Congress, journalists at a national news outlet, and others—are often shocked that their *friends* aren't interested in talking to them anymore once they're no longer in a position to help professionally.

Political journalists are often the worst purveyors of the Washington handshake, and insincerity generally. After all, members of Congress have risen to the top of the political ladder by knowing how to fake interest in other people. Reporters and pundits, not so much. . . .

Dog whistle: Political messaging using coded language that seems to mean one thing to the general population, but which to a targeted subgroup means something else entirely.

Conservatives are more frequently accused of using political dog whistles to talk past the general public. In his 2003 State of the Union speech, President George W. Bush spoke of "power, wonder-working power, in the goodness and idealism and faith of the American people." Evangelical Christians recognized the phrase "wonder-working power" as a line from the hymn "There is Power in the Blood."

Political scientist Bethany Albertson examined the impact of that phrase in a study for the University of Chicago and Princeton University's Center for the Study of Democratic Politics. She tested a group of Princeton students and found that just 9 percent were familiar with it, compared to 84 percent of Pentecostals that were sampled. "Amongst this group that was familiar with the coded language, they preferred the religious appeal when it was not made explicit," Albertson wrote. Her conclusion: "For religious appeals, coded communication is particularly persuasive in politics." . . .

More recently, Democrats attributed Newt Gingrich's resounding primary victory in South Carolina in 2012 to what they said was his dog-whistling depiction of Barack Obama as "the food-stamp president." Republicans, naturally, said Democrats read too much into such messages, and blasted Obama for what they called his own masked messaging. "When he says 'pay your fair share,' that's dog whistle, code for redistribution," Fox News talk show host Eric Bolling said in September 2012. "Redistribution is a code word, dog whistle for socialism." . . .

Droppin' the g's: An abrupt change in politicians' speech patterns in front of friendly crowds to sound informal.

The normally well-spoken President Barack Obama said in an April 2011 speech that without a new energy policy, "Folks will keep on makin' conventional cars." Better vehicles already exist, he added: "We don't have to create somethin' new." A year later, Mitt Romney wished one Southern audience "a fine Alabama mornin'."

When this happens, jokes abound and people wince. *Inside the Actor's*

Studio host James Lipton—himself a parody target by comedian Will Farrell for his uptightness—lashed out at Obama and his predecessor, George W. Bush. Lipton told conservative radio host Laura Ingraham about the Columbia- and Harvard Law-educated Obama, and Bush, who graduated from Yale and Harvard Business School: "I wanted to write a piece some time ago . . . called 'The Disappearing G.' It was inspired more by George W. Bush than by anybody else, where suddenly this man who comes from an upper-class family and comes from an upper-class world, but the 'g' in '-ing' vanished—'I'm goin',' 'We're talkin'.' And other politicians have taken it on. Obama does it there. I don't like it anywhere."

With the exception of Sarah Palin, the politician who has taken the most grief for dropping *g*'s is Hillary Clinton. Her speech patterns became an issue early in her 2008 Democratic presidential bid. During an appearance with Al Sharpton at a 2007 civil rights commemoration in Selma, Ala., Clinton laid on a rather transparently southern accent. But the criticism may have been unfair because in her case, the semi-drawl had something of an air of authenticity. Though reared in Chicago, Hillary spent nearly twenty years in Arkansas, where husband Bill Clinton was a rising political force. Early interviews from the 1992 election cycle feature Hillary speaking in a form of Southern drawl.

Even one of her most famous quotes drops some *g*'s: "You know, I'm not sittin' here like some little woman standing by my man, like Tammy Wynette. I'm sittin' here because I love him, and I respect him, and I honor what he's been through and what we've been through together."

"Elections have consequences": The political way for a winner to tell a loser, "Tough luck, you lost. Get over it."

President Barack Obama famously espoused this view shortly after his 2009 inauguration, during a widely reported meeting with congressional Republicans about economic proposals. Obama was quoted telling the GOP leaders that "elections have consequences," and, in case there was any doubt, "I won." Two years earlier, firebrand liberal Barbara Boxer of California upbraided fiery conservative James Inhofe of Oklahoma—her predecessor as chair of the Senate Environment and Public Works Committee—at a hearing about how ex-vice president Al Gore should respond to Inhofe's questions. Inhofe told her that Gore could respond when he was done talking, but Boxer bluntly retorted: "No, that isn't the rule. You're not making the rules. You used to, when you did this [chaired the committee]. Elections have consequences. So I make the rules."

It also was Senator Tom Harkin's view, if stated more elegantly, about the November 2013 curtailing of Senate filibusters. By that point the Iowa Democrat had been pushing to limit the filibuster for almost nineteen years. Harkin considered the filibuster an undemocratic abuse by the Senate minority. He was among the few lawmakers with the moral authority to make such a claim, having espoused the same argument for years even as the Senate majority seesawed back and forth. In an NPR interview, Harkin argued that Democrats, if back in the Senate minority, at some point, should have to live under the same rules. "If people vote for a Republican president that's going to nominate someone to the Supreme Court to overturn *Roe v. Wade,* listen, elections should have consequences. People should know, if they're going to vote that way, they better expect the results."

Of course, being on the losing end of an election often changes the view of politicos about how determinative elections should be. During the four-year tenure of Nancy Pelosi as the first female House Speaker, her Democrats didn't seem particularly interested in taking into account the viewpoints of minority Republicans. The Democrats routinely pushed through legislation with little, if any, support from Republicans. President Barack Obama's signature Affordable Care Act was only the most prominent example, along with a 2009 economic stimulus law and a cap-and-trade climate change bill that failed to become law. "Yes, we wrote the bill. Yes, we won the election," Pelosi said at one point in early 2009 as the stimulus bill ping-ponged between the Democratic-controlled House and Senate.

That was no different than her Republican predecessors as speaker, who approached their House majorities with *elections have consequences* confidence and bluster. But after House Democrats lost their majority in the 2010 midterm elections Pelosi, back on Capitol Hill in an encore performance as minority leader, seemed to take a different view. In April 2011, after a few months back in the minority, Pelosi told a Tufts University audience in Massachusetts that elections "shouldn't matter as much as they do." Pelosi seemed to urge Republicans to moderate their views so that the space between the parties is not so vast. Then, she imagined, elections wouldn't be so determinative. . . .

"I misspoke": An awkward all-purpose political excuse covering a multitude of sins, especially those that touch off an unintended furor. It is a close euphemistic relative of the time-honored chestnut "Mistakes were made."

As English journalist Steven Poole, author of the 2007 book *Unspeak: How Words Become Weapons, How Weapons Become a Message, and How That Message Becomes Reality,* wrote: "It is useful to say one 'misspoke.' You acknowledge that what you said was absolute balls [a Britishism for utter nonsense], but the fault is not your own, as it would be if you had lied or been wrong. No, the fault is somehow in the faculty of speech itself, something going wrong in the course of that complex magic between brain, lip and others' ears."

Though the phrase has been around for centuries, it entered the political lexicon in 1973 when Ronald Ziegler, Richard Nixon's press secretary, sought to atone for his previous inaccuracies about Watergate by declaring, "I misspoke myself."

When Mitt Romney told CNN in 2012, "I'm not concerned about the very poor," it was a line that fed the ongoing *meme* that he was out of touch. Two days later, he corrected himself: "It was a misstatement; I misspoke." That same year, Missouri GOP Senate candidate Todd Akin said after his remarks on "legitimate rape" caused a political firestorm: "In reviewing my off-the-cuff remarks, it's clear that I misspoke in this interview and it does not reflect the deep empathy I hold for the thousands of women who are raped and abused every year."

But Republicans aren't the only mis-spokespeople. Four years earlier, Hillary Clinton was found to have embellished a tale of her running from her plane to a vehicle because of threats of sniper fire. She sought to clarify: "What I was told was that we had to land a certain way and move quickly because of the threat of sniper fire. So I misspoke—I didn't say that in my book or other times, but if I said something that made it seem as though there was actual fire, that's not what I was told. I was told we had to land a certain way, we had to have our bulletproof stuff on because of the threat of sniper fire." . . .

Meme: A piece of political content with the potential to go *viral* online. Funny images and captions commenting on the day's events prove particularly infectious.

This distinctly twenty-first-century phenomenon provides new ways to view routine campaign events. Presidential debates, in particular, are meme-fodder. In 2012, even those who didn't watch the three in-person face-offs between President Barack Obama and Republican challenger Mitt Romney, would have been familiar with Big Bird, binders, and bayonets.

Those words were barely out of the candidates' mouths before Internet memes began appearing on Facebook, Twitter, and Tumblr feeds, where they quickly went viral. After threatening to defund PBS in the first debate, Big Bird became an albatross for Romney—though he was otherwise considered a winner in the faceoff against Obama.

Narrative: The all-important (at least to the media) way of framing a campaign, a presidency, or anything else in politics. The Austin, Texas-based Global Language Monitor declared "the narrative" the top political buzzword of 2010.

Narratives are the folklore of politics. Intellectual historian George Hoare sees narratives as "simplified but 'generally correct' aspects of popular knowledge which are used to identify, delineate and understand political phenomena. . . . The narrative of Left Versus Right is a signal example: it ranges over time and space as well as a multiplicity of different groups."

When a scandal or something unpleasant hits someone, it's automatically suggested that he or she "lost control of the narrative" and consequently isn't able to effectively convey his or her competence and/or trustworthiness. Nowhere was this more true than in the many problems accompanying the rollout of the Affordable Care Act (aka Obamacare) website in fall 2013. "At some level, the White House lost control of the narrative on this," said Democratic strategist Chris Lehane. "They, for whatever reason, continue to be playing defense on the subject."

But why has the narrative become so important? Observers see it as a result of the balkanization of the media in a highly polarized political climate. "Today's audiences are no longer satisfied with choosing their own news outlets," *Chicago Tribune* columnist Clarence Page wrote. "They also want to choose their own versions of the reality that news covers. Whether they realize it or not, they're shopping for their own 'narrative.'"

Nerd prom: The White House Correspondents' Association televised annual dinner, featuring big-name guests ranging from Henry Kissinger to *Hustler* mogul Larry Flynt, music or comedy from a well-known entertainer (Jay Leno, Ray Charles), and, generally, some well-scripted jokes from the commander in chief that are often in the *comic self-deprecation* vein. . . .

Walk back: Attempts by politicians and press handlers to limit the damage done by dumb, embarrassing, and stupid statements. It's a politely euphemistic way to address the subject of lying or deception without having to use those rather unseemly words.

Walk back is derived from "walking back the cat," which William Safire notes has been used in diplomatic circles to signify retreating from a previously held position in negotiations. In the spy world, it also means reexamining old analyses based on new information.

While lawmakers and candidates sometimes try to deny outright embarrassing words, in the age of cell-phone cameras and video and other recording devices, it's become increasingly difficult to pull that off. Sometimes, even anonymous quotes can force walk-backs. During the October

2013 government shutdown, the *Wall Street Journal* quoted about political tactics that Team Obama figured would bring congressional Republicans to heel. "We are winning," a senior administration official said, bragging that the length of the shutdown "doesn't really matter to us." The point: the political pain would be on the other side, and the president, who wasn't running for reelection, thought "what matters is the end result." But the White House quickly backed off the senior administration official's blind quote, with Press Secretary Jay Carney tweeting that "POTUS wants the shutdown to end NOW," and Obama himself later said "no one is winning" while the government is shut down. Republicans seized on the original quote in the *Journal*. "This isn't some damn game," House Speaker John Boehner said indignantly at a press conference.

Any discussion of political walk-backs must include Senate Democratic leader Harry Reid. The Nevada Democrat spent decades in politics, and by the time he ascended to the peak of his power during the Obama presidency he didn't particularly care who was offended by his tart tongue. Still, throughout the years Reid's staff made heroic, if mostly failed, efforts to walk back the senator's more controversial statements. During the same government shutdown, Reid drew flak after ineloquently responding to a question from CNN's Dana Bash about kids with cancer who, due to the government lockdown, were unable to undergo clinical trials run by the National Institutes of Health. (Bash: "But if you can help one child who has cancer, why wouldn't you do it?" Reid: "Why would we want to do that? I have 1,100 people at Nellis Air Force Base that are sitting home. They have a few problems of their own.") Reid's press aides quickly issued a clarifying statement, but Republicans knew a good sound bite when they heard it.

Reid himself has at times admitted to verbal excesses and walked back his own statements. On the Senate floor in October 2013, the Senate majority leader delivered a striking mea culpa, saying he and his colleagues had simply gotten too personal and nasty in their debates. A day earlier, Senator John Cornyn had scolded Reid for attacking Senator Ted Cruz, a fellow Texas Republican, by name as they debated the government shutdown. Cornyn read directly from the Senate rules that prohibit members from impugning each other's motives or conduct.

PART FIVE

The Presidency

27

RICHARD NEUSTADT

From *Presidential Power and the Modern Presidents*

From this often-read book comes the classic concept of presidential power as "the power to persuade." Richard Neustadt observed the essence of presidential power when working in the executive branch during Franklin Roosevelt's term as president. He stayed to serve under President Truman. It is said that President Kennedy brought Presidential Power *with him to the White House, and Neustadt worked briefly for JFK. The first half of the excerpt, in which he shows how presidents' well-developed personal characteristics permit successful persuasive abilities, comes from the book's first edition. The excerpt's closing pages reflect Neustadt's later musings on the nation, on world affairs, and on the challenges presidents face.*

IN THE EARLY summer of 1952, before the heat of the campaign, President [Harry] Truman used to contemplate the problems of the general-become-President should [Dwight David] Eisenhower win the forthcoming election. "He'll sit here," Truman would remark (tapping his desk for emphasis), "and he'll say, 'Do this! Do that!' *And nothing will happen.* Poor Ike—it won't be a bit like the Army. He'll find it very frustrating."

Eisenhower evidently found it so. "In the face of the continuing dissidence and disunity, the President sometimes simply exploded with exasperation," wrote Robert Donovan in comment on the early months of Eisenhower's first term. "What was the use, he demanded to know, of his trying to lead the Republican Party. . . . " And this reaction was not limited to early months alone, or to his party only. "The President still feels," an Eisenhower aide remarked to me in 1958, "that when he's decided something, that *ought* to be the end of it . . . and when it bounces back undone or done wrong, he tends to react with shocked surprise."

Truman knew whereof he spoke. With "resignation" in the place of "shocked surprise," the aide's description would have fitted Truman. The former senator may have been less shocked than the former general, but he was no less subjected to that painful and repetitive experience: "Do this, do that, and nothing will happen." Long before he came to talk of Eisenhower he had put his own experience in other words: "I sit here all day trying to persuade people to do the things they ought to have sense enough to do without my persuading them. . . . That's all the powers of the President amount to."

In these words of a President, spoken on the job, one finds the essence of the problem now before us: "powers" are no guarantee of power; clerkship is no guarantee of leadership. The President of the United States has an extraordinary range of formal powers, of authority in statute law and in the Constitution. Here is testimony that despite his "powers" he does not obtain results by giving orders—or not, at any rate, merely by giving orders. He also has extraordinary status, ex officio, according to the customs of our government and politics. Here is testimony that despite his status he does not get action without argument. Presidential power is the power to persuade. . . .

The limits on command suggest the structure of our government. The Constitutional Convention of 1787 is supposed to have created a government of "separated powers." It did nothing of the sort. Rather, it created a government of separated institutions *sharing* powers. "I am part of the legislative process," Eisenhower often said in 1959 as a reminder of his veto. Congress, the dispenser of authority and funds, is no less part of the administrative process. Federalism adds another set of separated institutions. The Bill of Rights adds others. Many public purposes can only be achieved by voluntary acts of private institutions; the press, for one, in Douglass Cater's phrase, is a "fourth branch of government." And with the coming of alliances abroad, the separate institutions of a London, or a Bonn, share in the making of American public policy.

What the Constitution separates our political parties do not combine. The parties are themselves composed of separated organizations sharing public authority. The authority consists of nominating powers. Our national parties are confederations of state and local party institutions, with a headquarters that represents the White House, more or less, if the party has a President in office. These confederacies manage presidential nominations. All other public offices depend upon electorates confined within the states. All other nominations are controlled within the states. The President and congressmen who bear one party's label are divided by dependence upon different sets of voters. The differences are sharpest at the stage of nomination. The White House has too small a share in nominating congressmen, and Congress has too little weight in nominating presidents for party to erase their constitutional separation. Party links are stronger than is frequently supposed, but nominating processes assure the separation.

The separateness of institutions and the sharing of authority prescribe the terms on which a President persuades. When one man shares authority with another, but does not gain or lose his job upon the other's whim, his willingness to act upon the urging of the other turns on whether he conceives the action right for him. The essence of a President's persuasive task is to convince such men that what the White House wants of them is what they ought to do for their sake and on their authority. (Sex matters not at all; for *man* read *woman*.)

Persuasive power, thus defined, amounts to more than charm or reasoned argument. These have their uses for a President, but these are not the whole of his resources. For the individuals he would induce to do what he wants done on their own responsibility will need or fear some acts by him on his responsibility. If they share his authority, he has some share in theirs. Presidential "powers" may be inconclusive when a President commands, but always remain relevant as he persuades. The status and authority inherent in his office reinforce his logic and his charm. . . .

A President's authority and status give him great advantages in dealing with the men he would persuade. Each "power" is a vantage point for him in the degree that other men have use for his authority. From the veto to appointments, from publicity to budgeting, and so down a long list, the White House now controls the most encompassing array of vantage points in the American political system. With hardly an exception, those who share in governing this country are aware that at some time, in some degree, the doing of *their* jobs, the furthering of *their* ambitions, may depend upon the President of the United States. Their need for presidential action, or their fear of it, is bound to be recurrent if not actually continuous. Their need or fear is his advantage.

A President's advantages are greater than mere listing of his "powers" might suggest. Those with whom he deals must deal with him until the last day of his term. Because they have continuing relationships with him, his future, while it lasts, supports his present influence. Even though there is no need or fear of him today, what he could do tomorrow may supply today's advantage. Continuing relationships may convert any "power," any aspect of his status, into vantage points in almost any case. When he induces other people to do what he wants done, a President can trade on their dependence now and later.

The President's advantages are checked by the advantages of others. Continuing relationships will pull in both directions. These are relationships of mutual dependence. A President depends upon the persons whom he would persuade; he has to reckon with his need or fear of them. They too will possess status, or authority, or both, else they would be of little use to him. Their vantage points confront his own; their power tempers his. . . .

The power to persuade is the power to bargain. Status and authority yield bargaining advantages. But in a government of "separated institutions sharing powers," they yield them to all sides. With the array of vantage points at his disposal, a President may be far more persuasive than his logic or his charm could make him. But outcomes are not guaranteed by his advantages. There remain the counter pressures those whom he would influence can bring to bear on him from vantage points at their disposal. Command has limited utility; persuasion becomes give-and-take. It is well that the White House holds the vantage points it does. In such a business any President may need them all—and more. . . .

When a President confronts divergent policy advisers, disputing experts, conflicting data, and uncertain outlooks, yet must choose, there plainly *are* some other things he can do for himself besides consulting his own power stakes. But there is a proviso—provided he has done that first and keeps clear in his mind how much his prospects may depend on his authority, how much on reputation, how much on public standing. In the world Reagan inhabited where reputation and prestige are far more intertwined than they had been in Truman's time, or even LBJ's, this proviso is no easy test of presidential expertise. It calls for a good ear and a fine eye. . . .

But when a President turns to others, regardless of the mode, he is dependent on their knowledge, judgment, and good will. If he turns essentially to one, alone, he puts a heavy burden on that other's knowledge. If he chooses not to read or hear details, he puts an even greater burden on the other's judgment. If he consents, besides, to secrecy from everyone whose task in life is to protect his flanks, he courts deep trouble. Good will should not be stretched beyond endurance. In a system characterized by separated institutions sharing powers, where presidential interests will diverge in some degree from those of almost everybody else, that suggests not stretching very far. . . .

Personally, I prefer Presidents . . . more skeptical than trustful, more curious than committed, more nearly Roosevelts than Reagans. I think the former energize our governmental system better and bring out its defects less than do the latter. Reagan's years did not persuade me otherwise, in spite of his appeal on other scores. Every scandal in his wake, for instance, must owe something to the narrow range of his convictions and the breadth of his incuriosity, along with all that trust. A President cannot abolish bad behavior, but he sets a tone, and if he is alert to possibilities he can set traps, and with them limits. Reagan's tone, apparently, was heard by all too many as "enrich yourselves," while those few traps deregulation spared appear to have been sprung and left unbaited for the most part. But this book has not been written to expound my personal preferences. Rather it endeavors to expose the problem for a President of either sort who seeks to buttress prospects for his future influence while making present choices—"looking toward tomorrow from today," as I wrote at the start. For me that remains a crucial enterprise. It is not, of course, the only thing a President should put his mind to, but it is the subject to which I have put my own throughout this book. It remains crucial, in my view, not simply for the purposes of Presidents, but also for the products of the system, whether effective policy, or flawed or none. Thus it becomes crucial for us all.

We now stand on the threshold of a time in which those separated institutions, Congress and the President, share powers fully and uncomfortably across the board of policy, both foreign and domestic. From the 1940s through the 1960s—"midcentury" in this book's terms—Congress, having been embarrassed at Pearl Harbor by the isolationism it displayed beforehand, gave successive Presidents more scope in defense budgeting and in the conduct of diplomacy toward Europe and Japan than was the norm between the two world wars. Once the Cold War had gotten under way, and then been largely militarized after Korea, that scope widened. With the onset of the missile age it deepened. Should nuclear war impend, the President became the system's final arbiter. Thus I characterized JFK against the background of the Cuban missile crisis. But by 1975 the denouement of Watergate and that of Vietnam, eight months apart, had put a period to what remained of congressional reticence left over from Pearl Harbor. And the closing of the Cold War, now in sight though by no means achieved, promises an end to nuclear danger as between the Soviet Union and the United States. Threats of nuclear attack could well remain, from Third World dictators or terrorists, but not destruction of the Northern Hemisphere. So in the realm of military preparations—even, indeed, covert actions—the congressional role waxes as the Cold War wanes, returning toward normality as understood in Franklin Roosevelt's first two terms.

In a multipolar world, crisscrossed by transnational relations, with economic and environmental issues paramount, and issues of security reshaped on regional lines, our Presidents will less and less have reason to seek solace in foreign relations from the piled-up frustrations of home affairs. Their foreign frustrations will be piled high too.

Since FDR in wartime, every President including Bush has found the role of superpower sovereign beguiling: personal responsibility at once direct and high, issues at once gripping and arcane, opposite numbers frequently intriguing and well-mannered, acclaim by foreign audiences echoing well at home, foreign travel relatively glamorous, compared with home, interest groups less clamorous, excepting special cases, authority always stronger, Congress often tamer. But the distinctions lessen—compare Bush's time with Nixon's to say nothing of Eisenhower's—and we should expect that they will lessen further. Telecommunications, trade, aid, banking and stock markets combined with AIDS and birth control and hunger, topped off by toxic waste and global warming—these are not the stuff of which the Congress of Vienna* was made, much less the summits of yore. Moreover, Europeans ten years hence, as well as Japanese, may not resemble much the relatively acquiescent "middle powers" we grew used to in the 1960s and 1970s. Cooperating with them may come to seem to Presidents no easier than cooperating with Congress. Our friends abroad will see it quite the other way around: How are they to cooperate with our peculiar mix of separated institutions sharing powers? Theirs are ordered governments, ours a rat race. Complaints of us by others in these terms are nothing new. They have been rife throughout this century. But by the next, some of the chief complainants may have fewer needs of us, while ours of them grow relatively greater, than at any other time since World War II. In that case foreign policy could cease to be a source of pleasure for a President. By the same token, he or she would have to do abroad as on the Hill and in Peoria: Check carefully the possible effects of present choices on prospective reputation and prestige—thinking of other governments and publics quite as hard as those at home. It is not just our accustomed NATO and Pacific allies who may force the pace here, but the Soviet Union, if it holds together, and potentially great powers—China, India, perhaps Brazil—as well as our neighbors, north and south.

From the multicentered, interdependent world now coming into being, environmentally endangered as it is, Presidents may look back on the Cold War as an era of stability, authority, and glamour. They may yearn for the simplicity they see in retrospect, and also for the solace. Too bad. The job of being President is tougher when incumbents have to struggle for effective influence in foreign and domestic spheres at once, with their

---

*After the 1814 defeat of the French leader Napoleon by Russia, Prussia, Austria, and Britain, these great powers met in Vienna, Austria, to ensure that the future of Europe would be peaceful. At the Congress of Vienna, they created a "balance of power" system so that no single European nation could dominate the continent.—Eds.

command of nuclear forces losing immediate relevance, and the American economy shorn of its former clout. There are, however, compensations, one in particular. If we outlive the Cold War,* the personal responsibility attached to nuclear weapons should become less burdensome for Presidents themselves, while contemplation of their mere humanity becomes less haunting for the rest of us. To me that seems a fair exchange.

*The Cold War refers to the hostility that existed between the United States and the Soviet Union from the end of World War II until recent times. The Cold War involved many forms of hostility: democracy versus communism; America's NATO allies versus the Soviet Union's Warsaw Pact military partners; the threat of nuclear war; economic competition; the dividing of Third World nations into pro-U.S. and pro-Soviet camps. With the demise of communism in Eastern Europe and the disintegration of the Soviet Union, the Cold War era has ended.—EDS.

28

ARTHUR SCHLESINGER

From *The Imperial Presidency*

Historian Arthur Schlesinger coined one of the most famous and often-quoted political phrases, used not just in academe but in the real world of government too. The demise of Richard Nixon, because of the Watergate scandal, inspired Schlesinger to look back in U.S. history to locate the roots of the tremendous power that the executive had accumulated. His observations led him to develop the idea of an "imperial Presidency," with all the connotations that phrase carries. The author believes that the imperial presidency initially evolved for a clear and identifiable reason; it then grew due to other secondary factors. Certain presidents—Roosevelt and especially Kennedy—garner praise from Schlesinger for their judicious use of imperial powers. Other presidents he condemns. Schlesinger's discussion of Richard Nixon, the ultimate imperial president, is a frank and unvarnished critique of the man who turned the imperial presidency homeward, against the American people. After Nixon left office, the phrase was little-used, until President George W. Bush responded to the terrorist attacks of September 11, 2001. To some, President Bush's response to 9/11, especially his "War on Terror" and the invasion of Iraq, signified a renewal of the "imperial presidency."

———

In the last years presidential primacy, so indispensable to the political order, has turned into presidential supremacy. The constitutional Presidency—as events so apparently disparate as the Indochina War and the Watergate affair showed—has become the imperial Presidency and threatens to be the revolutionary Presidency.

This book ... deals essentially with the shift in the *constitutional* balance—with, that is, the appropriation by the Presidency, and particularly by the contemporary Presidency, of powers reserved by the Constitution and by long historical practice to Congress.

This process of appropriation took place in both foreign and domestic affairs. Especially in the twentieth century, the circumstances of an increasingly perilous world as well as of an increasingly interdependent economy and society seemed to compel a larger concentration of authority in the Presidency. It must be said that historians and political scientists, this writer among them, contributed to the rise of the presidential mystique. But the imperial Presidency received its decisive impetus, I believe, from foreign policy; above all, from the capture by the Presidency of the most vital of national decisions, the decision to go to war.

This book consequently devotes special attention to the history of the war-making power. The assumption of that power by the Presidency was gradual and usually under the demand or pretext of emergency. It was as much a matter of congressional abdication as of presidential usurpation. . . .

The imperial Presidency was essentially the creation of foreign policy. A combination of doctrines and emotions—belief in permanent and universal crisis, fear of communism, faith in the duty and the right of the United States to intervene swiftly in every part of the world—had brought about the unprecedented centralization of decisions over war and peace in the Presidency. With this there came an unprecedented exclusion of the rest of the executive branch, of Congress, of the press and of public opinion in general from these decisions. Prolonged war in Vietnam strengthened the tendencies toward both centralization and exclusion. So the imperial Presidency grew at the expense of the constitutional order. Like the cowbird, it hatched its own eggs and pushed the others out of the nest. And, as it overwhelmed the traditional separation of powers in foreign affairs, it began to aspire toward an equivalent centralization of power in the domestic polity.

. . . We saw in the case of Franklin D. Roosevelt and the New Deal that extraordinary power flowing into the Presidency to meet domestic problems by no means enlarged presidential authority in foreign affairs. But we also saw in the case of FDR and the Second World War and Harry S. Truman and the steel seizure that extraordinary power flowing into the Presidency to meet international problems could easily encourage Presidents to extend their unilateral claims at home. . . . Twenty years later, the spillover effect from Vietnam coincided with indigenous developments that were quite separately carrying new power to the Presidency. For domestic as well as for international reasons, the imperial Presidency was sinking roots deep into the national society itself.

One such development was the decay of the traditional party system. . . . For much of American history the party has been the ultimate vehicle of political expression. Voters inherited their politics as they did their religion. . . . By the 1970s ticket-splitting had become common. Independent voting was spreading everywhere, especially among the young. Never had party loyalties been so weak, party affiliations so fluid, party organizations so irrelevant.

Many factors contributed to the decline of parties. The old political organizations had lost many of their functions. The waning of immigration, for example, had deprived the city machine of its classical clientele. The rise of civil service had cut off the machine's patronage. The New Deal had taken over the machine's social welfare role. Above all, the electronic revolution was drastically modifying the political environment. Two electronic devices had a particularly devastating impact on the traditional structure of politics—television and the computer. . . .

As the parties wasted away, the Presidency stood out in solitary majesty as the central focus of political emotion, the ever more potent symbol of national community. . . .

At the same time, the economic changes of the twentieth century had conferred vast new powers not just on the national government but more particularly on the Presidency. . . .

. . . The managed economy, in short, offered new forms of unilateral power to the President who was bold enough to take action on his own. . . .

. . . The imperial presidency, born in the 1940s and 1950s to save the outer world from perdition, thus began in the 1960s and 1970s to find nurture at home. Foreign policy had given the President the command of peace and war. Now the decay of the parties left him in command of the political scene, and the Keynesian revelation placed him in command of the economy. At this extraordinary historical moment, when foreign and domestic lines of force converged, much depended on whether the occupant of the White House was moved to ride the new tendencies of power or to resist them.

For the American Presidency was a peculiarly personal institution. It remained, of course, an agency of government, subject to unvarying demands and duties no matter who was President. But, more than most agencies of government, it changed shape, intensity and ethos according to the man in charge. . . . The management of the great foreign policy crisis of the Kennedy years—the Soviet attempt to install nuclear missiles in Cuba—came as if in proof of the proposition that the nuclear age left no alternative to unilateral presidential decision. . . .

. . . Time was short, because something had to be done before the bases became operational. Secrecy was imperative. Kennedy took the decision into his own hands, but it is to be noted that he did not make it in imperial solitude. The celebrated Executive Committee became a forum for exceedingly vigorous and intensive debate. Major alternatives received strong, even vehement, expression. Though there was no legislative consultation, there was most effective executive consultation. . . . But, even in retrospect, the missile crisis seems an emergency so acute in its nature and so peculiar in its structure that it did in fact require unilateral executive decision.

Yet this very acuteness and peculiarity disabled Kennedy's action in October 1962 as a precedent for future Presidents in situations less acute and less peculiar. For the missile crisis was unique in the postwar years in that it *really* combined all those pressures of threat, secrecy and time that the foreign policy establishment had claimed as characteristic of decisions in the nuclear age. Where the threat was less grave, the need for secrecy less urgent, the time for debate less restricted—i.e., in all other cases—the argument for independent and unilateral presidential action was notably less compelling.

Alas, Kennedy's action, which should have been celebrated as an exception, was instead enshrined as a rule. This was in great part because it so beautifully fulfilled both the romantic ideal of the strong President and the prophecy of split-second presidential decision in the nuclear age. The very brilliance of Kennedy's performance appeared to vindicate the idea that the President must take unto himself the final judgments of war and peace. The missile crisis, I believe, was superbly handled, and could not have been handled so well in any other way. But one of its legacies was the imperial conception of the Presidency that brought the republic so low in Vietnam. . . .

. . . Johnson talked to, even if he too seldom listened to, an endless stream of members of Congress and the press. He unquestionably denied himself reality for a long time, especially when it came to Vietnam. But in the end reality broke through, forcing him to accept unpleasant truths he did not wish to hear. Johnson's personality was far closer than Truman's to imperial specifications. But the fit was by no means perfect. . . .

Every President reconstructs the Presidency to meet his own psychological needs. Nixon displayed more monarchical yearnings than any of his predecessors. He plainly reveled in the ritual of the office, only regretting that it could not be more elaborate. What previous President, for example, would have dreamed of ceremonial trumpets or of putting the White House security force in costumes to rival the Guards at Buckingham Palace? Public ridicule stopped this. But Nixon saw no problem about using federal money, under the pretext of national security, to adorn his California and Florida estates with redwood fences, golf carts, heaters and wind screens for the swimming pool, beach cabanas, roof tiling, carpets, furniture, trees and shrubbery. . . . Nixon's fatal error was to institute within the White House itself a centralization even more total than that he contemplated for the executive branch. He rarely saw most of his so-called personal assistants. If an aide telephoned the President on a domestic matter, his call was switched to Haldeman's office.* If he sent the President a memorandum, Haldeman decided whether or not the President would see it. "Rather than the President telling someone to do something," Haldeman explained in 1971, "I'll tell the guy. If he wants to find out something from somebody, I'll do it."

Presidents like Roosevelt and Kennedy understood that, if the man at the top confined himself to a single information system, he became the prisoner of that system. Therefore they pitted sources of their own against the information delivered to them through official channels. They understood that contention was an indispensable means of government. But Nixon, instead of exposing himself to the chastening influence of debate, organized the executive branch and the White House in order to shield himself as far as humanly possible from direct question or challenge—i.e., from reality. . . .

As one examined the impressive range of Nixon's initiatives—from his appropriation of the war-making power to his interpretation of the appointing power, from his unilateral determination of social priorities to his unilateral abolition of statutory programs, from his attack on legislative privilege to his enlargement of executive privilege, from his theory of impoundment to his theory of the pocket veto, from his calculated disparagement of the cabinet and his calculated discrediting of the press to his carefully organized concentration of federal management in the White House—from all this a larger design ineluctably emerged. It was hard to know whether Nixon, whose style was banality, understood consciously where he was heading. He was not a man given to political philosophizing. But he was heading toward a new balance of constitutional powers, an audacious and imaginative reconstruction of the American Constitution. He did indeed contemplate, as he said in 1971 State of the Union message, a New American Revolution. But the essence of this revolution was not, as he said at the time, power to the people. The essence was power to the Presidency. . . . His purpose was probably more unconscious than conscious; and his revolution took direction and color not just from the external circumstances pressing new powers on the Presidency but from the needs and drives of his own agitated psyche. This was the fatal flaw in the revolutionary design. For everywhere he looked he saw around him hideous threats to the national security—threats that, even though he would not describe them to Congress or the people, kept his White House

---

*Robert Haldeman headed Richard Nixon's White House staff. He was a stern gatekeeper (the president wished it so) before his resignation in the face of the exploding Watergate scandals during the spring of 1973. He was subsequently convicted of criminal charges and imprisoned for his role in Watergate.—Eds.

in constant uproar and warranted in his own mind a clandestine presidential response of spectacular and historic illegality. If his public actions led toward a scheme of presidential supremacy under a considerably debilitated Constitution, his private obsessions pushed him toward the view that the Presidency could set itself, at will, *above* the Constitution. It was this theory that led straight to Watergate. . . .

Secrecy seemed to promise government three inestimable advantages: the power to withhold, the power to leak and the power to lie. . . .

The power to withhold held out the hope of denying the public the knowledge that would make possible an independent judgment on executive policy. The mystique of inside information—"if you only knew what we know"—was a most effective way to defend the national-security monopoly and prevent democratic control of foreign policy. . . .

The power to leak meant the power to tell the people what it served the government's purpose that they should know. . . .

The power to withhold and the power to leak led on inexorably to the power to lie. The secrecy system instilled in the executive branch the idea that foreign policy was no one's business save its own, and uncontrolled secrecy made it easy for lying to become routine. It was in this spirit that the Eisenhower administration concealed the CIA operations it was mounting against governments around the world. It was in this spirit that the Kennedy administration stealthily sent the Cuban brigade to the Bay of Pigs* and stealthily enlarged American involvement in Vietnam. It was in this spirit that the Johnson administration Americanized the Vietnam War, misrepresenting one episode after another to Congress and the people—Tonkin Gulf, the first American ground force commitment, the bombing of North Vietnam, My Lai and the rest.†

---

*In 1961, President John F. Kennedy accepted responsibility for the disaster at the Bay of Pigs in Cuba. Over a thousand Cuban exiles, trained by the U.S. Central Intelligence Agency (CIA), tried to land in Cuba to overthrow the communist government of Fidel Castro. The invasion was a complete failure, forcing Kennedy to reassess his foreign policy approach, especially toward Latin America.—EDS.

†The Tonkin Gulf incident involved two alleged attacks on American ships in the waters off the coast of Vietnam in 1964. President Lyndon Johnson may have exaggerated the extent of the attacks to gain support for widening the war. In response to the incident, the Senate voted 88 to 2 and the House of Representatives 416 to 0 to allow the president significant latitude in the use of American forces in Vietnam. No formal declaration of war was ever made concerning Vietnam, but the Gulf of Tonkin Resolution became the executive branch's "blank check" to expand the conflict. The 1968 My Lai massacre was a turning point in American public opinion concerning the Vietnam War. U.S. soldiers killed over a hundred Vietnamese villagers. One lieutenant was tried and convicted for the slaughter that had happened because of the inability of American troops to distinguish between enemy soldiers and civilians. Some Americans believed that those higher up in the military, not just Lieutenant William Calley, should have been prosecuted for the massacre.—EDS.

The longer the secrecy system dominated government, the more government assumed the *right* to lie. . . .

God, it has been well said, looks after drunks, children and the United States of America. However, given the number, the brazen presumption and the clownish ineptitude of the conspirators, if it had not been Watergate, it would surely have been something else. For Watergate was a symptom, not a cause. Nixon's supporters complained that his critics were blowing up a petty incident out of all proportion to its importance. No doubt a burglary at Democratic headquarters was trivial next to a mission to Peking. But Watergate's importance was not simply in itself. Its importance was in the way it brought to the surface, symbolized and made politically accessible the great question posed by the Nixon administration in every sector—the question of presidential power. The unwarranted and unprecedented expansion of presidential power, because it ran through the whole Nixon system, was bound, if repressed at one point, to break out at another. This, not Watergate, was the central issue. . . . Watergate did stop the revolutionary Presidency in its tracks. It blew away the mystique of the mandate and reinvigorated the constitutional separation of powers. If the independent judiciary, the free press, Congress and the executive agencies could not really claim too much credit as institutions for work performed within them by brave individuals, nonetheless they all drew new confidence as institutions from the exercise of power they had forgotten they possessed. The result could only be to brace and strengthen the inner balance of American democracy. . . .

If the Nixon White House escaped the legal consequences of its illegal behavior, why would future Presidents and their associates not suppose themselves entitled to do what the Nixon White House had done? Only condign punishment would restore popular faith in the Presidency and deter future Presidents from illegal conduct—so long, at least, as Watergate remained a vivid memory. We have noted that corruption appears to visit the White House in fifty-year cycles. This suggests that exposure and retribution inoculate the Presidency against its latent criminal impulses for about half a century. Around the year 2023 the American people would be well advised to go on the alert and start nailing down everything in sight.

29

THOMAS CRONIN
MICHAEL GENOVESE

From *The Paradoxes of the American Presidency*

The United States as a nation of paradoxes is a theme frequently used to explain the contradictions found throughout American life. In an earlier selection, Michael Kammen called Americans "people of paradox." Here, political scientists Thomas Cronin and Michael Genovese use the concept of paradox to explore the many images that citizens hold of their president. Each image they describe is accompanied by a contrary image. For example, Cronin and Genovese note, the president is supposed to be an average person just like us, while simultaneously being outstanding and extraordinary. With such paradoxical expectations of a president, is it any wonder that Americans judge the executive so harshly?

THE MIND SEARCHES FOR answers to the complexities of life. We often gravitate toward simple explanations for the world's mysteries. This is a natural way to try and make sense out of a world that seems to defy understanding. We are uncomfortable with contradictions so we reduce reality to understandable simplifications. And yet, contradictions and clashing expectations are part of life. "No aspect of society, no habit, custom, movement, development, is without cross-currents," says historian Barbara Tuchman. "Starving peasants in hovels live alongside prosperous landlords in featherbeds. Children are neglected and children are loved." In life we are confronted with paradoxes for which we seek meaning. The same is true for the American presidency. We admire presidential power, yet fear it. We yearn for the heroic, yet are also inherently suspicious of it. We demand dynamic leadership, yet grant only limited powers to the president. We want presidents to be dispassionate analysts and listeners, yet they must also be decisive. We are impressed with presidents who have great self-confidence, yet we dislike arrogance and respect those who express reasonable self-doubt.

How then are we to make sense of the presidency? This complex, multidimensional, even contradictory institution is vital to the American system of government. The physical and political laws that seem to constrain one president, liberate another. What proves successful in one, leads to failure in another. Rather than seeking one unifying theory of presidential politics that answers all our questions, we believe that the American presidency might be better understood as a series of paradoxes, clashing expectations and contradictions.

Leaders live with contradictions. Presidents, more than most people, learn to take advantage of contrary or divergent forces. Leadership situations commonly require successive displays of contrasting characteristics. Living with, even embracing, contradictions is a sign of political and personal maturity.

The effective leader understands the presence of opposites. The aware leader, much like a first-rate conductor, knows when to bring in various sections, knows when and how to turn the volume up and down, and learns how to balance opposing sections to achieve desired results. Effective presidents learn how to manage these contradictions and give meaning and purpose to confusing and often clashing expectations. The novelist F. Scott Fitzgerald once suggested that, "The test of a first-rate intelligence is the ability to hold two opposed ideas in the mind at the same time." Casey Stengel, long-time New York Yankee manager and occasional (if accidental) Zen philosopher, captured the essence of the paradox when he noted, "Good pitching will always stop good hitting, and vice versa."

Our expectations of, and demands on, the president are frequently so contradictory as to invite two-faced behavior by our presidents. Presidential powers are often not as great as many of us believe, and the president gets unjustly condemned as ineffective. Or a president will overreach or resort to unfair play while trying to live up to our demands.

The Constitution is of little help. The founders purposely left the presidency imprecisely defined. This was due in part to their fears of both the monarchy and the masses, and in part to their hopes that future presidents would create a more powerful office than the framers were able to do at the time. They knew that at times the president would have to move swiftly and effectively, yet they went to considerable lengths to avoid enumerating specific powers and duties in order to calm the then widespread fear of monarchy. After all, the nation had just fought a war against executive tyranny. Thus the paradox of the invention of the presidency: To get the presidency approved in 1787 and 1788, the framers had to leave several silences and ambiguities for fear of portraying the office as an overly centralized leadership institution. Yet when we need central leadership we turn to the president and read into Article II of the Constitution various prerogatives or inherent powers that allow the president to perform as an effective national leader.

Today the informal and symbolic powers of the presidency account for as much as the formal, stated ones. Presidential powers expand and contract in response to varying situational and technological changes. The powers of the presidency are thus interpreted so differently that they sometimes seem to be those of different offices. In some ways the modern presidency has virtually unlimited authority for almost anything its occupant chooses to do with it. In other ways, a president seems hopelessly ensnarled in a web of checks and balances.

Presidents and presidential candidates must constantly balance conflicting demands, cross pressures, and contradictions. It is characteristic of the American mind to hold contradictory ideas without bothering to resolve the conflicts between them. Perhaps some contradictions are best left unresolved, especially as ours is an imperfect world and our political system is a complicated one, held together by countless compromises. We may not be able to resolve many of these clashing expectations. Some of the inconsistencies in our judgments about presidents doubtless stem from the many ironies and paradoxes of the human condition. While difficult, at the least we should develop a better understanding of what it is we ask of our presidents, thereby increasing our sensitivity to the limits and possibilities of what a president can achieve. This might free presidents to lead and administer more effectively in those critical times when the nation has no choice but to turn to them. Whether we like it or not, the vitality of our democracy depends in large measure upon the sensitive interaction of presidential leadership with an understanding public willing to listen and willing to provide support. Carefully planned innovation is nearly impossible without the kind of leadership a competent and fair-minded president can provide.

The following are some of the paradoxes of the presidency. Some are cases of confused expectations. Some are cases of wanting one kind of presidential behavior at one time, and another kind later. Still others stem from the contradiction inherent in the concept of democratic leadership, which on the surface at least, appears to set up "democratic" and "leadership" as warring concepts. Whatever the source, each has implications for presidential performance and for how Americans judge presidential success and failure. . . .

Paradox #1. Americans demand powerful, popular presidential leadership that solves the nation's problems. Yet we are inherently suspicious of strong centralized leadership and especially the abuse of power and therefore we place significant limits on the president's powers.

We admire power but fear it. We love to unload responsibilities on our leaders, yet we intensely dislike being bossed around. We expect impres-

sive leadership from presidents, and we simultaneously impose constitutional, cultural, and political restrictions on them. These restrictions often
prevent presidents from living up to our expectations. . . .

Presidents are supposed to follow the laws and respect the constitutional procedures that were designed to restrict their power, yet still they
must be powerful and effective when action is needed. For example, we
approve of presidential military initiatives and covert operations when
they work out well, but we criticize presidents and insist they work more
closely with Congress when the initiatives fail. We recognize the need for
secrecy in certain government actions, but we resent being deceived and
left in the dark—again, especially when things go wrong, as in Reagan's
Iranian arms sale diversions to the Contras.

Although we sometimes do not approve of the way a president acts,
we often approve of the end results. Thus Lincoln is often criticized for
acting outside the limits of the Constitution, but at the same time he is
forgiven due to the obvious necessity for him to violate certain constitutional principles in order to preserve the Union. FDR was often flagrant-
ly deceptive and manipulative not only of his political opponents but also
of his staff and allies. FDR even relished pushing people around and toy-
ing with them. But leadership effectiveness in the end often comes down
to whether a person acts in terms of the highest interests of the nation.
Most historians conclude Lincoln and Roosevelt were responsible in the
use of presidential power, to preserve the Union, to fight the depression
and nazism. Historians also conclude that Nixon was wrong for acting
beyond the law in pursuit of personal power. . . .

Paradox #2. We yearn for the democratic "common person" and also
for the uncommon, charismatic, heroic, visionary performance.

We want our presidents to be like us, but better than us. We like to
think America is the land where the common sense of the common person reigns. Nourished on a diet of Frank Capra's "common-man-as-hero"
movies, and the literary celebration of the average citizen by authors such
as Emerson, Whitman, and Thoreau, we prize the common touch. The
plain-speaking Harry Truman, the up-from-the-log-cabin "man or woman of the people," is enticing. Few of us, however, settle for anything but
the best; we want presidents to succeed and we hunger for brilliant, uncommon, and semiregal performances from presidents. . . .

It is said the American people crave to be governed by a president
who is greater than anyone else yet not better than themselves. We are
inconsistent; we want our president to be one of the folks yet also something special. If presidents get too special, however, they get criticized and
roasted. If they try to be too folksy, people get bored. We cherish the myth

that anyone can grow up to be president, that there are no barriers and no elite qualifications, but we don't want someone who is too ordinary. Would-be presidents have to prove their special qualifications—their excellence, their stamina, and their capacity for uncommon leadership. Fellow commoner, Truman, rose to the demands of the job and became an apparently gifted decision maker, or so his admirers would have us believe.

In 1976 Governor Jimmy Carter seemed to grasp this conflict and he ran as local, down-home, farm-boy-next-door makes good. The image of the peanut farmer turned gifted governor contributed greatly to Carter's success as a national candidate and he used it with consummate skill. Early in his presidential bid, Carter enjoyed introducing himself as peanut farmer *and* nuclear physicist, once again suggesting he was down to earth but cerebral as well.

Ronald Reagan illustrated another aspect of this paradox. He was a representative all-American—small-town, midwestern, and also a rich celebrity of stage, screen, and television. He boasted of having been a Democrat, yet campaigned as a Republican. A veritable Mr. Smith goes to Washington, he also had uncommon star quality. Bill Clinton liked us to view him as both a Rhodes scholar and an ordinary saxophone-playing member of the high school band from Hope, Arkansas; as a John Kennedy and even an Elvis figure; and also as just another jogger who would stop by for a Big Mac on the way home from a run in the neighborhood. . . .

Paradox #3. We want a decent, just, caring, and compassionate president, yet we admire a cunning, guileful, and, on occasions that warrant it, even a ruthless, manipulative president.

There is always a fine line between boldness and recklessness, between strong self-confidence and what the Greeks called "hubris," between dogged determination and pigheaded stubbornness. Opinion polls indicate people want a just, decent, and intellectually honest individual as our chief executive. Almost as strongly, however, the public also demands the quality of toughness.

We may admire modesty, humility, and a sense of proportion, but most of our great leaders have been vain and crafty. After all, you don't get to the White House by being a wallflower. Most have aggressively sought power and were rarely preoccupied with metaphysical inquiry or ethical considerations.

Franklin Roosevelt's biographers, while emphasizing his compassion for the average American, also agree he was vain, devious, and manipulative and had a passion for secrecy. These, they note, are often the standard weaknesses of great leaders. Significant social and political advances are made by those with drive, ambition, and a certain amount of brash, irrational self-confidence. . . .

Perhaps Dwight Eisenhower reconciled these clashing expectations better than recent presidents. Blessed with a wonderfully seductive, benign smile and a reserved, calming disposition, he was also the disciplined, strong, no-nonsense five-star general with all the medals and victories to go along with it. His ultimate resource as president was this reconciliation of decency and proven toughness, likability alongside demonstrated valor. Some of his biographers suggest his success was at least partly due to his uncanny ability to appear guileless to the public yet act with ample cunning in private. . . .

One of the ironies of the American presidency is that those characteristics we condemn in one president, we look for in another. Thus a supporter of Jimmy Carter's once suggested that Sunday school teacher Carter wasn't "rotten enough," "a wheeler-dealer," "an s.o.b."—precisely the virtues (if they can be called that) that Lyndon Johnson was most criticized for a decade earlier. President Clinton was viewed as both a gifted Southern Baptist-style preacher by some of his followers and a man who was character challenged, by opponents. . . .

Paradox #4. We admire the "above politics" nonpartisan or bipartisan approach, yet the presidency is perhaps the most political office in the American system, a system in which we need a creative entrepreneurial master politician.

The public yearns for a statesman in the White House, for a George Washington or a second "era of good feelings"—anything that might prevent partisanship or politics as usual in the White House. Former French President Charles de Gaulle once said, "I'm neither of the left nor of the right nor of the center, but above." In fact, however, the job of president demands that the officeholder be a gifted political broker, ever attentive to changing political moods and coalitions. . . .

Presidents are often expected to be above politics in some respects while being highly political in others. Presidents are never supposed to act with their eyes on the next election, yet their power position demands they must. They are neither supposed to favor any particular group or party nor wheel and deal and twist too many arms. That's politics and that's bad! Instead, a president is supposed to be "president of all the people," above politics. A president is also asked to lead a party, to help fellow party members get elected or reelected, to deal firmly with party barons, interest group chieftains, and congressional political brokers. His ability to gain legislative victories depends on his skills at party leadership and on the size of his party's congressional membership. Jimmy Carter once lamented that "It's very difficult for someone to serve in this office and meet the difficult issues in a proper and courageous way and still maintain a combination of interest-group approval that will provide a clear majority at election time."

To take the president out of politics is to assume, incorrectly, that a president will be generally right and the public generally wrong, that a president must be protected from the push and shove of political pressures. But what president has always been right? Over the years, public opinion has usually been as sober a guide as anything else on the political waterfront. And, lest we forget, having a president constrained and informed by public opinion is what democracy is all about.

The fallacy of antipolitics presidencies is that only one view of the national interest is tenable, and a president may pursue that view only by ignoring political conflict and pressure. Politics, properly conceived, is the art of accommodating the diversity and variety of public opinion to meet public goals. Politics is the task of building durable coalitions and majorities. It isn't always pretty. "The process isn't immaculate and cannot always be kid-gloved. A president and his men must reward loyalty and punish opposition; it is the only way." . . .

Paradox #5. We want a president who can unify us, yet the job requires taking firm stands, making unpopular or controversial decisions that necessarily upset and divide us.

Closely related to paradox #4, paradox #5 holds that we ask the president to be a national unifier and a *harmonizer* while at the same time the job requires priority setting and *advocacy* leadership. The tasks are near opposites. . . .

Our nation is one of the few in the world that calls on its chief executive to serve as its symbolic, ceremonial head of state *and* as its political head of government. Elsewhere, these tasks are spread around. In some nations there is a monarch and a prime minister; in others there are three visible national leaders—a head of state, a premier, and a powerful party chief.

In the absence of an alternative office or institution, we demand that our president act as a unifying force in our lives. Perhaps it all began with George Washington, who so artfully performed this function. At least for a while he truly was above politics, a unique symbol of our new nation. He was a healer, a unifier, and an extraordinary man for several seasons. Today we ask no less of our presidents than that they should do as Washington did, and more.

We have designed a presidential job description, however, that often forces our contemporary presidents to act as national dividers. Presidents must necessarily divide when they act as the leaders of their political parties, when they set priorities to the advantage of certain goals and groups at the expense of others, when they forge and lead political coalitions, when they move out ahead of public opinion and assume the role of national educators, when they choose one set of advisers over another. A president, as a creative executive leader, cannot help but offend certain interests. When Franklin Roosevelt was running for a second term, some garment workers unfolded a great sign that said, "We love him for the enemies he has made." Such is the fate of a president on an everyday basis; if presidents choose to use power they will lose the goodwill of those who preferred inaction. . . .

Paradox #6. We expect our presidents to provide bold, visionary, innovative, *programmatic* leadership and at the same time to *pragmatically* respond to the will of public opinion majorities; that is to say, we expect presidents to lead and to follow, to exercise "democratic leadership."

We want both pragmatic and programmatic leadership. We want principled leadership and flexible, adaptable leaders. *Lead us*, but also *listen to us.*

Most people can be led only where they want to go. "Authentic leadership," wrote James MacGregor Burns, "is a collective process." It emerges from a sensitivity or appreciation of the motives and goals of both followers and leaders. The test of leadership, according to Burns, "is the realization of intended, real change that meets people's enduring needs." Thus a key function of leadership is "to engage followers, not merely to activate them, to commingle needs and aspirations and goals in a common enterprise, and in the process to make better citizens of both leaders and followers."

We want our presidents to offer leadership, to be architects of the future and to offer visions, plans, and goals. At the same time we want them to stay in close touch with the sentiments of the people. We want a certain amount of innovation, but we resist being led too far in any one direction.

We expect vigorous, innovative leadership when crises occur. Once a crisis is past, however, we frequently treat presidents as if we didn't need or want them around. We do expect presidents to provide us with bold, creative, and forceful initiatives "to move us ahead," but we resist radical new ideas and changes and usually embrace "new" initiatives only after they have achieved some consensus.

Most of our presidents have been conservatives or at best "pragmatic liberals." They have seldom ventured much beyond the crowd. They have followed public opinion rather than shaped it. John F. Kennedy, the author of the much-acclaimed *Profiles in Courage*, was often criticized for presenting more profile than courage. He avoided political risks where possible. Kennedy was fond of pointing out that he had barely won election in 1960 and that great innovations should not be forced on the public by a leader with such a slender mandate. President Kennedy is often credited with encouraging widespread public participation in politics, but he repeatedly reminded Americans that caution is needed, that the important issues are complicated, technical, and best left to the administrative and political experts. Seldom did Kennedy attempt to change the political context in which he operated. Instead he resisted, "the new form of politics emerging with the civil rights movement: mass action, argument on social fundamentals, appeals to considerations of justice and morality. Moving the American political system in such a direction would necessarily have been long range, requiring arduous educational work and promising substantial political risk."

Kennedy, the pragmatist, shied away from such an unpragmatic undertaking. . . .

Paradox #7. Americans want powerful, self-confident presidential leadership. Yet we are inherently suspicious of leaders who are arrogant, infallible, and above criticism.

We unquestionably cherish our three branches of government with their checks and balances and theories of dispersed and separated powers. We want our presidents to be successful and to share their power with their cabinets, Congress, and other "responsible" national leaders. In theory, we oppose the concentration of power, we dislike secrecy, and we resent depending on any one person to provide all of our leadership.

But Americans also yearn for dynamic, aggressive presidents—even if they do cut some corners. We celebrate the gutsy presidents who make a practice of manipulating and pushing Congress. We perceive the great presidents to be those who stretched their legal authority and dominated the other branches of government. It is still Jefferson, Jackson, Lincoln, and the Roosevelts who get top billing. Whatever may have been the framers' intentions for the three branches, most experts now agree that most of the time, especially in crises, our system works best when the presidency is strong and when we have a self-confident, assertive president.

There is, of course, a fine line between confidence and arrogance, between firmness and inflexibility. We want presidents who are not afraid to exert their will, but at what point does this become antidemocratic, even authoritarian? . . .

Paradox #8. What it takes to become president may not be what is needed to govern the nation.

To win a presidential election takes ambition, money, luck, and masterful public relations strategies. It requires the formation of an electoral coalition. To govern a democracy requires much more. It requires the formation of a *governing* coalition, and the ability to compromise and bargain.

"People who win primaries may become good presidents—but 'it ain't necessarily so'" wrote columnist David Broder. "Organizing well is important in governing just as it is in winning primaries. But the Nixon years should teach us that good advance men do not necessarily make trustworthy White House aides. Establishing a government is a little more complicated than having the motorcade run on time."

Ambition (in heavy doses) and stiff-necked determination are essential for a presidential candidate, yet too much of either can be dangerous. A candidate must be bold and energetic, but in excess these characteristics can produce a cold, frenetic candidate. To win the presidency obviously requires a single-mindedness, yet our presidents must also have a sense of proportion, be well-rounded, have a sense of humor, be able to take a joke, and have hobbies and interests outside the realm of politics.

To win the presidency many of our candidates (Lincoln, Kennedy, and Clinton come to mind) had to pose as being more progressive or even populist than they actually felt; to be effective in the job they are compelled to appear more cautious and conservative than they often want to be. One of Carter's political strategists said, "Jimmy campaigned liberal but governed conservative." And as Bill Clinton pointed out toward the end of his first year in office, "We've all become Eisenhower Republicans." . . .

We often also want both a "fresh face," an outsider, as a presidential candidate *and* a seasoned, mature, experienced veteran who knows the corridors of power and the back alleyways of Washington. That's why Colin Powell fascinated so many people. Frustration with past presidential performances leads us to turn to a "fresh new face" uncorrupted by Washington's politics and its "buddy system" (Carter, Reagan, Clinton). But inexperience, especially in foreign affairs, has sometimes led to blunders by the outsiders. . . .

Paradox #9. The presidency is sometimes too strong, yet other times too weak.

Presidents are granted wide latitude in dealing with events abroad. At times, presidents can act unilaterally, without the express consent of Congress. While the constitutional grounds for such action may be dubious, the climate of expectations allows presidents to act decisively abroad. This being the case, the public comes to think the president can do the same at home. But this is usually not the case. A clashing expectation is built into the presidency when strength in some areas is matched with weakness in other areas.

It often seems that our presidency is *always too strong* and *always too weak*. Always too powerful given our worst fears of tyranny and our ideals of a "government by the people." Always too strong, as well, because it now possesses the capacity to wage nuclear war (a capacity that doesn't permit much in the way of checks and balances and deliberative, participatory government). But always too weak when we remember nuclear proliferation, the rising national debt, the budget deficit, lingering discrimination, poverty, and the clutch of other fundamental problems yet to be solved.

The presidency is always too strong when we dislike the incumbent. Its limitations are bemoaned, however, when we believe the incumbent is striving valiantly to serve the public interest as we define it. The Johnson presidency vividly captured this paradox: many who believed he was too strong in Vietnam also believed he was too weak to wage his War on Poverty. Others believed just the opposite. . . .

Ultimately, being paradoxical does not make the presidency incomprehensible. Can we rid the presidency of all paradoxes? We couldn't, even if we wanted to do so. And anyway, what is wrong with some ambiguity? It is in embracing the paradoxical nature of the American presidency that we may be able to arrive at understanding. And with understanding may come enlightened or constructive criticism. This is the basis for citizen democracy.

30

CRAIG RIMMERMAN

From *The Rise of the Plebiscitary Presidency*

Scholars who examine American presidents look not only at individuals who have held the position but also at trends that mark different interpretations of the office. Here, Professor Craig Rimmerman builds on Theodore Lowi's concept of the "plebiscitary presidency," in which the president seeks to govern through the direct support of the American people. Likewise, citizens view the plebiscitary presidency as the focal point of government activity. Rimmerman believes this view to be vastly different from the Constitution's intent. He traces changes in the executive's power through several phases, mentioning the contributions of prominent scholars to an understanding of the presidency. From President Roosevelt onward, Rimmerman asks his readers to consider carefully the consequences of such an exalted and unrealistic vision of presidential power.

———

THE CONSTITUTIONAL framers would undoubtedly be disturbed by the shift to the presidentially centered government that characterizes the modern era. Their fear of monarchy led them to reject the concept of executive popular leadership. Instead, they assumed that the legislative branch would occupy the central policymaking role and would be held more easily accountable through republican government.

Congress has failed, however, to adhere to the framers' intentions and has abdicated its policymaking responsibility. The legislature, with support from the Supreme Court, has been all too willing to promote the illusion of presidential governance by providing the executive with new sources of power, including a highly developed administrative apparatus, and by delegating authority for policy implementation to the executive through vague legislative statutes. . . .

The president-centered government of the modern, plebiscitary era draws much of its power and legitimacy from the popular support of the citizenry, support that is grounded in the development of the rhetorical presidency and the exalted role of the presidency in the American political culture. Theodore Lowi is surely on target when he identifies "the refocusing of mass expectations upon the presidency" as a key problem of presidential governance since Franklin Delano Roosevelt and as a problem associated with the rise of the plebiscitary presidency.

The plebiscitary presidency is characterized by the following: presidential power and legitimacy emanates from citizen support as measured through public opinion polls; in the absence of coherent political parties, presidents forge a direct link to the masses through television; and structural barriers associated with the Madisonian governmental framework make it difficult for presidents to deliver on their policy promises to the citizenry. The framers of the Constitution would hardly have approved of these developments, for they had no intention of establishing a popularly elected monarch. Moreover, the nature of the governmental framework that they created actually prevents occupants of the Oval Office from meeting the heightened citizen expectations associated with the plebiscitary presidency in terms of concrete public policy, especially in the domestic policy arena. This has become particularly clear in the modern era as presidents confront a more fragmented and independent legislature, a decline in the importance of the political party as a governing and coalition-building device, an increase in the power of interest groups and political action committees that foster policy fragmentation, and a bureaucracy that resists centralized coordination. . . .

Throughout much of the nineteenth century, a passive president in domestic policymaking was deemed both acceptable and desirable. Congress took the lead in formulating public policy initiatives and expressed outright hostility toward presidential suggestions that particular legislation should be introduced. In fact, early in the nineteenth century it was commonly believed that the president should not exercise the veto to express policy preferences. The president's primary responsibility was to faithfully execute the laws passed by Congress. For the occupants of the Oval Office in the traditional period, the Constitution imposed "strict limitations on what a President could do." The constitutional separation of powers was taken seriously by all parties, and the prevailing view regarding the proper role of government was "the best government governed least." As opposed to the presidential government of the modern period, the traditional era was characterized by congressional leadership in the policy process.

In the foreign policy arena, however, the president did establish himself through the war-making power. Yet even here the president was restrained when compared to the occupants of the Oval Office in the twentieth century. A prevailing view in the nineteenth century was that the president should avoid involvement with foreign nations, although negotiation with foreign countries was occasionally required. The first president to travel abroad on behalf of the United States was Theodore Roosevelt. Prior to the twentieth century, some members of Congress even argued that the president lacked the necessary legal authority to travel in this manner.

Presidential speechmaking also reflected the largely symbolic chief-of-state roles played by presidents in the traditional era. Jeffrey Tulis's content analysis of presidential speeches reveals that presidents rarely gave the kind of official popular speeches that characterize speech-making in the modern era. When speeches were given, they were considered "unofficial," and they rarely contained policy pronouncements. Tulis concludes that William McKinley's rhetoric was representative of the century as a whole: "Expressions of greeting, inculcations of patriotic sentiment, attempts at building 'harmony' among the regions of the country, and very general, principled statements of policy, usually expressed in terms of the policy's consistency with that president's understanding of republicanism." Virtually all presidents of the time adhered to the same kind of presidential speechmaking. The only exception was Andrew Johnson, who attempted to rally support for his policies in Congress through the use of fiery demagoguery. Johnson's "improper" rhetoric fueled his impeachment charge; yet it is this same kind of rhetoric that today is accepted as "proper" presidential rhetoric.

The reserved role played by the president in the nineteenth century was clearly in keeping with the intention of the constitutional framers....

...Yet as the United States headed into its second full century, this situation was to change, as congressional government began to yield to the presidentially centered form of governance that has characterized the modern period.

Students of the presidency have identified a number of factors that have led to the development of the modern, personal, plebiscitary presidency as we know it today. The personal presidency is "an office of tremendous personal power drawn from the people—directly through Congress and the Supreme Court—and based on the new democratic theory that the presidency with all powers is the necessary condition for governing a large, democratic nation. Its development is rooted in changes in presidential rhetoric, the efforts of the progressive reformers of the early twentieth century, the Great Depression and Franklin Delano Roosevelt's New Deal, the role of Congress in granting the executive considerable discretionary power, and Supreme Court decisions throughout the twentieth century that have legitimated the central role that the president should play in the domestic and foreign policy arenas....

Presidential scholars have contributed to the presidentially centered government and the accompanying citizen expectations of presidential performance that characterize the development of presidential power since Franklin Roosevelt. The "cult of the presidency," "textbook presidency," or "savior model" was developed in response to FDR's leadership during the Great Depression, and it prevailed through the presidency of John F. Kennedy. Underlying this "cult" or model approach is a firm commitment to the presidency as a strong office and to the desirability of this condition for the political system as a whole. Political science texts written during this period concluded approvingly that the presidency was growing larger, while gaining more responsibilities and resources. The use of laudatory labels, such as "the Wilson years," "the Roosevelt revolution," "the Eisenhower period," and "the Kennedy Camelot years" also fostered the cult of the presidency and reinforced the notion that the president is the key figure in the American political system. . . .

Perhaps no other work contributed more to the development of this approach that Richard Neustadt's *Presidential Power*, which was first published in 1960. Representing a sharp break with the legalistic and constitutional approach that had dominated presidential scholarship up until that time, *Presidential Power* reinforced the notion that strong presidential leadership should be linked to good government. Neustadt eschewed strict legalistic interpretations of presidential power and instead conceived of power in the following way: "'Power' I defined as personal influence on governmental action. This I distinguished sharply—a novel distinction then—from formal powers vested in the Presidency." For Neustadt, the Franklin Delano Roosevelt activist presidency was the ideal model for presidential leadership and the exercise of power. Future presidents, according to Neustadt, should be evaluated on the basis of how well they achieved the standards set by Roosevelt. Like presidential scholars of his time and many since, Neustadt rejected the framers' view that the Congress should be the chief policymaking branch and that the president should be constrained by numerous checks and balances. Instead, Neustadt spoke of "separated institutions sharing powers."

As Neustadt and other scholars embraced a presidentially centered form of government, they failed to recognize the consequences of imposing a new interpretation of the political order on a governmental framework rooted in Madisonian principles. One such consequence has been that as presidents attempt to meet the heightened expectations associated with the modern presidency, they are sometimes driven to assert presidential prerogative powers in ways that threaten both constitutional and democratic principles. The Johnson and Nixon presidencies, in particular, provided empirical evidence to support this concern. In response, presidential scholars embraced a new model for evaluating presidential power: "the imperial presidency."

Concerns about excessive presidential power were articulated in light of Lyndon Johnson's legislative victories in the 1960s, Johnson's and Nixon's decisionmaking in the Vietnam War, the Nixon/Kissinger Cambodian debacle, and the Nixon presidency's disgrace in the wake of Watergate.* Presidential scholars began to question whether presidential strength would necessarily lead to the promotion of the general welfare. Scholars spoke of the pathological presidency, reinforcing many of the constitutional framers' fears regarding the consequences of concentrating excessive powers in the executive.

Writing in this vein and responding to presidential excesses in the conduct of the Vietnam War and the Watergate scandal, Arthur Schlesinger, Jr., developed the concept of the "imperial presidency." Schlesinger recognized that the system of checks and balances needed vigorous action by one of the three branches if the stalemate built into the system was to be overcome. Schlesinger believed that the presidency was best equipped to fill this role. Rather than rejecting centralized presidential power per se, he spoke of presidential abuses: "In the last years presidential primacy, so indispensable to the political order, has turned into presidential supremacy. The constitutional Presidency—as events so apparently disparate as the Indochina War and the Watergate affair showed—has become the imperial Presidency and threatens to be the revolutionary Presidency." Schlesinger placed much of the blame for the imperial presidency on presidential excesses in foreign policy.... Truman, Kennedy, Johnson, and Nixon interpreted the Constitution to permit the president to commit American combat troops unilaterally, and the prolonged Vietnam War encouraged foreign policy centralization and the use of secrecy. The imperial presidency, or "the presidency as satan model," can also be applied to the Nixon administration's domestic activities, including wiretapping, the use of impoundments, executive branch reorganization for political purposes, and expansive interpretations of executive privilege.

Schlesinger's analysis is an important contribution to the study of presidential power because it recognizes the limitations imposed by the framers and the potentially negative consequences of the plebiscitary presidency....

The plebiscitary presidency has been a key source of presidential power since 1933. For presidents such as Ford and Carter, however, the heightened expectations associated with the personal, plebiscitary presi-

*Set in motion by strong presidents, these three episodes—the prolonging of the war in Vietnam, the bombing of Vietnam's neutral neighbor, Cambodia, and a presidential administration's heavy involvement in and coverup of the burglary of the Democratic Party's Watergate Hotel-based election headquarters—all greatly divided the nation.—EDS.

dency have also led to citizen unhappiness and characterizations of presidential failure. The Carter presidency, in particular, reinforced elements of the plebiscitary presidency. As a "trustee" president, Jimmy Carter reinforced the notion that as the elected representative of all the people, "the president must act as the counterforce to special interests" and provide the leadership necessary in setting the policy agenda and introducing "comprehensive policy proposals." Charles Jones makes a persuasive case that Carter's vision of the trustee presidency was anathema to a Congress that had just passed a series of reforms designed to tame the imperial Nixon presidency. When Carter tried to introduce unpopular energy conservation policies and cut back "unnecessary dams and water projects" because they represented the "worst examples of the pork-barrel," he challenged Congress and the American people to reject politics as usual. In this sense, he was displaying a style of presidential leadership unseen in recent years, one that reinforced the plebiscitary presidency while at the same time challenging some of the assumptions on which it is based. Unlike his immediate predecessors and successors, Carter at least tried to heighten the level of dialogue around resource scarcity concerns. He soon learned, however, that his unwillingness to cultivate congressional support for his policies and his call for a shared sacrifice on the part of the American people undermined the plebiscitary foundations of the modern presidency. His 1980 presidential challenger understood Carter's problems quite well and was determined not to repeat them. Ronald Reagan's campaign and governing strategies accepted and extended the plebiscitary presidency. This helps to account for his victories in both 1980 and 1984....

In the American political system, presidents perform two roles that in other countries are often filled by separate individuals. As head of the nation, the president is required to play a unifying role of the kind played by monarchs in Britain, Norway, and the Netherlands or by presidents in France, Germany, and Austria. In addition, presidents serve as political leaders, "a post held in these other nations by a prime minister or chancellor." This dual role virtually guarantees that American presidents will occupy the central political and cultural role as the chief spokesperson for the American way of life. Political scientists, historians, and journalists have all reinforced and popularized the view that the presidency is an office of overwhelming symbolic importance.

Only recently have political scientists begun to challenge this perspective and discuss the negative consequences of such hero worship in a country that purports to adhere to democratic principles. Barbara Hinckley captures these issues well in her recent analysis:

It is the magic of symbolism to create illusion. But illusion has costs that must be considered by journalists, teachers of politics, and future presidents. Is the nation best served by carrying on the symbolism or by challenging it? Should the two contradictory pictures, in a kind of schizophrenic fashion, be carried on together? If so, what line should be drawn and what accommodation made between the two? The questions are compounded by the peculiar openness of the office to changing interpretations. By definition, all institutions are shaped by the expectations of relevant actors. The presidency is particularly susceptible to such influence.

As we have seen in our study of the Reagan and Bush presidencies, presidents attempt to build on their symbolic importance to enhance their public opinion ratings and to extend the plebiscitary presidency. The upshot of this activity over the past sixty years is that the public equates the president with the nation and the values associated with American exceptionalism. A president, such as Jimmy Carter, who attempts to challenge traditional elements of presidential symbolism and demystify the trappings of the White House, is treated with disdain by the public, the press, and to a certain extent by political scientists. . . .

This book suggests that Presidents Reagan and Bush turned to foreign policy when they encountered difficulties in translating their domestic campaign promises into concrete public policy and in meeting the demands of the plebiscitary presidency. Presidents who are caught between citizens' expectations and the constraints of the Madisonian policy-making process* look to the foreign policy arena in an effort to promote the values associated with American exceptionalism.

Any of the examples discussed . . . provide ample opportunity to explore these themes. The Iran–Contra affair,† in particular, raises compelling questions regarding presidential power in the foreign policy arena. In light of the aggrandizement of presidential power that characterized the Vietnam War period and Watergate and the resulting congressional response, it is important to ask students why a president and/or his staff would employ some of the same strategies in dealing with Congress, the media, and the American people. The role of covert activities in a democracy also deserves considerable attention.

If scholars of the presidency are truly concerned with developing a pedagogy and presidential evaluation scheme rooted in critical education

*James Madison's plan for American government limits each branch by checking and balancing the power of one branch against another.—EDs.
†During President Reagan's administration, members of his National Security Council (NSC) were charged with secretly selling arms to Iran in order to fund anti-communist Nicaraguan Contra activities.—EDs.

for citizenship, then their students must be asked to consider why so little questioning generally occurs regarding the role of the president in committing American troops to war. The Persian Gulf war was a case in point.* It begged for serious discussion, reflection, debate, and questioning about the Bush administration's foreign policy decisionmaking. Some argued that those who dissented from the president's foreign policy strategy were un-American and unpatriotic and were trying to undermine the troops who were already in the Middle East. In fact, if citizens fail to question a president's decisionmaking, then they are giving the president virtually unchecked power to do what he wants with their lives. The failure to question a president abdicates all of the principles of a meaningful and effective democracy and embraces the dictates of an authoritarian and totalitarian regime. This is, of course, the logical consequence of the plebiscitary presidency.

Alexis de Tocqueville spoke of a blind and unreflective patriotism that characterized the American citizenry during the nineteenth century. He would surely see evidence of such patriotism in America today. There is little doubt that such patriotism can be connected to the relationship of the citizenry to the state and the office of the presidency. No modern president can expect to succeed without the support of the public. Yet this support must be grounded in a firm rejection of the unrealistic notion of presidential power. Citizens who respond to the presidency in a highly personalized and reverential manner are likely to be disappointed by presidential performance and are also likely to embrace political passivity and acquiescence in the face of presidential power. In the words of Benjamin Barber, "democratic politics thus becomes a matter of what leaders do, something that citizens watch rather than something they do." As this book has pointed out, Ronald Reagan and George Bush heightened these expectations even further by using techniques that emphasize the plebiscitary, personal character of the modern presidency. Ross Perot's 1992 presidential campaign was firmly rooted in plebiscitary principles. His proposals for nation-wide town meetings and an electronic democracy scheme reflected support for government by plebiscite. To Perot, running

---

*The Persian Gulf War occurred within a two-month period in early 1991. Backed by House and Senate resolutions of support—not an actual declaration of war—President George H.W. Bush sent U.S. troops to the Persian Gulf as part of a multination coalition to force Iraqi President Saddam Hussein's military out of Kuwait. The United States experienced quick and dramatic success, with CNN's coverage bringing the war directly to Americans daily. Years later, questions remained about the long-term effectiveness of the military strikes in weakening the Iraqi threat. In 2003, President George W. Bush ordered an invasion of Iraq, claiming that Saddam Hussein possessed weapons of mass destruction, an allegation later found to be false.—EDS.

as an outsider, anti-establishment candidate, such a plan was desperately needed to challenge the gridlock growing out of the Madisonian policy process and two party system. His proposals also enabled him to emphasize his own leadership abilities and claim that he had the necessary leadership and entrepreneurial abilities to break governmental paralysis. In doing so, Perot reinforced the direct line between the presidency and the American people. Any course on the presidency should examine Perot's government-by-plebiscite proposals and the broader implications of his apparent willingness to bypass the congressional policy process and the two party system. The amount of attention and popularity that Perot's campaign garnered in a short period of time suggests once again that the plebiscitary presidency is an important explanatory construct. It also encourages political scientists to study, with renewed vigor, the relationship between the presidency and the citizenry.

For many students, the presidency is the personification of democratic politics and, as a result, monopolizes "the public space." This view impedes the development of the meaningful and effective participation needed by citizens as they attempt to control decisions that affect the quality and direction of their lives. Presidential scholars have been developing a more realistic understanding of the changing sources of presidential power and how individual presidents have used these powers through the years. We would also do well to consider Murray Edelman's claim that "leadership is an expression of the inadequate power of followers in their everyday lives." This is particularly important as we begin to evaluate the Bush presidency. It is also the first step toward challenging the plebiscitary presidency and achieving a more realistic and successful presidency, one that is grounded in principles of democratic accountability and the development of citizenship.

31

JACK GOLDSMITH

From *Power and Constraint*

Many of today's students of American government do not have a first-hand remembrance of September 11, 2001. Yet the events of that day—the attacks on the World Trade Center and the Pentagon and the crash of another hijacked airplane in Pennsylvania—marked the beginning of a War on Terror that has remained a key element of American foreign and defense policy in the years since. Jack Goldsmith looks at the ways that President Barack Obama's administration hoped to change the Bush-era response to terrorism. Obama planned to make significant policy shifts, but once in office, he continued certain tactics when he faced the reality of threats to the nation's security. Goldsmith points out that presidential candidates who campaigned on a reduced role for the executive branch in military involvement have often had to change course once in office. "The View from the Oval Office" is a unique one. Future candidates for the presidency might do well to consider Goldsmith's admonition. Toward the end of the excerpt, readers learn what a presidential "synopticon" is. Though the term might be new and a little dense, presidents today are aware that "many can watch one," as Goldsmith says, and that presidential actions are checked and balanced by many forces in the American polity: "power and constraint."

"TRAGICALLY, THE CURRENT ADMINISTRATION chose to respond [to the 9/11 attacks] with [a] series of unnecessary, self-inflicted wounds, which have gravely diminished our global standing and damaged our reputation for respecting the rule of law," said Harold Hongju Koh, two months before the election of 2008, in a Senate hearing on "Restoring the Rule of Law." Koh was at the time the dean of Yale Law School. He was also the former Assistant Secretary of State for Democracy, Human Rights and Labor during the Clinton administration; a passionate leader of the human rights movement; and a leading critic of the Bush administration's counterterrorism policies. After summing up his indictment of Bush-era sins, the man who the following year would become Barack Obama's top State Department lawyer looked to the future. "As difficult as the last seven years have been," Koh said, "they loom far less important in the grand scheme of things than the next eight, which will determine whether the pendulum of U.S. policy swings back from the extreme place to which it has been pushed, or stays stuck in a 'new normal' position under which our policies toward national security, law and human rights remain wholly subsumed by the 'War on Terror.'" Koh urged the next President to reject the Bush paradigm and "unambiguously reassert our historic commitments to human rights and the rule of law as a major source of our moral authority."

This is precisely what Barack Obama had promised to do. As a senator and on the campaign trail, Obama had blasted the Bush approach to military detention, military commissions, interrogation, rendition, surveillance, and more, suggesting that the Bush tactics were un-American. "I will make clear that the days of compromising our values are over," said the then Senator Obama in a typical campaign speech, in 2007, at the Woodrow Wilson International Center. "We cannot win a war unless we maintain the high ground." Obama pledged that if elected, "[w]e will again set an example for the world that the law is not subject to the whims of stubborn rulers, and that justice is not arbitrary." He reiterated these themes in his inaugural address on the first day of his presidency. "Our Founding Fathers, faced with perils that we can scarcely imagine, drafted a charter to assure the rule of law and the rights of man—a charter expanded by the blood of generations," he said to applause from supporters on the National Mall and around the country. "Those ideals still light the world, and we will not give them up for expedience sake."

Obama moved quickly to fulfill these promises. Within hours of his inaugural address, he suspended military commissions and reversed some Bush-era secrecy rules. Two days later, and to greater fanfare, he signed executive orders that banned torture, closed CIA black sites, pledged adherence to the Geneva Conventions, promised to close the detention center at Guantanamo Bay (commonly referred to as "GTMO") within a year, and established a task force to give him new options for the "apprehension, detention, trial, transfer, release, or other disposition" of terrorist detainees. "[O]ur ideals give us the strength and moral high ground" to combat terrorism, Obama said, just before signing the legal documents.

These events created a conspicuous sense of dramatic change in the nation's capital—a sense that the American people had rejected the counterterrorism policies of the Bush era, and that seven years of aggressive tactics had come to a screeching halt. "Bush's 'War' on Terror Comes to a Sudden End," announced the *Washington Post* the next day, in a typical headline. "With the stroke of his pen," the article reported, President Obama "effectively declared an end to the 'war on terror,' as President George W. Bush had defined it."

But it was not to be. Contrary to nearly everyone's expectations, the

Obama administration would continue almost all of its predecessor's policies, transforming what had seemed extraordinary under the Bush regime into the "new normal" of American counterterrorism policy....

In retrospect, what is remarkable about candidate Obama's criticisms of the Bush counterterrorism program is how much subtle wiggle room they left the future President. Once in office, the Obama administration exploited this wiggle room in some areas and departed from campaign pledges in others. The bottom line is that it copied most of the Bush counterterrorism program as it stood in January 2009, expanded some of it, and narrowed a bit....

... President Obama continued the Bush administration practice of targeting and killing enemy suspects in Pakistan and other places outside a traditional battlefield and inside countries with which the United States is not at war. But here one cannot charge Obama with any inconsistency, for he was clear on the campaign trail that he would target and kill members of al Qaeda and its affiliates wherever in the world they might be found. "The Bush administration has not acted aggressively enough to go after al-Qaeda's leadership," Obama said in a 2008 interview. "I would be clear that if Pakistan cannot or will not take out al-Qaeda leadership when we have actionable intelligence about their whereabouts, we will act to protect the American people. There can be no safe haven for al-Qaeda terrorists who killed thousands of Americans and threaten our homeland today."

Obama fulfilled this promise in dramatic fashion with his approval of Operation Neptune Spear, the daring and dangerous operation that killed Osama Bin Laden in Abbottabad, Pakistan, on May 2, 2011. But in truth he had adhered to this promise long before then. In a dozen nations outside of Afghanistan and Iraq, the Obama administration "has significantly increased military and intelligence operations, pursuing the enemy using robotic drones and commando teams, paying contractors to spy and training local operatives to chase terrorists," reported the *New York Times* in August 2010. The administration has been especially fond of using unmanned drones for "targeted killings" of enemy terrorists. It ramped up drone attacks quite a bit, using them more frequently during Obama's first year than Bush had in the previous seven combined. Many human rights groups criticized these attacks as illegal assassinations or "extrajudicial killings," and some accused the Obama administration of war crimes. But the administration has been unmoved. "[V]ery frankly, it's the only game in town in terms of confronting and trying to disrupt the al Qaeda leadership," said CIA Director Leon Panetta....

Barack Obama is not the first person to assume the office of presidency as a critic of executive power and then switch his position while on the job. President Thomas Jefferson, a fierce opponent of unilateral presidential war power before 1800, authorized military expeditions against Barbary Coast nations in the Mediterranean without congressional authorization. Congressman Abraham Lincoln opposed the broad presidential war powers that James K. Polk exercised in the run-up to the Mexican-American War. But as President during the Civil War, Lincoln would assert broader war powers than any President before or since. Woodrow Wilson believed in a strong presidency before entering office, but he also pledged an open and transparent one. When World War I came, however, he supported unprecedented secrecy restrictions. When Dwight D. Eisenhower became Chief Executive, he was determined to rein in the early Cold War presidency; instead he presided over the buildup of the modern secrecy system and the rise of covert action and executive privilege. Richard Nixon was a principled opponent of presidential power as a senator who saw matters differently as President. Candidate Bill Clinton berated George H. W. Bush's Haitian interception and detention policy but quickly embraced it as President.

President John F. Kennedy gave an eloquent explanation of the mismatch between pre-presidential beliefs and presidential actions during a television interview in the Oval Office in December 1962. Kennedy's "most penetrating answer on the President's attitudes and feelings about his job," as adviser Pierre Salinger later described it, was elicited by a question from ABC News White House correspondent Bill Lawrence. "As you look back upon your first two years in office, sir, has your experience in the office matched your expectations?" Lawrence asked. "You had studied a good deal the power of the presidency, the methods of its operations," he noted. "How has this worked out as you saw it in advance?"

Kennedy shifted from side to side in a rocking chair but answered confidently. "I would say that the problems are more difficult than I had imagined them to be. The responsibilities placed on the United States are greater than I imagined them to be, and there are greater limitations upon our ability to bring about a favorable result than I had imagined them to be," answered the President, who in his short time in office had suffered through the botched Bay of Pigs invasion, a disastrous meeting with Khrushchev in Vienna, the Cuban missile crisis, and the Berlin crisis. "And I think that is probably true of anyone who becomes President, because there is such a difference between those who advise or speak or legislate, and between the man who must select from the various alternatives proposed and say that this shall be the policy of the United States," added the former senator. "It is much easier to make the speeches than it is to finally make the judgments."

Barack Obama learned this lesson the hard way. He came to the presidency sincerely committed to bringing real change to America's counterterrorism policies. But he quickly encountered new information and significant limitations on his ability to bring about the result he had promised and that so many had expected. This information and these limitations reflected forces bigger than the pledges and inclinations of the President of the United States, forces that caused Obama to continue so many policies he once questioned or opposed.

The View From the Oval Office

The first force hit Obama in the days before he became President, when credible threat reports indicated that Somali terrorists were sneaking into the United States from Canada to detonate explosives during his inauguration. As senior Bush and Obama aides scrambled to figure out how to prevent the threat and how to react to it if it materialized, Obama became "more subdued than he had been," recalled David Axelrod, Obama's closest political adviser. "It's not as if you don't know what you're getting into," Axelrod said. "But when the reality comes and the baton is being passed and you're now dealing with real terrorism threats, it's a very sobering moment."

Sobering indeed, especially since the Somali threat paled in comparison to the larger threats the President-elect was reading about on a daily basis. Several Obama administration officials told me that reading these chilling threat reports led them to view Bush's counterterrorism policies differently. And it seemed to affect President Obama in the same way. "I want to end the politics of fear, the fever of fear," said candidate Obama, below an enormous "CHANGE WE CAN BELIEVE IN" banner, in a typical March 2008 campaign rally. But when he was personally confronted with reports of Islamist terrorists hiding among civilians and plotting to use ever-smaller and more deadly weapons to disrupt our way of life, the "hope over fear" meme quickly gave way to "the threat is real" meme. "[A]n extremist ideology threatens our people, and technology gives a handful of terrorists the potential to do us great harm," said the President in a May 2009 speech that explained why he would continue military detention without trial and military commissions. "We know that al Qaeda is actively planning to attack us again. We know that this threat will be with us for a long time, and that we must use all elements of our power to defeat it."

The reality of the threat was not the only new information the Obama team absorbed upon entering office. They also learned that the Bush policies were, in the words of Republican Senator Susan Collins, "better-thought-out than they realized." The Obama team came to office wanting to end the Bush "state secrets" practice but demurred after studying classified CIA declarations that convincingly explained why the adjudication of lawsuits about rendition and the Terrorist Surveillance Program would damage national security. "The declarations were really well done," one senior Obama official said, adding that "they persuaded me." The possibility of ending military detention without trial also foundered upon learning that the Bush administration was right that, in President Obama's words, there are terrorists "who pose a clear danger to the American people" but who "cannot be prosecuted for past crimes." Similarly, the main impetus for the Obama continuity on military commissions, according to the *Washington Post,* was that the new administration realized, just as its predecessor had claimed, that cases against many terrorists "would fail in federal courts or in standard military legal settings." And of course, closing Guantanamo was much harder than it looked from the outside, as the Bush administration had insisted all along.

Learning firsthand about the nature of the terror threat and the soundness of some of the Bush responses to it was a wake-up call for the young Obama administration. So too was the grim reality of presidential responsibility, which informed how these new facts would be interpreted. On January 20, 2009, Barack Obama went from a legislator and presidential candidate with no real national security experience or responsibility to the Commander in Chief whose counterterrorism decisions hold American lives in the balance. This intense, undelegable responsibility for the fate of the nation is "so personal as to be without parallel," said Harry Truman. It is a responsibility the President has "no moral right to shrink" from, or "even to count the chances of his own life" against, said Abraham Lincoln.

This new perspective had a profound impact on Obama, just as it does on every President. "[M]y single most important responsibility as President is to keep the American people safe," he said, three months into his presidency, sounding very much like George W. Bush. "It's the first thing that I think about when I wake up in the morning. It's the last thing that I think about when I go to sleep at night." The personal responsibility of the President for national security, combined with the continuing reality of a frightening and difficult-to-detect threat, unsurprisingly led Obama, like Bush, to use the full arsenal of presidential tools. "He is a different man now," said Washington sage David Broder, explaining the psychological dimension that underlies Obama's Bush-copying policies. "He has learned what it means to be commander in chief."

Another reason why Obama stuck with the Bush policies was that many of them were irreversibly woven into the fabric of the national security architecture. The Obama administration would not have faced the troubles of closing the Guantanamo detention facility if the Bush administration had not used the detention facility in the first place. And it would have had an easier time prosecuting some terrorist suspects in civilian courts had information about their crimes not been extracted through coercion (assuming, that is, that the suspects would have been nabbed in the absence of the information so gained). It is impossible to know how an Obama administration would have dealt with the manifold terrorist challenges beginning on 9/11, or how the world might look different today if the Bush administration had made different decisions. But some of the continuation of Bush policies no doubt reflects the fact that Obama inherited challenges traceable to decisions he might not have made had he been president in 2001. . . .

. . . The framers did not think of constraints on the presidency primarily in terms of fixed limits on its size and authorities. The Constitution was not designed to prevent the President from taking steps needed to keep the nation secure, including novel steps as the challenges facing the nation evolved. "The Founding Fathers were intensely practical men determined to charter a republic that would work and last in a dangerous world," noted Arthur Schlesinger Jr. They knew that the world would change and that the responsibilities and powers of the institutions it created would change as well. "In framing a system which we wish to last for the ages, we [should] not lose sight of the changes the ages will produce," Madison said in his notes on the Constitutional Convention.

Instead of placing fixed limits on presidential power, the framers sought to check presidential excesses by giving Congress and the courts, aided by a constitutionally protected press, the motives and tools to keep the presidency within contextualized limits measured by the national security challenge before the nation. This structure has grown more decentralized and today involves many actors beyond Congress, the courts, the traditional press, and voters. But the modern presidential synopticon* translates in a rough way the framers' original design of making presidential action accountable, both to the wishes of the people as expressed in

---

*Synopticon is a term used by sociologist Thomas Mathiesen to indicate a method whereby many different viewers can scrutinize one object. For example, the idea of a synopticon could be applied to television or to social media like Facebook or Twitter. Goldsmith, the author of the excerpt, mentions that a synopticon can be contrasted with a panopticon, originated in the late 1800s by Jeremy Bentham; in a prison, one guard can watch many prisoners. The American governmental system of checks and balances—a synopticon— means that the executive branch's power is "watched" by many others: the legislature, the judiciary, the citizenry.—EDS.

Congress and the press and elections, and to the law as enforced by congressional sanction and judicial action. Though many of the players in the modern accountability system are new, they combine with older ones to help ensure that the other institutions of government know about the President's actions, can require him to account for them, and can punish him if they think he is engaged in the wrong policy or acting unlawfully. . . .

In 1788, in the fifty-first Federalist Paper, James Madison famously announced that the U.S. Constitution embodied the "important idea" that a well-structured government is one in which "its several constituent parts may, by their mutual relations, be the means of keeping each other in their proper places." Madison believed that a properly designed government "would check interest with interest, class with class, faction with faction, and one branch of government with another in a harmonious system of mutual frustration," as Columbia historian Richard Hofstadter put it in his classic 1948 book, *The American Political Tradition.* If Madison were alive today, he would be astonished and probably appalled to see the gargantuan presidency exercising so much power, much of it in secret, in an endless global war against non-state actor terrorists. He would also be surprised by the reticulate presidential synopticon that has grown up to watch, check, and legitimate the presidency in war. But after adjusting to the modern world and studying the vitriolic clashes of the last decade between the presidency and its synopticon, Madison would discover a harmonious system of mutual frustration undergirding a surprising national consensus—a consensus always fruitfully under pressure from various quarters—about the proper scope of the President's counterterrorism authorities. And then the father of the Constitution would smile.

32

KENNETH MAYER

From *With the Stroke of a Pen*

Any study of American government leads us to a system of government based on separation of powers: three branches, checks and balances, bicameralism, the veto, war powers, Senate advice and consent, to mention a few key points. But there are important powers that are less visible and less checked. For example, "with the stroke of a pen," a president, without congressional involvement, can issue an executive order that can significantly shape policy. Kenneth Mayer introduces us to the little-known power of the executive order by citing the often-vague contours of the power. He then cites a policy area—civil rights—in which executive orders had great impact. Starting with President John Kennedy's executive order on affirmative action through President Lyndon Johnson's action, Mayer traces the development of the executive's power to affect policy. Even President Ronald Reagan, whose views may have differed from his predecessors in office, continued the policies created by the earlier executive orders. Ultimately, President Bill Clinton extended affirmative action to include gender discrimination, again by executive order. Though perhaps lacking in drama and excitement, executive orders can have great impact.

———

WHAT, PRECISELY, IS AN EXECUTIVE ORDER? In the most formal sense, an executive order is a directive issued by the president, "directing the executive branch in the fulfillment of a particular program," targeted at executive branch personnel and intended to alter their behavior in some way, and published in the *Federal Register*. Executive orders are instruments by which the president carries out the functions of the office, and every president has issued them (although there was no system for tracking them until the twentieth century). A 1974 Senate study of executive orders noted that "from the time of the birth of the Nation, the day-to-day conduct of Government business has, of necessity, required the issuance of Presidential orders and policy decisions to carry out the provisions of the Constitution that specify that the President 'shall take care that the laws be faithfully executed.'" The lack of any agreed-upon definition means that, in essence, an executive order is whatever the president chooses to call by that name.

Several authors have offered their own definitions and categories, but they tend to be contradictory. Robert Cash describes executive orders as presidential directives and orders "which are directed to, and govern actions of, governmental officials and agencies." William Neighbors notes that even though the terms "executive order" and "proclamation" are frequently interchanged, executive orders are "used primarily in the executive department, [issued] by the president directing federal government officials or agencies to take some action on specified matters"; in contrast, proclamations are "used primarily in the field of foreign affairs, for ceremonial purposes, and when required . . . by statute." Corwin described proclamations as "the social acts of the highest official of government, the best known example being the Thanksgiving Proclamation," which was first issued by Washington but which has been issued every year since 1863.

These distinctions, while accurate on average, are wrong enough of the time to make them less useful for a comprehensive classification. The argument that executive orders are targeted at the behavior of executive branch officials and not the public at large reflects a limited and formalistic perspective of public administration. One could hardly classify in this way Reagan's Executive Order 12291, which fundamentally reshaped the regulatory process, or the series of civil rights orders which directed executive branch officials to use their power and resources to effect substantial and dramatic social change. Presidents have used executive orders to significantly alter baseline "private rights," or the rights of individuals that are commonly understood to be part of an established landscape of private property and personal freedoms. Through executive orders, presidents have shaped the employment practices of government contractors, the travel rights of American citizens, foreign economic policy, private claims against foreign governments, and claims on natural resources on government-owned lands. Terry Eastland, a Justice Department official in the Reagan administration, has noted the blurred line between purely governmental and private effects: "In theory executive orders are directed to those who enforce the laws but often they have at least as much impact on the governed as the governors."

Nevertheless, it is possible to differentiate among the different executive instruments and identify some distinctive characteristics of executive orders. The major classes of presidential policy instruments are executive orders, proclamations, memoranda, administrative directives, findings and determinations, and regulations. Of these, executive orders combine the highest levels of substance, discretion, and direct presidential involvement. Compared with proclamations, which are usually, but not always, ceremonial, executive orders are a "more far reaching instrument for administrative legislation" and have more substantive effects. Presidential memoranda and directives more often address issues that are temporary or are used to instruct agency officials to take specified action in accordance with established regulatory or departmental processes. Determinations and findings refer to particular decisions the president must issue on the record in order to carry out specific authority that has been delegated by Congress to the executive branch. Although these boundaries are fluid, there is little doubt that presidents and their staffs consider executive orders to be the most important statements of executive policy. . . .

In previous chapters I have documented the ways in which presidents have used executive orders to create or alter institutions and processes that have grown central to executive leadership; to carve out new policy responsibilities in the face of congressional acquiescence and to protect those responsibilities from congressional encroachment; and to solidify their control over executive branch administration. All of these patterns are consistent with what the new institutional economics framework predicts. In each case presidents, by relying on their inherent or delegated legal authority and in some cases by exceeding it, have managed to outmaneuver Congress and take advantage of the discretion that inevitably accompanies broad and general grants of constitutional and statutory authority. In the competition for control over institutions, presidents have significant advantages stemming from their relative unity contrasted with Congress's collective processes, and from judicial readings that usually favor executive authority even when Congress tries to contain it.

But the ability to create and alter is a two-edged sword, since organizations, once they are established, may be able to deflect presidential pressure by creating their own constituencies and mobilizing political supporters. In other words, presidents might establish a new institution or process only to find that it resists their (and future presidents') efforts to direct it. This is the classic principal-agent problem at the core of economic institutionalism: how can a principal (a president, in this case) be sure that an agent (a policy or advisory organization) will faithfully implement his policy wishes? Or how can a president control structures and institutions left over from a previous administration? The existing theory of executive orders and presidential prerogative offers the stock answer that what was enacted by executive order can be undone by simply issuing another order. As the history of presidential involvement in civil rights shows, the process is not so simple. Over several decades, presidents expanded the scope of federal civil rights protections, using their constitutional and statutory powers to institute new policies by executive order. Not all of these policies were effective. Many, though, had a substantive impact on racial equality, and most helped shape the public debate on civil rights.

In making the case that the president played a key role in using executive orders to promote a civil rights agenda in the three decades before the Civil Rights Act of 1964, I do not wish to fall into the trap of historical determinism—of oversimplifying the convoluted and complex chain of events, issues, and personalities that shaped civil rights policy into a rigid cause-and-effect argument about presidential power. When explaining historical events political scientists, according to Russell Riley, are especially prone to attribute too much importance to individual initiative by presidents, and his work challenges the thesis that presidents were especially active in civil rights, in any case. "Presidential contributions toward the processes of black equality," he concludes, "have tended to be overstated, [while] presidential contributions to the process of suppressing movements for racial equality have tended to be understated." More specifically, Riley objects to the notion that presidents elevated civil rights out of a concern for justice and equality; rather, he argues, presidents were responding to shifts in political pressure that *forced* them to take seriously the demands of groups pushing for racial equality.

The progression of civil rights executive orders between 1941 and the 1970s also indicates that presidents may indeed have trouble controlling the institutions that they create by executive orders. The succession of civil rights orders tended to commit future presidents to the path that had already been established, and it is now impossible for a president to undo even the most controversial policies that have arisen through executive action. Affirmative action, or the taking of race into consideration in contracting, employment, and college admissions, emerged most sharply out of a 1965 executive order and the implementing regulations that followed over the next five years. In the 1980s, despite concerted opposition from the Justice Department under Ronald Reagan, affirmative action survived repeated attempts to scale it back. In the 1990s, as state-level action and federal court decisions narrowed the scope of permissible affirmative action (or eliminated it altogether), [President Bill] Clinton struggled to keep control of what had become an explosive political issue.

In other areas of presidential policy making, what was once controversial eventually became accepted as normal operating procedure. With affirmative action the pattern was reversed, as what was initially relatively noncontroversial has become the rallying point for opponents and a litmus test for supporters. Yet the programs and institutions endure, an object lesson in the structural politics of institutional control. . . .

In a recent analysis of affirmative action, sociologist John David Skrenty concludes that the emphasis on proportional hiring originated in the 1940s and 1950s, when the FEPC [Fair Employment Practices Committee] and its progeny focused on employment statistics as the only way to identify and root out discriminatory employment practices. "Throughout the 1950s and 1960s," he argues, "agencies in search of a useful tool for fighting discrimination were continually led to the affirmative action approach, monitoring numbers and percentages of African-Americans hired as a measure of discrimination." In his view, affirmative action was an administrative solution to the complex problem of discrimination.

Affirmative action—or the practice of granting preferences in employment, contracting, or education on the basis of race or gender—is largely a creature of executive action, even though the presidents who crafted the language showed no inkling that the concept would eventually become the lightning rod of civil rights policy. [President John] Kennedy's Executive Order 10925 contained the first use of the term at the presidential level, with its mandate that government contractors "take affirmative action to ensure that applicants are employed, and that employees are treated during employment, without regard to their race, creed, color, or national origin." There was, though, no indication that Kennedy had given much thought to this wording, and the term did not have the meaning that it would take on in the following decade.

Indeed, notes [historian Hugh Davis] Graham, the term "affirmative action" had long been used by civil rights groups to mean aggressive efforts to recruit minority applicants, instead of the "passive nondiscrimination" of the Eisenhower administration. The phrase was put into E.O. 10925 almost as an afterthought, and it was not considered especially controversial at the time. The vice president's aides spent far more time worrying about the administrative structure of the committee and resisting pressure to add sex and age to the list of prohibited grounds for discrimination. In 1982, James E. Jones, Jr., a staff lawyer in the Department of Labor who assisted in the initial organization of the PCEEO [President's Committee on Equal Employment Opportunity, headed by vice president Lyndon Johnson] referred to a "collective failure in 1961 to appreciate the overriding significance of the affirmative action element of Executive Order 10925."

Similarly, Johnson's Executive Order 11246, which is generally considered to have established the legal basis for a wider application and broader construction of affirmative action, was not intended to be a blueprint for such a policy but was instead motivated by a need to rationalize a compli-

cated administrative structure that had evolved since the Civil Rights Act
of 1964; the specific language about the goals was almost identical to what
Kennedy had used in Executive Order 10925: "The internal debate leading to Johnson's new executive orders in September 1965 focused almost
exclusively on structural arrangements, administrative jurisdictions, bureaucratic politics, and to some degree on questions of leadership and staff
personalities. Affirmative action had simply not been fundamentally at issue in the tortured evolution of E.O. 11246 . . . the potential sword was
mighty, as it had always been. But the language was vintage 1961." The
key differences between E.O. 11246 and its predecessors were the provisions that transferred enforcement authority from a presidential commission to the secretary of labor, gave the secretary of labor authority to require compliance reports on hiring practices before companies could bid
on government contracts, and required that contractors comply with the
order in all of their activities, not just those directly related to federal contract activities. Even civil rights groups failed to appreciate the potential
that this new authority created, and many criticized the order for not
doing more. Yet it "potentially possessed the awesome power of the federal contract purse." . . .

In the face of sustained controversy, however, even presidents firmly
opposed to affirmative action have resisted the idea of backing away from
E.O. 11246. As with the earlier orders, successive presidents have had the
authority to rescind or modify the specifics of 11246, but they have had to
take into consideration the symbolic problems in retreating from a well-
established precedent. By the 1980s affirmative action had become synonymous with "quotas," anathema to the Reagan administration; there were
moves both within the White House and the Department of Justice to
modify 11246 or change the administrative enforcement mechanisms.

Despite this strong opposition and repeated efforts, and despite considerable support in Congress, the Reagan administration was unable to
make any major changes to affirmative action programs or 11246. . . .

The resilience of affirmative action programs during the Reagan years
confirms a central premise of the new institutional economics paradigm:
institutions, once they are created, can resist attempts to impose significant
change. Institutional creation is a double-edged sword: presidents can create new administrative capabilities, and they will exert control over these
new capabilities more often than not, but there is no guarantee that they
will be able to do so. The case of affirmative action also demonstrates how
executive orders can bind successive presidents. In this instance, change
was blocked by the emergence of an institutional capacity to protect ex-

isting programs. Within the executive branch, those who favored altering
11246 ran into opposition from the Department of Labor and its congressional allies, the Equal Employment Opportunities Commission (EEOC,
created in the Civil Rights Act to enforce language in the act banning
workplace discrimination), and the broader civil rights community. Surprisingly, even the business community expressed ambivalence about
changing the 11246 program, with many CEOs indicating that their companies would retain affirmative action programs no matter what the government did (although some groups, such as the Chamber of Commerce,
favored repeal). The 1985–1986 dispute between Labor and Justice engendered a contentious, public, and cabinetwide split, and Reagan ultimately
refused to step in. This episode tells us that "intuition notwithstanding,
preexisting executive orders are not always so easy to change. Ronald
Reagan was a popular president whose view of civil rights was most definitely in conflict with an executive order program inherited from previous administrations. Yet despite having the legal and constitutional
wherewithal to bring the order into line with his own administration's
views on civil rights issues, [he] apparently felt obligated to maintain the
status quo." . . .

The language of Executive Orders 10925 and 11246 prohibited discrimination on the basis of race, color, religion, or national origin. Conspicuously absent in these provisions was any reference to sex. Far from
reflecting an oversight, the exclusion of gender from these early nondiscrimination orders was intentional. Gender issues were viewed as distinct from, and less important than, race discrimination, and civil rights
activists fought efforts to merge the two (in part because few people
truly saw sex discrimination as a serious issue, but also because there was
no broad pressure to "support the inclusion of a prohibition on sex-
based discrimination in an executive order to ban racial bias in private
employment").

Nevertheless Kennedy recognized the importance of political support
from women, and in December 1961 established (via Executive Order
10980) the President's Commission on the Status of Women (PCSW).
The commission quickly zeroed in on the president's power to extend the
nondiscrimination language in 10925 to sex, although members split on
the wisdom of the addition and the commission ultimately refused to recommend it. The PCSW, along with two other groups—the Citizens'
Advisory Council on the Status of Women, and the Interdepartmental
Committee on the Status of Women, both created by Executive Order

11126—played a key role in placing sex discrimination on the public agenda, and was instrumental in persuading Johnson to amend 11246 to include sex as a protected category, in October 1967. Cynthia Harrison describes the PCSW and its successors: "The president's commission and its state-level offspring helped to legitimize the issue of sex discrimination, made data available to support allegations that discrimination against women constituted a serious problem, drew up agendas to ameliorate inequities, raised expectations that responsible parties would take action, and, most important, sensitized a nationwide network of women to the problems women faced."

Clinton provides another example of how presidents have used executive orders to extend the protection of earlier civil rights orders, particularly when doing so offers a way around a recalcitrant Congress. In May 1998 Clinton issued Executive Order 13087, which prohibited federal agencies from discriminating in employment on the basis of sexual orientation. In doing so, Clinton continued the pattern of adding to the list of prohibited bases for discrimination first established by Kennedy's 1962 executive order establishing the PCEEO.

Clinton's order provoked an immediate reaction. Congressional Republicans and conservative religious organizations denounced Clinton for creating a new protected class eligible for affirmative action benefits. Donald Devine, who headed the Office of Personnel Management from 1981 to 1995, was especially critical of the way Clinton implemented the policy, arguing that Clinton had circumvented public deliberation and congressional involvement by resorting to an executive order and calling on Congress to overturn it:

President Clinton's Executive Order 13087 was issued out of the glare of public attention but can have far-reaching implications in both the short- and long-term. In my opinion, this order mandates a completely unwise, unworkable, and unenforceable policy that will make the government even more difficult to manage. Far-reaching policies such as these should be developed with the benefit of reasoned debate and public consensus, two things obviously lacking here. The courts are not properly situated to act decisively and quickly enough to prevent the damage this order will do. Congress alone is properly positioned to take action correcting this order before it can do much damage both to the orderly management of the government and to its equal employment policies generally.

Within a few months, legislators had introduced several bills and amendments designed to explicitly overturn 13087 or to prohibit agencies from using any public funds to enforce it. For all of the huffing and puffing about presidential imperialism, though, Congress did nothing about the order itself. On the one floor vote on the matter, a spending prohibition amendment to the Commerce, Justice, State, Judiciary, and Related Agencies appropriations bill, the proposal lost by a wide margin in early 1998, 176–252. The fate of 13087 offers yet another example of Congress's relative inability to counter executive orders through legislation. . . .

33

SAMUEL POPKIN

From *The Candidate*

A presidential campaign can sometimes go wrong when it must go right. In this excerpt Samuel Popkin invokes several analogies to explain successful campaign: boxer Mike Tyson responding to unexpected setbacks; the military adapting to unanticipated challenges; and finally, a ship captain and the crew. To win, a candidate must create a strong team. The team will help a presidential hopeful "be agile to balance conflicting demands," and have "endurance . . . to handle the setback" when things don't go as planned. Staffers on the team play many roles; certain candidates need particular advice. For those readers who plan to work on a presidential campaign, we recommend reading the entire book. For the rest, this excerpt will suffice to give a taste of what faces presidential hopefuls. Don't forget the JFK anecdote at the end.

———

IN EVERY PRESIDENTIAL ELECTION, there are three possible campaigns any candidate can run: He can run as a *challenger* trying to regain the White House for his party, an *incumbent* trying to stay in the White House, or a *successor* trying to retain the White House for the party in power.

The three campaigns repeat like movie roles: Challengers offer a fresh start, incumbents offer experience, and successors—the toughest campaign—offer continuity. Each role has different inherent vulnerabilities. Each role also experiences different organizational challenges during the campaign.

Candidates who don't understand which campaign they are waging make predictable strategic mistakes. For example, they misjudge how and when to fight. Like boxers, they forget they are facing, in the words of one crisis management expert, "the world according to Mike Tyson." When Tyson was the greatest boxer in the world, reporters would ask him about his opponent's strategy. "They all have a strategy," Tyson replied, "until they get hit."

There are effective attacks and effective counterattacks, even when a candidate is hit by a Tysonlike uppercut on the campaign trail. But counterattacks only succeed when a candidate knows the rules of engagement by which she will be judged. Figuring out how people will frame her fight makes all the difference between the candidate who gets knocked out and the one who picks herself up again. And that is the topic of this book.

It sounds simple . . . but it is not.

The sophisticated professionals, both strategists and legislators, who endorsed these losing candidates, all paid a price. They lost potential influence with the eventual winner, credibility with their supporters, and status within their party for backing a flop. And they wasted tens of millions of dollars.

Even the most sophisticated observers repeat the common mistake of falling for the person who seems to have all the inherent God-given traits of a leader—like charisma, popularity, and a powerful presence. The problem with this is that time and again we are usually wrong about which qualities a candidate must ultimately have.

Movie producers are "forever searching for heroes" because people look to winners for inspiration. Everyone thinking about running for president looks at the current president to see how he did it, and whether she can measure up to that campaign and use the same strategy and tactics. This is a near-certain road to defeat.

All too often, winners' stories are structured as fairy tales, populated with misleading magic formulas to vanquish enemies and right wrongs before reaching the promised land. There are no magic formulas or silver bullets, but many people claim to have one—that *this* time is different.

Candidates would be better off by examining losers. General William Westmoreland, commander of the American forces in Vietnam, explained to reporters why he had not read any books written by French generals after their devastating defeat there. "They lost," he explained. And so did we. . . .

Many presidents began as improbable candidates—before hindsight rewrote our memories. Richard M. Nixon lost to John F. Kennedy in 1960, then was humiliated in 1962 when he threw a famous tantrum at the press conference after losing the governor's race—and still managed to come back. Carter, a one-term governor of Georgia, started out in fifteenth place in the field of Democratic candidates for the presidency—yet won. Truman's defeat of Dewey is the most famous upset of the twentieth century. Young, inexperienced Senator Barack Obama, just two years removed from the Illinois Legislature, outmaneuvered Hillary Clinton, who had been in two presidential campaigns and two Senate campaigns.

When you write about war, Barbara Tuchman cautioned, write as if you "did not know who would win." Otherwise, as Michael Kinsley cleverly illustrates, what was simply one of many plausible outcomes becomes a predestined result:

Today, at the frenzied peak of the baroque phase, we debate the wisdom of a candidate's choice of ties—fueled by anonymous quotes from advisers who urged paisley and are damned if they're going down with the ship of a captain who listened to fools recommending stripes. A week from now, we'll be proclaiming the result as the foreordained culmination of trends since the Pleistocene era.

A presidential campaign, like a military campaign, is what Tuchman is credited with calling "the unfolding of miscalculations." They are always perilous. Charisma, money, and polls are not enough to make it through a campaign. . . .

In the beginning there is ambition.

A person who says "I should be president" is claiming the right to be the most powerful person in the world. Normal people do not make this claim. Only the truly audacious can imagine claiming the power of the American presidency. As Barack Obama admitted when he claimed the right to challenge other, more established politicians, "I recognize there is a certain presumptuousness—a certain audacity—to this announcement."

From the first moment anyone announces he is running for president, people size him up in a new way. Candidates face constant scrutiny, the way the men and women sitting around the saloon in old-time cowboy movies eye the new sheriff or the new gunslinger.

The men and women who run have spent years watching other candidates, biding their time, while professing no presidential ambitions. Only after they are in the maelstrom do they realize just how big a leap they have taken. They are on the biggest stage in the world, handling three jobs at once. And they cannot fail at any single one of the three and win.

The candidate has to persuade skeptical voters that she is "one of us," that she understands their lives and shares their values. She has to show everyone a vision of where she wants to take the country during the next four years and how she will lead us there. And the candidate has to oversee her campaign and show people that she can command the ship of state. . . .

There is an epic quality to the men and women who decide to run for president, but a candidate's psychological makeup is but one essential ingredient of a good campaign. I know of no scale or test by which to determine whether Barack Obama, Bill Clinton, and George W Bush all had more specific inner resources than Hillary Clinton, Robert Dole, or

Al Gore. Winners and losers alike had obvious flaws and displayed lapses of judgment; every single one of them made miscalculations and stumbled badly during his or her campaign.

As I said at the beginning of the book, even sophisticated politicos make the common mistake of falling for the person who seems to have all the inherent God-given leadership traits, including a powerful presence. Time and again we are wrong about which qualities that a candidate must ultimately have are present from birth and which can be learned.

I have concentrated not on individual character but on the one thing that is essential to *any* successful campaign: a team that works. Anyone audacious enough to run must also be agile and resilient, and it is the candidate's assembled team that determines the level of the candidate's agility and resilience. Candidates are made, not born, and they are made by the team that they—and only they—can build.

A candidate for president is like a captain preparing to take a perilous voyage through uncharted waters. A heroic image will help the captain find patrons and raise money, but in the end, the captains who go the farthest are the ones who prepare carefully, attract good sailors, and turn them into a strong crew. Candidates only get as far as their team can take them, and the strongest-looking candidates do not necessarily develop the strongest teams. . . .

Candidates have to be agile to balance conflicting demands, reconcile seemingly incompatible pledges, adjust to changing conditions, and show how an (inevitable) change of an old position is compatible with strong, consistent values. They have to know when to sound strong while being vague and when to sound vague while being strong.

Candidates can build coalitions and make credible commitments only if they know how far they can go without contradicting other commitments or compromising their values. This is harder than it sounds: so many people make so many demands about so many issues. Businessmen, union leaders, and the heads of dozens of religious, ethnic, racial, environmental, and social groups make incompatible demands and push for detailed commitments. A candidate must reconcile promises for smaller government with promises for increased defense spending, promises to cut energy consumption with promises to save jobs in manufacturing—all the while establishing her reliability and sincerity.

When a candidate can establish trust with one group without making specific promises that will alienate others, the job of juggling and balancing the coalition is easier. Each candidate will attempt to perform triangulation. Unless the candidacy has good balance, all the cleverness amounts to spitting into the wind.

A large part of establishing and maintaining trust requires the candidate to have clear core values. After working with five Republican presidents, Stu Spencer concluded it was inconceivable that anyone could be president who didn't know what he stood for well enough to know when he was about to compromise himself. He worked with potential candidates to see whether they knew where they stood:

> You test them. You take an issue and you ask them, "Where do you stand on this issue?" Once they tell you, you start playing devil's advocate. You start working them over, coming at them. . . . If you can move them . . . you know that they don't have a very hard-core value system. . . . [You know they have values if] at the end of the day they still smile and say, "All well and good, but this is where I stand."

A candidate's stand is the political equivalent of a dancer's spot. To avoid losing their bearings, dancers focus on a single spot and return to it as they dance and spin. If candidates know their stand well enough to keep it in focus, they can dance around their positions, adjusting their rhetoric to the audience and occasion without losing their balance. . . .

At some point along the trail, every candidate suffers major setbacks. They all have strategies before they got knocked down, but they cannot pass the Mike Tyson test—having a strategy after they get hit—without a team. Endurance will not get a candidate back on track without a team that is prepared to handle the setback. Increased effort will not suffice, because without an appropriate strategy "they'll just do the wrong thing with more gusto." . . .

There is no magic formula for an ideal team. Teams that work help the candidate in the same ways, but they have different kinds of skills because the mix that works depends upon the candidate, her family and friends, the terrain, the media, and the opponent. Every team that works well completes the candidate and includes: a chief of staff who is a near equal; a peer; an objective navigator; a "body man" or sidekick; a mediator between professionals and family and friends; and a protector of the candidate's brand name. A team completes the candidate by providing complementary expertise on the roles and subjects where candidates are in over their head (as every candidate is at some point).

No candidate can possibly be knowledgeable on all the issues, interest groups, and tactics. Ronald Reagan didn't need anyone to tell him how to stand or speak; George H. W. Bush did. George H. W. Bush didn't need anyone to tell him about foreign policy; Ronald Reagan did. Barack Obama didn't need anyone to tell him how to talk about law or the Constitution; John McCain did. John McCain didn't need anyone to tell him how to talk about military service; Barack Obama did.

None of them have all the necessary virtues and personal and interpersonal skills, either. Richard Nixon didn't need anyone watching out for women with a gleam in their eye; Bill Clinton did. Jimmy Carter didn't need a staffer to go through his suit pocket and find all the coasters and napkins on which he wrote down the promises he made drinking with his pals; Gerald Ford did. Barack Obama didn't need anyone to keep him from overeating on the campaign trail; Al Gore did. George W. Bush didn't need anyone to keep him away from craps tables and make sure photographers didn't catch him shooting dice with a friendly blonde standing next to him "for good luck"; John McCain did. . . .

Every candidate *wants* a team greater than the sum of its parts, a team where the principal decision-makers care more about victory than about their personal profits, status, glory, or policy choices. But dedication and loyalty to the candidate are neither necessary nor sufficient to assure mutual accountability, reciprocity, or efficiency. People who put victory first may not have adequate chemistry to work well with the candidate or with each other. People entirely loyal to the candidate may not understand imperatives of the terrain or media or new role the candidate is assuming.

On paper, it sounds simple and straightforward to customize a team for the next campaign. But developing chemistry and real teamwork is never simple, and upgrading the old staff for the new campaign is treacherous. Candidates have a difficult time separating their stakes in any proposed change from the personal stakes for their principal staffers. They continually must balance chemistry and competence: Do they keep the adequate staffer whom they know well and with whom they are comfortable, or do they bring in a more competent person with whom they have little familiarity?

Candidates always have to decide what the right choice is *this* time while surrounded by people who typically find reasons to favor the tactics or strategies that are good for their careers, bank accounts, or causes. At every step up the ladder, it gets harder and harder for candidates to become comfortable enough to trust staffers, because there are more opportunities for staffers to try to advance themselves at the expense of the candidate. And this makes it harder for candidates to ever move out of their comfort zone. . . .

It takes a long time to develop chemistry and integrate individuals into a team. In the National Football League, quarterbacks communicate with a coach for fifteen seconds before each play. There is no time for explanations, discussions, or arguments among the coaches or with the players. The brief communication is successful only if the team members have developed a shorthand language and a structure for decision-making. Someone has to decide what option to use; not every player can be the star at the end of the game.

As much as candidates need big talents and must learn how to handle their egos, they never need people who will make them look bad. It is one thing to be a game-saver who can use his bureaucratic black belt to help a president look better. It is quite another to be an expert who embarrasses the president to enhance his reputation.

Competence without discretion is as dangerous for a candidate as discretion without competence. The ideal, of course, is both at once. Myer Feldman, an aide to President Kennedy, was once profiled as "the White House's Anonymous Man." Helping with debate preparation in 1960, Feldman was resourceful enough to find Irish-sounding names among the Texans who died at the Alamo; these names came in handy when Kennedy gave a speech defending his Catholicism before religious leaders in Houston. Feldman was also an unheard, unnoticed liaison between the White House and business leaders, with enough connections to have obtained the lowest District of Columbia license plate number, a prestige symbol akin to playing touch football with the Kennedys or visiting Camp David. "If Mike ever turned dishonest," Kennedy told Sorensen, "we could all go to jail."

PART SIX

The Executive Branch

34

PAUL LIGHT

From *A Government Ill Executed*

Paul Light is one of the nation's leading authorities on the executive branch. The executive branch is made up of a lot more people than the president and his staff. Millions of civil service workers comprise the ever-growing bureaucracy that administers governmental policies. Light is concerned about the simultaneous growth in the bureaucracy's responsibilities and the decline in the commitment of those who work in the federal service. The fault is not easily assigned. With the impending retirement of many government workers who have been employed for decades, Light sees opportunities for reform. By citing several specific areas for change, the author suggests ways in which the federal workforce can be made more effective. Notable among them is the need to interest capable young citizens in working for the executive branch. Reform is not easy, Light acknowledges, especially when many responsibilities of the federal government are farmed out to a "hidden workforce" of private contractors and state and local employees. Ultimately, it is tough to even figure out what government does and what it costs taxpayers to get the job done.

THIS BOOK IS BASED on Alexander Hamilton's warning about the dangers of a government ill executed. As he argued in *Federalist No. 70,* "A feeble execution is but another phrase for a bad execution; and a government ill executed, whatever it may be in theory must be in practice, a bad government." A government well executed was essential to virtually every challenge that faced the new republic.

More than two hundred years later, however, the federal government seems plagued by bad execution.

The stories are all too familiar: taxpayer abuse by the Internal Revenue Service, security breaches at the nation's nuclear laboratories, missing laptops at the Federal Bureau of Investigation, the Challenger and Columbia space shuttle disasters, breakdowns in policing everything from toys to cattle, the sluggish response to Hurricane Katrina, miscalculations about the war in Iraq, a cascade of wasteful government contracts, continued struggles to unite the nation's intelligence services, agonizing backlogs at the Social Security Administration and the Passport Bureau, near misses on airport runways, staff shortages across the government, porous borders, mistakes on airline passenger screening lines, the subprime mortgage meltdown, destruction of the CIA interrogation tapes, and negligent medical care of veterans. As the stories have accumulated, the federal government's customer service ratings have plummeted, and now rank with those of the airlines and cable TV.

This is not to suggest that the federal government is a wasteland of failure. To the contrary, the federal government accomplishes the impossible every day. Yet, if the federal government is still far from being ill executed, it is not uniformly well executed, either.

Hamilton's warning reflected more than his own experience with a government ill executed during the Revolutionary War. He also recognized that the new government would fail unless it could execute the laws. After all, the Constitution said almost nothing about the administrative state beyond giving the president a role, checked and balanced, in appointing and overseeing the officers of government. Otherwise, it was up to the president to decide how to "take care" that the laws would be faithfully executed. According to Hamilton, that required an energetic executive and a federal service to match. . . .

As the federal government's agenda has expanded over the decades, Hamilton's energetic federal service eventually became the victim of his own vision. Its mission is far broader than its capability; its chains of command are complex and confused; its process for filling the senior offices of government has become a source of embarrassment and delay; its workforce is drawn more by pay, benefits, and security than the chance to make a difference; its future employees would not know how to find a federal job even if they wanted one; its reform agenda has become a destination for fads; and execution of the laws now involves a large and mostly hidden workforce that cannot be held accountable for results. . . .

This erosion of the federal service is no longer a quiet crisis easily dismissed. To the contrary, it is now deafening.

The nation has good reason to worry about the continued erosion. Global warming is working its will on the climate, a new generation of terrorists is flexing its muscle in the Middle East, Medicare is straining under rising health costs, Social Security is bending as the baby boomers prepare for retirement, water wars are rising in the western states, energy independence is decades beyond reach, the nation's infrastructure is rusting, many of its public schools are struggling, and many of its greatest achievements of the past sixty years are in jeopardy as an uncertain future bears down on government.

The question is whether the federal government can rise to the tasks ahead. It has never had a more complex agenda, but has never seemed so confused about its priorities. It has never had a greater need for agility, but has never seemed so thick with bureaucracy. It has never had a bigger budget, but has never been so short on the resources to do its job. It has never had a greater need for decisiveness, but has never seemed so dependent on its hidden workforce to execute decisions. It has never had greater cause for commitment, but has never faced so much reform. Although federal agencies such as the National Institutes of Health and Centers for Disease Control continue to perform at high levels, their laboratories are rusting and their workforces are aging ever closer to retirement.

This [essay] is about reversing the erosion in the capacity to produce a government well executed, whether by creating more flexible careers as the baby boomers leave, building a disciplinary process that actually remedies poor performance, giving federal employees the resources to do their jobs, eliminating layers of needless management, focusing federal agencies and employees on clear priorities, abandoning missions that no longer make sense, or creating an appointments process that makes it easier for America's most talented civic and corporate leaders to say "yes" to a post of honor.

Moreover, with nearly a million baby boomers about to retire from the federal service, the nation has a unique but brief opportunity for radical action to reshape the federal hierarchy, reduce layers of needless management, redistribute resources toward the front lines of government, address the increasing dependency on the hidden workforce of contractors and grantees, and restore student interest in federal careers.

The most powerful advocates for this kind of reform are not outside government, but inside. Federal employees know they do not have enough capacity to do their jobs, and are hungry for change. They also know the time for tinkering is long past. Improving the hiring process will not suffice if new recruits do not have the opportunity to grow; enhancing retention will not help if it produces more layers of management; providing new resources will not matter if they are spread too thin; and setting priorities will not generate clarity if appointees are not in office long enough to make the decisions stick.

There are many reasons to worry about these trends. . . .

At least for now, Americans have little interest in rebuilding the federal service, especially in light of seemingly unending stories of fraud, waste, and abuse. They want the federal government to be involved in great endeavors such as protecting voting rights, reducing disease, and providing health care to low-income Americans, but also think government wastes the vast majority of the money it spends. They think the federal government mostly has the right priorities, but also think federal employees take their jobs for the pay, benefits, and security, not the chance to accomplish something worthwhile, make a difference, or help people. They want the federal government to maintain its programs to deal with important problems, but believe it deserves most of the criticism it receives.

In a very real sense, Americans are getting the government they deserve. They demand more, yet create a climate that encourages their leaders to exploit their distrust. Although the current erosion of the federal service is not just the public's fault, it reflects the tension between what Americans want and what they are willing to pay for. . . .

The weakening of the federal service reflects a series of separate trends that come together to weaken the faithful execution of the laws as a whole. Based on the belief that government can always do more with less, these trends have created a cascade of failures that are harbingers of further, deeper distress.

Both by accident and intent, this belief has been nurtured by repeated campaigns against government, and is reflected in the seven trends embedded in the contemporary erosion. . . . Although each of the trends has contributed to the crisis separately, they have combined to create a desperate moment in bureaucratic time in which the lack of action can only condemn government to greater frustration and failure.

An Ever-Expanding Mission

The threat to the federal service would not be relevant if government did not have such a large list of significant missions. After all, the federal agenda includes many of the most difficult and important problems the nation faces, whether guaranteeing voting rights through decent technology and aggressive enforcement, reducing disease through continued research in modern laboratories, improving the quality of life for older Americans through Social Security and an expanded Medicare program, or protecting the environment through effective implementation of the Clean Air and Water Acts. Americans may not agree on every mission, but the federal government is given little choice but to implement them all. . . .

Still Thickening Government

The federal government's expanding hierarchy reflects its steadily expanding mission, as well as the constant mimicry of new titles. Both by inattention and intent, Congress and the president continue to build a towering monument to their addiction to leadership by layers.

As this book suggests, the federal government has never had more layers of management or more leaders per layer. Despite his promises of businesslike government, George W. Bush's administration now oversees sixty-four discrete titles at the top of the federal government, and almost 2,600 titleholders, up from fifty-one titles and 2,400 titleholders in the final years of the Clinton administration. Although some of the growth reflects the war on terrorism, every department has expanded. Presidents may think the titles create greater leadership, but this book suggests just the opposite—more leaders create more opportunity for delay and obfuscation. . . .

Innocent until Nominated

In theory, tight chains of command should increase executive control at all levels of government. However, the presidential appointments process has become so slow and cumbersome that many layers remain unoccupied for months at the start of a new presidential administration, and continue unoccupied as appointees exit with regularity after eighteen to twenty-four months on the job.

As the scrutiny has increased, the process has slowed. Whereas the Kennedy administration was up and running within three months of inauguration day, the second Bush administration waited more than eight months on average to complete its long list of cabinet and subcabinet appointments. The delays have raised the importance of the de facto subcabinet composed of appointees who serve solely at the pleasure of the president without Senate confirmation.

This . . . does not address the impact of zealous appointees on the erosion of an energetic federal service, though there appears to be an increase in such appointees in Democratic and Republican administrations alike, especially in the rapidly expanding public affairs offices that often seek to politicize unpleasant facts and scientific evidence. However, there is no question that the process itself increasingly discourages appointees, whatever their ideology and intensity, from accepting the call to service. Delays are common, even among highly-qualified appointees, and complaints about the Senate and White House are high. Past appointees report that neither institution acts responsibly, while potential appointees worry that the process will embarrass and confuse them.

Although potential appointees worry more about the process than the past experience of actual appointees suggests is necessary, they also see living in Washington, D.C., as a significant barrier to service, and report significant concerns about the impact of presidential service on their future careers, especially their ability to return to their previous jobs. The result is a dwindling pool of potential appointees, many of whom may be motivated more by the chance to make future contacts and increase their earning power than the chance to serve an admired president.

A Deafening Crisis

Whatever their motivation, presidential appointees oversee a federal workforce that reports serious obstacles to success, especially when compared with business and the nonprofit sector.

On full exertion for the public benefit, many federal employees said they took their jobs for the pay, benefits, and security instead of the chance to accomplish something worthwhile. Compared to nonprofit employees, who emphasize the chance to accomplish something worthwhile and the nature of the work, federal employees have taken Hamilton's model seriously, putting compensation at the top of the list for coming to work each day.

On work that matters, federal employees reported that they do not always receive the kind of work that encourages innovation and high performance. At first glance, the quality of work looks reasonably attractive, especially among employees who said they are surrounded by peers who are committed to the mission, given the chance to do the things they do best, and encouraged to take risks and try new ways of doing things. But when compared with business and nonprofit employment, the quality of federal work suffers.

On the adequate provision of support, federal employees were consistently dissatisfied with access to the tools they need, including training, technology, and enough employees to do the job. Nor did they rate their leadership and coworkers as competent as business and nonprofit employees. At least according to the 2001 and 2002 surveys, most federal employees rated their peers as not particularly competent and not getting better.

On rewards for a job well done and discipline for a job done poorly, most federal employees gave their organization's disciplinary process failing marks and blamed this poor performance in part on their organization's unwillingness to ask enough of all employees. Federal employees also gave their own organizations low ratings on basic tasks such as delivering programs and services, being fair, and spending money wisely.

Finally, on the respect of the public served, ordinary citizens are not the only ones who have come to distrust government. Federal employees themselves showed little trust in their own organizations, in no small part because the federal government has been so penurious with the basic resources they need to do their jobs well.

Ironically given the urgency of the war on terrorism, many of these indicators actually decayed following the 9/11 attacks, in part because federal employees may have become less tolerant of bureaucracy and red tape. The most surprising problems came at the Department of Defense, where employees simultaneously reported an increased sense of mission, but more layers of needless management, inadequate staffing levels, and less access to the technology and training they needed to succeed. Faced with an urgent mission, they became increasingly angry with the bureaucracy around them, and surprisingly less likely to report high morale among their colleagues.

The Spirit of Service

All of these trends have contributed to declining interest in federal service among young Americans, who rightly wonder whether the federal government can deliver on its promises of extensive and arduous enterprise without sacrificing each new generation of talent. In a very real sense, the federal government's reputation precedes it, whether on college campuses, in professional schools, or in the halls of government itself.

. . . [M]any college seniors would not want a federal job even if they knew how to get one, too many graduates of the nation's top professional schools see government as a destination for pay, benefits, and security rather than challenging work. . . . Having redefined the basic meaning of public service almost to the point of excluding government work, young Americans now view nonprofits as the destination of choice for making a difference and learning new skills. Asked to show them the work, the federal government too often shows young Americans the bureaucracy, including a hiring process that sends the instant message that life will be difficult at best once on the federal payroll. . . .

The Tides of Reform

The onslaught of reform over the decades has contributed to the federal government's reputation for administrative inertia. . . .

The level of federal reform appears to parallel the frenzy of management improvement fads in business. But as the pace of federal management reform has increased over the past thirty years, so has the mix of reforms. As Congress has become more involved in making government work, federal employees have faced one competing reform after another, leading to confusion, wasted motion, and frustration in setting priorities with fads and fashions that are now out of favor. . . .

The True Size of Government

The rising tides of reform speak to a general frustration with government's ability to perform, but much of that performance is now dependent on a hidden workforce of contractors, grantees, and state and local employees who labor under federal mandates. Although this workforce is essential to implementing the federal mission, there is cause for concern about the costs embedded in continued outsourcing, especially given the lack of an experienced cadre of federal employees to oversee the activity.

There is no question that this hidden workforce is growing. Although the true size of government dropped sharply in the years following the end of the cold war, it began rising in the late 1990s and has been growing ever since. In 1999, for example, the true size of government had reached its lowest level in more than a decade, dropping to just 11 million civil servants, postal workers, military personnel, and contract- and grant-generated employees. Six years later, in 2005, the true size of government had risen to 14.6 million, largely driven by the burgeoning war on terrorism and the Iraq War. Most of the increase did not come from the purchase of goods but from services such as computer programming, management assistance, and temporary labor. . . .

It is impossible to claim that the hidden workforce of contractors and grantees is not doing its job either effectively or at reasonable cost, if only because such a claim would require more information and oversight than overworked federal procurement officers now have. Nevertheless, the increasing use of contractors, grantees, and state and local employees suggests a significant substitution of hidden workers for fulltime federal employees. In turn, this substitution effect creates a series of illusions, including the notion that the federal government can actually track its large and increasing number of megacontracts and the labor they purchase. The hidden workforce may be mostly invisible to the public and press, but it exists nonetheless. . . .

Big problems demand big answers, which is why tinkering will no longer suffice. . . .

35

CORNELIUS KERWIN
SCOTT FURLONG

From *Rulemaking*

The legislative branch passes laws, the executive branch carries them out, and the judicial branch interprets the law when challenges arise. Straightforward? Not so, Cornelius Kerwin and Scott Furlong find. Congress passes laws, but those laws are subject to detailed and lengthy "rulemaking" by agencies within the executive branch. The rules that bureaucrats devise are often what determine a law's real impact on the American people. The authors illuminate key parts of the process of making the rules that give day-to-day meaning to a congressional act. Illumination is necessary because most Americans know little about how, when, who, where, and why rules are made. Bureaucrats, whether in a cabinet agency or in an independent regulatory commission, decide many details about the way a law is going to be implemented. They don't do this alone, Kerwin and Furlong explain. The process of writing rules involves many points of contact. The Congress can weigh in, since it passed the original legislation. The president has a say over how executive agencies operate. Most important, perhaps, are the comments from the public, whether in the form of individuals' views or of interest groups' inputs that represent factions within the population. Public input is crucial, but it can be lacking in technical understanding, overwhelming in amount and filled with contradictory opinions. Burdensome and convoluted though the rulemaking process may be, behind the scenes it's where the action is in the American lawmaking process.

"OUTCRY BUILDS IN WASHINGTON for Recovery of AIG Bonuses" read the March 17, 2009, headline in *The New York Times,* one of many that followed the recent and historic collapse of financial institutions, credit markets, and the larger economy. In a time when outrage had become commonplace, the reaction to this particular story was extraordinary. The American Insurance Group (AIG), a very large and established firm that required hundreds of billions of dollars of taxpayer money in 2008 to avoid a collapse feared to be catastrophic to the broader economy, had entered into contracts with employees that required the company to pay hundreds of millions of dollars in bonuses. When the news broke it threatened to undermine the credibility of all involved in the efforts to forestall systemic financial failure. How could people who ostensibly participated in one of the most astounding financial collapses in history and accepted unprecedented amounts of public assistance be rewarded in such a fashion? Congress had already enacted President Barack Obama's proposed framework for restoration of the American economy, the American Recovery and Reinvestment Act. With the new developments from AIG, one of the act's nonspending provisions—an amendment to the executive compensation provisions of 2008—took on new and compelling significance.

Just three months after news of the AIG bonuses was revealed the Department of the Treasury issued a set of regulations that severely restricted compensation for executives working in firms that received bailout funds from the Troubled Asset Relief Program (TARP). The rules were the direct result of the authority granted to the secretary of the Treasury through the American Recovery and Reinvestment Act. They provided specificity on the new requirements essential to the affected companies, the personnel covered by the new rules, and enforcement officials in the government. The Treasury-issued rules covered the full range of compensation issues raised in the statute, including limits on salary, bonuses, and payment of "golden parachutes and so-called 'clawback' regulations that allowed the federal government to recoup compensation awarded on the basis of" materially inaccurate performance criteria. In addition, they added a number of other requirements the department viewed as important to the goals Congress intended in the legislation but not specifically included in the statute. These included mandatory reporting of "perks" over $25,000; prohibition of the practice of providing additional compensation to cover tax liability and the appointment of a special master with broad powers to review and approve the compensation structure for the executive officers and one hundred top earners in any affected firm; and the authority to negotiate repayments by firms to the Treasury for improper payments made previously to covered employees. The Treasury rules covered 123 pages in the *Federal Register* on the day they were issued, including references to earlier rules they had issued on the same topic. This compares to the four pages devoted to the executive compensation issue in the parent legislation. The rules conclude with the qualification that some would consider a warning that Treasury would issue additional rules as conditions merit.

Throughout our history, in crisis and in the normal course of the public's business, Congress deferred to the expertise, management, and administrative capabilities of an agency to carry out what they, as elected representatives, perceived to be the will of the people.

Rulemaking has been used in this case, and countless others, because as an instrument of government it is unmatched in its potential for speed, specificity, quality, and legitimacy. Rulemaking is a ubiquitous presence in virtually all government programs. For a variety of reasons Congress is unwilling or unable to write laws specific enough to be implemented by government agencies and complied with by private citizens. The crucial intermediate process of rulemaking stands between the enactment of a law by Congress and the realization of the goals that both Congress and the people it represents seek to achieve by that law. Increasingly, rulemaking defines the substance of public programs. It determines, to a very large extent, the specific legal obligations we bear as a society. Rulemaking gives precise form to the benefits we enjoy under a wide range of statutes. In the process, it fixes the actual costs we incur in meeting the ambitious objectives of our many public programs.

Rulemaking is important for many reasons. The best place to begin a discussion of those reasons is with a definition of rulemaking and an explanation of why it is crucial to our system of government....

Colin Diver, former dean of the University of Pennsylvania Law School and one of the most thoughtful observers of rules and rulemaking, defines the term in a paraphrase of the great jurist Oliver Wendell Holmes: A "rule is the skin of a living policy . . . it hardens an inchoate normative judgment into the frozen form of words. . . . Its issuance marks the transformation of policy from the private wish to public expectation. . . . [T]he framing of a rule is the climactic act of the policy making process." This definition underscores the pivotal role that rules play in our system of government, but more light must be shed on their key characteristics.

More than sixty years after its enactment into law, the Administrative Procedure Act of 1946 (referred to henceforth as the APA) still contains the best definition of *rule*. The act was written by Congress to bring regularity and predictability to the decision-making processes of government agencies, which by the mid-1940s were having a profound influence on life in this country. Rules and rulemaking were already important parts of the administrative process in 1946. Both, however, required careful definition so that the procedural requirements established in the act would be applied to the types of actions Congress intended to affect.

The APA states: "[R]ule means the whole or part of an agency statement of general or particular applicability and future effect designed to implement, interpret, or prescribe law or policy." At first reading this statement does not appear to reveal much. On closer examination, however, it surrenders several elements crucial to understanding contemporary rulemaking. Not the first element mentioned but a good place to start is a single word—*agency*—because it identifies the source of rules. . . .

We learn first from this definition that rules do not come from the major institutions created by the Constitution. They are not products of Congress or some other legislature. Rules are by-products of the deliberations and votes of our elected representatives, but they are not themselves legislation. Congress does have its own institutional rules, but they apply only to its members and committees. Under the APA definition, rules do not originate with the president or some other chief executive. As we will see, the actions of the president of the United States and chief executives at the various levels of government have a profound effect on the rulemaking process. These officials employ executive orders and directives in the course of their management responsibilities, but rarely, if ever, do they write rules of the type considered in this book.

Various and sundry courts may have reason to consider rules. Their actions may result in rules being changed or eliminated. But judges do not write rules in the first instance either, except, like Congress, to establish procedures for their colleagues and the operation of the courts over which they preside.

Rules are produced by bureaucratic institutions entrusted with the implementation, management, and administration of our law and public policy. We view bureaucracies as inferior in status to the constitutional branches of government—Congress, the president, and the judiciary. We do so because the authority of these agencies is derived and patterned after and drawn from the three main branches. In one important respect, however, agencies are the equal of these institutions. The rules issued by departments, agencies, or commissions are law; they carry the same weight as congressional legislation, presidential executive orders, and judicial decisions. An important and controversial feature of our system of government is that bureaucratic institutions are vested with all three government powers established in the Constitution. Through a device called delegation of authority, government agencies perform legislative, executive, and judicial functions. Rulemaking occurs when agencies use the legislative authority granted them by Congress.

It is significant that agencies are the sources of rules, because it means that rulemaking is subjected to the external and internal influences that have been found to affect decision making in our public bureaucracies. Agencies behave differently from the constitutional branches of government. Their decisions cannot be explained simply by reference to the admittedly strong pressures they continually feel from Congress, the White House, the courts, interest groups, and the public at large. As one group of scholars put it, "Public agencies are major political actors in all phases of the policy process."

The organization, division of labor, culture, professional orientation, and work routines of bureaucracies affect the way they make decisions. So too do the motives of individual bureaucrats. These themes will be developed further in the book's final chapter. We must expect the law and policy embodied in rules written by agencies to be different from what would be developed by Congress, the president, or the courts. So the very source of rules makes them immediately distinctive from other instruments of law and public policy.

Agency can mean any one of a number of organizational arrangements used to carry out law and policy. Public bureaucracies have many names. There are departments, such as the Department of Transportation; commissions, such as the Federal Trade Commission (FTC); administrations, such as the Federal Aviation Administration (FAA); and agencies, such as the Environmental Protection Agency (EPA). However organized or named, most of these bodies have the authority to issue rules and use a rulemaking process to carry it out. . . .

Given the vast scope of rules and the importance of their content, it should not be surprising that the process used to write them draws attention. During the past sixty years rulemaking has been the focus of considerable professional and political controversy. The way rules are written profoundly affects what they contain, and the content of rules determines, to a very large extent, the quality of our lives.

The substance of rules and the process of rulemaking are linked in many important ways. The elements of the contemporary rulemaking process are reactions to great expansion in the substantive reach of rulemaking. We have seen that the New Deal and the 1970s and 1980s were periods of explosive growth in government programs that required massive rulemaking to meet ambitious objectives. Even the Bush II administration—reputed to be skeptical about, if not hostile to, regulation—found it useful to dramatically expand the use of rulemaking and the number of rules related to homeland security. These expansions of the subject matter of rulemaking stimulated intense interest in the manner in which rules were developed by the responsible agencies. In each period there was concern about how agencies were making decisions about the contents of rules. What were agencies taking into account? To whom were they listening? To whom were they responsible? These concerns led to many proposals—some successful, others not—to change the way rules were written. . . .

Participation in rulemaking poses problems for both the public and the agency. In order to become involved in rulemaking in a way that holds some prospects for success, individuals, groups, and firms need resources, organization, and sophistication. These prerequisites are not distributed evenly. Consequently, some fail to participate in rulemaking because they lack the ability to do so or have little awareness of the problems. Rulemaking demands a keen sense of timing and a grasp of the subtleties of bureaucratic decision making. These skills are not necessarily related to the size of an organization or the amount of money it has to spend on public affairs. Size and money help, to be sure, but an understanding of the process of rulemaking is more important.

Problems arise, however, even when participation is both extensive and balanced. Sometimes the quality of participation is poor; the agency solicits and receives the views of the public, but the results do little or nothing to improve the rule. This occurs for several reasons. First, the information provided by the agency about the rule under development may be misleading or insufficient to allow interested parties to comment intelligently. As noted in earlier chapters, however, legal requirements and inbred agency caution make this a relatively minor problem. Second, given the fact that most rulemaking requires detailed and often technical knowledge, commenting parties may not possess the requisite expertise to be able to offer any additional information or constructive advice on rules. Finally, parties are often uninterested in improving a rule. They use the opportunity to participate to challenge the rule, per se, or to make their opposition a matter of public record that can be referred to in subsequent challenges to the rule.

The sheer number of participants can be a significant problem for the agency developing the rule. A system for collecting the comments must be established, and the comments themselves must be read and analyzed. Then the agency must have some mechanism to decide which of the comments have merit, which require changes in the rule, and what those changes will be. Finally, if the agency revises the proposed rule based on the comments it receives, it must prepare an analysis of the changes and why they were made. The magnitude of the task presented to the agency obviously depends on the number, length, and complexity of the comments.

There are near-legendary examples of rules proposed by federal agencies that generated massive outpourings of public comment. Several ill-fated efforts by the Department of the Treasury's Bureau of Alcohol, Tobacco, and Firearms to regulate handguns were greeted by tens of thousands of postcard responses, orchestrated by the National Rifle Association and related groups. Initial publication of proposed rules by the

Department of Agriculture that would, among other things, define the term *organic* attracted more than 450,000 comments. More recently, in 2008 a proposed rule by the Federal Reserve System dealing with business practices of credit card firms attracted 56,000 public comments, a record for that agency. But lest it be thought that only politically charged issues like gun control, food labeling, or credit cards generate this level of interest, consider the proposed rule of the Animal and Plant Health Inspection Service (APHIS) on the importation of ostriches. When it was published it stimulated more than 2,000 written comments, an extraordinary number when one considers that ostriches are not normally considered an issue with high political salience. Massive volumes of public participation in rulemaking strain agencies' resources. The rise of electronic communication exacerbates the problem and highlights the paradox of participation in rulemaking. Because rules bring specific effects to easily identified parties, there is a strong incentive to participate; technology makes this relatively easy. The volume of public comment, however, can slow the process and interfere with decision making.

Participation in rulemaking displays the same proclivity for conflict and deadlock that characterizes other key elements of the public policy process. Phillip Harter, an important figure in efforts to reform the rulemaking process, catalogued the problems that can beset the development of major rules under the general title "adversary process." He viewed rulemaking as too often characterized by the taking of extreme positions, both by the agency and by affected parties; waves of "defensive research"; and an inability or unwillingness of parties to the rulemaking to state and deal with "true concerns." Formal mechanisms for participation, such as written comment and public hearings, become stylized rituals from which neither side expects much more than an affirmation of what is already known. He noted that these forms are not conducive to the resolution of "polycentric" issues, and they are not well suited to the give-and-take between parties that is so elemental to dispute resolution. Accommodation of contending positions, if it occurs at all, happens behind the scenes in quiet negotiations. When conflict persists and is not resolved, rules are issued, and the controversy spills into the federal courts, the halls of Congress, or the White House. Petitions for reconsideration are filed, and the initial rulemaking effort may be for naught.

Harter was careful to note that this description does not apply to all rulemaking. In fact, evidence will be presented . . . that disputes this general view of rulemaking. Some external parties who participate actively in the rulemaking process find it a valuable and fruitful activity and find the agencies they deal with responsive. Nevertheless, at least some of the dysfunctions in participation of the sort Harter identified persist, and still others have appeared. They will be examined at greater lengths presently.

Involvement of the public in rulemaking may be the most complex and important form of political action in the contemporary American political system. When it is blocked or otherwise does not occur, there are profound constitutional and practical implications. As we will detail . . . because rulemaking is a form of lawmaking, participation by the public is important to the maintenance of democracy. And because rule writers are not omniscient, the information that the public possesses is badly needed. . . .

Because we are a representative democracy and because lawmaking is the ultimate power granted our government under the Constitution, rulemaking presents us with a profound dilemma. On the one hand, we have established that in order for government to be truly responsive to the incessant demands of the American people for public programs to solve private problems, rulemaking by government agencies is essential. It frees Congress to attend to many more problems than it would otherwise have time to deal with. It relieves Congress of the burden of maintaining and managing enormous staffs who possess the expertise essential to refining the operating standards and procedures for myriad programs. Finally, it is the best means yet found to break legislative deadlocks and to avoid difficult political decisions, while still taking serious actions. On the other hand, as an indispensable surrogate to the legislative process, rulemaking has a fundamental flaw that violates basic democratic principles. Those who write the law embodied in rules are not elected; they are accountable to the American people only through indirect means. Our elected representatives have confronted this dilemma on numerous occasions and decided that one answer is direct participation by the public in rulemaking.

Implicit in the various discussions of participation in rulemaking is a fundamental debate analogous to the trustee/delegate dialectic* in the political science literature regarding the proper role of elected officials. With rulemaking, however, the arguments for each archetype are actually more pointed. Those who would dismiss either the value or constitutional need for public participation point to the fact that a statute is writ-

---

*The trustee/delegate contrast often refers to how a legislator views the job: to use the elected official's own best judgment about what is good for the constituents (a trustee); or to be guided by the views of the voters who elected the legislator to represent them (delegate). Here, the contrasting approaches refer to the weight that a bureaucrat gives to public input in formulating a rule, either not much or a lot.—EDS.

ten by duly elected representatives. Furthermore, the legislature's decision to entrust subsequent lawmaking needed to implement the goals of the statute contains a delegation of authority to agency-based experts who are fully capable of developing the information they need for a given rule without the input of the public, who are less well-informed, technically competent, and objective. And, given the grave implications of decisions made during the development of rules, do we truly wish to have the opinions and demands of an interested but inept public delay or, worse, color the decisions of those charged with protecting our health, safety, wealth, and general quality of life?

The opposing argument notes that lawmaking is the seminal power granted in our Constitution, and whether it is written by elected representatives or unelected bureaucratic experts, the voice of the people must be heard to confer legitimacy on the mandates the resultant laws contain. Why, they would ask, should the will of the people be confined to the enactment of legislation when it is widely accepted that the most specific statements of Americans' rights and responsibilities are to be found in rules and regulations? Advocates for participation would note that whatever the levels of expertise extant in government agencies, none are omniscient, and all face profound challenges in the face of growing responsibilities and expectations arising from new statutes or simply changing conditions. The "people" have access to vast expertise in the form of interest groups they comprise and support. Public participation is not, in their eyes, a trivial symbolic exercise but one often essential if agencies are going to function with the best and most current information when writing rules.

36

JAMES Q. WILSON

From *Bureaucracy*

It's been over twenty years since the "new" ice skating rink was built in New York's Central Park. Many skaters have enjoyed it since 1986. In that time, New York City has experienced much change. New mayors have come and gone. September 11, 2001, happened: The city mourned and then slowly recovered. But some things in New York City have remained the same, even if not exactly. Donald Trump still knows how to get things done. Back in the mid-1980s, before "The Apprentice," real estate developer Trump showed that the efficiency of the private sector could accomplish what no public bureaucracy seemed to be able to do: refurbish the Central Park skating rink, quickly and inexpensively. Today we'd say that the city fired itself and "privatized" the project by hiring Trump. Renowned political scientist James Q. Wilson looks at Trump's success with the skating rink project, but also explains why he had that success. The public sector has many limitations on its actions that the private sector does not have to consider. As privatization becomes increasingly popular on the state and local and even national level of government, it's important to remember Wilson's caveats: efficiency is not the only worthy goal and not all publicly run projects are inefficient.

ON THE MORNING OF MAY 22, 1986, Donald Trump, the New York real estate developer, called one of his executives, Anthony Gliedman, into his office. They discussed the inability of the City of New York, despite six years of effort and the expenditure of nearly $13 million, to rebuild the ice-skating rink in Central Park. On May 28 Trump offered to take over the rink reconstruction, promising to do the job in less than six months. A week later Mayor Edward Koch accepted the offer and shortly thereafter the city appropriated $3 million on the understanding that Trump would have to pay for any cost overruns out of his own pocket. On October 28, the renovation was complete, over a month ahead of schedule and about $750,000 under budget. Two weeks later, skaters were using it.

For many readers it is obvious that private enterprise is more efficient than are public bureaucracies, and so they would file this story away as simply another illustration of what everyone already knows. But for other readers it is not so obvious what this story means; to them, business is greedy and unless watched like a hawk will fob off shoddy or overpriced goods on the American public, as when it sells the government $435 hammers and $3,000 coffee-pots. Trump may have done a good job in this instance, but perhaps there is something about skating rinks or New York City government that gave him a comparative advantage; in any event, no larger lessons should be drawn from it.

Some lessons can be drawn, however, if one looks closely at the incentives and constraints facing Trump and the Department of Parks and Recreation. It becomes apparent that there is not one "bureaucracy problem" but several, and the solution to each in some degree is incompatible with the solution to every other. First there is the problem of accountability—getting agencies to serve agreed-upon goals. Second there is the problem of equity—treating all citizens fairly, which usually means treating them alike on the basis of clear rules known in advance. Third there is the problem of responsiveness—reacting reasonably to the special needs and circumstances of particular people. Fourth there is the problem of efficiency—obtaining the greatest output for a given level of resources. Finally there is the problem of fiscal integrity—assuring that public funds are spent prudently for public purposes. Donald Trump and Mayor Koch were situated differently with respect to most of these matters.

Accountability

The Mayor wanted the old skating rink refurbished, but he also wanted to minimize the cost of the fuel needed to operate the rink (the first effort to rebuild it occurred right after the Arab oil embargo and the attendant increase in energy prices). Trying to achieve both goals led city hall to select a new refrigeration system that as it turned out would not work properly. Trump came on the scene when only one goal dominated: get the rink rebuilt. He felt free to select the most reliable refrigeration system without worrying too much about energy costs.

Equity

The Parks and Recreation Department was required by law to give every contractor an equal chance to do the job. This meant it had to put every part of the job out to bid and to accept the lowest without much regard to the reputation or prior performance of the lowest bidder. Moreover, state law forbade city agencies from hiring a general contractor and letting him select the subcontractors; in fact, the law forbade the city from even discussing the project in advance with a general contractor who might later bid on it—that would have been collusion. Trump, by contrast, was free to locate the rink builder with the best reputation and give him the job.

Fiscal Integrity

To reduce the chance of corruption or sweetheart deals the law required Parks and Recreation to furnish complete, detailed plans to every contractor bidding on the job; any changes after that would require renegotiating the contract. No such law constrained Trump; he was free to give incomplete plans to his chosen contractor, hold him accountable for building a satisfactory rink, but allow him to work out the details as he went along.

Efficiency

When the Parks and Recreation Department spent over six years and $13 million and still could not reopen the rink, there was public criticism but no city official lost money. When Trump accepted a contract to do it, any cost overruns or delays would have come out of his pocket and any savings could have gone into his pocket (in this case, Trump agreed not to take a profit on the job).

Gliedman summarized the differences neatly: "The problem with government is that government can't say 'yes'. . . . . there is nobody in government that can do that. There are fifteen or twenty people who have to agree. Government has to be slower. It has to safeguard the process.". . . .

The government can't say "yes." In other words, the government is constrained. Where do the constraints come from? From us.

Herbert Kaufman has explained red tape as being of our own making: "Every restraint and requirement originates in somebody's demand for it." Applied to the Central Park skating rink Kaufman's insight reminds us that civil-service reformers demanded that no city official benefit personally from building a project; that contractors demanded that all be given an equal chance to bid on every job; and that fiscal watchdogs demanded that all contract specifications be as detailed as possible. For each demand a procedure was established; viewed from the outside, those procedures are called red tape. To enforce each procedure a manager was appointed; those managers are called bureaucrats. No organized group demanded that all skating rinks be rebuilt as quickly as possible, no procedure existed to enforce that demand, and no manager was appointed to enforce it. The political process can more easily enforce compliance with constraints than the attainment of goals.

When we denounce bureaucracy for being inefficient we are saying something that is half true. Efficiency is a ratio of valued resources used to valued outputs produced. The smaller that ratio the more efficient the production. If the valued output is a rebuilt skating rink, then whatever process uses the fewest dollars or the least time to produce a satisfactory rink is the most efficient process. By this test Trump was more efficient than the Parks and Recreation Department.

But that is too narrow a view of the matter. The economic definition of efficiency (efficiency in the small, so to speak) assumes that there is only one valued output, the new rink. But government has many valued outputs, including a reputation for integrity, the confidence of the people, and the support of important interest groups. When we complain about skating rinks not being built on time we speak as if all we cared about were skating rinks. But when we complain that contracts were awarded without competitive bidding or in a way that allowed bureaucrats to line their pockets we acknowledge that we care about many things besides skating rinks; we care about the contextual goals—the constraints—that we want government to observe. A government that is slow to build rinks but is honest and accountable in its actions and properly responsive to worthy constituencies may be a very efficient government, *if* we measure efficiency in the large by taking into account *all* of the valued outputs.

Calling a government agency efficient when it is slow, cumbersome, and costly may seem perverse. But that is only because we lack any objective way for deciding how much money or time should be devoted to maintaining honest behavior, producing a fair allocation of benefits, and generating popular support as well as to achieving the main goal of the project. If we could measure these things, and if we agreed as to their value, then we would be in a position to judge the true efficiency of a government agency and decide when it is taking too much time or spending too much money achieving all that we expect of it. But we cannot measure these things nor do we agree about their relative importance, and so government always will appear to be inefficient compared to organizations that have fewer goals.

Put simply, the only way to decide whether an agency is truly inefficient is to decide which of the constraints affecting its action ought to be ignored or discounted. In fact that is what most debates about agency behavior are all about. In fighting crime are the police handcuffed? In educating children are teachers tied down by rules? In launching a space shuttle are we too concerned with safety? In building a dam do we worry excessively about endangered species? In running the Postal Service is it important to have many post offices close to where people live? In the case of the skating rink, was the requirement of competitive bidding for each contract on the basis of detailed specifications a reasonable one? Probably not. But if it were abandoned, the gain (the swifter completion of the rink) would have to be balanced against the costs (complaints from contractors who might lose business and the chance of collusion and corruption in some future projects).

Even allowing for all of these constraints, government agencies may still be inefficient. Indeed, given the fact that bureaucrats cannot (for the most part) benefit monetarily from their agencies' achievements, it would be surprising if they were not inefficient. Efficiency, in the large or the small, doesn't pay. . . .

Inefficiency is not the only bureaucratic problem nor is it even the most important. A perfectly efficient agency could be a monstrous one, swiftly denying us our liberties, economically inflicting injustices, and competently expropriating our wealth. People complain about bureaucracy as often because it is unfair or unreasonable as because it is slow or cumbersome.

Arbitrary rule refers to officials acting without legal authority, or with that authority in a way that offends our sense of justice. Justice means, first, that we require the government to treat people equally on the basis of clear rules known in advance: If Becky and Bob both are driving sixty miles per hour in a thirty-mile-per-hour zone and the police give a ticket to Bob, we believe they also should give a ticket to Becky. Second, we believe that justice obliges the government to take into account the special needs and circumstances of individuals: If Becky is speeding because she is on her way to the hospital to give birth to a child and Bob is speeding for the fun of it, we may feel that the police should ticket Bob but not Becky. Justice in the first sense means fairness, in the second it means responsiveness. Obviously, fairness and responsiveness often are in conflict.

The checks and balances of the American constitutional system reflect our desire to reduce the arbitrariness of official rule. That desire is based squarely on the premise that inefficiency is a small price to pay for freedom and responsiveness. Congressional oversight, judicial review, interest-group participation, media investigations, and formalized procedures all are intended to check administrative discretion. It is not hyperbole to say that the constitutional order is animated by the desire to make the government "inefficient."

This creates two great tradeoffs. First, adding constraints reduces the efficiency with which the main goal of an agency can be attained but increases the chances that the agency will act in a nonarbitrary manner. Efficient police departments would seek out criminals without reading them their rights, allowing them to call their attorneys, or releasing them in response to a writ of habeas corpus. An efficient building department would issue construction permits on demand without insisting that the applicant first show that the proposed building meets fire, safety, sanitation, geological, and earthquake standards.

The second great tradeoff is between nonarbitrary governance defined as treating people equally and such governance defined as treating each case on its merits. We want the government to be both fair and responsive, but the more rules we impose to insure fairness (that is, to treat all people alike) the harder we make it for the government to be responsive (that is, to take into account the special needs and circumstances of a particular case).

The way our government manages these tradeoffs reflects both our political culture as well as the rivalries of our governing institutions. Both tend toward the same end: We define claims as rights, impose general rules to insure equal treatment, lament (but do nothing about) the resulting inefficiencies, and respond to revelations about unresponsiveness by adopting new rules intended to guarantee that special circumstances will be handled with special care (rarely bothering to reconcile the rules that require responsiveness with those that require equality). And we do all this out of the best of motives: a desire to be both just and benevolent. Justice inclines us to treat people equally, benevolence to treat them differently; both inclinations are expressed in rules, though in fact only justice can be. It is this futile desire to have a rule for every circumstance that led Herbert Kaufman to explain "how compassion spawns red tape." . . . .

In the meantime we live in a country that despite its baffling array of rules and regulations and the insatiable desire of some people to use government to rationalize society still makes it possible to get drinkable water instantly, put through a telephone call in seconds, deliver a letter in a day, and obtain a passport in a week. Our Social Security checks arrive on time. Some state prisons, and most of the federal ones, are reasonably decent and humane institutions. The great majority of Americans, cursing all the while, pay their taxes. One can stand on the deck of an aircraft carrier during night flight operations and watch two thousand nineteen-year-old boys faultlessly operate one of the most complex organizational systems ever created. There are not many places where all this happens. It is astonishing it can be made to happen at all.

37

ROBERT REICH

From *Locked in the Cabinet*

University professor Robert Reich was appointed to President Clinton's cabinet in 1993 to be his Secretary of Labor. Writing with all the candor and humor that is Reich's trademark, he gives readers three important criteria he considered in selecting his assistants and then concludes, "I'm flying blind." His daily schedule is packed, and he is motivated to escape from the "bubble" and actually tour the vast buildings of the Labor Department. Finally, Reich offers an instructive anecdote about an idea developed by an obscure civil servant in the department, an idea that turns out to be a real winner and becomes an important new government policy.

February 1, [1993] Washington

I INTERVIEW TWENTY people today. I have to find a deputy secretary and chief of staff with all the management skills I lack. I also have to find a small platoon of assistant secretaries: one to run the Occupational Safety and Health Administration (detested by corporations, revered by unions); another to be in charge of the myriad of employment and job training programs (billions of dollars), plus unemployment insurance (billions more); another to police the nation's pension funds (four trillion dollars' worth); another to patrol the nation's nine million workplaces to make sure that young children aren't being exploited, that workers receive at least a minimum hourly wage plus time and a half for overtime, that sweatshops are relegated to history.

The Department of Labor is vast, its powers seemingly endless. With a history spanning the better part of the twentieth century—involving every major controversy affecting American workers—it issues thousands of regulations, sends vast sums of money to states and cities, and sues countless employers. I can barely comprehend it all. It was created in 1913 with an ambitious mission: *Foster, promote, and develop the welfare of the wage earners of the United States, improve their working conditions, and advance their opportunities for profitable employment.* That about sums it up.

And yet here I am assembling my team before I've even figured it all out. No time to waste. Bill will have to sign off on my choices, then each of them will be nitpicked for months by the White House staff and the FBI, and if they survive those hurdles each must be confirmed by the Senate.

If I'm fast enough out of the starting gate, my team might be fully installed by June. If I dally now and get caught in the traffic jam of sub-cabinet nominations from every department, I might not see them for a year. And whenever they officially start, add another six months before they have the slightest idea what's going on.

No other democracy does it this way. No private corporation would think of operating like this. Every time a new president is elected, America assembles a new government of 3,000 or so amateurs who only sometimes know the policies they're about to administer, rarely have experience managing large government bureaucracies, and almost never know the particular piece of it they're going to run. These people are appointed quickly by a president-elect who is thoroughly exhausted from a year and a half of campaigning. And they remain in office, on average, under two years—barely enough time to find the nearest bathroom. It's a miracle we don't screw it up worse than we do.

Part of my problem is I don't know exactly what I'm looking for and I certainly don't know how to tell whether I've found it. Some obvious criteria:

1. *They should share the President-elect's values.* But how will I know they do? I can't very well ask, "Do you share the President's values?" and expect an honest answer. Even if they contributed money to the campaign, there's no telling. I've heard of several middle-aged Washington lawyers so desperate to escape the tedium of law practice by becoming an assistant secretary for Anything That Gets Me Out of Here that they've made whopping contributions to both campaigns.

2. *They should be competent and knowledgeable about the policies they'll administer.* Sounds logical, but here again, how can I tell? I don't know enough to know whether someone *else* knows enough. "What do you think about the Employee Retirement Income Security Act?" I might ask, and an ambitious huckster could snow me. "I've thought a lot about this," he might say, "and I've concluded that Section 508(m) should be changed because most retirees have 307 accounts which are treated by the IRS as Subchapter 12 entities." Uttered with enough conviction, bullshit like this could sweep me off my feet.

3. *They should be good managers.* But how to find out? Yesterday I phoned someone about a particular job candidate's management skills, at her suggestion. He told me she worked for him and was a terrific manager. "Ter-

rific?" I repeated. "Wonderful. The best," he said. "You'd recommend her?"
I asked. "Absolutely. Can't go wrong," he assured me. I thanked him, hung
up the phone, and was enthusiastic for about five minutes, until I realized
how little I had learned. How do I know *he* recognizes a good manager?
Maybe he's a lousy manager himself and has a bunch of bozos working for
him. Why should I trust that he's more interested in my having her on *my*
team than in getting her off his?

I'm flying blind. . . .

March 2 Washington

This afternoon, I mount a small revolution at the Labor Department.
The result is chaos.

Background: My cavernous office is becoming one of those hermeti-
cally sealed, germ-free bubbles they place around children born with immune deficiencies. Whatever gets through to me is carefully sanitized.
Telephone calls are prescreened, letters are filtered, memos are reviewed.
Those that don't get through are diverted elsewhere. Only [deputy secre-
tary] Tom [Glynn], chief of staff Kitty [Higgins], and my secretary walk
into the office whenever they want. All others seeking access must first be
scheduled, and have a sufficient reason to take my precious germ-free
time.

I'm scheduled to the teeth. Here, for example, is today's timetable:

6:45 A.M.	Leave apartment
7:10 A.M.	Arrive office
7:15 A.M.	Breakfast with MB from the *Post*
8:00 A.M.	Conference call with Rubin
8:30 A.M.	Daily meeting with senior staff
9:15 A.M.	Depart for Washington Hilton
9:40 A.M.	Speech to National Association of Private Industry Councils
10:15 A.M.	Meet with Joe Dear (OSHA enforcement)
11:15 A.M.	Meet with Darla Letourneau (DOL budget)
12:00	Lunch with JG from National League of Cities
1:00 P.M.	CNN interview (taped)
1:30 P.M.	Congressional leadership panel
2:15 P.M.	Congressman Ford
3:00 P.M.	NEC budget meeting at White House
4:00 P.M.	Welfare meeting at White House
5:00 P.M.	National Public Radio interview (taped)
5:45 P.M.	Conference call with mayors
6:15 P.M.	Telephone time

7:00 P.M. Meet with Maria Echeveste (Wage and Hour)
8:00 P.M. Kitty and Tom daily briefing
8:30 P.M. National Alliance of Business reception
9:00 P.M. Return to apartment.

I remain in the bubble even when I'm outside the building—ushered from place to place by someone who stays in contact with the front office by cellular phone. I stay in the bubble after business hours. If I dine out, I'm driven to the destination and escorted to the front door. After dinner, I'm escorted back to the car, driven to my apartment, and escorted from the car, into the apartment building, into the elevator, and to my apartment door.

No one gives me a bath, tastes my food, or wipes my bottom—at least not yet. But in all other respects I feel like a goddamn two-year-old. Tom and Kitty insist it has to be this way. Otherwise I'd be deluged with calls, letters, meetings, other demands on my time, coming from all directions. People would force themselves on me, harass me, maybe even threaten me. The bubble protects me.

Tom and Kitty have hired three people to handle my daily schedule (respond to invitations, cull the ones that seem most promising, and squeeze all the current obligations into the time available), one person to ready my briefing book each evening so I can prepare for the next day's schedule, and two people to "advance" me by making sure I get where I'm supposed to be and depart on time. All of them now join Tom and Kitty as guardians of the bubble.

"How do you decide what I do and what gets through to me?" I ask Kitty.

"We have you do and see what you'd choose if you had time to examine all the options yourself—sifting through all the phone calls, letters, memos, and meeting invitations," she says simply.

"But how can you possibly *know* what I'd choose for myself?"

"Don't worry," Kitty says patiently. "We know."

They have no way of knowing. We've worked together only a few weeks. Clare and I have lived together for a quarter century and even she wouldn't know.

I trust Tom and Kitty. They share my values. I hired them because I sensed this, and everything they've done since then has confirmed it. But it's not a matter of trust.

The *real* criterion Tom and Kitty use (whether or not they know it or admit it) is their own experienced view of what a secretary of labor with my values and aspirations *should* choose to see and hear. They transmit to me through the bubble only those letters, phone calls, memoranda, people, meetings, and events which they believe *someone like me* ought to have. But if I see and hear only what "someone like me" should see and hear, no original or out-of-the-ordinary thought will ever permeate the bubble. I'll never be surprised or shocked. I'll never be forced to rethink or reevaluate anything. I'll just lumber along, blissfully ignorant of what I *really* need to see and hear—which are things that don't merely confirm my preconceptions about the world.

I make a list of what I want them to transmit through the bubble henceforth:

1. The angriest, meanest ass-kicking letters we get from the public every week.

2. Complaints from department employees about anything.

3. Bad news about fuck-ups, large and small.

4. Ideas, ideas, ideas: from department employees, from outside academics and researchers, from average citizens. Anything that even resembles a good idea about what we should do better or differently. Don't screen out the wacky ones.

5. Anything from the President or members of Congress.

6. A random sample of calls or letters from real people outside Washington, outside government—people who aren't lawyers, investment bankers, politicians, or business consultants; people who aren't professionals; people without college degrees.

7. "Town meetings" with department employees here at headquarters and in the regions. "Town meetings" in working-class and poor areas of the country. "Town meetings" in community colleges, with adult students.

8. Calls and letters from business executives, including those who hate my guts. Set up meetings with some of them.

9. Lunch meetings with small groups of department employees, randomly chosen from all ranks.

10. Meetings with conservative Republicans in Congress.

I send the memo to Tom and Kitty. Then, still feeling rebellious and with nothing on my schedule for the next hour (the NEC meeting scheduled for 3:00 was canceled) I simply walk out of the bubble. I sneak out of my big office by the back entrance and start down the corridor.

I take the elevator to floors I've never visited. I wander to places in the department I've never been. I have spontaneous conversations with employees I'd never otherwise see. *Free at last.*

Kitty discovers I'm missing. It's as if the warden had discovered an escape from the state pen. The alarm is sounded: Secretary loose! Secretary escapes from bubble! Find the Secretary! Security guards are dispatched.

By now I've wandered to the farthest reaches of the building, to corridors never before walked by anyone ranking higher than GS-12. I visit the mailroom, the printshop, the basement workshop.

The hour is almost up. Time to head back. But which way? I'm at the northernmost outpost of the building, in bureaucratic Siberia. I try to retrace my steps but keep coming back to the same point in the wilderness.

I'm lost.

In the end, of course, a security guard finds me and takes me back to the bubble. Kitty isn't pleased. "You shouldn't do that," she says sternly. "We were worried."

"It was good for me." I'm defiant.

"We need to know where you *are*." She sounds like the mother of a young juvenile delinquent.

"Next time give me a beeper, and I'll call home to see if you need me."

"You *must* have someone with you. It's not safe."

"This is the Labor Department, not Bosnia."

"You might get lost."

"That's *ridiculous*. How in hell could someone get *lost* in this building?"

She knows she has me. "You'd be surprised." She smiles knowingly and heads back to her office. . . .

March 14 Washington

Tom and Kitty suggest I conduct a "town meeting" of Labor Department employees here at headquarters—give them an opportunity to ask me questions and me a chance to express my views. After all, I've been here almost eight weeks and presumably have a few answers and one or two views.

Some of the other senior staff think it unwise. They point to the risk of gathering thousands of employees together in one place with access to microphones. The cumulative frustrations from years of not being listened to by political appointees could explode when exposed to the open air, like a dangerous gas. Gripes, vendettas, personal slights, hurts, malfeasance, nonfeasance, mistreatments, slurs, lies, deceptions, frauds. Who knows what might be in that incendiary mix?

Secretaries of labor have come and gone, usually within two years. Assistant secretaries, even faster. Only a tiny fraction of Labor Department employees are appointed to their jobs because of who's occupying the White House. The vast majority are career employees, here because they got their jobs through the civil service. Most of them will remain here for decades, some for their entire careers. They have come as lawyers, accountants, economists, investigators, clerks, secretaries, and custodians. Government doesn't pay as well as the private sector, but the jobs are more secure. And some have come because they believe that public service is inherently important.

But for years they've been treated like shit. Republican appointees were often contemptuous of or uninterested in most of what went on here. The Reagan and Bush administrations didn't exactly put workplace issues at the top of their agenda. In fact, Reagan slashed the department's budget and reduced the number of employees by about a quarter. His first appointee as secretary of labor was a building contractor.

The career people don't harbor much more trust for Democrats. It's an article of faith among civil servants that political appointees, of whatever party, care only about the immediate future. They won't be here years from now to implement fully their jazzy ideas, or to pick up the pieces if the ideas fall apart. Career civil servants would prefer not to take short-term risks. They don't want headlines. Even if the headlines are positive, headlines draw extra attention, and in Washington attention can be dangerous.

There is a final reason for their cynicism. Career civil servants feel unappreciated by politicians. Every presidential candidate since Carter has run as a Washington "outsider," against the permanent Washington establishment. Almost every congressional and senatorial candidate decries the "faceless bureaucrats" who are assumed to wield unaccountable power. Career civil servants are easy targets. They can't talk back. This scapegoating parallels the public's mounting contempt for Washington. In opinion polls conducted during the Eisenhower administration, about seventy-five percent of the American public thought that their government "could be trusted to act in the public interest most of the time." In a recent poll, only twenty-five percent expressed similar sentiments. But career civil servants aren't to blame. The disintegration has come on the heels of mistakes and improprieties by political leaders—Vietnam, Watergate, the Iran-*contra* imbroglio, the savings-and-loan scandal. And it accelerated as the nation emerged from five decades of Depression, hot war, and cold war—common experiences that forced us to band together and support a strong government—into a global economy without clear borders or evil empires.

Our "town meeting" is set for noon. A small stage is erected on one side of a huge open hall on the first floor of the department. The hall is about the size of football field. On its walls are paintings of former secretaries of labor.

I walk in exactly at noon. Nervous (Wasn't President James Garfield assassinated by a disgruntled civil servant?)

The hall is jammed with thousands of people. Many are sitting on folding chairs, tightly packed around the makeshift stage. Others are standing. Several hundred are standing on risers around the outer perimeter, near the walls. Is it legal for so many employees to be packed so tightly in one place? Tomorrow's Washington *Post*: Labor Secretary Endangers Workers. Subhead: Violates the Occupational Safety and Health Act.

I make my way up to the small stage and face the crowd. I don't want to speak from behind a lectern, because to see over it I'd have to stand on a stool and would look ridiculous. So I hold the microphone. The crowd quiets.

"Hello."

"Hello!" they roar back in unison. Laughter. A good start, anyway. . . .

"Who's first?" I scan the crowd—left, center, right. No hands. I'm back in the classroom, first class of the semester. I've asked the question, but no one wants to break the ice. They have plenty to say, but no one dares. So I'll do what I always do: I'll just stand here silently, smiling, until someone gets up the courage. I can bear the silence.

I wait. Thirty seconds. Forty-five seconds. A minute. Thousands of people here, but no sound. They seem startled. I know they have all sorts of opinions about what should be done. They share them with each other every day. But have they ever shared them directly with the Secretary?

Finally, one timid hand in the air. I point to her. "Yes! You! What's your name?" All eyes on her. The crowd explodes into rumbles, murmurs, and laughs, like a huge lung exhaling. A cordless mike is passed to her.

"Connie," she answers, nervously.

I move to the front of the stage so I can see Connie better. "Which agency do you work in, Connie?"

"Employment Standards."

"What's your idea?"

Connie's voice is unsteady, but she's determined. "Well, I don't see why we need to fill out time cards when we come to work and when we leave. It's silly and demeaning."

Applause. Connie is buoyed by the response, and her voice grows stronger. "I mean, if someone is dishonest they'll just fill in the wrong times anyway. Our supervisors know when we come and go. The work has to get done. Besides, we're professionals. Why treat us like children?"

I look over at Tom. He shrugs his shoulders: Why not?

"Okay, done. Starting tomorrow, no more time cards."

For a moment, silence. The audience seems stunned. Then a loud roar of approval that breaks into wild applause. Many who were seated stand and cheer.

What have I done? I haven't doubled their salaries or sent them on all-expenses-paid vacations to Hawaii. All I did was accept a suggestion that seemed reasonable. But for people who have grown accustomed to being ignored, I think I just delivered an important gift.

The rest of the meeting isn't quite as buoyant. Some suggestions I reject outright (a thirty-five-hour workweek). Others I write down and defer for further consideration. But I learn a great deal. I hear ideas I never would have thought of. One thin and balding man from the Employment and Training Administration has a commonsensical one: When newly unemployed people register for unemployment insurance, why not determine whether their layoff is likely to be permanent or temporary— and if permanent, get them retraining and job-placement services right away instead of waiting until their benefits almost run out? He has evidence this will shorten the average length of unemployment and save billions of dollars. I say I'll look into it. . . .

September 20 Washington

Tom tells me that calls are pouring in from members of Congress demanding that unemployment benefits be extended beyond their normal six months. "We've got to find several billion dollars, quick," says Tom. But I don't know where to find the money other than taking it out of job counseling and training—which would be nuts.

"We *won't* extend unemployment benefits if it means less money for finding new jobs!" I'm defiant.

"I don't think you have a choice," says Tom. "People just don't believe there're new jobs out there. All they know is they had a job. They think it's coming back eventually, and they need money to live on in the meantime."

Kitty rushes in. "I've got it!"

"What?"

"The *answer*. Remember the fellow at the department town meeting who had the idea for fixing the unemployment system?"

"Vaguely." I recall a tall, hollow-eyed career employee who spoke toward the end.

"He suggested that when newly unemployed people apply for unemployment insurance they're screened to determine whether their layoff is temporary or permanent—and if *permanent* they immediately get help finding a new job. *Well* . . . " Kitty pauses to catch her breath. "I spoke with him at some length this morning. His name is Steve Wandner. Seems that a few years ago he ran a pilot project for the department, trying his idea out. Get *this*: Where he tried it, the average length of unemployment dropped two to four weeks! The poor guy has been trying to sell the idea since then, but no one has ever listened."

"I don't get it. How does this help us?"

"Think of it! Do what he did all over the country, and cut the average length of unemployment two to four weeks. This saves the government $400 million a year in unemployment benefits. That's $2 billion over the next five years, if you need help with the math."

"I understand the math. I just don't understand the *point*. So what? That's money saved in the *future*. How does that get us the money we need now?"

Kitty stares at me with her usual what-is-this-man-doing-as-a-cabinet-member expression. "If we can show that we'll save this money over the next five years, we can use it *now* to offset extra unemployment benefits. It's like extra *cash*!" She lunges toward a stack of paper on the corner of my desk and tosses the entire pile into the air. "Manna *from heaven*!"

"I still don't get it. And by the way, you're making a mess."

Kitty is excited, but she talks slowly, as if to a recent graduate of kindergarten. "Try to *understand*. The federal budget law requires that if you want to spend more money, you've got to get the money from somewhere else. Right? One place you can get it is from future savings, but only if the Congressional Budget Office believes you. Follow me?"

"I think so."

"Now comes our brilliant geek from the bowels of the Labor Department with *proof* that we can save around $2 billion during the next five years. And the true *beauty* of it"—Kitty beams—"is that this reform brings us a step closer to what *you've* been talking about. We get a law providing emergency extra unemployment benefits—$2 billion worth—covering the next few months. And *at the same time* we permanently change the whole system so that it's more focused on finding new jobs. It's a twofer! A win-win! Nobody can vote against it! I *love* it!"

I look at Tom. "Is she right?"

"Yup." Tom is impressed.

Kitty begins to dance around the office. She is the only person I have ever met who can fall in love with proposed legislation. . . .

November 24 *The White House*

B sits at his elaborately carved desk in the Oval Office before the usual gaggle of cameras and spotlights. Clustered tightly around him in order to get into the shot are five smiling senators and ten smiling House members. B utters some sentences about why people who have lost their jobs shouldn't have to worry that their unemployment benefits will run out. He signs the bill into law. The congressmen applaud. He stands and shakes each of their hands. The spotlights go out and the cameras are packed away. The whole thing takes less than five minutes.

Kitty is here, smiling from ear to ear. I congratulate her.

Against a far wall, behind the small crowd, I see Steve Wandner, the hollow-eyed Labor Department employee who first suggested the idea that was just signed into law. I made sure Steve was invited to this signing ceremony. I walk over to where he's standing.

"Good job." I extend my hand.

He hesitates a moment. "I never thought . . . " His voice trails off.

"I want to introduce you to the President."

Steve is reluctant. I pull his elbow and guide him toward where B is chatting energetically with several members of Congress who still encircle him. They're talking football—big men, each over six feet, laughing, telling stories, bonding. It's a veritable huddle. We wait on the periphery.

Several White House aides try to coax the group out of the Oval. It's early in the day, and B is already hopelessly behind schedule. Steve wants to exit, but I motion him to stay put.

The herd begins to move. I see an opening. "Mr. President!" B turns, eyes dancing. He's having fun. It's a good day: signing legislation, talking sports. It's been a good few months: the budget victory, the Middle East peace accord, the NAFTA victory. He's winning, and he can feel it. And when B is happy, the happiness echoes through the White House like a sweet song.

"Come here, pal." B draws me toward him and drapes an arm around my shoulders. I feel like a favorite pet.

"Mr. President, I want you to meet the man who came up with the idea for today's legislation." I motion Steve forward.

With his left arm still around my shoulders, B extends his right hand to Steve, who takes it as if it were an Olympic trophy.

"Good work," is all B says to Steve, but B's tight grip and his fleeting you-are-the-only-person-in-the-world-who-matters gaze into Steve's eyes light the man up, giving him a glow I hadn't thought possible.

It's over in a flash. B turns away to respond to a staffer who has urgently whispered something into his ear. But Steve doesn't move. The hand that had been in the presidential grip falls slowly to his side. He stares in B's direction. The afterglow remains.

I have heard tales of people who are moved by a profound religious experience, whose lives of torment or boredom are suddenly transformed, who actually *look* different because they have found Truth and Meaning. Steve Wandner—the gangly, diffident career bureaucrat who has traipsed to his office at the Labor Department every workday for twenty years, slowly chipping away at the same large rock, answering to the same career executives, coping with silly demands by low-level political appointees to do this or that, seeing the same problems and making the same suggestions and sensing that nothing will ever really change—has now witnessed the impossible. His idea has become the law of the land. . . .

PART SEVEN

The Judiciary

38

ALEXANDER HAMILTON

From *The Federalist* 78

The 1787 Federalist Papers have been quoted extensively in earlier sections of this book. The most famous selections belong to James Madison, writing about separation of powers and federalism. The Federalist actually had three authors: Madison, Alexander Hamilton, and John Jay. In No. 78, Hamilton expounds on the judicial branch. He makes a strong case for an independent judiciary, separate from the legislative and executive branches. He discusses the lifetime appointment of federal judges. Hamilton was a strong proponent of the courts' power, and as such, he believed that the Supreme Court should have the right to declare an act of Congress unconstitutional. This enormous power, termed judicial review, is explained and justified here by Hamilton, although it was not explicitly stated in the Constitution. In 1803, Chief Justice John Marshall established the precedent for the Supreme Court's use of judicial review in the landmark Marbury v. Madison *case. The year after Marshall's decision, Alexander Hamilton was killed in a duel with Vice-President Aaron Burr.*

No. 78: Hamilton

WE PROCEED now to an examination of the judiciary department of the proposed government. . . .

Whoever attentively considers the different departments of power must perceive that, in a government in which they are separated from each other, the judiciary, from the nature of its functions, will always be the least dangerous to the political rights of the Constitution; because it will be least in a capacity to annoy or injure them. The executive not only dispenses the honors but holds the sword of the community. The legislature not only commands the purse but prescribes the rules by which the duties and rights of every citizen are to be regulated. The judiciary, on the contrary, has no influence over either the sword or the purse; no direction either of the strength or of the wealth of the society, and can take no active resolution whatever. It may truly be said to have neither FORCE nor WILL but merely judgment; and must ultimately depend upon the aid of the executive arm even for the efficacy of its judgments.

This simple view of the matter suggests several important consequences. It proves incontestably that the judiciary is beyond comparison the weakest of the three departments of power;* that it can never attack with success either of the other two; and that all possible care is requisite to enable it to defend itself against their attacks. It equally proves that though individual oppression may now and then proceed from the courts of justice, the general liberty of the people can never be endangered from that quarter; I mean so long as the judiciary remains truly distinct from both the legislature and the executive. For I agree that "there is no liberty if the power of judging be not separated from the legislative and executive powers." And it proves, in the last place, that as liberty can have nothing to fear from the judiciary alone, but would have everything to fear from its union with either of the other departments; that as all the effects of such a union must ensue from a dependence of the former on the latter, notwithstanding a nominal and apparent separation; that as, from the natural feebleness of the judiciary, it is in continual jeopardy of being overpowered, awed, or influenced by its co-ordinate branches; and that as nothing can contribute so much to its firmness and independence as permanency in office, this quality may therefore be justly regarded as an indispensable ingredient in its constitution, and, in a great measure, as the citadel of the public justice and the public security.

The complete independence of the courts of justice is peculiarly essential in a limited Constitution. By a limited Constitution, I understand one which contains certain specified exceptions to the legislative authority; such, for instance, as that it shall pass no bills of attainder, no *ex post facto* laws, and the like. Limitations of this kind can be preserved in practice no other way than through the medium of courts of justice, whose duty it must be to declare all acts contrary to the manifest tenor of the Constitution void. Without this, all the reservations of particular rights or privileges would amount to nothing.

Some perplexity respecting the rights of the courts to pronounce legislative acts void, because contrary to the Constitution, has arisen from an imagination that the doctrine would imply a superiority of the judiciary to the legislative power. It is urged that the authority which can declare the acts of another void must necessarily be superior to the one whose acts may be declared void. As this doctrine is of great importance in all the American constitutions, a brief discussion of the grounds on which it rests cannot be unacceptable.

There is no position which depends on clearer principles than that

*The celebrated Montesquieu, speaking of them, says: "Of the three powers above mentioned, the JUDICIARY is next to nothing."—*Spirit of Laws*,Vol. I, page 186.

every act of a delegated authority, contrary to the tenor of the commission under which it is exercised, is void. No legislative act, therefore, contrary to the Constitution, can be valid. To deny this would be to affirm that the deputy is greater than his principal; that the servant is above his master; that the representatives of the people are superior to the people themselves; that men acting by virtue of powers may do not only what their powers do not authorize, but what they forbid.

If it be said that the legislative body are themselves the constitutional judges of their own powers and that the construction they put upon them is conclusive upon the other departments it may be answered that this cannot be the natural presumption where it is not to be collected from any particular provisions in the Constitution. It is not otherwise to be supposed that the Constitution could intend to enable the representatives of the people to substitute their *will* to that of their constituents. It is far more rational to suppose that the courts were designed to be an intermediate body between the people and the legislature in order, among other things, to keep the latter within the limits assigned to their authority. The interpretation of the laws is the proper and peculiar province of the courts. A constitution is, in fact, and must be regarded by the judges as, a fundamental law. It therefore belongs to them to ascertain its meaning as well as the meaning of any particular act proceeding from the legislative body. If there should happen to be an irreconcilable variance between the two, that which has the superior obligation and validity ought, of course, to be preferred; or, in other words, the Constitution ought to be preferred to the statute, the intention of the people to the intention of their agents.

Nor does this conclusion by any means suppose a superiority of the judicial to the legislative power. It only supposes that the power of the people is superior to both, and that where the will of the legislature, declared in its statutes, stands in opposition to that of the people, declared in the Constitution, the judges ought to be governed by the latter rather than the former. They ought to regulate their decisions by the fundamental laws rather than by those which are not fundamental. . . .

If, then, the courts of justice are to be considered as the bulwarks of a limited Constitution against legislative encroachments, this consideration will afford a strong argument for the permanent tenure of judicial offices, since nothing will contribute so much as this to that independent spirit in the judges which must be essential to the faithful performance of so arduous a duty.

This independence of the judges is equally requisite to guard the Constitution and the rights of individuals from the effects of those ill humors which the arts of designing men, or the influence of particular conjunctures, sometimes disseminate among the people themselves, and which, though they speedily give place to better information, and more deliberate reflection, have a tendency, in the meantime, to occasion dangerous innovations in the government, and serious oppressions of the minor party in the community. Though I trust the friends of the proposed Constitution will never concur with its enemies in questioning that fundamental principle of republican government which admits the right of the people to alter or abolish the established Constitution whenever they find it inconsistent with their happiness; yet it is not to be inferred from this principle that the representatives of the people, whenever a momentary inclination happens to lay hold of a majority of their constituents incompatible with the provisions in the existing Constitution would, on that account, be justifiable in a violation of those provisions; or that the courts would be under a greater obligation to connive at infractions in this shape than when they had proceeded wholly from the cabals of the representative body. Until the people have, by some solemn and authoritative act, annulled or changed the established form, it is binding upon themselves collectively, as well as individually; and no presumption, or even knowledge of their sentiments, can warrant their representatives in a departure from it prior to such an act. But it is easy to see that it would require an uncommon portion of fortitude in the judges to do their duty as faithful guardians of the Constitution, where legislative invasions of it had been instigated by the major voice of the community.

But it is not with a view to infractions of the Constitution only that the independence of the judges may be an essential safeguard against the effects of occasional ill humors in the society. These sometimes extend no farther than to the injury of the private rights of particular classes of citizens, by unjust and partial laws. Here also the firmness of the judicial magistracy is of vast importance in mitigating the severity and confining the operation of such laws. It not only serves to moderate the immediate mischiefs of those which may have been passed but it operates as a check upon the legislative body in passing them; who, perceiving that obstacles to the success of an iniquitous intention are to be expected from the scruples of the courts, are in a manner compelled, by the very motives of the injustice they meditate, to qualify their attempts. This is a circumstance calculated to have more influence upon the character of our governments than but few may be aware of. The benefits of the integrity and moderation of the judiciary have already been felt in more States than one; and though they may have displeased those whose sinister expectations they may have disappointed, they must have commanded the esteem and applause of all the virtuous and disinterested. Considerate men of every description ought to prize whatever will tend to beget or fortify that temper in the courts; as no man can be sure that he may not be to-morrow the victim of a spirit of injustice, by which he may be a gainer today. And every man must now feel that the inevitable tendency of such a spirit is to sap the foundations of public and private confidence and to introduce in its stead universal distrust and distress. . . . *Publius*

39

DAVID O'BRIEN

From *Storm Center*

Professor David O'Brien's fine book on the Supreme Court touches on many landmark cases in constitutional law. Few are more important than Brown v. Board of Education of Topeka, Kansas. *Today's students of American government often take* Brown *for granted, since they've lived with the Court's ruling their whole lives; thus they may forget the dramatic events surrounding the 1954 decision. In this excerpt O'Brien revisits the first* Brown *case, as well as* Brown II, *exploring the delicate relationship between the Court and public opinion. He then goes back to President Franklin Roosevelt's infamous 1937 "court-packing" scheme to illustrate another aspect of the impact of public opinion on the judiciary. Unlike the citizenry's direct and immediate reaction to Congress and the president, the communication of views between the public and the judiciary is less easy to measure, O'Brien acknowledges. Yet the Supreme Court lies, as it should, at the heart of the process that resolves the nation's monumental political issues.*

"WHY DOES the Supreme Court pass the school desegregation case?" asked one of Chief Justice Vinson's law clerks in 1952. *Brown v. Board of Education of Topeka, Kansas* had arrived on the Court's docket in 1951, but it was carried over for oral argument the next term and then consolidated with four other cases and reargued in December 1953. The landmark ruling did not come down until May 17, 1954. "Well," Justice Frankfurter explained, "we're holding it for the election"—1952 was a presidential election year. "You're holding it for the election?" The clerk persisted in disbelief. "I thought the Supreme Court was supposed to decide cases without regard to elections." "When you have a major social political issue of this magnitude," timing and public reactions are important considerations, and, Frankfurter continued, "we do not think this is the time to decide it." Similarly, Tom Clark has recalled that the Court awaited, over Douglas's dissent, additional cases from the District of Columbia and other regions, so as "to get a national coverage, rather than a sectional one." Such political considerations are by no means unique. "We often delay adjudication. It's not a question of evading at all," Clark concluded. "It's just the practicalities of life—common sense."

Denied the power of the sword or the purse, the Court must cultivate its institutional prestige. The power of the Court lies in the pervasiveness of its rulings and ultimately rests with other political institutions and public opinion. As an independent force, the Court has no chance to resolve great issues of public policy. *Dred Scott v. Sandford* (1857) and *Brown v. Board of Education* (1954) illustrate the limitations of Supreme Court policymaking. The "great folly," as Senator Henry Cabot Lodge characterized *Dred Scott*, was not the Court's interpretation of the Constitution or the unpersuasive moral position that blacks were not persons under the Constitution. Rather, "the attempt of the Court to settle the slavery question by judicial decision was simple madness." . . . A hundred years later, political struggles within the country and, notably, presidential and congressional leadership in enforcing the Court's school desegregation ruling saved the moral appeal of *Brown* from becoming another "great folly."

Because the Court's decisions are not self-executing, public reactions inevitably weigh on the minds of the justices. . . .

. . . Opposition to the school desegregation ruling in *Brown* led to bitter, sometimes violent confrontations. In Little Rock, Arkansas, Governor Orval Faubus encouraged disobedience by southern segregationists. The federal National Guard had to be called out to maintain order. The school board in Little Rock unsuccessfully pleaded, in *Cooper v. Aaron* (1958), for the Court's postponement of the implementation of *Brown's* mandate. In the midst of the controversy, Frankfurter worried that Chief Justice Warren's attitude had become "more like that of a fighting politician than that of a judicial statesman." In such confrontations between the Court and the country, "the transcending issue," Frankfurter reminded the brethren, remains that of preserving "the Supreme Court as the authoritative organ of what the Constitution requires." When the justices move too far or too fast in their interpretation of the Constitution, they threaten public acceptance of the Court's legitimacy.

The political struggles of the Court (and among the justices) continue after the writing of opinions and final votes. Announcements of decisions trigger diverse reactions from the media, interest groups, lower courts, Congress, the President, and the general public. Their reactions may enhance or thwart compliance and reinforce or undermine the Court's prestige. Opinion days thus may reveal something of the political struggles that might otherwise remain hidden within the marble temple. They may also mark the beginning of larger political struggles for influence in the country. . . .

When deciding major issues of public law and policy, justices must consider strategies for getting public acceptance of their rulings. When

striking down the doctrine of "separate but equal" facilities in 1954 in
Brown v. Board of Education (Brown I), for instance, the Warren Court waited a year before issuing, in *Brown II*, its mandate for "all deliberate speed"
in ending racial segregation in public education.

Resistance to the social policy announced in *Brown I* was expected. A
rigid timetable for desegregation would only intensify opposition. During
oral arguments on *Brown II*, devoted to the question of what kind of decree the Court should issue to enforce *Brown*, Warren confronted the hard
fact of southern resistance. The attorney for South Carolina, S. Emory
Rogers, pressed for an open-ended decree—one that would not specify
when and how desegregation should take place. He boldly proclaimed

> Mr. Chief Justice, to say we will conform depends on the decree handed
> down. I am frank to tell you, right now [in] our district I do not think that we will
> send—[that] the white people of the district will send their children to the Negro
> schools. It would be unfair to tell the Court that we are going to do that. I do not
> think it is. But I do think that something can be worked out. We hope so.

"It is not a question of attitude," Warren shot back, "it is a question of
conforming to the decree." Their heated exchange continued as follows:

> CHIEF JUSTICE WARREN: But you are not willing to say here that there
>   would be an honest attempt to conform to this decree, if we did leave
>   it to the district court [to implement]?
> MR. ROGERS: No, I am not. Let us get the word "honest" out of there.
> CHIEF JUSTICE WARREN: No, leave it in.
> MR. ROGERS: No, because I would have to tell you that right now we
>   would not conform—we would not send our white children to the
>   negro schools. . . .

Agreement emerged that the Court should issue a short opinion-
decree. In a memorandum, Warren summarized the main points of agreement. The opinion should simply state that *Brown I* held radically segregated public schools to be unconstitutional. *Brown II* should acknowledge
that the ruling creates various administrative problems, but emphasize that
"local school authorities have the primary responsibility for assessing and
solving these problems; [and] the courts will have to consider these problems in determining whether the efforts of local school authorities" are in
good-faith compliance. . . .

Enforcement and implementation required the cooperation and coordination of all three branches. Little progress could be made, as Assistant Attorney General Pollack has explained, "where historically there
had been slavery and a long tradition of discrimination [until] all three
branches of the federal government [could] be lined up in support of a

movement forward or a requirement for change." The election of Nixon in 1968 then brought changes both in the policies of the executive branch and in the composition of the Court. The simplicity and flexibility of *Brown*, moreover, invited evasion. It produced a continuing struggle over measures, such as gerrymandering school district lines and busing in the 1970s and 1980s, because the mandate itself had evolved from one of ending segregation to one of securing integration in public schools. . . .

"By itself," the political scientist Robert Dahl observed, "the Court is almost powerless to affect the course of national policy." *Brown* dramatically altered the course of American life, but it also reflected the justices' awareness that their decisions are not self-executing. The rulings [in] *Brown* . . . were unanimous but ambiguous. The ambiguity in the desegregation rulings . . . was the price of achieving unanimity. Unanimity appeared necessary if the Court was to preserve its institutional prestige while pursuing revolutionary change in social policy. Justices sacrificed their own policy preferences for more precise guidelines, while the Court tolerated lengthy delays in recognition of the costs of open defiance and the pressures of public opinion. . . .

Public opinion serves to curb the Court when it threatens to go too far or too fast in its rulings. The Court has usually been in step with major political movements, except during transitional periods or critical elections. It would nevertheless be wrong to conclude, along with Peter Finley Dunne's fictional Mr. Dooley, that "th' supreme court follows th' iliction returns." To be sure, the battle over FDR's "Court-packing" plan and the Court's "switch-in-time-that-saved-nine" in 1937 gives that impression. Public opinion supported the New Deal, but turned against FDR after his landslide reelection in 1936 when he proposed to "pack the Court" by increasing its size from nine to fifteen. In a series of five-to-four and six-to-three decisions in 1935–1936, the Court had struck down virtually every important measure of FDR's New Deal program. But in the spring of 1937, while the Senate Judiciary Committee considered FDR's proposal, the Court abruptly handed down three five-to-four rulings upholding major pieces of New Deal legislation. Shortly afterward, FDR's close personal friend and soon-to-be nominee for the Court, Felix Frankfurter, wrote Justice Stone confessing that he was "not wholly happy in thinking that Mr. Dooley should, in the course of history turn out to have been one of the most distinguished legal philosophers." Frankfurter, of course, knew that justices do not simply follow the election returns. The influence of public opinion is more subtle and complex.

Life in the marble temple is not immune from shifts in public opinion. . . . The justices, however, deny being directly influenced by public opinion. The Court's prestige rests on preserving the public's view that justices base their decisions on interpretations of the law, rather than on their personal policy preferences. Yet, complete indifference to public opinion would be the height of judicial arrogance. . . .

"The powers exercised by this Court are inherently oligarchic," Frankfurter once observed when pointing out that "[t]he Court is not saved from being oligarchic because it professes to act in the service of humane ends." Judicial review is antidemocratic. But the Court's power stems from its duty to give authoritative meaning to the Constitution, and rests with the persuasive forces of reason, institutional prestige, the cooperation of other political institutions, and, ultimately, public opinion. The country, in a sense, saves the justices from being an oligarchy by curbing the Court when it goes too far or too fast with its policy-making. Violent opposition and resistance, however, threaten not merely the Court's prestige but the very idea of a government under law.

Some Court watchers, and occasionally even the justices, warn of "an imperial judiciary" and a "government by the judiciary." For much of the Court's history, though, the work of the justices has not involved major issues of public policy. In most areas of public law and policy, the fact that the Court decides an issue is more important than what it decides. Relatively few of the many issues of domestic and foreign policy that arise in government reach the Court. When the Court does decide major questions of public policy, it does so by bringing political controversies within the language, structure, and spirit of the Constitution. By deciding only immediate cases, the Court infuses constitutional meaning into the resolution of the larger surrounding political controversies. But by itself the Court cannot lay those controversies to rest.

The Court can profoundly influence American life. As a guardian of the Constitution, the Court sometimes invites controversy by challenging majoritarian sentiments to respect the rights of minorities and the principles of a representative democracy. The Court's influence is usually more subtle and indirect, varying over time and from one policy issue to another. In the end, the Court's influence on American life cannot be measured precisely, because its policy-making is inextricably bound up with that of other political institutions. Major confrontations in constitutional politics, like those over school desegregation, school prayer, and abortion, are determined as much by what is possible in a system of free government and in a pluralistic society as by what the Court says about the meaning of the Constitution. At its best, the Court appeals to the country to respect the substantive value choices of human dignity and self-governance embedded in our written Constitution.

40

DAVID YALOF

From *Pursuit of Justices*

In selecting nominees to the Supreme Court, the president faces a daunting task. Legal scholar David Yalof takes readers inside the process, pointing out the many factions in the nation, in the branches of government, and even within the president's own circle that must be considered when making a nomination. The president today has access to large amounts of information about a potential justice, but so does everyone else in the political process. After all, remember that a Supreme Court justice is often the most significant and long lasting legacy that a president leaves behind.

ON JUNE 27, 1992, the Supreme Court inserted itself once again into the national debate over abortion with its surprising decision in *Planned Parenthood v. Casey*. Specifically, five of the nine justices refused to cast aside *Roe v. Wade*, the Court's controversial 1973 opinion establishing a constitutional right to abortion. Included among *Roe*'s saviors that day were Sandra Day O'Connor and Anthony Kennedy, both appointees of former President Ronald Reagan. As a candidate for the presidency in 1980 and 1984, Reagan had supported a constitutional amendment to overturn *Roe*, a ruling considered to be among the most vilified of public targets for social conservatives in his party. As president, Reagan had publicly promised to appoint justices to the Supreme Court willing to reverse *Roe v. Wade*. Yet just the opposite occurred in *Casey*: a majority of the Court reaffirmed the core right to privacy first discovered in *Roe*. And in a touch of irony, two of President Reagan's own nominees had played significant roles in safeguarding the decision from the Court's conservatives.

Obviously the selection of Supreme Court nominees is among the president's most significant duties. Yet as the outcome in *Casey* demonstrates, it is a task beset with difficulties and potential frustrations. On one hand, a president ordinarily tries to choose a nominee whose influence will reach beyond the current political environment. As a beneficiary of life tenure, a justice may well extend that president's legacy on judicial matters long into the future. Yet in selecting a nominee the president must also successfully maneuver through that immediate environment, lest he suffer politically or (as in some cases) see his nominee rejected by the Senate outright. In recent years internal strife and factionalism within the executive branch have only further complicated what was already a delicate undertaking. . . .

A central question remains: why were these particular candidates chosen over others possessing similar—and in some cases superior—qualifications? The classic "textbook" portrayal of the Supreme Court nomination process depicts presidents as choosing Supreme Court justices more for their judicial politics than for their judicial talents. By this version of events, presidents, by nominating justices whose political views appear compatible with their own, try to gain increased influence over the Supreme Court. Once on the Court, a justice may then satisfy or disappoint the appointing president by his decisions. Such an oversimplified view of nomination politics usually ignores the more complex political environment in which modern presidents must act, including the various intricacies and nuances of executive branch politics.

. . . I contend that modern presidents are often forced to arbitrate among factions within their own administrations, each pursuing its own interests and agendas in the selection process. At first glance, presidential reliance on numerous high-level officials equipped with a variety of perspectives might seem a logical response to the often hostile and unpredictable political environment that surrounds modern appointments to the Court. Yet conflicts within the administration itself may have a debilitating effect on that president's overall interests. High-level advisors may be sincerely pursuing their own conceptions of what makes up the administration's best interests; but to achieve their own maximum preferred outcomes, they may feel compelled to skew the presentation of critical information, if not leave it out altogether. In recent administrations the final choice of a nominee has usually reflected one advisor's hard-won victory over his rivals, without necessarily accounting for the president's other political interests. . . .

The New Deal marked the beginning of a fundamental transformation in American politics. A national economic crisis demanded national solutions, and the government in Washington grew exponentially to meet these new demands. Beginning in the 1930s, the federal government entered one policy area after another that had previously been the exclusive province of state governments. Emergency conditions required quick institutional responses, and the executive branch in particular was drawn into critical aspects of national policymaking. Just as the character of national politics changed dramatically, the Supreme Court was undergoing a transformation of its own. Fundamental changes in the political landscape affecting Supreme Court appointments were a by-product of these chang-es. At least ten critical developments in American politics substantially al-tered the character of the modern selection process for justices:

1. The *growth and bureaucratization of the Justice Department* facilitated the investment of considerable manpower and other resources towards the consideration of prospective Supreme Court candidates. As the size of the national government grew dramatically during the early twentieth cen-tury, the government's overall legal responsibilities quickly expanded. Congress reacted by increasing the size of the Justice Department and transferring to it most litigating functions from other federal agencies. Armed with a full staff of attorneys and more extensive bureaucratic sup-port, attorneys general in modern times have enjoyed more regular input into the selection of Supreme Court nominees, often consulting with the president well before a vacancy on the Court even arises. . . .

2. The *growth and bureaucratization of the White House* has also had an impact on the nomination process. The White House staff, once limited to a handful of personal assistants, was barely a factor in political decision-making for most of the nineteenth and early twentieth centuries. Starting with Franklin Roosevelt's administration, however, the White House staff experienced prodigious growth, expanding from just thirty-seven em-ployees in the early 1930s to more than nine hundred by the late 1980s. As the modern presidency has brought more policymaking activities within the White House, the White House staff has increasingly figured in mat-ters of high presidential priority.

Modern presidents often rely on the White House Counsel's Office to assist them in screening and selecting prospective Supreme Court nomi-nees. Thus, increasingly, the attorney general's most constant and genuine competitor for influence has been the White House Counsel. Theodore Sorenson, John Kennedy's special counsel, asserted that his duties did not overlap with the attorney general's; rather he was involved "as a policy advisor to the president with respect to legislation, with respect to his programs and messages, with respect to executive orders, and with respect to those few formally legal problems, which come to the White House." But those supposed lines of demarcation have blurred considerably dur-ing the past thirty years. Today, a president has at his disposal two distinct organizations, each with its own bureaucratic resources; the president may rely on either or both offices for counsel concerning the selection of Su-preme Court nominees.

3. Paralleling the increased role for national political institutions in American life has been the *growth in size and influence of federal courts.* Con-gress's willingness in the past to meet increased caseloads with new judge-

ships has steadily multiplied the president's opportunities to place his imprint on lower court policymaking. The total number of district and
circuit judgeships rose from under two hundred in 1930 to well over sev-
en hundred by the late 1980s. Thus between thirty and forty vacancies
may occur annually on the federal bench. These federal judges must be
counted on to interpret, enforce, and in some cases limit the expansion of
federal governmental authority. At times federal courts have even fash-
ioned national law and policy, serving as key facilitators of social, economic, and political growth.

Senatorial courtesy, to be sure, remains the dominant factor in lower
court selections, but the steady increase in the number of judgeships has
provided presidents with more than an occasional opportunity to nominate candidates of their own choosing after the preferences of individual
senators have been satisfied. The growing size and prestige of the D.C.
Circuit have given presidents additional opportunities to hand out plum
assignments: because senatorial courtesy does not apply to those seats,
presidents may freely nominate ideologically compatible law professors,
former administration officials, and others to positions of considerable
prestige in the federal judicial system. Thus more than ever before, the
federal courts today provide an especially useful "proving ground" for candidates who might one day be considered for a seat on the high court.

4. *Divided party government* has become a recurring theme in American
government since World War II. Between 1896 and 1946, opposing parties
controlled the White House and the Senate during just two sessions of
Congress. By contrast, split party conditions now seem almost routine. . . .

5. The *confirmation process has become increasingly public.* For much of our
nation's history the confirmation process unfolded largely behind closed
doors. Though the Senate Judiciary Committee often met and offered
recommendations on nominees during the nineteenth century, closed investigative hearings were not conducted until 1873 when President Ulys-
ses Grant unsuccessfully nominated George Williams to be chief justice.
Open hearings were held for the first time only in 1916, when the Senate
considered Louis Brandeis's candidacy. Nine years later Harlan Fiske Stone
became the first nominee in history to appear before the committee personally. Full-fledged public hearings were finally instituted on a regular
basis beginning in 1930 with President Hoover's nomination of John J.
Parker.

Since 1955, virtually all Supreme Court nominees have formally testified before the Senate Judiciary Committee. Hearings have been televised
live since 1981, insuring heightened public access to the process. The increasingly public nature of confirmation-stage politics has placed added

strain on senators, many of whom may be reluctant to spend their time and political capital on an arduous process that will only create enemies back home. Meanwhile, the president must now find nominees who, aside from meeting ideological or professional criteria, will fare well in front of television cameras when facing a barrage of senators' questions.

6. The *rise in power of the organized bar* has figured significantly in recent Supreme Court selections. The American Bar Association's Special Committee on the (federal) Judiciary (later renamed the "Standing Committee on Federal Judiciary") was founded in 1947 to "promote the nomination of competent persons and to oppose the nomination of unfit persons" to the federal courts. During the past half-century that committee has played a significant if uneven role in the appointment of lower federal court judges. Not surprisingly, the ABA has taken an especially strong interest in the nomination of Supreme Court justices as well. Beginning with Eisenhower's nomination of Harlan in 1954, the ABA has formally reviewed all Supreme Court nominees for the Senate Judiciary Committee. Thus in selecting nominees, presidents must incorporate into their calculations the possibility that a less-than-exceptional rating from the ABA could serve as a rallying point for opposition during the subsequent confirmation process. Still, the bar's actual influence over the choice of nominees has varied largely depending upon the administration in power. In 1956, the Eisenhower administration began to submit names of potential Supreme Court nominees to the ABA at the same time that the FBI began its background check. During this period the ABA exerted little direct influence during initial deliberations over prospective candidates. By contrast, subsequent administrations have often enlisted the committee's services during much earlier stages of the process. High-ranking officials in the Justice Department have consulted with committee members to gauge potential support for and opposition to a prospective candidate. . . .

7. *Increased participation by interest groups* has also altered the character of the Supreme Court nomination process. This is not an entirely new phenomenon. Organized interests (including the National Grange and the Anti-Monopoly League) figured significantly in defeating Stanley Matthews's nomination to the Court in 1881. Almost fifty years later, an unlikely coalition of labor interests and civil rights groups joined together to defeat the nomination of John Parker. Since World War II, interest groups have extended their influence into the early stages of nominee selection by virtue of their increased numbers and political power. Groups such as the Alliance for Justice, People for the American Way, and the Leadership Conference on Civil Rights have made Supreme Court appointments a

high priority in their respective organizations. Many interest groups now conduct their own research into the backgrounds of prospective nominees and inundate the administration with information and analysis about various individual candidates.

8. *Increased media attention* has further transformed nominee selection politics. Presidents in the nineteenth and early twentieth centuries, working outside the media's glare, could often delay the selection of a nominee for many months while suffering few political repercussions. By contrast, contemporary presidents must contend with daily coverage of their aides' ruminations concerning a Supreme Court vacancy. Reporters assigned to the "Supreme Court beat" often provide their readership with the most recent "shortlists" of candidates under consideration by the president. A long delay in naming a replacement may be viewed by the press as a sign of indecision and uncertainty on the part of the president. Delay may also work to an administration's benefit, especially if media outlets expend their own resources investigating prospective candidates and airing potential political liabilities prior to any formal commitment by the administration.

9. *Advances in legal research technology* have had a pronounced effect on the selection process. All modern participants in the appointment process, including officials within the White House and the Justice Department, enjoy access to sophisticated tools for researching the backgrounds of prospective Supreme Court candidates. Legal software programs such as LEXIS/NEXIS and WESTLAW allow officials to quickly gather all of a prospective candidate's past judicial opinions, scholarship, and other public commentary as part of an increasingly elaborate screening process. Computer searches may be either tailored around narrow subject issues or they may be comprehensive in scope. The prevalence of C-SPAN and other cable and video outlets has made it possible to analyze prospective candidates' speeches and activities that would have otherwise gone unnoticed. Of course, advanced research technology is a double-edged sword: media outlets and interest groups may just as effectively publicize negative information about prospective candidates, undermining the president's carefully laid plans for a particular vacancy.

10. Finally, the *more visible role the Supreme Court has assumed in American political life* has increased the perceived stakes of the nomination process for everyone involved. Several of the critical developments listed above, including increased media attention and interest group influence in the nominee selection process, stem from a larger political development involving the Court itself: during this century the Supreme Court has entrenched itself at the forefront of American politics. Prior to the New

Deal, the Court only occasionally tried to compete with other governmental institutions for national influence. For example, the Taney Court inserted itself into the debate over slavery with its decision in *Dred Scott v. Sanford* (1857). The Court's aggressive protection of property rights in the late nineteenth century pitted it first against state governments, and then later against Congress and the president during the early part of the twentieth century. In each instance the judiciary usually represented a political ideology in decline; after a period of time the Court eventually returned to its role as an essentially reaffirming institution.

Since the early 1940s, however, the Supreme Court has positioned itself at the center of major political controversies on a nearly continuous basis. Driven by a primarily rights-based agenda, the Court has found itself wrestling with matters embedded in the American psyche: desegregation, privacy rights, affirmative action, and law enforcement. With the Court's continuously high visibility in the American political system, each appointment of a new justice now draws the attention of nearly all segments of society. The stakes of Supreme Court appointments may only seem higher than before, but that perception alone has caused a veritable sea change in the way presidents . . . must treat the selection of Supreme Court nominees.

41

RICHARD FALLON

From *The Dynamic Constitution*

The Supreme Court always gets a lot of public attention when vacancies occur and a new president nominates replacements whom the Senate must confirm. Yet behind the media spotlight accorded to Court nominees lie several basic principles necessary to understand the role of the Supreme Court in American government. Constitutional law professor Richard Fallon raises the issue of interpreting "a very old constitution." He discusses the importance of precedent, in terms of the tension between maintaining and overturning past decisions. Giving guidance to lower courts by creating "rules and tests" is another responsibility of the Supreme Court. By selecting the cases it will hear, the Court determines what areas of the law it will influence. Fallon explores several controversial topics in constitutional law today: the Court's relationship to the majority of Americans and to elected officials, the philosophy of "originalism" held by some Supreme Court justices, and the "moral rights" approach to jurisprudence. Cases mentioned in the excerpt such as Brown v. Board of Education and Roe v. Wade are familiar to students of American government. Ultimately, Fallon writes, the resolution of the complicated set of controversies that swirl around the Supreme Court comes from a less lofty, more practical consideration: decisions need to "produce good results overall," results that the American people endorse.

WRITING IN 1936 IN AN IMPORTANT CASE invalidating the centerpiece of the New Deal's farm program, justice Owen Roberts tried to blunt criticism by saying that the Supreme Court's job was not to exercise any independent judgment about the wisdom or even the possibly urgent necessity of challenged legislation, but simply "to lay the article of the Constitution which is invoked beside the statute which is challenged and to decide whether the latter squares with the former." The Constitution's meaning, he implied, was almost invariably plain. In cases of doubt, others have suggested, research into the "original understanding" will ordinarily resolve any uncertainty.

... Roberts' portrait of the judicial role was more fanciful than realistic. (One wonders whether Roberts himself would not have acknowledged as much in less defensive moments—if not in 1936, then surely a year later, when his so-called "switch in time that saved nine" ended the constitutional crisis that had provoked Franklin Roosevelt's Court-packing plan.) Often the Constitution's plain text will give no simple answer to modern constitutional questions: Which utterances lie within and without "the freedom of speech"? When is a search or seizure "unreasonable" and thus forbidden (rather then reasonable and thus permissible)? Which governmental classifications are consistent and inconsistent with "the equal protection of the laws"?

When the text gives no obvious answer, few would deny that the original understanding of constitutional language is relevant, but it is often hard to apply eighteenth- and nineteenth-century understandings to modern problems....

What is more, many strands of judicial precedent seem inconsistent with the original understandings of constitutional language, and once precedents have been established, nearly everyone acknowledges that they, too, need to be reckoned with in constitutional adjudication. A particularly clear example involves the constitutionality of paper currency. The issuance of paper money very arguably exceeds the original understanding of Congress's power, conferred by Article I, Section 8, Clause 5 of the Constitution, to "coin Money." Had the framers wished to empower Congress to issue "greenbacks," they could easily have said so; the authorization to "coin Money" seems to speak more narrowly. But the Supreme Court held otherwise in 1871, and a reversal on this issue would provoke economic chaos.

Another example involves race-based discrimination by the federal government. Although it seems clear that no provision of the Constitution, even as amended, was originally understood to bar discrimination by Congress (as the Equal Protection Clause, enacted in the aftermath of the civil war, only limits action by the *states*), the Supreme Court has treated race-based discriminations by the federal government as "suspect" for more than sixty years now and has subjected such discriminations to "strict" or "searching" judicial scrutiny. Regardless of whether the earliest cases were rightly reasoned, the matter is now considered by nearly everyone to be settled by precedent and evolving moral understandings. Indeed, even Supreme Court Justices who maintain in other contexts that constitutional adjudication should reflect "the original understanding" of constitutional language have accepted judicial precedents applying equal protection norms to the federal government (and, more controversially, have cited those precedents as authority for condemning federal affirmative action programs).

It is true, of course, that the Supreme Court is not absolutely bound by precedent. Sometimes it chooses to "overrule" itself. But the largely discretionary judgment of when to follow precedent and when to over-rule it only adds a further judgmental element to constitutional adjudica-tion in the Supreme Court.

When the various relevant considerations are all put into play, I have suggested repeatedly now—largely following Professor Ronald Dworkin on this point—that Supreme Court Justices typically decide how the Constitution is *best* interpreted in light of history, precedent, and consid-erations of moral desirability and practical workability. All of these factors are relevant. No clear rule specifies which will be controlling in a particu-lar case. In this context, political scientists repeatedly emphasize that the voting patterns of Supreme Court Justices tend to be relatively (though not perfectly) predictable on the basis of their political ideology. In view of the judgmental character of constitutional adjudication, it would be astonishing if the results were otherwise.

To say this is not to imply that the decisions of Supreme Court Jus-tices are crudely political. The Justices function . . . as a constitutional "practice," which subjects them to a number of role-based constraints. They must reason like lawyers and take account of text and history as well as precedent. They work in the medium of constitutional law, not partisan politics, and the medium of law—with its characteristic techniques of reasoning—limits, shapes, and channels the Justices' search for the best interpretation of the Constitution. Nevertheless, the nature of constitu-tional interpretation leaves abundant room for the exercise of legal and sometimes moral imagination.

Nor, in assessing the scope of judicial power, is it always helpful or even strictly accurate to think of the Supreme Court as engaged solely in constitutional "interpretation." Among the Court's characteristic modern functions is to formulate rules and tests for application by lower courts in future cases. This process of course begins with an interpretive search for "the meaning of the Constitution." Before reaching a conclusion, how-ever, the Court frequently needs to make a lot of practical judgments, informed by its sense of likely consequences. In my view many of the Court's rules are better viewed as devices to "implement" constitutional values than as "interpretations" of constitutional language. Among the clearest examples of constitutional "implementation" as a function distinct from pure "interpretation" comes from *Miranda v. Arizona* (1966), which introduced the requirement that the police give so-called *Miranda* warn-ings. Although admittedly an extreme case, the *Miranda* decision exempli-fies a broader phenomenon. Many of the doctrinal tests . . . lack clear roots in either the Constitution's language or its history. The Supreme Court has devised them in order to implement constitutional values, but they do not emerge from the Constitution through a process that would naturally be described as one of interpretation.

One final detail about the role of the Supreme Court deserves mention in a discussion of judicial power. Under the current statutory scheme, the Supreme Court enjoys almost complete discretion about which cases to hear and not to hear. Courts in the United States decide tens of thousands of cases every year. The Supreme Court could not possibly review every decision involving a federal constitutional question. After experimenting with various other schemes, Congress, by statute, has provided that the Supreme Court simply gets to choose which cases decided by lower courts it would like to review. In a typical year, the Court is asked to review more than 7,000 cases, out of which it has recently selected fewer than 100. For the most part, the Court agrees to decide those cases that the Justices think most important. The Supreme Court's power to choose its own cases is an important one, which permits the Court to establish and pursue any agenda that it may wish to adopt—for example, by expanding constitutional rights or powers in some areas or pruning them in others. . . .

The breadth of the power exercised by courts, and especially by the Supreme Court, naturally gives rise to recurrent debates and anxiety. As lawyers and judges worry about whether and when it is legitimate for courts to invalidate legislation based on their interpretation (which others may not share) of a very old constitution, they have at least two concerns in mind. One involves public acceptance of judicial review: Under what circumstances, if any, might the American people simply refuse to put up with having courts invalidate legislation that popular majorities support? What would happen if a popular President defied a very unpopular judicial ruling? Might the people line up behind the President, rather than behind the Court? A second question involves the moral and political justifiability of judicial review, especially in light of the relatively freewheeling way in which it is sometimes practiced: How, if at all, should courts go about deciding constitutional issues such that the American people *ought* to put up with their doing so?

These are perennial questions in American constitutional law and American politics. But they have arisen with special sharpness at some times in constitutional history—for example, during the *Lochner* era and then when Richard Nixon promised to appoint "strict constructionist" Justices who would halt the excesses (as he saw them) of the Warren Court. In recent years conservative critics of the Supreme Court have found a focal point for criticism in the Court's 1973 decision in *Roe v. Wade,* which held that absolute prohibitions against abortion violate the

Constitution during the period before a fetus becomes viable or capable of surviving outside the womb. Although restrictions on abortion undoubtedly curtail "liberty," no one believes that the Due Process Clause—the provision on which the Court based its decision—was originally understood or intended to protect abortion rights. The Court based its ruling partly on precedent, partly on a contestable judgment that it is unreasonable to make women bear an unwanted fetus.

In objecting to decisions such as *Roe,* critics often maintain not just that the Court reached the wrong decision, but that it is not fair or "legitimate" for the unelected Justices of the Supreme Court to exercise a power to thwart the judgments of political majorities—at least when legislation is not in flat contravention of the Constitution's originally understood meaning. This challenge, to which Alexander Bickel gave the label of "the counter-majoritarian difficulty," deserves to be taken seriously. But it bears emphasis that charges of "countermajoritarianism" can be leveled at conservative as well as liberal judicial decisions. . . . [I]n recent years, the five Justices of the Supreme Court who are generally labeled most "conservative" have invalidated numerous pieces of federal regulatory legislation, including the so-called Violence Against Women Act, on the ground that Congress lacks authority to enact it. Conservative Justices have also voted to subject federal affirmative action programs to strict judicial scrutiny, even though no provision of the Constitution was originally understood to bar affirmative action (or other forms of race-based discrimination) by the federal government. Conservative Justices have also voted to strike down popularly enacted restrictions on commercial advertising, even though it seems highly doubtful, at best, that the First Amendment was originally understood to protect commercial advertising.

Against the background of the countermajoritarian difficulty and related anxieties, judges and Justices openly debate questions of judicial role and interpretive methodology, often in the course of opinions deciding actual cases. Nor are debates about constitutional methodology confined to the courts. When Presidential candidates talk about the kind of judges and Justices that they would like to appoint, issues of proper interpretive methodology enter a broader public arena. Similar debates occur when the Senate considers whether to approve the nominations of candidates put forward by the President to become federal judges.

In recent years, at least two (highly conservative) Justices of the Supreme Court, Antonin Scalia and Clarence Thomas, have occasionally maintained that judges and Justices should renounce interpretive methodologies that require them to decide how the Constitution would "best" or most fairly be applied to modern conditions and should decide cases

based solely on the original understanding of constitutional language—
what it was understood to mean by those who ratified it. Because virtually no one denies that the original understanding is *relevant* to constitutional adjudication, it is often hard to gauge the precise scope of the
difference between so-called originalists and their opponents. But originalists often claim that their methodology is sharply distinctive.

Insofar as originalism is sharply distinctive, however, critics urge two
forceful objections. First, the "original understanding" of some constitutional provisions may be far out of touch with current realities. For example, . . . the principal basis for claims of federal authority to regulate
the economy is a constitutional provision empowering Congress to regulate "Commerce . . . among the several States." It is highly questionable
whether Congress's regulatory authority in this vital area should depend
entirely on the understanding that prevailed in what President Franklin
Roosevelt, in championing the need for federal power to defeat the Great
Depression, referred to as "horse and buggy" days.

A second problem, to which I have called attention already, is that a
great deal of modern constitutional doctrine that is now too entrenched
to be given up seems impossible to justify by reference to the original
understanding. Originalists do not maintain otherwise. They generally
concede that their theory must make an *exception* for issues settled by past,
entrenched judicial decisions—or at least some of them. It is issues of
consistency that give originalists trouble, for they do not contend that all
erroneous precedents should be immune from correction. To take perhaps
the best known example, prominent originalists insist tirelessly that *Roe v.
Wade's* recognition of constitutional abortion rights ought to be overruled. But what distinguishes *Roe* from the precedents that originalists
would leave unaltered? In essence, originalists reserve the right to pick
which precedents to reject and which to accept, largely on the basis of
their own judgments concerning which are important, desirable, and undesirable. Once it is recognized that Justices must make judgments of this
kind, originalism fails in its own aspiration to exclude the Justices' moral
and political views from constitutional adjudication. It is a philosophy
available to be trotted out in some cases and ignored in others.

Confronted with objections such as these, originalists commonly insist that it takes a theory to beat a theory. Many originalists believe the
best defense of their method is that it is the least bad of an imperfect lot.
Others believe that alternative approaches to constitutional adjudication
are better.

Another prominent theory of constitutional adjudication rests on the
premise that the Constitution embodies "moral" rights. According to this

view, the Constitution's framers and ratifiers did not invent such rights as those to freedom of speech and religion and to the equal protection of the laws. Rather, they recognized that such rights already existed as moral rights, and they incorporated those moral rights into the Constitution. Those holding this view would say, for example, that the Equal Protection Clause extends as far as the moral right to treatment as an equal and thus justifies the result in *Brown v. Board of Education,* even if the framers and ratifiers of the Fourteenth Amendment would have thought otherwise. At its foundation, a "moral rights" approach to constitutional adjudication must posit that the courts are better at identifying moral truths than are members of Congress and the state legislatures, perhaps because the latter are subject to political pressures to which the former—who have more opportunity to be long-sighted and deliberative—are not. Critics of course maintain that this approach invites judges simply to impose their personal moral views. Judges, they insist, have no monopoly on, and indeed no special insight into, moral truth.

In view of the objections to both originalism and a "moral rights" approach, some observers call for greater "judicial restraint" in invalidating legislation. When members of Congress and state legislators enact statutes, they have presumably considered whether the legislation violates the Constitution and determined that it does not. In light of this presumption, advocates of judicial restraint have long contended—since the *Lochner* era and even before—that the Supreme Court should accord "deference" to the constitutional judgments of other branches of government. According to one famous formulation of this position, the Court should invalidate statutes only when Congress or a state legislature has made a "clear mistake" about what the Constitution permits. This is by no means a wholly implausible position, but it would call for a dramatically reduced judicial role. It would also cast retrospective doubt on many of the Supreme Court's most celebrated decisions, including some that have protected the rights of racial minorities, safeguarded political speech, and enforced voting rights.

Believing that the Court should retain a robustly protective role in these areas, the late constitutional scholar John Hart Ely argued for deference to majorities *except* in cases involving claims of minority rights or rights to participate in the political process. He justified this approach by arguing that the Constitution's predominant commitment is to political democracy, and that courts should therefore intervene to make sure that the processes of political democracy function fairly. Among its implications, Ely's theory would stop courts from invalidating affirmative action programs (which disadvantage the white majority, not a racial minority) and recently enacted statutes that discriminate against women (who are a numerical majority, not a minority, of the population). Ely did not claim that the Supreme Court actually follows his theory, only that it should.

Other participants in constitutional practice defend a more flexible approach to constitutional adjudication, such as they believe the Court has characteristically practiced, partly based on an analogy to the way that judges decided cases under the so-called common law. Well into the nineteenth century, Congress and the state legislatures still had enacted comparatively few statutes, and the most basic law—called the common law—was developed by judges on the basis of custom and reason. In deciding cases at common law, judges begin with the rules as formulated in prior judicial decisions, but they also enjoy some flexibility to adapt those rules as circumstances change or as custom and reason require. Under the approach advocated by common-law constitutionalists, Supreme Court Justices should employ a comparably flexible approach in deciding constitutional issues. They should always begin with the text of the written Constitution, with which any interpretation must at least be reconciled. And they should treat the original understanding as always relevant and often decisive. But, it is argued, judges and especially Justices should also give weight to previous judicial decisions, including those that depart from original constitutional understandings, and they should take express account of what is fair, reasonable, workable, and desirable under modern circumstances, because we will get better constitutional law if they do so than if they do not. Critics, notably including originalists, argue that the common-law approach gives too large a role to judges, who are invited to thwart the wishes of democratic majorities based on their personal notions of justice and workability.

As the seemingly endless debate perhaps suggests, it may well be that questions of appropriate interpretive methodology admit no *general* answer—and that there can be no categorically persuasive rejoinder to the countermajoritarian difficulty either. The justification of the Supreme Court's role and interpretive methodology, if any, may well depend on the substantive fairness and popular acceptability of the particular decisions that it makes across the sweep of time. For now, at least, the people of the United States appear to have accepted a judicial role in adapting the Constitution to changing perceptions of need and fairness. But their acceptance of a flexible judicial role should surely be regarded as contingent, based on an assumption—grounded in our traditions—that judicial review as historically practiced has tended to produce good results overall: It is a useful device for promoting substantive justice and for reaching results that are broadly acceptable to the American public in ways that are at least tolerably consistent with the constitutional ideal of "a government of laws, and not of men."

Alexander Bickel may have had a thought such as this in mind when he wrote, somewhat enigmatically, that the Court "labors under the obligation to succeed." If the Court must somehow succeed in order to justify the role that it plays, and if success depends on reconciling the contestable demands of substantive justice with sometimes competing imperatives of adhering to settled rules of law and of rendering decisions that the public deems acceptable, it is easy to understand why the practice of judicial review should provoke ongoing anxieties and debate. . . .

42

MARCIA COYLE

From *The Roberts Court*

Legal analyst Marcia Coyle offers an inside look into the U.S. Supreme Court and its nine justices. The Court's decision on the constitutionality of the Affordable Care Act (called, for short, controversially, "Obamacare") provides the backdrop for Coyle's narrative. She sets the scene by addressing the tension between the Court's legal role and its political role. Which is true? Both, maybe. The Bush v. Gore decision that determined the winner of the 2000 presidential election has relevance, Coyle notes, as she explores the complex debate over whether the Supreme Court is a political branch of government. Coyle then recounts the events of March 2010 when the ACA's constitutionality was argued before the Court. There's an interesting cast of characters and some memorable instances: frog in throat, at a critical moment. The justices ask questions, then deliberate among themselves. The players are many: Justices Scalia, Kennedy, Ginsburg, Breyer, Thomas, Alito, Kagan, Sotomayor, and Chief Justice Roberts, the key figure and at the center of the storm, to borrow David O'Brien's term (see #39). Although we all know that the Court upheld the ACA, Coyle's account is riveting, especially because of the unusual fault lines of the decision. Coyle's look at this important moment in the Roberts Court hints at the ongoing controversy throughout the nation in the years since the 5–4 decision in National Federation of Independent Business v. Sebelius.

—————

A BELL RINGS THROUGH the chambers of the nine justices of the Supreme Court just five minutes before they take their seats in the courtroom to hear arguments in the day's cases. The sound reminds them that it is time to go to the robing room, an oak-paneled room, containing nine closets, each with a brass nameplate of the justice whose robes are inside. As soon as more than one justice enters, the traditional handshake in which each justice shakes hands with each of the other eight begins. If someone is missed there, the next opportunity is the next stop: the main conference room off of the chief justice's chambers. Chief Justice John Roberts Jr. likes to be the first justice into the conference room in order to greet his colleagues as they enter.

The handshake is done before arguments and before each conference in which the justices discuss petitions for review and vote on cases. Chief

Justice Melvin Fuller started the tradition in the late nineteenth century as a reminder that although they may differ—sometimes passionately—in their opinions, they can find harmony in their common purpose.

When the justices leave the conference room on argument days, they wait in a small area behind the heavy maroon drapes that separate them from the courtroom for the buzzer announcing the 10 am start of court. On some days, the waiting public may hear muffled voices or laughter behind those drapes. On June 28, 2012, the day on which the Roberts Court would issue its most important decision in seven years, a decision with the potential to shape a presidential election and to alter the constitutional structure of government, no sound came from behind the curtains, and silence quickly descended upon a courtroom whose atmosphere was electric with anticipation.

All of the justices did shake hands that morning before the fate of the nation's new health care law was revealed, confirmed one justice, but the harmony of a shared purpose was harder for some to grasp. This was a bitterly divided Court.

In one sense, the Roberts Court had come full circle. The last day of the 2006–07 term (ironically also June 28), had been the high-water mark for intense emotion and disagreement on the Court. A 5–4 conservative majority, led by Roberts, rejected two school districts' attempts to maintain racial diversity in their public schools. The Court's four moderate-liberal justices, in passionate dissent, accused Roberts and the majority of distorting the meaning of the landmark *Brown v. Board of Education,* which ended school segregation, and of abandoning other important precedents on issues ranging from abortion to antitrust law. On the final day of the 2011–12 term, Roberts and the four moderate-liberal justices found common ground to save the linchpin of the new health care law—the individual mandate—while the four remaining conservatives, in angry dissent, skewered the majority for rewriting the law, they claimed, to make it constitutional. That day, one justice later said, was as intensely emotional for all of them as the day of the school race decision five years earlier.

Disparagingly dubbed "Obamacare" by its opponents, the Patient Protection and Affordable Care Act became the centerpiece of the latest struggle for ownership of the true meaning and scope of some of the U.S. Constitution's most significant grants of power. It is a struggle as old as the Constitution itself, and it engages public passions particularly when the nation faces pressing social or economic questions.

The struggle is not between one president and one chief justice, or between the Congress and the Supreme Court. It is a struggle within the Supreme Court itself and it reflects differing visions as well within the other branches of government, the political parties, and the American people themselves.

"However counterintuitive it may seem, the integrity and coherence of constitutional law are to be found in, not apart from, controversy," wrote one constitutional law scholar a decade ago. . . .

The health care challenge . . . arrived at the U.S. Supreme Court at a particularly sensitive time for the Roberts Court. In what one presidential and Supreme Court scholar has called an "unprecedented" phenomenon, the ideologies of the nine justices are aligned with the politics of the presidents who appointed them. The Court's five conservative justices were appointed by Republican presidents, and the four liberal justices by Democratic presidents. That was not the case when recently retired Justices John Paul Stevens and David Souter sat on the Court. Both were Republican appointees, but they sided most often with the Court's Democratic appointees, and so blurred the ideological and political lines.

As if sensing the coming political tornado embodied by the health care challenge, Justice Ruth Bader Ginsburg, in an interview in the summer of 2011, said: "What I care most about, and I think most of my colleagues do, too, is that we want this institution to maintain the position that it has had in this system, where it is not considered a political branch of government."

The Supreme Court, however, sits atop a political branch of government, one of three branches whose powers and duties are enshrined in the Constitution. Federal judges and justices get their jobs through a political process: political recommendations to the president, appointment by the president, and confirmation by the Senate. Ginsburg's real concern and fervent hope were that the Court not be considered a partisan institution.

"The Court survived one great danger—*Bush v. Gore*,"* said one justice, referring to charges that politics drove the outcome in the 2000 ruling by the Rehnquist Court that decided the presidential election. "At least to me that seemed highly political."

However, *Bush v. Gore* triggered an enduring cynicism about the Court among many Americans. That cynicism deepened with the Roberts Court's 2010 decision in *Citizens United v. Federal Election Commission*,

---

***Bush v. Gore* is a highly controversial case. The 2000 presidential election remained undecided for several weeks after the election with the 25 Electoral College votes of Florida— the votes that would determine the winner—in question. Recounts were begun in several counties, but the Supreme Court eventually ended the recounts, with the state's votes going to George W. Bush. Vice President Al Gore actually won the nationwide popular vote in 2000 creating a partisan controversy, a national political ordeal, and a once-in-a-nation's history political science class.—Eds.

which eliminated legal bans on the use of general treasury funds by corporations and unions for making independent expenditures in elections. "It's the most hated of any recent Supreme Court decision, even more than *Bush v. Gore*," said the lawyer who won both cases, Theodore Olson. And this cynicism was reflected in a number of public opinion polls taken shortly before the 2012 health care ruling in which a majority of voters said politics would influence the outcome of the challenge to the new law.

Whether the justices are practicing law or politics in their most controversial cases is a profoundly difficult question, but one that scholars and others have tried to define, measure, or answer in various ways. "Judicial activism" is by now an overused and mostly unsatisfactory way of answering the question and implying a political agenda. For many people, a charge of judicial activism today has come to mean a decision with which those making the charge disagree.

Yale Law School's Jack Balkin and others have written about "high politics" and "low politics" on the Supreme Court.

"It is ok for judges and Justices to have constitutional politics, to have larger visions of what the Constitution means or should mean and what rights Americans have or should have," explains Balkin. "That is what I mean by 'high politics,' and there's nothing wrong with judges having such views." Judges pursue "high politics," he adds, through their legal arguments.

On the other hand, judges should not pursue "low politics"—the manipulation of doctrine to give an advantage or power to a particular group or political party. For Balkin, the decision in *Bush v. Gore* was "low politics," and others would point to the *Citizens United* decision.

The justices themselves vehemently deny that politics, especially of the "low" kind, ever enters their deliberations.

"I don't think the Court is political at all," Justice Scalia said during a television interview a month after the health care decision. "People say that because at least in the recent couple of years since John Paul Stevens and David, Souter have left the Court, the breakout is often 5 to 4, with 5 [Republican-appointed judges] and 4 by Democrats on the other side. Why should they be surprised that after assiduously trying to get people with these philosophies, [presidents] end up with people with these philosophies?"

Politics is what happens "across the street," Justice Clarence Thomas has said, referring to Congress, which meets across the street from the U.S. Supreme Court Building.

Another justice, speaking only on background, explained, "I think when Justice *X* sits down and starts working on a case, that justice doesn't think, 'This is the result I want to reach because I'm a [liberal Democrat or a conservative Republican].' That justice does what I do: reads the briefs, reads the statute, reads the cases. And even if nine times out of ten looking back you see it in a certain way, we all know that's just not how the process works."

Justice Stephen Breyer too has chafed at what he considers to be the media's portrayal of the justices at times as "junior league politicians." Breyer has written that "[p]olitics in our decision-making process does not exist. By politics, I mean . . . will it help certain individuals be elected? Personal ideology or philosophy is a different matter. Judges have had different life experiences and different kinds of training, and they come from different backgrounds. Judges appointed by different presidents of different political parties may have different views about the interpretation of the law and its relation to the world." . . .

An exuberant crowd of about three hundred supporters filled the East Room of the White House shortly before noon on March 23, 2010. Just two months after the Roberts Court had jolted the political world with *Citizens United,* its blockbuster campaign finance ruling, the stakes in the upcoming midterm elections and beyond were about to soar again.

As Democratic congressional leaders, cabinet members, and friends hovered around him, President Barack Obama, using twenty-two different pens, signed into law the signature success of his domestic agenda—a success that many of his predecessors going back to Teddy Roosevelt had failed to achieve. The Patient Protection and Affordable Care Act (ACA for short, or Obamacare to its critics) had survived a contentious partisan battle in Congress to offer the hope of health insurance to 50 million uninsured Americans.

Seven minutes after Obama put down his pen, a lawyer in the office of Florida Republican attorney general Bill McCollum electronically filed the first lawsuit challenging the new law's constitutionality in a federal district court in Pensacola, Florida. By the 5 pm close of business that day, three additional challenges had been lodged with federal courts in Richmond, Virginia; Lynchburg, Virginia; and Detroit, Michigan. They had discharged the opening volley in a fierce legal and political battle over the most sweeping social legislation in decades.

Besides their legal arguments, those separate lawsuits shared a common pedigree: the architects of the four challenges were some of the most conservative members of the Republican Party and associated organizations.

There was McCollum, leading ten other Republican state attorneys general whose numbers eventually would swell to twenty-six; Tea Party favorite Ken Cuccinelli, the attorney general of Virginia; Liberty University, founded by the evangelical fundamentalist Jerry Falwell and run by his son, Jerry Falwell Jr.; and the Thomas More Law Center, a conservative Christian legal organization created in 1999 by a prominent Roman Catholic and the founder of Domino Pizza, Tom Monaghan.

Regardless of the courts in which the lawsuits were filed, all four had one ultimate, planned destination—the U.S. Supreme Court—and one time frame: as fast as possible. Although the lawsuits raised similar constitutional challenges, each of their leaders, anticipating a historic showdown with the White House, wanted to have the case that the justices would review. However, conventional wisdom favored the suit by the Republican attorneys general because of its broad attack on the law; and this time, conventional wisdom was right. . . .

Although the Court's marble-laden home has a remarkable insulating effect, figuratively and literally, the justices were acutely aware of the politically charged atmosphere surrounding the term, and the health care case in particular.

The weekend before the health care decision was issued, Ruth Bader Ginsburg delivered remarks at the annual convention of a liberal legal advocacy organization, the American Constitution Society. She noted that "No contest since the Court invited new briefs and argument in *Citizens United* has attracted more attention in the press, the academy and the ticket line outside the Supreme Court, a line that formed three days before the oral arguments commenced."

And another justice confided the day before the health care ruling that he had felt the political tensions surrounding the term more than in prior terms. "I felt it more this term," said the justice, adding, "I don't know why. Perhaps it was the many difficult issues [on the docket] and the political atmosphere coming together."

On the first day of the health care arguments, Monday, March 26, 2012, the action outside the Court was more energized than the arguments inside. Old-fashioned protests, complete with signs and chants, unfolded in front of the Supreme Court Building, and a long line of hopeful observers snaked around the corner. The Anti-Injunction Act of 1867 was the issue of the day, and it quickly became clear that the justices did not see that act as a bar to their reviewing the constitutionality of the health care law.

When [solicitor general] Donald Verrilli stood up to make the government's argument that the act did not apply, he faced little pushback. Although not evident at the time, the Court's relatively low-key questioning left Verrilli with extra time to fill, which he seized effectively by laying the groundwork for the government's argument on Congress's tax power. Justice Sotomayor provided the opening by asking if there were any collateral consequences of not having health insurance. Verrilli spent considerable time explaining how the penalty—tax—for not having insurance operated. That explanation, it would be seen later, had a keen impact on the chief justice.

Tuesday, March 27, the second day, was the main event—the constitutionality of the individual mandate. Outside, a near-circuslike atmosphere prevailed: demonstrators, music, even a belly dancer occupied the sidewalk below the building's plaza. Inside, the lawyers would play to a packed house. More than a dozen members of Congress from both sides of the aisle took seats in the courtroom, as did a number of Obama administration cabinet members, including the attorney general and the secretary of Health and Human Services. Bill McCollum, the former Florida attorney general who had spearheaded the health care lawsuit, had a special seat in the justices' guest section. The chief justice's wife, who works as a legal headhunter, had recruited him for the law firm where he then worked, and she gave him her seat since she was out of town that day. McCollum found himself sitting between two of the chief justice's physicians.

Verrilli was first at the podium and immediately encountered a freakish problem. Slightly hoarse with a frog in his throat, he struggled to begin his argument, took a sip of water, failed to clear his throat, and tried again. Roberts, looking concerned yet unsure what to do, leaned forward as if to say something, but Verrilli found his voice and started again. After that, his argument seemed disjointed and weak. Later, he was harshly criticized as having blown the most important argument of the century.

Various factors led to that criticism. Verrilli, according to a recent study of the arguments, was interrupted 180 times—an average of every twenty-two seconds—during his fifty-six minutes at the podium by questions primarily from the Court's conservative wing. He was able to speak roughly ten or fewer seconds more than 40 percent of the time before being interrupted. By contrast, his main opponent, [former solicitor general, attorney for the states attorneys general, Paul] Clement, was interrupted thirty-three times in thirty minutes and spoke for one minute or longer before being interrupted. He and [National Federation of Inde-

pendent Business attorney Michael] Carvin faced far fewer questions
from the conservative justices, even though they were the challengers.
Verrilli, Clement, and Carvin also have dramatically different styles.
The solicitor general is soft-spoken and deliberate. Clement, standing
with no papers to aid him, is quick, confident, and at ease with light ban-
tering with the justices. Carvin is aggressive and tenacious. The Court's
conservative justices, frankly, also are better questioners than their colleagues on the left, although that is slowly changing as Kagan and Sotomayor gain experience.

In the end, scholars and others who closely followed the mandate arguments agreed that Verrilli made the points that he needed to make.
Working off of Judge Jeffrey Sutton's opinion in the Sixth Circuit, Verrilli
stressed the unique features of the health insurance market. Because everyone would enter the market but there is no control over when, an insurance requirement in advance of the point of sale was justified. It was an
application of the commerce clause, not an extension of it. Based on their
later questions to Clement, both Roberts and Kennedy understood the
government's argument, if not persuaded by it. Verrilli also reinforced the
tax power argument from the previous day.

There was no question that it was a bad day for the government.
There also was a surprising partisan overtone to some of the questions by
Scalia and Alito. Scalia in particular seemed to be repeating the opponents'
talking points and was the first to raise the broccoli argument against the
individual mandate (if the government could force individuals to buy
health insurance, it also could require them to buy broccoli). He later also
referred to the so-called Cornhusker kickback amendment as if he believed it was still in the law, even though it had been removed two years
earlier. And he startled the audience when, after Verrilli explained that we
as a society had obligated ourselves to care for the uninsured when they
showed up in emergency rooms for care, the justice leaned forward to
retort, "Well, don't obligate yourself to that!"

The third and last day was not a good one either for the government.
At least four justices seemed inclined to strike down the entire law if the
mandate was unconstitutional, and the states' challenge to the Medicaid
expansion appeared to make headway with a number of the justices—a
remarkable reaction given the fact that the Supreme Court had never
found a federal funding condition to be coercive and the federal government was covering the cost of the Medicaid expansion at 100 percent in
the first three years and never less than 90 percent permanently.

The arguments ended on Wednesday, March 28, and the justices met
the following Friday to vote on the issues. . . .

On June 28, 2012, the term's last day, the courtroom again was filled to capacity. The spouses of some of the justices came, as did retired Justice John Paul Stevens. At 10 am, the justices emerged from behind the maroon velvet drapes that separate the courtroom from their chambers and stood at their chairs as the marshal of the Court gave the traditional "Oyez, Oyez" call. Absent were the usual smiles and nods by the justices to the audience that marked the end of the term. Sotomayor and Kagan, bookends on the bench, appeared exhausted. Scalia, Thomas, and Alito looked grim and leaned back in their chairs. Only Breyer looked, well, content.

After disposing of two cases, only health care—the most important decision in the history of the Roberts Court—remained. Not surprisingly, Roberts announced that he had the opinion. And then Chief Justice Roberts, clear-eyed and in matter-of-fact voice, delivered the most remarkable opinion of his career.

He began by restating the government's argument that the individual mandate was a proper exercise of Congress's power to regulate commerce and to tax. Roberts said that he and Justices Scalia, Kennedy, Thomas, and Alito had concluded that the individual mandate was an unconstitutional exercise of Congress's commerce power. That power only allows Congress to regulate activity, not inactivity. "The individual mandate, however, does not regulate existing commercial activity," he wrote. "It instead compels individuals to become active in commerce by purchasing a product, on the ground that their failure to do so affects interstate commerce. Construing the Commerce Clause to permit Congress to regulate individuals precisely because they are doing nothing would open a new and potentially vast domain to congressional authority. Every day individuals do not do an infinite number of things."

The mandate also could not be upheld under the necessary and proper clause, added the chief justice, because even if it were necessary to achieve the act's insurance reforms, the expansion of federal power is not a "proper" means for making the reforms effective.

Roberts then turned to the government's second argument: the tax power. He noted the "well established" judicial principle "that if a statute has two possible meanings, one of which violates the Constitution, courts should adopt the meaning that does not do so." Roberts, joined by Ginsburg, Breyer, Sotomayor, and Kagan, held that the mandate was a constitutional exercise of Congress's power to tax. Although the act calls the payment for not having insurance a "penalty" and not a "tax," Roberts said the label does not determine whether it falls within the tax power. What is determinative is how it functions, he explained, and this penalty functions like a tax in many respects. For example, it is paid into the Treasury by taxpayers when they file their tax returns, he said. The requirement to pay is in the Internal Revenue Code and is enforced by the Internal Revenue Service. The amount is determined by such familiar factors as taxable income, number of dependents, and joint filing status, and it produces some revenue for the government. He added, "Because the Constitution permits such a tax, it is not our role to forbid it, or to pass upon its wisdom or fairness."

On the Medicaid issue, all of the justices except Ginsburg and Sotomayor agreed that the expanded program exceeded Congress's authority under the spending clause. Congress unconstitutionally coerced the states to adopt the changes by threatening to withhold all of the states' Medicaid grants. Roberts called the threat "a gun to the head." The surprise here was the agreement by Breyer and Kagan, who had been particularly skeptical of the challengers' arguments.

However, Roberts, joined only by Ginsburg, Breyer, Sotomayor, and Kagan, held that the constitutional violation could be remedied by invalidating the unconstitutional condition—the threat to withhold all existing Medicaid funds for failure to comply—and not the entire program. States now have a real choice, he said, adding, "We are confident that Congress would have wanted to preserve the rest of the act."

An emotional Kennedy next summarized an unusual joint dissent written, he said, by himself, Scalia, Thomas, and Alito. "In our view, the Act before us is invalid in its entirety." They agreed that the mandate could not be justified as an exercise of the commerce power, but they also did not see it as a proper exercise of the tax power. Congress, he said, went to great lengths to structure the mandate as a penalty, not a tax, and he accused the majority of "judicial tax-writing."

The Medicaid expansion, he said, could not be saved by the majority's remedy because that is "rewriting the statute" and there is no judicial authority to do so. Finally, he concluded that the mandate and the Medicaid expansion were central to the law's design and operation, and the act's other provisions would not have been enacted without them. "It must follow that the entire statute is linked together, and without the mandate and Medicaid expansion, the entire Act is inoperative," he said.

Amazingly, Kennedy, the center of power on the Roberts Court for six years, had lost the most important case on power in more than sixty years. . . .

Roberts's decision was remarkable in that it gave the law's opponents a new limit on Congress's commerce clause power—the activity-inactivity distinction—as well as a new opportunity for states to challenge federal conditions on funding or regulations that they deem coercive. And yet, he upheld the mandate for the law's supporters and saved the Medicaid expansion. The decision also avoided an ideological split that would have made the Court vulnerable to charges of partisan politics since he and the liberal wing agreed on the tax power, and Kagan and Breyer joined the conservative wing on the Medicaid issue.

The boldest, most aggressive decision in the case, however, came from the four joint dissenters who would have struck down the entire, 2,700-page law, including many provisions that had nothing to do with the insurance reforms, such as amendments to the Black Lung Benefits Act that evened the playing field for dying coal miners or their widows seeking benefits from coal companies.

Just days after the decision, a CBS News correspondent reported that sources with specific knowledge of the deliberations had told her that Roberts initially voted to strike down the mandate but later switched his position. The leaks told of how hard the conservatives tried to win Roberts back and, upon failing, they decided to have nothing more to do with him. The rift in the Court, she reported, was "deep and personal."

Suddenly, Roberts was being attacked by some opponents of the mandate as not a true conservative, unprincipled and political, motivated less by law and more by the desire to remove the Court from the eye of a political storm.

For example, in an interview with *National Review,* Randy Barnett, the leading opponent of the health care law who previously had said the Court would not be influenced "one bit by politics or the election," said after the ruling: "The fact that this decision was apparently political, rather than legal, completely undermines its legitimacy as a precedent. Its result can be reversed by the people in November, and its weak-tax-power holding reversed by any future Court without pause."

The government's tax power argument had been rejected in the lower federal courts, but it was not considered a weak argument by some leading constitutional scholars and tax law experts, who wrote articles and amicus briefs advocating it from the beginning of the litigation through the Supreme Court. The Justice Department never waivered in raising the tax argument from the outset. Roberts himself mentioned that the penalty looked like a tax on the opening day of the health care arguments.

While the mandate's opponents were tearing down John Roberts, its supporters were comparing him to John Marshall, the Great Chief Justice, and how Marshall deftly avoided a constitutional showdown with President Thomas Jefferson. And, they suggested, Roberts was the modern Fe-lix Frankfurter, a leading proponent of judicial restraint.

Justices change their minds, or make up their minds, even after they vote in the privacy of their conferences, after they exchange draft opinions with back-and-forth comments, after they find that an opinion "just doesn't write." As Ginsburg said in a late summer interview, "It ain't over 'til it's over."

43

JEFFREY TOOBIN

From *The Oath*

Legal scholar Jeffrey Toobin takes readers inside the 2009 appointment of the first Hispanic to the Supreme Court, Sonia Sotomayor. He opens with an account of Sotomayor's humble family circumstances, her move from Puerto Rico to New York's South Bronx, and then to the gigantic Co-op City development. After Princeton University and Yale Law School, Sotomayor practiced law, and then became a federal district court judge. In 1995, Judge Sotomayor made an important decision in the major league baseball free-agency dispute. She moved up to the Second Circuit Appeals Court where President Obama found her in 2009. Her nomination to the Supreme Court was not without controversy as her critics focused attention on comments she made in a 2001 speech regarding affirmative action. Read them, along with her clarification at her confirmation hearings, and you'll see how important every small detail is when the Senate places a president's nominee on the high court, for life.

SONIA SOTOMAYOR COULD HAVE BEEN genetically engineered to be a Democratic nominee to the United States Supreme Court. She had impeccable credentials: Princeton, then Yale Law School. She had ideal experience: big-city prosecutor, six years as a federal district judge (nominated by George H. W. Bush), and then a decade on the federal appeals court. She had, above all, a great story: raised amid poverty in the Bronx, with juvenile diabetes no less, she would make history as the first Hispanic on the Supreme Court. In light of all this, it looked like political malpractice for Obama *not* to nominate her. . . .

In the brusque shorthand of political life, White House officials later described Sotomayor's story as "an American story." It was an extraordinary one.

Celina Báez and Juan Sotomayor were both born in Puerto Rico and came to the United States as part of the great migration that transformed New York during and after World War II. Celina worked as a telephone operator at a hospital, Juan as a tool-and-die maker in a factory. Their daughter, Sonia, was born in 1954, and they moved into an unfinished Bronxdale housing project in the South Bronx with the poetic name of Building 28. (Her brother, Juan, was born three years later.) Their lives were hard and soon got even harder. When Sonia was eight, she was diagnosed with type 1 diabetes. The following year, Juan Sotomayor Sr. died suddenly of a heart attack at the age of forty-two.

Celina was a striver, committed to bettering herself and making sure that her children could do the same. After her husband's death, she started speaking English at home; as a consequence, Sonia speaks Spanish fluently but her younger brother barely speaks it at all. Celina obtained a GED and then trained to become a practical nurse. The job paid better, and it taught Celina to manage her daughter's illness. She placed Sonia and Juan in highly regarded Catholic schools. The reasons were educational, not religious. In an oft-told tale, Celina invested in an expensive set of encyclopedias—supposedly the only one in the building—for her two children. The neighborhood was deteriorating, and Celina moved her family to Co-op City, the sprawling development near the Westchester border. While keeping her job at the hospital, caring for her own kids, and serving as a kind of unofficial doctor for her neighbors, Celina commenced studies to be a registered nurse. (The exodus of middle-class families like the Sotomayors in the seventies helped turn the South Bronx into a national symbol of urban decay.)

Sonia won a scholarship to Princeton, where she experienced immediate culture shock. After a rocky freshman year, she settled in and became successful, socially and academically. She wrote a thesis about Puerto Rico's independence movement, graduated summa cum laude, and won acceptance to Yale Law School. (Her younger brother became a physician.) For all her achievements, Sotomayor held no illusions about one of the reasons for her success. As she said in a speech after she became a judge, "I am a product of affirmative action. I am the perfect affirmative action baby. My test scores were not comparable to that of my colleagues at Princeton or Yale, but not so far off the mark that I wasn't able to succeed at those institutions." In any case, she thrived at Yale, too.

Toward the end of law school, Sotomayor happened to show up at a career-day presentation by Robert Morgenthau, the legendary Manhattan district attorney. After sizing her up, Morgenthau arranged for a job interview the next day, and she was quickly hired. Sotomayor worked her way up in the office and capped her career there with a victory in the tabloid-ready Tarzan Murderer case. Richard Maddicks was a familiar New York type in the seventies and eighties—the desperate junkie who preyed on his neighbors to support his habit. What distinguished Maddicks was his ability to jump from building to building while making his rounds, a circuit that produced seven shootings and four murders. In 1983, thanks to Sotomayor and a fellow prosecutor, Maddicks was convicted and received a life sentence.

Sotomayor tired of the never-ending misery in the criminal justice system and left the office after only five years to join a small private firm. (After graduating from Princeton, she had married her college boyfriend, whom she had known since high school; he was in graduate school in molecular biology for much of the marriage, and their commuting relationship didn't last. They divorced after seven years. She was later engaged, but did not marry again.) Like many other young lawyers, Sotomayor was guided both by altruism and by ambition. In 1980, she joined the Puerto Rican Legal Defense and Education Fund—a leading civil rights organization. While in private practice, Sotomayor was named to the State of New York Mortgage Agency board; the next year, thanks to Morgenthau, she gained a seat on the New York City Campaign Finance Board. In 1986, she toured Israel with a group of Latino activists. When George H. W. Bush was president, the New York senators divided the judicial appointments so that Al D'Amato received three appointments for every one for Daniel Patrick Moynihan. In 1992, Moynihan heard about Sotomayor and put up her name; at the age of thirty-eight, she was confirmed unanimously for a federal judgeship in lower Manhattan.

As with the Tarzan Murderer, a celebrated case brought Sotomayor wide public notice on the district court. A labor dispute had destroyed the 1994 major league baseball season, including the World Series, and the 1995 season was in jeopardy when the battle between the players and the owners wound up in her courtroom. On March 30, 1995, the union demanded that the owners continue free-agent negotiations and salary arbitrations while the two sides negotiated an agreement. Sotomayor told the lawyers that she didn't know the history of their case, but "I hope none of you assumed . . . that my lack of knowledge of any of the intimate details of your dispute meant I was not a baseball fan. You can't grow up in the South Bronx without knowing about baseball." She issued an injunction reinstituting free agency, the players went back to work, and the 232-day dispute soon ended. It was a classic Sotomayor moment—decisive and unequivocal. It was the kind of behavior that generally wins praise for male judges, if not always for their female counterparts. Certainly, it did not hurt that Sotomayor became famous as the judge who saved baseball.

Bill Clinton nominated her to the Second Circuit two years later, and she soon became known—even to Barack Obama, whom she had never met—as the Democrats' leading Supreme Court justice-in-waiting.

But that was only part of the story, especially for Obama. Although Sotomayor flourished on the Second Circuit, she kept her ties to the Bronx. She remained a frequent visitor to her grammar school and high school; she was godmother of five children, including the son of her dentist; she gave talks to Hispanic student groups all over the country. As a public figure, Sotomayor had a stump speech of sorts. The one she gave in 2001 at the University of California, Berkeley, was typical. These kinds of inspirational talks often consist of banalities, but not Sotomayor's. Her talk was serious and substantive—with a quietly radical message.

Sotomayor began with the customary paean to her roots, in her case as a "Nuyorican." "For me, a very special part of my being Latina is the *muchos platos de arroz, gandules y pernil*—rice, beans, and pork—that I have eaten at countless family holidays and special events," she said. "My Latina identity also includes, because of my particularly adventurous taste buds, *morcilla*—pig intestines—*patitas de cerdo con garbanzos*—pigs' feet with beans—and *la lengua y orejas de cuchifrito*—pigs' tongue and ears."

Soon enough, Sotomayor took aim at one of the hardest questions surrounding affirmative action. *Why* does it matter if there are more women, or minorities, on the bench? She quoted a former colleague on the Manhattan federal trial court, Miriam Cedarbaum, who "sees danger in presuming that judging should be gender or anything else based. She rightly points out that the perception of the differences between men and women is what led to many paternalistic laws and to the denial to women of the right to vote." Sotomayor went on, "Judge Cedarbaum nevertheless believes that judges must transcend their personal sympathies and prejudices and aspire to achieve a greater degree of fairness and integrity based on the reason of law."

But that wasn't Sotomayor's opinion. She embraced the view that women and minorities brought something different to the bench. "Our experiences as women and people of color affect our decisions," she said. "The aspiration to impartiality is just that—it's an aspiration because it denies the fact that we are by our experiences making different choices than others." She continued, "Whether born from experience or inherent physiological or cultural differences, a possibility I abhor less or discount less than my colleague Judge Cedarbaum, our gender and national origins may and will make a difference in our judging. Justice O'Connor has often been cited as saying that a wise old man and wise old woman will reach the same conclusion in deciding cases." But in the crucial passage in the speech, Sotomayor said she *disagreed* with O'Connor's view. "I would hope that a wise Latina woman with the richness of her experiences would more often than not reach a better conclusion than a white male who hasn't lived that life." According to Sotomayor, gender and ethnicity among judges made a substantive difference in results. "Personal experiences affect the facts that judges choose to see," she said. "My hope is that I will take the good from my experiences and extrapolate them further into areas with which I am unfamiliar. I simply do not know exactly what that difference will be in my judging. But I accept there will be some based on my gender and my Latina heritage." . . .

Heading into Memorial Day weekend, Sotomayor had been told she was the likely nominee but that she would hear the official word from the president probably on Monday. (White House officials had consulted several doctors and were assured that Sotomayor's diabetes would not prevent her from living a normal life span.) On the afternoon of the holiday, Obama called [an aide, Ron] Klain, and asked him to run the negatives on Sotomayor one more time. Klain rehearsed the expected attacks: intemperate, too liberal, too pro–affirmative action. Obama was unpersuaded by the case against her and told Klain he would make the formal offer that night.

In the meantime, Sotomayor—nervous and unable to tell anyone what was going on—went to her chambers on Memorial Day, if only to fill the time. Relatives called for updates, and there were none. Finally, she decided to return to her apartment in Greenwich Village and pack for the trip to Washington—just in case. At 8:10 p.m., Obama called her cell phone. When he made the offer official, Sotomayor began to cry.

"I want you to make me two promises," Obama said. "First, you have to remain the person you are. And second, to stay connected to your community." Happy to oblige, the nominee told the president.

Obama and his staff had been so caught up in the details of the selection process that they weren't prepared for what happened the next day, when he announced Sotomayor's nomination in the East Room. There were people, lots of them, weeping with joy. Many of them did not even know Sotomayor personally. Supreme Court nominations are cultural markers in the United States—Louis Brandeis in 1916, Thurgood Marshall in 1967, Sandra Day O'Connor in 1981. The dates are not coincidental, for they mark coming-of-age moments for Jewish Americans, African Americans, and women. May 26, 2009 was such a date for Hispanic Americans. In a White House hallway afterwards, Obama told Ron Klain, his designated naysayer, "I feel great about this now." . . .

[During the Senate Judiciary Committee hearings,] on the "wise Latina" issue, Sotomayor caved. When questioned closely on the matter by Jeff Sessions, the senior Republican on the committee, she first dodged the central contention of her speeches: "My record shows that at no point or time have I ever permitted my personal views or sympathies to influence an outcome of a case. In every case where I have identified a sympathy, I have articulated it and explained to the litigant why the law requires a different result."

"Well, Judge . . . ," Sessions interrupted.

"I do not permit my sympathies, personal views, or prejudices to influence the outcome of my cases," she said, ignoring the interruption.

In the end, Sotomayor just walked away from her previous position. "I was using a rhetorical flourish that fell flat. I knew that Justice O'Connor couldn't have meant that if judges reached different conclusions—legal conclusions—that one of them wasn't wise. That couldn't have been her meaning, because reasonable judges disagree on legal conclusions in some cases. So I was trying to play on her words. My play was—fell flat.

"It was bad, because it left an impression that I believed that life experiences commanded a result in a case, but that's clearly not what I do as a judge," she went on. "It's clearly not what I intended in the context of my broader speech, which was attempting to inspire young Hispanic, Latino students and lawyers to believe that their life experiences added value to the process."

From the perspective of the White House, Sotomayor's hearing was a clear success. Above all, she did nothing to jeopardize her chances of being confirmed. In a way, it was an Obama-like performance—progressive by implication, biographical rather than ideological. Sotomayor was a highly qualified nominee whose views appeared to mirror the careful inclinations of the president who appointed her. That's what Obama wanted in a Supreme Court justice, and that's what he received. On July 28, the Judiciary Committee voted 13–6 in her favor. (Only Lindsey Graham, Republican of South Carolina, crossed party lines to vote for her.) On August 6, the full Senate confirmed Sotomayor by a vote of 68–31. (Nine Republicans voted for her.)

PART EIGHT

Civil Liberties
and
Civil Rights

44

ANTHONY LEWIS

From *Gideon's Trumpet*

Written in 1964, Gideon's Trumpet *is one of the most-assigned books in American government courses. The excerpt presented here touches on all the major points in the legal and personal story of Clarence Earl Gideon, the Florida prisoner whose case,* Gideon v. Wainwright *(1963), transformed American justice. As Gideon's story unfolds, notice the following elements in journalist Anthony Lewis's account of the landmark case that ensured all defendants legal counsel in state criminal cases:* in forma pauperis; *writ of certiorari;* Betts v. Brady; *stare decisis; Attorney Abe Fortas; Fourteenth Amendment; selective incorporation of the Bill of Rights; "a great marble temple"; "Oyez, oyez, oyez"; Justice Black; 9-0; court-appointed attorney Fred Turner; public defenders; not guilty; the Bay Harbor Poolroom.*

IN THE MORNING MAIL of January 8, 1962, the Supreme Court of the United States received a large envelope from Clarence Earl Gideon, prisoner No. 003826, Florida State Prison, P.O. Box 221, Raiford, Florida. Like all correspondence addressed to the Court generally rather than to any particular justice or Court employee, it went to a room at the top of the great marble steps so familiar to Washington tourists. There a secretary opened the envelope. As the return address had indicated, it was another petition by a prisoner without funds asking the Supreme Court to get him out of jail—another, in the secretary's eyes, because pleas from prisoners were so familiar a part of her work. . . .

. . . A federal statute permits persons to proceed in any federal court *in forma pauperis,* in the manner of a pauper, without following the usual forms or paying the regular costs. The only requirement in the statute is that the litigant "make affidavit that he is unable to pay such costs or give security therefor."

The Supreme Court's own rules show special concern for *in forma pauperis* cases. Rule 53 allows an impoverished person to file just one copy of a petition, instead of the forty ordinarily required, and states that the Court will make "due allowance" for technical errors so long as there is substantial compliance. In practice, the men in the Clerk's Office—a half dozen career employees, who effectively handle the Court's relations with the outside world—stretch even the rule of substantial compliance.

Rule 53 also waives the general requirement that documents submitted to the Supreme Court be printed. It says that *in forma pauperis* applications should be typewritten "whenever possible," but in fact handwritten papers are accepted.

Gideon's were written in pencil. They were done in carefully formed printing, like a schoolboy's, on lined sheets evidently provided by the Florida prison. Printed at the top of each sheet, under the heading Correspondence Regulations, was a set of rules ("Only 2 letters each week . . . written on one side only . . . letters must be written in English . . . ") and the warning: MAIL WILL NOT BE DELIVERED WHICH DOES NOT CONFORM TO THESE RULES. Gideon's punctuation and spelling were full of surprises, but there was also a good deal of practiced, if archaic, legal jargon, such as "Comes now the petitioner . . . ".

Gideon was a fifty-one-year-old white man who had been in and out of prisons much of his life. He had served time for four previous felonies, and he bore the physical marks of a destitute life: a wrinkled, prematurely aged face, a voice and hands that trembled, a frail body, white hair. He had never been a professional criminal or a man of violence; he just could not seem to settle down to work, and so he had made his way by gambling and occasional thefts. Those who had known him, even the men who had arrested him and those who were now his jailers, considered Gideon a perfectly harmless human being, rather likeable, but one tossed aside by life. Anyone meeting him for the first time would be likely to regard him as the most wretched of men.

And yet a flame still burned in Clarence Earl Gideon. He had not given up caring about life or freedom; he had not lost his sense of injustice. Right now he had a passionate—some thought almost irrational—feeling of having been wronged by the State of Florida, and he had the determination to try to do something about it. Although the Clerk's Office could not be expected to remember him, this was in fact his second petition to the Supreme Court. The first had been returned for failure to include a pauper's affidavit, and the Clerk's Office had enclosed a copy of the rules and a sample affidavit to help him do better next time. Gideon persevered. . . .

Gideon's main submission was a five-page document entitled "Petition for a Writ of Certiorari Directed to the Supreme Court State of Florida." A writ of certiorari is a formal device to bring a case up to the Supreme Court from a lower court. In plain terms Gideon was asking the Supreme Court to hear his case.

What was his case? Gideon said he was serving a five-year term for "the crime of breaking and entering with the intent to commit a misdemeanor, to wit, petty larceny." He had been convicted of breaking into the Bay Harbor Poolroom in Panama City, Florida. Gideon said his conviction violated the due-process clause of the Fourteenth Amendment to the Constitution, which provides that "No state shall . . . deprive any person of life, liberty, or property, without due process of law." In what way had Gideon's trial or conviction assertedly lacked "due process of law"? For two of the petition's five pages it was impossible to tell. Then came this pregnant statement:

"When at the time of the petitioners trial he ask the lower court for the aid of counsel, the court refused this aid. Petitioner told the court that this Court made decision to the effect that all citizens tried for a felony crime should have aid of counsel. The lower court ignored this plea."

Five more times in the succeeding pages of his penciled petition Gideon spoke of the right to counsel. To try a poor man for a felony without giving him a lawyer, he said, was to deprive him of due process of law. There was only one trouble with the argument, and it was a problem Gideon did not mention. Just twenty years before, in the case of *Betts v. Brady*, the Supreme Court had rejected the contention that the due-process clause of the Fourteenth Amendment provided a flat guarantee of counsel in state criminal trials.

Betts v. Brady was a decision that surprised many persons when made and that had been a subject of dispute ever since. For a majority of six to three, Justice Owen J. Roberts said the Fourteenth Amendment provided no universal assurance of a lawyer's help in a state criminal trial. A lawyer was constitutionally required only if to be tried without one amounted to "a denial of fundamental fairness." . . .

Later cases had refined the rule of *Betts v. Brady*. To prove that he was denied "fundamental fairness" because he had no counsel, the poor man had to show that he was the victim of what the Court called "special circumstances." Those might be his own illiteracy, ignorance, youth, or mental illness, the complexity of the charge against him or the conduct of the prosecutor or judge at the trial. . . .

But Gideon did not claim any "special circumstances." His petition made not the slightest attempt to come within the sophisticated rule of *Betts v. Brady*. Indeed, there was nothing to indicate he had ever heard of the case or its principle. From the day he was tried Gideon had had one idea: That under the Constitution of the United States he, a poor man, was flatly entitled to have a lawyer provided to help in his defense. . . .

Gideon was wrong, of course. The United States Supreme Court had not said he was entitled to counsel; in *Betts v. Brady* and succeeding cases it had said quite the opposite. But that did not necessarily make Gideon's

petition futile, for the Supreme Court never speaks with absolute finality
when it interprets the Constitution. From time to time—with due solem-
nity, and after much searching of conscience—the Court has overruled its
own decisions. Although he did not know it, Clarence Earl Gideon was
calling for one of those great occasions in legal history. He was asking the
Supreme Court to change its mind. . . .

Clarence Earl Gideon's petition for certiorari inevitably involved, for
all the members of the Court, the most delicate factors of timing and
strategy. The issue he presented—the right to counsel—was undeniably of
first-rank importance, and it was an issue with which all of the justices
were thoroughly familiar. . . .

. . . Professional comment on the Betts case, in the law reviews, had
always been critical and was growing stronger, and within the Supreme
Court several justices had urged its overruling. On the other hand, a majority might well draw back from so large a step. . . . At the conference of
June 1, 1962, the Court had before it two jurisdictional statements asking
the Court to hear appeals, twenty-six petitions for certiorari on the Appellate Docket, ten paupers' applications on the Miscellaneous Docket
and three petitions for rehearing. . . .

The results of the deliberations at this conference were made known
to the world shortly after ten A.M. the following Monday, June 4th, when
a clerk posted on a bulletin board the mimeographed list of the Supreme
Court's orders for that day. One order read:

Gideon v. Cochran 890 Misc.

The motion for leave to proceed *in forma pauperis* and the petition for writ of
certiorari are granted. The case is transferred to the appellate docket. In addition
to other questions presented by this case, counsel are requested to discuss the following in their briefs and oral argument:

"Should this Court's holding in *Betts v. Brady*, 316 U.S. *455*, be reconsid-
ered?" . . .

In the Circuit Court of Bay County, Florida, Clarence Earl Gideon
had been unable to obtain counsel, but there was no doubt that he could
have a lawyer in the Supreme Court of the United States now that it had
agreed to hear his case. It is the unvarying practice of the Court to appoint a lawyer for any impoverished prisoner whose petition for review
has been granted and who requests counsel.

Appointment by the Supreme Court to represent a poor man is a
great honor. For the eminent practitioner who would never, otherwise,
dip his fingers into the criminal law it can be an enriching experience,

making him think again of the human dimensions of liberty. It may provide the first, sometimes the only, opportunity for a lawyer in some distant corner of the country to appear before the Supreme Court. It may also require great personal sacrifice. There is no monetary compensation of any kind—only the satisfaction of service. The Court pays the cost of the lawyer's transportation to Washington and home, and it prints the briefs, but there is no other provision for expenses, not even secretarial help or a hotel room. The lawyer donates that most valuable commodity, his own time. . . .

The next Monday the Court entered this order in the case of *Gideon v. Cochran:*

"The motion for appointment of counsel is granted and it is ordered that Abe Fortas, Esquire, of Washington, D.C., a member of the Bar of this Court be, and he is hereby, appointed to serve as counsel for petitioner in this case.

Abe Fortas is a high-powered example of that high-powered species, the Washington lawyer. He is the driving force in the firm of Arnold, Fortas and Porter. . . . A lawyer who has worked with him says: "Of all the men I have met he most knows why he is doing what he does. I don't like the s.o.b., but if I were in trouble I'd want him on my side. He's the most resourceful, the boldest, the most thorough lawyer I know." . . .

. . . "The real question," Fortas said, "was whether I should urge upon the Court the special-circumstances doctrine. As the record then stood, there was nothing to show that he had suffered from any special circumstances. . . .

When that transcript was read at Arnold, Fortas and Porter, there was no longer any question about the appropriateness of this case as the vehicle to challenge *Betts v. Brady.* Plainly Gideon was not mentally defective. The charge against him, and the proof, were not particularly complicated. The judge had tried to be fair; at least there was no overt bias in the courtroom. In short, Gideon had not suffered from any of the special circumstances that would have entitled him to a lawyer under the limited rule of *Betts v. Brady.* And yet it was altogether clear that a lawyer would have helped. The trial had been a rudimentary one, with a prosecution case that was fragmentary at best. Gideon had not made a single objection or pressed any of the favorable lines of defense. An Arnold, Fortas and Porter associate said later: "We knew as soon as we read that transcript that here was a perfect case to challenge the assumption of *Betts* that a man could have a fair trial without a lawyer. He did very well for a layman, he acted like a lawyer. But it was a pitiful effort really. He may have committed this crime, but it was never proved by the prosecution. A lawyer—not a great lawyer, just an ordinary, competent lawyer—could have made ashes of the case." . . .

As Abe Fortas began to think about the case in the summer of 1962, before Justice Frankfurter's retirement, it was clear to him that overruling *Betts v. Brady* would not come easily to Justice Frankfurter or others of his view. This was true not only because of their judicial philosophy in general, but because of the way they had applied it on specific matters. One of these was the question of precedent.

"In most matters it is more important that the applicable rule of law be settled than that it be settled right." Justice Brandeis thus succinctly stated the basic reason for *stare decisis*, the judicial doctrine of following precedents. . . .

Another issue . . . cut even deeper than *stare decisis*, and closer to Gideon's case. This was their attitude toward federalism—the independence of the states in our federal system of government. . . .

The Bill of Rights is the name collectively given to the first ten amendments to the Constitution, all proposed by the First Congress of the United States in 1789 and ratified in 1791. The first eight contain the guarantees of individual liberty with which we are so familiar: freedom of speech, press, religion and assembly; protection for the privacy of the home; assurance against double jeopardy and compulsory self-incrimination; the right to counsel and to trial by jury; freedom from cruel and unusual punishments. At the time of their adoption it was universally agreed that these eight amendments limited only the Federal Government and its processes. . . .

There matters stood until the Fourteenth Amendment became part of the Constitution in 1868. A product of the Civil War, it was specifically designed to prevent abuse of individuals by state governments. Section 1 provided: "No State shall make or enforce any law which shall abridge the privileges or immunities of citizens of the United States; nor shall any State deprive any person of life, liberty, or property, without due process of law; nor deny to any person within its jurisdiction the equal protection of the laws." Soon the claim was advanced that this section had been designed by its framers to *incorporate*, and apply to the states, all the provisions of the first eight amendments.

This theory of wholesale incorporation of the Bill of Rights has been adopted by one or more Supreme Court justices from time to time, but never a majority. . . .

But if wholesale incorporation has been rejected, the Supreme Court has used the Fourteenth Amendment to apply provisions of the Bill of Rights to the states *selectively*. The vehicle has been the clause assuring individuals due process of law. The Court has said that state denial of any right deemed "fundamental" by society amounts to a denial of due process and hence violates the Fourteenth Amendment. . . .

The difficult question has been which provisions of the first eight amendments to absorb. . . .

Grandiose is the word for the physical setting. The W.P.A. Guide to Washington* called the Supreme Court building a "great marble temple" which "by its august scale and mighty splendor seems to bear little relation to the functional purposes of government." Shortly before the justices moved into the building in 1935 from their old chamber across the street in the Capitol, Justice Stone wrote his sons "The place is almost bombastically pretentious, and thus it seems to me wholly inappropriate for a quiet group of old boys such as the Supreme Court." He told his friends that the justices would be "nine black beetles in the Temple of Karnak."

The visitor who climbs the marble steps and passes through the marble columns of the huge pseudo-classical facade finds himself in a cold, lofty hall, again all marble. Great bronze gates exclude him from the area of the building where the justices work in private—their offices, library and conference room. In the courtroom, which is always open to the public, the atmosphere of austere pomp is continued: there are more columns, an enormously high ceiling, red velvet hangings, friezes carved high on the walls. The ritual opening of each day's session adds to the feeling of awe. The Court Crier to the right of the bench smashes his gavel down sharply on a wooden block, everyone rises and the justices file in through the red draperies behind the bench and stand at their places as the Crier intones the traditional opening: "The honorable, the Chief Justice and the Associate Justices of the Supreme Court of the United States. Oyez, oyez, oyez. All persons having business before the honorable, the Supreme Court of the United States, are admonished to draw near and give their attention, for the Court is now sitting. God save the United States and this honorable Court."

But then, when an argument begins, all the trappings and ceremony seem to fade, and the scene takes on an extraordinary intimacy. In the most informal way, altogether without pomp, Court and counsel converse. It is conversation—as direct, unpretentious and focused discussion as can be found anywhere in Washington. . . .

*The WPA, the Works Progress Administration, was started by President Franklin Roosevelt as part of the New Deal in 1935. WPA projects, designed to put people back to work during the Depression, included school and park building, theater and music performances, and map and guidebook writing.—EDS.

Chief Justice Warren, as is the custom, called the next case by reading aloud its full title: Number 155, Clarence Earl Gideon, petitioner, versus H. G. Cochran, Jr., director, Division of Corrections, State of Florida. . . .

The lawyer arguing a case stands at a small rostrum between the two counsel tables, facing the Chief Justice. The party that lost in the lower court goes first, and so the argument in *Gideon v. Cochran* was begun by Abe Fortas. As he stood, the Chief Justice gave him the customary greeting, "Mr. Fortas," and he made the customary opening: "Mr. Chief Justice, may it please the Court. . . . "

This case presents "a narrow question," Fortas said—the right to counsel—unencumbered by extraneous issues. . . .

"This record does not indicate that Clarence Earl Gideon was a person of low intelligence," Fortas said, "or that the judge was unfair to him. But to me this case shows the basic difficulty with Betts versus Brady. It shows that no man, however intelligent, can conduct his own defense adequately." . . .

"I believe we can confidently say that overruling Betts versus Brady at this time would be in accord with the opinion of those entitled to an opinion. That is not always true of great constitutional questions. . . . We may be comforted in this constitutional moment by the fact that what we are doing is a deliberate change after twenty years of experience—a change that has the overwhelming support of the bench, the bar and even of the states." . . .

It was only a few days later, as it happened, that *Gideon v. Wainwright* was decided. There was no prior notice; there never is. The Court gives out no advance press releases and tells no one what cases will be decided on a particular Monday, much less how they will be decided. Opinion days have a special quality. The Supreme Court is one of the last American appellate courts where decisions are announced orally. The justices, who divide on so many issues, disagree about this practice, too. Some regard it as a waste of time; others value it as an occasion for descending from the ivory tower, however briefly, and communicating with the live audience in the courtroom. . . .

Then, in the ascending order of seniority, it was Justice Black's turn. He looked at his wife, who was sitting in the box reserved for the justices' friends and families, and said: "I have for announcement the opinion and judgment of the Court in Number One fifty-five, Gideon against Wainwright."

Justice Black leaned forward and gave his words the emphasis and the drama of a great occasion. Speaking very directly to the audience in the courtroom, in an almost folksy way, he told about Clarence Earl Gideon's case and how it had reached the Supreme Court of the United States.

"It raised a fundamental question," Justice Black said, "the rightness of a case we decided twenty-one years ago, Betts against Brady. When we granted certiorari in this case, we asked the lawyers on both sides to argue to us whether we should reconsider that case. We do reconsider Betts and Brady, and we reach an opposite conclusion."

By now the page boys were passing out the opinions. There were four—by Justices Douglas, Clark and Harlan, in addition to the opinion of the Court. But none of the other three was a dissent. A quick look at the end of each showed that it concurred in the overruling of *Betts v. Brady*. On that central result, then, the Court was unanimous. . . .

That was the end of Clarence Earl Gideon's case in the Supreme Court of the United States. The opinions delivered that Monday were quickly circulated around the country by special legal services, then issued in pamphlets by the Government Printing Office. Eventually they appeared in the bound volumes of Supreme Court decisions, the United States Reports, to be cited as *Gideon v. Wainwright*, 372 U.S. 335—meaning that the case could be found beginning on page 335 of the 372nd volume of the reports.

Justice Black, talking to a friend a few weeks after the decision, said quietly: "When *Betts v. Brady* was decided, I never thought I'd live to see it overruled." . . .

The reaction of the states to *Gideon v. Wainwright* was swift and constructive. The most dramatic response came from Florida, whose rural-dominated legislature had so long refused to relieve the problem of the unrepresented indigent such as Gideon. Shortly after the decision Governor Farris Bryant called on the legislature to enact a public-defender law. . . .

Resolution of the great constitutional question in *Gideon v. Wainwright* did not decide the fate of Clarence Earl Gideon. He was now entitled to a new trial, with a lawyer. Was he guilty of breaking into the Bay Harbor Poolroom? The verdict would not set any legal precedents, but there is significance in the human beings who make constitutional-law cases as well as in the law. And in this case there was the interesting question whether the legal assistance for which Gideon had fought so hard would make any difference to him. . . .

. . . After ascertaining that Gideon had no money to hire a lawyer of his own choice, Judge McCrary asked whether there was a local lawyer whom Gideon would like to represent him. There was: W. Fred Turner.

"For the record," Judge McCrary said quickly, "I am going to appoint Mr. Fred Turner to represent this defendant, Clarence Earl Gideon." . . .

The jury went out at four-twenty P.M., after a colorless charge by the judge including the instruction—requested by Turner—that the jury must believe Gideon guilty "beyond a reasonable doubt" in order to convict him. When a half-hour had passed with no verdict, the prosecutors were less confident. At five twenty-five there was a knock on the door between the courtroom and the jury room. The jurors filed in, and the court clerk read their verdict, written on a form. It was *Not Guilty*.

"So say you all?" asked Judge McCrary, without a flicker of emotion. The jurors nodded. . . .

After nearly two years in the state penitentiary Gideon was a free man. . . . That night he would pay a last, triumphant visit to the Bay Harbor Poolroom. Could someone let him have a few dollars? Someone did.

"Do you feel like you accomplished something?" a newspaper reporter asked.

"Well I did."

45

RICHARD KLUGER

From *Simple Justice*

No Supreme Court case has so changed the United States as did Brown v. Board of Education of Topeka, Kansas *(1954). Volumes have been written on* Brown *and the aftermath of* Brown, *but the best place to start is with Richard Kluger's classic work. The selection here focuses on Earl Warren, the chief justice who wrote the landmark decision. The case that would reverse* Plessy v. Ferguson *(1896) and the "separate but equal" doctrine that the Court had upheld for half a century, was waiting to be heard when the death of Chief Justice Fred Vinson put Warren on the Court. Kluger quotes Justice Frankfurter as saying on hearing of Vinson's death, "This is the first indication I have ever had that there is a God." Kluger explores the intricate process Warren faced in forging a majority, and eventually unanimity, for overturning "separate but equal." While those Americans who were born after* Brown *cannot remember a time when it was not the law of the land, Kluger takes us back to that thrilling moment of change.*

———

IN THE TWO AND A HALF YEARS since they had last sat down to decide a major racial case, the Justices of the Supreme Court had not grown closer. Indeed, the philosophical and personal fissures in their ranks had widened since they had agreed—unanimously—to side with the Negro appellants in *Sweatt, McLaurin*, and *Henderson* in the spring of 1950. That had been a rare show of unanimity. By the 1952 Term, the Court was failing to reach a unanimous decision 81 percent of the time, nearly twice as high a percentage of disagreement as it had recorded a decade earlier. . . .

It was perhaps the most severely fractured Court in history—testament, on the face of it, to Vinson's failure as Chief Justice. Selected to lead the Court because of his skills as a conciliator, the low-key, mournful-visaged Kentuckian found that the issues before him were far different from, and far less readily negotiable than, the hard-edged problems he had faced as Franklin Roosevelt's ace economic troubleshooter and Harry Truman's Secretary of the Treasury and back-room confederate.

Fred Vinson's lot as Chief Justice . . . had not proven a happy one. . . .

What, then, could be expected of the deeply divided Vinson Court as it convened on the morning of December 13, 1952, to deliberate on the

transcendent case of *Brown v. Board of Education*? The earlier racial cases—
Sweatt and *McLaurin*—they had managed to cope with by chipping away
at the edges of Jim Crow but avoiding the real question of *Plessy*'s continued validity.* The Court could no longer dodge that question, though it
might continue to stall in resolving it. Hovering over the Justices were all
the repressive bugaboos of the Cold War era. The civil rights of Negroes
and the civil liberties of political dissenters and criminal defendants were
prone to be scrambled together in the public mind, and every malcontent
was a sitting target for the red tar of anti-Americanism. No sector of the
nation was less hospitable to both civil-liberties and civil-rights claimants
than the segregating states of the South, and it was the South with which
the Justices had primarily to deal in confronting *Brown*. . . .

    And so they were divided. But given the gravity of the issue, they
were willing to take their time to try to reconcile their differences. They
clamped a precautionary lid on all their discussions of *Brown* as the year
turned and Fred Vinson swore in Dwight David Eisenhower as the thirty-
fourth President of the United States. The Justices seemed to make little
headway toward resolving the problem, but they all knew that a close vote
would likely be a disaster for Court and country alike. The problem of
welding the disparate views into a single one was obviously complicated
by the ambivalence afflicting the Court's presiding Justice. As spring came
and the end of the Court's 1952 Term neared, Fred Vinson seemed to be
in increasingly disagreeable and edgy spirits. Says one of the people at the
Court closest to him then: "I got the distinct impression that he was dis-
tressed over the Court's inability to find a strong, unified position on such
an important case."

    What evidence there is suggests that those on or close to the Court
thought it was about as severely divided as it could be at this stage of its
deliberations. . . .

    During the last week of the term in June, the law clerks of all the
Justices met in an informal luncheon session and took a two-part poll.
Each clerk was asked how he would vote in the school-segregation cases
and how he thought his Justice would vote. According to one of their
number, a man who later became a professor of law: "The clerks were al-

---

*The Supreme Court in *Plessy v. Ferguson* (1896) interpreted the equal protection clause of
the Fourteenth Amendment to mean that the states could require separation of the races in
public institutions if these institutions were equal (the "separate but equal doctrine"). From
1937 until 1954 the Court subjected "separate but equal" to increasingly rigorous scrutiny. In
Sweatt v. Painter (1950) and *McLaurin v. Oklahoma State Regents* (1950), for example, the Court
invalidated specific state racial segregationist practices in higher education on grounds that
they did not permit truly equal access to black students. Yet, the Court had not overturned
Plessy.—EDS.

most unanimous for overruling *Plessy* and ordering desegregation, but, according to their impressions, the Court would have been closely divided if it had announced its decision at that time. Many of the clerks were only guessing at the positions of their respective Justices, but it appeared that a majority of the Justices would not have overruled *Plessy* but would have given some relief in some of the cases on the ground that the separate facilities were not in fact equal." . . .

All such bets on the alignment of the Court ended abruptly a few days later when the single most fateful judicial event of that long summer occurred. In his Washington hotel apartment, Fred M. Vinson died of a heart attack at 3:15 in the morning of September 8 [1953]. He was sixty-three.

All the members of the Court attended Vinson's burial in Louisa, Kentucky, his ancestral home. But not all the members of the Court grieved equally at his passing. And one at least did not grieve at all. Felix Frankfurter had not much admired Fred Vinson as judge or man. And he was certain that the Chief Justice had been the chief obstacle to the Court's prospects of reaching a humanitarian and judicially defensible settlement of the monumental segregation cases. In view of Vinson's passing just before the *Brown* reargument, Frankfurter remarked to a former clerk, "This is the first indication I have ever had that there is a God." . . . Fred Vinson was not yet cold in his grave when speculation rose well above a whisper as to whom President Eisenhower would pick to heal and lead the Supreme Court as it faced one of its most momentous decisions in the segregation cases. . . .

Dwight Eisenhower's principal contribution to the civil rights of Americans would prove to be his selection of Earl Warren as Chief Justice—a decision Eisenhower would later say had been a mistake. The President was on hand, at any rate, on Monday, October 5, when just after noon the clerk of the Supreme Court read aloud the commission of the President that began, "Know ye: That reposing special trust and confidence in the wisdom, uprightness and learning of Earl Warren of California, I do appoint him Chief Justice of the United States. . . . " Warren stood up at the clerk's desk to the side of the bench and read aloud his oath of office. At the end, Clerk Harold Willey said to him, "So help you God." Warren said, "So help me God." Then he stepped quickly behind the velour curtains and re-emerged a moment later through the opening in the center to take the presiding seat. His entire worthy career to that moment would be dwarfed by what followed. . . . At the reargument, Earl Warren had said very little. The Chief Justice had put no substantive questions to any of the attorneys. Nor is it likely that he had given any indication of his views to the other Justices before they convened at the Saturday-morning conference on December 12. But then, speaking first, he made his views unmistakable.

Nearly twenty years later, he would recall, "I don't remember having any great doubts about which way it should go. It seemed to me a comparatively simple case. Just look at the various decisions that had been eroding *Plessy* for so many years. They kept chipping away at it rather than ever really facing it head-on. If you looked back—to *Gaines*, to *Sweatt*, to some of the interstate-commerce cases—you saw that the doctrine of separate-but-equal had been so eroded that only the *fact* of segregation itself remained unconsidered. On the merits, the natural, the logical, and practically the only way the case could be decided was clear. The question was *how* the decision was to be reached."

At least two sets of notes survive from the Justices' 1953 conference discussion of the segregation cases—extensive ones by Justice Burton and exceedingly scratchy and cryptic ones by Justice Frankfurter. They agree on the Chief Justice's remarks. The cases had been well argued, in his judgment, Earl Warren told the conference, and the government had been very frank in both its written and its oral presentations. He said he had of course been giving much thought to the entire question since coming to the Court, and after studying the briefs and relevant history and hearing the arguments, he could not escape the feeling that the Court had "finally arrived" at the moment when it now had to determine whether segregation was allowable in the public schools. Without saying it in so many words, the new Chief Justice was declaring that the Court's policy of delay, favored by his predecessor, could no longer be permitted.

The more he had pondered the question, Warren said, the more he had come to the conclusion that the doctrine of separate-but-equal rested upon the concept of the inferiority of the colored race. He did not see how *Plessy* and its progeny could be sustained on any other theory—and if the Court were to choose to sustain them, "we must do it on that basis," he was recorded by Burton as saying. He was concerned, to be sure, about the necessity of overruling earlier decisions and lines of reasoning, but he had concluded that segregation of Negro schoolchildren had to be ended. The law, he said in words noted by Frankfurter, "cannot in 'this day and age' set them apart." The law could not say, Burton recorded the Chief as asserting, that Negroes were "not entitled to *exactly same* treatment of all others." To do so would go against the intentions of the three Civil War amendments.

Unless any of the other four Justices who had indicated a year earlier their readiness to overturn segregation—Black, Douglas, Burton, and

Minton—had since changed his mind, Warren's opening remarks meant that a majority of the Court now stood ready to strike down the practice.

But to gain a narrow majority was no cause for exultation. A sharply divided Court, no matter which way it leaned, was an indecisive one, and for Warren to force a split decision out of it would have amounted to hardly more constructive leadership on this transcendent question than Fred Vinson had managed. The new Chief Justice wanted to unite the Court in *Brown*. . . .

He recognized that a number of Court precedents of long standing would be shattered in the process of overturning *Plessy*, and he regretted that necessity. It was the sort of reassuring medicine most welcomed by Burton and Minton, the least judicially and intellectually adventurous members of the Court.

He recognized that the Court's decision would have wide repercussions, varying in intensity from state to state, and that they would all therefore have to approach the matter in as tolerant and understanding a way as possible. Implicit in this was a call for flexibility in how the Court might frame its decree.

But overarching all these cushioning comments and a tribute to both his compassion as a man and his persuasive skills as a politician was the moral stance Earl Warren took at the outset of his remarks. Segregation, he had told his new colleagues, could be justified only by belief in the inferiority of the Negro; any of them who wished to perpetuate the practice, he implied, ought in candor to be willing to acknowledge as much. These were plain words, and they did not have to be hollered. They cut across all the legal theories that had been so endlessly aired and went straight to the human tissue at the core of the controversy. . . .

The Warren opinion was "finally approved" at the May 15 conference, Burton noted in his diary. The man from California had won the support of every member of the Court.

. . . Not long before the Court's decision in *Brown* was announced, Warren told *Ebony* magazine twenty years later, he had decided to spend a few days visiting Civil War monuments in Virginia. He went by automobile with a black chauffeur.

At the end of the first day, the Chief Justice's car pulled up at a hotel, where he had made arrangements to spend the night. Warren simply assumed that his chauffeur would stay somewhere else, presumably at a less expensive place. When the Chief Justice came out of his hotel the next morning to resume his tour, he soon figured out that the chauffeur had spent the night in the car. He asked the black man why.

"Well, Mr. Chief Justice," the chauffeur began, "I just couldn't find a place—couldn't find a place to . . . "

Warren was stricken by his own thoughtlessness in bringing an employee of his to a town where lodgings were not available to the man solely because of his color. "I was embarrassed, I was ashamed," Warren recalled. "We turned back immediately. . . . "

. . . In the press room on the ground floor, reporters filing in at the tail end of the morning were advised that May 17, 1954, looked like a quiet day at the Supreme Court of the United States.

All of the opinions of the Court were announced on Mondays in that era. The ritual was simple and unvarying. The Justices convened at noon. Lawyers seeking admission to the Supreme Court bar were presented to the Court by their sponsors, greeted briefly by the Chief Justice, and sworn in by the clerk of the Court. Then, in ascending order of seniority, the Justices with opinions to deliver read them aloud, every word usually, without much effort at dramaturgy. Concurrences and dissents were read after the majority opinion. And then the next case, and then the next. There was no applause; there were no catcalls. There were no television or newsreel cameras. There were no questions from the newsmen in the audience. There was no briefing session in the press room or the Justices' chambers after Court adjourned. There were no weekly press conferences. There were no appearances on *Meet the Press* the following Sunday. There were no press releases elaborating on what the Court had said or meant or done. The opinions themselves were all there was. . . .

Down in the press room, as the first three routine opinions were distributed, it looked, as predicted, like a very quiet day at the Court. But then, as Douglas finished up, Clerk of the Court Harold Willey dispatched a pneumatic message to Banning E. Whittington, the Court's dour press officer. Whittington slipped on his suit jacket, advised the press-room contingent, "Reading of the segregation decisions is about to begin in the courtroom," added as he headed out the door that the text of the opinion would be distributed in the press room afterward, and then led the scrambling reporters in a dash up the marble stairs.

"I have for announcement," said Earl Warren, "the judgment and opinion of the Court in No. 1—*Oliver Brown et al. v. Board of Education of Topeka.*" It was 12:52 P.M. In the press room, the Associated Press wire carried the first word to the country: "Chief Justice Warren today began reading the Supreme Court's decision in the public school segregation cases. The court's ruling could not be determined immediately." The bells went off in every news room in America. The nation was listening.

It was Warren's first major opinion as Chief Justice. He read it, by all accounts, in a firm, clear, unemotional voice. If he had delivered no other opinion but this one, he would have won his place in American history. Considering its magnitude, it was a short opinion. During its first part, no one hearing it could tell where it would come out. . . .

Without in any way becoming technical and rhetorical, Warren then proceeded to demonstrate the dynamic nature and adaptive genius of American constitutional law. . . . Having declared its essential value to the nation's civic health and vitality, he then argued for the central importance of education in the private life and aspirations of every individual. . . . That led finally to the critical question: "Does segregation of children in public schools solely on the basis of race . . . deprive the children of the minority group of equal educational opportunities?"

To this point, nearly two-thirds through the opinion, Warren had not tipped his hand. Now, in the next sentence, he showed it by answering that critical question: "We believe that it does." . . .

This finding flew directly in the face of *Plessy*. And here, finally, Warren collided with the 1896 decision. . . .

The balance of the Chief Justice's opinion consisted of just two paragraphs. The first began: "We conclude"—and here Warren departed from the printed text before him to insert the word "unanimously," which sent a sound of muffled astonishment eddying around the courtroom—"that in the field of public education the doctrine of 'separate but equal' has no place. Separate educational facilities are inherently unequal." The plaintiffs and others similarly situated—technically meaning Negro children within the segregated school districts under challenge—were therefore being deprived of the equal protection of the laws guaranteed by the Fourteenth Amendment.

The concluding paragraph of the opinion revealed Earl Warren's political adroitness both at compromise and at the ready use of the power of his office for ends he thought worthy. "Because these are class actions, because of the wide applicability of this decision, and because of the great variety of local conditions," he declared, "these cases present problems of considerable complexity. . . . In order that we may have the full assistance of the parties in formulating decrees," the Court was scheduling further argument for the term beginning the following fall. The attorneys general of the United States and all the states requiring or permitting segregation in public education were invited to participate. In a few strokes, Warren thus managed to (1) proclaim "the wide applicability" of the decision and make it plain that the Court had no intention of limiting its benefits to a handful of plaintiffs in a few outlying districts; (2) reassure

the South that the Court understood the emotional wrench desegregation would cause and was therefore granting the region some time to get
accustomed to the idea; and (3) invite the South to participate in the en-
tombing of Jim Crow by joining the Court's efforts to fashion a temper-
ate implementation decree—or to forfeit that chance by petulantly ab-
staining from the Court's further deliberations and thereby run the risk of
having a harsh decree imposed upon it. It was such dexterous use of the
power available to him and of the circumstances in which to exploit it
that had established John Marshall as a judicial statesman and political
tactician of the most formidable sort. The Court had not seen his like
since. Earl Warren, in his first major opinion, moved now with that same
sure purposefulness. . . .

It was 1:20 P.M. The wire services proclaimed the news to the nation.
Within the hour, the Voice of America would begin beaming word to
the world in thirty-four languages: In the United States, schoolchildren
could no longer be segregated by race. The law of the land no longer
recognized a separate equality. No Americans were more equal than any
other Americans.

46

CHARLES OGLETREE

From *All Deliberate Speed*

The impact of the Supreme Court case, Brown v. Board of Education, *certainly did not end in 1954 when the decision was handed down. Legal scholar Charles Ogletree picks up the story of* Brown *with the events after the landmark decision. Ogletree looks at* Brown II, *the subsequent decision that required school desegregation "with all deliberate speed." Contrary to common belief, the real meaning of this phrase, Ogletree asserts, is that change could come slowly, not right away. Ogletree then takes readers decades ahead to three classic civil rights cases based on affirmative action. He explores the 1978* Bakke *decision and the more recent 2003* Gratz *and* Grutter *cases from the University of Michigan: the issues in all three involve the value of diversity and the means to achieve it. To close the excerpt, Ogletree looks ahead to the way in which all these cases may affect education in the United States in the coming decades. The meaning of "all deliberate speed" has proven crucial to the lives of millions of American young people.*

ON MAY 17, 1954, AN OTHERWISE UNEVENTFUL Monday afternoon, fifteen months into Dwight D. Eisenhower's presidency, Chief Justice Earl Warren, speaking on behalf of a unanimous Supreme Court, issued a historic ruling that he and his colleagues hoped would irrevocably change the social fabric of the United States. "We conclude that in the field of public education the doctrine of 'separate-but-equal' has no place. Separate educational facilities are inherently unequal." Thurgood Marshall, who had passionately argued the case before the Court, joined a jubilant throng of other civil rights leaders in hailing this decision as the Court's most significant opinion of the twentieth century. The *New York Times* extolled the *Brown* decision as having "reaffirmed its faith and the underlying American faith in the equality of all men and all children before the law." . . .

At the time, no one doubted the far-reaching implications of the Court's ruling. The *Brown* lawyers had apparently accomplished what politicians, scholars, and others could not—an unparalleled victory that would create a nation of equal justice under the law. The Court's decision seemed to call for a new era in which black children and white children would have equal opportunities to achieve the proverbial American Dream. It did not come too soon for the families whose children were victims of segregation. . . .

Having broadly proclaimed its support of desegregating public schools, the Supreme Court shortly thereafter issued [a second] opinion [*Brown II*]—the opinion that legitimized much of the social upheaval that forms the central theme of this book. Fearful that southern segregationists, as well as the executive and legislative branches of state and federal governments, would both resist and impede this courageous decision, the Court offered a palliative to those opposed to *Brown*'s directive. Speaking again with one voice, the Court concluded that, to achieve the goal of desegregation, the lower federal courts were to "enter such orders and decrees consistent with this opinion as are necessary and proper to admit to public schools on a racially nondiscriminatory basis *with all deliberate speed* the parties to these cases."

As Thurgood Marshall and other civil rights lawyers pondered the second decision, they tried to ascertain what the Court meant in adding the crucial phrase "all deliberate speed" to its opinion. It is reported that, after the lawyers read the decision, a staff member consulted a dictionary to confirm their worst fears—that the "all deliberate speed" language meant "slow" and that the apparent victory was compromised because resisters were allowed to end segregation on their own timetable. These three critical words would indeed turn out to be of great consequence, in that they ignore the urgency on which the *Brown* lawyers insisted. When asked to explain his view of "all deliberate speed," Thurgood Marshall frequently told anyone who would listen that the term meant S-L-O-W. . . .

Nearly twenty-five years after the landmark *Brown* decision, a major challenge to its underlying principles of equality in education was emerging. The timing was significant for me in that I was among the large wave of first-generation African-Americans going to college and graduate school. Even though *Brown* paved the way by removing the barrier of segregated educational systems, it remained to be seen who would now have the opportunity to attend the prestigious institutions that had been substantially, if not completely, closed to African-Americans. While the battle for integration continued in the courtrooms around America, the shocking assassination of Martin Luther King, Jr., in April 1968, triggered a chain reaction of nationwide black protest; it also forced many institutions to open their doors much faster than they had contemplated. Harvard Law School was no different. A private institution, it claimed that its doors had always been open to people regardless of color (although women were not admitted until 1953), and it could point out that George Lewis Ruffin, an African-American, had graduated from the law school in 1869 (which, coincidentally, was the year that Howard Law School was founded), but there was still no real effort to seek out and admit African-Americans. . . .

When I arrived in the fall of 1975, Harvard Law School was admitting fifty to sixty African-American students each year, nearly 10 percent of its entering class. Harvard was, in fact, admitting more African-American students than any of its peer institutions and, with the exception of Howard Law School, was at the top of all law schools in the number of minority students enrolled. Some twenty-five years after *Brown*, diversity appeared to be a permanent part of Harvard's educational mission. Our sense of comfort was nearly shattered, however, when Allan Bakke, a white student who had applied to the University of California at Davis Medical School and been rejected, filed a suit challenging an admissions program that affirmatively recruited and admitted African-American and Chicano applicants. The lawsuit called the *Brown* case into question, and squarely raised the issue of what public institutions could do, or not do, to increase the deplorably low representation of minorities in their universities and graduate schools. . . .

In *Bakke*, Justice Powell asserted that Title VI of the Civil Rights Act of 1964 proscribed only racial classifications that would be unconstitutional if used by a state. He applied strict scrutiny and concluded that, although achieving a diverse student body constituted a compelling state interest, the California program was not narrowly tailored to meet that end. He upheld the aspect of the UC Davis plan as that allowed the consideration of diversity, as articulated in the Harvard plan, as one factor, in selecting a class of students to pursue higher education. . . .

What differentiates *Brown* from *Bakke* is the forced abandonment of a legal and intellectual justification of integration based on remedying past discrimination. *Bakke* placed the legitimacy of affirmative action in universities squarely on educational diversity rather than on remedial aims. . . .

I routinely discuss legal, personal, and social issues with my friend John Payton, and in 1997, John called with some exciting news. His law firm had been approached by the University of Michigan to represent it in a lawsuit filed by some white applicants who had unsuccessfully applied to Michigan's law school and undergraduate program. The white applicants were represented by the Center for Individual Rights (CIR), a conservative Washington, D.C.-based organization. . . .

The Michigan lawsuits demanded, among other things, the end to any program that considered an applicant's race, the immediate admission of those whites who were allegedly qualified and denied admission, and money damages. . . .

The civil rights community and those private and public universities committed to maintaining a diverse pool of applicants for their institutions learned some painful lessons from the *Bakke* case, and they decided to develop a more focused effort this time around. More than 150 groups filed briefs in support of the Michigan diversity plan; they included law schools, universities, members of Congress, and corporations. Retired members of the armed forces, reporting that the military could not have credibility without an affirmative action plan that recruited minority officers into its ranks, filed a highly influential brief. Their brief caused a stir, in that it went against the public position of President George W. Bush, who filed a brief opposing the Michigan plan and labeled it a quota. There were further splits within the Republican ranks, as the highest-ranked and best-known African-Americans in the Bush administration, Colin Powell and Condoleezza Rice, also supported diversity and, in Powell's case, supported Michigan explicitly. Despite all of this external agitation, only nine votes counted, and I was carefully counting to see whether we could muster five votes. . . .

In *Gratz v. Bollinger* and *Grutter v. Bollinger*, the Supreme Court answered the central question, debated since *Bakke*, of the propriety of university or college affirmative action programs. The results were, at best, a moderate success for affirmative action. They remain, in the context of the Court's jurisprudence on race- and economic-based educational programs, an important setback to the mission established in *Brown*. By a vote of 5 to 4, the Court upheld the Michigan Law School's affirmative action plan. By a vote of 6 to 3, it held that the undergraduate program was tantamount to a quota system, and unconstitutional. It was a day to celebrate, largely because a contrary decision in the law school case would have been unfathomable.

In *Grutter*, O'Connor presented a robust endorsement of the principle of diversity as a factor in university admissions. Justice O'Connor not only endorsed Justice Powell's broad mandate in *Bakke* but went even further in embracing the significance of diversity in the *Grutter* decision:

Justice Powell emphasized that *nothing less* than the "nation's future depends upon leaders trained through wide exposure to the ideas and mores of students as diverse as this Nation of many peoples."

So long as the admissions program does not constitute the type of quota system of "racial balancing" outlawed by *Bakke*, it may admit a "critical mass" of minority students in an effort to obtain a racially diverse student body. Educational institutions are permitted to use race as a factor (in the words of *Bakke*, quoted in *Grutter*, as a "plus") in minority admissions, so long as the decision to admit the student is "flexible enough to ensure that each applicant is evaluated as an individual and not in a way that makes an applicant's race or ethnicity the defining feature of his or her application."

In the *Gratz* opinion, Chief Justice Rehnquist, writing for a 6-to-3 majority, found the undergraduate admissions program unconstitutional. He was joined by the conservative justices Scalia, Kennedy, O'Connor, and Thomas. The centrist justice Breyer concurred in the judgment of the Court while not joining the chief justice's opinion. The chief justice found that awarding a blanket score—in this case, 20 points, or just over 13 percent of the maximum 150 points used to rank applicants—ensured that the university would admit all qualified minority applicants. He held that the scoring system, "by setting up automatic, predetermined point allocations for the soft variables [including race], ensures that the diversity contributions of applicants cannot be individually assessed." The university's failure to consider individualized features of the diversity of each applicant rendered its affirmative action plan unconstitutional and required the Court to strike it down.

Grutter held that attainment of the educational benefits flowing from diversity (such as promoting cross-racial understanding that breaks down racial stereotypes) constitutes a compelling interest, and deferred to the university's determination that diversity is essential to its educational mission. The law school's position was further bolstered by numerous expert studies and reports, as well as the experience of major American businesses, retired military officers, and civilian military officials. Finally, universities and, more especially, law schools are training grounds for future leaders, and "the path to leadership must be visibly open to talented and qualified individuals of every race and ethnicity."

Moreover, the individualized consideration, the absence of quotas, and the recognition of diversity stemming from sources other than race (all of which resemble the Harvard approach that Justice Powell praised in *Bakke*) render the plan narrowly tailored. However, affirmative action must be limited in time, and the Court expects it will no longer be necessary twenty-five years from now. . . .

Collectively, *Grutter* and *Gratz* preserved the institution of affirmative action in American higher education and, to that extent, are important. Nonetheless, both cases—*Grutter* by what it did *not* say and *Gratz* by what it *did* say—are troubling in that they will likely fail to be the catalysts for dispensing with the "all deliberate speed" mentality adopted in *Brown*. With the decisions, the Court did not erect a further barrier in the path of the struggle to true integration and equality; it also did little to promote that struggle. . . .

. . . My fear that *Brown's* vision is being accomplished only with "all deliberate speed" is now supplanted by my greater fear that resegregation of public education is occurring at a faster pace. While we celebrate the Michigan decision as a vindication of the principles articulated in *Brown*, we must also be vigilant to make sure that the progress of fifty years is not compromised any further. . . .

Racial segregation today is the result of a complicated mix of social, political, legal, and economic factors, rather than the result of direct state commands ordering racial separation. Yet, whatever the causes, it remains overwhelmingly true that black and Latino children in central cities are educated in virtually all-minority schools with decidedly inferior facilities and educational opportunities. Even when students in suburban and rural schools are included, a majority of black and Latino students around the country still attend predominantly minority schools.

The effective compromise reached in the United States at the close of the twentieth century is that schools may be segregated by race as long as it is not due to direct government fiat. Furthermore, although *Brown I* emphasized that equal educational opportunity was a crucial component of citizenship, there is no federal constitutional requirement that pupils in predominantly minority school districts receive the same quality of education as students in wealthier, largely all-white suburban districts. Although these suburban districts appear as healthy as ever, the public school system in many urban areas is on the brink of collapse. Increasing numbers of parents who live in these urban areas are pushing for charter schools, home schooling, or vouchers for private schools in order to avoid traditional public school education. At the start of the twenty-first century, the principle of *Brown* seems as hallowed as ever, but its practical effect seems increasingly irrelevant to contemporary public schooling.

Indeed, the United States has been in a period of resegregation for some time now. Resegregation is strongly correlated with class and with poverty. Today, white children attend schools where 80 percent of the student body is also white, resulting in the highest level of segregation of any group. Only 15 percent of segregated white schools are in areas of concentrated poverty; over 85 percent of segregated black and Latino schools are. Schools in high-poverty areas routinely show lower levels of educational performance; even well-prepared students with stable family backgrounds are hurt academically by attending such schools.

U.S. public schools as a whole are becoming more nonwhite as minority enrollment approaches 40 percent of all students, nearly twice the percentage in the 1960s. In the western and southern regions of the country, almost half of all students are minorities. In today's schools, blacks make up only 8.6 percent of the average white student's school, and just over 10 percent of white students attend schools that have a predominantly minority population. Even more striking is the fact that over 37 percent of black and Latino students attend 90-100 percent minority schools.

This trend has led to the emergence of a substantial number of public schools where the student body is almost entirely nonwhite. The 2000 United States Department of Calculation data showed that there has been a very rapid increase in the number of multiracial schools where three different racial groups comprise at least one-tenth of the total enrollment. However, these schools are attended by only 14 percent of white children. Most of the shrinking white enrollment occurs in the nation's largest city school systems.

Minority segregated schools have much higher concentrations of poverty and much lower average test scores, lower levels of student and teacher qualifications, and fewer advanced courses. They are often plagued by limited resources and social and health problems. High-poverty schools have been shown to increase educational inequality for the students who attend them because of such problems as a lack of resources, shortage of qualified teachers, lower parent involvement, and higher teacher turnover. Almost half of the students in schools attended by the average black or Latino student are poor or nearly poor. By contrast, less than one student in five in schools attended by the average white student is classified as poor. As Gary Orfield, co-director of the Civil Rights Project (CRP) at Harvard University, and Susan E. Eaton, researcher at CRP, note, "Nine times in ten, an extremely segregated black and Latino school will also be a high-poverty school. And studies have shown that high-poverty schools are overburdened, have high rates of turnover, less qualified and experienced teachers, and operate a world away from mainstream society." . . .

Certainly, there must be some form of social change on the education front. Whether this occurs through separation or in an integrated environment is a matter of great consequence for American society. Our experiment with integration started with a pronouncement, half a century ago in *Brown*, that integration was an important value with positive social consequences that should be embraced by all Americans. Twenty years later, real action to integrate our schools had only just started. We are but one generation into an integrated society, and the signs are that the majority of the population is tired with the process. Those at the top want to stay there, and those in the middle would rather hold on to what they have than give a little to get a lot. We have to decide whether this is a country that is comfortable with discrimination. Are we satisfied with the fact that many whites find minorities so repellent that they will move and change their children's schooling to avoid us? For, make no mistake, that is what underpins the supposedly "rational" decisions based on racial stereotyping: an inability on the part of the majority of Americans to acknowledge that minority citizens are "just like us."

There is little surprise in acknowledging that there was substantial resistance by the white community to integration and later to affirmative action. But the theory of interest convergence suggests that most Americans cannot be bothered to engage that problem unless it directly affects them. They would rather turn away, uninterested, and perpetuate racial disadvantage than acknowledge it, let alone confront it. We have witnessed the *Brown* decision, followed by *Bakke* and, more recently, *Grutter v. Bollinger*. We have witnessed Dr. King's historic "I Have a Dream" speech and his subsequent assassination. We have heard the powerful words of President Johnson in his commitment to affirmative action, and President Bush's criticism of the Michigan plan as a program promoting racial preferences. We have seen diversity plans approved by the Supreme Court and, in the same year, some HBCUs [historically black colleges and universities] lose their accreditation and close. We continue to make progress, and suffer setbacks, in grappling with the persistent problem of race in America. But we must remain vigilant in our commitment to confront racial inequalities, even when we face persistent, even increasing resistance. . . .

The decision in *Brown I*, ending segregation in our public schools—and by implication de jure segregation everywhere—is justly celebrated as one of the great events in our legal and political history. Precedent did not compel the result, nor was the composition of the Court indicative of a favorable outcome. There is no doubt that the circumstances of many African-Americans are better now than they were before the *Brown* decision. But the speed with which we have embraced the society made possible by *Brown I* has indeed been all too deliberate. It has been deliberate meaning "slow," "cautious," "wary," as if Americans remained to be convinced of the integration ideal. It has been deliberate in the sense of "ponderous" or "awkward," as if each step had been taken painfully and at great cost. Yet the speed with which we have embraced integration has not been deliberate in the sense of "thoughtful" or "reflective"—on the contrary, our response has been emotional and instinctive, perhaps on both sides of the debate. These reactions, anticipated and epitomized in *Brown II*, I suggest, are the real legacy of *Brown I*.

It would be foolhardy to deny that progress has been made, or to dismiss the reality that *Brown I* is a momentous decision both for what it says and for what it has achieved. But there is more yet to do. *Brown I* should be celebrated for ending de jure segregation in this country—a blight that lasted almost four hundred years and harmed millions of Americans of all races. Far too many African-Americans, however, have been left behind, while only a relative few have truly prospered. For some, the promise of integration has proved ephemeral. For others, short-term gains have been replaced by setbacks engendered by new forms of racism. School districts, briefly integrated, have become resegregated. Some distinctively African-American institutions have been permanently destroyed and others crippled. As we stand near the end or the transformation of affirmative action, things look set to get worse, not better.

For all their clear vision of the need to end segregation, *Brown I* and *II* stand as decisions that see integration as a solution that is embraced only grudgingly. Subsequent courts do not even seem to recognize integration as an imperative. And that, perhaps, is the worst indictment of the *Brown* decisions: their faith in progress and their failure to see how quickly people of a different mind could not only resist but, once the tide had turned, even reverse the halting progress toward a fully integrated society....

47

Obergefell v. Hodges (2015) and
Chief Justice Roberts' Dissent

In June of 2015, the U.S. Supreme Court ruled that same-sex marriage was constitutional in all fifty states under the Fourteenth Amendment. James Obergefell was only one of the litigants in this landmark case, since cases from Ohio, Tennessee, Michigan and Kentucky were decided together. Before this decision was handed down by the Supreme Court, same-sex marriage had been made legal by eleven states and by the District of Columbia, based on state legislation. The majority of the Court, led by Justice Anthony Kennedy, found that the Due Process and Equal Protection Clauses of the Fourteenth Amendment extend to all states the right of same-sex couples to marry, and thus, to have marriages performed in one state be acknowledged by all other states. Justice Kennedy begins his majority opinion with historical and philosophical observations about the institution of marriage. He discusses human liberty and personal identity. Kennedy writes about the "new dimensions of freedom" that have emerged over time resulting in many changes in American society's views on gender and sexual identification. Marriage is a fundamental right guaranteed by the Fourteenth Amendment, Kennedy explains, developing the majority's argument in several interesting ways. Chief Justice Roberts' dissent is built not on opposition to the idea of same-sex marriage, but on the Supreme Court's role in bringing about this change. "Five lawyers have closed the debate and enacted their own vision of marriage as a matter of constitutional law." The dissenters would have allowed the American people through their state legislatures to make the decision on a state-by-state basis. It would have been slower, less uniform, messier; but it would have been more respectful of differing views—particularly religious views—and of the power of the public's opinion, Roberts believes. The decision in Obergefell v. Hodges *was 5–4.*

Obergefell v. Hodges
576 U.S.___(2015)

JUSTICE KENNEDY delivered the opinion of the Court.

The Constitution promises liberty to all within its reach, a liberty that includes certain specific rights that allow persons, within a lawful realm, to define and express their identity. The petitioners in these cases seek to find that liberty by marrying someone of the same sex and having their marriages deemed lawful on the same terms and conditions as marriages between persons of the opposite sex.

I

These cases come from Michigan, Kentucky, Ohio, and Tennessee, States that define marriage as a union between one man and one woman. See, *e.g.,* Mich. Const., Art. I, §25; Ky. Const. §233A; Ohio Rev. Code Ann. §3101.01 (Lexis 2008); Tenn. Const., Art. XI, §18. The petitioners are 14 same-sex couples and two men whose same-sex partners are deceased. The respondents are state officials responsible for enforcing the laws in question. The petitioners claim the respondents violate the Fourteenth Amendment by denying them the right to marry or to have their marriages, lawfully performed in another State, given full recognition.

Petitioners filed these suits in United States District Courts in their home States. Each District Court ruled in their favor. Citations to those cases are in Appendix A, *infra.* The respondents appealed the decisions against them to the United States Court of Appeals for the Sixth Circuit. It consolidated the cases and reversed the judgments of the District Courts. *DeBoer v. Snyder,* 772 F. 3d 388 (2014). The Court of Appeals held that a State has no constitutional obligation to license same-sex marriages or to recognize same-sex marriages performed out of State.

The petitioners sought certiorari. This Court granted review, limited to two questions. 574 U. S. ___ (2015). The first, presented by the cases from Michigan and Kentucky, is whether the Fourteenth Amendment requires a State to license a marriage between two people of the same sex. The second, presented by the cases from Ohio, Tennessee, and, again, Kentucky, is whether the Fourteenth Amendment requires a State to recognize a same-sex marriage licensed and performed in a State which does grant that right.

II

Before addressing the principles and precedents that govern these cases, it is appropriate to note the history of the subject now before the Court.

A

From their beginning to their most recent page, the annals of human history reveal the transcendent importance of marriage. The lifelong union of a man and a woman always has promised nobility and dignity to all persons, without regard to their station in life. Marriage is sacred to those who live by their religions and offers unique fulfillment to those who find meaning in the secular realm. Its dynamic allows two people to find a life that could not be found alone, for a marriage becomes greater than just the two persons. Rising from the most basic human needs, marriage is essential to our most profound hopes and aspirations.

The centrality of marriage to the human condition makes it unsurprising that the institution has existed for millennia and across civilizations. Since the dawn of history, marriage has transformed strangers into relatives, binding families and societies together. Confucius taught that marriage lies at the foundation of government. 2 Li Chi: Book of Rites 266 (C. Chai & W. Chai eds., J. Legge transl. 1967). This wisdom was echoed centuries later and half a world away by Cicero, who wrote, "The first bond of society is marriage; next, children; and then the family." See De Officiis 57 (W. Miller transl. 1913). There are untold references to the beauty of marriage in religious and philosophical texts spanning time, cultures, and faiths, as well as in art and literature in all their forms. It is fair and necessary to say these references were based on the understanding that marriage is a union between two persons of the opposite sex.

That history is the beginning of these cases. The respondents say it should be the end as well. To them, it would demean a timeless institution if the concept and lawful status of marriage were extended to two persons of the same sex. Marriage, in their view, is by its nature a gender-differentiated union of man and woman. This view long has been held— and continues to be held—in good faith by reasonable and sincere people here and throughout the world.

The petitioners acknowledge this history but contend that these cases cannot end there. Were their intent to demean the revered idea and reality of marriage, the petitioners' claims would be of a different order. But that is neither their purpose nor their submission. To the contrary, it is the enduring importance of marriage that underlies the petitioners' contentions. This, they say, is their whole point. Far from seeking to devalue marriage, the petitioners seek it for themselves because of their respect—and need—for its privileges and responsibilities. And their immutable nature dictates that same-sex marriage is their only real path to this profound commitment. . . .

B

The ancient origins of marriage confirm its centrality, but it has not stood in isolation from developments in law and society. The history of marriage is one of both continuity and change. That institution—even as confined to opposite-sex relations—has evolved over time. . . . These new insights have strengthened not weakened, the institution of marriage. Indeed, changed understandings of marriage are characteristic of a Nation where new dimensions of freedom become apparent to new generations, often through perspectives that begin in pleas or protests and then are considered in the political sphere and the judicial process. This dynamic can be seen in the Nation's experiences with the rights of gays and lesbians. Until the mid-20th century, same-sex intimacy long had been condemned as immoral by the state itself in most Western nations, a belief often embodied in the criminal law. For this reason, among others, many persons did not deem homosexuals to have dignity in their own distinct identity. A truthful declaration by same-sex couples of what was in their hearts had to remain unspoken. Even when a greater awareness of the humanity and integrity of homosexual persons came in the period after World War II, the argument that gays and lesbians had a just claim to dignity was in conflict with both law and widespread social conventions. Same-sex intimacy remained a crime in many States. Gays and lesbians were prohibited from most government employment, barred from military service, excluded under immigration laws, targeted by police, and burdened in their rights to associate. See Brief for Organization of American Historians as *Amicus Curiae* 5–28.

For much of the 20th century, moreover, homosexuality was treated as an illness. When the American Psychiatric Association published the first Diagnostic and Statistical Manual of Mental Disorders in 1952, homosexuality was classified as a mental disorder, a position adhered to until 1973. See Position Statement on Homosexuality and Civil Rights, 1973, in 131 Am. J. Psychiatry 497 (1974). Only in more recent years have psychiatrists and others recognized that sexual orientation is both a normal expression of human sexuality and immutable. See Brief for American Psychological Association et al. as *Amici Curiae* 7–17.

In the late 20th century, following substantial cultural and political developments, same-sex couples began to lead more open and public lives and to establish families. This development was followed by a quite extensive discussion of the issue in both governmental and private sectors and by a shift in public attitudes toward greater tolerance. As a result, questions about the rights of gays and lesbians soon reached the courts, where the issue could be discussed in the formal discourse of the law.

Numerous cases about same-sex marriage have reached the United States Courts of Appeals in recent years. In accordance with the judicial duty to base their decisions on principled reasons and neutral discussions, without scornful or disparaging commentary, courts have written a substantial body of law considering all sides of these issues. That case law helps to explain and formulate the underlying principles this Court now must consider. With the exception of the opinion here under review and one other, see *Citizens for Equal Protection* v. *Bruning*, 455 F. 3d 859, 864–868 (CA8 2006), the Courts of Appeals have held that excluding same-sex couples from marriage violates the Constitution. There also have been many thoughtful District Court decisions addressing same-sex marriage—and most of them, too, have concluded same-sex couples must be allowed to marry. In addition the highest courts of many States have contributed to this ongoing dialogue in decisions interpreting their own State Constitutions. These state and federal judicial opinions are cited in Appendix A, *infra*.

After years of litigation, legislation, referenda, and the discussions that attended these public acts, the States are now divided on the issue of same-sex marriage. See Office of the Atty. Gen. of Maryland, The State of Marriage Equality in America, State-by-State Supp. (2015).

III

Under the Due Process Clause of the Fourteenth Amendment, no State shall "deprive any person of life, liberty, or property, without due process of law." The fundamental liberties protected by this Clause include most of the rights enumerated in the Bill of Rights. See *Duncan* v. *Louisiana*, 391 U. S. 145, 147–149 (1968). In addition these liberties extend to certain personal choices central to individual dignity and autonomy, including intimate choices that define personal identity and beliefs. See, *e.g.*, *Eisenstadt* v. *Baird*, 405 U. S. 438, 453 (1972); *Griswold* v. *Connecticut*, 381 U. S. 479, 484–486 (1965).

The identification and protection of fundamental rights is an enduring part of the judicial duty to interpret the Constitution. That responsibility, however, "has not been reduced to any formula." *Poe* v. *Ullman*, 367 U. S. 497, 542 (1961) (Harlan, J., dissenting). Rather, it requires courts to exercise reasoned judgment in identifying interests of the person so fundamental that the State must accord them its respect. See *ibid.* That process is guided by many of the same considerations relevant to analysis of other constitutional provisions that set forth broad principles rather than specific requirements. History and tradition guide and discipline this inquiry but do not set its outer boundaries. See *Lawrence, supra*, at 572. That method respects our history and learns from it without allowing the past alone to rule the present.

The nature of injustice is that we may not always see it in our own times. The generations that wrote and ratified the Bill of Rights and the Fourteenth Amendment did not presume to know the extent of freedom in all of its dimensions, and so they entrusted to future generations a charter protecting the right of all persons to enjoy liberty as we learn its meaning. When new insight reveals discord between the Constitution's central protections and a received legal stricture, a claim to liberty must be addressed. . . .

It cannot be denied that this Court's cases describing the right to marry presumed a relationship involving opposite-sex partners. The Court, like many institutions, has made assumptions defined by the world and time of which it is a part. . . .

This analysis compels the conclusion that same-sex couples may exercise the right to marry. The four principles and traditions to be discussed demonstrate that the reasons marriage is fundamental under the Constitution apply with equal force to same-sex couples.

A first premise of the Court's relevant precedents is that the right to personal choice regarding marriage is inherent in the concept of individual autonomy. This abiding connection between marriage and liberty is why *Loving* invalidated interracial marriage bans under the Due Process Clause. See 388 U. S., at 12; see also *Zablocki, supra*, at 384 (observing *Loving* held "the right to marry is of fundamental importance for all individuals"). Like choices concerning contraception, family relationships, procreation, and childrearing, all of which are protected by the Constitution, decisions concerning marriage are among the most intimate that an individual can make. See *Lawrence, supra*, at 574. Indeed, the Court has noted it would be contradictory "to recognize a right of privacy with respect to other matters of family life and not with respect to the decision to enter the relationship that is the foundation of the family in our society." *Zablocki, supra*, at 386. . . .

A second principle in this Court's jurisprudence is that the right to marry is fundamental because it supports a two-person union unlike any other in its importance to the committed individuals. This point was central to *Griswold v. Connecticut*, which held the Constitution protects the right of married couples to use contraception. 381 U. S., at 485. Suggesting that marriage is a right "older than the Bill of Rights," *Griswold* described marriage this way:

"Marriage is a coming together for better or for worse, hopefully enduring, and intimate to the degree of being sacred. It is an association that promotes a way of life, not causes; a harmony in living, not political faiths; a bilateral loyalty, not commercial or social projects. Yet it is an association for as noble a purpose as any involved in our prior decisions." *Id.*, at 486.

And in *Turner*, the Court again acknowledged the intimate association protected by this right, holding prisoners could not be denied the right to marry because their committed relationships satisfied the basic reasons why marriage is a fundamental right. See 482 U. S., at 95–96. The right to marry thus dignifies couples who "wish to define themselves by their commitment to each other." *Windsor, supra*, at ___ (slip op., at 14). Marriage responds to the universal fear that a lonely person might call out only to find no one there. It offers the hope of companionship and understanding and assurance that while both still live there will be someone to care for the other. . . .

A third basis for protecting the right to marry is that it safeguards children and families and thus draws meaning from related rights of child-rearing, procreation, and education. See *Pierce* v. *Society of Sisters*, 268 U. S. 510 (1925); *Meyer*, 262 U. S., at 399. The Court has recognized these connections by describing the varied rights as a unified whole: "[T]he right to 'marry, establish a home and bring up children' is a central part of the liberty protected by the Due Process Clause." *Zablocki*, 434 U. S., at 384 (quoting *Meyer, supra*, at 399). Under the laws of the several States, some of marriage's protections for children and families are material. But marriage also confers more profound benefits. By giving recognition and legal structure to their parents' relationship, marriage allows children "to understand the integrity and closeness of their own family and its concord with other families in their community and in their daily lives." *Windsor, supra*, at ___ (slip op., at 23). Marriage also affords the permanency and stability important to children's best interests. See Brief for Scholars of the Constitutional Rights of Children as *Amici Curiae* 22–27.

As all parties agree, many same-sex couples provide loving and nurturing homes to their children, whether biological or adopted. And hundreds of thousands of children are presently being raised by such couples. See Brief for Gary J. Gates as *Amicus Curiae* 4. Most States have allowed gays and lesbians to adopt, either as individuals or as couples, and many adopted and foster children have same-sex parents, see *id.*, at 5. This provides powerful confirmation from the law itself that gays and lesbians can create loving, supportive families. . . .

Fourth and finally, this Court's cases and the Nation's traditions make clear that marriage is a keystone of our social order. Alexis de Tocqueville recognized this truth on his travels through the United States almost two centuries ago:

"There is certainly no country in the world where the tie of marriage is so much respected as in America . . . [W]hen the American retires from the turmoil of public life to the bosom of his family, he finds in it the image of order and of peace. . . . [H]e afterwards carries [that image] with him into public affairs." 1 Democracy in America 309 (H. Reeve transl., rev. ed. 1990).

In *Maynard* v. *Hill*, 125 U. S. 190, 211 (1888), the Court echoed de Tocqueville, explaining that marriage is "the foundation of the family and of society, without which there would be neither civilization nor progress." Marriage, the *Maynard* Court said, has long been "'a great public institution, giving character to our whole civil polity.'" *Id.*, at 213. This idea has been reiterated even as the institution has evolved in substantial ways over time, superseding rules related to parental consent, gender, and race once thought by many to be essential. See generally N. Cott, Public Vows. Marriage remains a building block of our national community. . . .

The right of same-sex couples to marry that is part of the liberty promised by the Fourteenth Amendment is derived, too, from that Amendment's guarantee of the equal protection of the laws. The Due Process Clause and the Equal Protection Clause are connected in a profound way, though they set forth independent principles. Rights implicit in liberty and rights secured by equal protection may rest on different precepts and are not always coextensive, yet in some instances each may be instructive as to the meaning and reach of the other. In any particular case one Clause may be thought to capture the essence of the right in a more accurate and comprehensive way, even as the two Clauses may converge in the identification and definition of the right. See *M. L. B.*, 519 U. S., at 120–121; *id.*, at 128–129 (KENNEDY, J., concurring in judgment); *Bearden* v. *Georgia*, 461 U. S. 660, 665 (1983). This interrelation of the two principles furthers our understanding of what freedom is and must become. . . .

These considerations lead to the conclusion that the right to marry is a fundamental right inherent in the liberty of the person, and under the Due Process and Equal Protection Clauses of the Fourteenth Amendment couples of the same-sex may not be deprived of that right and that liberty. The Court now holds that same-sex couples may exercise the fundamental right to marry. No longer may this liberty be denied to them. *Baker* v. *Nelson* must be and now is overruled, and the State laws challenged by Petitioners in these cases are now held invalid to the extent they exclude same-sex couples from civil marriage on the same terms and conditions as opposite-sex couples. . . .

. . . The Court, in this decision holds same-sex couples may exercise the fundamental right to marry in all States. It follows that the Court also must hold—and it now does hold—that there is no lawful basis for a State to refuse to recognize a lawful same-sex marriage performed in another State on the ground of its same-sex character.

No union is more profound than marriage, for it embodies the highest ideals of love, fidelity, devotion, sacrifice, and family. In forming a marital union, two people become something greater than once they were. As some of the petitioners in these cases demonstrate, marriage embodies a love that may endure even past death. It would misunderstand these men and women to say they disrespect the idea of marriage. Their plea is that they do respect it, respect it so deeply that they seek to find its fulfillment for themselves. Their hope is not to be condemned to live in loneliness, excluded from one of civilization's oldest institutions. They ask for equal dignity in the eyes of the law. The Constitution grants them that right.

The judgment of the Court of Appeals for the Sixth Circuit is reversed.

It is so ordered.

CHIEF JUSTICE ROBERTS, with whom JUSTICE SCALIA and JUSTICE THOMAS join, dissenting.

Petitioners make strong arguments rooted in social policy and considerations of fairness. They contend that same-sex couples should be allowed to affirm their love and commitment through marriage, just like opposite-sex couples. That position has undeniable appeal; over the past six years, voters and legislators in eleven States and the District of Columbia have revised their laws to allow marriage between two people of the same sex.

But this Court is not a legislature. Whether same-sex marriage is a good idea should be of no concern to us. Under the Constitution, judges have power to say what the law is, not what it should be. The people who ratified the Constitution authorized courts to exercise "neither force nor will but merely judgment." The Federalist No. 78, p. 465 (C. Rossiter ed. 1961) (A. Hamilton) (capitalization altered).

Although the policy arguments for extending marriage to same-sex couples may be compelling, the legal arguments for requiring such an extension are not. The fundamental right to marry does not include a right to make a State change its definition of marriage. And a State's decision to maintain the meaning of marriage that has persisted in every culture throughout human history can hardly be called irrational. In short, our Constitution does not enact any one theory of marriage. The people of a State are free to expand marriage to include same-sex couples, or to retain the historic definition.

Today, however, the Court takes the extraordinary step of ordering every State to license and recognize same-sex marriage. Many people will rejoice at this decision, and I begrudge none their celebration. But for those who believe in a government of laws, not of men, the majority's approach is deeply disheartening. Supporters of same-sex marriage have achieved considerable success persuading their fellow citizens—through the democratic process—to adopt their view. That ends today. Five lawyers have closed the debate and enacted their own vision of marriage as a matter of constitutional law. Stealing this issue from the people will for many cast a cloud over same-sex marriage, making a dramatic social change that much more difficult to accept.

The majority's decision is an act of will, not legal judgment. The right it announces has no basis in the Constitution or this Court's precedent. The majority expressly disclaims judicial "caution" and omits even a pretense of humility, openly relying on its desire to remake society according to its own "new insight" into the "nature of injustice." *Ante*, at 11, 23. As a result, the Court invalidates the marriage laws of more than half the States and orders the transformation of a social institution that has formed the basis of human society for millennia, for the Kalahari Bushmen and the Han Chinese, the Carthaginians and the Aztecs. Just who do we think we are?

It can be tempting for judges to confuse our own preferences with the requirements of the law. But as this Court has been reminded throughout our history, the Constitution "is made for people of fundamentally differing views." *Lochner* v. *New York*, 198 U. S. 45, 76 (1905) (Holmes, J., dissenting). Accordingly, "courts are not concerned with the wisdom or policy of legislation." *Id.*, at 69 (Harlan, J., dissenting). The majority today neglects that restrained conception of the judicial role. It seizes for itself a question the Constitution leaves to the people, at a time when the people are engaged in a vibrant debate on that question. And it answers that question based not on neutral principles of constitutional law, but on its own "understanding of what freedom is and must become." *Ante*, at 19. I have no choice but to dissent.

Understand well what this dissent is about: It is not about whether, in my judgment, the institution of marriage should be changed to include same-sex couples. It is instead about whether, in our democratic republic, that decision should rest with the people acting through their elected representatives, or with five lawyers who happen to hold commissions authorizing them to resolve legal disputes according to law. The Constitution leaves no doubt about the answer. . . .

Those who founded our country would not recognize the majority's conception of the judicial role. They after all risked their lives and fortunes for the precious right to govern themselves. They would never have imagined yielding that right on a question of social policy to unaccountable and unelected judges. And they certainly would not have been satisfied by a system empowering judges to override policy judgments so long as they do so after "a quite extensive discussion." *Ante,* at 8. In our democracy, debate about the content of the law is not an exhaustion requirement to be checked off before courts can impose their will. "Surely the Constitution does not put either the legislative branch or the executive branch in the position of a television quiz show contestant so that when a given period of time has elapsed and a problem remains unresolved by them, the federal judiciary may press a buzzer and take its turn at fashioning a solution." Rehnquist, The Notion of a Living Constitution, 54 Texas L. Rev. 693, 700 (1976). As a plurality of this Court explained just last year, "It is demeaning to the democratic process to presume that voters are not capable of deciding an issue of this sensitivity on decent and rational grounds." *Schuette* v. *BAMN,* 572 U. S. __, __–__ (2014) (slip op., at 16–17).

The Court's accumulation of power does not occur in a vacuum. It comes at the expense of the people. And they know it. Here and abroad, people are in the midst of a serious and thoughtful public debate on the issue of same-sex marriage. They see voters carefully considering same-sex marriage, casting ballots in favor or opposed, and sometimes changing their minds. They see political leaders similarly reexamining their positions, and either reversing course or explaining adherence to old convictions confirmed anew. They see governments and businesses modifying policies and practices with respect to same-sex couples, and participating actively in the civic discourse. They see countries overseas democratically accepting profound social change, or declining to do so. This deliberative process is making people take seriously questions that they may not have even regarded as questions before.

When decisions are reached through democratic means, some people will inevitably be disappointed with the results. But those whose views do not prevail at least know that they have had their say, and accordingly are—in the tradition of our political culture—reconciled to the result of a fair and honest debate. In addition, they can gear up to raise the issue later, hoping to persuade enough on the winning side to think again. "That is exactly how our system of government is supposed to work." *Post*, at 2–3 (SCALIA, J., dissenting).

But today the Court puts a stop to all that. By deciding this question under the Constitution, the Court removes it from the realm of democratic decision. There will be consequences to shutting down the political process on an issue of such profound public significance. Closing debate tends to close minds. People denied a voice are less likely to accept the ruling of a court on an issue that does not seem to be the sort of thing courts usually decide. As a thoughtful commentator observed about another issue, "The political process was moving . . . , not swiftly enough for advocates of quick, complete change, but majoritarian institutions were listening and acting. Heavy-handed judicial intervention was difficult to justify and appears to have provoked, not resolved, conflict." Ginsburg, Some Thoughts on Autonomy and Equality in Relation to *Roe v. Wade*, 63 N. C. L. Rev. 375, 385–386 (1985) (footnote omitted). Indeed, however heartened the proponents of same-sex marriage might be on this day, it is worth acknowledging what they have lost, and lost forever: the opportunity to win the true acceptance that comes from persuading their fellow citizens of the justice of their cause. And they lose this just when the winds of change were freshening at their backs.

Federal courts are blunt instruments when it comes to creating rights. They have constitutional power only to resolve concrete cases or controversies; they do not have the flexibility of legislatures to address concerns of parties not before the court or to anticipate problems that may arise from the exercise of a new right. Today's decision, for example, creates serious questions about religious liberty. Many good and decent people oppose same-sex marriage as a tenet of faith, and their freedom to exercise religion is—unlike the right imagined by the majority—actually spelled out in the Constitution. Amdt. 1.

Respect for sincere religious conviction has led voters and legislators in every State that has adopted same-sex marriage democratically to include accommodations for religious practice. The majority's decision imposing same-sex marriage cannot, of course, create any such accommodations. The majority graciously suggests that religious believers may continue to "advocate" and "teach" their views of marriage. *Ante*, at 27. The First Amendment guarantees, however, the freedom to "*exercise*" religion. Ominously, that is not a word the majority uses. . . .

Perhaps the most discouraging aspect of today's decision is the extent to which the majority feels compelled to sully those on the other side of the debate. The majority offers a cursory assurance that it does not intend to disparage people who, as a matter of conscience, cannot accept same-sex marriage. *Ante*, at 19. That disclaimer is hard to square with the very next sentence, in which the majority explains that "the necessary consequence" of laws codifying the traditional definition of marriage is to "demea[n] or stigmatiz[e]" same-sex couples. *Ante*, at 19. The majority reiterates such characterizations over and over. By the majority's account, Americans who did nothing more than follow the understanding of marriage that has existed for our entire history—in particular, the tens of millions of people who voted to reaffirm their States' enduring definition of marriage—have acted to "lock . . . out," "disparage," "disrespect and subordinate," and inflict "[d]ignitary wounds" upon their gay and lesbian neighbors. *Ante*, at 17, 19, 22, 25. These apparent assaults on the character of fairminded people will have an effect, in society and in court. See *post*, at 6–7 (ALITO, J., dissenting). Moreover, they are entirely gratuitous. It is one thing for the majority to conclude that the Constitution protects a right to same-sex marriage; it is something else to portray everyone who does not share the majority's "better informed understanding" as bigoted. *Ante*, at 19.

In the face of all this, a much different view of the Court's role is possible. That view is more modest and restrained. It is more skeptical that the legal abilities of judges also reflect insight into moral and philosophical issues. It is more sensitive to the fact that judges are unelected and unaccountable, and that the legitimacy of their power depends on confining it to the exercise of legal judgment. It is more attuned to the lessons of history, and what it has meant for the country and Court when Justices have exceeded their proper bounds. And it is less pretentious than to suppose that while people around the world have viewed an institution in a particular way for thousands of years, the present generation and the present Court are the ones chosen to burst the bonds of that history and tradition.

If you are among the many Americans—of whatever sexual orientation—who favor expanding same-sex marriage, by all means celebrate today's decision. Celebrate the achievement of a desired goal. Celebrate the opportunity for a new expression of commitment to a partner. Celebrate the availability of new benefits. But do not celebrate the Constitution. It had nothing to do with it.

I respectfully dissent.

48

DAVID BERNSTEIN

From *You Can't Say That!*

Not all attacks on civil liberties, such as free speech, come from groups on the right side of the political spectrum, claims law professor David Bernstein. The author cites several memorable examples of the application of laws that prohibit discrimination against groups of people to situations that seem extreme. The results are sometimes bizarre, Bernstein believes, and civil liberties are sacrificed. Of particular interest is the author's examination of speech codes on college campuses. There are two sides to every issue, and especially to this issue, so you, the readers, will have to find your own position. "Idle chatter of a sexual nature," the "South of the Border party" T-shirt, and the "friend, lover, or partner" terminology are up for debate. How should the First Amendment's right to free speech fit into everyday life in school or at work?

INTOLERANT ACTIVISTS ARE DETERMINED to impose their moralistic views on all Americans, regardless of the consequences for civil liberties. These zealots are politically well organized and are a dominant force in one of the two major political parties. They have already achieved many legislative victories, especially at the local level, where they often wield disproportionate power. Courts have often acquiesced to their agenda, even when it conflicts directly with constitutional provisions protecting civil liberties. Until the power of these militants is checked, the First Amendment's protection of freedom of speech and freedom of religion will be in constant danger.

To many civil libertarians, the preceding paragraph reads like a description of the Christian right. But it also describes left-wing egalitarian activists, many of whom are associated with the "civil rights" establishment. Their agenda of elevating antidiscrimination concerns above all others poses an acute threat to civil liberties. The First Amendment prohibits the government from interfering with freedom of expression, which includes free exercise of religion, freedom of speech, freedom of the press, and the right to petition the government for a redress of grievances. All of these civil libertarian restrictions on government power are at risk from antidiscrimination laws. For example:

• In Berkeley, the federal Department of Housing and Urban Development threatened to sanction three neighborhood activists for organizing community opposition to a plan to turn a rundown hotel into a homeless center. HUD alleged that the activists had violated the Fair Housing Act by interfering with a project that would serve a group of people who would be disproportionately mentally ill or recovering substance abusers, protected groups under the Act. HUD spokesperson John Phillips, trying to parry free speech concerns raised by the media, instead stoked them. "To ask questions is one thing," Phillips told reporters. "To write brochures and articles and go out and actively organize people to say, 'We don't want those people in those structures,' is another."

• In San Francisco, Krissy Keefer is using an antidiscrimination law to challenge the artistic autonomy of the San Francisco Ballet. She is suing the ballet for height and weight discrimination for refusing to accept her daughter Fredrika into its preprofessional program. Fredrika is of average height and weight, while modern ballet's aesthetic standards require that dancers be tall and lithe.

• In Denver, the city government refused to issue a Columbus Day parade permit unless the organizers signed an agreement stating that "there will be no references, depictions, or acknowledgment of Christopher Columbus during the parade; and no speeches or wreath laying for Christopher Columbus will be conducted." The city was responding to pressure from American Indian activists, who alleged that a parade celebrating Columbus would create an illegal "hostile public environment."

• In New York City, Michelle Ganzy sued the Allen Christian School for firing her after she became pregnant out of wedlock. Ganzy, like all of the school's teachers, had agreed to serve as a role model for her students, in part by behaving in accordance with the school's conservative moral beliefs. Nevertheless, Ganzy sued for sex discrimination. A federal court, seemingly oblivious to the threat this lawsuit posed to the autonomy of religious institutions, ruled in her favor, holding that "[r]estrictions on pregnancy are not permitted because they are gender discriminatory by definition."

• In Minneapolis, a group of librarians complained of sexual harassment because patrons using the library computers viewed images the librarians saw and found offensive. The Equal Employment Opportunity Commission found that the librarians had "probable cause" to pursue their claim. Because of this and similar cases, public and private libraries throughout the United States are under pressure to install filtering software on their computers, lest a librarian inadvertently view offensive material and file a sexual harassment lawsuit. Defining the issue precisely backwards, a representative of the National Organization for Women told the *New York Times* that she wondered "how far First Amendment rights may go before they infringe on sexual harassment laws."

• In Eugene, Oregon, the state Newspaper Publishers Association published a list of 80 words and phrases that its members should ban from real estate advertisements to avoid liability under federal, state, or local fair housing laws. The forbidden words and phrases include language that signifies an obvious intent to violate fair housing laws (e.g., "no Mexicans"), but also language that is merely descriptive, such as "near church" or "walking distance to synagogue." Fair housing officials overzealously interpret such phrases as expressing an illicit preference for Christians and Jews, respectively. The list also includes phrases that some fair housing officials believe are used as codes to discourage minorities ("exclusive neighborhood," "board approval required") or families with children ("quiet tenants," "bachelor pad"). There are a number of other phrases that did not make the Oregon list, but that some realtors avoid nonetheless for fear of liability, including the following: master bedroom (either sexist or purportedly evocative of slavery and therefore insulting to African Americans), great view (allegedly expresses preference for the nonblind), and walk-up (supposedly discourages the disabled).

• Religious conservatives have also jumped on the antidiscrimination bandwagon. In Wellsville, Ohio, Dolores Stanley celebrated her new job as manager of the local Dairy Mart by removing *Playboy* and *Penthouse* from the store's shelves. "It goes against everything I believe in as a Christian," Stanley said. "There's no way I could participate in that." Stanley's superiors at corporate headquarters, attempting to exercise Dairy Mart's First Amendment right to sell legal magazines, told Stanley to replace the periodicals. She refused and was fired. The American Family Association, a conservative antipornography organization, represented Stanley in a lawsuit against Dairy Mart for sex and religious discrimination and for subjecting her to a "hostile workplace environment." The case settled before trial for a sum "well into the six figures."

These anecdotes are just a few examples of the growing threat antidiscrimination laws pose to civil liberties. Some civil libertarians have attempted to finesse the issue by redefining civil liberties to include protection from the discriminatory behavior of private parties. Under this view, conflicts between freedom of expression and antdiscrimination laws could be construed as clashes between competing civil liberties. For purposes of this book, however, civil liberties retains its traditional definition, referring to constitutional rights protected by the First Amendment and related constitutional provisions.

The clash of civil liberties and antidiscrimination laws has emerged due to the gradual expansion of such laws to the point at which they regulate just about all aspects of American life. This expansion of antidiscrimination laws, in turn, reflects a shift in the primary justification for such laws from the practical, relatively limited goal of redressing harms visited upon previously oppressed groups, especially African Americans, to a moralistic agenda aimed at eliminating all forms of invidious discrimination. Such an extraordinarily ambitious goal cannot possibly be achieved—or even vigorously pursued—without grave consequences for civil liberties. . . .

By the mid-1980s, antidiscrimination laws had emerged as a serious threat to civil liberties. Courts found that these laws punished everything from refusing to cast a pregnant woman as a bimbo in a soap opera, to giving speeches extolling the virtues of stay-at-home mothers, to expressing politically incorrect opinions at work, to refusing to share one's house with a gay roommate, to refusing to fund heretical student organizations at a Catholic university. Defendants protested that their First Amendment rights were being trampled on, but to no avail. Through the early 1990s, courts consistently refused to enforce First Amendment rights and other constitutionally protected civil liberties when their enforcement would have limited the reach of antidiscrimination laws. The trend of recent court decisions seems more friendly to civil liberties, largely because the courts have been populated with conservatives less committed to the antidiscrimination agenda. However, the final outcome of the conflict between civil liberties and antidiscrimination laws remains unresolved. Meanwhile, the fear of litigation—fear not only of actually losing a lawsuit, but also fear of being vindicated only after a protracted, expensive legal battle—is having a profound chilling effect on the exercise of civil liberties in workplaces, universities, membership organizations, and churches throughout the United States. . . .

Given the moral authority of antidiscrimination law in a society still recovering from a viciously racist past, writing a book critical of many of antidiscrimination law's applications is necessarily perilous, the law professor's equivalent of a politician disparaging mom and apple pie. The laudable goal of the ever-broadening antidiscrimination edifice is to achieve a fairer, more just society. Yet even—or perhaps especially—well-meaning attempts to achieve a praiseworthy goal must be criticized when the means used to achieve that goal become a threat to civil liberties.

The student who callously utters a racial epithet, the business executive who excludes Jews from his club, the coworker who tells obnoxious sexist jokes, the neighbor who lobbies against housing for the mentally ill—the actions of these individuals can be infuriating, especially to those who, like the author of this book, have been personally victimized by bigots. But the alternative to protecting the constitutional rights of such scoundrels is much worse: the gradual evisceration of the pluralism, autonomy, and check on government power that civil liberties provide. . . .

Public universities, like all government entities, must comply with the First Amendment. Nevertheless, many public universities have established speech codes to censor expression potentially offensive to women, African Americans, or other groups protected by civil rights laws. Universities commonly justify these rules as being necessary to prevent the creation of an illegal "hostile environment" on campus. University officials have not, however, been able to reconcile suppression of potentially offensive expression with the First Amendment.

The first wave of public university speech codes appeared in the late 1980s, with the rise of censorious political correctness. The University of Michigan's code, for example, banned speech "that stigmatizes or victimizes an individual on the basis of race" or that "has the purpose or reasonably foreseeable effect of interfering with an individual's academic efforts." Another part of the code prohibited speech relating to sex or sexual orientation that "creates an intimidating, hostile or demeaning environment for educational pursuits."

In furtherance of its code, the university distributed a handbook with examples of illicit speech. For example, a student organization, the book stated, would violate the speech code if it "sponsors entertainment that includes a comedian who slurs Hispanics." The handbook also noted that expression of certain politically incorrect opinions, such as remarks by male students that "women just aren't as good in this field as men," were prohibited. Beyond these two examples, students could only guess at what speech was forbidden. A federal court concluded "that the University had no idea what the limits of the [p]olicy were and it was essentially making up the rules as it went along." . . .

In any case, many public universities retain speech codes despite the lurking First Amendment issues. Some codes are so broad that, when taken literally, they are absurd. The University of Maryland's sexual harassment policy, for example, bans "idle chatter of a sexual nature, sexual innuendoes, comments about a person's clothing, body, and/or sexual activities, comments of a sexual nature about weight, body shape, size, or figure, and comments or questions about the sensuality of a person." So, at the University of Maryland, saying "I like your shirt, Brenda" is a punishable instance of sexual harassment. Further, because under Maryland's code the prohibited speech need not be specifically directed at an individual to constitute harassment, even saying "I really like men who wear bow ties" is out of bounds, at least if a man who wears bow ties hears about it.

Public university censorship to prevent a hostile environment extends well beyond the sex discrimination issues raised in the Santa Rosa case. Federal law also bans discrimination in education on the basis of race, religion, veteran status, and other criteria, and universities argue that they must censor speech to prevent a hostile environment for groups protected by those laws, as well. As a measure of just how far the law extends, consider the actions of the Office of Federal Contract Compliance Programs. That office charged illegal harassment based on Vietnam-era veteran status when an exhibit at Ohio State University displayed pictures and postings criticizing the actions of American military personnel during the Vietnam War. So much for academic freedom and the spirit of open debate in higher education.

A more typical case arose when a member of Phi Kappa Sigma at the University of California, Riverside, designed a T-shirt advertising a "South of the Border" party. The shirt featured a figure wearing a serape and sombrero sitting on a beach looking at the setting sun and holding a bottle of tequila, along with a picture of a set of steel drums and a wooden tiki head, in which was carved the word "Jamaica." The bottom of the shirt depicted a smiling Rastafarian carrying a six-pack of beer while standing in a Mexican cantina frequented by Riverside students, humming a lyric from an antiracist song by Bob Marley: "It doesn't matter where you come from long as you know where you are going." Although not exactly a brilliant artistic gem, the shirt was nonetheless a little more creative and diverse than the average frat party ad.

Campus Latino activists, however, were not favorably impressed. They charged that the shirt "dehumanizes and promotes racist views of Mexican people" and they formally accused the fraternity of violating university rules by circulating "offensive racial stereotypes." The fraternity president, Rich Carrez, apologized to the activists and pointed out that he was part Native American, the vice president of the fraternity was Latino, the T-shirt creator was Latino, and the fraternity was the most racially diverse on campus, with 25 white and 22 nonwhite members. The activists were unmoved and stubbornly clung to their view that the innocuous T-shirt promoted offensive stereotypes.

Ultimately, the university required fraternity members to destroy all of the T-shirts, apologize in writing, engage in community service, and attend two seminars on multiculturalism—an ironic punishment given that almost half the fraternity members were themselves minorities. The university also stripped the fraternity of its charter and expelled it from campus for three years. The university eventually lifted all of the sanctions, but only after legal intervention by the Individual Rights Foundation, a national network of lawyers that responds to threats to the First Amendment by college administrators and government officials.

Lawsuits, or even the threat of lawsuits, certainly seem to get campus officials' attention. At some public universities, civil libertarians have used the threat of legal action to persuade school officials to abandon their speech codes. For example, in 1997, the Office of Social Justice at West Virginia University published a brochure defining illicit discriminatory behavior as, among other things, expression of politically incorrect sentiments. An example of such forbidden discrimination was provided: claiming that "women never do well" in a particular science class regardless, apparently, of whether the statement is true. With such strict limits on what thoughts and feelings could be publicly shared, WVU students might well have had trouble finding anything neutral and sensitive enough to say to each other. But not to worry, the brochure provided helpful "advice" for encouraging a welcome environment, such as substituting "friend, lover, or partner" for the word boyfriend or girlfriend. The brochure further cheerfully suggested that failure to comply with its advice would be punishable.

Concerned faculty members wrote to the president of the university, David Hardesty Jr., seeking assurance that the brochure was not a speech and behavior code for students and faculty. Hardesty instead confirmed his correspondents' fears by writing that "[t]he right to free speech and the concept of academic freedom do not exist in isolation," and that freedom of speech does not include the right "to create a hostile environment on campus." The university ultimately withdrew the brochure, but, as is no doubt becoming a familiar theme in these tales, only after the West Virginia Civil Liberties Union threatened to sue. . . .

Regardless of whether their universities have formal speech codes, public university officials frequently restrict "offensive" student speech on an ad hoc basis. For example, UCLA suspended an editor of the student newspaper for running an editorial cartoon ridiculing affirmative action preferences. In the cartoon, a student asks a rooster on campus how it got into UCLA. The rooster responds, "affirmative action." After the editor was sanctioned by UCLA, student editor James Taranto reproduced the cartoon in the California State University, Northridge, student newspaper and criticized UCLA officials for suspending the paper's editor for engaging in constitutionally protected expression. Northridge officials suspended Taranto from his editorial position for two weeks for publishing controversial material "without permission." However, when Taranto threatened a lawsuit, the school removed the suspension from his transcript. Taranto continued to pursue a career in journalism and currently edits Opinionjournal.com.

In another incident, administrators at the University of Minnesota, Twin Cities, prohibited the College Republicans from distributing at the school's orientation fliers critical of then-president Bill Clinton. Several fliers contained R-rated humor, and one of them vulgarly satirized the president's views on gay rights. University officials argued that the fliers violated the university's nondiscrimination policy, violated orientation guidelines that require orientation to provide students with an "appreciation of diversity," and were not "consistent with the goals of the university."

After severe criticism from the American Civil Liberties Union and the local media—especially the *Minneapolis Star Tribune*—the university relented and permitted the distribution of the fliers. However, university president Nils Hasselmo stubbornly insisted that the flyer incident had only had the "appearance of" suppressing speech. He maintained that the orientation regulations that the fliers had violated were constitutional and had only been suspended, not repealed. Subsequently, an outraged Minnesota law student sued the university for violating its students' constitutional rights. The university capitulated, agreeing not only to stop censoring student materials but also, in a welcome twist on the usual forced sensitivity training ritual, to have its administration attend a lecture on the protection of freedom of speech afforded by the First Amendment. . . .

PART NINE

Public Opinion and the Media

49

V. O. KEY

From *Public Opinion and American Democracy*

Professor V. O. Key was a pioneer in the study of many facets of modern American politics, including elections, political parties, and public opinion. His detailed study of public opinion attempted to explain the relationship between the people's opinions and the political leadership's opinions. Key's analysis is complicated but clear in its recognition of both elite and mass influence. A particularly useful concept is Key's "opinion dike." He believed that the public's opinion keeps leaders from straying too far outside the parameters acceptable to the people in the making of policy. Most important, Key lifted the blame for "indecision, decay, and disaster" from the shoulders of the public onto the leadership stratum where, he alleged, it really belongs.

———

THE EXPLORATION of public attitudes is a pursuit of endless fascination—and frustration. Depiction of the distribution of opinions within the public, identification of the qualities of opinion, isolation of the odd and of the obvious correlates of opinion, and ascertainment of the modes of opinion formation are pursuits that excite human curiosity. Yet these endeavors are bootless unless the findings about the preferences, aspirations, and prejudices of the public can be connected with the workings of the governmental system. The nature of that connection has been suggested by the examination of the channels by which governments become aware of public sentiment and the institutions through which opinion finds more or less formal expression.

When all these linkages are treated, the place of public opinion in government has still not been adequately portrayed. The problem of opinion and government needs to be viewed in an even broader context. Consideration of the role of public opinion drives the observer to the more fundamental question of how it is that democratic governments manage to operate at all. Despite endless speculation on that problem, perplexities still exist about what critical circumstances, beliefs, outlooks, faiths, and conditions are conducive to the maintenance of regimes under which public opinion is controlling, at least in principle, and is, in fact, highly influential. . . . Though the preceding analyses did not uncover the secret of the conditions precedent to the practice of democratic politics, they pointed to a major piece of the puzzle that was missing as we sought to assemble the elements that go into the construction of a democratic regime. The significance of that missing piece may be made apparent in an indirect manner. In an earlier day public opinion seemed to be pictured as a mysterious vapor that emanated from the undifferentiated citizenry and in some way or another enveloped the apparatus of government to bring it into conformity with the public will. These weird conceptions, some of which were mentioned in our introductory chapter, passed out of style as the technique of the sample survey permitted the determination, with some accuracy, of the distribution of opinions within the population. Vast areas of ignorance remain in our information about people's opinions and aspirations; nevertheless, a far more revealing map of the gross topography of public opinion can now be drawn than could have been a quarter of a century ago.

Despite their power as instruments for the observation of mass opinion, sampling procedures do not bring within their range elements of the political system basic for the understanding of the role of mass opinion within the system. Repeatedly, as we have sought to explain particular distributions, movements, and qualities of mass opinion, we have had to go beyond the survey data and make assumptions and estimates about the role and behavior of that thin stratum of persons referred to variously as the political elite, the political activists, the leadership echelons, or the influentials. In the normal operation of surveys designed to obtain tests of mass sentiment, so few persons from this activist stratum fall into the sample that they cannot well be differentiated, even in a static description, from those persons less involved politically. The data tell us almost nothing about the dynamic relations between the upper layer of activists and mass opinion. The missing piece of our puzzle is this elite element of the opinion system. . . .

While the ruling classes of a democratic order are in a way invisible because of the vagueness of the lines defining the influentials and the relative ease of entry to their ranks, it is plain that the modal norms and standards of a democratic elite have their peculiarities. Not all persons in leadership echelons have precisely the same basic beliefs; some may even regard the people as a beast. Yet a fairly high concentration prevails around the modal beliefs, even though the definition of those beliefs must be imprecise. Fundamental is a regard for public opinion, a belief that in some way or another it should prevail. Even those who cynically humbug the people make a great show of deference to the populace. The basic doctrine goes further to include a sense of trusteeship for the people generally and an adherence to the basic doctrine that collective efforts should be dedicated to the promotion of mass gains rather than of narrow class advantage; elite elements tethered to narrow group interest have no slack for maneuver to accommodate themselves to mass aspirations. Ultimate expression of these faiths comes in the willingness to abide by the outcome of popular elections. The growth of leadership structures with beliefs including these broad articles of faith is probably accomplished only over a considerable period of time, and then only under auspicious circumstances.

If an elite is not to monopolize power and thereby to bring an end to democratic practices, its rules of the game must include restraints in the exploitation of public opinion. Dimly perceptible are rules of etiquette that limit the kinds of appeals to public opinion that may be properly made. If it is assumed that the public is manipulable at the hands of unscrupulous leadership (as it is under some conditions), the maintenance of a democratic order requires the inculcation in leadership elements of a taboo against appeals that would endanger the existence of democratic practices. Inflammation of the sentiments of a sector of the public disposed to exert the tyranny of an intolerant majority (or minority) would be a means of destruction of a democratic order. Or by the exploitation of latent differences and conflicts within the citizenry it may at times be possible to paralyze a regime as intense hatreds among classes of people come to dominate public affairs. Or by encouraging unrealistic expectations among the people a clique of politicians may rise to power, a position to be kept by repression as disillusionment sets in. In an experienced democracy such tactics may be "unfair" competition among members of the politically active class. In short, certain restraints on political competition help keep competition within tolerable limits. The observation of a few American political campaigns might lead one to the conclusion that there are no restraints on politicians as they attempt to humbug the people. Even so, admonitions ever recur against arousing class against class, against stirring the animosities of religious groups, and against demagoguery in its more extreme forms. American politicians manifest considerable restraint in this regard when they are tested against the standards of behavior of politicians of most of those regimes that have failed in the attempt to establish or maintain democratic practices. . . .

. . . Certain broad structural or organizational characteristics may need to be maintained among the activists of a democratic order if they are to perform their functions in the system. Fundamental is the absence of sufficient cohesion among the activists to unite them into a single group dedicated to the management of public affairs and public opinion. Solidification of the elite by definition forecloses opportunity for public choice among alternative governing groups and also destroys the mechanism for the unfettered expression of public opinion or of the opinions of the many subpublics. . . .

. . . Competitive segments of the leadership echelons normally have their roots in interests or opinion blocs within society. A degree of social diversity thus may be, if not a prerequisite, at least helpful in the construction of a leadership appropriate for a democratic regime. A series of independent social bases provide the foundations for a political elite difficult to bring to the state of unification that either prevents the rise of democratic processes or converts them into sham rituals. . . .

Another characteristic may be mentioned as one that, if not a prerequuisite to government by public opinion, may profoundly affect the nature of a democratic order. This is the distribution through the social structure of those persons highly active in politics. By various analyses, none founded on completely satisfactory data, we have shown that in the United States the political activists—if we define the term broadly—are scattered through the socio-economic hierarchy. The upper-income and occupational groups, to be sure, contribute disproportionately; nevertheless, individuals of high political participation are sprinkled throughout the lesser occupational strata. Contrast the circumstances when the highly active political stratum coincides with the high socioeconomic stratum. Conceivably the winning of consent and the creation of a sense of political participation and of sharing in public affairs may be far simpler when political activists of some degree are spread through all social strata. . . .

Allied with these questions is the matter of access to the wider circles of political leadership and of the recruitment and indoctrination of these political activists. Relative ease of access to the arena of active politics may be a preventive of the rise of intransigent blocs of opinion managed by those denied participation in the regularized processes of politics. In a sense, ease of access is a necessary consequence of the existence of a somewhat fragmented stratum of political activists. . . .

This discussion in terms of leadership echelons, political activists, or elites falls painfully on the ears of democratic romantics. The mystique of democracy has in it no place for ruling classes. As perhaps with all powerful systems of faith, it is vague on the operating details. Yet by their nature governing systems, be they democratic or not, involve a division of social labor. Once that axiom is accepted, the comprehension of democratic practices requires a search for the peculiar characteristics of the political influentials in such an order, for the special conditions under which they work, and for the means by which the people keep them in check. The vagueness of the mystique of democracy is matched by the intricacy of its operating practices. If it is true that those who rule tend sooner or later to prove themselves enemies of the rights of man—and there is something to be said for the validity of this proposition—then any system that restrains that tendency however slightly can excite only awe. . . . Analytically it is useful to conceive of the structure of a democratic order as consisting of the political activists and the mass of people. Yet this differentiation becomes deceptive unless it is kept in mind that the democratic activists consist of people arranged along a spectrum of political participation and involvement, ranging from those in the highest posts of official leadership to the amateurs who become sufficiently interested to try to round up a few votes for their favorite in the presidential campaign. . . . It is in the dynamics of the system, the interactions between these strata, that the import of public opinion in democratic orders becomes manifest. Between the activists and the mass there exists a system of communication and interplay so complex as to defy simple description; yet identification of a few major features of that system may aid in our construction of a general conception of democratic processes.

Opinion Dikes

In the interactions between democratic leadership echelons and the mass of people some insight comes from the conception of public opinion as a system of dikes which channel public action or which fix a range of discretion within which government may act or within which debate at official levels may proceed. This conception avoids the error of personifying "public opinion" as an entity that exercises initiative and in some way functions as an operating organism to translate its purposes into governmental action.

In one of their aspects the dikes of opinion have a substantive nature in that they define areas within which day-to-day debate about the course of specific action may occur. Some types of legislative proposals, given the content of general opinion, can scarcely expect to attract serious attention. They depart too far from the general understandings of what is proper. A scheme for public ownership of the automobile industry, for example, would probably be regarded as so far outside the area of legitimate public action that not even the industry would become greatly concerned. On the other hand, other types of questions arise within areas of what we have called permissive consensus. A widespread, if not a unanimous, sentiment prevails that supports action toward some general objective, such as the care of the ill or the mitigation of the economic hazards of the individual. Probably quite commonly mass opinion of a permissive character tends to develop in advance of governmental action in many areas of domestic policy. That opinion grows out of public discussion against the background of the modal aspirations and values of people generally. As it takes shape, the time becomes ripe for action that will be generally acceptable or may even arouse popular acclaim for its authors. . . .

The idea of public opinion as forming a system of dikes which channel action yields a different conception of the place of public opinion than does the notion of a government by public opinion as one in which by some mysterious means a referendum occurs on very major issue. In the former conception the articulation between government and opinion is relatively loose. Parallelism between action and opinion tends not to be precise in matters of detail; it prevails rather with respect to broad purpose. And in the correlation of purpose and action time lags may occur between the crystallization of a sense of mass purpose and its fulfillment in public action. Yet in the long run majority purpose and public action tend to be brought into harmony. . . .

The argument amounts essentially to the position that the masses do not corrupt themselves; if they are corrupt, they have been corrupted. If this hypothesis has a substantial strain of validity, the critical element for the health of a democratic order consists in the beliefs, standards, and competence of those who constitute the influentials, the opinion-leaders, the political activists in the order. That group, as has been made plain, refuses to define itself with great clarity in the American system; yet analysis after analysis points to its existence. If a democracy tends toward indecision, decay, and disaster, the responsibility rests here, not in the mass of the people.

50

THOMAS CRONIN

From *Direct Democracy*

Although the United States is a representative—republican—system of government, elements of direct democracy have been introduced on the state and local levels over time, especially in the early twentieth century during the Progressive era. Initiative, referendum, and recall give citizens an immediate and direct voice in their government, beyond just electing officials. Professor Thomas Cronin explains these instruments of direct democracy and cites California's 1978 tax-cutting Proposition 13 as a leading example of an important statewide ballot question. Controversy swirls over the wisdom of such exercises in direct democracy. Cronin weighs the advantages against the potential problems of allowing voters to have a direct say in policy-making. His conclusion is that initiative, referendum, and recall will neither destroy American government nor save it. Yet in the twenty-first century, with voters' openly-expressed distrust of public officials, direct democracy will surely become more and more a part of the state and local political scene.

FOR ABOUT A hundred years Americans have been saying that voting occasionally for public officials is not enough. Political reformers contend that more democracy is needed and that the American people are mature enough and deserve the right to vote on critical issues facing their states and the nation. During the twentieth century, American voters in many parts of the country have indeed won the right to write new laws and repeal old ones through the initiative and referendum. They have also thrown hundreds of state and local officials out of office in recall elections.

Although the framers of the Constitution deliberately designed a republic, or indirect democracy, the practice of direct democracy and the debate over its desirability are as old as English settlements in America. Public debate and popular voting on issues go back to early seventeenth-century town assemblies and persist today in New England town meetings.

Populist democracy in America has produced conspicuous assets and conspicuous liabilities. It has won the support and admiration of many enthusiasts, yet it is also fraught with disturbing implications. Its most important contributions came early in this century in the form of the initiative, referendum, and recall, as a reaction to corrupt and unresponsive state legislatures throughout the country. Most of us would not recognize what then passed for representative government. "Bills that the machine and its backers do not desire are smothered in committee; measures which they do desire are brought out and hurried through their passage," said Governor Woodrow Wilson at the time. "It happens again and again that great groups of such bills are rushed through in the hurried hours that mark the close of the legislative sessions, when everyone is withheld from vigilance by fatigue and when it is possible to do secret things." The threat, if not the reality, of the initiative, referendum, and recall helped to encourage a more responsible, civic-minded breed of state legislator. These measures were not intended to subvert or alter the basic character of American government. "Their intention," as Wilson saw it, was "to restore, not to destroy, representative government."

The *initiative* allows voters to propose a legislative measure (statutory initiative) or a constitutional amendment (constitutional initiative) by filing a petition bearing a required number of valid citizen signatures.

The *referendum* refers a proposed or existing law or statute to voters for their approval or rejection. Some state constitutions require referenda; in other states, the legislature may decide to refer a measure to the voters. Measures referred by legislatures (statutes, constitutional amendments, bonds, or advisory questions) are the most common ballot propositions. A *popular* or *petition referendum* (a less frequently used device) refers an already enacted measure to the voters before it can go into effect. States allowing the petition referendum require a minimum number of valid citizen signatures within a specified time. There is confusion about the difference between the initiative and referendum because *referendum* is frequently used in a casual or generic way to describe all ballot measures.

The *recall* allows voters to remove or discharge a public official from office by filing a petition bearing a specified number of valid signatures demanding a vote on the official's continued tenure in office. Recall procedures typically require that the petition be signed by 25 percent of those who voted in the last election, after which a special election is almost always required. The recall differs from impeachment in that the people, not the legislature, initiate the election and determine the outcome with their votes. It is a purely political and not even a semijudicial process.

American voters today admire and respect the virtues of representative government, yet most of them also yearn for an even greater voice in how their laws are made. They understand the defects of both representative and direct democracy and prefer, on balance, to have a mixture of the two. Sensible or sound democracy is their aspiration.

Although Americans cannot cast votes on critical national issues, voters in twenty-six states, the District of Columbia, and hundreds of localities do have the right to put measures on their ballots. Legislatures can also refer measures to the public for a general vote. And constitutional changes in every state except Delaware must be approved by voters before becoming law. Voters in fifteen states and the District of Columbia can also recall elected state officials, and thirty-six states permit the recall of various local officials.

When Americans think of their right to vote, they think primarily of their right to nominate and elect legislators, members of school boards and of city councils, and the American president. Yet California's famous Proposition 13 in June 1978 focused nationwide attention on the public's right to participate in controversial tax decision making, as Californians voted to cut their property taxes by at least half. More voters participated in this issue contest than in the same day's gubernatorial primaries.

California's Proposition 13 had two additional effects. It triggered similar tax-slashing measures (both as bills and as direct legislation by the people) in numerous other states, and it encouraged conservative interest groups to use the initiative and referendum processes to achieve some of their goals. In the past decade conservative interests have placed on state and local ballots scores of measures favoring the death penalty, victims' rights, English-only regulations, and prayer in schools, and opposing taxation or spending, pornography, abortion, and homosexuality. Several states have regularly conducted referenda on issues ranging from a nuclear freeze to seat-belt laws. Citizens are now voting on hundreds of initiatives and referenda at state and local levels. . . .

Skeptics, however, worry about tyranny by the majority and fear voters are seldom well enough informed to cast votes on complicated, technical national laws. People also worry, and justifiably, about the way well-financed special interest groups might use these procedures. Corruption at the state level is much less common today than it was early in the century, but special interests are surely just as involved as ever. The power of campaign contributions is clear. The advantages to those who can afford campaign and political consultants, direct mail firms, and widespread television and media appeals are very real. Although in theory Americans are politically equal, in practice there remain enormous disparities in individuals' and groups' capacities to influence the direction of government. And although the direct democracy devices of the initiative, referendum, and recall type are widely available, the evidence suggests it is generally the organized interests that can afford to put them to use. The idealistic notion that populist democracy devices can make every citizen a citizen-legislator and move us closer to political and egalitarian democracy is plainly an unrealized aspiration.

The initiative, referendum, and recall were born in an era of real grievances. They made for a different kind of democracy in those areas that permitted them. At the very least, they signaled the unacceptability of some of the most corrupt and irresponsible political practices of that earlier era. It is fashionable among political analysts today to say that although they have rarely lived up to their promises, neither have they resulted in the dire outcomes feared by critics. Yet they have had both good and questionable consequences. . . .

By examining direct democracy practices we can learn about the strengths and weaknesses of a neglected aspect of American politics, as well as the workings of representative democracy. We seek to understand it so we can improve it, and to improve it so it can better supplement rather than replace our institutions of representative government. . . .

A populist impulse, incorporating notions of "power to the people" and skepticism about the system has always existed in America. Americans seldom abide quietly the failings and deficiencies of capitalism, the welfare state, or the political decision rules by which we live. We are, as historian Richard Hofstadter wrote, "forever restlessly pitting ourselves against them, demanding changes, improvements, remedies." Demand for more democracy occurs when there is growing distrust of legislative bodies and when there is a growing suspicion that privileged interests exert far greater influences on the typical politician than does the common voter.

Direct democracy, especially as embodied in the referendum, initiative, and recall, is sometimes viewed as a typically American political response to perceived abuses of the public trust. Voters periodically become frustrated with taxes, regulations, inefficiency in government programs, the inequalities or injustices of the system, the arms race, environmental hazards, and countless other irritations. This frustration arises in part because more public policy decisions are now made in distant capitals, by remote agencies or private yet unaccountable entities—such as regulatory bodies, the Federal Reserve Board, foreign governments, multinational alliances, or foreign trading combines—instead of at the local or county level as once was the case, or as perhaps we like to remember.

Champions of populist democracy claim many benefits will accrue from their reforms. Here are some:

- Citizen initiatives will promote government responsiveness and accountability. If officials ignore the voice of the people, the people will have an available means to make needed law.

- Initiatives are freer from special interest domination than the legislative branches of most states, and so provide a desirable safeguard that can be called into use when legislators are corrupt, irresponsible, or dominated by privileged special interests.

- The initiative and referendum will produce open, educational debate on critical issues that otherwise might be inadequately discussed.

- Referendum, initiative, and recall are nonviolent means of political participation that fulfill a citizen's right to petition the government for redress of grievances.

- Direct democracy increases voter interest and election-day turnout. Perhaps, too, giving the citizen more of a role in governmental processes might lessen alienation and apathy.

- Finally (although this hardly exhausts the claims), citizen initiatives are needed because legislators often evade the tough issues. Fearing to be ahead of their time, they frequently adopt a zero-risk mentality. Concern with staying in office often makes them timid and perhaps too wedded to the status quo. One result is that controversial social issues frequently have to be resolved in the judicial branch. But who elected the judges?

For every claim put forward on behalf of direct democracy, however, there is an almost equally compelling criticism. Many opponents believe the ordinary citizen usually is not well enough informed about complicated matters to arrive at sound public policy judgments. They also fear the influence of slick television advertisements or bumper sticker messages.

Some critics of direct democracy contend the best way to restore faith in representative institutions is to find better people to run for office. They prefer the deliberations and the collective judgment of elected representatives who have the time to study complicated public policy matters, matters that should be decided within the give-and-take process of politics. That process, they say, takes better account of civil liberties.

Critics also contend that in normal times initiative and referendum voter turnout is often a small proportion of the general population and so the results are unduly influenced by special interests: big money will win eight out of ten times.

A paradox runs throughout this debate. As the United States has aged, we have extended the suffrage in an impressive way. The older the country, the more we have preached the gospel of civic participation. Yet we also have experienced centralization of power in the national government and the development of the professional politician. The citizen-politician has become an endangered species.

Representative government is always in the process of development and decay. Its fortunes rise and fall depending upon various factors, not least the quality of people involved and the resources devoted to making it work effectively. When the slumps come, proposals that would reform and change the character of representative government soon follow. Direct democracy notions have never been entirely foreign to our country—countless proponents from Benjamin Franklin to Jesse Jackson, Jack Kemp, and Richard Gephardt have urged us to listen more to the common citizen. . . .

The American experience with direct democracy has fulfilled neither the dreams and expectations of its proponents nor the fears of its opponents.

The initiative and referendum have not undermined or weakened representative government. The initiative, referendum, and recall have been no more of a threat to the representative principle than has judicial review or the executive veto. Tools of neither the "lunatic fringe" nor the rich, direct democracy devices have become a permanent feature of American politics, especially in the West.

The initiative, referendum, and recall have not been used as often as their advocates would have wished, in part because state legislatures have steadily improved. Better-educated members, more-professional staff, better media coverage of legislative proceedings, and longer sessions have transformed the legislative process at the state level, mostly for the better. Interest groups once denied access to secret sessions now regularly attend, testify, and participate in a variety of ways in the legislative process. Although individuals and some groups remain frustrated, the level and intensity of that frustration appear to be lower than the discontent that prompted the popular democracy movements around the turn of the century.

Still, hundreds of measures have found their way onto ballots in states across the country, and 35 to 40 percent of the more than 1,500 citizen-initiated ballot measures considered since 1904 have won voter approval. About half of these have been on our ballots since World War II. A few thousand legislatively referred measures have also been placed on the ballot, and at least 60 percent of these regularly win voter approval. Popular, or petition, referenda, placed on the ballot by citizens seeking a voter veto of laws already passed by state legislatures, have been used infrequently. . . .

Recall, used mainly at the local and county level, is seldom used against state officials. The marvel is that all these devices of popular democracy, so vulnerable to apathy, ignorance, and prejudice, not only have worked but also have generally been used in a reasonable and constructive manner. Voters have been cautious and have almost always rejected extreme proposals. Most studies suggest that voters, despite the complexity of measures and the deceptions of some campaigns, exercise shrewd judgment, and most students of direct democracy believe most American voters take this responsibility seriously. Just as in candidate campaigns, when they give the benefit of the doubt to the incumbent and the burden of proof is on the challenger to give reasons why he or she should be voted into office, so in issue elections the voter needs to be persuaded that change is needed. In the absence of a convincing case that change is better, the electorate traditionally sticks with the status quo.

Few radical measures pass. Few measures that are discriminatory or would have diminished the rights of minorities win voter approval, and most of the exceptions are ruled unconstitutional by the courts. On balance, the voters at large are no more prone to be small-minded, racist, or sexist than are legislators or courts.

A case can be made that elected officials are more tolerant, more educated, and more sophisticated than the average voter. "Learning the arguments for freedom and tolerance formulated by notables such as Jefferson, Madison, Mill, or the more libertarian justices of the Supreme Court is no simple task," one study concludes. "Many of those arguments are subtle, esoteric, and difficult to grasp. Intelligence, awareness, and education are required to appreciate them fully." Yet on the occasional issues affecting civil liberties and civil rights that have come to the ballot, voters have generally acted in an enlightened way. This is in part the case because enlightened elites help shape public opinion on such occasions through endorsements, news editorials, talk-show discussions, public debates, and legislative and executive commentary. Further, those voting on state and local ballot measures are usually among the top 30 or 40 percent in educational and information levels.

The civic and educational value of direct democracy upon the electorate has been significant, but this aspect of the promise of direct democracy was plainly overstated from the start. Most voters make up their minds on ballot issues or recall elections in the last few days, or even hours, before they vote. The technical and ambiguous language of many of these measures is still an invitation to confusion, and about a quarter of those voting in these elections tell pollsters they could have used more information in making their decisions on these types of election choices.

Like any other democratic institution, the initiative, referendum, and recall have their shortcomings. Voters are sometimes confused. On occasion an ill-considered or undesirable measure wins approval. Large, organized groups and those who can raise vast sums of money are in a better position either to win, or especially to block, approval of ballot measures. Sometimes a recall campaign is mounted for unfair reasons, and recall campaigns can stir up unnecessary and undesirable conflict in a community. Most of these criticisms can also be leveled at our more traditional institutions. Courts sometimes err, as in the *Dred Scott* decision and in *Plessy v. Ferguson* or *Korematsu*. Presidents surely make mistakes (FDR's attempt to pack the Supreme Court, 1937; Kennedy's Bay of Pigs fiasco, 1961; Nixon's involvement in the Watergate break-in and subsequent coverup, 1972–1974; Reagan's involvement in the Iran-contra arms deal, 1986). And legislatures not only make mistakes about policy from time to time but wind up spending nearly a third of their time amending, changing, and correcting past legislation that proved inadequate or wrong. In short, we pay a price for believing in and practicing democracy—whatever the form.

Whatever the shortcomings of direct democracy, and there are several, they do not justify the elimination of the populist devices from those state constitutions permitting them. Moreover, any suggestion to repeal the initiative, referendum, and recall would be defeated by the voters. Public opinion strongly supports retaining these devices where they are allowed. . . .

In sum, direct democracy devices have not been a cure-all for most political, social, or economic ills, yet they have been an occasional remedy, and generally a moderate remedy, for legislative lethargy and the misuse and nonuse of legislative power. It was long feared that these devices would dull legislators' sense of responsibility without in fact quickening the people to the exercise of any real control in public affairs. Little evidence exists for those fears today. When popular demands for reasonable change are repeatedly ignored by elected officials and when legislators or other officials ignore valid interests and criticism, the initiative, referendum, and recall can be a means by which the people may protect themselves in the grand tradition of self-government.

51

LARRY SABATO

From *Feeding Frenzy*

*When political scientist Larry Sabato published his 1991 book on the me-
dia's role in campaigning, he gave a term to a phenomenon others had already seen: a feeding frenzy. The press en masse attacks a wounded politician
whose record—or more accurately, his or her character—has been questioned.
Every network and cable station participates, often without any real evidence
to back up the rumor. Sabato's list of thirty-six examples ends in 1990;
knowledgeable readers will be able to update the list. Paradoxically, the spectacular success of the* Washington Post's *Bob Woodward and Carl Bernstein in investigating Watergate set the stage for recent feeding frenzies. Today, just the fear of being a media target may deter many qualified people
from entering public service, Sabato notes.*

IT HAS BECOME a spectacle without equal in modern American politics: the news media, print and broadcast, go after a wounded
politician like sharks in a feeding frenzy. The wounds may have been self-
inflicted, and the politician may richly deserve his or her fate, but the
journalists now take center stage in the process, creating the news as much
as reporting it, changing both the shape of election-year politics and the
contours of government. Having replaced the political parties as the
screening committee for candidates and officeholders, the media propel
some politicians toward power and unceremoniously eliminate others.
Unavoidably, this enormously influential role—and the news practices
employed in exercising it—has provided rich fodder for a multitude of
press critics.

These critics' charges against the press cascade down with the fury of
rain in a summer squall. Public officials and many other observers see
journalists as rude, arrogant, and cynical, given to exaggeration, harassment, sensationalism, and gross insensitivity. . . .

Press invasion of privacy is leading to the gradual erasure of the line
protecting a public person's purely private life. This makes the price of
public life enormously higher, serving as an even greater deterrent for
those not absolutely obsessed with holding power—the kind of people
we ought least to want in office. Rather than recognizing this unfortunate
consequence, many in journalism prefer to relish their newly assumed

role of "gatekeeper," which, as mentioned earlier, enables them to substitute for party leaders in deciding which characters are virtuous enough to merit consideration for high office. As ABC News correspondent Brit Hume self-critically suggests:

> We don't see ourselves institutionally, collectively anymore as a bunch of journalists out there faithfully reporting what's happening day by day. . . . We have a much grander view of ourselves: we are the Horatio at the national bridge. We are the people who want to prevent the bad characters from crossing over into public office.

Hume's veteran ABC colleague Sander Vanocur agrees, detecting "among some young reporters a quality of the avenging angel: they are going to sanitize American politics." More and more, the news media seem determined to show that would-be emperors have no clothes, and if necessary to prove the point, they personally will strip the candidates naked on the campaign trail. The sheer number of journalists participating in these public denudings guarantees riotous behavior, and the "full-court press" almost always presents itself as a snarling, unruly mob more bent on killing kings than making them. Not surprisingly potential candidates deeply fear the power of an inquisitorial press, and in deciding whether to seek office, they often consult journalists as much as party leaders, even sharing private vulnerabilities with newsmen to gauge reaction. The *Los Angeles Times's* Washington bureau chief, Jack Nelson, had such an encounter before the 1988 campaign season, when a prospective presidential candidate "literally asked me how long I thought the statute of limitations was" for marital infidelity. "I told him I didn't know, but I didn't think [the limit] had been reached in his case!" For whatever reasons, the individual chose not to run.

As the reader will see later in this volume, able members of the news corps offer impressive defenses for all the practices mentioned thus far, not the least of which is that the press has become more aggressive to combat the legions of image makers, political consultants, spin doctors, and handlers who surround modern candidates like a nearly impenetrable shield. Yet upon reflection, most news veterans recognize that press excesses are not an acceptable antidote for consultant or candidate evils. In fact, not one of the interviewed journalists even attempted to justify an increasingly frequent occurrence in news organizations: the publication of gossip and rumor *without convincing proof.* Gossip has always been the drug of choice for journalists as well as the rest of the political community, but as the threshold for publication of information about private lives has been lowered, journalists sometimes cover politics as "Entertainment Tonight" reporters cover Hollywood. A bitter Gary Hart* observed: "Rumor and gossip have become the coins of the political realm," and the *New York Times*'s Michael Oreskes seemed to agree: "1988 was a pretty sorry year when the *National Enquirer* was the most important publication in American journalism." With all the stories and innuendo about personal vice, campaigns appear to be little more than a stream of talegates (or in the case of sexual misadventures, tailgates).

The sorry standard set on the campaign trail is spilling over into coverage of governmental battles. Ever since Watergate,† government scandals have paraded across the television set in a roll call so lengthy and numbing that they are inseparable in the public consciousness, all joined at the Achilles' heel. Some recent lynchings such as John Tower's failure to be confirmed as secretary of defense,‡ rival any spectacle produced by colonial Salem. At the same time more vital and revealing information is ignored or crowded off the agenda. *Real* scandals, such as the savings-and-loan heist or the influence peddling at the Department of Housing and Urban Development in the 1980s, go undetected for years. The sad conclusion is inescapable: The press has become obsessed with gossip rather than governance; it prefers to employ titillation rather than scrutiny; as a result, its political coverage produces trivialization rather than enlightenment. And the dynamic mechanism propelling and demonstrating this decline in news standards is the "feeding frenzy." . . .

The term *frenzy* suggests some kind of disorderly, compulsive, or agitated activity that is muscular and instinctive, not cerebral and thoughtful. In the animal world, no activity is more classically frenzied than the feeding of sharks, piranhas, or bluefish when they encounter a wounded prey. These attack-fish with extraordinarily acute senses first search out weak, ill, or injured targets. On locating them, each hunter moves in quickly to gain a share of the kill, feeding not just off the victim but also off its fellow hunters' agitation. The excitement and drama of the violent encounter builds to a crescendo, sometimes overwhelming the creatures' usual inhi-

*Former Senator (D-Col.) Gary Hart's 1988 presidential candidacy ended after media revelations about his extramarital relations with Donna Rice.—Eds.

†Watergate began with the 1972 break-in at the Democratic National headquarters by several men associated with President Nixon's re-election committee. Watergate ended two years later with the resignation of President Nixon. Nixon and his closest aides were implicated in the coverup of the Watergate burglary. Tapes made by President Nixon of his Oval Office conversations revealed lying and obstruction of justice at the highest levels of government.—Eds.

‡In 1989, the Senate rejected President Bush's nominee for secretary of defense, former Texas Senator John Tower. Senate hearings produced allegations that Tower was an excessive drinker and a womanizer.—Eds.

bitions. The frenzy can spread, with the delirious attackers wildly striking any object that moves in the water, even each other. Veteran reporters will recognize more press behavior in this passage than they might wish to acknowledge. This reverse anthropomorphism can be carried too far, but the similarity of piranha in the water and press on the campaign trail can be summed up in a shared goal: If it bleeds, try to kill it.

The kingdom of politics and not of nature is the subject of this volume, so for our purposes, a feeding frenzy is defined as the press coverage attending any political event or circumstance where a critical mass of journalists leap to cover the same embarrassing or scandalous subject and pursue it intensely, often excessively, and sometimes uncontrollably. No precise number of journalists can be attached to the term *critical mass*, but in the video age, we truly know it when we see it; the forest of cameras, lights, microphones, and adrenaline-choked reporters surrounding a Gary Hart, Dan Quayle, or Geraldine Ferraro is unmistakable. [The following table] contains a list of thirty-six events that surely qualify as frenzies. They are occasions of sin for the press as well as the politicians, and thus ideal research sites that will serve as case studies for this book. A majority (twenty-one) are drawn from presidential politics, while seven examples come from the state and local levels, with the remaining eight focused on government scandals or personal peccadilloes of nationally recognized political figures. . . .

Conditions are always ripe for the spawning of a frenzy in the brave new world of omnipresent journalism. Advances in media technology have revolutionized campaign coverage. Handheld miniature cameras (minicams) and satellite broadcasting have enabled television to go live anywhere, anytime with ease. Instantaneous transmission (by broadcast and fax) to all corners of the country has dramatically increased the velocity of campaign developments today, accelerating events to their conclusion at breakneck speed. Gary Hart, for example, went from front-runner to ex-candidate in less than a week in May 1987. Continuous public-affairs programming, such as C-SPAN and CNN, helps put more of a politician's utterances on the record, as Senator Joseph Biden discovered to his chagrin when C-SPAN unobtrusively taped Biden's exaggeration of his résumé at a New Hampshire kaffeeklatsch in 1987. (This became a contributing piece of the frenzy that brought Biden down.) C-SPAN, CNN, and satellite broadcasting capability also contribute to the phenomenon called "the news cycle without end," which creates a voracious news appetite demanding to be fed constantly, increasing the pressure to include marginal bits of information and gossip and producing novel if distorting "angles" on the same news to differentiate one report from an-

FEEDING FRENZIES: CASE STUDIES USED FOR THIS BOOK

From Presidential Politics
1952	Richard Nixon's "secret fund"
1968	George Romney's "brainwashing" about Vietnam
1968	Spiro Agnew's "fat Jap" flap
1969	Ted Kennedy's Chappaquiddick
1972	Edmund Muskie's New Hampshire cry
1972	Thomas Eagleton's mental health
1976	Jimmy Carter's "lust in the heart" *Playboy* interview
1976	Gerald Ford's "free Poland" gaffe
1979	Jimmy Carter's "killer rabbit"
1980	Billygate (Billy Carter and Libya)
1983	Debategate (Reagan's use of Carter's debate briefing books)
1984	Gary Hart's age, name, and signature changes
1984	Jesse Jackson's "Hymietown" remark
1984	Geraldine Ferraro's family finances
1985/86	Jack Kemp's purported homosexuality
1987	Gary Hart and Donna Rice
1987	Joseph Biden's plagiarism and Michael Dukakis's "attack video"
1987	Pat Robertson's exaggerated résumé and shotgun marriage
1988	Dukakis's mental health
1988	Dan Quayle (National Guard service, Paula Parkinson, academic record, rumors such as plagiarism and drugs)
1988	George Bush's alleged mistress

From the State and Local Levels
1987/88	Governor Evan Mecham on the impeachment trail (Arizona)
1987/88	Chuck Robb and the cocaine parties (Virginia)
1983/90	Mayor Marion Barry's escapades (District of Columbia)
1987	Governor Dick Celeste's womanizing (Ohio)
1988	Mayor Henry Cisneros's extramarital affair (San Antonio, Texas)
1989/90	Governor Gaston Caperton's "soap opera" divorce (West Virginia)
1990	Texas governor's election: drugs, rape, and "honey hunts"

Noncampaign Examples
1973/74	The Watergate scandals
1974	Congressman Wilbur Mills and stripper Fanne Foxe
1986/87	The Iran-Contra affair
1987	Supreme Court nominee Douglas Ginsburg's marijuana use (and campaign repercussions)
1989	John Tower's losing fight to become secretary of defense
1989	Speaker Jim Wright's fall from power
1989	Tom Foley's rocky rise to the Speakership
1989/90	Barney Frank and the male prostitute

other. The extraordinary number of local stations covering national politics today—up to several hundred at major political events—creates an
echo chamber producing seemingly endless repetitions of essentially the
same news stories. This local contingent also swells the corps traveling the
campaign trail. In 1988 an estimated two thousand journalists of all stripes
flooded the Iowa caucuses, for instance. Reporters not infrequently outnumber participants at meetings and whistlestops. . . .

Whether on the rise or not, the unfortunate effects of pack journalism are apparent to both news reporters and news consumers: conformity,
homogeneity, and formulaic reporting. Innovation is discouraged, and the
checks and balances supposedly provided by competition evaporate. Press
energies are devoted to finding mere variations on a theme (new angles
and wiggle disclosures), while a mob psychology catches hold that allows
little mercy for the frenzy victim. CNN's Frank Sesno captures the pack
mood perfectly:

I've been in that group psychology; I know what it's like. You think you're on to
something, you've got somebody on the run. How dare they not come clean? How
dare they not tell the full story? What are they trying to hide? Why are they
hiding it? And you become a crusader for the truth. Goddammit, you're going to
get the truth! . . .

Sesno's crusader spirit can be traced directly to the lingering effects of
the Watergate scandal, which had the most profound impact of any modern event on the manner and substance of the press's conduct. In many
respects Watergate began the press's open season on politicians in a chain
reaction that today allows for scrutiny of even the most private sanctums
of public officials' lives. Moreover, coupled with Vietnam and the civil
rights movement, Watergate shifted the orientation of journalism away
from mere description—providing an accurate account of happenings—
and toward prescription—helping to set the campaign's (and society's)
agendas by focusing attention on the candidates' shortcomings as well as
certain social problems.

A new breed and a new generation of reporters were attracted to
journalism, and particularly its investigative arm. As a group they were
idealistic, though aggressively mistrustful of all authority, and they shared
a contempt for "politics as usual." Critics called them do-gooders and
purists who wanted the world to stand at moral attention for them. Twenty years later the Vietnam and Watergate generation dominates journalism:
They and their younger cohorts hold sway over most newsrooms, with
two-thirds of all reporters now under the age of thirty-six and an ever-
increasing share of editors and executives drawn from the Watergate-era

class. Of course, many of those who found journalism newly attractive in the wake of Watergate were not completely altruistic. The ambitious saw the happy fate of the *Washington Post*'s young Watergate sleuths Bob Woodward and Carl Bernstein, who gained fame and fortune, not to mention big-screen portrayals by Robert Redford and Dustin Hoffman in the movie *All the President's Men*. As *U.S. News & World Report*'s Steven Roberts sees it:

A lot of reporters run around this town dreaming of the day that Dustin Hoffman and Robert Redford are going to play them in the movies. That movie had more effect on the self-image of young journalists than anything else. Christ! Robert Redford playing a journalist? It lends an air of glamour and excitement that acts as a magnet drawing young reporters to investigative reporting.

The young were attracted not just to journalism but to a particular *kind* of journalism. The role models were not respected, established reporters but two unknowns who refused to play by the rules their seniors had accepted. "Youngsters learned that deductive techniques, all guesswork, and lots of unattributed information [were] the royal road to fame, even if it wasn't being terribly responsible," says Robert Novak. After all, adds columnist Mark Shields, "Robert Redford didn't play Walter Lippmann and Dustin Hoffman didn't play Joseph Kraft." (Kraft, like Lippmann, had a long and distinguished career in journalism.) . . .

A clear consequence of Watergate and other recent historical events was the increasing emphasis placed by the press on the character of candidates. As journalists reviewed the three tragic but exceptionally capable figures who had held the presidency since 1960, they saw that the failures of Kennedy, Johnson, and Nixon were not those of intellect but of ethos. Chappaquiddick, Spiro Agnew, and the Eagleton affair reinforced that view. The party affiliations and ideology of these disappointing leaders varied, but in common they possessed defects of personality, constitution, and disposition. In the world of journalism (or academe), as few as two data points can constitute a trend; these six together constituted an irrefutable mother lode of proof. "We in the press learned from experience that character flaws could have very large costs," says David Broder, "and we couldn't afford to ignore them if we were going to meet our responsibility." . . .

[A] troubling consequence of modern media coverage for the political system has to do with the recruitment of candidates and public servants. Simply put, the price of power has been raised dramatically, far too high for many outstanding potential officeholders. An individual contemplating a run for office must now accept the possibility of almost unlimited intrusion into his or her financial and personal life. Every investment made, every affair conducted, every private sin committed from college years to the present may one day wind up in a headline or on television. For a reasonably sane and moderately sensitive person, this is a daunting realization, with potentially hurtful results not just for the candidate but for his or her immediate family and friends. To have achieved a nongovernmental position of respect and honor in one's community is a source of pride and security, and the risk that it could all be destroyed by an unremitting and distorted assault on one's faults and foibles cannot be taken lightly. American society today is losing the services of many exceptionally talented individuals who could make outstanding contributions to the commonweal, but who understandably will not subject themselves and their loved ones to abusive, intrusive press coverage. Of course, this problem stems as much from the attitudes of the public as from those of the press; the strain of moral absolutism in portions of the American people merely finds expression in the relentless press frenzies and ethicsgate hunts. . . . *New York Times* columnist Anthony Lewis is surely correct when he suggests, "If we tell people there's to be absolutely nothing private left to them, then we will tend to attract to public office only those most brazen, least sensitive personalities. Is that what we want to do?"

52

CASS SUNSTEIN

From *Republic.com 2.0*

Law professor Cass Sunstein challenges conventional wisdom about the Internet as a tool to enhance open debate and the exchange of ideas in a democratic society. Yes, individuals have great freedom to gather information, he writes, but often that freedom is exercised in very narrow, particularistic ways that end up limiting an individual's exposure to a few favorite topics and a few favorite points of view. Each individual finds her or his cyber-niche and settles into it. Sunstein points to the danger of this personalized world of information. The author also underscores the importance of "shared experiences" in a diverse society; they'll become less and less common as people carve out their own narrow spheres of interest. Sunstein then discusses the blogosphere, in which limitless numbers of Internet opinion leaders share views with their web readers. A chance for a more open democracy? Yes, in a sense, Sunstein thinks, but also a chance for error and for extreme, polarized views to flourish. The "echo chamber" is hardly Sunstein's ideal vision for the new communications technologies. The author's critique of the new media is especially interesting because early in President Barack Obama's administration, Professor Sunstein was selected as the head of the Office of Information and Regulatory Affairs within the president's Office of Management and Budget.

IN A DEMOCRACY, people do not live in echo chambers or information cocoons. They see and hear a wide range of topics and ideas. They do so even if they did not, and would not, choose to see and to hear those topics and those ideas in advance. These claims raise serious questions about certain uses of new technologies, above all the Internet, and about the astonishing growth in the power to choose—to screen in and to screen out.

Louis Brandeis, one of America's greatest Supreme Court justices, insisted that the greatest threat to freedom is "an inert people." To avoid inertness, a democratic public must certainly be free from censorship. But the system of free expression must do far more than avoid censorship; it must ensure that people are exposed to competing perspectives. The idea of free speech has an affirmative side. It imposes constraints on what government may do, but it requires a certain kind of culture as well. (George

Orwell's *Nineteen Eighty-Four*, with its omnipresent, choice-denying Big Brother, is the most familiar vision of democracy's defeat; a more subtle vision is Aldous Huxley's *Brave New World*, with its pacified, choice-happy, formally free citizenry.) Members of a democratic public will not do well if they are unable to appreciate the views of their fellow citizens, or if they see one another as enemies or adversaries in some kind of war....

In many respects, our communications market is rapidly moving in the direction of this [personalized news]. As of this writing, many newspapers, including the *Wall Street Journal*, allow readers to create "personalized" electronic editions, containing exactly what they want, and excluding what they do not want.

If you are interested in getting help with the design of an entirely individual paper, you can consult an ever-growing number of sites, including individual.com (helpfully named!) and crayon.com (a less helpful name, but evocative in its own way). Reddit.com "learns what you like as you vote on existing links or submit your own!" Findory.com will help you to personalize not only news, but also blogs, videos, and podcasts. In its own enthusiastic words, "The more articles you click on, the more personalized Findory will look. Our Personalization Technology adapts the website to show you interesting and relevant information based on your reading habits."

If you put the words "personalized news" in any search engine, you will find vivid evidence of what is happening. Google News provides a case in point, with the appealing suggestion, "No one can read all the news that's published every day, so why not set up your page to show you the stories that best represent your interests?" And that is only the tip of the iceberg. Consider TiVo, the television recording system, which is designed to give "you the ultimate control over your TV viewing." TiVo will help you create "your personal TV line-up." It will also learn your tastes, so that it can "suggest other shows that you may want to record and watch based on your preferences." In reality, we are not so very far from complete personalization of the system of communications.

In 1995, MIT technology specialist Nicholas Negroponte prophesied the emergence of "the Daily Me"—a communications package that is personally designed, with each component fully chosen in advance. Negroponte's prophecy was not nearly ambitious enough. As it turns out, you don't need to create a Daily Me. Others can create it for you. If people know a little bit about you, they can discover, and tell you, what "people like you" tend to like—and they can create a Daily Me, just for you, in a matter of seconds.

Many of us are applauding these developments, which obviously increase fun, convenience, and entertainment. But in the midst of the applause, we should insist on asking some questions. How will the increasing power of private control affect democracy? How will the Internet and the explosion of communications options alter the capacity of citizens to govern themselves? What are the social preconditions for a well-functioning system of democratic deliberation, or for individual freedom itself?

My purpose . . . is to cast some light on these questions. I do so by emphasizing the most striking power provided by emerging technologies, *the growing power of consumers to "filter" what they see.* In the process of discussing this power, I will attempt to provide a better understanding of the meaning of freedom of speech in a democratic society.

A large part of my aim is to explore what makes for a well-functioning system of free expression. Above all, I urge that in a diverse society, such a system requires far more than restraints on government censorship and respect for individual choices. For the last decades, this has been the preoccupation of American law and politics, and in fact the law and politics of many other nations as well, including, for example, Germany, France, England, Italy, Russia, and Israel. Censorship is indeed the largest threat to democracy and freedom. But an exclusive focus on government censorship produces serious blind spots. In particular, a well-functioning system of free expression must meet two distinctive requirements.

First, people should be exposed to materials that they would not have chosen in advance. Unplanned, unanticipated encounters are central to democracy itself. Such encounters often involve topics and points of view that people have not sought out and perhaps find quite irritating. They are important partly to ensure against fragmentation and extremism, which are predictable outcomes of any situation in which like-minded people speak only with themselves. I do not suggest that government should force people to see things that they wish to avoid. But I do contend that in a democracy deserving the name, lives should be structured so that people often come across views and topics that they have not specifically selected.

Second, many or most citizens should have a range of common experiences. Without shared experiences, a heterogeneous society will have a much more difficult time in addressing social problems. People may even find it hard to understand one another. Common experiences, emphatically including the common experiences made possible by the media, provide a form of social glue. A system of communications that radically diminishes the number of such experiences will create a number of problems, not least because of the increase in social fragmentation.

As preconditions for a well-functioning democracy, these requirements hold in any large country. They are especially important in a heterogeneous nation, one that faces an occasional risk of fragmentation. They have all the more importance as each nation becomes increasingly global and each citizen becomes, to a greater or lesser degree, a "citizen of the world." Consider, for example, the risks of terrorism, climate change, and avian flu. A sensible perspective on these risks, and others like them, is impossible to obtain if people sort themselves into echo chambers of their own design. . . .

One of the more striking developments of the early twenty-first century has been the rise of weblogs, which can serve to elicit and aggregate the information held by countless contributors. Weblogs, or "blogs," have been growing at a truly astounding rate—so much so that any current account will rapidly grow out of date. As of the present writing, there are over 55 million blogs, and over 40,000 new ones are created each day, with a new one every 2.2 seconds. (Question: How many blogs are created in the time it takes to read a short book?) In recent years, the most highly rated political blogs—including Atrios, Instapundit, and the Daily Kos—have received over tens of thousands of visitors *each day.*

You can easily find blogs on countless subjects. Often, of course, the real topic is the life of the author, in an unintended reimagining of the idea of the Daily Me; one survey finds that "the typical blog is written by a teenage girl who uses it twice a month to update her friends and classmates on happenings in her life." Political blogs are a small percentage of the total, but they are plentiful, and they seem to be having a real influence on people's beliefs and judgments. In my own field of law, there are numerous blogs, and some of them are often quite good. For example, the Volokh Conspiracy and Balkinization offer clear and illuminating analyses of legal questions, often with amazing speed.

For most of those who write and read them, blogs can be a lot of fun. And if countless people are maintaining their own blogs, they should be able to act as fact-checkers and as supplemental information sources, not only for one another but also for prominent members of the mass media. If hundreds of thousands of people are reading the most prominent blogs, then errors should be corrected quickly. No one doubts that the blogosphere enables interested readers to find an astounding range of opinions and facts.

If the blogosphere is working well, we might understand it in two different ways. First, we might believe that the blogosphere serves as a huge market, in a way that supports the claims of those who claim that free markets can help society to obtain the widely dispersed information that individuals have. Second, we might think that the blogosphere operates as a kind of gigantic town meeting, in a way that fits well with the claims of those who speak of the operation of the well-functioning public sphere. On this second view, the world of blogs is helping to improve the operation of deliberative democracy, because it involves a great deal of citizen involvement and because arguments are often supported by facts and reasons.

These two understandings of the blogosphere lie behind many of the contemporary celebrations. Are the celebrations warranted? . . .

True enough, many blogs aggregate a lot of information; instapundit .com, for example, assembles material from many sources. We might even consider the most elite bloggers, who gather material from elsewhere in the blogosphere, as an aggregating mechanism of sorts. Daniel Drezner and Henry Farrell have shown that because of the networked structure of the blogosphere, "only a few blogs are likely to become focal points," but those few blogs "offer both a means of filtering interesting blog posts from less interesting ones, and a focal point at which bloggers with interesting posts and potential readers of these posts can coordinate." But . . . some of the elite or "focal point" bloggers have their own biases. Many of them are primarily interested in cherry-picking items of opinion or information that reinforce their preexisting views. In other words, we lack a blog that succeeds in correcting errors and assembling truths. Those who consult blogs will learn a great deal, but they will have a tough time separating falsehoods from facts.

There is another point. Participants in the blogospere often lack an economic incentive. If they spread falsehoods, or simply offer their opinion, they usually sacrifice little or nothing. Maybe their reputation will suffer, but maybe not; maybe the most dramatic falsehoods will draw attention and hence readers. True, some bloggers attract advertising, and they have a stake in preserving their credibility. But most bloggers do not, and it is hardly clear that the best way to attract advertising revenues is to tell the truth. Many advertisers on political blogs are themselves trying to sell products designed to appeal to those with strong partisan beliefs. They are unlikely to object to exaggerations and semifalsehoods that appeal to the prejudices of their target audiences.

By their very nature, blogs offer rival and contentious positions on facts as well as values. In many ways, this is a virtue. People who are curious can find a wide range of views, including those that oppose their own. But if truth is to emerge, it is because of the competition of the marketplace of ideas, and this particular marketplace is far from perfect. One of the undeniable effects of blogs is to spread misunderstandings and mistakes. This point leads to another possible understanding of blogs, closely connected to my central concerns here—an understanding that is rooted in the idea of deliberative democracy. . . .

. . . Certainly it can be said that as compared to many alternatives, the blogosphere is both "public and inclusive," and grants communication rights to countless participants. Perhaps the blogosphere can be said to operate, at least to some degree, in this idealized fashion, in a way that will promote the emergence of "the better argument."

In view of what we know about group polarization, however, it should be clear that this happy view of the blogosphere faces a big problem. Drezner and Farrell emphasize its networked structure, in which ideas from less popular blogs can "bubble up" to much larger audiences. But a serious question is whether people are mostly reading blogs that conform to their own preexisting beliefs. If so, the truth is not likely to emerge, and polarization is nearly inevitable. Liberals, reading liberal blogs, will end up being more liberal; conservatives will become more conservative if they restrict themselves to conservative blogs. . . .

It is entirely reasonable to think that something of this kind finds itself replicated in the blogosphere every day. Indeed some bloggers, and many readers of blogs, try to create echo chambers. Because of self-sorting, people are often reading like-minded points of view, in a way that can breed greater confidence, more uniformity within groups, and more extremism. Note in this regard that shared identities are often salient on the blogosphere, in a way that makes polarization both more likely and more likely to be large. On any day of any year, it is easy to find unjustified rage, baseless attacks on people's motivations, and ludicrous false statements of fact in the blogosphere. From the democratic point of the view, this is nothing to celebrate.

Of course the quality of bloggers is immensely variable, and some of them are very good, in part because they take account of reasonable counterarguments. . . . Information aggregation is likely to work best when many minds are involved, but it is also important that reasons and information are being exchanged in a way that can lead to corrections and real creativity. To some extent, this is happening already. I have not denied that we are better off with blogs than without them. But it is a big stretch to celebrate blogs as an incarnation of deliberative ideals. . . .

One study explores the degree to which conservative and liberal bloggers are interacting with each other. Focusing on 1,400 blogs, the study finds that 91 percent of the links are to like-minded sites. Hence the two sides sort themselves into identifiable communities. For example, power lineblog.com, a conservative blog, has links from only twenty-five liberal blogs—but from 195 conservative blogs. Dailykos.com, a liberal blog, has links from 46 conservative blogs—but from 292 liberal blogs. In the aggregate, the behavior of conservative bloggers is more noteworthy in this regard; they link to one another far more often and in a denser pattern. The study's authors also examined about 40 "A-List" blogs, and here too they found a great deal of segregation. Sources were cited almost exclusively by one side or the other. Those sites with identifiable political commitments, such as Salon.com and NationalReview.com, were almost always cited by blogs on the same side of the political spectrum. . . .

The general conclusion is that in the blogosphere, there is a significant divide between politically identifiable communities. Liberals link mostly to liberals and conservatives link mostly to conservatives. Much of the time, they do not even discuss the same topics. Of course, it is true that many people are using the blogosphere not to strengthen their antecedent convictions, and not to waste their time, but to learn about different views and new topics. The blogosphere increases the range of available information and perspectives, and this is a great virtue, above all for curious and open-minded people. There are networks here with multiple connections, not entirely segregated communities. But if linking behavior on blogs can be taken as a proxy for how people are using the blogosphere, it is reasonable to think that many readers are obtaining one-sided views of political issues. For many people, blunders, confusion, and extremism are highly likely, not in spite of the blogosphere but because of it.

53

DIANA MUTZ

How the Mass Media Divide Us

How the mass media divide us is by entertaining us with TV shows that are built on bitter debate, sharp disagreement, and angry confrontation. This makes for exciting shows but has negative consequences for American politics. When people watch these uncivil exchanges, Professor Diana Mutz believes, they become more extreme in their political views. Mutz, an expert in communications and political psychology, has conducted some interesting studies to substantiate her thesis. Perhaps you don't remember when former Senator Zell Miller told commentator Chris Matthews that he'd like to meet him in a duel: Hardball *was definitely memorable that night! Perhaps* C-SPAN's *talking heads, who discuss issues calmly and drone on too long, are not very entertaining, but they would be more beneficial to political dialogue. There are many factors behind the polarization that has characterized American politics in the past decades, and Mutz has identified an important one.*

"Shout-show" television has been the target of a tremendous amount of criticism from many quarters, academic and otherwise. The world of political disagreement as witnessed through the lens of political talk shows is quite polarized. Increased competition for audiences has led many programs on political topics to liven themselves up in order to increase audience size. Thus, political talk shows such as *The McLaughlin Group, The O'Reilly Factor, Meet the Press, Capital Gang, Hardball,* and many others tend to involve particularly intense and heated exchanges.

The issue of contentiousness and incivility in political discourse was brought to a head in October 2004, when *Daily Show* host Jon Stewart appeared on *Crossfire* and openly criticized this program (and others like it) for its "partisan hackery," which Stewart said was "hurting America." Is there any truth to Stewart's claim? Aside from the obvious distastefulness some find in watching politicians scream, yell, and interrupt one another for thirty minutes or more, how is this kind of in-your-face politics implicated as a potential cause of mass polarization?

The tendency on television is to highlight more emotionally extreme and less polite expressions of opinion, and research suggests that these expressions of incivility may have important consequences for attitudes

toward the opposition. These consequences flow from the fact that polite-
ness and civility are more than mere social norms; they are means of demonstrating mutual respect. In other words, uncivil discourse increases polarization by helping partisans think even less of their opponents than
they already did.

And yet market forces seem to favor the kind of television that encourages polarization. Polarized political discourse and an angry opposition makes for compelling television. Viewers may claim that they find it
disgusting, but they cannot help watching—just as passing motorists cannot help "rubbernecking" when there is an accident alongside the highway. It is not that people actually *enjoy* what they are seeing, but there is
something about information of this kind—information about life and
death, about conflict and warring tribes in a dispute—that makes it difficult to ignore. Evolutionary psychologists have pointed to the adaptive
advantage of having brains that automatically pay attention to conflict as
a means of staying alive in an earlier era. At a cognitive level, of course,
no one really expects to be caught in the "crossfire" of a televised partisan shout-fest. But even when it is "only television," and thus poses no
real threat of bodily harm, people cannot help but watch and react to
incivility.

My own research suggests that psychologists are correct about the
demands of incivility on human attentional processes. To examine the difference that incivility makes independent of political content, I produced
a mock political talk show—on a professional television set using professional actors as congressional candidates. The candidates espoused the
same issue positions and made exactly the same arguments for and against
various issue positions in two different versions of the program. In one
discussion, however, they raised their voices, rolled their eyes, and engaged
in an impolite, uncivil exchange. In the civil version of the program, they
spoke calmly, refrained from interrupting one another, and showed mutual respect simply by obeying the social norms for polite discourse.

The differences in viewer reactions to the two programs were startling. The group randomly assigned to the uncivil version of the political
discussion came away with roughly the same feelings toward their preferred candidate as those in the civil group. But attitudes toward the "other side" became much more intensely negative when the two exchanged
views in an uncivil manner. The more dramatic, uncivil exchanges encouraged a more black-and-white view of the world: their candidate was
not just the best; the alternative was downright evil.

This effect was evident for partisans on both sides of the political
spectrum and regardless of which candidate they liked best. Interestingly,

watching the uncivil version led to greater polarization in perceptions of "us" versus "them," relative to a control group, but watching the civil version of the exchange led to *decreased* levels of polarization. This pattern of findings suggests that political television has the potential to *improve* as well as to exacerbate the divide among partisans of opposing views; it simply depends upon how those differences of opinion are aired. When differences of opinion are conveyed in a manner that suggests mutual respect, viewers are able to understand and process the rationales on the other side and are less likely to see the opposition in starkly negative terms. Differences of opinion are perceived as having some legitimate and reasonable basis. But when those same views and rationales are expressed in an uncivil manner, people respond with an emotional, gut-level reaction, rejecting the opposition as unfairly and viciously attacking one's cherished views.

Using indicators of physiological response, my studies also demonstrate that televised incivility causes viewers' levels of emotional arousal to increase, just as they do when people encounter face-to-face incivility. In the face of real-world conflict, this reaction supposedly serves a functional purpose—participants are given the rush of adrenaline they may need to flee the situation. But with televised incivility, this kind of reaction serves no purpose; it is simply a remnant of brains that have not adapted to twentieth-century representational technology.

Even though viewers are just third-party observers of other people's conflicts on television, they show heightened levels of emotional arousal, just as people do when encountering face-to-face disagreement. This is not so surprising if one considers how it feels to be a third-party observer of a couple's argument at a dinner party. The same discomfort, awkwardness, and tension exist, even for those not directly involved in the conflict. Likewise, when political commentator Robert Novak stormed off the set of a live broadcast of CNN's *Inside Politics* in August 2004, viewers were uncomfortable—and they paid attention. The tension was palpable to viewers, even though few may be able to remember what the substance of the conflict was.

The heightened arousal produced by incivility can make it difficult to process the substance of the exchange. Some arousal helps to call attention to what otherwise might be considered bland and uninteresting. But at extremely high levels of arousal, people will remember only the emotional content of the program (who screamed at whom, who stomped off in a pique) and recall little of the substance of the disagreement. As anyone who has ever had an argument knows, there is a point at which the emotional content of the exchange overwhelms any potential for rational discourse. As a result, viewers gain little understanding of the other side. They perceive their own side of the debate as unfairly attacked, and thus the incivility their own candidate displays is simply an appropriate level of righteous indignation in reaction to an unprovoked attack. The incivility demonstrated by the opponent demonstrates that he is a raving lunatic, wholly unfit for office.

In addition to this disdain for the opposing side, incivility produces a second important reaction—heightened attention. As Bill O'Reilly, host of *The O'Reilly Factor,* suggests, "If a radio producer can find someone who eggs on conservative listeners to spout off and prods liberals into shouting back, he's got a hit show. The best host is the guy or gal who can get the most listeners extremely annoyed—over and over and over again." Evidently, these sorts of shows have hooked Senator Hillary Rodham Clinton (D-N.Y.), who indicated that she and her husband Bill now have TiVo, a technology that allows a viewer to record and replay television programs. And for what purpose do the senator and the former president use TiVo? According to Senator Clinton, they use it to record the most outrageous statements made by their political opponents so they can play them over and over and yell back at the television. An optimist might regard this vignette as an example of how viewers are *not* necessarily selectively exposing themselves to politically compatible media. But the pessimist would undoubtedly point out that yet another media mechanism of polarization has kicked in to take its place. Uncivil political discourse that produces such strong emotional reactions is unlikely to further the cause of political moderation.

Controlled laboratory studies suggest, for better or worse, that O'Reilly is correct: incivility is extremely entertaining and people like to watch it, even if it is just to scream back. Despite the fact that many viewers claim to be repulsed by it, the respondents who viewed the identical but uncivil version of the same program always rated it as more entertaining, found it more exciting to watch, and indicated a greater desire to see the uncivil program again than the civil version. Polite conversation is boring, and the deliberative ideal for political discourse makes for dull television. "I acknowledge there are some good points on my opponent's side" will probably never make good television, whereas "These evil people must be stopped!" always will.

With these findings in mind, it is important to consider the extent to which the rise of televised political incivility can help explain mass polarization. Is political discourse truly any more uncivil now than in the past? Some have suggested that the United States is in the midst of a "civility crisis" in its public life. As then University of Pennsylvania president Judith Rodin argued in 1996, "Across America and increasingly around the world, from campuses to the halls of Congress, to talk radio and network TV, social and political life seem dominated today by incivility. . . . No one seems to question the premise that political debate has become too extreme, too confrontational, too coarse." Similar calls for greater civility in political discourse have come from a wide array of scholars, as well as from philanthropic organizations. . . .

Clearly, there is a widespread perception that political discourse is much more uncivil now than in the past, but there is little historical evidence to confirm such a trend. As then senator Zell Miller (D-Ga.) implied when he wistfully said he would like to challenge *Hardball* host Chris Matthews to a duel, violence among political opponents was once far more common than it is now. Senator Miller's statement was made during an uncivil exchange between himself and a journalist during the 2004 Republican National Convention. It made headlines, precisely because the idea of using weapons to resolve political differences seemed absurd. We have not had a duel to the death among politicians for many years, and thus one could easily characterize today's political talk shows as mild by comparison.

So is it fair to say that incivility is on the rise in political discourse? There is no definitive answer to this question, but the increased *visibility* of uncivil conflicts on television seems indisputable. Although politicians of past eras may frequently have exchanged harsh words, without television cameras there to record these events and to replay them for a mass audience their impact on public perceptions was probably substantially lower. The dominance of television as a source of exposure to politics suggests that public exposure to uncivil political discourse has increased. Moreover, it is one thing to read about political pundits' or candidates' contrary views in the press, and quite another to witness them directly engaged in vituperative argument. The sensory realism of television conveys a sense of intimacy with political actors that people were unlikely to encounter in the past, even among the few lucky enough to have face-to-face meetings.

Television provides a uniquely intimate perspective on conflict. In the literature on human proxemics, the distance deemed appropriate for face-to-face interactions with public figures in American culture is more than twelve feet. Yet exposure to politicians on television gives the appearance of being much closer. When people are arguing, the tendency is to back off and put greater space between those who disagree. Instead, when political conflicts flare up on television, cameras tend to go in for tighter and tighter close-ups. This creates an intense experience for the viewers, one in which they view conflict from an unusually intimate perspective. Political scientist Jane J. Mansbridge has noted that when open political conflict occurs in real life, bringing people together in one another's presence can intensify their anger and aggression. To the extent that a television presence has similar effects, incivility is likely to encourage polarization. . . .

The underlying question that still needs to be confronted—by scholars as well as those in the media business—is how to make a topic that is not inherently interesting to many Americans nonetheless exciting to watch. And if the answer is not behind-the-scenes coverage of election strategy, or mudslinging on political talk shows, or partisan extremists rallying the troops, then what will keep those politically marginal citizens from watching movies on cable instead?

PART TEN

Interest Groups

54

ALEXIS DE TOCQUEVILLE

From *Democracy in America*

Interest-group politics remains a big part of U.S. government today—for good and bad. But it is not as new a part as it may seem. Young French aristocrat Alexis de Tocqueville, visiting in 1831, observed how naturally Americans formed "associations." Just like today, groups were formed "to promote the public safety, commerce, industry, morality, and religion." In a country that emphasized individuality, Tocqueville thought, group allegiances gave people the power to work together to reach shared goals. American interest groups were out in the open, meeting freely to advance their viewpoints. Tocqueville, whose earlier selection from Democracy in America *opened this book, placed great faith in interest groups as a way that minorities could protect themselves from "tyranny of the majority." Today, one wonders how he would suggest that the nation protect itself from the tyranny of interest groups.*

IN NO COUNTRY IN the world has the principle of association been more successfully used, or more unsparingly applied to a multitude of different objects, than in America. Besides the permanent associations, which are established by law under the names of townships, cities, and counties, a vast number of others are formed and maintained by the agency of private individuals.

The citizen of the United States is taught from his earliest infancy to rely upon his own exertions, in order to resist the evils and the difficulties of life; he looks upon the social authority with an eye of mistrust and anxiety, and he only claims its assistance when he is quite unable to shift without it. This habit may even be traced in the schools of the rising generation, where the children in their games are wont to submit to rules which they have themselves established, and to punish misdemeanors which they have themselves defined. The same spirit pervades every act of social life. If a stoppage occurs in a thoroughfare, and the circulation of the public is hindered, the neighbors immediately constitute a deliberative body; and this extemporaneous assembly gives rise to an executive power, which remedies the inconvenience, before anybody has thought of recurring to an authority superior to that of the persons immediately concerned. If the public pleasures are concerned, an association is formed to provide for the splendor and the regularity of the entertainment. Societies are formed to resist enemies which are exclusively of a moral nature, and to diminish the vice of intemperance: in the United States associations are established to promote public order, commerce, industry, morality, and religion, for there is no end which the human will seconded by the collective exertions of individuals, despairs of attaining. . . .

An association consists simply in the public assent which a number of individuals give to certain doctrines; and in the engagement which they contract to promote the spread of those doctrines by their exertions. The right of associating with such views is very analogous to the liberty of unlicensed writing; but societies thus formed possess more authority than the press. When an opinion is represented by a society, it necessarily assumes a more exact and explicit form. It numbers its partisans, and compromises their welfare in its cause: they, on the other hand, become acquainted with each other, and their zeal is increased by their number. An association unites the efforts of minds which have a tendency to diverge in one single channel, and urges them vigorously towards the one single end which it points out.

The second degree in the right of association is the power of meeting. When an association is allowed to establish centres of action at certain important points in the country, its activity is increased, and its influence extended. Men have the opportunity of seeing each other; means of execution are more readily combined; and opinions are maintained with a warmth and energy which written language cannot approach.

Lastly, in the exercise of the right of political association, there is a third degree: the partisans of an opinion may unite in electoral bodies, and choose delegates to represent them in a central assembly. This is, properly speaking, the application of the representative system to a party.

Thus, in the first instance, a society is formed between individuals professing the same opinion, and the tie which keeps it together is of a purely intellectual nature: in the second case, small assemblies are formed which only represent a faction of the party. Lastly, in the third case, they constitute a separate nation in the midst of the nation, a government within the Government. . . .

It cannot be denied that the unrestrained liberty of association for political purposes is the privilege which a people is longest in learning how to exercise. If it does not throw the nation into anarchy, it perpetually augments the chances of that calamity. On one point, however, this perilous liberty offers a security against dangers of another kind; in countries where associations are free, secret societies are unknown. In America, there are numerous factions, but no conspiracies. . . .

The most natural privilege of man, next to the right of acting for himself, is that of combining his exertions with those of his fellow-creatures, and of acting in common with them. I am therefore led to conclude that the right of association is almost as inalienable as the right of personal liberty. . . .

55

E. E. SCHATTSCHNEIDER

From *The Semisovereign People*

The late 1950s and early 1960s was a time when political scientists placed their focus on the interest group theory of American politics. Although hardly a new idea, interest group politics was studied intensely, sometimes to be idealized as the perfect model of government and other times critiqued as the downfall of democracy. Scholar E. E. Schattschneider's much-cited book explored the "pressure system" in American politics, dominated by "organized" (as opposed to informal), "special-interest" (not public-interest) groups. Schattschneider's conclusion was that "the pressure system has an upper-class bias." Decades later, political scientists might not use the exact same language as Schattschneider, who relied on the concept of class in his analysis. Today, vastly different degrees of organization, financial resources, and intensity separate interest group claimants in the competition for getting their issues heard by the government.

———

MORE THAN any other system American politics provides the raw materials for testing the organizational assumptions of two contrasting kinds of politics, *pressure politics* and *party politics*. The concepts that underlie these forms of politics constitute the raw stuff of a general theory of political action. The basic issue between the two patterns of organization is one of size and scope of conflict; pressure groups are small-scale organizations while political parties are very large-scale organizations. One need not be surprised, therefore, that the partisans of large-scale and small-scale organizations differ passionately, because the outcome of the political game depends on the scale on which it is played.

To understand the controversy about the scale of political organization it is necessary first to take a look at some theories about interest-group politics. Pressure groups have played a remarkable role in American politics, but they have played an even more remarkable role in American political theory. Considering the political condition of the country in the first third of the twentieth century, it was probably inevitable that the discussion of special interest pressure groups should lead to development of "group" theories of politics in which an attempt is made to explain everything in terms of group activity, i.e., an attempt to formulate a universal group theory. Since one of the best ways to test an idea is to ride it into the ground, political theory has unquestionably been improved by the heroic attempt to create a political universe revolving about the group. Now that we have a number of drastic statements of the group theory of politics pushed to a great extreme, we ought to be able to see what the limitations of the idea are. . . .

One difficulty running through the literature of the subject results from the attempt to explain *everything* in terms of the group theory. On general grounds it would be remarkable indeed if a single hypothesis explained everything about so complex a subject as American politics. Other difficulties have grown out of the fact that group concepts have been stated in terms so universal that the subject seems to have no shape or form.

The question is: Are pressure groups the universal basic ingredient of all political situations, and do they explain everything? To answer this question it is necessary to review a bit of rudimentary political theory.

Two modest reservations might be made merely to test the group dogma. We might clarify our ideas if (1) we explore more fully the possibility of making a distinction between public interest groups and special-interest groups and (2) if we distinguished between organized and unorganized groups. . . .

As a matter of fact, the distinction between *public* and *private* interests is a thoroughly respectable one; it is one of the oldest known to political theory. In the literature of the subject the public interest refers to general or common interests shared by all or by substantially all members of the community. Presumably no community exists unless there is some kind of community of interests, just as there is no nation without some notion of national interests. If it is really impossible to distinguish between private and public interests the group theorists have produced a revolution in political thought so great that it is impossible to foresee its consequences. For this reason the distinction ought to be explored with great care.

At a time when nationalism is described as one of the most dynamic forces in the world, it should not be difficult to understand that national interests actually do exist. It is necessary only to consider the proportion of the American budget devoted to national defense to realize that the common interest in national survival is a great one. Measured in dollars this interest is one of the biggest things in the world. Moreover, it is difficult to describe this interest as special. The diet on which the American leviathan feeds is something more than a jungle of disparate special interests. In the literature of democratic theory the body of common agreement found in the community is known as the "consensus" without which it is believed that no democratic system can survive.

The reality of the common interest is suggested by demonstrated capacity of the community to survive. There must be something that holds people together.

In contrast with the common interests are the special interests. The implication of this term is that these are interests shared by only a few people or a fraction of the community; they *exclude* others and may be *adverse* to them. A special interest is exclusive in about the same way as private property is exclusive. In a complex society it is not surprising that there are some interests that are shared by all or substantially all members of the community and some interests that are not shared so widely. The distinction is useful precisely because conflicting claims are made by people about the nature of their interests in controversial matters. . . .

Is it possible to distinguish between the "interests" of the members of the National Association of Manufacturers and the members of the American League to Abolish Capital Punishment? The facts in the two cases are not identical. First, *the members of the A.L.A.C.P. obviously do not expect to be hanged.* The membership of the A.L.A.C.P. is not restricted to persons under indictment for murder or in jeopardy of the extreme penalty. *Anybody* can join A.L.A.C.P. Its members oppose capital punishment although they are not personally likely to benefit by the policy they advocate. The inference is therefore that the interest of the A.L.A.C.P. is not adverse, exclusive or special. It is not like the interest of the Petroleum Institute in depletion allowances. . . .

We can now examine the second distinction, the distinction between organized and unorganized groups. The question here is not whether the distinction can be made but whether or not it is worth making. Organization has been described as "merely a stage or degree of interaction" in the development of a group.

The proposition is a good one, but what conclusions do we draw from it? We do not dispose of the matter by calling the distinction between organized and unorganized groups a "mere" difference of degree because some of the greatest differences in the world are differences of degree. As far as special-interest politics is concerned the implication to be avoided is that a few workmen who habitually stop at a corner saloon for a glass of beer are essentially the same as the United States Army because the difference between them is merely one of degree. At this point we have a distinction that makes a difference. . . .

If we are able, therefore, to distinguish between public and private interests and between organized and unorganized groups we have marked out the major boundaries of the subject; *we have given the subject shape and scope.* We are now in a position to attempt to define the area we want to explore. Having cut the pie into four pieces, we can now appropriate the piece we want and leave the rest to someone else. For a multitude of reasons *the most likely field of study is that of the organized, special-interest groups.* The advantage of concentrating on organized groups is that they are known, identifiable and recognizable. The advantage of concentrating on special-interest groups is that they have one important characteristic in common: they are all exclusive. This piece of the pie (the organized special-interest groups) we shall call the *pressure system.* The pressure system has boundaries we can define; we can fix its scope and make an attempt to estimate its bias. . . .

The organized groups listed in the various directories (such as *National Associations of the United States,* published at intervals by the United States Department of Commerce) and specialty yearbooks, registers, etc., and the *Lobby Index,* published by the United States House of Representatives, probably include the bulk of the organizations in the pressure system. All compilations are incomplete, but these are extensive enough to provide us with some basis for estimating the scope of the system. . . .

When lists of these organizations are examined, the fact that strikes the student most forcibly is that *the system is very small.* The range of organized, identifiable, known groups is amazingly narrow; there is nothing remotely universal about it. There is a tendency on the part of the publishers of directories of associations to place an undue emphasis on business organizations, an emphasis that is almost inevitable because the business community is by a wide margin the most highly organized segment of society. Publishers doubtless tend also to reflect public demand for information. Nevertheless, the dominance of business groups in the pressure system is so marked that it probably cannot be explained away as an accident of the publishing industry. . . .

The business or upper-class bias of the pressure system shows up everywhere. Businessmen are four or five times as likely to write to their congressmen as manual laborers are. College graduates are far more apt to write to their congressmen than people in the lowest educational category are. . . .

Broadly, the pressure system has an upper-class bias. There is overwhelming evidence that participation in voluntary organizations is related to upper social and economic status; the rate of participation is much higher in the upper strata than it is elsewhere. . . .

The bias of the system is shown by the fact that *even nonbusiness organizations reflect an upper-class tendency.* . . .

The class bias of associational activity gives meaning to the limited scope of the pressure system, because *scope and bias are aspects of the same tendency.* The data raise a serious question about the validity of the proposition that special-interest groups are a universal form of political organization reflecting *all* interests. As a matter of fact, to suppose that everyone participates in pressure-group activity and that all interests get themselves organized in the pressure system is to destroy the meaning of this form of politics. The pressure system makes sense only as the political instrument of a segment of the community. It gets results by being selective and biased; *if everybody got into the act the unique advantages of this form of organization would be destroyed, for it is possible that if all interests could be mobilized the result would be a stalemate.*

Special-interest organizations are most easily formed when they deal with small numbers of individuals who are acutely aware of their exclusive interests. To describe the conditions of pressure-group organization in this way is, however, to say that it is primarily a business phenomenon. Aside from a few very large organizations (the churches, organized labor, farm organizations, and veterans' organizations) the residue is a small segment of the population. *Pressure politics is essentially the politics of small groups.*

The vice of the groupist theory is that it conceals the most significant aspects of the system. The flaw in the pluralist heaven is that the heavenly chorus sings with a strong upper-class accent. Probably about 90 percent of the people cannot get into the pressure system.

The notion that the pressure system is automatically representative of the whole community is a myth fostered by the universalizing tendency of modern group theories. *Pressure politics is a selective process* ill designed to serve diffuse interests. The system is skewed, loaded and unbalanced in favor of a fraction of a minority. . . .

The competing claims of pressure groups and political parties for the loyalty of the American public revolve about the difference between the results likely to be achieved by small-scale and large-scale political organization. Inevitably, the outcome of pressure politics and party politics will be vastly different.

56

ANTHONY NOWNES

From *Interest Groups in American Politics*

The 2010 oil well disaster in the Gulf of Mexico sets the stage for Anthony Nownes's examination of interest groups in American politics. "In short, what was a disaster for many people was a boon to lobbyists." The author points to the paradoxical view that we hold about interest groups: hating them but supporting those whose interests we identify with. While Nownes assures us that lobbyists who employ outright corruption (bribes, sex, alcohol!) are the exception not the rule, he does give readers a few colorful reminders. He then goes on to the more usual "drinking, schmoozing, going out for lunch or dinner, playing golf, . . . providing gifts and doing favors" as standard lobbying techniques. All of these methods lead to personal relationships between public officials and lobbyists. Some students who study political science hope to become lobbyists, and here, Nownes gives us a look at the salary and work requirements for such. His final topic is the "revolving door" that brings many former government officials—elected and appointed—into the world of interest group lobbying after their government service has ended. It's all about "access."

FAMOUS FRENCHMAN Alexis de Tocqueville remarked in 1834 that nowhere in the world were associations more ubiquitous and more important than they were in the United States. Over 175 years later, evidence that de Tocqueville's point still is incisive is everywhere. In Washington, DC, as well as in states, cities, counties, and everywhere else government decisions are made, interest groups are omnipresent. Their lobbyists roam the halls of government buildings, their advertisements fill the airwaves during election season, their membership pleas clutter our mailboxes, and their influence is blamed for everything from global warming and the financial crisis, to high gas prices and protracted war in the Middle East. . . .

On April 20, 2010, *The Deepwater Horizon*, an offshore oil drilling rig, blew up. The rig, which was located approximately 400 miles off the Louisiana coast in the Gulf of Mexico, was drilling what is called an "exploratory well" almost one mile below the ocean's surface. Just before 10 a.m. on the 20th, highly pressurized methane gas burst out of the drill column and then caught fire. Most of the people who were working on the rig were rescued. But eleven people were never found. They are presumed dead. The fire raged for a day and a half, until on the morning of April 22nd, the crippled rig sank. On April 23rd, the company that leased the well, BP (formerly known as British Petroleum), reported that there was no oil leaking from either the sunken rig or the well. By the 24th, however, it was clear that BP was mistaken. No one knows for certain how many gallons of oil leaked from the wellhead before it was finally capped on July 15, 2010. But experts agree that the spill was the largest in U.S. history, far surpassing the *Exxon Valdez* spill that dominated headlines for a time in 1989. In all, hundreds of millions of gallons of oil spewed into the Gulf of Mexico. In the weeks and months after the explosion, the effects of the spill became obvious. Thousands of square miles of ocean were soiled with oil, endangering fish and other wildlife. In June, oil reached the Louisiana coast. By early July, oil had reached Alabama, Mississippi, and Texas.

The oil spill was disastrous for many people. It was most disastrous, of course, for the eleven workers who lost their lives. It was also disastrous for many of the people who live and work near the coastal areas of the Gulf states. But for some people the oil spill was a boon. Who? The answer is *lobbyists*. In the wake of the oil spill, BP, many environmental interest groups, and interest groups representing oil companies substantially ramped up their lobbying activities. Environmental groups hoped to use the spill as a justification for policies they had long championed—policies that would tighten regulations on oil drilling. Transocean Ltd., the company that owned the rig and leased it to BP, retained the services of a lobbying firm called Capitol Hill Consulting Group to help it stave off stricter federal regulations and to rehabilitate its image with the public and government decision-makers. For its part, BP hired a slew of well-connected lobbyists in an effort to preempt punitive policies proposed by various Washington decision-makers intent on punishing the company for the spill. The American Petroleum Institute, which represents energy producers including BP, stepped up its lobbying operations to make sure the federal government did not adopt new and onerous regulations that would add to the cost of doing business. Other organizations stepped up their lobbying efforts as well, including shallow water oil drilling companies that used the spill as an opportunity to tout their method of drilling as a safer and preferable alternative to the deep water drilling that led to the disaster. In short, what was a disaster for many people was a boon to lobbyists. . . .

Oil spills do not happen every day. And a gigantic oil spill is a once-in-a-generation phenomenon. Thus, it is certainly *not* the case that the events that took place during the summer of 2010 represented "business as usual" in the nation's capital. Yet in one way the lobbying that took place *did* embody "business as usual"; for Washington, DC is a place where frenzied lobbying activity takes place almost all the time. For better or worse, in Washington as well as in cities, counties, towns, and states across America, interest groups and their lobbyists are everywhere government decisions are made.

The ubiquity of interest groups and their lobbyists worries many Americans. Lobbyists—the people who represent interest groups in front of government decision-makers—are not popular. Public opinion polls show that most Americans hold them in lower esteem even than auto mechanics, lawyers, and members of Congress. Americans believe that lobbyists are about as ethical and honest as car salespeople. Interest groups themselves are similarly despised by the public. While the military, the police, and small businesses generally are well respected by most Americans, interest groups are scorned.

Ordinary Americans are not the only ones who disdain interest groups. Politicians scorn them as well. Hardly a day passes without some high-ranking public official decrying the impact of "special interests" on government decisions. Presidents have proven especially contemptuous of interest groups. Every president since George Washington has taken time out from his busy schedule to castigate lobbyists and the organizations they represent. Even before the Constitution was adopted, for example, future president James Madison warned that interest groups posed a great danger to the republic because they worked to gain advantage for themselves at the expense of others. Similarly, upon retiring from office, President Dwight Eisenhower warned of the pernicious influence of powerful organizations that were part of "the military-industrial complex." More recently, throughout the 1990s, President Clinton regularly denounced conservative groups that dredged up allegations of philandering. And President Barack Obama, frustrated by slow action on some of his signature initiatives, has repeatedly taken special interest groups to task.

Why all the fuss? What's *wrong* with interest groups attempting to influence government decisions? After all, most of us support *some* sort of interest group—be it conservative, liberal, moderate, or "none of the above." In fact, many of us actually *belong* to interest groups, and few of us can deny that there are at least some interest groups working to further our political goals. In the aftermath of the BP oil spill, for example, almost all possible viewpoints were represented by interest groups. As the vignette that opened this chapter attests, some interest groups lobbied for strict punishment of the people and companies responsible for the spill.

438 ANTHONY NOWNES

And some groups lobbied for more regulations on oil drilling, while others lobbied for a more measured approach to punishment and less onerous regulations. This is the case in many political battles—there are groups on all sides of the issue.

The theme of this book is that there is something paradoxical about the way Americans view interest groups. On the one hand, all of us are sympathetic to *some* interest groups. On the other hand, most of us say we hate lobbyists and the interest groups they represent. Why the contradiction? What explains this paradox—a paradox I call "the paradox of interest groups"? The answer lies in the complicated nature of interest group politics in the United States. . . .

It would be an exaggeration to say that interest groups are at the very center of American politics. In the end, the elected and appointed decision-makers who represent us in government are at the center of most political storms. And this is as it should be; for the founders of this country designed a democratic republic in which most authoritative decisions are left to government decision-makers. Yet government decision-makers are hardly the *only* players in the American political process. As the storm brewed over how to react to the BP oil spill, all sorts of interest groups got themselves involved. They met with government decision-makers, they mobilized citizens, they advertised on television and radio, they circulated petitions, and they held protests and rallies. What all these interest groups had in common is this: they participated in the American political process. And this is why we study interest groups—because they are important players in the American political process. . . .

For many years the conventional wisdom was that lobbying was all about giving government decision-makers free stuff and, to put it bluntly, "sucking up" to them. Lobbying was viewed by scholars and the media alike primarily as a personal business that involved favors and corruption rather than information. Today the conventional wisdom is quite the opposite. Lobbying, most scholars agree, is mostly about providing accurate and timely information to government decision-makers. "Sucking up" does not get you anywhere if you don't know what you're talking about. Nevertheless, there is no question that wining and dining, doing favors, and just "hanging out" are staples of the lobbying business. How common are such practices? What forms do they take? How often do they mutate into unethical and illegal practices? . . .

Throughout American history interest groups and their lobbyists have sometimes resorted to questionable practices to achieve their goals. As political scientists Larry J. Sabato and Glenn R. Simpson have pointed out, political corruption "is truly a staple of our Republic's existence." Among the most common questionable lobbying practices are bribery, and the use of sex and/or alcohol to gain favorable treatment from government decision-makers.

Bribing government decision-makers is not a common lobbying technique. Nonetheless, the use of bribery by lobbyists is not unheard of. Perhaps the most outrageous example of lobbyist bribery in our history took place in the early 1920s, in an incident known as the "Teapot Dome Affair." Shortly after his election in 1920, President Warren G. Harding began to distinguish himself as one of the nation's worst presidents. He was particularly notorious for his disastrous political appointments. His worst appointment was Interior Secretary Albert B. Fall of New Mexico. Fall, who left the Senate to join Harding's cabinet, was financially strapped when he took over the Interior Department. In short order, however, Fall began buying huge and expensive chunks of land around his modest ranch in New Mexico. These purchases raised some eyebrows at the time, in light of his $12,000 annual salary. The money, it turns out, came from oil companies that wanted favors from Fall. In late 1921, Fall asked the president to transfer control of some naval petroleum reserves from the Department of the Navy to the Department of the Interior. Fall then turned around and sold the drilling rights to two millionaire oilmen. The oilmen received immensely valuable land at a fraction of its value, and Fall received over $400,000 for his work on their behalf. Eventually Fall was tried and convicted of graft. He was the first cabinet officer in history to go to prison.

Unfortunately, this is not the only example of lobbyist bribery in our history. Fifty years before Teapot Dome, a company called Credit Mobilier, which was hired to construct America's first transcontinental railroad, staved off congressional inquiries about questionable billing practices by illegally distributing stock and cash to members of Congress. Ultimately a congressional investigation uncovered evidence that Vice-President Schuyler Colfax, Speaker of the House James G. Blaine, and others had received payoffs from the company. More recently, in the midst of his Watergate troubles, Richard Nixon asked for and received massive and illegal cash contributions from business lobbyists. In the last few decades, state legislators in Arizona, California, Kentucky, and South Carolina have been convicted of receiving bribes from lobbyists. And the last decade has been one of spectacular lobbying scandals. For example, in 2005, former Member of Congress Bob Ney (R-Ohio) pleaded guilty to corruption charges involving bribes from lobbyists. His Republican colleague, Randall Cunningham (R-California), is currently serving out a prison term for accepting millions of dollars in bribes from defense contractors. And of course there is Jack Abramoff, the Republican über-lobbyist who spent time in prison for a variety of charges including tax evasion, fraud, and corruption.

Sex and alcohol have also featured prominently in some lobbying scandals. Though lobbyists understandably often decline to discuss the role of either in public, periodic scandals show that both can be used as lobbying tools. For example, in one of the more bizarre political scandals ever, lobbyist Paula Parkinson reported that she regularly traded sex for votes in Congress in the late 1970s and early 1980s. Parkinson, a contract lobbyist and political consultant, admitted to wining, dining, and servicing several Republican members of Congress in exchange for their votes on legislation. Parkinson claims that one member paid for her 1980 abortion. No legislators have ever acknowledged having sex with Parkinson. As for alcohol, it has always been in ample supply in locales where government decisions are made. The relationship between alcohol and lobbying was particularly apparent in a 1986 episode in Tallahassee, Florida. It was there that after a night of carousing and drinking a state legislator and a lobbyist were involved in a hit and run accident. When the police caught up with the duo, the lobbyist quickly confessed that he was driving the car. The legislator later admitted that he had been driving the car. When asked about the incident, the lobbyist replied, "You know, I am a lobbyist, and you have to take the fall when you work for a legislator." More recently, reports indicate that disgraced lobbyist Jack Abramoff regularly entertained government decision-makers at his own restaurant (called Signatures), and alcohol was regularly served.

Despite the examples cited in this section, interest group scholars agree that bribery, sexual and substance-related misconduct, and illegal lobbying activities are not common. The public perception that lobbyists are sleazy, disreputable characters who regularly violate the law is mistaken. Like all professions, the lobbying profession has its "bad apples." These bad apples have occasionally engaged in behavior that has brought the worst aspects of the lobbying business to light. But virtually every scholarly study of lobbying ever conducted has concluded that most lobbyists abide by the law and conduct themselves in a thoroughly professional manner. Why, then, does the lobbying profession have such a bad reputation? There are two answers to this question.

First, media tend to focus on the bad apples rather than the "good eggs." Most of the time news media ignore lobbying. Covering lobbying extensively would be difficult and boring. There is nothing particularly

From *Interest Groups in American Politics*   441

noteworthy about professional lobbyists testifying before legislative committees, filing lawsuits, or commenting on proposed federal regulations. However, lobbying becomes newsworthy and interesting when illegal behavior is involved. Bribery, sexual peccadilloes, and other unsavory practices—even if they occur infrequently—make the news. Thus, when the public at large hears about lobbying, it tends to hear things that make lobbying seem much dirtier than it is. Second, lobbying has a bad reputation because sometimes it takes place "behind the scenes." In other words, lobbyists sometimes meet with government decision-makers in informal settings outside of the halls of government. Many Americans seem to think that this shows a disregard for the law and democratic process. As we shall see, however, most informal contacts between lobbyists and government decision-makers are quite harmless. In fact, they generally entail the exchange of information and little more. However, the widespread use of informal lobbying techniques does raise legitimate questions about democracy, representative government, and the role of lobbyists in politics. . . .

Occasional scandal is the inevitable result of a political system that allows lobbyists such high levels of access to government decision-makers. For better or worse, government decision-makers in the United States generally develop close relationships with lobbyists. These relationships generally develop from extensive informal contacts between lobbyists and government decision-makers. Both parties to the exchange of information between a lobbyist and a government official benefit from this closeness. For their part, government decision-makers obtain valuable information that helps them make decisions. As for lobbyists, closeness allows them access to the people who make the decisions that affect them and their clients.

One form of direct informal lobbying entails drinking, schmoozing, going out for lunch or dinner, playing golf, and otherwise hanging out with government decision-makers. These types of interactions are undeniable parts of lobbying. . . . [L]arge majorities of state lobbyists report engaging in these sorts of informal contacts with government decision-makers. Studies of Washington lobbyists suggest that engaging in informal contacts with government decision-makers is quite common among Washington lobbyists as well. Informal contacts often take place in bars and restaurants. Most state capitals have well-known watering holes, pubs, and grills at which lobbyists and government decision-makers mingle. In Washington, restaurants and bars along the "K Street corridor" serve as meeting places for government decision-makers, lobbyists, journalists, and others involved in Washington politics.

What happens at informal meetings between lobbyists and government decision-makers? First of all, lobbyists provide information. In other
words, informal get-togethers, meetings, and encounters are forums at
which lobbyists pass on policy analytical, political, and/or legal information to government decision-makers. In other words, informal meetings
over food, coffee, or liquor are yet other avenues through which lobbyists
provide information to government decision-makers. Second, lobbyists
receive information from government decision-makers. In their roles as
monitors, lobbyists often use informal meetings to gather information
about political happenings. A lobbyist may, for example, inquire about the
status of a given piece of legislation. Or he/she might ask a legislative
staffer when a certain piece of legislation is "going to the floor" for a vote.
Alan Rosenthal, the preeminent scholar of state lobbying, has noted that
lobbying often "comes down to basic human relationships." He concludes:
"Whatever the political system or culture, the lobbyist's goal is to make
connections and develop close relationships" with as many government
decision-makers as possible. According to Rosenthal, building relationships allows lobbyists to prove their credibility, honesty, and reliability. He
concludes that lobbyists try to develop relationships "that allow them
to demonstrate the worthy attributes they themselves possess, which is
prerequisite for promoting their client's wares." Developing relationships
is also important because it leads to increased access to government
decision-makers. For example, if a lobbyist strikes up a friendship with a
legislator, it may translate into more invitations to congressional hearings
or greater input during the markup of a bill.

Drinking and eating are not the only ways lobbyists informally lobby
government decision-makers. There is also *providing gifts* and *doing favors*
for government decision-makers. . . . [Fifty-four] percent of state lobbyists
say that they do favors for legislators. Again, studies of Washington lobbyists suggest that a similar proportion of Washington lobbyists engage in
this sort of behavior. More specific survey items aimed at state government decision-makers show that 15 percent do favors for executive agency personnel and 14 percent do favors for the governor. As for gifts, we do
not have good data on how often Washington lobbyists provide them to
government decision-makers, but the results of the state lobbyist survey
. . . show that 19 percent of state lobbyists report giving gifts to legislators,
while only 2 percent report giving gifts to the governor. As for specific
gifts, studies show that lobbyists provide everything from perishables such
as flowers, candy, cigars, and peanuts, to free babysitting, tickets to athletic
events, and rides to work.

While most gifts and favors are small and apolitical, lobbyists agree that they help build relationships. Gifts and small favors help government decision-makers see a lobbyist's clients in a favorable light. One of the most popular gifts is the "junket," which is a free trip. Junkets are generally provided to legislators and their aides, as many other government decision-makers are barred from accepting them. Junkets can take many forms. Until 1995, when Congress adopted a law that banned some types of junkets, the typical federal junket consisted of an all-expenses-paid trip to a "conference" or "forum." Expenses included airfare, luxury hotel accommodations, meals, drinks, and incidentals. Interest groups that could afford to, usually held these conferences or forums at well-equipped hotels and resorts in Hawaii, the Virgin Islands, Las Vegas, San Diego, or Florida. Members of Congress defended such junkets, of course, saying that they provided them the opportunity to listen to their constituents and learn about important issues. Though Congress banned some types of junkets for its members in 1995, they are alive and well in the form of trips for "fact-finding missions" and "conferences" at which legislators serve as panelists or speakers. Junkets are also common in the states. While some states and localities have laws that essentially prohibit junkets, many others have laws that allow them. Moreover, even in places where junkets are banned, some government decision-makers, especially legislators and their aides, find ways to go on trips with lobbyists. . . .

In sum, informal lobbying techniques—wining, dining, schmoozing, gift-giving, and providing travel—are alive and well wherever lobbying takes place. Surveys suggest that chatting with government decision-makers over food or coffee is the most common form of informal lobbying. Giving gifts, doing favors, and providing travel are not unheard of. However, it is important to realize that despite the disproportionate media attention given to these types of lobbyist–government-decision-maker interactions, they are quite uncommon compared to other techniques of lobbying. While informal interaction is common, it is arguably less common than the kind of formal interaction that takes place in the actual halls of government. It is important to keep this in mind as we evaluate the worth and appropriateness of informal lobbying. . . .

Like the interest groups they represent, lobbyists are ubiquitous in the United States. . . . The number has been in the 10–15,000 range for the past fifteen years. Because some lobbyists are not required to register, there are probably closer to 25,000 professional lobbyists working in Washington. There are tens of thousands of additional lobbyists operating in states and localities across the country. For example, in 2010, over 1,500 lobbyists were registered to lobby in Texas, over 800 were registered in Montana, and over 500 were registered in Iowa. And most big cities and counties have hundreds of lobbyists, and even small cities and counties have dozens (and in some cases hundreds).

The term "lobbyist" evolved from the term "lobby agent," which was first used in the early 1800s to describe association representatives active in New York state politics. Popular mythology has it that lobby agents were deemed so because they waited in the corridors of power to buttonhole legislators. The term was subsequently shortened to "lobbyist." Political scientists generally distinguish between two basic types of lobbyists: *association lobbyists* and *contract lobbyists*. An association lobbyist is *one who works for, and is employed by, a single interest group*. In contrast, a contract lobbyist is *a lobbyist who has a number of clients and works for whomever hires him/her*. Newspaper and magazine stories on lobbyists tend to focus on powerful contract lobbyists. Yet while these "super lobbyists" make for fascinating copy, they are the exceptions rather than the rule in national, state, and local politics. Studies show that between 75 and 80 percent of lobbyists are association lobbyists. It is important to note, however, that many interest groups have their own lobbyists *and* "hire out" for special lobbying services. Thus, though association lobbyists outnumber contract lobbyists, the latter are used at one time or another by many interest groups.

One reason why the media focus on contract lobbyists is that their numbers have increased in recent decades. The recent proliferation has produced a new player in interest group politics: the *lobbying law firm,* which is a law firm that employs a number of contract lobbyists. The number of lobbying law firms is on the rise in Washington and state capitals and big cities. A lobbying law firm provides "one-stop shopping" for its clients. Today's all-purpose lobbying law firm provides a wide variety of services to interest groups including public relations, fundraising, direct lobbying, indirect lobbying, media services, and political consulting. The trend toward all-purpose lobbying shops has seemingly accelerated as lobbying has become increasingly technological.

As for the question of who lobbyists actually are, over 40 years ago political scientist Lester Milbrath found that the typical lobbyist was a well-educated, upper- or middle-class, 40–60-year-old white male. Virtually every subsequent study of lobbyists has painted a similar picture. There is some evidence, however, that the lobbying community is becoming more diverse, as women and ethnic and racial minorities invade previously inaccessible "good ol' boy" lobbying networks.

Many lobbyists make a pretty good living. One recent study found that the average lobbyist makes a little over $98,000 annually. It is not unusual for a high-profile Washington lobbyist to make between $500,000 and $1 million per year, while some particularly well-connected lobbyists (especially former members of Congress) make well over $1 million. Many state lobbyists are similarly well paid. Some of the top lobbyists in big states such as California and Texas, for example, make over $1 million annually. Moreover, even in smaller states such as Colorado and Arkansas a number of lobbyists make six-figure salaries, while the average lobbyist makes approximately $50,000.

Though lobbying is an elite occupation, few children grow up aspiring to lobby for a living. Most people who become lobbyists do so via other jobs. Government is the primary training ground for Washington, state, and local lobbyists. Studies suggest that over half of all Washington lobbyists and a similar proportion of state lobbyists have some sort of government experience. Among the most common government positions previously held by lobbyists are legislator, legislative aide, chief executive aide, and executive agency official. Not all lobbyists come from government. Many association lobbyists, for example, serve their employers in other capacities before they become lobbyists. Excluding public service, the two occupations that produce the most lobbyists are law and business. All told, lobbying is an elite profession. Many of its practitioners are well educated, well off, well paid, and well traveled. There's a reason for this: lobbying is not a job for slackers—as the communications theory of lobbying implies, it requires expertise. Policy analytical information, for example, often requires substantive knowledge about the "ins and outs" of a specific policy area. Similarly, most political analysis requires an intimate understanding of the powers, roles, and motives of government decision-makers, as well as the intricacies of the government decision-making process. Finally, legal analysis requires legal expertise—familiarity with the law and the legal process. Where does one get expertise? The career paths of lobbyists tell the story. Both policy and political expertise come from a combination of education and government experience. Not surprisingly, legal expertise often comes from going to law school and subsequently practicing law.

Expertise is essential if a lobbyist is to make his/her case. But valuable as expertise is, it may be less valuable than *access*—having the opportunity to present your case to government decision-makers. Access is the ability to put your expertise to work for you. Virtually all forms of direct lobbying require some level of access. And, of course, access is critical if a lobbyist wishes to have face-to-face contact with any government decision-maker. The importance of access explains why most lobbyists have government experience. As the previous section notes, having a close relationship with government decision-makers is important to lobbyists.

And building a relationship with government decision-makers is not necessary if you already have a relationship with government decision-makers. Interest groups, realizing the importance of access and closeness, often go out of their way to hire ex-government decision-makers as lobbyists. One recent study showed that "in the past 10 years" alone, "Nearly 5,400 former congressional staffers have left Capitol Hill to become federal lobbyists." Another study showed that "Of the 352 members of Congress who . . . left office" between 1998 and 2011, a whopping 79 percent became lobbyists. In fact, all manner of high-profile erstwhile government decision-makers are the subject of bidding wars by lobbying firms and interest groups wishing to cash in on their connections. Some of the most influential and important government decision-makers of the past twenty-five years are working as lobbyists. For example, former Senator Chris Dodd (D-Connecticut) now works for the Motion Picture Association of America; former House Majority Leader Dick Armey (R-Texas) works for an interest group called FreedomWorks; former Attorney General of the United States John Ashcroft has his own lobbying law firm called the Ashcroft Group; and former Senator Tom Daschle (D-South Dakota) works for the lobbying law firm DLA Piper. Wherever lobbying takes place, lobbying firms and interest groups pay big bucks to land ex-government decision-makers. The reason they do this is clear—they believe that erstwhile government decision-makers have the connections and/or expertise that make them more effective lobbyists.

The prevalence of "in and outers"—government decision-makers who become lobbyists after they quit or are removed from government—has raised eyebrows among critics who fear that this "revolving door" may harm the integrity of government. The revolving door issue raises a number of ethical questions. First, like informal lobbying, junkets, and gifts, it may bias interest group representation in favor of the few. Because ex-government decision-makers are very expensive to hire, the richest interest groups are generally the ones that can afford to hire them. Second, many critics believe that the revolving door may make government decision-makers, while they are in office, more responsive to potential future employers than to their constituents. For example, a member of Congress who plans to retire before the next election may make decisions while in office that are designed to make him/her attractive to certain interest groups that may hire him/her after the election. Similarly, a bureaucrat at the Department of Defense may do what he/she can while employed by the agency to curry the favor of weapons manufacturing companies in hopes of receiving a lucrative job offer after he/she quits.

Finally, the revolving door raises questions about the propriety of selfishly parlaying a government job into a lucrative lobbying career. Political analyst Pat Choate once imagined the following scenario. An individual is working for the Department of Commerce on trade issues. He/she is doing so at the taxpayers' expense. While working for the U.S. government, he/she receives invaluable experience in matters of international trade. After a few years on the job, the government employee quits. He/she is then quickly hired at a salary several times higher than that he/she received at the Department of Commerce by a foreign business firm. As the head lobbyist for the company, this person works hard to help the firm compete more effectively against American companies. The scenario, says Choate, is played out on a daily basis in Washington. Choate asks: Why should taxpayers subsidize interest groups by training their future employees, especially when these employees often work against the interests of vast numbers of Americans?

Over the years, a number of government decision-makers have paid lip-service to ending the revolving door. When he first took office, for example, President Clinton issued new rules that forbade former presidential appointees from lobbying their former employers for five years after they left government. These rules, like most others designed to thwart the revolving door, proved ineffective. One of Clinton's first appointees, deputy chief of staff Roy Neel, left the White House in late 1993 to take a job with the United States Telephone Association—a trade association. Technically Neel was not a lobbyist and did not directly contact the White House. He did, however, begin immediately to supervise lobbyists who regularly contacted the White House. More recently, when President Barack Obama took office, he announced that he would make all of his top political appointees sign a pledge saying that if they left the White House to become lobbyists they would not lobby the White House at all while Obama was in office. However, since Obama took office many of his aides have left government to become lobbyists, avoiding running afoul of the pledge they signed by lobbying other parts of the government (e.g., Congress) instead of the White House, and "supervising" other lobbyists who *do* lobby the White House. In short, the revolving door continues to spin unabated. The real reason the revolving door continues to operate is that government decision-makers like it. Ex-government decision-makers believe they should be able to do whatever they want with their lives when they leave government. Moreover, many government decision-makers enjoy politics and become lobbyists to remain involved and active. . . .

448 ANTHONY NOWNES

Public opinion polls and surveys show that overwhelming majorities of Americans believe that "special interests" dominate government decision-making. Are the public's perceptions accurate? *Do* interest groups get what they want from government while the views of ordinary citizens are virtually ignored? My answer to this question represents a bit of an anti-climax. For in the end, I must answer with a resounding: *It depends.*

The primary message of this chapter is this: sometimes interest groups get what they want from government and sometimes they don't. Anyone who tells you that interest groups always win or that ordinary citizens always "get the shaft" is wrong. The real world of politics, as scholars of policy domains have noted, is too messy, contentious, and unpredictable to support broad and sweeping generalizations about the power and influence of interest groups. Each and every government decision is the result of an exceedingly complex and multifaceted process that involves many factors. Interest group lobbying is one of these factors. In some battles—those, for example, where the public is unengaged and uninvolved—interest groups typically exert some (often a great deal of) influence over government decisions. In other battles—those, for example, that involve highly salient, ideologically charged issues or those where the public is heavily involved and highly engaged—interest groups typically exert little or no influence.

In the end, it is clear that interest groups are powerful players in American politics. As pluralists noted fifty years ago, interest groups are left out of very few important political battles. It is just as clear, however, that interest groups do *not* dominate and control American politics. Despite considerable public cynicism, there is plenty of evidence that "when push comes to shove," government decision-makers do what their constituents want them to do—even if this conflicts with the desires of powerful "special interests."

57

Citizens United v. Federal Election Commission
Justice Stevens' Concurrence and Dissent
Commentary by Jack Fruchtman Jr.

Supreme Court decisions often create strong reactions among people. Here's a case that is a particular source of controversy among Americans who follow politics closely. Citizens United v. Federal Election Commission *deals with the financing of campaigns, in particular, the right of corporations and labor unions to use their money in ways that go well beyond federal campaign finance rules. Some Americans love the decision. Others hate the decision. To understand the Court's stance, we first get some needed background and analysis from Professor Jack Fruchtman. With his clear and careful guidance, we can then read excerpts from Justice Anthony Kennedy's majority opinion and Justice John Paul Stevens's dissent. First Amendment, Hillary: The Movie, campaign spending, McCain-Feingold—still unsure where you stand? The decision was 5–4 and maybe it's not the last word on the subject.*

CONGRESS FIRST RESTRICTED corporate contributions in federal elections in 1907 with the passage of the Tillman Act, named for Democratic Senator Benjamin Tillman of South Carolina, who was an avowedly white supremacist. Although President Theodore Roosevelt had accepted corporate contributions for his reelection in 1904, he strongly supported the act: he also advocated prohibiting corporate funding of state elections and the use of corporate money to influence legislation. The Supreme Court upheld such limitations as recently as 2003 when the justices reviewed various provisions of the Bipartisan Campaign Reform Act of 2002, also known as the McCain-Feingold Campaign Reform Act (*McConnell v. Federal Election Commission*, 540 U.S. 93). *McConnell* was largely based on a 1990 decision when the Court outlawed corporate funding of campaign advertisements, *Austin v. Michigan Chamber of Commerce*, 494 U.S. 652.

The Bipartisan Campaign Reform Act, co-sponsored by Republican Senator John McCain of Arizona and Democratic Senator Russell Feingold of Wisconsin, was designed to regulate so-called "soft money," which is unregulated funding that wealthy contributors and corporations use for advertisements to attack candidates they wished to see defeated. Contributors did not direct money to official campaign organizations, but rather to Political Action Committees or PACs, set up for the purpose of skirting federal limitations on campaign contributions. Some sixty percent of the total amount of soft money spent in the 2000 election—

around $500 million—came from 800 individuals, corporations, and labor unions.

The Court concentrated on Sections 203 and 441b of McCain-Feingold, which is how the Act is also known, because those two provisions directly addressed soft money that corporations and labor unions used to finance campaign advertisements. The case focused on the use of money by Citizens United, a conservative, non-profit organization. In 2008, the organization opposed the candidacy of Senator Hillary Rodham Clinton of New York, the wife of former President Bill Clinton, for the Democratic nomination for the presidency. At issue was whether the organization's distribution of a ninety-minute political film called *Hillary: The Movie* violated the McCain-Feingold Act or whether its distribution was protected by the First Amendment.

Fearing that McCain-Feingold prohibited a corporation from directly encouraging citizens to vote against a candidate, Citizens United sought, but failed to receive, declaratory and injunctive relief against the Federal Election Commission in U.S. district court. That court held that the provisions prohibiting *Hillary* from being funded by a corporation were constitutional because it was "susceptible of no other interpretation than to inform the electorate that Senator Clinton is unfit for office, that the United States would be a dangerous place in a President Hillary Clinton world, and that viewers should vote against her." Citizens United appealed to the Supreme Court, and on re-argument, the Court asked the parties to address whether it should overrule the part of *McConnell* that addressed the facial* validity of McCain-Feingold.

Voting five to four, the Court overruled the district court's decision. In so doing, it also overruled *Austin* and found the McCain-Feingold Sections 203 and 441b unconstitutional. Justice Kennedy wrote the opinion for the Court. He was joined by Chief Justice Roberts and Justices Scalia, Alito, and Thomas. Justice Stevens dissented in an opinion joined by Justices Ginsburg, Breyer, and Sotomayor.

Citizens United v. Federal Election Commission
558 U.S. 50, 130 S.Ct. 876 (2010)

JUSTICE KENNEDY delivered the opinion of the Court.

The law before us is an outright ban, backed by criminal sanctions. It makes it a felony for all corporations—including nonprofit advocacy cor-

---

*The legal term "facial" means that the law is being challenged in terms of its overall constitutionality, not just that the law is unconstitutional in this particular instance.—EDS.

porations—either to expressly advocate the election or defeat of candidates or to broadcast electioneering communications within 30 days of a primary election and 60 days of a general election. Thus, the following acts would all be felonies under 441b: The Sierra Club runs an ad, within the crucial phase of 60 days before the general election, that exhorts the public to disapprove of a Congressman who favors logging in national forests; the National Rifle Association publishes a book urging the public to vote for the challenger because the incumbent U. S. Senator supports a handgun ban; and the American Civil Liberties Union creates a Web site telling the public to vote for a Presidential candidate in light of that candidate's defense of free speech. These prohibitions are classic examples of censorship.

441b is a ban on corporate speech notwithstanding the fact that a PAC [political action committee] created by a corporation can still speak. A PAC is a separate association from the corporation. So the PAC exemption from [the law's] expenditure ban does not allow corporations to speak. Even if a PAC could somehow allow a corporation to speak—and it does not—the option to form PACs does not alleviate the First Amendment problems with 441b. PACs are burdensome alternatives; they are expensive to administer and subject to extensive regulations. For example, every PAC must appoint a treasurer, forward donations to the treasurer promptly, keep detailed records of the identities of the persons making donations, preserve receipts for three years, and file an organization statement and report changes to this information within 10 days. . . .

We find no basis for the proposition that, in the context of political speech, the Government may impose restrictions on certain disfavored speakers. Both history and logic lead us to this conclusion.

The Court has recognized that First Amendment protection extends to corporations. This protection has been extended by explicit holdings to the context of political speech. Under the rationale of these precedents, political speech does not lose First Amendment protection "simply because its source is a corporation." The Court has thus rejected the argument that political speech of corporations or other associations should be treated differently under the First Amendment simply because such associations are not "natural persons." . . .

There is simply no support for the view that the First Amendment, as originally understood, would permit the suppression of political speech by media corporations. The Framers may not have anticipated modern business and media corporations. Yet television networks and major newspapers owned by media corporations have become the most important means of mass communication in modern times. The First Amendment was certainly not understood to condone the suppression of political speech in society's most salient media. It was understood as a response to the repression of speech and the press that had existed in England and the heavy taxes on the press that were imposed in the colonies. The great debates between the Federalists and the Anti-Federalists over our founding document were published and expressed in the most important means of mass communication of that era—newspapers owned by individuals. At the founding, speech was open, comprehensive, and vital to society's definition of itself; there were no limits on the sources of speech and knowledge. The Framers may have been unaware of certain types of speakers or forms of communication, but that does not mean that those speakers and media are entitled to less First Amendment protection than those types of speakers and media that provided the means of communicating political ideas when the Bill of Rights was adopted. . . .

When Government seeks to use its full power, including the criminal law, to command where a person may get his or her information or what distrusted source he or she may not hear, it uses censorship to control thought. This is unlawful. The First Amendment confirms the freedom to think for ourselves. . . . For the reasons explained above, we now conclude that independent expenditures, including those made by corporations, do not give rise to corruption or the appearance of corruption. . . . The appearance of influence or access, furthermore, will not cause the electorate to lose faith in our democracy. By definition, an independent expenditure is political speech presented to the electorate that is not coordinated with a candidate. See *Buckley* [424 U.S. 1 (1976)]. The fact that a corporation, or any other speaker, is willing to spend money to try to persuade voters presupposes that the people have the ultimate influence over elected officials. This is inconsistent with any suggestion that the electorate will refuse "'to take part in democratic governance'" because of additional political speech made by a corporation or any other speaker. *McConnell*.

Austin is overruled, so it provides no basis for allowing the Government to limit corporate independent expenditures. As the Government appears to concede, overruling *Austin* "effectively invalidate[s] not only BCRA Section 203, but also 2 U.S.C. 441b's prohibition on the use of corporate treasury funds for express advocacy." Section 441b's restrictions on corporate independent expenditures are therefore invalid and cannot be applied to *Hillary*.

Given our conclusion we are further required to overrule the part of *McConnell* that upheld BCRA §203's extension of §441b's restrictions on corporate independent expenditures. The *McConnell* Court relied on the antidistortion interest recognized in *Austin* to uphold a greater restriction on speech than the restriction upheld in *Austin*, and we have found this interest unconvincing and insufficient. This part of *McConnell* is now overruled. . . .

When word concerning the plot of the movie *Mr. Smith Goes to Washington* reached the circles of Government, some officials sought, by persuasion, to discourage its distribution. Under *Austin*, though, officials could have done more than discourage its distribution—they could have banned the film. After all, it, like *Hillary*, was speech funded by a corporation that was critical of Members of Congress. *Mr. Smith Goes to Washington* may be fiction and caricature; but fiction and caricature can be a powerful force. . . .

The judgment of the District Court is reversed with respect to the constitutionality of §441b's restrictions on corporate independent expenditures.

JUSTICE STEVENS, concurring in part and dissenting in part.

The majority's approach to corporate electioneering marks a dramatic break from our past. Congress has placed special limitations on campaign spending by corporations ever since the passage of the Tillman Act in 1907. We have unanimously concluded that this "reflects a permissible assessment of the dangers posed by those entities to the electoral process," *FEC v. National Right to Work Comm.*, 459 U.S. 197 (1982), and have accepted the "legislative judgment that the special characteristics of the corporate structure require particularly careful regulation." The Court today rejects a century of history when it treats the distinction between corporate and individual campaign spending as an invidious novelty born of *Austin v. Michigan Chamber of Commerce* (1990). Relying largely on individual dissenting opinions, the majority blazes through our precedents, overruling or disavowing a body of case law. . . .

In a democratic society, the longstanding consensus on the need to limit corporate campaign spending should outweigh the wooden application of judge-made rules. The majority's rejection of this principle "elevates corporations to a level of deference which has not been seen at least since the days when substantive due process was regularly used to invalidate regulatory legislation thought to unfairly impinge upon established economic interests." At bottom, the Court's opinion is thus a rejection of the common sense of the American people, who have recognized a need to prevent corporations from undermining self-government since the founding, and who have fought against the distinctive corrupting potential of corporate electioneering since the days of Theodore Roosevelt. It is a strange time to repudiate that common sense. While American democracy is imperfect, few outside the majority of this Court would have thought its flaws included a dearth of corporate money in politics. I would affirm the judgment of the District Court.

58

MATT BARRETO
GARY SEGURA

From *Latino America*

Matt Barreto and Gary Segura head a research group called Latino Decisions which provides opinion research data about the Latino population in the U.S. Their findings touch on many varied aspects of Latino life, but as political scientists, Barreto and Segura are clear: ". . . in the twenty-first century American politics will be shaped, in large measure, by how Latinos are incorporated into the political system." All candidates for political office, national, state, and local, know this by now, or have learned it the hard way. The authors provide some demographic data to open the selection. Then, they move into the partisan implications of the Latino wave. A liberal tendency is evident in Latino Decisions research. The news for the Republican Party in upcoming elections is not so good, the authors contend. "Demography may not be destiny, but it dramatically constrains the range of the possible." We, the readers, have the chance to test out the two scholars' thesis in real-life politics: election years 2016 and 2020, for starters.

———

SOMETIME IN APRIL 2014, somewhere in a hospital in California, a Latino child was born who tipped the demographic scales of California's new plurality. Latinos displaced non-Hispanic whites as the largest racial/ethnic group in the state. And so, 166 years after the Treaty of Guadalupe Hidalgo brought the Mexican province of Alta California into the United States, Latinos once again became the largest population in the state.

Surprised? Texas will make the same transition sometime before 2020, and Latinos have had a plurality in New Mexico for some time. Latinos are already over 17% of the population of the United States, and that number will grow toward a national plurality over the course of this century. The America that today's infants will die in is going to look very different from the nation in which they were born. Oh, and by the way, more than half of today's children under age five are nonwhite.

The pace of demographic change and its impact on both the racial structure of American society and the future makeup of the electorate are illustrated clearly in Table 1. In the 1950 census, the white share of the population reached its peak at just under 90%. And in 1980, when Ron-

Table 1 HISTORICAL TRENDS IN WHITE IDENTIFICATION IN THE US CENSUS

Year	White	Non-Hispanic White	Hispanic (Any Race)	Non-Hispanic, not in Combination	Non-Hispanic, Two or More Races
1800*	81.1%	—	—	—	—
1850	84.3%	—	—	—	—
1900	87.9%	—	—	—	—
1950	89.5%	—	—	—	—
1960	88.8%	—	—	—	—
1970	87.5%	83.2%	4.7%	—	—
1980	83.1%	79.6%	6.4%	—	—
1990	80.3%	75.6%	9%	—	—
2000	77.1%	70.9%	12.5%	70.4%	1.6%
2010	74.8%	65.3%	16.4%	63.7%	1.9%

Source: US Bureau of the Census. For 1800, see US Bureau of the Census, "Table 1. United States—Race and Hispanic Origin: 1790 to 1990," available at: www.census.gov/population /www/documentation/twps0056/tab0l.pdf. For 2010, see US Census Bureau, "Overview of Race and Hispanic Origin 2010 Census Briefs," March 2011, available at: http://www. census.gov/prod/cen2010/briefs/c2010br-02.pdf (accessed June 1, 2011).

ald Reagan was elected president, nearly 80% of all Americans were white. Meanwhile, in 1970, just 4.7% of Americans identified themselves as being of Hispanic ancestry. These populations were concentrated in New York and Chicago (Puerto Rican), Miami (Cuban), and the Southwest, from Texas to California (Mexican). Since 1980, however, the share of all Americans identifying themselves, unambiguously, as white has fallen precipitously, and Latinos, at 17%, are now present in every state and are the largest minority group in more than half of them. Nationally, the Latino population includes not just Mexicans, Puerto Ricans, and Cubans but also large numbers of Salvadorans, Guatemalans, Dominicans, Hondurans, Colombians, and countless others.

The ethnicity question in the census allowed us to count Hispanics separately from others answering "white" to the race question. It is ironic in the extreme that Latinos had been previously classified as "white" since that nominal status did not prevent them from being sent to segregated schools, kept off juries, being refused burial in local cemeteries, and other indignities historically reserved for the nonwhites in American society. White privilege clearly did *not* extend to Latinos.

The rapid growth of the Latino population will change America in profound ways. In the 1990s, Latino activists were fond of citing the 1992 report that salsa had displaced ketchup as America's most frequently purchased condiment, but that change really just scratches the cultural surface. Latin food, music, and dance have gone fully mainstream. Lin-Manuel Miranda won the Tony Award for Best Musical in 2008 for *In the Heights,* a story set in the largely Dominican community of Washington Heights, New York, almost exactly fifty years after *West Side Story* introduced Americans to Puerto Ricans living in the same city. Yet at the same time, English-language television continues to feature very few Latino lead characters. And although Latinos outnumber African Americans overall in the United States (and in more than half the states), African Americans are far more visible, both culturally and politically. Latinos may have restructured the race discussion in this country, once so powerfully dominated by the black-white dyadic relationship, but it is clear that the Latino story is very much a work in progress.

The central argument of this book is that in the twenty-first century American politics will be shaped, in large measure, by how Latinos are incorporated into the political system. The Latino electoral history of significant inter-election movement over time suggests that Latino population growth will combine with growth in the Latino electorate to present both political parties with new opportunities in their approaches to Latino voters. Such opportunities are not, of course, without precedent—the large-scale incorporation of urban immigrants in the early twentieth century played a significant role in realigning the American electorate and establishing the New Deal coalition, which dominated national politics for two generations.

If the past is prologue, the more than 53 million souls who make up this (mostly) new American community may well rewrite the political history of the United States. The demography is relentless—live births contribute more to population growth among Latinos now than immigration does, and over 93% of Latinos under age eighteen are citizens of the United States. More than 73,000 of these young people turn eighteen and become eligible to vote every month! There will be no stunning reversal of these numbers—there will be neither a sudden surge in white immigration and live births nor a Latino exodus. Each day every congressional district in the United States, and nearly every census tract, becomes more Latino than it was the day before.

If these new Americans represent political opportunity, they also represent political peril. For Republicans, the current numbers look grim. These new Americans enter the electorate two-to-one Democratic. In 2012 they voted nearly three-to-one Democratic. It wasn't always so. Ronald Reagan and George W. Bush both performed significantly better among Latinos in their reelection fights. But those days appear to be long gone, and as we discuss later in this book, it's high time for the GOP to get to work on rebuilding its brand with the Latino electorate. The Democrats face perils of their own. The party's failure to provide meaningful outreach and effectively mobilize voters has led Democrats to leave millions of votes on the table, and they will continue to do so if nothing changes in their approach. Moreover, with the Democratic Party's reliance on minority voters—most notably African American voters—and rainbow racial coalitions, it must carefully nurture policy agreement and strategic partnerships between the minority groups. Rivalry—or worse, direct conflict—could undo the Democratic demographic advantage.

The complexity of Latinos as a group makes for a politics more nuanced and less lockstep than the political behavior often described by the media and casual observers. Nevertheless, over the last several elections there can be little question that Latinos have become a political force—a force whose potential may not yet have been realized, but a force nonetheless. . . .

Before we delve into the diverse and dynamic world of Latino America, it is important to establish some baseline demographic information on the 53 million Latinos presently living in the United States. Longtime observers of Latino politics can recall a time when Latinos flew under the political radar because they were considered demographically and politically insignificant. The rapid growth of the Latino population in the late twentieth century, however (see Figure 1), coupled with a political awakening in the mid-1990s, propelled them into the national spotlight.

Figure 1 THE LATINO POPULATION IN THE UNITED STATES (IN MILLIONS)

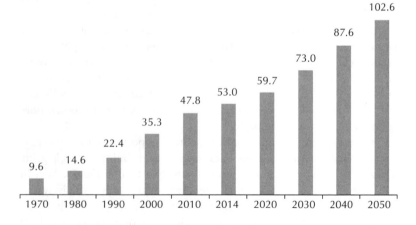

Figure 2 THE LATINO POPULATION AS A PERCENTAGE OF THE TOTAL US
POPULATION

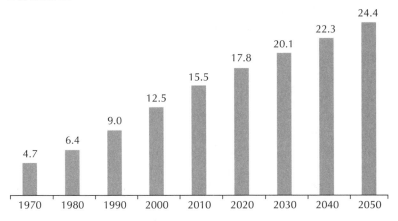

Although Mexican Americans and Puerto Ricans, the two largest Latino groups, were active in the 1960s civil rights struggles, by and large
Latinos were not significant nationwide political actors in the 1970s and
1980s. But by the 2000 census, Latinos had grown to over 35 million (or
12.5% of the US population; see Figure 2) and were on the verge of becoming the nation's largest minority. In the last decade, their size and
growing political clout have come to the notice of political pundits and
politicians, many of whom proclaim that the "sleeping giant" has finally
"awakened." No doubt, Latinos' political strength will only continue to
surge in the coming decades, given the population growth forecasts
shown in Figures 1 and 2. . . .

In the coming years, Latinos will exert greater electoral and policy
influence in states and communities across the country and in national
politics as well. They have come to prominence in the American political
realm as many before them have done—by making their way down a difficult path and going against the occasionally active resistance of the existing majority. What sets Latinos apart is their rapid rate of growth, which
has led them to surpass all previous newcomer populations in size and, by
extension, potential for political and social influence. The spasms of racial
and xenophobic antagonism toward Latinos can in some ways be better
understood if viewed from a perspective that accounts for how rapidly
this population has changed socially and demographically.

Latino Decisions has devoted the last seven years to watching these political developments, and all our polling suggests that major political change will follow from the demographic changes we have observed. In California such change is already a reality, and as Latinos across the country continue to show up at the polls in ever greater numbers, the rest of America, we believe, will quickly catch up.

59

MARK LEIBOVICH

From *This Town*

Mark Leibovich's 2013 best seller is filled with a myriad of stories and gossip about the Washington, D.C. crowd. Yet in some ways, his book reads like an American government textbook. In this excerpt, Leibovich looks at the lobbying industry in the nation's capital, much of it populated by former members of Congress and former executive branch appointees. He discusses the "revolving door," with no shortage of examples. For public servants who come to D.C. to serve the folks back home, the lure of the city is strong and few ever leave. Instead they settle in on K Street where experience, expertise, and personal connections pay off.

RELATIONSHIPS ARE TO WASHINGTON what computer chips are to Silicon Valley (or casino chips are to Vegas). Unlike computer chips, relationships are not grounded in exact science. But that does not stop people from trying, or paying a lot, to create and nurture them. Corporations have figured out that despite the exorbitant costs of hiring lobbyists, the ability to shape or tweak or kill even the tiniest legislative loophole can be worth tens of millions of dollars.

Harry Reid [former Senate Democratic majority leader] tells a favorite story about his friendship with the late Forrest Mars, the billionaire candy magnate who kept a home in Nevada and struck up a friendship with Reid. Reid liked Mars because he was an odd character, and he likes odd characters. He never gave Reid any money, but Reid kept visiting him because he liked talking to Mars. Finally, Mars wrote Reid a check for $1,000. "I'm doing this because I like you, not because I think it will do me any good," Mars told Reid. "I learned a long time ago, if you give your money to lobbyists, they will do a lot more good for you." His reasoning is that the lobbyists, rather than individual donors, are far more likely to get meaningful access to the elected official.

Lobbyists were present in the Capitol even before the Capitol was in Washington. When the first session of Congress gathered in New York in 1789, business representatives showed up bent on thwarting a tariff bill. The American tradition of lobbying the government dates back four centuries to the Virginia colony, according to the former *Washington Post* managing editor Bob Kaiser in his book on the modern lobbying culture, *So Much Damn Money: The Triumph of Lobbying and the Corrosion of American Government*. But until recently these "lobbyists"—supposedly named for the area of the buildings in which they congregated—did not constitute the critical mass they do now. In the sixties, businesses often avoided and even ignored the city altogether, believing it was not relevant or was counterproductive to their fortunes.

Now, nearly every major corporation, trade association, and union either employs their own lobbyist or army of lobbyists, or pays handsome retainers—often in the neighborhood of $50,000 a month, regardless of what work they actually do—to a lobbying practice. Corporations will routinely pay large sums to D.C.-based trade associations and also hire their own lobbying teams to hedge their bets in case the trade association is not effective.

Lobbying is a thriving example of Washington's middleman economy in which a third party (the lobbyist) facilitates a relationship or some illusion thereof between a client and a government official. Even those who do not formally register to lobby the government can market lucrative services via a "strategic communications" or "strategic public affairs" practice (everyone here has a "practice" now, as if they're doctors performing surgery). One way or another, almost every engine of new wealth in the region has derived from the federal government, or at least the desire to be close to it.

Calculations vary on how many former members of Congress have joined the influence-peddling set. By the middle of 2011, at least 160 former lawmakers were working as lobbyists in Washington, according to First Street, a website that tracks lobbying trends in D.C., in April 2013. The Center for Responsive Politics listed 412 former members who are influence peddling, 305 of whom are registered as federal lobbyists. Hundreds more were reaping huge, often six- and seven-figure salaries as consultants or "senior advisers," those being among the noms de choice for avoiding the scarlet L.

In addition, tens of thousands of Hill and administration staff people move seamlessly into lobbying jobs. In a memoir by disgraced Republican lobbyist Jack Abramoff, the felon wrote that the best way for lobbyists to influence people on the Hill is to casually suggest they join their firm after they complete their public service. "Now, the moment I said that to them or any of our staff said that to them, that was it, we owned them," said Abramoff, who spent forty-three months in the federal slammer after being convicted on fraud and conspiracy charges. "And what does that mean?" Abramoff continued. "Every request from our office, every request of our clients, everything that we want, they're gonna do. And not only that, they're gonna think of things we can't think of to do." Lobbyists can offer, in other words, an implicit preemptive payoff to powerful government officials. It happens not only on the Hill but in the boastfully antilobbyist, anti-revolving-door Obama White House. Scores of administration officials had by 2010 left the administration for K Street jobs without anyone so much as pointing out that they were defying a central tenet of the Obama political enterprise. If it was noted at all, the news was treated as a natural turn within the revolving door. After five legislative affairs staffers left the White House in the first part of 2011— three of whom went to K Street—Politico reporter Amie Parnes presented the trend as a natural by-product of administration staffers working hard for a period of time and then getting rewarded. "There are good jobs waiting at the end of the tunnel," Parnes quoted Stephen Hess, an oft-cited "governance studies" expert at the Brookings Institution. Parnes made no mention of Obama's public antipathy to K Street and his vow to slow the city's revolving door. Still, the work can be a grind, Parnes wrote sympathetically, with the plum lobbying gigs awaiting them as just rewards. "There's a payoff," Hess concluded, using the word "payoff" with no apparent wryness.

As Dodd was finishing up his financial regulatory bill in the summer of 2010, I spoke about him with outgoing senator Robert Bennett, a Republican of Utah who had been defeated in his reelection bid by a Tea Party favorite, Mike Lee. Bennett said he was surprised by how personally the voters of Connecticut had felt betrayed by Dodd. "They seemed to think Chris was actually corrupt," Bennett said, adding that this was not fair and that he certainly did not believe this about Dodd. He said the people of Utah were more pleasant to him when they tossed him aside than the cranky voters of Connecticut were to poor Dodd.

Bennett and another retiring senator, Byron Dorgan, Democrat of North Dakota, announced on the same day they would be joining Arent Fox, a major downtown law firm that includes a large lobbying component. Both Bennett and Dorgan had served on the Senate Committee on Appropriations, which gave them vast knowledge of how Congress allocates cash. It also made them coveted recruits for K Street.

Technically, former senators are forbidden from lobbying their old colleagues by a two-year "cooling-off period," so Bennett and Dorgan joined Arent Fox as "senior policy advisers" in the government relations department. There is little practical difference between what a former officeholder who lobbies does and what a former officeholder who "senior advises" does. For instance, someone like Dorgan could correctly say he has not formally registered to lobby even though he also owns the title of co-chair of the firm's government relations practice. In other words, he essentially oversees a staff of lobbyists. He talks all the time to his former lawmaking colleagues, and he can also use his specialized knowledge and access to call on old colleagues, friends, and fund-raisers to advance his clients' interests in bending a law or provision to their favor. He knows not only whom to call but also the phone number and who hired the staffer and precisely what to say to make things "happen."

While in the Senate, Dorgan was often quick to get all contemptuously righteous about people on the Hill cashing in their public service. When Jack Abramoff testified before the Senate Committee on Indian Affairs, Dorgan beat him up over the "cesspool of greed" that surrounded Abramoff's lobbying practice. In his subsequent memoir, Abramoff wrote of Dorgan, "I guess it wasn't a cesspool when he had his hand out to take over $75,000 in campaign contributions from our team and clients." (The *Washington Post* reported in 2005 that Dorgan said he would return $67,000 in donations from Indian tribes that Abramoff represented.)

When asked if his career change could be classified as "cashing in," Robert Bennett replied, "Is there anything in the Constitution that forbids me from earning a living?"

Representative David Obey, the cantankerous liberal appropriator from Wisconsin, retired in 2010 and—to the shock of many—joined the lobbying shop run by former colleague Richard Gephardt, the former Democratic majority leader whose willingness to reverse long-held positions in the service of paying clients was egregious even by D.C.'s standards of hired-gun opportunism. Examples abound in the case of Gephardt, a Teamster's son who represented a working-class district in eastern Missouri for twenty-eight years and was known as one of Congress's great champions of organized labor. But that was when he was in Congress and twice ran for president, in 1988 and 2004, with the substantial backing of labor. He would don a union windbreaker and blow out Teamsters' halls. "I'm fighting for *yoouuu,*" he would boom over raucous crowds, and he was always convincing. His dad drove a milk truck, even.

Gephardt was praised by AFL-CIO head John Sweeney as "a real friend of working people and a powerful voice for working families on issue after issue." But after leaving Congress in 2005, Gephardt became a powerful force for Dick Gephardt on issue after issue. He joined the Washington offices of DLA Piper as a "senior counsel" before starting his own lobbying shop in 2007. By 2010, Gephardt Government Affairs was listing his annual billings at $6.59 million, up from a pittance of $625,000 in 2007. In addition to having a top-drawer roster of corporate clients that included Goldman Sachs ($200,000 in 2010), the Boeing Company ($440,000), and Visa Inc. ($200,000), Gephardt became a "labor consultant" for Spirit AeroSystems, where he oversaw a tough antiunion campaign; also while in Congress, he supported a House resolution condemning the Armenian genocide of 1915, only to oppose the resolution as a lobbyist who was being paid about $70,000 a month by the Turkish government, according to the *Washington Post*. Genocide goes down a little easier at those rates.

Some Einstein in the White House decided to christen these sticky months of July and August 2010 in Washington the "Recovery Summer." It was a sweet turn of branding indeed, given the still-sputtering economy. The phrase was meant to highlight the "surge in Recovery Act infrastructure projects" and all of the "jobs they'll create well into the fall and through the end of the year," according to the White House website. As it turned out, the economy wasn't recovering much at all, though the D.C. economy, which was humming right along, had nothing to recover from. And the sector of lame-duck lawmakers was recovering quite nicely from the collective dings and indignities they had suffered as Washington officeholders circa 2010.

Evan Bayh, for instance, was in dire need of a Recovery Summer. He was worn down and burned out. In announcing his retirement from the Senate earlier in 2010, the Indiana Democrat was extravagant in his grief over what Washington had become. Like Dodd and Bennett, Bayh was a senator's son: daddy Birch Bayh served from 1963 to 1981. Evan was savaged in the most personal ways during the debate over health care. His wife, Susan, sat on numerous corporate boards, making more than $1 million a year since leaving as first lady of Indiana, from numerous corporate interests. (The Fort Wayne *Journal Gazette* described Susan Bayh as a "professional board member," having been a director of fourteen corporations since 1994, eight since 2006.)

Evan's insistence that his wife's deep financial stake in the industry would have no bearing on his role in overhauling it was met with open derision. Salon's Glenn Greenwald called Bayh the "perfectly representative face for the rotted Washington establishment," while Matt Yglesias, writing for ThinkProgress, said Bayh was "acting to entrench the culture of narcissism and hypocrisy that's killing the United States Congress."

On the way out, Evan Bayh wrote a much-discussed op-ed in the *New York Times* cataloguing his many frustrations with politics and how the overall spirit of Washington was "certainly better in my father's time."

He complained about the "unyielding ideology" of the Senate. He took the critique several steps further when he declared, "I want to be engaged in an honorable line of work," a remark that predictably rankled many of his former colleagues. Bayh also elicited eye rolls from senators who wondered where this man had been for the last twelve years—or eye rolls because they could predict precisely what was coming next.

But Bayh didn't stop there, soothing his deep despair over institutional conditions in Washington with dreams of "giving back" on the outside. He talked about joining a foundation. He waxed nostalgic for a previous chapter of his life in which he taught business students at the University of Indiana. He yearned to once again feel that tangible end-of-the-day satisfaction in his work. He fantasized lavishly to the *Washington Post*'s Ezra Klein about coming home to his wife after a long day of work and saying, "Dear, do you know what we got done today? I've got this really bright kid in my class, and do you know what he asked me, and here's what I told him, and I think I saw a little epiphany moment go off in his mind."

Bayh's valedictory lament and corollary yearnings might have been the most memorable statements he made in an otherwise ordinary two terms in the Senate. And if he had followed through on trying to fix the ills he had described on his way out ("the corrosive system of campaign financing," "the strident partisanship"), Bayh's post-Senate life could have made a greater impact than his time in office did. He might have made a tiny dent in how politicians in Washington are perceived by the general public, which he characterized this way: "They look at us like we're worse than used-car salesmen."

He then showed just the shameless opportunism that would repel any used-car buyer ("Make Crazy Evan an offer!").

After decrying "strident partisanship" and "unyielding ideology," Bayh joined Fox News as a commentator. The man who called upon members of Congress and their constituents to engage in "a new spirit of devotion to the national welfare beyond party or self-interest" signed on as a highly paid "senior adviser" to a large private equity firm (Apollo Global Management) and to a massive law and lobbying firm (McGuireWoods). Bayh, who was a finalist to be Barack Obama's running mate in 2008, vacuumed up as many sweet gigs as he could fit into his Club-issued trick-or-treat bag. He would eventually join the most potent business lobby in Washington, the U.S. Chamber of Commerce—arguably the most fervent opponent of the Obama administration's agenda. Bayh and Andrew Card, the former White House chief of staff under George W. Bush, embarked on a summer "road show" on behalf of the chamber's interest in stopping certain regulations on business. Think *Thelma & Louise* without the headscarves. Or think, as Steve Benen wrote in the *Washington Monthly*, a former senator who is "practically a caricature of what a sell-out looks like." . . .

The dynamic fairly glared with the outgoing Senate and House classes of 2010. Big numbers of them were announcing their retirements, saying they were worn down by the city and the gridlock and the bushels of resentment they were getting from the voters and shouting demagogues on cable and talk radio. One after another, lawmakers would grieve over the state of things and gallantly announce that they were stepping away, washing their hands of all the affectation and hypocrisy and invective and blame. It had all become so personal. All those Tea Partyers, they rued, or the "professional left," as Robert Gibbs dismissed impatient liberal activists. The haters were all being so unfair and indiscriminate in lumping all of Washington together as a cache of smooth-talking sellouts.

And then, with light-headed speed, so many of the departing office-holders would settle into the retainer class. Even if they really hated Washington—in their bones, not just their sound bites—they can't leave, because they are institutionalized, and the reality of it shines upon them soon enough: that maybe it's not so bad in Washington after all. In fact, maybe it's the greatest city in the world.

PART ELEVEN

Voting and Elections

60

DANTE SCALA

From *Stormy Weather*

It's the fall of 2011. You're in school. Congress and the president are at work in Washington, D.C. A presidential election is a year away, far into the future. But for the candidates, the future is now and the place is New Hampshire. How can a tiny northern non-demographically representative locale be the critical focus of American politics? The New Hampshire primary, held early in the winter of a presidential election year, can become the source of "momentum," explains Dante Scala: that precious and unmeasurable quality that can make or break a campaign. Scala points to the realities of momentum and the media attention it garners; with media attention come donations. Scala takes readers through the Exhibition Season, a bizarre combination of grassroots politics based on winning over local activists and simultaneously catering to the national press corps. Then comes the Media Fishbowl, the New Hampshire primary that occurs right after the Iowa caucuses. New Hampshire has had its moment in the spotlight. It has given and taken away candidates' momentum. All too soon, the fall of 2015 will be here.

THE FACT THAT CANDIDATES for the highest office in the land must pass muster with the residents of New Hampshire, a small New England state, is one of the greatest eccentricities of the American electoral calendar. This eccentricity is embraced by those who consider New Hampshire the last bastion of grassroots politics in the presidential selection process, a place where a politician seeking the highest office in the land must look a voter in the eye, shake hands, and answer questions on a one-to-one basis. Critics dismiss the New Hampshire primary as an annoying appendix to the presidential nomination process, a model of grassroots democracy now much more myth than reality. They charge that the primary gives vastly disproportionate influence to a relatively small group of voters who are unrepresentative of the national electorate, pointing to the Granite State's peculiarly libertarian brand of conservatism, its aversion to taxes, and its homogeneous, white population.

That such a small state came to play such a large role in choosing major-party nominees for president—and thus a significant role in choosing the next occupant of the White House—is a uniquely American story

of the idiosyncrasies of local politics mixing with national trends to produce an unforeseen development. When the state's political elites scheduled the presidential primary to coincide with Town Meeting Day in
March, they did so in order to save the money and trouble of holding two
separate events. Not in their wildest dreams did the frugal Yankees realize
that they were gaining squatter's rights to the most valuable real estate in
presidential nomination politics. . . .

The fuel New Hampshire has provided, in a word, is "momentum."
Momentum sometimes takes on a mystical, ill-defined quality for observers and participants in a campaign, something akin to "team chemistry" in
sports. A losing team is often said to suffer from bad chemistry among its
members, but that chemistry magically transforms when the same team
has a winning streak. Candidates often claim to have momentum until
results at the polls prove otherwise. . . .

. . . In the presidential primaries, a candidate's momentum is judged
on a weekly, even daily, basis by the answer to a single question: What is
the likelihood that the candidate will go on to win the support of a majority of the delegates to the party's national convention and the nomination? A candidate is said to have momentum if that likelihood is on the
rise. In the course of the campaign, that likelihood will rise and fall as
political handicappers compare a candidate's progress in relation to his
competitors and consider what opportunities are left for the candidate to
pick up more delegates. . . .

. . . Media attention along with financial contributions and standings
in the polls are the three main measurements of momentum. Often these
measures all affect one another in a cyclical manner. A flurry of stories on
a candidate boosts name recognition; increased name recognition leads to
better standings in the polls; and better showings in the polls prompt more
contributors to send funds to the campaign. . . . At a certain point, the
momentum may be seen as ineluctable as the candidate takes on, or is
given, an "aura of success."

A candidate gains that aura by exceeding expectations or a series of
markers that observers such as the national media lay down as criteria for
successful results. The media's expectations are often criticized as arbitrary,
especially by those candidates who fail to meet them or feel that the media have been too lenient on their opponents. Expectations, however, do
have their roots in a comparison of assumptions about how a candidate
will do—based on evidence such as historical precedents, poll standings,
results from neighboring states, and the efforts of campaigns—with how a
candidate actually does. Expectations and momentum are a zero-sum
game: a *better than expected performance* fuels momentum, increasing the

candidate's likelihood of winning the nomination while reducing that of the opponent; *performing no better than expectations but no worse* means the candidate remains moving at the same pace toward the nomination, with little advantage for either the candidate or the opponent; *performing worse than expectations* puts the brakes on a candidate's momentum, harming his chances of winning the nomination and advancing those of the opponent.

Momentum can thus be fleeting, an important consideration given that the presidential nomination "process" is really more a series of loosely connected electoral contests held at irregular intervals over a prolonged period of time. Each state has its own peculiarities, its own set of factions and differing proportions of factions, so that momentum created in one primary can be dashed as the successful message employed there backfires in subsequent states.

Momentum can be a valuable addition to the other types of resources that a candidate carries with him into the presidential nomination process. Some of these, such as a candidate's ideological reputation or his inherent abilities as a campaigner, are established prior to the beginning of the campaign. A candidate's liberalism, for example, will aid him in a liberal state but harm him in a conservative one. The availability of vital resources—money, attention from the media, and overall popularity—may depend on the success of the candidate's campaign, such as a strong performance in a competitive primary that attracts media coverage. With all other factors equal, candidates with more resources will do better than candidates with fewer resources, and early success can generate increased resources, such as the backing of donors who prefer to send their donations to perceived winners. . . .

First Stage: The Exhibition Season

Also referred to as the invisible primary, this is the period that extends from the morning after a general presidential election, until the first contests in Iowa and New Hampshire more than three years later. "The exhibition season is a building and testing period," Cook wrote, "in which candidates are free to fashion campaign themes and to discover which constituencies are receptive to their appeals." Key tasks include fundraising; the early stages of organization building in various primary states; and seeking the support of key interest groups such as labor unions. Although no votes are cast in the exhibition season, the games played at this time clearly count on the candidate's record.

The ability to raise money is one of the chief benchmarks for a successful campaign during the exhibition season. Conventional political wisdom places the prerequisite amount for a viable primary campaign at roughly $20 million. Candidates with lots of cash on hand have obvious advantages in a nomination campaign, including the capability to pay for staffers, to put advertising on the airwaves, and to garner valuable data from polling. Money alone may not necessarily decide a nomination, but money does make it possible for a candidate to employ certain means that help to secure a victory, such as advance polling.

The task of raising campaign funds, however, has been greatly complicated by the campaign finance reforms of the 1970s. Prior to these reforms, a presidential candidate was able to rely on a small group of wealthy donors to provide invaluable seed money for the initial stages of a campaign. After the reforms, which placed a ceiling of $1,000 on individual donations (now raised to $2,000 for the 2004 election cycle, after the passage of the McCain-Feingold campaign finance reform legislation), reliance on a few fat-cat donors was no longer possible. In order to run a viable campaign, presidential candidates instead have to collect thousands upon thousands of donations, in addition to obtaining matching public funding. Campaigns employ a variety of strategies to accomplish this daunting task. While insurgent ideological candidates can patch together a viable campaign by using direct mail or even 1-800 numbers, candidates who can raise money in thousand-dollar increments, as opposed to hundred-dollar increments, undoubtedly are able to raise large amounts of money more efficiently while still being eligible for matching public financing as well. The ability to raise funds is, in many ways, the first real contest of the nomination season. . . .

Much media speculation inevitably focuses on how candidates are doing in the first-in-the-nation primary in New Hampshire. Thus, in addition to fundraising trips to money centers such as New York and California, New Hampshire's Manchester International Airport is a frequent stop for candidates playing in the exhibition season. One weekend in fall 2002, for instance, Senator John Edwards of North Carolina did no fewer than a dozen events in a three-day tour of the state, beginning with a speech at the state Democratic Party's annual Jefferson-Jackson dinner Friday night in Manchester. The events ranged widely in size and were held all over the state, from the smallest, a coffee with four or five people, to house parties with dozens of people, including one at the home of Peter Burling, leader of the Democratic delegation in the New Hampshire House of Representatives. At one point during Edwards's whirlwind weekend, the van taking the candidate from Claremont to Cornish in western New Hampshire got lost. Edwards's political consultant, Nick Baldick, himself a New

Hampshire primary veteran, chalked this up as par for the course: "This is New Hampshire," he said. "There are no signs. People are going to get lost."

For many aspiring presidential candidates, a trip to New Hampshire is indeed similar to an educated business traveler's first voyage to a far-off land. The traveler needs to accomplish a number of things on his first visit. He needs to make acquaintances and discover friends. He needs a base of operations that will run and expand while he is away on business elsewhere. Most of all, though, the traveler needs a guide from among the natives. But how should he choose? Dayton Duncan, veteran New Hampshire activist and author of *Grass Roots*, a book on activists in the 1988 presidential campaign, described the dilemma of finding good advice this way:

You're a wealthy Englishman going big-game hunting in a foreign country.... [You] might be very good at firing your big gun. But you're in a foreign country, and [depending on] which guides you hire when you arrive, they might lead you to where you get a good shot off, or they might lead you to where all you get is malaria. And part of it is, before you made your choice of guides, had you done some previous work on that, of trying to determine who the guides ought to be? Or, do you also just have innate, common sense or innate political ability to figure it out?

Answering these questions, Duncan said, is key to this first stage of the New Hampshire primary: the competition among the candidates to lure activists and build an organization. This contest ends by the close of September or early October, months before the primary; by this time, the courtship of activists is mostly complete, and organizations are well along in their setup. Courting activists is more an art than a science, in part because there are as many motivations that draw activists to candidates as there are activists, said Manchester Democratic party chair Ray Buckley:

Some people just like personal attention. If you're running for president, and you call this person once a week for six months, you've got him. Other people, they want you to be the ... craziest liberal. Another person, it's because you're on a particular committee in the Senate, and so you did something on an issue, they're attracted on the issue.... They happened to have been at an event, and you gave an amazing speech, and you showed charisma, so the person was excited by that. You get this one person in, because they know forty other activists, you happen to get that whole clique.

Unlike the early days of the New Hampshire primary, candidates must now undertake this competition in the media spotlight, knowing that their every move is scrutinized by the political cognoscenti. When the

New Hampshire Democratic Party held a fund-raising dinner in February 2003, for instance, the list of presidential candidate attendees made not just the *Manchester Union Leader* but also ABCNews.com's "The Note," a daily must-read for the national political elite. American politics today, including media coverage of politics, "lends itself to endless speculation, and gum-chewing, and thumb-sucking about what's going to happen, versus real reporting on what actually is happening," Duncan said. In that type of environment, grassroots campaigning in New Hampshire is important in part because of the image such action conveys to the watching media. "Having that as your backdrop to how you're campaigning is a good backdrop to have. It also saves you from getting a rap going, particularly early on, that you're doing it wrong." ...

Second Stage: The Media Fishbowl

The seemingly interminable exhibition season finally ends in January of the year of the presidential election, when Iowa holds its caucuses and, soon after, New Hampshire its primary.

The Iowa caucuses are both inconclusive and definitive for candidates' fortunes. On one hand, the January caucuses held in precincts across the state do not actually award convention delegates to candidates; this occurs months later at state party conventions. On the other hand, and more important, the Iowa caucuses are "the gateway to a long and complex nomination process, and all players and all observers very much want whatever information they can glean" from the results, however transitory they may be. The media turn their attention from speculation on a candidate's prospects to analysis of the verdict from actual voters: "Iowa results, plus media spin" set the story line for New Hampshire and establish the roles of front runner, lead challenger (or challengers), and the remaining bit players who have the unenviable parts of long shots or also-rans.

For the week between the Iowa caucuses and New Hampshire's first-in-the-nation primary, the attention of the national political media descends on New Hampshire in a deluge. "That week is full of electricity," said Pat Griffin, executive vice president for the advertising firm O'Neil Griffin Bodi and a veteran of several political campaigns. In jest, he compared the last week before the primary to being on the set of *Doctor Zhivago*:

All these Washington types buy their mukluks ... to come up once every four years. ... They come up and say, "My God, where can I get my hair done? Where can I find arugula salad?" ... Go to [Manchester restaurant] Richard's Bistro at night, they're all at the same places, [saying] "My goodness, can you believe this tundra where these people live?"

The national political media venture into the tundra—at least as far as Manchester and its environs, if not the seacoast or the Connecticut River valley or the North Country—because the people who live there possess something they want dearly: information on how actual voters feel about the presidential candidates. The Iowa caucuses, in which participants have to devote hours of time on a single evening, are usually low-turnout events attended by party faithful, in which strong organizations are often vital to a good showing. The New Hampshire primary, in contrast, turns out a much higher percentage of voters, and candidates must therefore be able to appeal to a variety of constituencies. Iowa and New Hampshire together, plus the media's interpretations of those two contests, winnow the field to a front runner and one or, at most, two or three challengers. . . .

Perhaps one of the reasons New Hampshire has been and remains an indicator is that it is an early testing ground of candidates' organizational skills, charisma, and appeal to the broad range of the relevant electorate. For, notwithstanding its idiosyncrasies—and what state is not idiosyncratic?—New Hampshire's populace is composed of various factions that have their analogues in the rest of the nation. How a candidate crafts a message to appeal to those factions or constituencies in New Hampshire does affect how he or she will be perceived thereafter. New Hampshire's ability to determine the nomination may be in question; that it is an early indicator of how a candidate plans on running a campaign and the likely chances of the success of that message, however, is not.

61

ROBERT BOATRIGHT

From *Getting Primaried*

The Democratic and Republican political parties' primary elections to select candidates used to get media attention only in presidential years when one or both parties had several hopefuls vying for the top nomination. Now, Robert Boatright reveals, primaries have taken on a new dimension. Some candidates have been identified by ideologically extreme groups as not taking positions pure enough, and thus, worthy of being challenged from within their own party. Many groups have been instrumental in leading primary challenges, among them, the Club for Growth (challenging Republican incumbents thought to be too moderate) and MoveOn.org (taking on Democrats not sufficiently liberal). These outside groups have been influential mostly by sending large sums of money into the primary races they've targeted. An addendum to this book would include the new Super PAC money that flows into a few selected primary races as well as the involvement of high profile groups like the Tea Party. Ironically, these primary challenges sometimes backfire at the general election handing the win over to the other party's candidate. "So, in the end, do congressional primary challenges matter?" asks the author. The political junkies among us enjoy the excitement in a usually calm pre-election period. More seriously, "getting primaried"—or just the threat of getting primaried—only adds to the further polarization of party politics in the U.S.

———

DURING THE 2004 AND 2006 ELECTIONS, a new word entered the American political lexicon: the verb "to primary," meaning to mount a primary campaign against an incumbent member of Congress. Conservative and liberal bloggers spent much time discussing incumbent members of Congress who, in their opinion, needed to be primaried. Calls for primarying reached a fever pitch during the 2008 election cycle; a quick search of blogs such as DailyKos, firedoglake, and Free Republic turns up numerous calls for politicians to be primaried, based on their overall record or on one or two high-profile votes. In a few cases, the bloggers took aim at incumbents who were ineffective or had been accused of corruption. More often, however, these incumbents were criticized for being insufficiently partisan. In 2008, candidates who were threatened with being primaried tended to be Democrats who had supported some of President Bush's priorities or Republicans who had not supported them. In

2010, liberal groups took aim at Democratic incumbents who had not supported President Obama's agenda, and conservative groups, most notably those associated with the Tea Party movement, took aim at Republican incumbents who had.

Primary challenges to incumbent members of Congress are hardly unheard of, but they have rarely been a subject of national discussion. Congressional primary elections have received little scholarly attention, and the literature on primaries has generally concluded that they are either a minor irritant to incumbents in lopsidedly partisan districts—a byproduct of districts in which winning the primary is tantamount to winning the general election—or the consequence of scandalous misbehavior on the part of incumbents. Until recently, congressional primaries were mostly treated as low-visibility affairs, elections that tell one next to nothing about national politics.

All of this has changed during the past decade. A casual perusal of political websites and of the major American newspapers provides much evidence that primarying (or at least the threat of primarying) has become widespread and is becoming a standard weapon for activists on both the political left and right. After organized labor and progressive groups combined to back primary challenger Donna Edwards in her 2008 defeat of Maryland incumbent Al Wynn, the *Baltimore Sun* quoted a spokesperson for one liberal think tank as speculating that "it is possible that this is part of a larger, anti-incumbent trend." Likewise, an article in *Politico* noted that Wynn's defeat "had nothing to do with the more customary reasons why incumbents fail to win nomination"—that is, he was done in not by redistricting or scandal but by being insufficiently partisan. The *Politico* article went on to predict that 2008 would be "a rough election cycle for incumbents facing serious intraparty challenges." Similar predictions were made in 2010 following [incumbent Arkansas Democratic] Senator Blanche Lambert Lincoln's narrow primary win over a challenger backed by the same liberal-labor coalition.

Despite the prominence of such challenges from the left, however, progressive groups have taken their cues from the Club for Growth's strategy of bundling contributions for primary challengers to "RINOs," or Republicans in Name Only. Since 2000, the Club for Growth,* a conservative advocacy group, has raised money for and run television advertise-

---

*The Club for Growth is an influential, well-funded group that supports candidates who favor free market economic policies. As Boatright describes the club, it bundles money for the candidates it supports, and also has a big-spending super PAC. In particular, the Club for Growth has focused its efforts in primaries helping candidates who take on Republicans deemed too moderate by its standards.—Eds.

ments on behalf of several prominent primary challengers to moderate Republican incumbents, including challengers to New Jersey representative Marge Roukema, New York representative Sherwood Boehlert, Pennsylvania senator Arlen Specter, and Rhode Island senator Lincoln Chafee. The club did not succeed in defeating an incumbent until 2006, however, when a conservative challenger ousted moderate first-term Republican Joe Schwarz in Michigan, and it did not succeed in ousting an established Republican until Maryland representative Wayne Gilchrest was defeated in his 2008 primary.

Although the Club for Growth has, by its own admission, been most successful in helping candidates in open-seat primaries, its campaigns against incumbent Republicans have attracted more attention than its open-seat campaigns. In a well-publicized interview with the *New York Times* in 2003, the club's founder, Stephen Moore, claimed that incumbents "start wetting their pants" when the Club for Growth threatens to run a candidate against them and that it planned to "scalp" Arlen Specter. By 2006, many on the left openly admitted that the club had inspired them to mount similar challenges. *The Nation* called for challenges to pro-war Democrats, and MoveOn.org* singled out prominent Democrats who it claimed were insufficiently liberal or were enabling President Bush's policies, particularly in Iraq. Among the most celebrated such challenges on the left was Ned Lamont's victory in the Connecticut Senate primary over incumbent senator Joseph Lieberman.

It is easy to see why primarying makes for an irresistible story line. In a pop culture sense, primarying resembles a common trope in the gangster movie genre—a prominent gang member is suspected of secretly consorting with a rival gang or with the police, and some within the gang seek to bump him off in order to weed out traitors and make an example of him, to keep others in line, and perhaps in order to strengthen their own position in the gang. In a game-theoretic sense, primarying is an example of the "grim trigger" strategy: in order to keep adversaries in line, one must be able not only to make threats but to demonstrate the ability to carry out threats, even when doing so is to one's own disadvantage. Primarying represents a threat not only to the incumbent who is primaried but to those who might support the primary challenge—there is always the danger that, for instance, a liberal challenger to a moderate Democrat will be a weaker candidate in the general election and that the

---

*"Ambition must be made to counteract ambition," wrote James Madison in *The Federalist* 51. Thus, MoveOn.org provides the counterpoise to groups like the Club for Growth. MoveOn.org has been active in primaries and general election contests on behalf of extremely liberal, progressive Democratic candidates.—Eds.

primary challenge will result in the opposition party winning the seat because either the successful primary challenger loses the general election or the incumbent is sufficiently weakened in the primary that he cannot win the general election.

The story behind primary challenges thus requires that the challenger and his or her supporters take on an almost cartoonish quality, as exemplified by Moore's over-the-top claims, the delicious irony of former Democratic vice presidential candidate Lieberman being parodied in advertisements for literally embracing President Bush, or the allegations by the Club for Growth that moderate Republicans Olympia Snowe and George Voinovich were "Franco-Americans" for occasionally putting the brakes on Republican proposals (they were said to be such not on the basis of their ethnicity but on account of the club's equation of their suspect patriotism with the surrender by the French to the Germans in World War II). Such preposterous allegations are absolutely ideal for garnering media attention during the early months of an election year. When the general election is far off, stories such as these offer a better diet for political junkies seeking to gain insight into the fall's elections than does, say, parsing fundraising figures for candidates. . . .

Earlier chapters of this book showed that congressional primary challenges are still somewhat rare but that there has been a change in the fundraising base of many ideological challengers over the past few decades. There is more money coming in to ideological primary challengers in small amounts, and there is more money coming into their campaigns from out of state than was once the case. It is virtually impossible to imagine this happening without the existence of some sort of entity coordinating the efforts of donors nationwide. To return to the example of the Arkansas Senate primary [challenging incumbent Democrat Blanche Lambert Lincoln in 2010] . . . it is inconceivable that citizens from around the country could be motivated to care about the Arkansas race unless someone convinced them to care, and the challenger in that race showed no sign of having the ability to single-handedly make the non-Arkansan public care. In short, the financial data suggest that nonparty groups are increasingly focusing their efforts on congressional primaries.

Traditional theories on interest groups provide little insight into why groups would do this, and as I argued . . . direct group contributions are a negligible part of challengers' funds. As we shall see . . . the task of nationalizing primary challenges has been taken up in many instances by interest groups such as MoveOn.org or the Club for Growth. Less formal political movements, such as the Tea Party movement, can also fulfill this function, as can such blogs as DailyKos or RedState. Even an individual political actor—such as [former] South Carolina senator Jim DeMint or former Alaska governor Sarah Palin—can call the attention of a nationwide audience to a primary challenge. It is difficult to take fingerprints from an individual primary challenger's donor file to see who has drawn the attention of donors to that campaign. Yet the undeniable fact that some combination of groups, online communities, and individual political activists has touted the campaigns of several primary candidates over the past few election cycles indicates that we should narrow our focus somewhat. While it is evident that most PACs are skittish about becoming involved in congressional primaries, the decisions of one or two interest groups or other political actors can elevate the profile of a small number of primary challengers.

The broad generalizations frequently drawn about politicians' motives do not apply to all politicians or all groups. To say that, as a rule, incumbent members of Congress will not support primary challengers to their colleagues is not to say that there will not be one or two renegade members who throw caution to the wind and get involved in primaries. To say that most interest groups do not get involved in primaries is not to say that one or two groups will not seek to distinguish themselves by focusing on primaries. Because of the rarity of such steps, a group or politician doing this draws attention. Some groups or politicians may benefit from this attention; most will not. For the Club for Growth or MoveOn to do this is to serve notice of their independence from the parties; likewise, for Sarah Palin to do this is to serve notice of being a different kind of politician, of seeking reform above and beyond party labels. . . .

The 2010 Alaska Republican Primary

More than any other election considered in this book, however, it is the 2010 Alaska Senate primary that represents the "perfect storm" for outside activity in primary elections. In Susan Dunn's history of Franklin Delano Roosevelt's attempted "purge" of the Democratic Party in the 1938 primaries, Roosevelt advisor Jim Farley, who disagreed with Roosevelt's decision to get involved in primaries, decamped for Alaska during the election, saying, "As I surveyed the coming primaries, I wondered if Alaska was far enough." Alaska was, of course, not a state at the time. But since gaining statehood, Alaska has been a state where primary challenges can flourish. Former senator Mike Gravel faced primary challengers in each of his reelection bids; and in 2008, Senator Ted Stevens and the state's lone House member, Don Young, faced primary challengers. Alaska's incumbent senior senator going into the 2010 election, Lisa Murkowski, has been a conventional Alaska Republican in many ways. She has touted her ability to procure federal funds for Alaska, while at the same time siding with Democrats in the Senate on many social issues. Murkowski was, for instance, among the eight Republicans who voted to repeal the military's "Don't Ask, Don't Tell" policy during the 2010 lame-duck session.

Murkowski also came into office under unusual circumstances. She was appointed to the Senate by her father, veteran senator Frank Murkowski, in December of 2002, after her father ran successfully for the state's governorship. Although Lisa Murkowski had served in the Alaska House of Representatives for two terms, her ascension to the Senate was widely seen as a gift from her father. She was challenged in the 2004 Republican primary, winning with 58 percent of the vote. Her father, meanwhile, lost his 2006 primary for reelection to the governorship to political neophyte Sarah Palin, following one term marred by a scandal that touched several other Alaska politicians, including the state's other senator, Ted Stevens. Although Alaska politics has often featured infighting within both parties, the developing split between party regulars such as Murkowski and Stevens and a more conservative reformist faction led by Palin indicated that Murkowski would be vulnerable. The state's small population, low voter turnout, and relatively concentrated population (half of the state's residents live in the Anchorage area) also can make campaigning in Alaska a relatively inexpensive proposition, which may work to the advantage of primary challengers.

Joe Miller, an obscure lawyer from Fairbanks with little prior political experience, mounted a challenge to Murkowski in 2010. Miller raised only $284,000 during the primary, compared with $3.4 million raised by Murkowski. Miller was aided, however, by an independent expenditure of $300,000 by the Club for Growth and by an estimated $600,000 spent by the Tea Party Express on his behalf. Miller's challenge to Murkowski was clearly ideological in nature; Miller called for eliminating Medicare, Social Security, the Department of Education, and anything else that he claimed is not "constitutionally authorized." Miller also criticized Murkowski's support for cap and trade legislation (tepid though it was), her pro-choice stance on abortion rights, and even her aggressive effort to procure federal funds for Alaska. Although Miller developed several clever YouTube videos that received national attention, his campaign on the ground in Alaska was largely funded by others. Miller narrowly won the Alaska primary by a 51 to 49 percent margin, a margin of approximately 2,000 of the 110,000 votes cast. Murkowski, who still had $1.9 million on hand after the primary, eventually mounted a write-in campaign and defeated Miller in the general election.

What did outside groups do for Miller? Media reports indicate that the Tea Party Express funded extensive volunteer training exercises, sending volunteers to Alaska to help locals coordinate get-out-the-vote efforts, craft press releases and letters to newspapers editors, and maintain a "war room" on a cruise ship docked in an Alaska harbor. Of the money spent by the Tea Party Express, $150,000 was spent on advertisements in the final week of the campaign. The fact that Murkowski had led in all of the preprimary polls indicated that this effort must have been effective. The Club for Growth, noting Miller's nearly depleted treasury after the primary election, mounted an aggressive effort after the election to bundle contributions for Miller, who ultimately raised $3.2 million by the end of the general election. The club had made several ad buys for Miller during the primary. It also mounted a campaign to encourage fifteen hundred donors to Murkowski to request refunds after the primary. The club reported that a similar effort in the wake of Arlen Specter's party switch had cost Specter over $800,000.

During the general election, several other groups would weigh in on Miller's behalf, including the National Republican Senatorial Committee and Senator Jim DeMint's Senate Conservatives Fund. Apart from several small independent expenditures on Murkowski's behalf, however, the field was dominated by the Club for Growth and the Tea Party Express, and the size of these groups' expenditures, although they do stand out, seem less important for their financial clout than simply as signals of these groups' interest in the race.

The other outside actor in this race who may well have mattered was Sarah Palin. Palin endorsed Miller on her Facebook page in June and recorded several robocalls describing Murkowski as "another Democrat in the Senate voting for the Obama agenda which is bankrupting us." This surely came as no surprise to Murkowski—Palin had, after all, run against Murkowski's father for governor and had endorsed Murkowski's primary opponent in 2004—but Murkowski apparently decided that it would be unwise to take Palin on in the race and did not directly criticize her until after the primary. Murkowski sought to separate Miller from Palin and focus instead on Miller's inexperience, while increasing her criticism of the Obama administration and presenting herself as an independent. It is hard to quantify the effect of Palin's involvement in the race, especially since the sorts of numbers available for interest groups are not available for Palin, but her involvement, like that of the Tea Party Express and the Club for Growth, had the effect of making the race more about Lisa Murkowski than about Joe Miller.

The Alaska Republican primary represents a confluence of features we have seen elsewhere in this book. The incumbent was someone who raised the ire of ideological activists. The geography of Alaska was conducive to a well-run campaign on the part of one or two outside groups. The political culture of Alaska is such that the major party organizations are weak, and Alaskans have a history of supporting unconventional politicians. The race was about ideology, but other concerns, about Lisa Murkowski's appointment to the seat and the ethical troubles of her father's gubernatorial administration, ensured that there was more to the race than simply ideology. Miller's lack of a political pedigree may have ultimately made him a problematic general election candidate, and he never fully stepped out of the shadow of the groups supporting him. But his relative anonymity made him a good vehicle for a group-sponsored primary challenge. While the Club for Growth may have been willing to run the risk of sacrificing the seat to the Democrats as a result of their campaign . . . the relative weakness of the Democrat in the race made it unlikely that this would happen.

In other words, the Alaska race was a good race for conservative groups to use to lay down a marker, and they arguably did this despite Murkowski's ultimate victory. The long-term consequences for Murkowski herself are not clear—her subsequent votes in the Senate do not indicate that she has moved to the right as a result of her narrow escape, and she does not have to face the Alaska voters again until 2016. The Republican Party's decision to support Miller in the general election put her in a situation analogous to that of [former Connecticut Senator] Joe Lieberman following his 2006 primary defeat. But the rhetoric from the Club for Growth following the election—as well as that of Jim DeMint's group—made it clear that many Republicans up for reelection in 2012 would now have reason to fear similar efforts. . . .

So, in the end, do congressional primary challenges matter? They do, but they matter largely because politicians and those who follow politics have been told repeatedly that they do. They are an instance of belief becoming reality. They are not more numerous than they were in the past, but they draw more national attention and more money. There are no easily measurable effects on incumbents' voting, but it is certainly plausible that they affect the behavior of incumbents who are not ultimately challenged—that the fear of being primaried is a crucial source of party discipline. There is always the possibility that the *belief* that primary challenges are becoming more frequent and that centrist incumbents are becoming more vulnerable will prompt potential candidates to come out of the woodwork, so that we will see more challenges in the future. Perhaps this began to happen in 2010. It is hard to argue that more competition would be bad for democracy, but it is certainly a concern for advocates of bipartisanship, centrism, civility and so forth in Congress.

62

DENNIS JOHNSON

From *No Place for Amateurs*

Behind the scenes of every political campaign today is a political consultant. Political consulting is a thriving business whose skills are employed not just by candidates for national office, but those running for state and local positions, too. No race is too small or too obscure to be aided by consulting firms, whether big-time ones led by the famous (James Carville, Dick Morris) or the anonymous one- or two-person basement operation. Dennis Johnson reveals the multitude of tasks that consultants perform for a campaign. He also gives some good tips on movies to rent on the topic: The War Room and Wag the Dog are particularly good choices for those who enjoy the blend of fact and fiction.

———

I don't want to read about you in the press.
I'm sick and tired of consultants getting famous at my expense.
Any story that comes out during the campaign undermines my candidacy.

—BILL CLINTON to his new 1996 reelection consultants
Dick Morris and Doug Schoen

JUST DAYS BEFORE THE 1996 Democratic National Convention, a smiling, confident Bill Clinton was featured on the cover of *Time* magazine. Pasted on Clinton's right shoulder was a cut-out photo of political consultant Dick Morris, "the most influential private citizen in America," according to *Time*. On the eve of Clinton's renomination, *Time* was sending its readers a backhanded pictorial message: here is the most powerful man in the world, who fought his way back from political oblivion, and perched on his shoulder is the reason why. Suddenly the once-secretive, behind-the-scenes consultant was a household name. In the early months of the reelection campaign, Morris worked hard at being the unseen political mastermind and strategist. "Being a man of mystery helps me work better," he confided to George Stephanopoulos. While Bill Clinton's 1992 consultants were talk-show regulars, wrote best-sellers, and traveled the big-dollars lecture circuit, Morris was the backroom schemer. Many media outlets had trouble even finding a file photo of the elusive Dick Morris, adding to the mystery and illusion of power.

Morris had been Clinton's earliest political adviser back in Arkansas during the first run for governor. They had a rocky relationship over the years, but following the Republican takeover of Congress in November 1994, Bill Clinton began meeting secretly with Morris. Working out of the Jefferson Hotel in Washington, using the code name "Charlie," Morris plotted the president's comeback. He was the anonymous, behind-the-scenes consultant who would retool Clinton's image, reposition his policies, and help revive his faltering presidency.

Throughout his career, Bill Clinton had a reputation for discarding political consultants. Those who helped him capture the White House in 1992—Mandy Grunwald, Stanley Greenberg, Paul Begala, and James Carville—were nowhere to be seen following the 1994 election upheaval. By the spring of 1995, Morris had assembled his own team, including veteran media consultants Bob Squier, Bill Knapp, and Hank Sheinkopf, and pollsters Mark Penn and Doug Schoen. They met regularly with several White House insiders to plan the remarkable political comeback of Bill Clinton.

Morris's anonymity was shattered when he was caught with his longtime prostitute companion by the supermarket tabloid the *Star*. The tabloid deliberately timed its bombshell story for maximum effect on the Democratic convention, with the scandal erupting on the day that Bill Clinton accepted his party's renomination for the presidency. Morris and his wife immediately left the Chicago convention and the Clinton campaign, retreating to their Connecticut home, besieged by reporters and photographers. Morris, the political consultant turned nefarious celebrity, had become a late-night dirty joke, damaged goods, and certainly a political liability. There were rumors that he was sharing sensitive White House information with his prostitute girlfriend, and Morris shocked many by announcing that months earlier he had signed a secret book deal to write the inside story of Clinton's reelection comeback. Morris now had plenty of free time to write his version of the 1996 campaign, work the talk-show circuit, join a twelve-step sex addiction program, retool his tarnished image, and pocket his $2.5 million book advance. Though the Morris scandal scarcely damaged the Clinton campaign, it ended up being everything President Clinton objected to: Dick Morris was getting famous—and rich—at his expense. For the moment, Morris joined a short list of celebrity political consultants who became as famous and often far more handsomely paid than their clients.

For years Americans had been unwittingly exposed to campaign posturing and manipulation engineered by political consultants. In the 1990s they grew curious about the manipulators. Suddenly, political consultants were hot properties. Movies, documentaries, and books gave us a glimpse of consultants at work. A film documentary, *The War Room*, made media stars of James Carville and George Stephanopoulos in Bill Clinton's 1992 presidential campaign headquarters. Reporter Joe Klein's best-selling roman à clef, *Primary Colors*, detailed with unnerving accuracy the seamy side of the presidential quest by an ambitious young Southern governor and his avaricious campaign team. Later John Travolta starred as the silver-haired young presidential candidate in the inevitable movie version. *Vote for Me*, a PBS documentary, showed hard-charging New York media consultant Hank Sheinkopf patiently coaching his candidate, an Alabama Supreme Court judge, on the fine points of camera angles and voice projection. Another film documentary, *The Perfect Candidate*, chronicled the highly charged campaign of conservative lightning rod Oliver North and his consultant Mark Goodin as they battled and lost to the uninspiring, wooden Charles Robb in the 1994 Virginia Senate race.

In the movie *Wag the Dog*, the president's spin doctor (Robert De Niro) and a high-powered Hollywood myth-maker (Dustin Hoffman) conjure up a wartime incident in Albania to cover up the president's sexual indiscretions with a twelve-year-old girl. Michael J. Fox portrayed the energetic, earnest young White House aide, a George Stephanopoulos clone, in the film *An American President* (1995), and later reprised the role in a television series, *Spin City*, with Fox serving as an aide to an unprincipled, vacuous mayor of New York City.

The bookshelf was suddenly filling up with insider accounts by political consultants. Well-traveled, controversial Republican consultant Ed Rollins skewered many of his campaign rivals and former clients in a book entitled *Bare Knuckles and Back Rooms*. On the dust jacket was the middle-aged, balding Rollins, poised with his boxing gloves, ready to take on the rough and tumble of politics. Carville and his Republican-operative wife, Mary Matalin, teamed up on the lecture circuit, hawked credit cards and aspirin in television commercials, and wrote a best-selling memoir, *All's Fair: Love, War, and Running for President*.

Carville, Stephanopoulos, and Paul Begala reappeared during the Lewinsky scandal* and the impeachment hearings. Begala returned as the loyal defender inside the White House bunker, while Carville attacked special prosecutor Kenneth Starr on television talk shows and through an angry book. . . . *And the Horse He Rode in On: The People v. Kenneth Starr*.

---

*The Lewinsky scandal led to President Bill Clinton's 1998-99 impeachment by the House of Representatives and subsequent acquittal in a Senate trial. Clinton was charged with being untruthful, in legal proceedings, about revealing his sexual relationship with Monica Lewinsky, a White House intern.—Eds.

Stephanopoulos, meanwhile, singed by the president's betrayal, distanced himself from the White House and publicly criticized Clinton's behavior in his 1999 book, *All Too Human*. Morris, too, resurfaced on talk shows, wrote political columns, advised Clinton on how to deflect criticism during the Lewinsky scandal, and penned another book, immodestly titled *The New Prince: Machiavelli Updated for the Twenty-first Century*.

Despite the notoriety and self-promotion of Morris, Carville, and others, the celebrity consultant is the exception, not the rule. Most political consultants toil in the background, content to ply their craft in anonymity. Even at the presidential campaign level, consultants generally labor in obscurity. Few Americans had ever heard of Don Sipple or Bill McInturff, consultants in Bob Dole's dysfunctional 1996 presidential race, or Bill Clinton's 1996 consultants Bill Knapp, Doug Schoen, and Marius Penczner. Very few have ever heard of George W. Bush's chief strategist Karl Rove, Al Gore's media consultant Carter Eskew, or John McCain's consultant Mike Murphy.

Political consultants, both controversial and anonymous, have become essential players in the increasingly technological, fast-paced, often brutal world of modern elections. Through it all, they have changed the face of modern American politics.

Political Consultants at Work

In earlier decades, campaigns were financed and run by local or state political parties. They were fueled by local party activists and volunteers, by family, friends, and close political supporters. By the early 1960s presidential campaigns and statewide campaigns for governor and senator began seeking out media and polling firms to help deliver their messages to voters. During the next two decades, there emerged both a new industry, political management, and a new professional, the campaign consultant. By the 1980s every serious presidential candidate, nearly every statewide candidate, and a large number of congressional candidates were using the services of professional political consultants.

The 1990s witnessed yet another transformation. Candidates for office below the statewide level were beginning to seek the advice of professional political consultants. For many candidates, the dividing line was the $50,000 campaign: those who could not raise that kind of money had to rely solely on volunteer services, and those above this threshold usually sought professional assistance. In some local political jurisdictions, record amounts of campaign funds were being raised to pay for campaign services, and races for medium-city mayor, county sheriff, or local judge took on the techniques and tactics once seen only in statewide, professionally managed contests. Professional consulting services, such as phone banks, telemarketing, and direct mail, were supplanting the efforts once provided by volunteers and party loyalists. This multibillion-dollar industry is now directed by professional consultants who make the key decisions, determine strategy, develop campaign communications, and carry out campaign tactics for their clients.

The influence of political consultants goes well beyond getting candidates elected to office. They play an increased role in ballot measures by helping clients determine ballot strategy, framing issues, and even providing the campaign foot soldiers who gather signatures for ballot petitions. Consultants use marketing and mobilization skills to orchestrate pressure on legislators. Political telemarketers link angered constituents directly with the telephones of members of Congress. Overnight, they can guarantee five thousand constituent telephone calls patched directly to a legislator's office. Political consultants are also finding lucrative markets internationally, serving presidential and other candidates throughout the world.

In the commercial world, a business that generates less than $50 million is considered a small enterprise. By that measure, every political consulting firm, except for some of the vendors, is a small business. Most of the estimated three thousand firms that specialize in campaigns and elections have ten or fewer staffers and generate just several hundred thousand dollars in revenue annually. Only a few firms, such as media consultant Squier, Knapp, and Dunn, generate millions of dollars in revenue; most of this money, however, passes through the consultants' hands to pay television advertising costs.

Leading polling firms, such as the Tarrance Group or Public Opinion Strategies, may have forty to eighty employees; most are support staff working the telephones and part of the back office operations. Quite a few firms are cottage enterprises—one- or two-person boutiques, often in speciality markets such as event planning, opposition research, fundraising, or media buying. Many political consulting firms operate out of the basement of the principal's home with no more than telephone lines, computers, fax machines, and online access. For example, even after he became famous as Clinton's principal political adviser, James Carville and his assistants worked out of the "bat cave," a basement studio apartment on Capitol Hill that served as Carville's home and nerve center for his far-flung political operations.

Firms that rely solely on campaign cycles are exposed to the rollercoaster of cash flow: many lean months, with very little money coming in from clients, countered by a few fat months, when the bulk of the revenue

pours in. In addition to the on-off flow of cash, the firms must deal with
the logistical difficulties of juggling many candidates during the crucial
last weeks of the campaign cycle and the enormous time pressures of a
busy campaign season. Some consulting firms have around-the-clock operations during critical weeks of the campaign. These political emergency
rooms are geared to handle any last-minute crisis. During long stretches
when there are few campaign opportunities, professionals and support
staff may have to be let go until the cycle picks up again.

One of the most difficult but necessary tasks is to even out the steep
curves in the election cycle so that money and resources flow more regularly. Consultants have developed several strategies for this: convincing
candidates to hire consultants earlier in the cycle, stretching out the
amount of time they stay with campaigns, and seeking out off-year races,
especially down the electoral ladder, such as mayoral races, general assembly, and other local contests, many of which in past years would not have
sought professional assistance. Consultants are becoming more involved in
the growing business of initiatives, referenda, and issues management.
Many of these campaigns are tied to the same election cycle as candidate
campaigns, but others are tied to local, state, or congressional issue cycles.
Political consulting firms also pursue clients from the corporate and trade
association world and international clients. By spreading out business,
consulting firms are able to stay competitive, smooth out the peaks and
valleys of the election cycle, and keep their heads above water.

In the 1980s firms began to shift away from heavy reliance on candidate campaigns. For example, the late Matt Reese, one of the founders of
the political consulting business, who had worked for more than four
hundred Democratic candidates, changed direction after the 1982 elections to concentrate on corporate and trade association clients. Republican consultant Eddie Mahe shifted his business from 100 percent candidate-based in 1980 to about fifteen percent candidate-based in the early
1990s, picking up corporate and other clients. In the mid-1970s Wally
Clinton's pioneering political telemarketing firm, the Clinton Group,
gained 90 percent of its work from candidates, but has since moved away
from reliance on candidates to issues and corporate work. Many successful
consulting firms have followed this pattern and now have much of their
business coming from noncandidate campaigns.

As corporations have discovered the value of grassroots lobbying and
issues management, consultants who specialize in direct mail and political
telemarketing have shifted focus to legislative and issues work. Corporate
and trade association organizations took special notice of the successful
political consultant-orchestrated grassroots campaign run against President

Clinton's 1993–94 health care proposal. For political consultants, such
work is often far more lucrative, more reliable, and less stress-inducing
than working for candidates in competitive election cycles. Some of the
most successful political consulting firms have less than half of their revenue coming from candidate campaigns. . . .

What Consultants Bring to Campaigns

Candidates, not consultants, win or lose elections. In 1996 voters chose
Bill Clinton, not media consultant Bob Squier; they rejected Bob Dole,
not pollster Bill McInturff. Candidates alone face the voters and ultimately bear the responsibility for the tone and expression of their campaign. Sometimes reputations are diminished and images tarnished by the
campaign itself. For example, George Bush will be remembered for permitting a down-and-dirty campaign that included the infamous "Revolving Door" and Willie Horton* commercials in his 1988 presidential campaign. In that same year, Michael Dukakis will be remembered for his ride
in a military vehicle, hunkered down in an oversized battle helmet, looking goofy. Alphonse D'Amato and Charles Schumer will be remembered
for the abusive, in-your-face campaigns they waged in the 1998 New York
Senate race.

While candidates are ultimately responsible for their campaigns, there
is no way they can compete, let alone win, without professional help. Professional consultants bring direction and discipline to the campaign. Few
enterprises are as unpredictable, vulnerable, and chaotic as a modern campaign. So much can go wrong: the candidate might go "off message," in
which case the campaign loses focus; internal party feuds might threaten
the success of the entire campaign; fund-raising might fall short of expectations, choking the life out of the entire enterprise. All the while, the
opponent's campaign is raising more money, attacking with a sharp, clear
message, redefining the race in its own terms, grabbing media attention,
and efficiently mobilizing its resources. Campaign professionals are needed to bring order out of chaos, maintain message and strategy discipline,
and keep the campaign focused.

The best consultants are able to define the race on their own terms—

*The Willie Horton ad is a famous—or infamous—negative ad from the 1988 Bush-Duka-
kis presidential campaign. An independent PAC created the initial ad that accused Democratic candidate, Gov. Michael Dukakis of Massachusetts, of allowing convicted murderer
William Horton out of prison on a weekend furlough; Horton committed several violent
crimes while on furlough. Because Horton was black and his victims were white, the ad
stirred up racial tensions that lurked not too far beneath the surface of the 1988 Bush-
Dukakis campaign.—EDS.

not the terms set by the opposition, the media, or outside third parties. In the end, the campaign boils down to letting voters know the answers to some very simple questions: who the candidate is, what the issues are, and why this race is important. Following are some examples of defining issues and messages.

From the 1996 Clinton-Gore reelection campaign:

DEFINING ISSUE: Who is better prepared to lead this country into the next century?
MESSAGE: "Building a bridge to the twenty-first century."

From the 1980 Reagan-Bush campaign:

DEFINING ISSUE: The shortcomings of the Carter administration's policies.
MESSAGE: "Are you better off today than you were four years ago?"

Republican consultant Lee Atwater was fond of saying that he knew that the message of his campaign was hitting home when he would go to a local Kmart and ask shoppers what they thought of the contest, and they'd simply parrot the message he had developed.

Professionals also take campaign burdens off the candidate. Campaigns are exhausting, placing extraordinary physical and emotional demands upon the candidate. The campaign staff, and especially the campaign manager, absorb as much of the stress of the campaign as possible. A campaign manager may serve as official campaign optimist, psychologist, and handholder for the candidate or, often, the candidate's spouse. The manager will make the tough personnel and tactical choices when the campaign starts going bad, and be the unofficial heavy (or whipping boy) when needed.

Consultants, particularly those in niche or vendor industries, provide legal, tax, and accounting services for the increasingly complex financial disclosure reporting requirements. They provide expertise in buying television time and placing radio and television commercials. Consulting firms capture and analyze television commercials aired by opponents and other races, and offer both quantitative and qualitative analysis from survey research, focus-group, and dial-group findings. Increasingly campaigns depend on specialists who also can provide a technological edge. Consultants provide online retrieval systems and websites, computer-assisted telephone technology, voter and demographic databases, and geo-mapping and sophisticated targeting techniques so that a campaign can know, block by block and house by house, who is likely to vote and for whom they would cast a ballot. Strategists are able to use predictive technologies, traditional statistical techniques such as regression analysis, and new artificial intelligence technologies such as neural nets and genetic algorithms to target potential voters.

Above all, consultants bring experience from other campaigns. Every campaign has its unique circumstances, events, and dynamics. But campaigns are also great recycling bins. When a consultant has worked for fifteen or twenty-five races, campaigns begin to fall into predictable patterns: messages and themes, issues, and tactics reappear, taking on slight variations—new twists to old challenges. Veteran consultants can save a candidate from making mistakes, spot opportunities quickly, and take advantage of changing circumstances. As veteran consultant Joseph R. Cerrell put it, tongue in cheek, we need consultants—"to have someone handy who has forgotten more about media, mail, fund-raising and strategy than most candidates will ever know."

Growing reliance on professional consultants is costly: the price of admission to elections has risen substantially. The campaign, for many candidates, becomes a perverse full-time game of chasing dollars. Consultants have seen business grow because of the superheated fund-raising activities of the national Democratic and Republican parties, the explosion of soft money, and issues advocacy.

The best consultants aren't afraid of a fight. They know that in many cases an election can be won only if they drop the pretense of reasoned, civilized campaigning and take the gloves off. Campaigns engage in rough tactics because they work. Opposition researchers dig deep into personal lives, seeking out misdeeds and character flaws. Pollsters test-market negative material before focus and electronic dial meter groups. Then the media team cuts slash-and-burn thirty-second clips, using all the tricks of the trade: unflattering black-and-white photos of the opponent, ominous music and sound effects, and distorted features, salted with authentic-sounding textual material, often taken out of context. The direct mail pieces may get even uglier. The goal is to drive up the opponent's negatives, to paint the opponent in such unflattering ways that enough voters have only a negative view of that candidate.

Certainly not all campaigns use negative tactics. Candidates are often very reluctant to engage in mudslinging or demagoguery. Voters are turned off by negative campaigns and feel alienated from the democratic process. But campaign consultants see negative campaigning as a tool, not so much a question of political ethics or morality. If the only way to win is to go negative, then negative it is.

Professional consultants bring many weapons to a campaign. The campaign's theme and message are communicated through television and radio commercials, through direct mail pieces, and increasingly through campaign websites. Those communications are developed and honed through the use of sophisticated research analyses, especially survey research, focus groups, and dial meter sessions. Even more fundamental is the campaign's deadliest weapon, candidate and opposition research. . . .

Professional campaigns and the political consulting industry will flourish in the decades to come. Candidates for public office—both incumbents and challengers—will not hesitate to raise increasingly larger sums of campaign funds to pay for professional consultants and their services. Despite the occasional outburst from elected officials or the public, candidates need, want, and for the most part appreciate the assistance they receive from professional consultants. We may see profound changes in campaign financing, communications, and technology. Through it all, professional consulting will endure, adapt, and prosper. Professionals have become indispensable players in modern campaigns.

63

DAVID MARK

From *Going Dirty*

Don't assume that negative campaigning is new, or that it is worse now than ever, or that only today's YouTube technology encourages it. Negative campaigning has a long history, much of it even before David Mark starts his story in 1964. When you finish reading the excerpt, go to YouTube for a trip down negative advertising's memory lane: look at the 1964 Lyndon Johnson "Daisy Girl" ad against Barry Goldwater; the 1988 "Willie Horton" ad that George H.W. Bush used against Michael Dukakis (a classic negative ad mentioned briefly in the excerpt); and the 2004 Swift Boat Vets' ad against John Kerry. We learn about 527 groups and about the campaign finance reform of 2002 (McCain-Feingold). The 527s are not confined to any one political party's loyalists or to any one ideological position. Democrat, Republican, liberal, conservative: with strong views, lots of money, and a good ad writer, the 527s are on the scene.

FIRST, I WANT TO DISTINGUISH negative campaigning—charges and accusations that, while often distorted, contain at least a kernel of truth—from dirty tricks or cheating. Examples abound of campaign dirty tricks, most famously the tactics of Richard M. Nixon's 1972 Committee to Reelect the President (CREEP), which were exposed in the Watergate proceedings of 1973 to 1974. Perhaps the most notorious dirty trick was a letter planted in a New Hampshire newspaper alleging that a leading Democratic presidential candidate, Senator Edmund Muskie of Maine, had approved a slur that referred to Americans of French-Canadian descent as "Canucks." On a snowy New Hampshire day, standing outside the offices of the newspaper, Muskie gave a rambling denial in which tears seemed to drip from his eyes (some contend they were actually melting snowflakes). His emotional conduct, replayed on television, caused him to drop in the New Hampshire polls shortly before the presidential primary. Senator George McGovern of South Dakota, considered a weaker candidate by Nixon political strategists, eventually won the 1972 Democratic nomination and lost the general election to the Republican president in a landslide. . . .

Yet even beyond dirty tricks, many people still recoil at legitimate negative political ads on television, radio, the Internet, and in other forms.

Negative campaigning has become a catchall phrase that implies there is something inherently wrong with criticizing an opponent. Negative campaigning is one of the most bemoaned aspects of the American political system, particularly by academics and journalists who say it diminishes the level of political discourse and intensifies the divisions among voters.

These complaints emerge each election cycle, partly because political spots are so different in content, style, and form than ads for commercial products. Anyone peddling breakfast cereal needs to be careful about criticizing competitors too overtly or else run the risk of turning off consumers so much that they'll start their day with another form of breakfast food. Rarely do product advertisements include hard-hitting direct comparisons to competitors. (And when they do, the contrasts are usually mild and fleeting.)

The goal of political marketing is entirely different, whether in a Republican versus Democrat match or a tough party primary. Unlike product campaigns, political campaigns do not mind at all turning off some "consumers," the voters. In fact, political operatives often *prefer* to keep voter participation down among those inclined to vote for the opposition. They are perfectly happy to drive down turnout, as long as those who do show up vote for them. And then there's the timing. The stakes of elections are higher than everyday consumer purchases. Consumers do not have to live with the same cereal or beer for the next few years, but they do have to live with the same president, governor, or member of Congress. . . .

For better or worse, aggressive campaign tactics have been a vital part of the American political system from the very start. . . . [The] tenor of modern political campaigns is actually considerably milder than that of old. And, . . . negative campaign tactics have been constantly reinvented, to adapt to the latest technologies and to fit the prevailing mood of the electorate during different eras of American history. . . .

Few candidates have needed to employ negative campaigning less than President Lyndon Baines Johnson in 1964. The assassination of President John F. Kennedy in November 1963 ensured that the Republicans would face an up-hill battle no matter whom they pitted against the Texas Democrat. After all, the new president had ridden a wave of goodwill after the tragic events of Dallas, toward swift passage of much of his predecessor's idling legislative agenda. Most notably, LBJ, the former Senate majority leader, muscled through a recalcitrant Congress the landmark Civil Rights Act of 1964, which guaranteed blacks access to all public facilities and accommodations and banned discrimination because of race, religion, national origin, or sex. The Vietnam War, later to be Johnson's downfall, was escalating. But on Election Day' of 1964, it had yet to become a real liability.

The ambitious Johnson did not just want to win his own term as president; he craved a resounding victory that would establish a new White House power base. Then he could push forward his own legislative agenda, which included creation of Medicare and Medicaid, aid to education, regional redevelopment and urban renewal, and scores of other proposals to establish a "Great Society." . . .

So as he looked toward a victory of historic proportions as president in 1964, Johnson approved his campaign's launch of the first media campaign centered on the rapidly growing medium of television, much of it an assault on the Republican presidential nominee, Senator Barry Goldwater of Arizona. Johnson adviser Bill Moyers said the president "was determined to roll up the biggest damned plurality ever and he felt that anything that could help—and he believed advertising could help—was worth the price."

Goldwater himself became the focus of the election, not foreign policy, taxation, or other issues. According to Johnson's ads, Goldwater would destroy Social Security, end government programs to aid the poor, and potentially launch a nuclear war that could endanger all humanity. While LBJ's victory was never really in doubt, his campaign set the precedent for the television attack ads Americans now take for granted. Many of the spots seem tame and downright quaint compared to the commercials that followed forty years later, but at the time the massive television onslaught of political commercials stunned the Republican opposition.

The 1964 presidential race also offers a vivid illustration of how effectively negative campaigning has worked when it has played into voters' preconceived notions about candidates. The Johnson ads did a masterful job of using Goldwater's words against him, which typecast the Republican. The vaunted "Daisy Girl" ad that suggested Goldwater would start a nuclear war (it never mentioned his name) was consistent with many voters' views of the Republican candidate. "The commercial evoked a deep feeling in many people that Goldwater might actually use nuclear weapons," wrote Tony Schwartz, creator of the famous ad. "This distrust was not in the Daisy spot. It was in the people who viewed the commercial." . . .

A couple of ads by the Johnson campaign aired only one time each. The "Daisy Girl" spot, perhaps the most famous campaign ad of all time, ran during NBC's *Monday Night at the Movies* on September 7; it turned Goldwater's outspokenness on military action and nuclear weapons into a story of nuclear apocalypse (he had once joked about tossing a nuclear weapon into the men's room of the Kremlin.) The 30-second ad showed a little girl in a field picking petals from a daisy. As she counted, the camera moved closer, finally freezing on a close-up of her eye. At the same, time, an announcer started to intone a countdown. Suddenly, the screen erupted in a nuclear mushroom. The voiceover of Lyndon Johnson then admonished: "These are the stakes; to make a world in which all God's children can live, or to go into the darkness. Either we must love each other or we must die." Then words appeared on the screen: "On November 3rd, vote for President Johnson."

The ad served to remind American voters of Goldwater's propensity for warlike statements, even though the spot never mentioned the Republican or made reference to him. More than forty years after the ad ran, its creator, Tony Schwartz, said it was fair game based on Goldwater's record. "He had made two speeches" on the use of nuclear weapons, Schwartz recalled. "It was a very effective commercial." The Goldwater campaign actually filed a complaint with the Fair Campaign Practices Committee to stop the ad, which didn't go through when the Johnson team made it clear the commercial would only be run once. (Even Senator Hubert Humphrey, the Democratic vice-presidential candidate, publicly disapproved of the spot.) Still, for many Republicans, the Daisy Girl ad eviscerated whatever goodwill existed toward LBJ after he assumed office in place of Kennedy, the martyred president. "That's negative campaigning carried to an unbelievable excess," said Bill Brock, who in 1964 was a freshman Republican House member from Tennessee and later won election to the U.S. Senate.

Though the ad ran only once on commercial television, it earned tremendous airtime through repetition and discussion on news shows. In a sense, the ad served as a precursor of the "free media" effect the Swift Boat Vets would have forty years later, when the group's spots, purchased on an initially small budget, attacked the military record of Senator John F. Kerry, the 2004 Democratic presidential nominee. In 1964 most of the Daisy Girl ad's repetitious playing came from three television networks' nightly news shows. Forty years later, the ability to post such controversial ads on the Internet and send them by e-mail had increased their visibility exponentially. . . .

During the heated 2004 campaign season, television viewers in Ohio, Florida, and other presidential battleground states learned that Senator John Kerry had once accused American servicemen in Vietnam of committing war crimes. Viewers were also told, in another commercial, that a former officer in the Alabama Air National Guard and his friends never saw George W. Bush at their unit in 1972, when he was temporarily assigned there.

Such accusations, hurled against Kerry by the Swift Vets and POWs for Truth (originally known as the Swift Boat Veterans for Truth) and toward Bush by Texans for Truth, made liberal use of facts on the public record. But the ads didn't tell the whole truth. In testimony before a Senate committee in 1971, Kerry did not accuse specific people of war crimes; he said he was describing atrocities alleged by other veterans. And Bush pointed to his honorable discharge from the Air National Guard as evidence that he had fulfilled his service.

Such nuances and finer points were lost on many television viewers. That was exactly the point. The ads played on viewers' emotions and aimed to drive true believers to the polls on Election Day. The spots were among a slew of hard-edged television attacks aired during the 2004 presidential election cycle, the first to operate under the rules of the 2002 Bipartisan Campaign Finance Reform Act (BCRA), also known as McCain-Feingold, for its sponsors, Senators John McCain (R-Ariz.) and Russ Feingold (D-Wis.).

Notably, neither Bush nor Kerry sponsored the ads. Instead, they came from independent groups bankrolled by wealthy individuals who wanted to affect the election outcome. Ironically, their donations were the very things BCRA sought to block, or at least reduce. Unlimited fat-cat donations simply shifted from national party organizations—the Republican National Committee and Democratic National Committee—to private groups that aimed not just to support their favored candidate but to tear down the opposition with the bluntest possible words and images as well.

The biggest recipients of the campaign cash were 527 groups,* named for the federal tax code provision that governed their operations. These organizations eagerly threw out charges and criticized the opposition more virulently than the candidates themselves did. Bush's campaign did not criticize Kerry for his decorated service while in Vietnam because that could have easily brought a backlash, considering the president had

*So-called 527 groups first appeared in the 2004 election, in response to changes in campaign finance law. The Bipartisan Campaign Finance Reform Act of 2002 (McCain-Feingold) closed a loophole that had allowed political parties to use wealthy donors' money to create campaign ads and spend for other campaign activities above and beyond what the candidates themselves could raise and spend. In the place of party spending, private 527s appeared. Named for their designation in the tax code, 527s were independent of the campaigns and therefore could spend whatever "soft money" amount they wanted, on whatever they wanted: negative ads were their contribution of choice. Prominent 527s include groups of all political viewpoints, from ultra-liberal to ultra-conservative.—EDS.

stayed stateside during the war. The Swift Vets, Kerry's key critics among the 527 groups, felt no such restraints. "The Bush campaign would never have said the things the Swift Boat Vets said noted Chris LaCivita, the group's chief strategist. "If people want to complain about 527s, thank McCain-Feingold."

The new, complex campaign finance rules—upheld virtually in their entirety by the U.S. Supreme Court'—helped spawn a dramatic increase of negative campaigning over the airwaves, on the Internet, and through direct mail. The 527s ratcheted up the shrillness, nastiness, and outright distortions in political ads, all the while injecting massive sums of money into the political process. According to a postelection study by the non-partisan Campaign Finance Institute, 527 committees raised $405 million in 2004, up dramatically from the $151 million they collected in 2002. GOP Senator Trent Lott of Mississippi—who had voted against BCRA—called contributions to 527s "sewer money" after the election. . . .

The stakes in the 2004 election were huge: Executing the global war on terror in the post–9/11 world; a costly, divisive war in Iraq; and an economy in recovery that still lost hundreds of thousands of jobs. Adding to the intensity was the near even split between registered Republicans and Democrats, lingering bitterness over the disputed 2000 election, and the deep, personal dislike many Democrats had for the president, along with the disdain Republicans held for the Democratic challenger.

So it was no surprise that big money would find a way into the system, especially to opponents of the legislation who predicted just such an outcome. Recent campaign history showed outside organizations would seek to fill in the gaps where candidates were limited in collecting donations. The 527s that proliferated during the 2004 election cycle were only the latest type of independent-expenditure group to be active in national politics. During the 1980 election cycle, the National Conservative Political Action Committee (NCPAC) spent more than $1 million on independent-expenditure ads in an effort to defeat several Democratic U.S. senators. After sending out millions of direct mail pieces and running scores of television commercials knocking the Democratic incumbents, NCPAC succeeded wildly; the Republicans won control of the Senate for the first time in 26 years. NCPAC also ran several independent ads in favor of Republican presidential candidate Ronald Reagan that criticized President Jimmy Carter's handling of the Iranian hostage crisis and other matters. And the most memorable ad of the 1988 presidential election—one that linked Democratic nominee and Massachusetts Governor Michael Dukakis with furloughed criminal Willie Horton—came from an independent group called the National Security Political Action Committee. (The independent ad showed a picture of Horton, who was black, while a spot by the campaign of Vice President George H. W. Bush focused solely on the Massachusetts prison-furlough program and did not feature the criminal's image or name.)

Even two of the Supreme Court justices whose decision upheld the constitutionality of BCRA acknowledged that large amounts of money would still find a way into the political system, which Congress would eventually have to regulate again: "[We are] under no illusion that this will be the last congressional statement on the matter. Money, like water, will always find an outlet. What problems will arise, and how Congress will respond, are concerns for another day," wrote John Paul Stevens and Sandra Day O'Connor. . . .

In tone, the outside groups were much more likely to connect the dots in a conspiratorial fashion and draw the worst possible conclusions about the opposition. "You had both sides feeling essentially the world was going to turn into a black hole if the other side won," said Brooks Jackson, director of FactCheck.org, an authoritative website that monitors the veracity of campaign ads. . . .

Arguably no ads were more memorable—or controversial—than those run by the Swift Vets. The group consisted of Vietnam veterans who patrolled the Mekong Delta in Swift boats similar to those that Kerry piloted. Kerry had tried to inoculate himself on national security issues by making his heroism in Vietnam the centerpiece of his nominating convention and a reason he was fit to be commander in chief. To critics, that strategy opened Kerry up to the torrent of criticism about his military service that followed.

The Swift Vets wanted to destroy Kerry's heroic image and raise questions about his ability to lead the nation during a time of war. Their ads started with an initially small media buy, $500,000, in Wisconsin, Ohio, and West Virginia. But cable shows played the ads repeatedly, and pundits chewed them over on air for weeks. Senator Kerry's critics furiously e-mailed the spots to anyone they could. Even criticisms of the Swift Vets' charges helped increase their exposure. "We wanted to generate controversy," said Chris LaCivita, the Swift Vets' chief strategist. That strategy succeeded wildly. The ads had the effect of confronting Kerry on one of his perceived strong issues, said LaCivita, a combat Marine veteran from the Gulf War, who said he was drawn to the group by their disgust with Kerry for criticizing active-duty troops after he returned from Vietnam.

The commercials were a milestone in the history of negative campaigning in presidential politics. Candidates had long been chastised for avoiding combat service, whether it was Grover Cleveland for hiring a substitute during the Civil War or Bill Clinton for pulling strings to avoid going to Vietnam. But the Swift Vets' ads in 2004 marked the first time a candidate's active-duty military service had been used *against* him during a campaign, rather than in his own favor....

The issues and themes of negative campaigning will vary by decade and era, but the use of those tactics by ambitious politicians is not going away. Nor should it. Voters should be given as many facts about potential officeholders as possible, so they can make up their own minds about what is and is not important and relevant. Positive ads can be more misleading because candidates omit key pieces of information about themselves. What a candidate chooses *not* to discuss is usually as important as what he or she prefers to emphasize. If a candidate has a deep character flaw, voters should know that before casting their votes.

Further, despite claims that negative campaigning turns voters off, it's the most partisan races that often bring more people to the polls. The 2004 presidential campaign, one of the most heated in recent memory, produced a voter turnout of roughly 60 percent, the highest in 36 years. Senator John Kerry's vote total was up 16 percent from Vice President Al Gore's; President George W. Bush's vote total was up 23 percent from what it had been four years before. That fits a historical pattern, as turnout rose during the years following the Civil War, when campaigns were very biting; Republicans were accused of "waving the bloody shirt" and Democrats labeled "disloyal." "Enthusiasm in politics usually contains a large element of hatred," noted political commentator Michael Barone, coauthor of the biannual *The Almanac of American Politics.*

Finally, the way candidates respond to negative campaign tactics can be indicative of how they would perform in office. In a democratic society, public officials must be willing to accept a tremendous amount of criticism about their public actions and personal lives—much of it unfair. If they wilt under attacks or fail to respond to negative charges, it may be a sign they would not perform particularly well in the rough and tumble of elected office. "Part of what people look for is how he answers it. Does he stand up to it? Does he hide from it?" said Carter Wrenn, the veteran North Carolina Republican political consultant and former captain of Senator Jesse Helms's old political machine, the Congressional Club.

Ultimately, much of the responsibility for the tone of American political campaigns rests with voters themselves. In the Internet age, with news sources legion, voters have no excuse for not finding sufficient information to make decisions on whether to support or oppose political candidates. Yes, votes in a legislative body can be twisted to make it seem something they are not. But there's plenty of information available to overcome such distortions, if voters only make minimal efforts to educate themselves.

64

SASHA ISSENBERG

From *The Victory Lab*

As a journalist, Sasha Issenberg knows a lot about political campaigns in the U.S.—the mass media attention, the big-money ad buys, the high profile candidate appearances. He also knows a lot about the less glitzy techniques of a campaign, ones that happen invisibly and quietly behind the scenes. As the pursuit of political office has become more high tech, some of those high tech tactics are being applied in remarkably simple, old-style ways. Issenberg first explains the way that Hal Malchow used direct mail letters to encourage Democratic voters to show up at the polls for a Colorado Senate election. His letter contained an unusual appeal, resulting in a few percentage points of added turnout, just enough for a Democratic victory. Malchow's plan was not a random shot in the dark, reveals Issenberg. Ever since the very narrowly-decided 2000 presidential election, campaign professionals have used "microtargeting" data to get certain voters to turn out on election day. We learn about the mysterious Analyst Institute, a key developer of new techniques to influence voters, as well as other direct mail firms and their microtargeting. Maybe you don't know what the PennySaver is, but microtargeters do.

THE ADS AIRED BY THE TWO CANDIDATES in the 2010 Colorado U.S. Senate race told the story of the ideological war that defined that midterm election. Michael Bennet, a freshman Democrat appointed to replace a man who had become one of Barack Obama's cabinet secretaries, was deeply in hock to a liberal White House. Tea Party Republican challenger Ken Buck was—or so went the punditry and Bennet's attacks—too conservative for the moderate, suburbanizing state.

Meanwhile, one million letters being delivered to Democratic-leaning Coloradoans in the last days of the race made no mention of either candidate, their allegiances, or the issues that separated them. They lacked any allusion to the ideological split riving the nation or reference to the policy consequences of a change in party control of the Senate. The folded pieces of laser-printed white paper were designed to be ugly, with a return address referring to a sender whose name voters were unlikely to recognize. The sender thanked the recipient by first name for having voted in 2008, and then said she looked forward to being able to express such gratitude again after the coming elections. The letter, dispassionate in tone and startlingly personal in content, might have inspired most recipients to dispatch it to a trash can with no strong feeling other than being oddly unsettled by its arrival.

It was not only in Colorado where communications in the last days before the 2010 elections seemed out of whack with such a feral season in American politics. Across the country on the Sunday night before the election, millions of Democrats received an e-mail from Obama's seemingly dormant campaign apparatus, Organizing for America, with a gently worded reminder that they had "made a commitment to vote in this election" and that "the time has come to make good on that commitment. Think about when you'll cast your vote and how you'll get there."

The voters who received either the Colorado letter or the Organizing for America message had likely never encountered anything like them before. At a moment when many candidates, admen, pundits, and organizers thought that the way to get their allies to the polls was to implore them through television ads to consider the election's high stakes and respond in kind, these tactics, designed to go undetected by media coverage, aimed to push buttons that many voters didn't even know they had. The people who had scripted the messages and carefully selected their recipients aimed to exploit eternal human vulnerabilities—such as the desire to fit in or not to be seen as a liar—in order to turn layabouts into voters.

The man who had sent the million letters in white envelopes did the quick math after the Colorado election from his post thousands of miles away. Hal Malchow was a middle-aged Mississippian who had spent his life conniving new ways to win elections, except for a brief detour into securities law that ended when he realized that writing the contracts to guard against complex financial schemes was less fun than trying to hatch them. Now he was playing a different angle, and calculated that the psychological influence he had exerted through his letters would improve turnout among recipients by 2.5 percent. That would mean that his language had created 25,000 new voters, most of them carefully selected to be likely votes for the incumbent. Bennet had lagged Buck for much of the year and had never approached the 50 percent threshold that many experts say is necessary in pre-election polls for an incumbent to expect victory. There was further evidence of a gap in partisan enthusiasms: at the time the polls opened, 74,000 fewer Democrats had returned their early-vote ballots than Republicans. But on election day, something was pushing Bennet even with Buck, and by the time Malchow turned in for the night the two candidates were separated by only hundreds of votes.

The next morning, he awoke to good news from the west. Bennet had pulled ahead of Buck, and was on his way to winning the race by

15,000 votes. His victory would help to keep the Senate in Democratic control. Malchow was having fun.

Colorado was one of the rare sources of cheer for Democrats in an otherwise disastrous set of midterm elections in 2010. Party wise men were eager to mine grand lessons from the Rockies; if only they could figure out what made Colorado resist a national conservative wave, they could use Bennet's strategy as a model for Obama's reelection two years later. "The Bennet thing was pretty instructive," Obama's chief strategist, David Axelrod, told the *National Journal* in a postmortem. "The contrast he drew with Buck was very meaningful."

The people who explain politics for a living—the politicians themselves, their advisers, the media who cover them—love to reach tidy conclusions like this one. Elections are decided by charismatic personalities, strategic maneuvers, the power of rhetoric, the zeitgeist of the political moment. The explainers cloak themselves in loose-fitting theories because they offer a narrative comfort, unlike the more honest acknowledgment that elections hinge on the motivations of millions of individual human beings and their messy, illogical, often unknowable psychologies. In fact, Bennet could have won the Senate seat because of major demographic changes and ideological fault lines around delicate cultural issues, or because of a single letter that exerted a subtle dose of peer pressure on its recipients—or hundreds of other factors big and small that played a part in changing people's minds or getting them to vote.

The political craft thrives on that ambiguity. It allows just about anyone involved to take credit for good results or attribute blame for poor ones, confident of never being proven wrong. After a positive result on election night, everything a winning campaign did looks brilliant. When a campaign loses, consultants usually blame the candidate or the moment—and there rarely seem to be professional consequences for those who had set the strategy or tactics. Longevity, as well as the aura of wisdom that comes from it, is a political operative's most valued trait.

Over a generation, helping Americans choose their leaders has grown into a $6-billion-per-year industry. But the new profession hums along on a mixture of tradition and inertia, unable to learn from its successes or its failures. The tools available to campaign operatives can do little to explain what makes someone vote—and few of the people toiling inside campaign war rooms seem disturbed by this gap in their knowledge. "It's probably the only industry in the world where there's no market research," says Dave Carney, the top strategist on the launch of Texas governor Rick Perry's presidential campaign. "Most things are done with only one check," says Steve Rosenthal, a Democratic consultant who works closely on campaigns with many of the left's top interest groups. "People's guts."

The unheralded arrival of the gently threatening letters in Colorado mailboxes marked the maturation of a tactical revolution against that kind of gut politics. The first stirrings had come a decade earlier, in the wake of the 2000 presidential vote, which shifted on election night from a contest between electoral strategists to a tussle among lawyers. What seemed at the time to be a low-stakes election would have a major effect on the way campaigns were waged. The narrow, almost accidental quality of George W. Bush's victory—decided by 537 votes in Florida, or really just one on the Supreme Court—provoked a reexamination of where votes come from.

Seemingly small boosts of two or three percentage points quickly became indispensable components of a victory formula, and the intellectual hierarchy of thinking about campaigns changed accordingly. Turnout, the unsexy practice of mobilizing known supporters to vote, could no longer be dismissed by campaign leadership as little more than a logistically demanding civics project to be handled by junior staff or volunteers. Campaigns could not obsess only over changing minds through mass media. "Many strategists had been believers that 'big things are all that matter in campaigns'—the big events, the big TV spots, the debates, the convention and the VP pick," says Adrian Gray, who worked in the Bush White House and on both of Bush's campaigns. "After 2000, for the first time a lot of people who shared that sentiment started to believe that there is a lot that can be done on the margins."

The result has been an ongoing, still unsettled battle between the two parties for analytical supremacy, a fight that Bush data analyst Alex Gage likens to an "information arms race." A new era of statistical accountability has been introduced to a trade governed largely by anecdote and lore. Each side has its own sobriquets for the intellectual rebels—Karl Rove boasted of his "propellerheads" and Rick Perry's campaign of its "eggheads," while those on the left were happy to call themselves "geeks." They have made their cases in the PowerPoint palimpsest that inevitably arrives when an industry quickly learns to appreciate its own data. Suddenly, the crucial divide within the consulting class is not between Democrats and Republicans, or the establishment and outsiders, but between these new empiricists and the old guard.

The latter can be found in both parties, and it was a constellation of new-guard academics and political consultants on the left who had mastered the psychological tool used in the Colorado mailer. Six years before, one of them had first had the idea of ominously reminding citizens that whether or not they vote is a matter of public record. In the next few elections, the language and presentation had been refined through serendipitous collaboration unusual in politics, flowing effortlessly between operatives and academic researchers who previously had neither the opportunity nor inclination to work together. Functioning in a growing laboratory culture, they had jerry-rigged a research-and-design function onto an industry that long resisted it. And by the summer of 2010, they had perfected the politics of shame. It was only a matter of time before a desperate campaign, or interest group, would summon the audacity to deploy it,

Two days after the 2010 election, while Colorado election officials were still counting ballots, Hal Malchow sat in his office in Washington, D.C., pleased to see Bennet on his way to victory. A sign hanging on the wall neatly summarized the self-satisfaction Malchow felt at moments like these: *All progress in the world depends on the unreasonable man.* He had spent more than three years obsessing over the technique he had used in his mailers. He had pored over the scholarly research that supported the use of what psychologists called social pressure, and he had finally persuaded the liberal group Women's Voices Women's Vote to overcome its fear of a backlash and send out letters to Colorado households likely to support Bennet but requiring an extra push to get to the polls.

The research had begun five years earlier. In 2005, a Michigan political consultant named Mark Grebner—whose glasses, stringy parted hair, eccentric polymathy, and relentless tinkering earned him comparisons to Ben Franklin—had written to two Yale political science professors who he knew were interested in finding new ways to motivate people to vote. The next year, they collaborated on an experiment in Michigan in which they sent voters a copy of their own public vote histories, along with their neighbors', and a threat to deliver an updated set after the election. It was marvelously effective, increasing turnout among those who received it by 20 percent. But no candidate or group wanted to be associated with a tactic that looked a lot like bullying—and a bit like blackmail.

How to muffle such a potent weapon so that it could be used in the course of regular campaigns became an obsession of the Analyst Institute, a consortium quietly founded in 2006 by liberal groups looking to coordinate their increasingly ambitious research agendas. The Analyst Institute was a hybrid of classic Washington traits: the intellectual ambition of a think tank, the legal privacy of a for-profit consulting firm, and the hush-hush sensibility of a secret society. But its culture derived from the laboratory. The Analyst Institute was founded on a faith in the randomized-control experiment, which had migrated in the middle of the twentieth century from agriculture to medicine as a unique instrument for isolating the effects of individual fertilizers and vaccines. Social scientists later adopted field experiments, transforming research in everything from credit-card marketing to developing-world economics. Around 2000, such experiments found their way into politics, with voters as their unwitting guinea pigs. Over a decade these "prescription drug trials for democracy," in the words of Rock the Vote president Heather Smith, have upended much of what the political world thought it knew about how voters' minds work, and dramatically changed the way that campaigns approach, cajole, and manipulate them.

The Analyst Institute's founding director, a psychologist named Todd Rogers, always liked to remind people that these behavioral science interventions couldn't alter a race's fundamental dynamics. No technique could do that; a good candidate or a bad economy would still set the conditions of an election. But experimental insights could decide close races—by nudging turnout up two points here, six points there—and none has proven as powerful and promising as Grebner's social-pressure breakthrough.

It took three years of trial and error by academics and operatives, including Malchow, until he settled on softer, more friendly language—thanking people for having voted in the past as opposed to threatening them if they didn't in the future—that delivered impressive results in a randomized experiment. During a test conducted during New Jersey's 2009 gubernatorial elections, such a letter had increased turnout among voters who received it by 2.5 percent. Through other tests, Malchow had found that many political messages were most effective when delivered in understated white typed envelopes, as opposed to multicolor glossy mailers, and so he packaged the Colorado social-pressure letters in a way he hoped would resemble an urgent notice from the taxman. "People want information, they don't want advertising," Malchow said. "When they see our fingerprints on this stuff, they believe it less."

The fact that Americans were tiring of political communication was, in many ways, a testament to the success of a profession Malchow had done much to develop. His métier was the direct-mail piece, the postbox-stuffing brochure so often dismissed as junk mail. That form, and Malchow's career, had emerged in the long mid-1980s shadow of television and relegated Malchow to a second-class status in the consulting world's star system. Direct mail is a staple of the category of campaign activity known as "voter contact," distinguished—as compared with media advertising—by its ability to hit a preselected individual with precision. This is the way most voters interact directly with campaigns: the phone calls that interrupt dinner, the knock on the door from a young canvasser, leaflets stuffing the mailbox as election day approaches, personalized text-message blasts. Even as these voter-contact activities often go ignored by the people who write about politics, campaigns continue to spend money on these tactics, and lavishly—as much as a half-billion dollars per presidential campaign season.

Political mail has been perhaps the least glamorous of all the voter-contact tools. At a young age, however, Malchow was drawn to the fact that brochures, unlike broadcast ads or rally coverage on the nightly news, could be unexpectedly personal. Working with mail gave him a distinctive perspective on the electorate—which he saw as an array of individuals rather than a puzzle of blocs and zones—and the ambition to measure the effect of his work on a similar scale. As a result, Malchow had ended up playing a key role in the two most radical innovations in political communication: the use of field experiments to measure cause and effect, and the so-called microtargeting that allows campaigns to confidently address individual voters instead of the broader public.

But even as Malchow found a growing circle of allies in academia and liberal interest groups, partisan campaigns remained skeptical of ideas that would radically disrupt the way they thought about how votes are won. For years, when Malchow couldn't convince campaigns to use the microtargeting techniques he said would help them locate otherwise unidentifiable pockets of persuadable voters, he paid for them himself, at a total loss of around eight hundred thousand dollars. The challenge of innovation came to excite him more than the predictable terms of partisan conflict. In fact, Malchow's giddiness—perceptible as his eyes open wide behind his glasses, and his words break into a gallop—emerged most readily not when he was plotting how to win a specific race for a candidate but when he was figuring out a way to run all campaigns more intelligently. . . .

By 2012, it has become impossible to correctly interpret campaign strategy without understanding the revolution in tactics. Some of the early decisions that shaped how the presidential race would be run were built on technical innovations invisible to the outside world. Texas governor Rick Perry considered withdrawing from select primary-season debates in part because the social scientists he had invited to run large-scale randomized-control experiments in an earlier race concluded that the candidate could have his biggest impact not through media appearances but through localized travel to targeted states. (In retrospect, no social scientist could have calculated how atrocious a debater Perry turned out to be.) Former Massachusetts governor Mitt Romney, who a decade earlier had been the first candidate in the country to use microtargeting formulas, knew he could hold back on committing resources to identify voters in Iowa because he had algorithms that would instantly tell him how every caucus-goer would be likely to vote even before they had made up their minds. And in Chicago, Barack Obama's aides looking to expand the playing field against their Republican opponent thought they might be able to use psychological tricks—which had significantly reduced the cost of registering new voters—to remake the electorate in certain states in a way that could permanently confuse red and blue.

Electoral politics has quietly entered the twenty-first century by undoing its greatest excesses of the late twentieth. Just as architects have atoned for the vainglories of their field's high-modernist period by pummeling its concrete superblocks and putting sleeping porches and Main Street–style shopping strips in their place, some electioneers are starting to conclude that political campaigns lost something when they became warped by broadcast waves. The campaign world's most sophisticated new thinking about who votes and why, informed by an intuitive understanding of the political brain, has naturally turned attention to the individual as the fundamental unit of our politics. The revolutionaries are taking a politics distended by television's long reach and restoring it to a human scale—even delivering, at times, a perfectly disarming touch of intimacy.

Our campaigns have not grown more humanistic because our candidates are more benevolent or their policy concerns more salient. In fact, over the last decade, public confidence in institutions—big business, the church, media, government—has declined dramatically. The political conversation has privileged the nasty and trivial. Yet during that period, election seasons have awakened with a new culture of volunteer activity. This cannot be credited to a politics inspiring people to hand over their time but rather to campaigns, newly alert to the irreplaceable value of a human touch, seeking it out. Finally campaigns are learning to quantify the ineffable—the value of a neighbor's knock, of a stranger's call, the delicate condition of being undecided—and isolate the moment where a behavior can be changed, or a heart won. Campaigns have started treating voters like people again. . . .

The buses running along the number 6 line in Akron's Metro Regional Transit Authority system often begin their inbound morning trips completely empty. The line's eastern terminus sits along the southwestern edge of that Ohio city, on the sidewalk in front of a Goodwill store in a forlorn shopping plaza so perfectly placeless that the pollster Peter Hart has maintained a permanent storefront facing the JCPenney to host focus groups monitoring a microcosm of the changing American mind.

The bus pulls out of the parking lot and turns past the Akron Springfield Assembly of God church, whose vast grass lawn can often find itself studded with alternating signs promising such varied civic activities as a local Oktoberfest and a Red Cross blood drive. The 6 bus ascends past the oaks and maples that canopy the single-family homes of middle-class, largely white Ellet, and down less verdant stretches of East Market Street that mark the southern edge of Middlebury, one of the city's oldest and most racially mixed neighborhoods. Farther on, the route passes the world headquarters of Goodyear, the tire maker that once made Akron an industrial boomtown, where salarymen pace the sidewalk as they savor their rationed minutes in nicotine's company.

Along the way, the bus gathers passengers—hospital orderlies in teal scrubs, elderly shoppers, students with backpacks and collapsing eyelids— as it rumbles toward the modest skyline of Ohio's fifth-largest city. Two-thirds of the way along its forty-minute route to the Akron Transit Center, the 6 begins to descend the gentle slope that pulls Akron's downtown toward the Ohio & Erie Canal, on which it was founded. The bus disgorges its commuters at the major institutions that keep Akron alive—the orderlies report for their shifts at the Akron City Hospital, students stumble out at the University of Akron, office workers scurry toward the municipal building and courthouse—even as the factories that once sustained the "Rubber Capital of the World" have relocated elsewhere.

In the fall of 2008, riders who didn't devote their commutes to their newspaper or mobile phone might have noticed Barack Obama traveling with them each day. The Democratic presidential nominee gazed triumphantly from one of the 11-by-28-inch cardboard advertisements that lined the bus's interior overhead, accompanied by a message rendered in his campaign's familiar sans serif typeface: "Don't Wait. Vote Early. Our Moment Is Now." In smaller type were a Ohio-specific phone number and website that could offer directions on early-voting procedures, which allowed state residents to cast a vote at their leisure as early as five weeks before the November election.

Obama was at that moment perhaps the most dynamic brand in the country—as omnipresent and approachable as Starbucks, as much an embodiment of the American now as Apple—but the company he kept in the interior of Akron's buses was far less inspiring. Most of the interior ads

on Akron's buses are for the Metro system itself, or public service announcements like "Keep Your Baby Sleeping Safe" and "Schizophrenia?
Accepting Research Patients Now." In fact, it is rare these days to find any
consumer advertising in buses anywhere; those for private businesses
speak to a whole different hierarchy of needs, like mental health services
or personal-injury law. And yet Obama was there, and it was far from an
accident.

Weeks earlier, a data analyst at Obama's Chicago headquarters was
reviewing the hundreds of individual-level variables thrown into microtargeting algorithms and realized that one—mass-transit ridership—played
an outsized role in predicting which Wisconsin voters were most likely to
support Obama. The analyst knew the campaign would already try to
mobilize these turnout targets through mail and phone calls, but he
thought his new finding pointed to yet one more medium in which it
should be able to reach them where they spent time—provided it could
be done as efficiently. The analyst alerted one of the campaign's media
planners, who called each of the public transit agencies in Wisconsin to
see which of them allowed advertisers to target particular routes, stops, or
depots instead of covering the whole system at once. Milwaukee did, and
so the media planner called over someone from the campaign's graphics
department, and together they made a map showing Milwaukee precincts
where individuals with high support scores were clustered, and a series of
transparencies for each of the city's bus routes. They laid the transparencies
atop the support map until they found lines that intersected their target
precincts, and sent an order to GMMB, the campaign's lead advertising
agency.

Danny Jester, a GMMB vice president and media director responsible
for the Obama account, had never processed a request quite like this.
Jester placed many of Obama's ads, as his agency had for John Kerry's
campaign four years earlier. For a presidential campaign, this typically
meant broadcast or cable television, or sometimes radio. Maybe a candidate for city council or county commission would buy bus ads, because
they were easier to produce than television spots and intuitively made
sense when thinking about geographically constrained electorates, but no
one at this level ever proposed putting outdoor advertising on the schedule. Among those who placed political ads, progress had been treated as
effectively synonymous with the introduction of new delivery devices.
The half-century-long history of refinements in media targeting were a
story of technological innovation: moving from buying national ads to
local ones in key markets, and then shifting from broadcast waves to cable

television, where narrow audiences could be more easily pinpointed. Internet advertising, with its ability to track users' movements through cookies and interests through search engines, was the latest breakthrough. Obama aggressively bought ads in all of those media, including $16 million in online advertising, among it deep reaches into mobile devices. With no hoopla, however, the campaign also bought bus ads. Milwaukee didn't have the inventory available on the routes Jester requested, but other cities did, and Jester started writing checks. Soon Obama's ads were rolling through select buses in ten cities nationwide, including Philadelphia, Miami, Denver, Flint, and Akron. The most technologically advanced campaign in history had so thoroughly mastered the politics of individual data and testing that it found new value in electioneering tactics many had abandoned as hopelessly last-century. "There's all this shit we used to say no to in campaigns—bus benches, mass-transit advertising, *PennySavers*, what's that sock they stick the newspaper in?—because we used to do it before TV got dominant," says Larry Grisolano, who coordinated all of the campaign's public-opinion research and media buys. "Now if I know that there are twenty-seven people I want to reach and they all cluster around this bus bench, I'll buy that bus bench. And if I know these twenty-seven people read the *PennySaver*, I'll buy an ad in the *Penny-Saver*." . . .

   Malchow had spent a quarter century living off the mail, but not until his revelatory steakhouse dinner with [social scientist and Yale academician Alan] Gerber did he give much thought to envelopes. After he had overcome his initial awe at the power of the social-pressure tool used in Michigan, Malchow looked closely at the mailers themselves. They were simple copy paper, laser-printed and crudely folded, the result of Grebner scrambling to produce them cheaply in his own office rather than hiring a professional copy shop for the job. They looked appropriately amateurish, unlike anything Malchow had put out in his years of sending political mail to raise money, persuade voters, or turn them out. By the traditional standards articulated by direct-mail vendors, valuing high-impact visuals that "cut through the clutter" of the mailbox, Grebner's bland letters should have been a dud. But, of course, they hadn't been, and now Malchow began to wonder whether their success owed something not only to psychological tricks but to their humble packaging as well.

   One of Grebner's letters didn't even try to exercise social pressure, instructing a voter merely, "Remember your rights and responsibilities as a citizen. Remember to vote." Such generic "civic duty" messages rarely made any impact on turnout, starting with the first Gerber-Green experiment in New Haven. In fact, the only reason they had included it in the Michigan test was as a baseline against which they could measure the various social-pressure effects. Yet in Grebner's hands the civic-duty message increased turnout by nearly two points over the control group, and the only reason Malchow could find to explain it was the primitive format. He thought about the other pieces of paper that shared those aesthetics: a jury-duty summons, a letter from the taxman, the homeowner's association announcing a policy change. What if, Malchow wondered, an unstylized simplicity had become a signal at the mailbox that something was to be taken seriously?

So he started testing. He ran experiments pitting letters against glossy brochures, black-and-white against full color, slick against clunky. The evidence piled up, all pointing in the same direction: toward plain, official-looking communications. Others at the Analyst Institute reported experimental findings that seemed to confirm the virtues of simplicity. A group called Our Oregon, which runs state ballot initiative campaigns for progressive causes, found that it could increase its vote tally in select precincts by five points by replacing its glossy mail with a bland, text-heavy voter guide devoid of endorsements from politicians but instead featuring the validating logos of groups like the PTA and the League of Women Voters. Rock the Vote found that e-mail and text messages arriving from unexciting senders like "Election Center" often do better than those with livelier "from" lines, like the names of celebrities. "If you believe this, it says we're doing everything wrong," says Malchow. "There's a principle underneath this. When people see the fingerprint of Madison Avenue, it becomes advertising—and advertising is not important to them."

65

KENNETH VOGEL

From *Big Money*

In this piece Kenneth Vogel takes us along as he crashes a fancy convocation of conservatives in the California desert. They're planning ways to raise large—very large—amounts of money for political campaigns. Not only are the Koch brothers doing this, but also, powerful liberal fund-raisers are doing the same thing. Central to Vogel's discussion is how the Supreme Court's decision in Citizens United v. Federal Election Commission *opened the floodgates for big—very big—money in politics. Super PACs and mega-donors dominate the scene. Vogel shows us how political operatives encourage donors to contribute large sums. What is the reward for such generous donations? Photos, breakfasts, briefings, sit-downs, dessert receptions, and more await those who write the big checks. As unsavory as an over-$1 billion-presidential campaign might be, the stakes are too great for any presidential hopeful to ignore.*

IT WAS 105 DEGREES ON A LATE APRIL AFTERNOON in the California desert town of Indian Wells. A blazing sun was beating down on the manicured grounds of the Renaissance Esmeralda Resort. A contingent of several dozen guests trickled into the hotel from the broiling outdoors wearing slacks and long sleeves, the women in silk blouses, the men sweating under sport coats. They were older and almost entirely white, and they had that well-kempt look that only privilege can bring. It was clear they were all together, both because they wore small black tags engraved only with their names and because they stuck out conspicuously from another set of guests who were about a third their age and were toned, tanned, tattooed, and quite fond of the poolside bar.

The boozier crowd was in town for the spring 2013 Stagecoach country music festival. The more groomed group had been invited by the billionaire industrialists Charles and David Koch to attend the latest in a running series of secretive political gatherings of the big-money conservative elite. Since 2003, twice a year the Koch brothers have brought together some of the top Republican politicians in the country, leading political operatives, and a hundred or more of the party's most generous donors for closed-door "seminars" on how, as an invitation to Indian Wells put it, "to advance a plan to defend our free-enterprise system." I had decided to travel to the California desert to try to get as close as I could to some of the most important—but least known—donors and operatives in politics. My aim was to get a sense of whether the Kochs and their donors were discouraged by the 2012 election six months earlier. After all, their political network had spent an estimated $400 million—an astounding and historic sum—in the run-up to Election Day, mostly beating up on President Barack Obama and his Democratic allies in Congress. Yet Obama had won handily and the Democrats gained seats in Congress.

But the election seemed not to be weighing on the Koch guests congregating in the hotel's eight-story atrium lobby before the seminar's opening dinner. One after another they made their way down a grand, curved double staircase built of tropical African hardwood, as if arriving for their coronation into politics' most elite ranks. A few hours later, with the Stagecoach posse mostly off-site, the Koch invitees had the run of the place. Some rimmed the lobby bar, while others gathered in a private lounge. Hotel and Koch security roamed the lobby anxiously and stood sentry by the double glass doors to the lounge, talking through earpieces and watching over their prized guests. State troopers buzzed about—a sure sign that governors were present. I tried my best to blend in, pulling up a seat at the bar next to a middle-aged fellow with the creased tan skin and shaggy blond hair of an aging beach bum. He was not, in my best estimation, a likely Koch seminar participant. Turns out he was a marketing executive for Toyota, the main sponsor of Stagecoach, and he wasn't particularly talkative. We watched the end of an NBA playoff game between the Oklahoma City Thunder and Houston Rockets, and I tried to make small talk during breaks in the action while keeping my eyes peeled for any circling big-name Republicans. I feigned disinterest in a conversation that Sen. Ron Johnson of Wisconsin was having with a group of donors as they walked by. Ken Ellegard, an Arizona car dealer and Republican donor, sidled up to the bar next to the Toyota marketing guy and me and ordered a vodka soda with a splash of cranberry. The conservative pundit Erick Erickson pulled up a seat at the far end of the bar and ordered food. Behind us, South Carolina governor Nikki Haley joined a small group at a high-top table near the bar. Nursing a glass of red wine, she held court for an hour about politics and stock car racing.

"That's the governor of South Carolina," I informed the Toyota guy in hushed tones, perhaps out of a subconscious desire to enlist an ally in my reconnaissance. I told him he was surrounded by masters of the universe, whose wealth the Koch brothers hoped to tap to reshape American politics, and that I was a reporter hoping to learn about their exclusive world. "The only Koch I know is Coca-Cola," the Toyota guy said, shaking his head and chuckling (the brothers' last name is pronounced "Coke.") Turning back to his cabernet, he conceded it was a relief to find out why everyone else was so much better dressed than he.

Not all the Koch summit attendees had followed the business casual dress code for daytime sessions. Billionaire tech entrepreneur Rob Ryan ambled through the Renaissance lobby in a rumpled white polo shirt, wrinkled khakis, and scuffed white sneakers. Rick Sharp, the former chairman of Crocs, Inc. and a regular at Koch seminars, regularly sported the ultra-casual, ultra-comfortable, and ultra-dorky foam clogs manufactured by the company at seminars. The point of the dress code is to suggest the aesthetic of an investors' conference. And that's pretty much what the Koch seminars are—political investors' conferences. Prospective donors sit through jargon-laden presentations and get up close with politicians and operatives in whom they might invest money. The summits are designed to help donors "effectively achieve what we believe to be your policy, political and philanthropic goals," as an email sent to attendees two months prior by senior Koch aide Kevin Gentry put it. Gentry promised an exclusive opportunity to engage with "several hundred of America's top business owners and CEOs" to discuss "short-term policy threats in 2013 while building toward free-market gains in 2014 and beyond."

The seminars are a brilliant way to raise political cash. For politicians and operatives, invitations are coveted. You got the closest thing to an endorsement from Koch World, plus a chance to go fishing in a stocked pond full of some the biggest donors in the land. It is the Kochs' ability to pool donations from wealthy attendees—rather than just Charles's and David's personal fortunes (estimated at $36 billion each in 2013)—that has put them among the leading forces in the increasingly competitive world of big-money politics. The more cash the Koch political network could raise in Indian Wells, the more influence it would have in setting the course for the then-rudderless Republican Party. Among the attendees at Indian Wells were Sens. Ted Cruz of Texas and Rand Paul of Kentucky and Govs. Bobby Jindal of Louisiana and John Kasich of Ohio, all prospective contenders for the party's 2016 presidential nomination.

Just like an investor conference, the Indian Wells gathering included presentations from experts on a range of subjects: How to use elaborate databases to mobilize voters. How to craft messages that appeal to young, female, and Hispanic voters (though in Indian Wells those demographics appeared to be represented primarily by the hotel staff). How to recruit and train candidates who adhere to the Kochs' small-government, anti-regulation philosophy.

Before the Kochs could shape the future of American politics, though, they needed to convince donors that they had learned from the bust that was 2012. That was perhaps the major task at Indian Wells. And it was the one facing all the well-funded operations on the right, from the Republican National Committee (RNC) to the groups powering the anti-establishment tea party to Koch World's most direct rival for big-money supremacy—the American Crossroads operation, steered by veteran GOP operative Karl Rove.

The Democrats had their own issues. They had nowhere near the big-money network that the conservative side did. Rich liberals like George Soros and Peter Lewis had spent more than $200 million a decade earlier trying to elect John Kerry president, and after that failure, many remained leery about tossing their millions into electoral politics. Democrats were trying to rally the major donors they did have into a cohesive group that could keep the party united post-Obama, or at least avoid the toxic factionalism being fueled by deep-pocketed conservative groups. It wasn't going to be easy. Lone-wolf liberal billionaires such as Michael Bloomberg and Tom Steyer were signaling a willingness to challenge the Democratic Party and its candidates on tricky issues like gun control and energy production. Some of the left's most influential leaders were trying to head off deeper divisions by uniting the deepest Democratic pockets behind Hillary Clinton, but several major donors were bristling at the idea that Hillary represented the future of the party. They were signaling willingness to invest serious cash to boost a more progressive alternative to carry the party's banner in 2016—and were actively looking for such a candidate.

The big-money jockeying on both sides would go a long way toward determining the shape of American politics for years to come. It was a striking departure from recent political history. A few dozen rich donors were now helping set the course of the two major political parties, challenging the power of elected and appointed party leaders who for decades had ruled politics with an iron grip. It used to be that if the party thought a particular politician would be a good soldier for them in Washington, they could use their recruiting, fund-raising, and networking infrastructure to propel that person to victory, if not in every case, then in many. Now, all it took to throw that into disarray was one affluent activist with a favorite candidate different from the party's. Things could really get messy if multiple wealthy partisans had different ideas about the best candidate. . . .

Indian Wells was a snapshot of an extraordinary shift: the reordering of the political system by an elite fraternity of the superrich and a small brain trust of consultants who cater to them. Starting in 2010, a few dozen of the wealthiest donors turned on a gusher of mega-checks that have made them more important than the thousands of grassroots activists, small individual donors, and even party leaders put together. Together, these donors have injected into campaigns sums that were once unimaginable, even as recently as the 2008 presidential election. During that election cycle, so-called outside spending of the sort that can be funded by massive checks totaled $338 million. In 2012, it was $1 billion, and that didn't include hundreds of millions in additional spending by more secretive groups like those in the Koch network that don't have to disclose as much information to the Federal Election Commission (FEC).

Intentionally or not, this new system has eroded the power of the official parties that have rigidly controlled modern politics for decades by doling out or withholding pork-barrel spending earmarks and campaign cash. Suddenly, party leaders have none of the former to offer (the result of symbolic belt-tightening reforms), and far less of the latter than big donors operating outside the party system. The result is the privatization of a system that we'd always thought of as public—a hijacking of American politics by the ultra-rich.

The foundation of this new system was laid ten years before the 2012 election, ironically by those working to *diminish* the role of big money in politics. These legislators and activists had pushed through a 2002 bill limiting mega-checks—parties could no longer accept them, and political committees could no longer spend them on certain campaign ads. That sparked a brief period in which bold donors and operatives steered money further outside the system, into groups that spent on ads and political organizing (some of which drew legal scrutiny). Then in 2010, a pair of federal court decisions came down that freed the ultra-rich to legally spend with even more impunity, and secrecy, than they'd had even before 2002. The catch was, they couldn't give the unlimited money directly to candidates or political parties. It had to go to independent groups that aren't allowed to coordinate their efforts with politicians or parties. The most impactful of the decisions was the Supreme Court's now-famous January 2010 ruling in a case called *Citizens United vs. Federal Election Commission* that struck down restrictions on corporate- and union-funded political ads. The restrictions, which had been reinforced by the 2002 law, had limited how explicit ads could be in supporting or attacking candidates. But a 5–4 majority of justices ruled the restrictions to be an unconstitutional infringement on free speech, and without such limitations, corporations and labor unions could spend as much as they wanted on aggressive campaign advertising. Two months later, the D.C. Circuit Court of Appeals issued a decision that was lower-profile but profound in impact. It allowed individuals (as well as unions and corporations) to give as much as they wanted to a new breed of independent political committee that came to be known as a super PAC, which could spend unlimited sums boosting or attacking candidates—again, as long as those new groups remained separate from the candidates' campaigns and parties.

The result? In 2012, the amount parties and candidates could accept was downright insignificant compared to what the super PACs and other big-money groups were allowed to take. The most an individual or group could donate was $5,000 to candidates and $30,800 to the national party committees. That may not sound paltry, but it was nothing compared with the unlimited checks pouring into the super PACs and other outside groups empowered by the court decisions. *Citizens United* did more than change the rules. It changed the mind-set of big donors and big-money operatives. Perhaps more importantly, it introduced the idea that a single ultra-donor, or a well-connected consultant with the ears of a handful of mega-donors, could fundamentally shift a campaign for the US presidency, not to mention a handful of Senate or governors' races or dozens of House races.

It's not just the politicians who've benefited from the mega-donors. The gusher of checks has sparked a gold rush among Washington's private political class. All manner of consultants jockey to tap this new vein of big money coursing into the system, knowing that all it takes to succeed is the ear of a single donor. Those who rise to the top gain wealth and power, pretty much irrespective of how their candidates fare. This secretive and hypercompetitive world, largely unregulated, has attracted a mix of accomplished political operators and young innovators offering new services, along with a fair number of scammers. The common thread is this: almost everyone now recognizes that the action—and the money—is outside the party system. . . .

Beyond the tone, it was telling that big-money Democratic outside groups like the governors association and Priorities USA—rather than the party committees or the Obama campaign—were behind some of the most exclusive, hottest, and most closely guarded soirees in Charlotte [site of the 2012 Democratic national convention]. The super PACs that had organized the Roosters fund-raiser held what was billed as an "intimate" brunch at the suburban Charlotte home of billionaire hedge fund manager Jim Simons, who ended up donating $9.5 million to the three PACs, making him one of the party's biggest super PAC whales. Making the schlep to Simons's place were Jim Messina, congressional leaders Harry Reid, Nancy Pelosi, Dick Durbin, Chuck Schumer, Steny Hoyer, and Steve Israel, and Chicago mayor Rahm Emanuel. During the convention,

Emanuel, revered by donors for his bare-knuckle persona, officially left his
honorary post as cochair of the Obama campaign to lead a fund-raising
push for Priorities USA in the run-up to the general election. On the final night of the convention, the group and its congressional partners also
threw a gala emceed by the actress Jessica Alba, with performances by the
New York pop band Scissor Sisters and the Miami rapper Pitbull. According to a sponsorship brochure, donors who gave a combined $100,000 to
the three super PACs got six tickets to the brunch at Simons's home,
twenty tickets to the [trendy restaurant] Roosters event featuring [leading
Democratic consultant and Priorities USA advisor, Paul] Begala, and fifty
tickets to the party. The convention fund-raising extravaganza, cheesily
coined "Super-O-Rama" in the sponsorship brochure, made some Democrats I talked to nervous. A showy super PAC presence created tricky
optics for Obama and congressional Democrats, many of whom had long
track records of opposing big money. Also, the notoriously control-
obsessed Obama campaign, even after embracing super PACs, was still
leery of having outside groups, no matter how closely aligned, assuming
such a presence at its convention.

In Charlotte, Obama's campaign finally rolled out a comprehensive
donor fulfillment program that would have made Romney's team proud.
The biggest donors got to choose from a veritable buffet of perks of the
sort Obama's top aides privately sneered at, with the most generous getting the best stuff. It was all laid out in a glossy pocket-sized booklet, the
"Obama Victory Fund Finance Guests Passport to the 2012 Democratic
National Convention," which was emblazoned with a holographic stamp
of the Obama campaign's rising sun logo on the cover. The booklet was
distributed to designated guests as part of welcome packets containing
"SEIU for Obama" thundersticks and various other trinkets as they
checked in at a handful of fine downtown Charlotte hotels that had been
reserved for donors—the "OVF Finance hotel block," according to the
passport. The passport began with an introduction signed by the campaign's national finance chairman, Matthew Barzun, who had been
Obama's ambassador to Sweden from 2009 until 2011, and the DNC's
national finance chair, Jane Stetson. It promised that "OVF Finance Guests
will be treated to a week of exciting and informative events."

Donors got the chance to pose for professional photos behind the
podium at the Time Warner Arena, where Obama would later accept his
party's nomination for reelection, followed by a dessert reception in the
arena's self-described "fine dining" restaurant. That podium sneak peak
was available to donors who qualified for the OBX Package (a designation given to those who pledged to raise $1 million or more by Election

Day) or the Kitty Hawk Package (between $500,000 and $1 million). Even lower-tier bundlers and donors were entitled to attend "an exclusive campaign briefing" on Tuesday morning with [President Obama's campaign manager, Jim] Messina, as well as a Wednesday "toast to the South with President Bill Clinton" and a Thursday rally with Vice President Joe Biden at the NASCAR Hall of Fame. A morning National Finance Committee breakfast meeting with Michelle Obama was open to members of the committee and "Presidential Partners"—those who gave the maximum $75,800 donation to the Obama Victory Fund.

Making sure donors felt like players at the convention—or, more important, did not feel overshadowed by other players—was a major preoccupation for politicians, super PACs, and other groups. Handled right, the donors would only be nominally aware of the transactional cottage industry that existed to keep them giving, consuming hundreds of staffers and volunteers full-time. Democracy Alliance staffers had been dispatched to the convention to serve as concierges for the group's donors, getting them tickets to parties and access to exclusive briefings. The Obama campaign, the Victory Fund, and the convention host committee each stationed a team of staff and volunteers in conference rooms at the donors' hotels to handle all manner of needs and complaints, and senior "fixers" wandered the lobbies, asking donors if they had had a good time at whatever shindig they had attended the preceding evening, and dispensing coveted party tickets or VIP party suite passes to the next night's fun to top donors or to panicked lieutenants who couldn't placate irate donors on their own.

"My advice to donors: throw a fit," one such fixer was overheard confiding in the lobby of the Westin on the first morning of the convention. "You'll get whatever you want."

Complaints from donors unhappy with their level of access were common and, depending on the importance of the donor, were sometimes leveraged to get them to cough up more cash. Donors could "write a check to get a higher package," according to a handbook distributed to Obama campaign staffers and volunteers. "Have the donor call the [Obama Victory Fund] hotline," the handbook instructed, listing an organizational chart with phone numbers for the donor fulfillment staff at each hotel. Volunteers could expect to "interact with industry moguls, diplomats, and ambassadors," advised the handbook. "Keep the relationship formal. Use titles or last names. When addressing dignitaries use titles (i.e. Madame Secretary, Mr. Ambassador, Doctor, Professor)." And no matter what happened, donor handlers were to "keep a positive attitude, especially when met with a negative attitude. DO NOT take someone's frustration personally. Try to keep the conversation focused on accomplishing the task at hand. Whenever possible, please present guests with an alternative," according to the handout. "ALL Finance guests are VIPs," it instructed.

Democrats, it seemed, had come to the conclusion that Jim Messina was right. There comes a time when populist rhetoric needs to take a backseat to big-money reality, and that time is two months before Election Day. . . .

Things can change fast in big-money politics—faster than through the party system, with its rigid and slow-to-adapt hierarchies. Another emerging trend that seemed to bode well for Republicans was the fissures developing among Democrats. Some of these appeared to have the potential to turn into major chasms given the right combination of primary challenges and big money. There was the Michael Bloomberg super PAC crusade targeting anti-gun-control Democrats and the Tom Steyer pledge to spend heavily to defeat candidates he deemed insufficiently supportive of environmental measures. But there was a bigger threat to Democratic unity starting to make itself apparent, one that threatened to pit its leading figures against each other. It was a divide between the party's populist wing and its centrist, business-friendly wing. In some ways the rift mirrored the one splitting the right, except instead of the tea party's populist demand for less government and taxes, populist Democrats saw more of both as the solution. Democratic elites worried such a movement could pull the party to the left in a way that would jeopardize its chances of cobbling together a winning electoral coalition—if not in 2014, then certainly in 2016. Their concerns coincided with the quiet swelling of a Democratic big-money tidal force that was very much the antithesis of the populist trend. It was a force that was both new, in that it would capitalize on the *Citizens United* era in a way that Obama never did, and also quite familiar and comforting to many of the rich Democrats who had yearned for Obama to do more in the big-money arena. It was the return of the Clinton cash machine.

The huge network of mega-donors fostered by Bill and Hillary Clinton, first in the White House and then during her Senate and presidential campaigns, had largely gone untended after Obama dispatched her in the long and brutal 2008 presidential primary. Many turned away from big giving dispirited, wondering if they'd seen the last of the political dynasty that, more than perhaps any other operation in American politics, knew how to inspire the wealthiest of supporters. While some eventually threw in with Obama, especially after he tapped Hillary to be his secretary of state, it just wasn't the same. There were none of the late-night bull sessions after fund-raisers that there had been with the Clintons, no White

House sleepovers. There was no spark. But once Hillary stepped down from a mostly well-received tenure helming the State Department, the magic started to come back. Her richest supporters—many of whom the family counted among their close friends—were whispering in her ear, telling her that the White House would be hers to lose in 2016. She said nothing to discourage them, and that was signal enough for many of the donors and operatives to begin building a big-money network that they hoped would put even Bill's vaunted soft-money machine to shame. The gang was getting back together. And there was no gang in politics that seemed as uniquely prepared to cash in on the new *Citizens United* era as the Clintons—not even Mitt Romney's family and friends. If Mitt was the big-money prototype candidate, Hillary seemed more like the finished product.

In some ways, the Clintons' network never totally went away. It was just idling during Obama's first term, with some of its energy shifted toward a less electoral footing. But during Obama's reelection campaign there were signs it was coming back to life. While some Clinton skeptics saw Bill's aggressive work rallying his old big donors for Obama as a self-interested attempt to prime the pump for his wife in 2016, few questioned its impact. When Bill started raising for Obama's campaign or the supportive Priorities USA, the big checks really started flowing.

66

RASMUS KLEIS NIELSEN

From *Ground Wars*

High school and college students may be able to identify with Rasmus Kleis Nielsen's research approach for his book about "ground wars," to him, the person-to-person techniques of campaigning. He knocked on doors and made phone calls for several 2008 congressional candidates. Maybe you've done what the excerpt's volunteers have done, or maybe you plan to take part in this unglamorous, behind-the-scenes part of a future campaign. Regardless, don't be discouraged. Sometimes people on your list are home and even willing to listen. Occasionally, a phone is answered with positive results. Nielsen notes that face-to-face (or voice-to-voicemail) contact can have a significant impact on undecided voters. It can encourage loyal partisans to turn out to vote. And in two years or four years, the information gleaned from all those personal contacts may help at the next election. Still, the lists are long, the days tiring, and the expletives aplenty. Welcome to politics at the very deepest of grassroots.

Episode 1.1

Charlene is in her late thirties, African American, and looking for a job. Her home is in Bridgeport, Connecticut, a decaying, de-industrialized city with an unemployment rate over 10 percent and about 20 percent of the population living below the poverty line. Right now she is making ten dollars an hour canvassing for the Connecticut Democrats' coordinated campaign—and gets a gas card every week too. "It helps pay the bills," she says. She finished her Microsoft Office User Specialist class at Workforce, Inc., this afternoon, and since then we have been out walking door-to-door, talking to voters.

Charlene knocks on the door, holding her clipboard with the Jim Himes for Congress flyers and a map of the area in one hand and a PalmPilot with our script, walk sheet, and talking points in her other hand. I stand a couple of yards behind her, clutching my own clipboard and PDA (personal digital assistant), watching the house for any signs of life. We are about to leave when an elderly white woman opens the door. We know from our list that she is probably Anna Rizzo, a seventy-seven-year-old registered Democrat who lives here. She is our target because she is an infrequent voter. Ms. Rizzo leaves the door chain on, and asks, "What do you want?" Charlene says, "We're here to tell you about Jim Himes, the Democratic congregational candidate." I flinch as she says "congregational." She has done it before, just as she again ignored the script we have been instructed to use. Ms. Rizzo closes the door without a word. We write her down as "Not

Home." She will be contacted again soon because she has been identified as a part of one of the target universes—sometimes called "lazy Democrats"—and because the campaign has her phone number and address.

"This is a bad list," Charlene says to me as we walk toward our next target, a couple of houses down the street. "I can't believe they've sent us out here. What a waste of time. Well, well—that's their problem."

Episode 1.2

It is late afternoon in Fanwood, New Jersey, Linda Stender's hometown, a town she has served as mayor and state assemblywoman for years and now hopes to represent in Congress. Her campaign office is in a worn-down demolition-slated building just across from the train station. Today we are four people working the phones, calling voters to tell them about Stender and ask them a few questions about where they stand on the upcoming election. Everyone on the phones is a volunteer. All are well over sixty (except me). We sit in a room separate from where the staff works.

Paula gets what she calls "a live one," her first since she arrived twenty minutes ago. So far she has just been leaving messages. She reads the first lines of her script to the voter, asking who he plans to vote for in the fall. It turns out he is leaning toward Stender's opponent, state senator Leonard Lance. Paula immediately gets into an argument with him. "I can't believe you want to vote for a Republican after what Bush has done to our country! Dragged us into a criminal war for oil, undermined the Constitution, handed over billions in tax cuts to the wealthiest!" They talk for a few minutes. From what we can hear, it is a spirited discussion.

After she puts down the phone, Paula says to the rest of us, "I can't believe there are people out there who aren't Democrats." We all chuckle. Clearly, Stender's campaign staffers and her outside consultants have an inkling that there are some voters in the district who aren't Democrats. Stender ran as a progressive in 2006 and lost narrowly to the incumbent Republican, Mike Ferguson. This cycle she is running as a moderate for what is now an open seat, without using her party affiliation or the name of the Democratic presidential nominee in her literature and advertisements. But many of the volunteers still see her—and present her to voters—as the woman they support, "the old Linda."

Episode 1.3

Election Day is only a week away, and the field organizers are struggling to whip the GOTV (Get Out the Vote) program into shape. People are on the phones constantly, calling paid part-time canvassers and potential volunteers, trying to get them to confirm their availability over the weekend. There are thousands of shifts to be filled, walk packets to be assembled, call sheets to be printed. This is a major logistical operation, with many moving parts, pursued under intense time pressure.

One of the field organizers complains that his volunteers are "flaky" and won't commit. The field director is stressed out: "We need more bodies!" He makes a call and then shouts to one of his deputies—who is technically employed by the state party and not the candidate—"We've got twenty more labor guys coming in. I need you to cut more turf. I'll send you the lists." Jack, the volunteer coordinator, is calmer, almost serene. He leans back and comments on the commotion around us: "We'll have to close some locations; it'll never work with all those phone banks. Multiple locations: great in theory, bad in practice. But they won't listen. We don't have time for this."

AROUND 100 MILLION AMERICANS were contacted at the door or over the phone by various political organizations during the 2008 elections. Millions of volunteers and tens of thousands of paid part-time workers did the contacting. Thousands of full-time staffers organized their efforts. At the surface it looked like nothing new under the sun. Even if the number of contacts made varies over time (and it has increased dramatically from 2000 onward), canvassing voters, by foot or by phone, is a staple of American politics. In some ways the conversations among people in 2008 probably were not all that different from those of 1988 or 1968: "Who do you plan to vote for?" "Here is why you should support my guy." "Now, remember to go and vote." That is the basic blueprint as campaigns try to identify where people stand, sway the undecided, and bring out their supporters. Volunteers who cut their teeth on Michael Dukakis's or even Hubert Humphrey's campaign for the presidency can still use their experience at the door many years later when confronted with an uninterested, unfriendly, or otherwise unapproachable voter who does not care much for "that one," the man who later became President Obama. At the face of things, on the front stage, canvassing seems largely unchanged.

But behind the scenes hundreds of specialists toiled at their computers to make it all possible, to maximize the instrumental impact, and to try to keep it all under control. Away from the doors and off the phones, staffers, volunteers, and part-timers used new information and communication technologies ranging from by now mundane things like cell phones and email, to emerging tools like social networking sites, and to specialized technologies like tailor-made campaign Web pages and dedicated software solutions for targeting and management. In Washington, D.C., and in innumerable offices and coffee shops around the country, consultants crunched numbers to make sure their client campaigns made the most of it all. The work done to sort index cards with voter information and to physically cut and paste the walk sheets for a canvass in 1968 or 1988 had little to do with what it took to update detailed Web-accessible voter files, synchronize personal digital assistants, and print turf maps in 2008. In political campaigns new technologies have not replaced older forms of communication as much as they have revived them.

The backstage changes are not only technological, they are also institutional. When Barack Obama topped the ticket in 2008, many of the organizations that had provided much of the manpower to knock on doors for Dukakis and Humphrey—most importantly labor unions and local Democratic Party organizations—were no longer what they used to be. Candidates and their staffers today have to piece together their own campaign operations from a wider, less structured, and more unruly universe of allies, volunteers, and paid part-timers. The supposedly old-fashioned practice of contacting voters directly on behalf of a candidate or party is deeply intertwined with the most recent advances in online-integrated software and database management; it is also deeply influenced by contemporary changes in how the major parties and their closest allies organize and are organized. Like campaign practices in general, these various forms of voter contact are characterized by both change and continuity.

This book deals with how American political campaigns pursue what I call "personalized political communication"—premeditated practices that use *people* as media for political communication. The main forms of this method of communication are door-to-door canvassing and phone banking, central parts of what political operatives call the "ground war." I analyze this subject not to assess its impact on electoral behavior, but to identify the implications that ground war practices have for how we understand processes of political communication, for how we understand campaigns, and for how we understand what it means to take part in them—an important form of political participation, a part of what it means to have a government that is created at least partially "by the people." How campaigns are waged matters, not only for electoral outcomes but also for what democratic politics *is*.

Personalized political communication on the large scale we have seen in recent elections requires resources that are well beyond those commanded by campaign organizations built around individual candidates. I show how this type of communication is pursued instead by wider "campaign assemblages" that include not only staffers and consultants but also allied interest groups and civic associations, numerous individual volunteers and paid part-timers, and a party-provided technical infrastructure for targeting voters. Close scrutiny of how such campaign assemblages engage in personalized political communication leads me to challenge the dominant view of political communication in contemporary America—that it is a tightly scripted, controlled, and professionalized set of practices that primarily represses turnout and turns people off politics in its cut-throat pursuit of victory. I highlight how even as they bankroll negative advertisements, feed the horserace coverage, and resort to direct mail attacks, campaigns also work hard to get out (especially partisan) voters and get people involved in (instrumental) forms of political participation. Analysis of how campaign assemblages wage ground wars leads me to dispute the widespread idea that American politics is increasingly the province of a small coterie of professionals as well as the romantic notion that canvassing and the like represents some purer form of "grassroots politics." I demonstrate how even well-funded competitive campaigns for federal office continue to rely on a wide range of nonprofessional elements, how the campaign organizations themselves are at most unevenly professionalized, and also how even the most seemingly innocent volunteer canvass is tied in with specialized targeting technologies and staff expertise.

Finally, attention to campaigns' and staffers' instrumental need for people to engage in the labor-intensive work of personalized political communication, of contacting voters one at a time, at the door or over the phone, leads me to suggest that when elections are competitive and ambition is thus still made to counteract ambition, today's political operatives and political organizations have a renewed self-interest in getting people to participate in the political process as volunteers and voters. Ground war campaigns are highly instrumental in their orientation; they pick and choose who they talk to and try to turn out, discriminate consciously and unconsciously in who they mobilize as volunteers, and have not even a semblance of internal democracy. But they actively encourage participation and generate higher turnout, and that is a good thing for a democracy plagued by widespread indifference and a sense of disconnect between people and politics.

Ground war campaigns and practices of personalized political communication offer a privileged point for observing American democracy in action. Working for a candidate or a party at election time is a paradigmatic form of political participation, something millions of people do every year. Most of them, whether they are volunteers or part-timers, will be asked to knock on doors or make calls and talk to voters. Canvassing and phone banking are intensely social, organized, and outward-oriented activities; they cannot easily be done in isolation from the privacy of one's living room like making an online donation to a candidate or writing out a check to be mailed to a campaign committee. Personal contacts confront participants with parts of the electorate, bring them together with others who are involved, and introduce them to the organizational and technological intricacies of contemporary campaigns. They offer an opportunity to try to influence (however slightly) electoral outcomes; meet people with a passion for, or a professional commitment to, politics; and, as one volunteer put it, "take a real-life lesson in practical politics." To understand practices of personalized political communication is therefore to understand a crucial component in civic and political life.

My analysis of recent ground wars is based primarily on ten months of ethnographic fieldwork on the Democratic side in two competitive congressional districts during the 2008 elections: Connecticut's 4th district and New Jersey's 7th district. . . .

Every single one of the countless knocks and calls made served one or more of the same three instrumental purposes: to persuade swing voters (those who have no fixed political allegiances and whose votes can thus determine election results), to motivate base voters to turn out, and to gather more information about the electorate for further contacts. Every call or knock was predicated upon the participation of players well beyond the core of full-time staffers in the campaign organization itself. Every one of these contacts entailed potentially fraught encounters with voters, came with numerous organizing challenges, and had to be effectively targeted to be worth the effort.

To demonstrate what such ambitious ground war campaigns mean for political communication and for how we understand contemporary forms of political organization and political participation in America, the rest of this book deals not only with the act of contacting voters but also with the organizing and targeting that make these countless conversations possible. Together, processes of contacting, organizing, and targeting define how personalized political communication works. The episodes scattered throughout the text include some of the elements that must be considered in this type of communication—the different communities of staffers, volunteers, and part-timers involved; the various technologies they use; the data their work is based on; the different motivations and conceptions of politics at play; and the whole heterogeneous edifice that is constructed around candidates in competitive districts to conduct field operations, to wage ground wars, to pursue personalized political communication.

Political practice on the ground does not single-handedly decide elections or define levels of political participation. Political scientists have long demonstrated the importance of broad economic trends, demographic developments, and party identification for electoral outcomes. Sociologists have established the importance of socioeconomic status and social ties for civic engagement. But campaigns matter—at the margin for who wins and who loses, and in terms of political participation because they constitute one of the pathways by which people can get involved in politics. The central role played by formal and informal intermediaries in encouraging, shaping, and sustaining civic engagement has led to detailed studies of, for example, antiabortion activism, environmentalist groups, and movements for urban renewal, but, curiously, not of political parties and campaigns.

Close attention to the work that goes into fighting ground wars brings to light an everyday life in campaigns that is far from the glamour that some associate with politics. Personalized political communication is rarely covered by journalists, who are more interested in who said what to whom and who is ahead. It plays no part in television drama series like *The West Wing* (1999–2006; much loved by many campaign staffers). It receives little breathless commentary on cable channels or political blogs. Field operations belong to the electoral backstage, where people who are not candidates, policy specialists, or high-profile consultants work hard in relative obscurity to bring about these countless contacts. To make visible the daily practices that make personalized political communication possible on a large scale, this book focuses on what I actually saw people say and do on the ground in the campaigns, and not on how canvassing and phone banking are depicted in the press or by prominent political operatives marketing themselves and their work. It is only on the basis of such firsthand evidence that a clear analysis of the logics at play, and the implications they have, becomes possible. . . .

Episode 3.1

Since four o'clock on this warm and sunny August afternoon, I have been canvassing with Allen in affluent, suburban Trumbull, Connecticut. He is a college senior doing an internship with Himes for Congress over the summer. We are walking a list with about a hundred targeted voters distributed across roughly eighty households. It will take us something like four hours to knock on every door in a terrain like this. We expect to speak to maybe thirty people. The canvassing director will come back to pick us up around eight.

Three more canvassing teams are working in pairs to "knock through" other parts of the area. We are staying out of some parts of Trumbull to avoid getting the candidate entangled in a primary fight between two well-connected local Democrats who both want a shot at the state Senate.

Allen walks up to a large, well-kept house, looking for signs of life. He rings the bell and waits for about twenty seconds. He pounds on the solid wood door and shouts, "Hello?" Ten seconds later, he sticks a Himes for Congress flyer under a potted plant next to the doorstep and walks back down toward me. As he reaches the road, where I'm waiting, he says, "Not home," and wipes the sweat off of his increasingly sunburned face.

Episode 3.2

I am phone banking with Paula and the other volunteers in Fanwood, New Jersey. Most of us have been on the phones for more than an hour, and the pace is increasingly sluggish. It is around five in the afternoon. Today we are calling women over sixty-five who are registered as Independents. The first hour, I made forty calls and had five contacts. I am on my second hour, and I have lost some pace. I have made fewer than thirty calls and have had only one contact. I feel no particular urge to punch in the number for the voter next on my list.

But I do it. And I sit with the phone in my hand listening to the dial tone while I count toward twenty in my head. After about fifteen seconds, I hear a robotic voice: "The person you have called is not available to take your call at this moment. Your call has been forwarded to an automatic voice-mail service. At the tone, please record your message. When you have finished recording, you may hang up or press one for more options."

I look down on the script in front of me, wait for the tone, then start reading. "Hi, my name is Rasmus. I'm a volunteer with Victory '08. I just wanted to call you to tell you about Linda Stender and the Democratic ticket. Linda Stender believes that the Bush administration has led our country in the wrong direction, and she will fight to get us back on the right track. Linda Stender will work to jump-start our economy and create good, new jobs; stop the war in Iraq and bring our troops home safely and soon; fight for affordable health care for every American; and develop a national energy policy that ends our dependence on foreign oil and brings down the price at the pump. Linda Stender will bring the change that New Jersey families need. If you would like to know more or perhaps to get involved in the campaign, please contact the Victory '08 office at 908-490-1380. This call was paid for by the New Jersey State Democratic Committee and Linda Stender for Congress. It is authorized by Linda Stender for Congress. Thank you, and have a good day."

This takes about forty seconds. I've read it into something like forty voicemail systems today.

Episode 3.3

It is October and late in the game. Linda Stender's opponent has been upping his game recently with a new television ad, and the Republican Congressional Campaign Committee has just sent out an aggressive direct mail piece to potentially undecided voters.

Kevin is on the phones, calling through a list of people who previously have been identified as undecided by other callers or canvassers, or are believed to be so on the basis of statistical analysis of the data available to the campaign. He has been in to "help out" a few times, being, as he puts it, "between things" right now. Given his previous experience working in telemarketing, it is no surprise that he is good on the phones—polite but firm, usually unwavering, and hardworking.

He dials the next person on the list and waits. The second he hears the "Hello?" at the other end, his whole body language changes. He straightens his back, brandishes a dazzling smile, and launches into his spiel: "Good evening, sir. My name is Kevin, and I'm a volunteer calling you on behalf of Linda Stender. She is a—" He stops speaking and hesitates for a second, then holds out the receiver while looking at it. He turns to me and says, "He told me to go fuck myself."

Episode 3.4

Charlene and I are canvassing together in the outskirts of Bridgeport, Connecticut. While not quite as depressed as the inner city, the area we are in is still poor, especially by Fairfield County standards. A few houses are vacant, many are for sale, and most are somewhat worse for wear. Though we are nowhere near the end of our list and are supposed to go on until eight-thirty, Charlene has announced that she wants to call it a day at seven-thirty. "Nobody wants to talk later anyway," she says. I know the canvassing director won't approve, but I say nothing. The part-timers seem to work slightly shorter hours with each passing week.

With ten minutes to go, I have a couple of houses left on the street we are on, so I have been rushing things a bit, knocking on doors and leaving after ten seconds or so if I sense no reaction. I have skipped some of the houses that seemed obviously empty to me, though maybe I shouldn't—it is sometimes hard to balance between acting like my fellow canvassers and following staff instructions. I sort of want to finish this row, but I half dread running into a "talker" who will go on forever and make Charlene have to wait for me in the car.

I need not fear. The only person I speak to on this street is a man in his late seventies who has even less time for me than I have for him. I ring the bell next to his open front door and say "hello" as he is watching television in his living room. He turns toward me in his chair without getting up and shouts to me, over the loud chatter of CNN pundits, "What is it?" I speak as loudly as I can without shouting, trying to get through to him while Dr. Sanjay Gupta is making some point in a faraway studio: "Hi, my name is Rasmus. I'm just out walking the streets for the Democratic Party, talking to folks about the fall elections. Have you thought about—" The man interrupts me: "Yeah, yeah, you don't need to read me the whole speech. I'll vote the ticket." He turns away and fidgets with the remote control. I hesitate for a moment, then turn around and walk away. On my PDA I put him down as a "solid Democrat" and a "definite supporter" of the various Democrats running. . . .

This is what personalized political communication looks like up close. Episodes like these are likely familiar to anyone who has been part of the field side of an American campaign. For those who have not, they provide a glimpse of what the countless contacts made are actually like. It is easy to lose sight of the texture of this in the face of political operatives and their talk of so-and-so many "knocks" and "calls." In the quantitative terms that campaign staffers favor, individual encounters are all alike and can be recorded in the clear-cut categories used to gather response data for further targeting: "not home," "undecided," "solid Democrat," and so on. But for people like Kevin, . . . Charlene, and millions more like them, who have taken it upon themselves to serve as media for personalized political communication, there is something more at stake in every attempt to contact a voter. Staffers in both campaigns were puzzled that I continued to take part in both canvassing and phone banking throughout my fieldwork. As one said, "You knock on the door and deliver the script. What's the big deal?" The big deal is what personalized political communication entails for those who are directly involved: uninvited interactions with total strangers. What is at stake here is not simply a chance to deliver a message and gather some information about voters, all on behalf of a campaign, but also the right to assume a certain role while doing so. The challenges involved make it difficult to keep personalized political communication "on message" and make it a draining and sometimes unpleasant experience for those involved. . . .

Canvassing voters and working the phones is widely seen as stressful. Almost everyone seems to be in agreement on this. One staffer remarked, "Honestly, I hate making phone calls." Some volunteers, clearly anticipating what they will be asked to do, arrive at campaign offices announcing, "I don't do phones, and I don't do doors, but I'll do anything else I can to help." (This is quite a headache for staffers who need help with "doing" phones and doors more than they need help with anything else.) Other volunteers are more stoic: "I don't like this, but if that's what I can do to help, so be it." Part-timers voice their concerns too: "I don't know how long I can continue doing this" (a remarkable verdict on a part-time job that will last at most two months). During my fieldwork I have seen everyone from senior staffers supervising dedicated volunteers to the most conscientiously loyal part-timers shirk from the job at hand. Some people fake phone calls by punching in imaginary numbers and holding the receiver while the error message sounds at the other end. Dozens admitted in private conversations to not actually knocking on doors they have walked up to and to sometimes fabricating response data about contacts that did not take place. No one stands by such behavior, but most of those who admitted to it explain it with reference to the wear and tear of seemingly endless numbers of often unpleasant conversations with voters. This is what most of those involved found most draining, uncomfortable, and ultimately stressful about personalized political communication. Not the hours spent on the phone or walking the streets, but the interactions themselves. (This helps explain why people strongly dislike productivity-enhancing technologies like auto-dialing systems for phone banking.

Most people are reluctant to make calls for more than an hour or two at the normal rate of thirty or so calls an hour. Computerized systems can ramp that up to a hundred or more, making the work even more taxing.)

The stress that people feel surely has multiple roots. Some battle a sense of futility, despite staffers' protestations to the contrary: "Personal contacts have been shown to be one of the most effective ways of influencing voters!" As made clear, much research suggests that staffers are right, and yet people wonder, "Why are we doing this?" "Does this make any difference?" Brought up on mass-mediated politics, it may be counterintuitive even to the people involved that talking to people one at a time may actually add up in a demonstrably effective way. Others complain of the tedious work involved: "I'm soo bored. . . ." "One more phone call and I'm going to shoot myself!" And though the interactions with voters are rarely the same, the work of contacting them surely is repetitive and a long way from the drama some news coverage and fictionalized accounts suggest surrounds politics. As one college intern put it, "I didn't realize how much hard work goes into campaigns!"

PART TWELVE

Political Parties

67

SEAN TRENDE

Are We in an Electoral Realignment?

The challenge of political science is to offer clear-cut theories of how politics works. But because of the variable of human nature as well as the difficulty of measuring and predicting political events with exactness, political science seems often less a "science" and more an "art." One of the attempts to develop a major theory to explain and predict politics is the theory of "critical elections." V.O. Key was the first to propose that certain presidential elections throughout American history mark significant long-term changes in the social and economic direction of the nation. Walter Dean Burnham, citing the elections of 1800, 1828, 1860, 1896 and 1932, described the characteristics of a critical or realigning election. But more recently, David Mayhew has challenged the whole theory of realignment. In this article web journalist Sean Trende opens his analysis with a discussion of the basics of realignment theory along with a critique of its validity. Regardless of whether or not the theory is valid, Trende measures recent political developments against the claims of realignment. There is no new set of major issues. No third party has appeared. There has not been long-term control by one political party. States have not dramatically changed their party loyalties. Trende considers the impact on future elections of coming demographic trends, ethnic, racial, and gender-based. Looking back to past predictions about realignment, Trende shows the futility of trying to anticipate such unpredictable shifts. While students of American government should be well versed in what realignment theory posits, we must be wary of such speculative, overarching views. What happened a few years or a few months ago might be a better predictor of electoral outcomes.

———

IN 1955, V. O. KEY WROTE a short article in *The Journal of Politics* entitled "A Theory of Critical Elections." Key examined the elections of 1896 and 1928 in New England, and concluded that there were certain elections that could be described as "critical" elections. These critical elections are marked by changes in the electorate that are, in Key's memorable phrase, "sharp and durable."

This wasn't an entirely new idea. Journalists such as Samuel Lubell had described certain elections as "realigning" elections several years earlier. But Key provided quantitative proof that suggested Lubell really was onto something.

Key's article spawned hundreds of others, as political scientists sought to identify what a realigning election looked like, categorize certain elections as realigning, and ascertain what drives these realigning elections. Opinion eventually more or less coalesced around the idea that a few important elections formed what we might call the "canonical" realignments: 1800, 1828, 1860, 1896, and 1932. Political scientists further speculated that there was a "periodicity" to realignments: They occurred roughly every thirty years or so.

The problem here should be immediately obvious: The list stops in 1932. There are no agreed-upon realignments after the 1932 election. Years like 1968, 1980, 1992, 1994, 1996, and the entire series from 2000 through 2010 have been proposed as potentially realigning elections. But none of these elections truly fits the definition of realignments set forth by political scientists.

So one possible answer to the question of whether 2012 is a realigning election is to critique the underlying question. Instead, perhaps the question should be "do realignments exist at all?" In 2004, Yale's David Mayhew wrote a blistering, controversial critique of realignment theory, *Electoral Realignments: A Critique of an American Genre*, which argues that American elections from 1828 through 1932 actually fit the realignment narrative much worse than realignment theorists allow. In *The Lost Majority*, the author of this chapter sought to pick up where Mayhew's work left off and to suggest that realignment theory fails to explain post-1932 elections well.

Nothing has changed that would suggest realignment is anything less than a false concept that should be abandoned. Political coalitions are constantly in flux, and confining our expectations of major change to particular elections cramps our understanding of history, condescends to the American people, and even encourages bad policymaking. This chapter focuses on the five most common claims of realignment theory.

But, recognizing that this is a minority view, this chapter will largely devote itself to engaging realignment theory on its own terms. Even with this broad concession, 2012 is a poor fit for a realignment. Indeed, even if we reframe the idea of realignment to be a sort of slow-moving, "secular" realignment later posited by Key, we would still struggle to explain the relevant time period in terms of realignment theory. . . .

We first must set some boundaries as to what constitutes a "realignment." Sloppy usage of the term is one of the main reasons that every election is seemingly followed by a claim of realignment. As John Sides has aptly observed, "The term 'realignment' gets thrown around casually, sometimes suggesting nothing more than 'something big is happening.'

But the term has a more precise meaning—indeed, it must have a precise meaning in order for it to mean anything."

Most accept the basic definition of a "critical," or realigning election as set forth by Key: that there be a "sharp and durable" change in the electorate. Beyond that, there is little agreement. For purposes of this chapter, we can turn to Mayhew's book, which helpfully collects fifteen broad claims made by various realignment theorists over the years. This chapter focuses on what we might consider the five "major" claims of realignment theory.

A realignment gives rise to new dominant voter cleavage over interests, ideological tendencies, or issues. For example, in 1828, we see the rise of the Second-Party System and the beginnings of the "Bank War." In 1860, the Third-Party System arrives, along with the Civil War. Then the 1896 election sees the end of the debate over the Civil War and the rise of the populist wing of the Democratic Party. Lastly, 1932 obviously brings about the New Deal and its eponymous coalition.

What new dominant voter interest, ideological tendency, or issue arose in the recent election? Perhaps we could say the Democrats' health care law. But this has been a goal of liberals for almost one hundred years, and has been a part of the Democratic Party platform for over sixty years. While it is an extremely important law, it isn't the type of fundamental redefinition of the relationship between the individual and the state that we find with, say, the New Deal or the onset of the Civil War.

Perhaps the fight over the Bush tax cuts for high earners? This is a variant of a fight we've been having since 1993, or even since 1980. If anything, the fact that both sides remain engaged in a death match over whether the top rate should be 39.6 percent or 35 percent illustrates just how little change we're really talking about. Perhaps we might find a fundamental issue-shift in Americans' increasing acceptance of marriage equality? This is certainly an important change in our country's attitude, but wasn't particularly a focal point of the campaign.

While we need to be careful not to diminish Obama's achievement in being reelected, it is also noteworthy that he will be the first president re-inaugurated with a lower share of the popular vote, smaller number of Electoral College votes, and lower number of total votes in our nation's history. The contrast with the other critical elections and their immediate successors is stark.

The polling also suggests that there has been very little change in Americans' attitude toward government. Gallup found that only 39 percent of Americans believed that government should do more to solve our country's problems. This is consistent with the long-term trend in Gallup, which has found 50 percent support for a more active government only a handful of times since the early 1990s. Likewise, the Pew Center has asked various questions regarding people's attitudes toward business, government, and society, which exhibit little movement since the late 1980s (again, outside of a handful of social issues). This doesn't mean that America is center-right or center-left or anything of that nature. It just suggests that its attitudes today aren't that different than they were even a few decades ago.

A realignment is preceded by—or contemporaneous with—a good showing by a third party, such as the rise of Free Soilers in the 1840s and 1850s, the People's Party in 1892, and the Progressive/Republican split of 1924. Of course, nothing of the sort has happened recently. The most recent third-party campaign to garner a significant share of the vote was Ross Perot's in the 1990s; his focus on the debt and deficit, his economic nationalism, and his strength among working-class whites make him an ill-suited candidate for a precursor to the Obama campaign.

Turnout is up in a realigning election. Because a realigning electorate shifts to address previously unmet needs, we see an increase in turnout. As of this writing, all the votes cast in 2012 have not yet been counted, so it is difficult to know precisely what percent of the voting eligible population voted. Regardless, the following chart proceeds under the assumption that there will be 129 million votes counted when the final vote counts are certified.

PERCENT OF ELIGIBLE VOTERS TURNING OUT

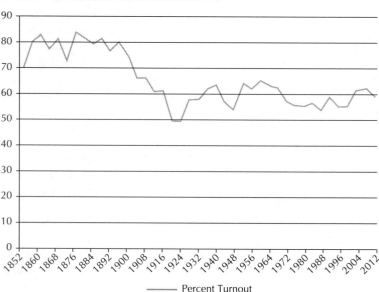

Percent Turnout

As you can see, turnout was actually down this election. Even 2008 shows a modest increase in turnout, at best. The big spike in turnout occurs in 2004, which would have actually suggested a realignment pointing toward Republicans.

Electoral realignments bring about long spans of unified party control of the government. The twelve years from 1828 through 1840 are the shortest period of unified control to follow a canonical realignment. This tendency makes any Democratic realignment in the past two decades problematic. Republicans have controlled the House now for eight of the past ten Congresses. Included in this list are Republicans' second-biggest and third-biggest House wins since 1928, which they achieved in the 2010 and 2012 elections. Given that no president since the Civil War has seen his party gain more than ten House seats in a midterm election, it seems unlikely that this streak will be broken in the near future.

This is a major problem for proponents of the "Obama realignment" thesis. Years like 2010 simply don't occur in the early stages of a realignment. While we could arguably be arriving at a time where separate "presidential" and "midterm" electorates result in alternative good and bad years for each party, that does not help the realignment case. As Sides aptly observed, "a realignment doesn't take midterm elections off."

A realignment brings about sharp and durable changes in the electorate. This is really the central claim of realignment theory. The First-, Second-, and Third-Party Systems are the major outcomes of the 1800, 1828, and 1860 elections. The solidification of Republican strength in the Northeast is the aftermath of the 1896 election, which helped enable the party to win seven of the nine succeeding elections. The Democrats became a truly national party in 1932, in turn winning seven of the next nine elections.

This is also the claim that most proponents of the "Obama realignment" hypothesis are really making. Under this narrative, the superficial closeness of the 2012 election belies a changing electorate. Obama's coalition of African American, Latino, liberal, and white suburban voters propelled him to victory, and will propel future Democratic candidates to victory in similar fashion.

It is possible. But from a realignment perspective, there are two problems. First, the recent changes in the electorate are not sharp. Second, it is far from certain that they will be durable. . . .

. . . [O]nly a few states have dramatically changed their partisan orientation, even in the twenty-four-year time frame [from 1988–2012]. Missouri, Montana, and South Dakota went from having marginal Democratic leans to having solid Republican leans. . . . West Virginia was the biggest mover of all the states, going from a solidly Democratic lean to a solidly Republican lean. Delaware, Maine, and New Jersey went from having mildly Republican leans to having solid Democratic leans, while New Hampshire, Virginia, Florida, and Nevada transformed from solidly Republican states to swing states. Other than that, we've mostly seen red states become redder, and blue states become bluer.

If the changes marked by the past few elections were not sharp, then perhaps they are durable? Maybe Obama's reelection marks a new era where Democrats continue to win elections narrowly, akin to the 1876 to 1896 period for Republicans? Perhaps the influx of young voters, single women, and minorities into the electorate creates something of a "Big Blue Wall" that now extends to the "tipping point" state—that state which gives the winner electoral vote number 270—to Democrats?

This demographic argument is necessarily speculative. But it runs into three potential problems. The first is that what we're seeing might be Obama's coalition, rather than a Democratic coalition. While it is incorrect (and more than a little condescending) to suggest that Obama's strong showing with blacks, Latinos, and other groups is due to his standing as the nation's first African American president, for African Americans to make up 13 percent of the electorate and to give 95 percent of their votes to a Democratic presidential candidate is an historical anomaly. The traditional numbers are more like 11 percent and 90 percent, respectively.

Could African American participation sink back to pre-2008 levels without Obama atop the ticket? It's by no means a given, but it is a possibility. Political scientist Matt Barreto notes that 79 percent of African Americans are "very enthusiastic" about the Democratic Party now, but only 47 percent say they will be after Obama's presidency ends. Obviously a lot can change in four years. But the substantial drop-off in African American participation that occurred from 2009 through 2011 is at least a warning sign that this could happen.

What would this mean? It would have potentially crippling effects on the Democrats. Assume, for a moment, that with Obama off the top of the ticket, the African American vote returns to 2004 levels of turnout and support for Democrats. Even if everything else in the electorate stayed exactly the same as 2012, Florida and Ohio would flip to Republican support, and Pennsylvania would be less than a point away from giving the Republican candidate electoral vote number 270.

Second, the demographic hypothesis immediately runs into the reality of 2009 through 2011. During this time, the "coalition of the ascendant" simply failed to show up, even in many of the "red-to-blue" states. In 2009, Bob McDonnell won the Virginia governorship by the same margin that Republican George Allen had enjoyed twenty years earlier in a similar political environment. In 2011, Republicans won control of the

Virginia State Senate under a map that had been gerrymandered by Democrats. In New Hampshire in 2010, Kelly Ayotte won a Senate race by twenty points. Richard Burr of North Carolina won by the largest margin of any North Carolina Senate candidate since 1974. Nevada and New Mexico both elected Latino Republican governors; Nevada did so by a healthy margin. Republicans swept most of the competitive races in the upper Midwest that year.

In the 2010 race for Congress there was a huge gender gap of twelve points. But Republicans actually carried women by two points, the first time that they had done so in House races on record. African Americans fell back to 10 percent of the electorate, and Republicans captured 9 percent of their vote. Republicans won college graduates by sixteen points, suburbanites by twelve points, and Independents by eighteen points— all groups that are supposed to be a part of the emerging Democratic majority.

Put differently, 2008 and 2012 happened, but so did everything in between, and the idea that we have necessarily distinct midterm and presidential electorates now is only a theory that hasn't really been tested. Even after the intervening 2012 elections, Republicans find themselves with an unusually high number of House, Senate, gubernatorial, and statehouse seats to be at the beginning of a realignment; they are proving more durable than the Democratic gains from 2006 and 2008. . . .

So it is far too early to declare that the Republican Party, at least as we know it, is about to become overwhelmed by a demographic tide that makes elections like 2012 the norm. At the very least, we need to wait until 2016 to find out (a) if minority participation continues at historically outsized rates with Obama off the ticket; (b) if whites' voting rate increases in 2016; and (c) if the anti-Democratic trend in white voting persists. All of these may well turn out in Democrats' favor. But we've already seen that simply changing (a) would have almost handed the election to Mitt Romney. If (b) and (c) change as well, a lot of these predictions of durability will look pretty weak. . . .

Up until now, we've engaged realignment on its own terms. But I think a lot of this discussion is beside the point. Even if Republicans win the presidency in 2016, it is still important that Obama won reelection by a nice margin in 2012, from both historical, policy and, not least of all, social perspectives.

More importantly, the historical record suggests that our ability to predict what elections will look like even two years in the future is weak at best. The 2004 and 2008 elections were both accompanied by a burst of triumphalist analysis proclaiming realignments that seemed to rule out the possibility that elections such as 2006 and 2010 were lurking around the corner.

A lot of these predictions came from partisans. But consider 1977, when political scientist Everett Carll Ladd, probably the most prominent election analyst of his day, had this to say about the 1976 elections:

The Republican party cannot find, outside of the performance of its presidential nominee, a single encouraging indicator of a general sort from its 1976 electoral performance. . . . We have criticized the common tendency of political commentators to overreact to the last election, but . . . [t]he Democrats have emerged almost everywhere outside the presidential arena as the "everyone party."

This assessment was not without support. Democrats had massive majorities in the House and Senate. Jimmy Carter had swept the South, suggesting that the Republicans' wins in the 1950s and early 1970s had more to do with Eisenhower's popularity and the fights over civil rights than actual Republican strength. Perhaps most ominously for the GOP, eighteen- to twenty-nine-year-olds—the most numerous demographic group in that election—had given Carter a 51 percent to 47 percent win. Ford's strongest group? Voters over sixty, who were half as numerous as the eighteen- to twenty-nine-year-olds.

Of course, 1976 reflected a low point for the GOP, and was actually followed by a steady progression of improving electoral fortunes. Because humans are very bad at predicting the short-term contingencies that truly drive elections a few months in advance, much less four years in advance, Ladd's projections fell apart. There was simply no way that he could see stagflation, the Iran hostage crisis, or killer bunnies. While an observer in 2004 might see the downturn in the Iraq war coming, the 2008 implosion of the economy, timed six weeks before the election, was outside the realm of foreseeability. An analyst in 2009 could be excused for missing the stagnant economy of 2010, the rise of the Tea Party, the unpopularity of the health care bill, or the Obama administration's inability to reenergize its base.

But this is just exactly the point. Realignment theory tells us that these sorts of things don't matter much, and that elections are more driven by demographics and the medium-term orientation of the parties. This doesn't square with the wild swings of the past few election cycles. For that matter, realignment theory doesn't even square up well with the parameters it has set for itself. When viewed across the broad expanse of American history, realignment theory becomes simultaneously overinclusive and underinclusive. That is to say, the canonical elections don't fit into the various realignment requirements that we sketched out particularly well. At the same time, other, noncanonical elections fit the requirements equally well, if not better. . . .

Rather than looking for broad, lasting wins in a vain attempt to scry the future, perhaps we should content ourselves with the realization that elections are governed largely by short-term forces that are largely unpredictable. Yes, Republicans won seven of ten elections from 1952 through 1988, and now Democrats have won the popular vote in five of six. But which of those elections, really, were the victorious parties supposed to lose? Do we need a construct regarding lasting majorities to explain them adequately?

Indeed, most elections, including the last one, can be projected reasonably well given a few structural data points, such as economic growth and whether an incumbent is seeking reelection. But if realignment theory were true, our econometric models should cease functioning at some point. In present terms, that means that Republicans should start running substantially behind what the models project. Instead, Republicans ran ahead of the models in 2000 and 2002, slightly behind in 2004 and 2006, about even in 2008 and 2012, and well ahead in 2010. We simply don't see any evidence that demographics or voter preferences are overriding short-term contingencies in the medium term, in a way that systematically harms either party.

None of this would matter if the concept of realignments didn't distort our understanding of elections. Realignment projects an apathetic electorate, one that comes alive only once every three decades to demand change. On the contrary, the record reflects an electorate that is active and constantly in flux, even if the shifts aren't always as dramatic as what we saw from 1924 through 1932.

Perhaps most perniciously, realignments can drive bad policy. Republicans famously sought a realignment in 2000 and 2004, and believed they had achieved it in the latter election. This encouraged a fair bit of hubris, which led to their pursuit of unpopular policies and arguably delayed the realization that something needed to change in the Iraq War. In 2008, Democrats were convinced that the Republicans were headed the way of the Whigs, and came across as absorbed with health care reform when most people were concerned with the economy. This has fed the overall impression that Washington is out of touch with the American people, and that our leaders are incapable of governing in a way that reflects the concerns of the American people.

In short, we should always be mindful of two things. First, as E. E. Schattschneider famously put it, "The people are a sovereign whose vocabulary is limited to two words, 'Yes' and 'No.' This sovereign, moreover, can speak only when spoken to." Second, the Founders set our government up such that the people get to speak relatively frequently. In other words, it is often difficult to translate the verdict rendered by the people, and probably impossible to do so at a level that would allow us to determine a realignment is taking place. Perhaps more importantly, another election is always just twenty-two months away from the swearing in, so even if we could translate accurately what an election "means," the people can always decide they want something else in fairly short order. That they exercised that option so frequently between 2004 and 2012 should give pause to anyone seeking to give an upper hand to either party. That they have exercised it so frequently, so consistently, with such sensitivity to short-term forces across history probably means that we should not confine our caution to the present day.

68

RONALD BROWNSTEIN

From *The Second Civil War*

Writing before President Barack Obama's 2008 election, journalist Ronald Brownstein described a political party system that is locked in nearly mortal combat, with no middle path possible. In his campaign, Obama suggested a post-partisan approach in which he would go beyond the two parties' clashing positions to find common ground. But Brownstein's view may prove to be the more valid one. He describes the loyalty that politicians owe to their "base," adding to the influence of the most extreme partisans in both parties. While clear-cut differences between the parties have been a mark of American politics at certain times in our history, the willingness to forge compromise solutions has been just as important. Those compromises are missing from Washington, D.C., today, Brownstein believes. Quoting several high-profile Democratic and Republican political figures, Brownstein makes the case that American government was not always so polarized. "Hyperpartisanship," as Brownstein terms it, does have positive byproducts, such as much more citizen participation. But at what price? Despite the fact that issues are no more divisive now than in the past, the cost of so much partisanship is paid by the American people. Perhaps the nation will find a post-partisan solution. Or perhaps there'll be a "second civil war."

AMERICA IS THE RICHEST and most powerful country in the world. It may be the richest and most powerful country in the history of the world.

But it cannot agree on a plan to reduce its dependence on foreign oil. Nor can it balance its federal budget.

It can't provide health insurance for the nearly one in six Americans without it, either.

It can't agree on a plan to improve security at its borders and provide a humane way to deal with the estimated twelve million illegal immigrants working in its fields and factories and restaurants.

It can't align the promises it has made to seniors through Social Security and Medicare with the tax burdens that future generations realistically can bear.

It can't agree on the steps to rebuild economic security for middle-class Americans in the age of global economic competition. It can't for-

mulate a strategy for reducing the emissions of the gases that contribute
to global warming and potentially disruptive changes in the climate.

It cannot agree on an approach to fight the threat of Islamic terrorism,
at home and abroad, in a way that unites the country with shared purpose.

None of these problems are new. All have been discussed for years in
the media. All are the subject of constant debate in Washington. In most
cases the options for dealing with them are limited and familiar.

Why, then, has America failed to make more progress against these
challenges?

The answer, above all, is that the day-to-day functioning of American
politics now inhibits the constructive compromises between the parties
required to confront these problems. The political system has evolved to a
point where the vast majority of elected officials in each party feel comfortable only advancing ideas acceptable to their core supporters—their
"base," in the jargon of modern campaigns. But progress against these
problems, and almost all other challenges facing America, requires comprehensive solutions that marry ideas favored by one party and opposed
by the other. It's implausible, for instance, to imagine that we can address
the long-term challenge of Social Security and Medicare without both
reducing benefits and increasing taxes. Or that we can regain control of
our borders without significantly toughening enforcement and creating a
legal framework for the millions of illegal immigrants already in the United States. Or that we can reduce our dependence on foreign oil without
reducing consumption and increasing domestic production. Yet in each of
those cases, and all the others listed above, most elected officials in one of
the two major parties will not accept half of that solution. The result is to
prevent us from using all of the tools available to attack our problems.
One side proposes to control the deficit solely through spending cuts; the
other side almost entirely through tax increases. One party proposes to
produce more energy, the other to conserve more energy. In fact, to make
meaningful progress against any of these problems, the answer is almost
always that we will need to do both. Yet because each party seeks to impose its will on the other—and recoils from actions that might challenge
its core supporters—it cannot propose comprehensive solutions. We are
left with either-or alternatives—increase production or reduce consumption, cut benefits or raise taxes—when the challenges demand that we
apply solutions built on the principle of both-and.

This book examines how we have reached this dangerous impasse. It
rests on an unambiguous conclusion: The central obstacle to more effective action against our most pressing problems is an unrelenting polariza-

tion of American politics that has divided Washington and the country into hostile, even irreconcilable camps. Competition and even contention between rival parties has been part of American political life since its founding. That partisan rivalry most often has been a source of energy, innovation, and inspiration. But today the parties are losing the capacity to recognize their shared interest in placing boundaries on their competition—and in transcending it when the national interest demands. On some occasions—notably efforts to balance the federal budget and reform the welfare system under Bill Clinton, and an initiative to rethink federal education policy in George W. Bush's first year—they have collaborated on reasonable compromises. But for most of the past two decades the two sides have collided with such persistent and unwavering disagreement on everything from taxes to Social Security to social and foreign policy that it sometimes seems they are organizing not only against each other, but against the idea of compromise itself.

Against this backdrop of perpetual conflict, America is living through a transformation of its political life. For most of our history American political parties have functioned as loose coalitions that lightly tether diverse ideological views. Because the parties were so diverse, they have usually operated as a force that synthesized the diverse interests in American society. As the great political historian Richard Hofstadter once wrote, "In our politics, each major party has become a compound, a hodgepodge, of various and conflicting interests; and the imperatives of party struggle, the quest for victory and for offices, have forced the parties to undertake the business of conciliation and compromise among such interests."

That definition is obsolete. From Congress and the White House through the grassroots, the parties today are becoming less diverse, more ideologically homogeneous, and less inclined to pursue reasonable agreements. American government . . . usually has worked best when it is open to a broad array of views and perspectives, and seeks to harmonize a diverse range of interests. Today the dynamics of the political competition are narrowing the perspectives of each party in a manner that pushes them toward operating as the champion of one group of Americans against another—with dangerous results for all Americans. Reconfigured by the large forces we will explore, . . . our politics today encourages confrontation over compromise. The political system now rewards ideology over pragmatism. It is designed to sharpen disagreements rather than construct consensus. It is built on exposing and inflaming the differences that separate Americans rather than the shared priorities and values that unite them. It produces too much animosity and too few solutions.

Political leaders on both sides now feel a relentless pressure for party discipline and intellectual conformity more common in parliamentary systems than through most of American history. Any politician who attempts to build alliances across party lines is more likely to provoke suspicion and criticism than praise. "People want you to choose sides so badly in modern politics, there is no ability to cross [party lines]," said Senator Lindsey Graham, a conservative but iconoclastic Republican from South Carolina. "You are one team versus the other and never shall the twain meet. If it's a Democratic idea, I have to be against it because it came from a Democrat. And vice versa."

Richard A. Gephardt of Missouri, the former Democratic leader in the House of Representatives, used almost the exact same terms to describe the changes he experienced during the twenty-eight years he served in the House before retiring after 2004. "There is no dialogue [between the parties]," he said. "You are either in the blue team or the red team, and you never wander off. It's like the British Parliament. And I never thought about it that much when I came, but it was very different then. It wasn't a parliamentary system, and people wandered off their side and voted in committee or on the floor with the other side. There was this understanding that we were there to solve problems."

The wars between the two parties that take place every day in Washington may seem to most Americans a form of distant posturing, like border clashes between two countries they could not find on the map. But this polarization of political life imposes a tangible cost on every American family—a failure to confront all of the problems listed above with sensible solutions that could improve life for average Americans. Less tangibly but as importantly, extreme partisanship has produced a toxic environment that empowers the most adversarial and shrill voices in each party and disenfranchises the millions of Americans more attracted to pragmatic compromise than to ideological crusades. The reflexive, even ritualized, combat of modern politics leaves fewer and fewer attractive choices for all Americans who don't want to be conscripted into a battle between feuding ideologues or forced to link arms with Michael Moore or Ann Coulter.* . . .

. . . [T]he trends in election results over the past several decades add to the portrait of a political system increasingly divided between stable, di-

---

*Michael Moore and Ann Coulter—on the left and right, respectively—represent the more extreme sides of the political spectrum. Moore is a television and movie producer, famous for films such as *Bowling for Columbine* and *Capitalism: A Love Story.* Coulter, a prolific author, is known for her books including *Godless: The Church of Liberalism* and *Guilty: Liberal "Victims" and Their Assault on America.*—Eds.

vergent, and antagonistic camps. Ideologically, culturally, and geographically, the electoral coalitions of the two major parties have dispersed to the point where they now represent almost mirror images of each other. As this resorting has proceeded, each party has established powerful regional strongholds in which it dominates the presidential vote as well as House and Senate races. Each party, in other words, is consolidating its control over a formidable sphere of influence that provides it a stable foundation of support. The flip side is that each party is losing the ability to speak for the entire nation as it loses the capacity to effectively compete in large sections of the country. . . .

The polarization of American politics is an enormously complex, interactive phenomenon. Its roots trace into factors far beyond the workings of the political system itself, into changes in social life, cultural attitudes, and America's place in the world. The tendency toward polarization has been fueled, on the one hand, by the rise of feminism and the gay rights movement, and on the other by the increasing popularity of fundamentalist and evangelical churches. It draws strength from the questions about America's international role opened by the end of the cold war. And it has been influenced by changes in residential patterns that appear to have increased the tendency of Americans to settle among neighbors who share their political views.

This book, though, will focus on the changes within the political system that have carried America into the age of hyperpartisanship: the changing nature of the party coalitions; the role of organized constituency groups in shaping the political debate; the shifts in the way the media interacts with political life; the changes in the rules and practices of Congress; and the strategies pursued by presidents and other political leaders. All of these changes are diminishing our capacity to resolve conflicts. Indeed, . . . almost every major force in American political life now operates as an integrated machine to push the parties apart and to sharpen the disagreements in American life.

The consequences of hyperpartisanship are not all negative. The new alignment offers voters clear, stark choices. As recently as 1980 less than half of Americans told pollsters they saw important differences between the Republican and Democratic parties. Today, three fourths of Americans say they see important differences. With the choices so vividly clarified, more Americans are participating in the political system. Over 122 million people voted in 2004 [and over 130 million in 2008], nearly 17 million more than just four years earlier. The number of people who volunteered and contributed money to campaigns has soared too. One study found that the number of small donors to the presidential campaign increased at least threefold, and perhaps even fourfold, from 2000 to 2004. Many of those small donors made their contributions through the Internet, which has demonstrated an extraordinary ability to connect ordinary citizens to politics. . . .

American politics isn't breaking down because the country's disagreements are inherently more difficult to bridge today. . . . It is breaking down because too few political leaders resist the rising pressures inside the parties for ideological and partisan conformity that make it more difficult to bridge our disagreements. Ideological voices are louder than perhaps ever before in all aspects of American politics, from Congress to the media, but that isn't because deeply ideological voters now dominate the American electorate. At its core, the problem isn't too many ideologues but too few conciliators willing to challenge the ideologues, and partisan warriors on each side demanding a polarized politics. The first step toward lowering the temperature in American politics is a political leadership that would rather douse fires than start them.

Today, though, the impulse to harmonize divergent interests has almost vanished from the capital. Rather than promoting consensus, Washington manufactures disagreement. In both parties, many politicians see it in their interests to widen, not narrow, the underlying divisions in society. Americans today are sincerely divided over the role of government in the economy, foreign policy (especially the Iraq War), and perhaps most intractably, cultural and social issues. But no one would say Americans are divided as violently and passionately as they were over civil rights and the Vietnam War in the 1960s, or the rise of the corporate economy in the 1890s, much less slavery in the 1850s. In each of those periods, the differences between Americans were so profound that they were expressed not just with words, but with fists, and clubs, and ultimately guns. (Think Kent State, the Homestead Steel strike, and John Brown, not to mention the Civil War.) Clearly the *country* has been more polarized than it is today. What's unusual now is that the *political system* is more polarized than the country. Rather than reducing the level of conflict, Washington increases it. That tendency, not the breadth of the underlying divisions itself, is the defining characteristic of our era and the principal cause of our impasse on so many problems.

The road to this point has been paved by the long list of factors. . . . It has been manifest in hundreds, even thousands, of discrete decisions, yet the overall direction has been unwavering. The center in American politics is eroding. Confrontation is rising. The parties are separating. And the conflict between them is widening.

With so many centrifugal forces at work, this era of hyperpartisanship won't unwind easily or quickly. No one any time soon will confuse American politics with the era of good feeling that virtually eradicated partisan competition early in the nineteenth century. The forces encouraging polarization are now deeply entrenched, and they are unlikely to be entirely neutralized: Many of the most antagonistic features of American politics over the past fifteen years are likely to endure indefinitely. But that doesn't mean the country has to be as sharply and relentlessly divided as it is today. The parties have cooperated before to reach commonsense solutions that advance the national interest and could do so again. . . .

69

BILL BISHOP

From *The Big Sort*

Although Americans are not aware of it, we are "forming tribes," observes Bill Bishop. If he were writing about people getting their news from cable television or the Internet, he'd call it narrowcasting. If Bishop's topic involved political parties, he'd use the term party polarization. But the author is commenting about a "sort" that's much more measurable and spatial. Americans choose to move to states, cities, towns, neighborhoods that contain people who are similar to them in attitudes. Aided by the demographic analysis of Robert Cushing, Bishop finds that places differ in their likes and dislikes. Maybe it's not a 100% conscious choice when loading the moving van to head out to a new locale. But for many folks, moving to another part of the nation—even to a particular neighborhood—is not heading out to parts unknown. Perhaps the U.S. embraces diversity in a broad way, but in individuals' own lives, alikeness is sought. How do people know where to find those who share their norms and values? Bishop says that people just know: ". . . you get a vibe." The implications of this "big sort" are, well, big for politics, with many fewer competitive congressional districts now than in the past. For example, in mid-2015, The Cook Political Report *found that only 56 out of 435 House of Representatives seats could be termed competitive for 2016, with Larry Sabato's* Crystal Ball *citing a similar number of seats that are up for grabs. Returning to the demographic facts, you can test Bishop's thesis by looking at the university you chose to attend, the city you moved to, and the neighborhood in which you settled. Is it a good fit for your attitudes and beliefs? Cats and dogs figure into the statistics, too.*

———

THE "RED" AND "BLUE" STATES shown on television maps during the past several national elections depict a country in a static standoff. On this scale, politics is a game of Risk. What will it take for Republicans to capture Michigan? For Democrats to regain Ohio? But people don't live in states. They live in communities. And those communities are not close to being in equipoise, even within solidly blue or red states. They are, most of them, becoming even more Democratic or Republican. As Americans have moved over the past three decades, they have clustered in communities of sameness, among people with similar ways of life, beliefs, and, in the end, politics. Little, if any, of this political migration was by design, a conscious effort by people to live among like-voting neighbors. When my wife and I moved to Austin, we didn't go hunting for the most Democratic neighborhood in town. But the result was the same: moving to Travis Heights, we took a side and fell into a stark geographic pattern of political belief, one that has grown more distinct in presidential elections since 1976.

Over the past thirty years, the United States has been sorting itself, sifting at the most microscopic levels of society, as people have packed children, CDs, and the family hound and moved. Between 4 and 5 percent of the population moves each year from one county to another—100 million Americans in the past decade. They are moving to take jobs, to be close to family, or to follow the sun. When they look for a place to live, they run through a checklist of amenities: Is there the right kind of church nearby? The right kind of coffee shop? How close is the neighborhood to the center of the city? What are the rents? Is the place safe? When people move, they also make choices about who their neighbors will be and who will share their new lives. Those are now political decisions, and they are having a profound effect on the nation's public life. It wasn't just my neighborhood that had tipped to become politically monogamous. In 1976, less than a quarter of Americans lived in places where the presidential election was a landslide. By 2004, nearly half of all voters lived in landslide counties.

In 2004, the press was buzzing about polarization, the inability of the leaders of the two political parties to find even a patch of common ground. All the measures of political ideology showed widening divisions between Democratic and Republican political leaders, and unbridled partisanship in national politics became a topic for Sunday news shows and newspaper columnists. Meanwhile, unnoticed, people had been reshaping the way they lived. Americans were forming tribes, not only in their neighborhoods but also in churches and volunteer groups. That's not the way people would describe what they were doing, but in every corner of society, people were creating new, more homogeneous relations. Churches were filled with people who looked alike and, more important, thought alike. So were clubs, civic organizations, and volunteer groups. Social psychologists had studied like-minded groups and could predict how people living and worshiping in homogeneous groups would react: as people heard their beliefs reflected and amplified, they would become more extreme in their thinking. What had happened over three decades wasn't a simple increase in political partisanship, but a more fundamental kind of self-perpetuating, self-reinforcing social division. The like-minded neighborhood supported the like-minded church, and both confirmed the image and beliefs of the tribe that lived and worshiped there. Americans were busy creating social resonators, and the hum that filled the air was the reverberated and amplified sound of their own voices and beliefs.

This was not an area of concern for most of those who wrote about politics. Migration wasn't thought to be much of a factor in politics. People moved, sure, and some states gained votes while others lost. But the effects were thought to be essentially a wash. Frankly, I only stumbled upon this trend in American politics—and that was only after I stumbled upon Robert Cushing.

I had previously worked for a small paper in the coalfields of Eastern Kentucky, and my wife and I had owned a weekly newspaper in rural Texas. From my experience living in small towns, I had become interested in why some communities develop vibrant economies while others stagnate, and I had written about this question as a newspaper columnist in Kentucky and then a reporter in Austin. Cushing was a sociologist and statistician who had recently retired from the University of Texas. My parents were friends with a cousin of Bob's wife, Frances. Through that tenuous connection, we met for breakfast one morning.

I remember telling Bob I had some data about Austin's economy but didn't know quite what to do with it. "I do," Bob responded. That was typical Bob, a guy who had paid his way through graduate school by working summers fighting forest fires as a Smokejumper in Montana. He did know what to do with the pile of data I had collected, and we began collaborating on projects for the *Austin American-Statesman*. We would decide on a question we wanted to answer, and Bob would begin clicking, programming, and calculating. Often in the middle of the night, a new set of charts and Excel files would arrive in my e-mail inbox, and I'd see that Bob had made another remarkable discovery. . . .

People don't check voting records before deciding where to live. Why would anyone bother? In a time of political segregation, it's simple enough to tell a place's politics just by looking. Before the 2006 midterm elections, marketing firms held focus groups and fielded polls, scouring the countryside to find the giveaway to a person's political inclination. Using the most sophisticated techniques of market profiling, these firms compiled a rather unsurprising list of attributes.

Democrats want to live by their own rules. They hang out with friends at parks or other public places. They think that religion and politics shouldn't mix. Democrats watch Sunday morning news shows and late-night television. They listen to morning radio, read weekly newsmagazines, watch network television, read music and lifestyle publications, and are inclined to belong to a DVD rental service. Democrats are more likely than Republicans to own cats.

Republicans go to church. They spend more time with family, get their news from Fox News or the radio, and own guns. Republicans read sports and home magazines, attend Bible study, frequently visit relatives, and talk about politics with people at church. They believe that people should take more responsibility for their lives, and they think that over-whelming force is the best way to defeat terrorists. Republicans are more likely than Democrats to own dogs.

None of this is particularly shocking. We've all learned by now that Republicans watch Fox News and Democrats are less likely to attend church. Okay, the DVD rental clue is a surprise, and Democrats in my part of town own plenty of dogs, but basically we all know these differences. What is new is that some of us appear to be *acting* on this knowledge. An Episcopal priest told me he had moved from the reliably Republican Louisville, Kentucky, suburbs to an older city neighborhood so that he could be within walking distance of produce stands, restaurants, and cof-fee shops—and to be among other Democrats. A journalism professor at the University of North Carolina told me that when he retired, he moved to a more urban part of Chapel Hill to escape Republican neighbors. A new resident of a Dallas exurb told a *New York Times* reporter that she stayed away from liberal Austin when considering a move from Wisconsin, choosing the Dallas suburb of Frisco instead. "Politically, I feel a lot more at home here," she explained. People don't need to check voting records to know the political flavor of a community. They can smell it. . . .

To explain how people choose which political party to join, Donald Green, a Yale political scientist, described two social events. Imagine that you are walking down a hall, Green said. Through one door is a cocktail party filled with Democrats. Through another is a party of Republi-cans. You look in at both, and then you ask yourself some questions: "Which one is filled with people that you most closely identify with? Not necessarily the people who would agree were you to talk policy with them. Which group most closely reflects your own sense of group self-conception? Which ones would you like to have your sons and daughters marry?" You don't compare party platforms. You size up the groups, and you get a vibe. And then you pick a door and join a party. Party attach-ments are uniquely strong in the United States. People rarely change their affiliation once they decide they are Democrats or Republicans. No won-der. Parties represent ways of life. How do you know which party to join?

Well, Green says, it *feels* right. The party is filled with your kind of people.*

How do you know which neighborhood to live in? The same way: because it feels right. It looks like the kind of place with boys and girls you'd like your children to marry. You just know when a place is filled with your kind. That's where you mentally draw a little smiley face of approval, just as my wife did as we moved from Kentucky to Austin in 1999.

Texas voted in 2005 on whether to make marriage between people of the same sex unconstitutional. Statewide, the anti–gay marriage amendment passed with ease. More than seven out of ten Texans voted for it. In my section of South Austin, however, the precincts voted more than nine to one *against* the measure. The difference between my neighborhood and Texas as a whole amounted to more than 60 percentage points. It's not coincidence that in our narrow slice of Austin, a metropolitan area of more than 1.4 million people filling five counties, the liberal writer Molly Ivins lived just five blocks from the liberal writer Jim Hightower—and at one time we lived five blocks from both of them.

During the same years that Americans were slowly sorting themselves into more ideologically homogeneous communities, elected officials polarized nationally. To measure partisan polarization among members of Congress, political scientists Howard Rosenthal, Nolan McCarty, and Keith Poole track votes of individual members, who are then placed on an ideological scale from liberal to conservative. In the 1970s, the scatter plot of the 435 members of the House of Representatives was decidedly mixed. Democrats tended toward the left and Republicans drifted right, but there was a lot of mingling. Members from the two parties overlapped on many issues. When the scholars fast-forward through the 1970s, 1980s, and 1990s, however, the votes of the 435 representatives begin to split left and right and then coalesce. The scatter plot forms two swarms on either side of the graph's moderate middle. By 2002, Democratic members of Congress were buzzing together on the left, quite apart from a tight hive of Republicans on the right. In the mid-1970s, moderates filled 37 percent of the seats in the House of Representatives. By 2005, only 8 percent of the House could be found in the moderate middle.

---

*Sociologist Paul Lazarsfeld, working in the 1940s, saw the same kind of policy-free connection between parties and people. In his book *Voting: A Study of Opinion Formation in a Presidential Campaign* (Chicago: University of Chicago Press, 1954), Lazarsfeld wrote: "The preference for one party rather than another must be highly similar to the preference for one kind of literature or music rather than another, and the choice of the same political party every four years may be parallel to the choice of the same old standards of conduct in new social situations. In short, it appears that a sense of fitness is a more striking feature of political preference than reason and calculation" (p. 311).

Members from the two parties used to mingle, trade votes, and swap confidences and allegiances. (In 1965, half the Republicans in the Senate voted for President Lyndon Johnson's Medicare bill.) That kind of congressional compromise and cross-pollination is now rare. More common is discord. The *Washington Post's* Dana Milbank and David Broder reported in early 2004 that "partisans on both sides say the tone of political discourse is as bad as ever—if not worse." Former Oklahoma congressman Mickey Edwards said that on a visit to Washington, D.C., he stopped at the barbershop in the Rayburn House Office Building. "And the barber told me, he said, 'It's so different, it's so different. People don't like each other; they don't talk to each other,'" Edwards recalled. "Now, when the barber in the Rayburn Building sees this, it's very, very real." . . .

Is the United States polarized? Maybe that's the wrong term. What's happening runs deeper than quantifiable differences in a grocery list of values. Despite the undeniable sameness of places across America—is a PetSmart in a Democratic county different from a PetSmart in a Republican county?—communities vary widely in how residents think, look, and live. And many of those differences are increasing. There are even increasing differences in the way we speak.* Over the past thirty years, communities have been busy creating new and different societies, almost in the way isolated islands foster distinct forms of life, but without a plan or an understanding of the consequences.

The first half of the twentieth century was an experiment in economic specialization, as craft production gave way to assembly lines; cabinetmakers became lathe operators or door assemblers. The second half of the century brought social specialization, the displacement of mass culture by media, organizations, and associations that were both more segmented and more homogeneous. We now worship in churches among like-minded parishioners, or we change churches, maybe even denominations, to find such persons. We join volunteer groups with like-minded companions. We read and watch news that confirms our existing opinions. Politics, markets, economies, culture, and religion have all moved along the same trajectory, from fragmentation in the nineteenth century to conglomeration in the twentieth century to segmentation today. Just as coun-

---

*Linguist William Labov of the University of Pennsylvania, one of the authors of *The Atlas of North American English*, told National Public Radio in February 2006 that "the regional dialects of this country are getting more and more different. So that people in Buffalo, St. Louis and Los Angeles are now speaking much more differently from each other than they ever did" (Interview, *All Things Considered*, National Public Radio, February 16, 2006, http://www.npr.org/templates/story/story.php?storyId=5220090).

ties have grown more distant from one another politically, regional economies are also separating—some booming and vibrant, others weak and dissipating. Mainline religious denominations gained parishioners through the first half of the twentieth century, the age of mass markets, but lost members beginning in the mid-1960s to independent churches designed for homogeneous communities. Media, advertising, city economies—they've all segmented, specialized, and segregated. . . .

The tale we've been told and have come to tell ourselves is that society cracked in 1968 as a result of protests, assassinations, and the melee in the streets of Chicago. Informed by the Big Sort, we can now see 1968 more as a consequence of gradual change than as a cause of the changes that followed. Old political, social, religious, and cultural relationships had begun to crumble years earlier. American culture had slowly shifted as people simultaneously grew richer and lost faith in the old institutions that had helped create that wealth: the Democratic Party, the Elks, the daily newspaper, the federal government, the institution of marriage, the Presbyterian Church. Party membership, newspaper circulation, trust in government, and the number of people in the pews of mainline churches all declined at the same time.

The old systems of order—around land, family, class, tradition, and religious denomination—gave way. They were replaced over the next thirty years with a new order based on individual choice. Today we seek our own kind in like-minded churches, like-minded neighborhoods, and like-minded sources of news and entertainment. As we will see later in this book, like-minded, homogeneous groups squelch dissent, grow more extreme in their thinking, and ignore evidence that their positions are wrong. As a result, we now live in a giant feedback loop, hearing our own thoughts about what's right and wrong bounced back to us by the television shows we watch, the newspapers and books we read, the blogs we visit online, the sermons we hear, and the neighborhoods we live in.

Politicians and parties have exploited this social evolution, and in doing so, they have exacerbated partisanship and division. Elites have always been more partisan, more extreme, and more ideological than regular voters. But today moderates on all sides are rebuffed, and those who seek consensus or compromise are squeezed out. Paul Maslin, Democratic presidential hopeful Howard Dean's pollster in 2004, explained it this way:

> If I had to say one true statement about the entire process you are describing, I think that at the national or state level, it's making life increasingly difficult for people who are trying to thread the needle, to find the swing voter. In a way Karl Rove and Howard Dean and [Dean campaign manager] Joe Trippi were all right here. It's probably one of the things that's driving our politics into a more polar-

ized situation. While the swing vote and the classic vote in the middle still matter, you are much more willing to say now that you ignore at your peril your own base. Because as everything spreads apart, the base becomes more important because they are demographically more together. You don't have a whole bunch of 51–49 communities out there. You have more and more 60–40, 65–35, 70–30 places. Well, you better damn well be sure you maximize your 70–30 votes, whether it's inner-city African Americans or liberal, educated Democrats or whether it's suburban, conservative Republicans or small-town, main-street, or Evangelical Republicans. We have to maximize our base, and they have to maximize their base. Ergo, polarization.

The country may be more diverse than ever coast to coast. But look around: our own streets are filled with people who live alike, think alike, and vote alike. This social transformation didn't happen by accident. We have built a country where everyone can choose the neighborhood (and church and news shows) most compatible with his or her lifestyle and beliefs. And we are living with the consequences of this segregation by way of life: pockets of like-minded citizens that have become so ideologically inbred that we don't know, can't understand, and can barely conceive of "those people" who live just a few miles away.

70

WILLIAM FREY

From *Diversity Explosion*

The United States is a demographer's delight: a lot is changing and changing quickly. Minority groups including Hispanics, Asians, and those of mixed racial backgrounds, are growing. A large mostly-white cohort is aging. African Americans are moving from Northern cities to new locales. William Frey explains how and why all of these changes are occurring and what the results will be. Then, Frey turns to the political effects of demographic change as he considers the 2008 and 2012 elections, and beyond. The so-called battleground states are Frey's special focus. It's by no means clear whether Democrats or Republicans will emerge from the nation's "diversity explosion" as the dominant political party in the coming decades.

AMERICA REACHED AN IMPORTANT MILESTONE in 2011. That occurred when, for the first time in the history of the country, more minority babies than white babies were born in a year. Soon, most children will be racial minorities: Hispanics, blacks, Asians, and other nonwhite races. And, in about three decades, whites will constitute a minority of all Americans (see figure 1). This milestone signals the beginning of a transformation from the mostly white baby boom culture that dominated the nation during the last half of the twentieth century to the more globalized, multiracial country that the United States is becoming.

Certainly in the past, the specter of a "minority white" nation instilled fear among some Americans, and to some extent it continues to do so today—fear of change, fear of losing privileged status, or fear of unwanted groups in their communities. These fears were especially evident during the decades following World War II, when immigration was low and phrases such as "invasion," "blockbusting," and "white flight" were commonly used in the context of black-white segregation. Such fears are evident today in the public backlashes that sometimes occur against more permissive immigration and voter registration laws.

Yet if demography is truly destiny, then these fears of a more racially diverse nation will almost certainly dissipate. In many communities, a broad spectrum of racial groups already is accepted by all, particularly among the highly diverse youth population. Moreover, as this book illustrates, a growing diverse, globally connected minority population will be

Figure 1 U.S. WHITE AND MINORITY POPULATIONS, 1970–2050

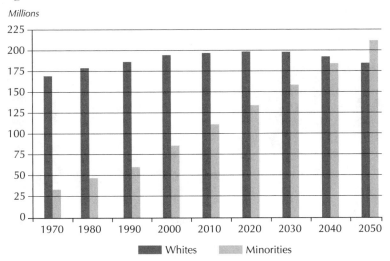

Source: U.S. censuses and Census Bureau projections, various years.

absolutely necessary to infuse the aging American labor force with vitality and to sustain populations in many parts of the country that are facing population declines. Rather than being feared, America's new diversity—poised to reinvigorate the country at a time when other developed nations are facing advanced aging and population loss—can be celebrated.

The sweep of diversity that has just begun to affect the nation is the theme of this book, which draws from my examination of the most recent U.S. census, census projections, and related sources. As a demographer who has followed U.S. population trends for decades, even I was surprised by the sheer scope of racial change that came to light with the 2010 census. The story that the data tell is not just more of the same. I am convinced that the United States is in the midst of a pivotal period ushering in extraordinary shifts in the nation's racial demographic makeup. If planned for properly, these demographic changes will allow the country to face the future with growth and vitality as it reinvents the classic American melting pot for a new era. In my experiences speaking publicly and answering press inquiries, I have seen the intensity of Americans' questions and thoughts about issues surrounding race. After having absorbed these startling census results and their implications, I wanted to interpret and expound on the dramatic shifts that they illustrate so that a general audience of readers can appreciate their force, promise, and challenges.

Figure 2 U.S. Race Groups and Projected Growth

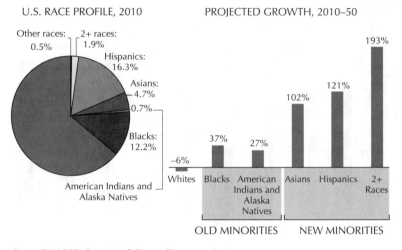

U.S. RACE PROFILE, 2010   PROJECTED GROWTH, 2010–50

Source: 2010 U.S. Census and Census Bureau projections.

Key among these changes are

• *the rapid growth of "new minorities": Hispanics, Asians, and increasingly multi-racial populations.* During the next 40 years, each of these groups is expected to more than double (see figure 2). New minorities have already become the major contributors to U.S. population gains. These new minorities—the products of recent immigration waves as well as the growing U.S.–born generations—contributed to more than three-quarters of the nation's population growth in the last decade. That trend will accelerate in the future.

• *the sharply diminished growth and rapid aging of America's white population.* Due to white low immigration, reduced fertility, and aging, the white population grew a tepid 1.2 percent in 2000–10. In roughly 10 years, the white population will begin a decline that will continue into the future. This decline will be most prominent among the younger populations. At the same time, the existing white population will age rapidly, as the large baby boom generation advances into seniorhood.

• *black economic advances and migration reversals.* Now, more than a half-century after the civil rights movement began, a recognizable segment of blacks has entered the middle class while simultaneously reversing historic population shifts. The long-standing Great Migration of blacks out of the South has now turned into a wholesale evacuation from the

North—to largely prosperous southern locales. Blacks are abandoning cities for the suburbs, and black neighborhood segregation continues to decline. Although many blacks still suffer the effects of inequality and segregation is far from gone, the economic and residential environments for blacks have improved well beyond the highly discriminatory, ghettoized life that most experienced for much of the twentieth century.

• *the shift toward a nation in which no racial group is the majority.* The shift toward "no majority" communities is already taking place as the constellation of racial minorities expands. In 2010, 22 of the nation's 100 largest metropolitan areas were minority white, up from just 14 in 2000 and 5 in 1990. Sometime after 2040, there will be no racial majority in the country. This is hardly the America that large numbers of today's older and middle-aged adults grew up with in their neighborhoods, workplaces, and civic lives. One implication of these shifts will be larger multiracial populations as multiracial marriages become far more commonplace.

The "diversity explosion" the country is now experiencing will bring significant changes in the attitudes of individuals, the practices of institutions, and the nature of American politics. Racial change has never been easy, and more often than not it has been fraught with fear and conflict. Yet for most of the nation's history, nonwhite racial groups have been a small minority. Partly because of that, blacks and other racial minorities were historically subjected to blatant discrimination, whether through Jim Crow laws, the Asian Exclusion Act, or any of the many other measures that denied racial minorities access to jobs, education, housing, financial resources, and basic rights of civic participation.

What will be different going forward is the sheer size of the minority population in the United States. It is arriving "just in time" as the aging white population begins to decline, bringing with it needed manpower and brain power and taking up residence in otherwise stagnating city and suburban housing markets. Although whites are still considered the mainstream in the United States, that perception should eventually shift as more minority members assume positions of responsibility, exert more political clout, exercise their strength as consumers, and demonstrate their value in the labor force. As they become integral to the nation's success, their concerns will be taken seriously. . . .

The sweeping diversity explosion that is now under way in the United States will continue to change the social and demographic personalities of all parts of the country in ways that would not have been anticipated 20 or 30 years ago. Its impact on national politics is one of these. This is nothing new. Since the nation's founding, significant episodes of demographic change have shaped and reshaped regional interests and voting blocs in unforeseen ways. The country is now in the midst of one of these episodes. The election of the nation's first black president, Barack Obama, a progressive Democrat, would have been unthinkable to voters in the Reagan Republican–dominated 1980s. Obama's election, largely on the shoulders of a growing young minority electorate—in some previously Republican-leaning New Sun Belt states—is probably the most visible symbol of how the diversity explosion has already made its mark.

The racial demographics that brought about this change are still evolving, in a way that makes it difficult to predict future election outcomes. The "browning" of America, from the bottom of the age structure upward, has already been manifested in the politics of the younger millennial generation. Yet their views will be countered by those of the aging, mostly white senior population, whose size will mushroom as the large baby boom generation ages. The new diversity is also affecting the nation's political geography by blurring the sharply separated Democratic "blue" and Republican "red" parts of the country as Democratic-leaning new minorities disperse from blue to red states and as blacks continue to flow into the heavily Republican South.

This chapter examines the impacts of the nation's new racial demographics on presidential politics. There is a considerable delay between purely demographic change and its effect on votes and elections. Despite this lag, minorities were responsible for giving Barack Obama the popular vote in both 2008 and 2012, and minorities will be an important—though not necessarily decisive—voice in future elections. These shifts are affecting states and electoral votes in presidential elections by expanding the number of battleground states, where minorities can make a difference. . . .

The 2012 election clearly validated the importance of minorities on the national political stage. But it also was an extremely polarizing election, with the Republican candidate gaining nine of his 10 votes from whites and the Democratic candidate capturing eight of every 10 minority votes. In addition to their potential for increasing racial divisions, future elections such as this one will not be demographically sustainable. If Romney could have eked out a victory, perhaps with greater white voter turnout, it would probably have been the "last hurrah" for a party strategy that relied primarily on whites as its base. Yet Obama's win, which required supersized minority outreach and turnout efforts while losing historically large numbers of white votes, is not a viable long-term strategy either. The projected rise in the minority portion of the electorate—from more than 30 percent in 2016 to nearly 40 percent in 2028—demands that both parties cross the racial divide to succeed in the future. Hispanics will contribute the most to this gain as they overtake blacks among eligible voters in 2020—two decades after Hispanics overtook blacks in the total population.

Potential crossover voting blocs also are on the horizon. Republican strategists such as Karl Rove, who engineered George W. Bush's relatively strong showing among Hispanics in 2004, have long advocated for greater GOP outreach to minorities, Hispanics in particular. Although not completely successful in his efforts, Bush supported initiatives that would appeal to Hispanic voters, like education and immigration reform. Such initiatives received far less emphasis in the subsequent unsuccessful presidential bids of Republicans John McCain and Mitt Romney, but they are likely to be revisited as the GOP attempts to expand its reach to minorities. They may find some openings. The 2012 General Social Survey indicates that for both blacks and Hispanics, those under age 30 were more likely than their elders to call themselves independents and less likely to identify as Democrats.

Democrats, for their part, have continued to eye potentially winnable segments of the white electorate. In their 2002 book *The Emerging Democratic Majority,* John B. Judis and Ruy Teixeira show that although the Democrats have lost their advantage with the white working class, their focus on progressive issues is increasing the party's appeal to rising white demographic segments in a postindustrial economy—professionals and women who, along with minorities, could reinvigorate the party's base. More recently, political writer Ronald Brownstein coined the term "coalition of the ascendant" to identify key growing voting blocs that Democrats could cultivate to their advantage. These include minorities, white college graduates—particularly women—and the younger millennial generation. Although minorities are clearly a cornerstone of the party's future, Brownstein points out that white college graduates are demographically significant. Among voters, they are becoming as numerous as traditional blue-collar whites and, especially among women, could become a solid Democratic constituency.

The millennial generation, in its overlap with the previous two blocs, could hold the most long-term promise. As young adults in both the 2008 and 2012 election, millennials propelled the strong 18- to 29-year-old vote for Obama. They are the most minority-dominant generation, and Pew Research Center polls show them to be more socially tolerant, liberal, open to larger government, and inclined to vote Democratic. If this generation, born between 1982 and 2003, continues to hold fast to those attitudes as they advance into middle age, Democrats would benefit greatly. Yet not all generations have held onto their youthful visions, as evidenced by many early baby boomers, who shifted politically to the right as they aged. The challenge for Democrats will be to retain the loyalties of millennials over the long term.

Given these trends, the country could be on the cusp of an emerging generation gap in voting patterns and in politics more broadly. As discussed, . . . the browning of America, starting with the younger generations, has caused a cultural generation gap between the young and the old. That became evident in past debates over immigration reform and in the competition for government resources between the young and the aged, as the largely white older generation feels disconnected from the increasingly diverse younger population. These kinds of divisions will emerge in national politics and in future presidential elections. Although the new racial shifts introduced by the millennial generation may very well drive current and future Democratic vote advantages, the national electorate will also include a large and growing senior population as the baby boom population continues to age. . . .

It might seem safe to assume that the popular vote scenario presented for future presidential elections will easily translate into actual election outcomes. But because presidents are elected on the basis of state-specific Electoral College votes, those outcomes could be muddied by state geography. The 2000 presidential election, in which Democrat Al Gore won the national popular vote but George W. Bush won the Electoral College vote, is a recent reminder that the two kinds of votes can differ. This is especially important to consider as the nation's racial makeup shifts across regions and states. In particular, the New Sun Belt region . . . is becoming part of an enlarged battleground of states as minorities become increasingly represented there.

The dispersal of the overall minority population . . . is also occurring—with a lag—in the eligible voter population. . . . Clearly, minorities are a sizable presence in many states, including those that are not in traditional coastal settlement areas. Minorities constitute nearly one-half or more of the electorate in Hawaii, New Mexico, California, Texas, and Washington, D.C., and at least one-third or more in a swath of additional states in the South and interior West.

Hispanics account for a substantial and increasing portion of the electorate in many western states as well as in Texas, Florida, New Jersey, New York, and Connecticut; in the latter states, they may soon approach blacks in electoral clout. Minorities constitute more than one-quarter of the electorate in most southern states, where blacks are the largest group (Florida, Texas, and Oklahoma excepted). Blacks still dominate the small minority populations in whiter Heartland states such as Michigan, Ohio, and Pennsylvania, although their much smaller Hispanic populations are rising, as in other parts of that region. Therefore, although the nation's electorate is still divided somewhat between whiter Heartland states and heavily minority coastal states, states in the New Sun Belt stand at the forefront of electorate change. These include fast-growing western interior states that are receiving Hispanics and other minorities and prosperous southern states that are attracting blacks along with Hispanics from other regions. . . .

The geographic dispersion of new minorities and the southward migration of blacks work to the advantage of the Democrats by enlarging the number of battleground states and allowing Democrats to cut into electoral turf that Republicans held steadily over a long period. . . .

It should not go unnoticed that minorities also were responsible for winning battleground states for Obama in the slowly growing Heartland, such as Ohio and Pennsylvania. Voters in both of these states were primarily white (83 and 85 percent, respectively) with modest recent minority gains. Obama won these states for two reasons: both Democratic margins and the turnout of their small minority populations, especially blacks, were high; and the white Republican voting margins were smaller than in other states. Even so, these were among the closest states in the 2012 election and point up a potential geographic fissure that may play out more vividly in future elections. That is, Democrats may become more successful at garnering fast-growing populations—millennials, minorities, and college graduates—as they open new geographic opportunities in the Sun Belt. Yet the older, whiter, slowly growing battlegrounds will be more open to Republicans if current party voting proclivities persist.

Despite their slow growth, the Heartland battleground states of Ohio, Pennsylvania, and Wisconsin—along with potential battlegrounds in Michigan, Minnesota, and Iowa—contain an impressive 80 votes in the Electoral College. As a group, their November 2012 eligible voter population was composed of 18 percent whites age 65 and over; 47 percent working-age, blue-collar whites; and 15 percent minorities. That contrasts with 16 percent whites age 65 and over; 34 percent working-age, blue-collar whites; and 31 percent minorities in the combined New Sun Belt battlegrounds of Virginia, North Carolina, Florida, Nevada, New Mexico, and Colorado, which together represent 77 Electoral College votes.

Although the six northern Heartland states voted for Obama in 2012, their future demographics are likely to consist of voters who are open to

Republican messages tailored to older baby boomers and blue-collar workers. These demographic and voting trends contrast with those in previous Republican-leaning Sun Belt states, in which blacks, Hispanics, and youth are open to the Democrats' outreach efforts. Thus, the cultural generation gap that both parties face nationally divides along a geographic dimension. Each party has to find ways to compete for both younger and older voting blocs in future presidential elections as the battleground expands into the Sun Belt.

71

ROBERT PUTNAM
DAVID CAMPBELL

From *American Grace*

"Congress shall make no law respecting an establishment of religion, or prohibiting the free exercise thereof . . . ," proclaims the U.S. Constitution in the first phrase of the First Amendment, ratified in 1791. By no means has this phrase been the end of the story. Robert Putnam and David Campbell often integrate sociology with political science and here, they examine the changed and changing place that religion has had in American lives and politics over several hundred years, and more specifically, over the past fifty years. The 1960s altered a lot in American politics with religion's role in people's lives and in their political preferences among the changes. Putnam and Campbell look at the paradox of easily-shifting religious loyalties alongside polarization based on religious beliefs: we're more accepting of differences AND less accepting of differences. In politics, the authors contrast political party positions on two high profile contemporary issues, abortion and same-sex marriage. In the recent past, Democrats and Republicans have had clearly differentiated views on these issues, but that might be changing. Young voters may hold attitudes on these two issues that re-shape the partisan divide. Religion can affect the polarization between the two major political parties, Putnam and Campbell contend, but it will not eliminate the tension that the First Amendment acknowledges.

———

IN THE 1950s, the Fraternal Order of Eagles teamed up with movie director Cecil B. DeMille for a unique promotion of the epic movie *The Ten Commandments*. In a form of reverse product placement, the Eagles and DeMille donated monuments of the biblical Ten Commandments to communities all around the country. Rather than putting a product in the movie, the primary symbol of the movie was instead placed in prominent locations—in public parks, in front of courthouses, and in the case of Texas on the grounds of the state capitol. These monuments reflected the zeitgeist, as the 1950s brought public, even government-sanctioned, expression of religion to the fore in many ways. This was also the decade in which "In God We Trust" was added to American currency, and the Pledge of Allegiance was amended to include the words "under God."

Those monuments stood for decades without causing a fuss. In recent years, however, they have led to court battles over whether their location on publicly owned land violates the constitutional prohibition on a government establishment of religion. In other words, fifty years ago these displays were so noncontroversial that they could safely be used as a marketing ploy for a big-budget Hollywood movie. Now they are the subject of litigation all the way to the Supreme Court.

Something has changed. . . .

This book is about what has changed in American religion over the past half century. Perhaps the most noticeable shift is how Americans have become polarized along religious lines. Americans are increasingly concentrated at opposite ends of the religious spectrum—the highly religious at one pole, and the avowedly secular at the other. The moderate religious middle is shrinking. Contrast today's religious landscape with America in the decades following the Second World War, when moderate—or mainline—religion was booming. In the past, there were religious tensions, but they were largely between religions (Catholic vs. Protestant most notably), rather than between the religious and irreligious. Today, America remains, on average, a highly religious nation, but that average obscures a growing secular swath of the population.

The nation's religious polarization has not been an inexorable process of smoothly unfolding change. Rather, it has resulted from three seismic societal shocks, the first of which was the sexually libertine 1960s. This tumultuous period then produced a prudish aftershock of growth in conservative religion, especially evangelicalism, and an even more pronounced cultural presence for American evangelicals, most noticeably in the political arena. As theological and political conservatism began to converge, religiously inflected issues emerged on the national political agenda, and "religion" became increasingly associated with the Republican Party. The first aftershock was followed by an opposite reaction, a second aftershock, which is still reverberating. A growing number of Americans, especially young people, have come to disavow religion. For many, their aversion to religion is rooted in unease with the association between religion and conservative politics. If religion equals Republican, then they have decided that religion is not for them.

Religious polarization has consequences beyond the religious realm, because being at one pole or the other correlates strongly with one's worldview, especially attitudes relating to such intimate matters as sex and the family. Given that American politics often centers on sex and family issues, this religious polarization has been especially visible in partisan politics. A "coalition of the religious" tends to vote one way, while Americans who are not religious vote another.

The current state of religious polarization has led social commentators to use heated, even hyperbolic, language to describe the state of American society. The bestseller lists are full of books highly critical of religion, countered by pundits whose rhetoric decries a public square made "naked" by religion's absence. In an overused metaphor, America is supposedly in the midst of a war over our culture.

And yet, when one ignores these venomous exchanges, and looks instead at how Americans of different religious backgrounds interact, the United States hardly seems like a house divided against itself. America peacefully combines a high degree of religious devotion with tremendous religious diversity—including growing ranks of the nonreligious. Americans have a high degree of tolerance for those of (most) other religions, including those without any religion in their lives.

Religion's role in America thus poses a puzzle. *How can religious pluralism coexist with religious polarization?*

The answer lies in the fact that, in America, religion is highly fluid. The conditions producing that fluidity are a signal feature of the nation's constitutional infrastructure. The very first words of the Bill of Rights guarantee that Congress—later interpreted to mean any level of government—will favor no particular religion, while ensuring that Americans can freely exercise their religious beliefs. In the legal arena, debates over such matters as whether the Ten Commandments can be displayed on public property hinge on the interpretation of the Constitution's words. More broadly, the absence of a state-run religious monopoly combined with a wide sphere of religious liberty has produced an ideal environment for a thriving religious ecosystem. Religions compete, adapt, and evolve as individual Americans freely move from one congregation to another, and even from one religion to another. In the United States, it seems perfectly natural to refer to one's religion as a "preference" instead of as a fixed characteristic.

This state of flux has actually contributed to religious polarization. A fluid religious environment enables people seeking something different to leave one religion for another, to find religion for the first time, or to leave religion altogether. This churn means that people gradually, but continually, sort themselves into like-minded clusters—their commonality defined not only by religion, but also by the social and political beliefs that go along with their religion.

The malleable nature of American religion, however, means that these clusters are not bunkers. Instead, the same fluidity that contributes to religious polarization means that nearly all Americans are acquainted with people of a different religious background. Even if you personally have never gone through a religious change, you likely know someone who has. Furthermore, that someone is likely to be more than a passing acquaintance, but rather a co-worker, a close friend, a spouse, or a child. All of this religious churn produces a jumble of relationships among people of varying religious backgrounds, often within extended families and even households, which keeps religious polarization from pulling the nation apart. . . .

Over the last fifty years, American religion has thus experienced two countervailing transformations. The first is the emergence of a new religious fault line in American society. Left on its own, such a fault line could split open and tear the nation apart. The second change, however, is precisely why the fault line has not become a gaping chasm. Polarization has not been accompanied by religious segregation—either literally or even metaphorically. To the contrary, rather than cocooning into isolated religious communities, Americans have become increasingly likely to work with, live alongside, and marry people of other religions—or people with no religion at all. In doing so, they have come to accept people with a religious background different from theirs. It is difficult to demonize the religion, or lack of religion, of people you know and, especially, those you love. Indeed, interreligious relationships are so common that most Americans probably pay them little mind, and consider them unremarkable. But their very commonness makes them remarkable indeed. . . .

Perhaps the most visible change in American religion over the last generation is the role it has come to play in the nation's politics. Religiosity has partisan overtones now that it did not have in the past. While there are notable exceptions, the most highly religious Americans are likely to be Republicans; Democrats predominate among those who are least religious. Among the punditry, this connection between religiosity and the vote has been given the unfortunate but alliterative label of the God gap—the gap in question referring to the political differences between people at varying levels of religiosity. It is thus like the so-called gender gap, the difference in the partisan tendencies of men and women. And, like the gender gap, the coupling between religiosity and partisanship has become one of those unquestioned generalizations of American political life—an election day fault line endlessly discussed by political pundits and shrewdly exploited by political operatives. . . .

We will first show that the glue which holds religiosity and partisanship together is the political salience of two issues in particular: abortion and same-sex marriage. Attitudes on both are tightly connected to religiosity—which is not a new development. The new part is that they have become politically salient, as the Democratic and Republican parties have taken opposing positions on both abortion and homosexual rights. As the parties have moved apart on these issues, religious and nonreligious voters have moved apart also. But, we suggest, should attitudes on these issues change, the religious divide in politics would likely also change. For while attitudes on same-sex marriage are moving sharply in a liberal direction, those on abortion are becoming somewhat more conservative— with both shifts most pronounced among young people.

Because of its longevity as a shaper of the partisan landscape, changes in abortion attitudes are especially portentous. Abortion has long been a wedge pulling more religious and less religious voters apart from one another. However, if unease with abortion becomes relatively common even among secular voters and comfort with gays relatively common even among religious voters, religiosity could cease to be a source of political division. If so, we could be headed toward a period of political "creative destruction," an opening for political entrepreneurs to forge new coalitions. . . .

We begin by confirming the conventional wisdom: Religious and nonreligious voters differ dramatically in their partisan preferences. While the extent and endurance of the religious divide between the parties easily can be exaggerated, as a broad generalization it is accurate to say that religiosity and support for the Republican Party are bound together. While there are many ways to make this point, it is instructive to focus on the frequency of saying grace as a good tracer of religiosity. The more often you say grace, the more likely you are to find a home in the Republican Party, and the less likely you are to identify with the Democrats. Being a political independent, though, is unrelated to grace saying. Indeed, few things about a person correspond as tightly to partisanship as grace saying. We stress that the connection between grace and the GOP is not a fluky result owing to the fact that grace saying is somehow an idiosyncratic measure of religiosity. No matter the yardstick of religious devotion or practice, the story comes out the same. . . . When using our more complete index of religiosity (which does not actually include saying grace as one of its components), the picture looks virtually identical: The highly religious are far more likely to be Republicans than Democrats, those who are low on our religiosity scale largely favor Democrats over the GOP, and religiosity has no bearing on partisan independence.

Even when we account statistically for other things that often go along with religiosity—such as marital status, age, region of the country—the connection between religiosity and partisanship remains. . . .

We began by affirming that the oft-discussed God gap in American politics is real. The Republicans have forged a coalition of the religious—although with exceptions, notably Black Protestants. Over roughly the last three decades, sex and family issues like abortion and same-sex marriage have brought this religious-political coalition together. The coalition will likely hold when sex and family issues are at stake in an election, and as long as the Republicans maintain their religion-friendly image. However, should sex and family issues recede in political significance, religion—or religiosity—will gradually cease to be such a salient political division. The data suggest that abortion and gay marriage may recede as political issues.

There has been a liberalizing trend on same-sex marriage, with younger Americans far more accepting of homosexuality generally, and same-sex unions specifically, than their elders. On abortion, though, we see evidence of a conservative tilt among young people, even though they are also the most secular age group in the population (because of the Juno Generation*—secular young people who are nonetheless uncomfortable with abortion).

Each of these trends has a different implication for the future of American politics. The trend on homosexual rights is likely to follow the same pattern as attitudes toward women's rights. Religiosity will remain a predictor of more conservative attitudes, but the floor for those attitudes will keep moving higher and higher. Recall that, in 2008, the most religious young person is just as likely to support gay marriage as the most secular member of his or her grandparents' generation. As the floor rises, opposition to homosexuality, like opposition to women's rights, will cease to be politically viable.

The trend on attitudes toward abortion among young people likely has a different, but no less portentous, implication. First, acceptance of abortion and same-sex marriage differ in that they are moving in opposite directions. For that reason, it would seem less likely that these issues would continue to share the same political platform. And since today's young people will constitute an ever greater share of the future electorate, continuation of this trend would lead aggregate opinion on abortion to shift modestly in a pro-life direction.

*The term Juno Generation comes from a 2007 movie about a teenage girl who decides against having an abortion.—EDS.

Secondly, and more subtly, abortion attitudes appear to have a weakening connection to religiosity among the rising generation. Since it was the tie between abortion and religiosity that brought the coalition of the religious together, any loosening of the abortion-religiosity connection has the potential to pull it apart. This would not necessarily mean that abortion ceases to be contentious, only that the debate over abortion is less likely to be waged along religious lines.

If we are reading the tea leaves right, these trends would not mean the immediate breakup of the coalition of the religious. Nor would they mean the immediate demise of the Religious Right as a political movement, as we are reminded that past rumors of the death of the Religious Right have been greatly exaggerated. Instead, we expect the Republicans' image as the religion-friendly party to endure, as images outlast issues. But party images can change. Adding to the potential for change, more and more Democratic candidates have begun using religious rhetoric and symbolism in an effort to neutralize the Republican advantage among churchgoers. In the short term, these efforts have had little effect, especially with the most religious voters, but over time they might lead to a change in whether the Republicans continue to be identified as the most religion-friendly party.

If sex and family issues fade from the political agenda and the Democrats successfully counterbalance the Republicans' association with religion—admittedly, two big ifs—it is tempting to predict that religion would cease to matter much in American politics. History, however, suggests that religion would still matter, just differently than it does now. . . .

Given the dynamism of American religion, we should not be surprised that over time the ways in which it intersects with politics change. Going all the way back to the election of 1800, Thomas Jefferson's opponents accused him of being an atheist intent on confiscating the Bibles of New England housewives. Later in the 1800s, there were sharp divisions between the liturgical (Episcopalians, Lutherans, Catholics) and pietistic (Baptists, Methodists) religions. As Catholic immigration swelled, tensions between Catholics and Protestants rose, fanned by Al Smith's candidacy in 1928 but then largely extinguished by Kennedy in 1960.* The demise of Catholic–Protestant conflict brought us a new source of religious division

---

*When Massachusetts senator John F. Kennedy ran for president in 1960, his Catholicism was anticipated to be a key issue in the campaign. Kennedy addressed the matter with an important speech stressing his independence, politically, from any religious loyalties he possessed. His opponent, Vice President Richard Nixon, did not make Kennedy's religion a campaign issue. Kennedy was narrowly elected in November 1960 and became the nation's first—and at least for over half a century after, the only—Catholic president occupying the White House until his assassination in 1963.

between the religious and the secular. Sex and family issues have now united a historically unique coalition of (most of) the religious but, we suggest, should the salience of those issues diminish, the coalition would likely unravel slowly. If so, we would not expect religion to cease to be a significant factor in American politics.

The particular constellation of religion and politics in contemporary America is the product of a particular set of historical contingencies—the shock and aftershocks that realigned the world of morality and religion and the strategic decisions of party leaders about how to respond to that new cleavage. History teaches us that if the current God gap were to fade, we should expect religion and politics to align in new ways, as political entrepreneurs work to construct new coalitions. The change will be in *how* religion affects our politics, not *whether* it does.

72

LINDA KILLIAN

From *The Swing Vote*

Why does required reading about American political parties include an excerpt from The Swing Vote, *a book about Independent voters? The answer, journalist Linda Killian asserts, is that Independent voters decide who wins most elections. They are a mix of seemingly contradictory views: they're liberal (on social issues) and conservative (on economic issues); they call themselves Democrats or Republicans or Independents; they care about politics, but see political solutions as nearly hopeless to achieve. Killian talks with Adam Gray, Jeanna Grasso and Michael Sciulla, Independents who are like people you might know. The excerpt only looks at three swing voters, but there are lots of them out there. At election time, the more polarized base of each major political party gets most of the attention from the media, but it's Independents who count. Killian sympathizes with their plight. The Democrats and the Republicans want their votes, but have little interest in their centrist views. After the election, it's back to the great partisan divide.*

. . . I HAVE COVERED AMERICAN POLITICS and government at the local, state, and national levels for many years, and increasingly I have become more concerned about the partisanship, the mounting influence of special interests and money on the legislative process, and the inability of the two parties to work together to solve our problems. I have also become aware that a great many Americans don't feel truly represented by their politicians and the system, especially the Independent voters, who now account for a larger portion of the electorate than either Democrats or Republicans. This disconnect between so many voters and the people elected to represent them is eroding trust in our political system and its effectiveness.

This nation faces so many serious problems: unemployment at its highest level in twenty-five years, a shrinking manufacturing base, a dependence on foreign oil and high energy prices, a crumbling infrastructure, a failing education system, and a federal debt and deficit that are driving the nation to the edge of a cliff. Our financial system and tax code serve those at the top but penalize the middle class and have increased the income gap between rich and middle-class wage earners to the largest disparity since the Census Bureau began keeping records, more than forty years ago. In 2010, CEO pay of Fortune 500 companies was up an astronomical 24 percent, at a higher level than in 2007, before our near economic collapse, and corporate profits were up 81 percent. But most Americans weren't feeling the benefits of this economic success—it was reserved for those at the top.

Our political system and elected officials seem incapable of dealing with these serious issues. In the eyes of the Independent voters, our politicians are fiddling while Rome burns. They can't seem to stop fighting long enough to do anything and aren't willing to make the compromises and tough choices that might solve some of our problems but might also jeopardize their own political careers.

Why has this happened, and what can be done about it? I hope that this book helps to answer those questions.

I wanted to tell the story of the Independent/Swing voters—the centrist voters who decide elections and represent more voters than those at the conservative and liberal ends of the political spectrum. Most of them are undeclared or unaffiliated—Independent voters. Some of them still remain registered Democrats and Republicans but they feel disconnected from the political parties and the government. They are not hard left or hard right and don't consistently identify with one political party. They are fiscally conservative and socially tolerant. They are in the middle. They "swing" back and forth, voting for candidates from both parties, largely because they are seeking change, aren't getting it from their elected leaders, and are increasingly disgusted with a system they don't believe truly represents them. I use the term *Independent/Swing voter* here to refer to those centrist voters who are Independents as well as to swing voters still belonging to a political party. Throughout the book, for clarity and simplicity, I will use the term *Independent voters* in referring to this group.

I was determined to talk with as many Independent voters as I could and use their own words to explain how they feel let down by the system. I wanted to give voice to these voters—the people to whom American politics should also belong.

Journalists from time to time interview or hold focus groups with "average voters" and feature them in stories. But this is mostly just a garnish. The meat and potatoes of political coverage are the political parties, their leaders, and the horse race—who's up and who's down, who's going to win either the next fight in Congress or the next election. Media stories about the presidential campaign begin long before any politicians have even declared their candidacies and dominate political coverage.

Republicans and Democrats, the left and right, are whom the American people consistently hear from even though a plurality of voters don't consider themselves one or the other. And the fundamental structural problems in our political system, the disenfranchisement of many of these Independent voters, gets ignored.

If a minority group were getting shut out of full participation in the political process, there would be a huge outcry. But Independent voters are far from a minority group. There are more of them than either Democrats or Republicans. Yet they are still woefully unrepresented within the political system. And they are just expected to take it. To sit back and enjoy the scraps thrown to them by the two political parties who have a stranglehold on the electoral and political process.

The conventional wisdom is that these voters pay less attention and participate less frequently, not to mention that they tend not to be regular or large financial donors to campaigns. Politicians and academics say they tune in and out. Some of that may be true, but the reason for that relative lack of engagement is our flawed political system.

What I heard over and over from the Independent voters I interviewed, who were by and large extremely politically aware and well informed, is that our current politics doesn't give them much of a reason to care. They don't see much difference between the two political parties, and they don't see things changing, no matter who gets elected.

To be sure, in addition to the Independent voters I talked with, I also interviewed hundreds of local, state, and national officials, party leaders, academics, and policy experts for this book. Not to have done so would have been like writing a book about baseball and interviewing only the fans and not the players and managers. But I talked to these politicians to understand how they operate in the system, the frustrations they also have, and what they think can be done to improve things.

I decided the best way to get at this story was to focus on four key swing states from different regions of the country, each representing a crucial group of Independent/Swing voters I wanted to describe. There were many states I considered, including Florida, Indiana, Missouri, Nevada, North Carolina, and Pennsylvania. But after much deliberation, I finally determined that New Hampshire, Virginia, Ohio, and Colorado were the best and most interesting examples of the nation's important swing states. Each state is unique to its region and illustrates a key swing voter demographic, and together they effectively tell the story of Independent/Swing voters throughout the country.

I reached out to Independent voters in those states in a variety of ways—I obtained lists of registered unaffiliated voters from voter registration offices and polling organizations and called up strangers on the telephone to ask them about their politics. Amazingly, most of them were willing to talk with me, even eager to do so. They were happy someone was listening. I also contacted universities and civic groups to find the perfect blend of Independent voters. I am incredibly grateful for all the time these voters shared with me. This book wouldn't have been possible without their cooperation. . . .

Twenty-five-year-old Adam Gray lives in Broomfield, Colorado, located between Denver and Boulder. He's an engineer who works for a small composite technology company that does advanced applications for the aerospace industry with clients including NASA and the Department of Defense.

Like so many young people, he moved to Colorado to attend college and never left. His parents are Republicans, and Gray says he started out as a Republican, voting for George W. Bush and John McCain for president, but then became an Independent. In 2010, he voted for Democrat John Hickenlooper for governor. "I thought when I first started to vote that you had to pick a side, but I got a little older and found myself disappointed with both sides."

Gray says he is more economically Republican but more socially Democratic. "This whole debt thing scares the hell out of me. . . . People my age get it. You're just starting out on your own, you know you can't spend more than you make. It's something most people my age can relate to—not overspending your bank account."

Gray is pro-choice, and believes gays should have the right to marry. "I think those are human rights," he explains. He watches Fox News, but also likes to check out the websites of CNN and the BBC. Like a lot of young people, he also picks up a lot of his political ideas from talking with his friends.

He doesn't understand why there should be only two parties in the United States and has some frustration about being a registered Independent because "You don't really have a voice if you don't side with one of the two big dogs."

But he is sick of what he sees going on in Washington. "There's no real compromise. It's like this tug-of-war match—it's not constructive. It's all a power play."

Gray has friends who worked on the Obama campaign who now say they are a bit disappointed, and he thinks "the Obama sheen has worn off." When I ask if he can see himself voting for a Democrat for president, he instantly responds, "Oh, sure," and says what he is really looking for in a candidate is, "Someone willing to admit their mistakes. I really hate that no one owns up to any mistake they make. I really want someone to be honest, tell it straight, and move forward. Candidates always make the safe play. I'd like to see someone just throwing it out there."

Jeanna Grasso, who lives in Denver, is a twenty-nine-year-old single mother of a six-year-old boy. She says she has already had some ups and downs in her life. Her father is a carpenter, and the grandmother who raised her is a receptionist at a car dealership. She took time off when her son was born to be with him but has since gone back to school at the University of Colorado–Denver and was on track to finish her political science degree in 2011.

She knows a lot of people who are unemployed and looking for work, and she is worried about finding a job when she graduates. She has been an Independent voter since she first registered to vote at eighteen and says it's because she has both liberal and conservative views. Some of her family members supported Ross Perot when he ran for president, and she says her favorite politicians are Bill Clinton and Colorado Governor John Hickenlooper. Grasso mostly votes for Democrats, although she's not always sure exactly what they stand for and usually doesn't think the options offered by either party are all that good.

I first met Grasso a few weeks before the 2010 election when she participated in a focus group I held in Denver and she expressed very negative feelings about Congress. "I don't feel a connection between them and real people. I definitely don't think they're relatable," she told me.

Grasso is concerned about the corrupting influence of money in politics and thinks being in Congress is "a purchased job. Who spends a hundred million dollars to get a job that pays a hundred fifty thousand? There's a reason why.

"All they are concerned about is, How do I stay in office? They are worried about protecting themselves and making sure they have a job rather than doing what's right."

Michael Sciulla is a sixty-year-old retired lobbyist who lives in Vienna, Virginia, in the suburbs just outside Washington, D.C. He's married, with two teenage children, and says he has been an Independent all his life. In 1980, he voted for John Anderson, an Independent candidate who was running for president. Usually, when he's trying to decide whom to vote for, Sciulla feels like he is forced to pick "the lesser of two evils."

"Economically I should be voting Republican, but I can't seem to do it because of their social agenda and their hypocrisy about the budget deficit and all of the spending they did for all of those years."

As a lobbyist, Sciulla ran a political action committee (PAC) and says, "I gave out thousands of dollars in campaign contributions and I became so disgusted with the system, I threw up my hands and got out." Sciulla says he thinks both parties are more interested in getting and holding on to power than in working on real solutions, and the cost of campaigns and the fund-raising politicians have to do to finance them are some of the biggest problems with the system.

Even though a lot of his friends and neighbors make their living working for or with the government, Sciulla says most of them, no matter their political philosophy, believe government spending and waste, fraud, and abuse are huge problems.

Sciulla says he thinks most people voted for Barack Obama because they wanted hope and change and "We haven't had much of either and that is so disappointing.

"Politics is an emotional sport as well as an intellectual endeavor. There's a keg of dynamite under a lot of people, and it can be set off if provided the right match." . . .

These are the Independent/Swing voters.

They are not reliably conservative or liberal. Many of them never registered with a party and have been Independent voters their entire lives. Others are former Republicans and Democrats who became disaffected with the parties because of social or economic policies. Many Independents say they have been driven from the two parties by their extremism and a failure to focus on the nation's most important issues. Independent voters think the parties care more about winning elections than about solving the nation's problems, and they have largely lost faith in the two-party system. Nearly two-thirds of these voters say they believe both parties care more about special interests than about average Americans.

These voters swing back and forth, supporting candidates from both parties, often in the same election. They live all over the country but are most important and sought after when they reside in swing states that also move back and forth from the Democratic to Republican column—especially the battleground states of New Hampshire, Colorado, Ohio, Virginia, Florida, and Pennsylvania. In closely contested elections, their votes usually determine the winner. The 2000 presidential contest was famously one of the closest elections in U.S. history with Al Gore winning the popular vote and, after a partial recount in Florida, George W. Bush winning the electoral vote and the state of Florida by fewer than one thousand votes. In 2008, Barack Obama carried North Carolina by only fourteen thousand votes and Virginia by a little more than five thousand votes. In congressional and local elections, the margin of victory can be as low as triple and even double digits in tight races in swing districts.

The number of Independent voters, along with their disaffection with the two-party political system, is growing exponentially. About 40 percent of all American voters now call themselves Independents, which is a bigger group than those who say they are either Democrats or Republicans and is the largest number of Independent voters in seventy years. In some states, Independents are a majority of the voters.

Polling by various organizations from Gallup to Pew verifies the significance and growth of the Independent voters. The American National Election Studies at the University of Michigan has been charting voting behavior and party identification in this country since 1952. Back then, about 25 percent of those polled identified themselves as Independent or Independent leaning. In 2008, the figure was up to 40 percent. The Pew Research Center in its most recent surveys also puts the number of Independents at around 40 percent.

Among these Independent voters, about half say they have not thought of themselves either a Democrat or Republican in the last five years. I believe this figure comes close to the true number of Independent/Swing voters in this country—about 20 percent of the electorate. And the role of this 20 percent of swing voters, especially in recent presidential elections, has been critical. Every election since World War II has been determined by voters in the middle. They are the voters who cast their ballots on issues and in favor of the candidate rather than for the party; and it is these voters who determine who will be president and which party will control Congress. . . .

The crucial Independent voters that I am describing here are ideologically "middle of the road" or centrist, and their views reflect the feelings of more Americans on national issues than either liberals or conservatives. They tend to be fiscally conservative, more skeptical about government, and more concerned about deficits, which is more in line with Republican Party positions. But they do believe some government programs are important and agree more with the positions of the Democratic Party on issues like abortion and gay rights. They want the government to stay out of their personal lives and they want Congress and the president to spend their tax dollars wisely and conduct foreign policy and defense in a way that will protect American interests and keep the country safe.

In several Pew Research Center polls over the past few years, more Independents say the Republican Party comes closer to their views on foreign policy, national security, and economic issues. But they say the Democratic Party is closer to their views on social issues.

In this regard, more than twice as many Independent voters than Republican voters favor allowing gays and lesbians to marry legally (45% vs. 20%).

As a group, independents remain difficult to pin down. They are clearly left-of-center when it comes to religiosity and issues of moral values—independents' views on homosexuality, gender roles, censorship and the role of religion in politics are clearly closer to those of Democrats than Republicans. At the same time, their views on broader economic issues have taken a turn to the right. In particular, they are now more conservative on questions relating to the role of government in providing a social safety net and the government's overall effectiveness and scope.

They are concerned about the federal deficit, government spending, and the American economy. They are extremely angry with Congress, frustrated with the way things are going in Washington, and mistrustful of a Democratic expansion of government. . . .

But even as the number of voters who consider themselves at the ideological center of American political opinion continues to grow, the number of moderates in both parties in Congress, the ones needed to achieve compromise, shrinks with every passing election, and the political parties become ever more extreme.

Political scientist Morris Fiorina of Stanford has written about this in several books—*Culture War? The Myth of a Polarized America* and *Disconnect: The Breakdown of Representation in American Politics.* "There is little doubt that the political class in the United States is significantly more polarized today than it was a generation ago. But a close examination of the general population finds little or no sign of a comparable increase in polarization," writes Fiorina. "In both red and blue states a solid majority of voters see themselves as positioned between two relatively extreme parties."

Most Americans are in the center and actually agree on a great deal. We're not so deeply divided a nation as either the two parties or the political pundits would have us believe. They just need to listen to the Independent voters. These voters at the ideological center of national political thought represent the way forward for the political parties and a new way of thinking and trying to solve problems. These voters want compromise and common sense, and they want Republicans and Democrats to work together on centrist solutions to the most difficult issues we face as a nation. Only by listening to these voters and reforming the political process can we revitalize our politics and our country.

PART THIRTEEN

Political Economy and Public Welfare

73

MICHAEL HARRINGTON

From *The Other America*

Poverty in the United States is not new, but it took social critic Michael Harrington's acclaimed book, published in 1962, to bring the reality of "the other America" in the midst of the "affluent society" to the nation's attention. Harrington's study of the middle class's withdrawal from the problems of poor city-dwellers marked the philosophical start of the "war on poverty," which was to begin later in the 1960s. Harrington explored the situation of people who were poor within a society of plenty. His characterization of the poor as "socially invisible" and "politically invisible" led to wide public recognition of the problem of poverty in America. President Lyndon B. Johnson's "war on poverty" legislation has faded, but the "invisible" poor do, from time to time, reappear, never more poignantly than in the film footage of New Orleans's residents, many of them poor, calling out for help from the Superdome, from the Convention Center, and from city rooftops day after day while waiting in vain for a response from the Federal Emergency Management Agency (FEMA) following the disastrous 2005 Hurricane Katrina.

━━━━

THERE IS A FAMILIAR AMERICA. It is celebrated in speeches and advertised on television and in the magazines. It has the highest mass standard of living the world has ever known.

In the 1950s this America worried about itself, yet even its anxieties were products of abundance. The title of a brilliant book was widely misinterpreted, and the familiar America began to call itself "the affluent society." There was introspection about Madison Avenue and tail fins*; there was discussion of the emotional suffering taking place in the suburbs. In all this, there was an implicit assumption that the basic grinding economic problems had been solved in the United States. In this theory the nation's problems were no longer a matter of basic human needs, of food, shelter, and clothing. Now they were seen as qualitative, a question of learning to live decently amid luxury.

While this discussion was carried on, there existed another America.

---

*Madison Avenue, in New York City, is the traditional home of the advertising industry. It is there that plans have been hatched for selling Americans products that they may not yet really know they want—like, in the 1950s, cars with tail fins.—EDS.

In it dwelt somewhere between 40,000,000 and 50,000,000 citizens of this land. They were poor. They still are.

To be sure, the other America is not impoverished in the same sense as those poor nations where millions cling to hunger as a defense against starvation. This country has escaped such extremes. That does not change the fact that tens of millions of Americans are, at this very moment, maimed in body and spirit, existing at levels beneath those necessary for human decency. If these people are not starving, they are hungry, and sometimes fat with hunger, for that is what cheap foods do. They are without adequate housing and education and medical care.

The Government has documented what this means to the bodies of the poor, and the figures will be cited throughout this book. But even more basic, this poverty twists and deforms the spirit. The American poor are pessimistic and defeated, and they are victimized by mental suffering to a degree unknown in Suburbia.

This book is a description of the world in which these people live; it is about the other America. Here are the unskilled workers, the migrant farm workers, the aged, the minorities, and all the others who live in the economic underworld of American life....

The millions who are poor in the United States tend to become increasingly invisible. Here is a great mass of people, yet it takes an effort of the intellect and will even to see them....

...The other America, the America of poverty, is hidden today in a way that it never was before. Its millions are socially invisible to the rest of us. No wonder that so many misinterpreted [economist John Kenneth] Galbraith's title and assumed that "the affluent society" meant that everyone had a decent standard of life. The misinterpretation was true as far as the actual day-to-day lives of two-thirds of the nation were concerned. Thus, one must begin a description of the other America by understanding why we do not see it.

There are perennial reasons that make the other America an invisible land.

Poverty is often off the beaten track. It always has been....

...The American city has been transformed. The poor still inhabit the miserable housing in the central area, but they are increasingly isolated from contact with, or sight of, anybody else. Middle-class women coming in from Suburbia on a rare trip may catch the merest glimpse of the other America on the way to an evening at the theater, but their children are segregated in suburban schools. The business or professional man may drive along the fringes of slums in a car or bus, but it is not an important experience to him. The failures, the unskilled, the disabled, the aged, and the minorities are right there, across the tracks, where they have always been. But hardly anyone else is.

In short, the very development of the American city has removed poverty from the living, emotional experience of millions upon millions of middle-class Americans. Living out in the suburbs, it is easy to assume that ours is, indeed, an affluent society.

This new segregation of poverty is compounded by a well-meaning ignorance. A good many concerned and sympathetic Americans are aware that there is much discussion of urban renewal. Suddenly, driving through the city, they notice that a familiar slum has been torn down and that there are towering, modern buildings where once there had been tenements or hovels. There is a warm feeling of satisfaction, of pride in the way things are working out: the poor, it is obvious, are being taken care of. . . .

And finally, the poor are politically invisible. It is one of the cruelest ironies of social life in advanced countries that the dispossessed at the bottom of society are unable to speak for themselves. The people of the other America do not, by far and large, belong to unions, to fraternal organizations, or to political parties. They are without lobbies of their own; they put forward no legislative program. As a group, they are atomized. They have no face; they have no voice.

Thus, there is not even a cynical political motive for caring about the poor, as in the old days. Because the slums are no longer centers of powerful political organizations, the politicians need not really care about their inhabitants. The slums are no longer visible to the middle class, so much of the idealistic urge to fight for those who need help is gone. Only the social agencies have a really direct involvement with the other America, and they are without any great political power. . . .

Indeed, the paradox that the welfare state benefits those least who need help most is but a single instance of a persistent irony in the other America. Even when the money finally trickles down, even when a school is built in a poor neighborhood, for instance, the poor are still deprived. Their entire environment, their life, their values, do not prepare them to take advantage of the new opportunity. The parents are anxious for the children to go to work; the pupils are pent up, waiting for the moment when their education has complied with the law.

Today's poor, in short, missed the political and social gains of the thirties. They are, as Galbraith rightly points out, the first minority poor in history, the first poor not to be seen, the first poor whom the politicians could leave alone. . . .

What shall we tell the American poor, once we have seen them? Shall we say to them that they are better off than the Indian poor, the Italian poor, the Russian poor? That is one answer, but it is heartless. I should put it another way. I want to tell every well-fed and optimistic American that it is intolerable that so many millions should be maimed in body and in spirit when it is not necessary that they should be. My standard of comparison is not how much worse things used to be. It is how much better they could be if only we were stirred. . . .

First and foremost, any attempt to abolish poverty in the United States must seek to destroy the pessimism and fatalism that flourish in the other America. In part, this can be done by offering real opportunities to these people, by changing the social reality that gives rise to their sense of hopelessness. But beyond that (these fears of the poor have a life of their own and are not simply rooted in analyses of employment chances), there should be a spirit, an élan, that communicates itself to the entire society.

If the nation comes into the other America grudgingly, with the mentality of an administrator, and says, "All right, we'll help you people," then there will be gains, but they will be kept to the minimum; a dollar spent will return a dollar. But if there is an attitude that society is gaining by eradicating poverty, if there is a positive attempt to bring these millions of the poor to the point where they can make their contribution to the United States, that will make a huge difference. The spirit of a campaign against poverty does not cost a single cent. It is a matter of vision, of sensitivity. . . .

Second, this book is based upon the proposition that poverty forms a culture, an interdependent system. In case after case, it has been documented that one cannot deal with the various components of poverty in isolation, changing this or that condition but leaving the basic structure intact. Consequently, a campaign against the misery of the poor should be comprehensive. It should think, not in terms of this or that aspect of poverty, but along the lines of establishing new communities, of substituting a human environment for the inhuman one that now exists. . . .

There is only one institution in the society capable of acting to abolish poverty. That is the Federal Government. In saying this, I do not rejoice, for centralization can lead to an impersonal and bureaucratic program, one that will be lacking in the very human quality so essential in an approach to the poor. In saying this, I am only recording the facts of political and social life in the United States. . . .

[However] it is not necessary to advocate complete central control of such a campaign. Far from it. Washington is essential in a double sense: as a source of the considerable funds needed to mount a campaign against the other America, and as a place for coordination, for planning, and the establishment of national standards. The actual implementation of a program to abolish poverty can be carried out through myriad institutions, and the closer they are to the specific local area, the better the results. There are, as has been pointed out already, housing administrators, welfare workers, and city planners with dedication and vision. They are working on the local level, and their main frustration is the lack of funds. They could be trusted actually to carry through on a national program. What they lack now is money and the support of the American people....

There is no point in attempting to blueprint or detail the mechanisms and institutions of a war on poverty in the United States. There is information enough for action. All that is lacking is political will....

These, then, are the strangest poor in the history of mankind.

They exist within the most powerful and rich society the world has ever known. Their misery has continued while the majority of the nation talked of itself as being "affluent" and worried about neuroses in the suburbs. In this way tens of millions of human beings became invisible. They dropped out of sight and out of mind; they were without their own political voice.

Yet this need not be. The means are at hand to fulfill the age-old dream: poverty can now be abolished. How long shall we ignore this underdeveloped nation in our midst? How long shall we look the other way while our fellow human beings suffer? How long?

74

JOSEPH STIGLITZ

From *The Price of Inequality*

The price of economic inequality has been and will be felt in the political arena, economist Joseph Stiglitz opines. He applies his analysis both to nations abroad, especially Egypt, Spain, and Greece, and within the U.S. At home, the 2011 Occupy Wall Street demonstrations garnered much attention, largely as a result of the recession's impact on low socioeconomic status [SES] Americans. Stiglitz indicts the American free market system: the big banks, the lack of legal repercussions after the 2008 collapse, and the overall inequality of wealth that pits the "99%" against the "1%." Underneath the economic inequality, Stiglitz writes, lies political inequality. Things are the way they are because the few who are wealthy dominate the political system. Stiglitz enthusiastically urges on the 99%, here and abroad. Agree or disagree, the author has hit upon a theme that figures powerfully in contemporary American elections.

THERE ARE MOMENTS in history when people all over the world seem to rise up, to say that *something is wrong*, to ask for change. This is what happened in the tumultuous years 1848 and 1968. Each of these years of upheaval marked the beginning of a new era. The year 2011 may prove to be another such moment.

A youth uprising that began in Tunisia, a little country on the coast of North Africa, spread to nearby Egypt, then to other countries of the Middle East. In some cases, the spark of protest seemed at least temporarily doused. In others, though, small protests precipitated cataclysmic societal change, taking down long-established dictators such as Egypt's Hosni Mubarak and Libya's Muammar Qaddafi. Soon the people of Spain and Greece, the United Kingdom, and the United States, and other countries around the world, had their own reasons to be in the streets.

Throughout 2011, I gladly accepted invitations to Egypt, Spain, and Tunisia and met with protesters in Madrid's Buen Retiro Park, at Zuccotti Park in New York, and in Cairo, where I spoke with young men and women who had been at Tahrir Square.

As we talked, it was clear to me that while specific grievances varied from country to country and, in particular, that the political grievances in the Middle East were very different from those in the West, there were some shared themes. There was a common understanding that in many ways the economic and political system had failed and that both were fundamentally unfair.

The protesters were right that something was wrong. The gap between what our economic and political systems are supposed to do—what we were told they did do—and what they actually do became too large to be ignored. Governments around the world were not addressing key economic problems, including that of persistent unemployment; and as universal values of fairness became sacrificed to the greed of a few, in spite of rhetoric to the contrary, the feeling of unfairness became a feeling of betrayal.

That the young would rise up against the dictatorships of Tunisia and Egypt was understandable. The youth were tired of aging, sclerotic leaders who protected their own interests at the expense of the rest of society. They had no opportunities to call for change through democratic processes. But electoral politics had also failed in Western democracies. U.S. president Barack Obama had promised "change you can believe in," but he subsequently delivered economic policies that, to many Americans, seemed like more of the same.

And yet in the United States and elsewhere, there were signs of hope in these youthful protesters, joined by their parents, grandparents, and teachers. They were not revolutionaries or anarchists. They were not trying to overthrow the system. They still believed that the electoral process *might* work, if only governments remembered that they are accountable to the people. The protesters took to the streets in order to push the system to change.

The name chosen by the young Spanish protesters in their movement that began on May 15 was "los indignados," the indignant or outraged. They were outraged that so many would suffer so much—exemplified by a youth unemployment rate in excess of 40 percent since the beginning of the crisis in 2008—as a result of the misdeeds of those in the financial sector. In the United States the "Occupy Wall Street" movement echoed the same refrain. The unfairness of a situation in which so many lost their homes and their jobs while the bankers enjoyed large bonuses was grating.

But the U.S. protests soon went beyond a focus on Wall Street to the broader inequities in American society. Their slogan became "the 99 percent." The protesters who took this slogan echoed the title of an article I wrote for the magazine *Vanity Fair*, "Of the 1%, for the 1%, by the 1%," which described the enormous increase in inequality in the United States and a political system that seemed to give disproportionate voice to those at the top.

Three themes resonated around the world: that markets weren't working the way they were supposed to, for they were obviously neither efficient nor stable; that the political system hadn't corrected the market failures; and that the economic and political systems are fundamentally unfair. While this book focuses on the excessive inequality that marks the United States and some other advanced industrial countries today it explains how the three themes are intimately interlinked: the inequality is cause and consequence of the failure of the political system, and it contributes to the instability of our economic system, which in turn contributes to increased inequality—a vicious downward spiral into which we have descended, and from which we can emerge only through concerted policies that I describe below.

Before centering our attention on inequality, I want to set the scene, by describing the broader failures of our economic system.

The Failure of Markets

Markets have clearly not been working in the way that their boosters claim. Markets are supposed to be stable, but the global financial crisis showed that they could be very unstable, with devastating consequences. The bankers had taken bets that, without government assistance, would have brought them and the entire economy down. But a closer look at the *system* showed that this was not an accident; the bankers had incentives to behave this way

The virtue of the market is supposed to be its efficiency. But the market obviously is *not* efficient. The most basic law of economics—necessary if the economy is to be efficient—is that demand equals supply. But we have a world in which there are huge unmet needs—investments to bring the poor out of poverty, to promote development in less developed countries in Africa and other continents around the world, to retrofit the global economy to face the challenges of global warming. At the same time, we have vast underutilized resources—workers and machines that are idle or are not producing up to their potential. Unemployment—the inability of the market to generate jobs for so many citizens—is the worst failure of the market, the greatest source of inefficiency, and a major cause of inequality.

As of March 2012, some 24 million Americans who would have liked a full-time job couldn't get one.

In the United States, we are throwing millions out of their homes. We have empty homes and homeless people.

But even before the crisis, the American economy had not been delivering what had been promised: although there was growth in GDP,

most citizens were seeing their standards of living erode. . . . [For] most American families, even before the onset of recession, incomes adjusted for inflation were lower than they had been a decade earlier. America had created a marvelous economic machine, but evidently one that worked only
for those at the top.

So Much at Stake

This book is about why our economic system is failing for most
Americans, why inequality is growing to the extent it is, and what the
consequences are. The underlying thesis is that we are paying a high
price for our inequality—an economic system that is less stable and less
efficient, with less growth, and a democracy that has been put into peril.
But even more is at stake: as our economic system is seen to fail for most
citizens, and as our political system seems to be captured by moneyed interests, confidence in our democracy and in our market economy will
erode along with our global influence. As the reality sinks in that we
are no longer a country of opportunity and that even our long-vaunted
rule of law and system of justice have been compromised, even our sense
of national identity may be put into jeopardy.

In some countries the Occupy Wall Street movement has become
closely allied with the antiglobalization movement. They do have some
things in common: a belief not only that something is wrong but also that
change is possible. The problem, however, is not that globalization is bad
or wrong but that governments are managing it so poorly—largely for the
benefit of special interests. The interconnectedness of peoples, countries,
and economies around the globe is a development that can be used as effectively to promote prosperity as to spread greed and misery. The same
is true for the market economy: the power of markets is enormous, but
they have no inherent moral character. We have to decide how to manage
them. At their best, markets have played a central role in the stunning increases in productivity and standards of living in the past two hundred
years—increases that far exceeded those of the previous two millennia.
But government has also played a major role in these advances, a fact that
free-market advocates typically fail to acknowledge. On the other hand,
markets can also concentrate wealth, pass environmental costs on to society, and abuse workers and consumers. For all these reasons, it is plain that
markets must be tamed and tempered to make sure they work to the
benefit of most citizens. And that has to be done repeatedly, to ensure that
they continue to do so. That happened in the United States in the Progressive Era, when competition laws were passed for the first time. It hap-

pened in the New Deal, when Social Security, employment, and minimum-wage laws were passed. The message of Occupy Wall Street—and of so many other protesters around the world—is that markets once again must be tamed and tempered. The consequences of not doing so are serious: within a meaningful democracy, where the voices of ordinary citizens are heard, we cannot maintain an open and globalized market system, at least not in the form that we know it, if that system year after year makes those citizens worse-off. One or the other will have to give—either our politics or our economics.

Inequality and Unfairness

Markets, by themselves, even when they are stable, often lead to high levels of inequality, outcomes that are widely viewed as unfair. Recent research in economics and psychology . . . has shown the importance that individuals attach to fairness. More than anything else, a sense that the economic and political systems were unfair is what motivates the protests around the world. In Tunisia and Egypt and other parts of the Middle East, it wasn't merely that jobs were hard to come by but that those jobs that were available went to those with connections.

In the United States and Europe, things seemed more fair, but only superficially so. Those who graduated from the best schools with the best grades had a better chance at the good jobs. But the system was stacked because wealthy parents sent their children to the best kindergartens, grade schools, and high schools, and those students had a far better chance of getting into the elite universities.

Americans grasped that the Occupy Wall Street protesters were speaking to *their* values, which was why, while the numbers protesting may have been relatively small, two-thirds of Americans said that they supported the protesters. If there was any doubt of this support, the ability of the protesters to gather 300,000 signatures to keep their protests alive, almost overnight, when Mayor Michael Bloomberg of New York first suggested that he would shut down the camp at Zuccotti Park, near Wall Street, showed otherwise. And support came not just among the poor and the disaffected. While the police may have been excessively rough with protesters in Oakland—and the thirty thousand who joined the protests the day after the downtown encampment was violently disbanded seemed to think so—it was noteworthy that some of the police themselves expressed support for the protesters.

The financial crisis unleashed a new realization that our economic system was not only inefficient and unstable but also fundamentally unfair. Indeed, in the aftermath of the crisis (and the response of the Bush and the Obama administrations), almost half thought so, according to a recent poll. It was rightly perceived to be grossly unfair that many in the financial sector (which, for shorthand, I will often refer to as "the bankers") walked off with outsize bonuses, while those who suffered from the crisis brought on by these bankers went without a job; or that government bailed out the banks, but was reluctant to even extend unemployment insurance for those who, through no fault of their own, could not get employment after searching for months and months; or that government failed to provide anything except token help to the millions who were losing their homes. What happened in the midst of the crisis made clear that it was *not* contribution to society that determined relative pay, but something else: bankers received large rewards, though their contribution to society—and even to their firms—had been *negative*. The wealth given to the elites and to the bankers seemed to arise out of their ability and willingness to take advantage of others.

One aspect of fairness that is deeply ingrained in American values is opportunity. America has always thought of itself as a land of *equal opportunity*. Horatio Alger stories, of individuals who made it from the bottom to the top, are part of American folklore. But . . . increasingly, the American dream that saw the country as a land of opportunity began to seem just that: a dream, a myth reinforced by anecdotes and stories, but not supported by the data. The chances of an American citizen making his way from the bottom to the top are less than those of citizens in other advanced industrial countries.

There is a corresponding myth—rags to riches in three generations—suggesting that those at the top have to work hard to stay there; if they don't, they (or their descendants) quickly move down. But . . . this too is largely a myth, for the children of those at the top will, more likely than not, remain there.

In a way, in America and throughout the world, the youthful protesters took what they heard from their parents and politicians at face value—just as America's youth did fifty years ago during the civil rights movement. Back then they scrutinized the values *equality, fairness,* and *justice* in the context of the nation's treatment of African Americans, and they found the nation's policies wanting. Now they scrutinize the same values in terms of how our economic and judicial system works, and they have found the system wanting for poor and middle-class Americans—not just for minorities but for *most* Americans of all backgrounds.

If President Obama and our court system had found those who brought the economy to the brink of ruin "guilty" of some malfeasance, then perhaps it would have been possible to say that the system was functioning. There was at least some sense of accountability. In fact, however, those who should have been so convicted were often not charged, and when they were charged, they were typically found innocent or at least not convicted. A few in the hedge fund industry have been convicted subsequently of insider trading, but this is a sideshow, almost a distraction. The hedge fund industry did not cause the crisis. It was the banks. And it is the bankers who have gone, almost to a person, free.

If no one is accountable, if no individual can be *blamed* for what has happened, it means that the problem lies in the economic and political system.

From Social Cohesion to Class Warfare

The slogan "we are the 99 percent" may have marked an important turning point in the debate about inequality in the United States. Americans have always shied away from class analysis; America, we liked to believe, is a middle-class country, and that belief helps bind us together. There should be no divisions between the upper and the lower classes, between the bourgeoisie and the workers. But if by a class-based society we mean one in which the prospects of those at the bottom to move up are low, America may have become even more class-based than old Europe, and our divisions have now become even greater than those there. Those in the 99 percent are continuing with the "we're all middle class" tradition, with one slight modification: they recognize that we're actually not all moving up together. The vast majority is suffering together, and the very top—the 1 percent—is living a different life. The "99 percent" marks an attempt to forge a new coalition—a new sense of national identity, based not on the fiction of a universal middle class but on the reality of the economic divides within our economy and our society.

For years there was a deal between the top and the rest of our society that went something like this: we will provide you jobs and prosperity, and you will let us walk away with the bonuses. You all get a share, even if we get a bigger share. But now that tacit agreement between the rich and the rest, which was always fragile, has come apart. Those in the 1 percent are walking off with the riches, but in doing so they have provided nothing but anxiety and insecurity to the 99 percent. The majority of Americans have simply not been benefiting from the country's growth....

Failure of Political System

The political system seems to be failing as much as the economic system. Given the high level of youth unemployment around the world— near 50 percent in Spain and 18 percent in the United States—it was perhaps more surprising that it took so long for the protest movements to begin than that protests eventually broke out. The unemployed, including young people who had studied hard and done everything that they were supposed to do ("played by the rules," as some politicians are wont to say), faced a stark choice: remaining unemployed or accepting a job far below that for which they were qualified. In many cases there was not even a choice: there simply were no jobs, and hadn't been for years.

One interpretation of the long delay in the arrival of mass protests was that, in the aftermath of the crisis, there was hope in democracy, faith that the political system would work, that it would hold accountable those who had brought on the crisis and quickly repair the economic system. But years after the breaking of the bubble, it became clear that our political system had failed, just as it had failed to prevent the crisis, to check the growing inequality, to protect those at the bottom, to prevent the corporate abuses. It was only then that protesters turned to the streets.

Americans, Europeans, and people in other democracies around the world take great pride in their democratic institutions. But the protesters have called into question whether there is a *real* democracy. Real democracy is more than the right to vote once every two or four years. The choices have to be meaningful. The politicians have to listen to the voices of the citizens. But increasingly, and especially in the United States, it seems that the political system is more akin to "one dollar one vote" than to "one person one vote." Rather than correcting the market's failures, the political system was reinforcing them.

Politicians give speeches about what is happening to our values and our society, but then they appoint to high office the CEOs and other corporate officials who were at the helm in the financial sector as the system was failing so badly. We shouldn't have expected the architects of the system that has not been working to rebuild the system to make it work, and especially work for most citizens—and they didn't.

The failures in politics and economics are related, and they reinforce each other. A political system that amplifies the voice of the wealthy provides ample opportunity for laws and regulations—and the administration of them—to be designed in ways that not only fail to protect the ordinary citizens against the wealthy but also further enrich the wealthy at the expense of the rest of society.

This brings me to one of the central theses of this book: while there may be underlying economic forces at play, politics have shaped the market, and shaped it in ways that advantage the top at the expense of the rest. Any economic system has to have rules and regulations; it has to operate within a legal framework. There are many different such frameworks, and each has consequences for distribution as well as growth, efficiency, and stability. The economic elite have pushed for a framework that benefits them at the expense of the rest, but it is an economic system that is neither efficient nor fair. I explain how our inequality gets reflected in every important decision that we make as a nation—from our budget to our monetary policy, even to our system of justice—and show how these decisions themselves help perpetuate and exacerbate this inequality.

Given a political system that is so sensitive to moneyed interests, growing economic inequality leads to a growing imbalance of political power, a vicious nexus between politics and economics. And the two together shape, and are shaped by, societal forces—social mores and institutions—that help reinforce this growing inequality.

What the Protesters Are Asking for, and What They Are Accomplishing

The protesters, perhaps more than most politicians, grasped what was going on. At one level, they are asking for so little: for a chance to use their skills, for the right to decent work at decent pay, for a fairer economy and society, one that treats them with dignity. In Europe and the United States, their requests are not revolutionary, but evolutionary. At another level, though, they are asking for a great deal: for a democracy where people, not dollars, matter; and for a market economy that delivers on what it is supposed to do. The two demands are related: unfettered markets do not work well, as we have seen. For markets to work the way markets are supposed to, there has to be appropriate government regulation. But for that to occur, we have to have a democracy that reflects the general interests—not the special interests or just those at the top.

The protesters have been criticized for not having an agenda, but such criticism misses the point of protest movements. They are an expression of frustration with the political system and even, in those countries where there are elections, with the electoral process. They sound an alarm.

In some ways the protesters have already accomplished a great deal: think tanks, government agencies, and the media have confirmed their allegations, the failures not just of the market system but of the high and *unjustifiable* level of inequality. The expression "we are the 99 percent" has entered into popular consciousness. No one can be sure where the movements will lead. But of this we can be sure: these young protesters have already altered public discourse and the consciousness of ordinary citizens and politicians alike.

75

MILTON FRIEDMAN

From *Free to Choose*

Conservative economists are numerous today. But none can compete for style and consistency of viewpoint with Nobel Prize-winning Economics Professor Milton Friedman. Friedman has been the voice of conservative economics over the past half-century, during times when his ideas received little public acceptance. Free to Choose, written with his wife Rose Friedman, became the basis for an informative, entertaining—and controversial—TV series. Friedman's central theme is "freedom," both in economics and in politics. He advocates that the maximum amount of economic power be left to individual citizens, to make their own choices, with the least possible control placed in the central government's province. Big government is Friedman's target. In the excerpt, Friedman mentions his heroes, classical economists Adam Smith and Friedrich Hayek. The name of Milton Friedman will join that list for future generations of conservatives.

———

THE STORY of the United States is the story of an economic miracle and a political miracle that was made possible by the translation into practice of two sets of ideas—both, by a curious coincidence, formulated in documents published in the same year, 1776.

One set of ideas was embodied in *The Wealth of Nations*, the masterpiece that established the Scotsman Adam Smith as the father of modern economics. It analyzed the way in which a market system could combine the freedom of individuals to pursue their own objectives with the extensive cooperation and collaboration needed in the economic field to produce our food, our clothing, our housing. Adam Smith's key insight was that both parties to an exchange can benefit and that, *so long as cooperation is strictly voluntary*, no exchange will take place unless both parties do benefit. No external force, no coercion, no violation of freedom is necessary to produce cooperation among individuals all of whom can benefit. That is why, as Adam Smith put it, an individual who "intends only his own gain" is "led by an invisible hand to promote an end which was no part of his intention. Nor is it always the worse for the society that it was no part of it. By pursuing his own interest he frequently promotes that of the society more effectually than when he really intends to promote it. I have never known much good done by those who affected to trade for the public good."

The second set of ideas was embodied in the Declaration of Independence, drafted by Thomas Jefferson to express the general sense of his fellow countrymen. It proclaimed a new nation, the first in history established on the principle that every person is entitled to pursue his own values: "We hold these truths to be self-evident, that all men are created equal, that they are endowed by their Creator with certain unalienable Rights; that among these are Life, Liberty, and the pursuit of Happiness." . . .

Economic freedom is an essential requisite for political freedom. By enabling people to cooperate with one another without coercion or central direction, it reduces the area over which political power is exercised. In addition, by dispersing power, the free market provides an offset to whatever concentration of political power may arise. The combination of economic and political *power* in the same hands is a sure recipe for tyranny. . . .

Ironically, the very success of economic and political freedom reduced its appeal to later thinkers. The narrowly limited government of the late nineteenth century possessed little concentrated power that endangered the ordinary man. The other side of that coin was that it possessed little power that would enable good people to do good. And in an imperfect world there were still many evils. Indeed, the very progress of society made the residual evils seem all the more objectionable. As always, people took the favorable developments for granted. They forgot the danger to freedom from a strong government. Instead, they were attracted by the good that a stronger government could achieve—if only government power were in the "right" hands. . . .

These views have dominated developments in the United States during the past half-century. They have led to a growth in government at all levels, as well as to a transfer of power from local government and local control to central government and central control. The government has increasingly undertaken the task of taking from some to give to others in the name of security and equality. . . .

These developments have been produced by good intentions with a major assist from self-interest. [Yet] even the strongest supporters of the welfare and paternal state agree that the results have been disappointing. . . .

The experience of recent years—slowing growth and declining productivity—raises a doubt whether private ingenuity can continue to overcome the deadening effects of government control if we continue to grant ever more power to government, to authorize a "new class" of civil servants to spend ever larger fractions of our income supposedly on our behalf. Sooner or later—and perhaps sooner than many of us expect—an ever bigger government would destroy both the prosperity that we owe to the free market and the human freedom proclaimed so eloquently in the Declaration of Independence.

We have not yet reached the point of no return. We are still free as a people to choose whether we shall continue speeding down the "road to serfdom," as Friedrich Hayek entitled his profound and influential book, or whether we shall set tighter limits on government and rely more heavily on voluntary cooperation among free individuals to achieve our several objectives. Will our golden age come to an end in a relapse into the tyranny and misery that has always been, and remains today, the state of most of mankind? Or shall we have the wisdom, the foresight, and the courage to change our course, to learn from experience, and to benefit from a "rebirth of freedom"? . . . If the cresting of the tide . . . is to be followed by a move toward a freer society and a more limited government rather than toward a totalitarian society, the public must not only recognize the defects of the present situation but also how it has come about and what we can do about it. Why are the results of policies so often the opposite of their ostensible objectives? Why do special interests prevail over the general interest? What devices can we use to stop and reverse the process? . . .

. . . Whenever we visit Washington, D.C., we are impressed all over again with how much power is concentrated in that city. Walk the halls of Congress, and the 435 members of the House plus the 100 senators are hard to find among their 18,000 employees—about 65 for each senator and 27 for each member of the House. In addition, the more than 15,000 registered lobbyists—often accompanied by secretaries, typists, researchers, or representatives of the special interest they represent—walk the same halls seeking to exercise influence.

And this is but the tip of the iceberg. The federal government employs close to 3 million civilians (excluding the uniformed military forces). Over 350,000 are in Washington and the surrounding metropolitan area. Countless others are indirectly employed through government contracts with nominally private organizations, or are employed by labor or business organizations or other special interest groups that maintain their headquarters, or at least an office, in Washington because it is the seat of government. . . .

... Both the fragmentation of power and the conflicting government policies are rooted in the political realities of a democratic system that operates by enacting detailed and specific legislation. Such a system tends to give undue political power to small groups that have highly concentrated interests, to give greater weight to obvious, direct, and immediate effects of government action than to possibly more important but concealed, indirect, and delayed effects, to set in motion a process that sacrifices the general interest to serve special interests, rather than the other way around. There is, as it were, an invisible hand in politics that operates in precisely the opposite direction to Adam Smith's invisible hand. Individuals who intend only to promote the *general interest* are led by the invisible political hand to promote a *special interest* that they had no intention to promote. . . .

The benefit an individual gets from any one program that he has a special interest in may be more than canceled by the costs to him of many programs that affect him lightly. Yet it pays him to favor the one program, and not oppose the others. He can readily recognize that he and the small group with the same special interest can afford to spend enough money and time to make a difference in respect of the one program. Not promoting that program will not prevent the others, which do him harm, from being adopted. To achieve that, he would have to be willing and able to devote as much effort to opposing each of them as he does to favoring his own. That is clearly a losing proposition. . . .

Currently in the United States, anything like effective detailed control of government by the public is limited to villages, towns, smaller cities, and suburban areas—and even there only to those matters not mandated by the state or federal government. In large cities, states, Washington, we have government of the people not by the people but by a largely faceless group of bureaucrats.

No federal legislator could conceivably even read, let alone analyze and study, all the laws on which he must vote. He must depend on his numerous aides and assistants, or outside lobbyists, or fellow legislators, or some other source for most of his decisions on how to vote. The unelected congressional bureaucracy almost surely has far more influence today in shaping the detailed laws that are passed than do our elected representatives.

The situation is even more extreme in the administration of government programs. The vast federal bureaucracy spread through the many government departments and independent agencies is literally out of control of the elected representatives of the public. Elected Presidents and senators and representatives come and go but the civil service remains.

Higher-level bureaucrats are past masters at the art of using red tape to delay and defeat proposals they do not favor; of issuing rules and regulations as "interpretations" of laws that in fact subtly, or sometimes crudely, alter their thrust; of dragging their feet in administering those parts of laws of which they disapprove, while pressing on with those they favor. . . .

Bureaucrats have not usurped power They have not deliberately engaged in any kind of conspiracy to subvert the democratic process. Power has been thrust on them. . . .

The growth of the bureaucracy in size and power affects every detail of the relation between a citizen and his government. . . . Needless to say, those of us who want to halt and reverse the recent trend should oppose additional specific measures to expand further the power and scope of government, urge repeal and reform of existing measures, and try to elect legislators and executives who share that view. But that is not an effective way to reverse the growth of government. It is doomed to failure. Each of us would defend our own special privileges and try to limit government at someone else's expense. We would be fighting a many-headed hydra that would grow new heads faster than we could cut old ones off.*

Our founding fathers have shown us a more promising way to proceed: by package deals, as it were. We should adopt self-denying ordinances that limit the objectives we try to pursue through political channels. We should not consider each case on its merits, but lay down broad rules limiting what government may do. . . .

We need, in our opinion, the equivalent of the First Amendment to limit government power in the economic and social area—an economic Bill of Rights to complement and reinforce the original Bill of Rights. . . .

The proposed amendments would alter the conditions under which legislators—state or federal, as the case may be—operate by limiting the total amount they are authorized to appropriate. The amendments would give the government a limited budget, specified in advance, the way each of us has a limited budget. Much special interest legislation is undesirable, but it is never clearly and unmistakably bad. On the contrary, every measure will be represented as serving a good cause. The problem is that there are an infinite number of good causes. Currently, a legislator is in a weak position to oppose a "good" cause. If he objects that it will raise taxes, he will be labeled a reactionary who is willing to sacrifice human need for base mercenary reasons—after all, this good cause will only require raising

---

*The Hydra was a mythical Greek monster that grew two heads for each one that was chopped off. It was killed by the hero Hercules.—Eds.

taxes by a few cents or dollars per person. The legislator is in a far better position if he can say, "Yes, yours is a good cause, but we have a fixed budget. More money for your cause means less for others. Which of these others should be cut?" The effect would be to require the special interests to compete with one another for a bigger share of a fixed pie, instead of their being able to collude with one another to make the pie bigger at the expense of the taxpayer. . . .

. . . The two ideas of human freedom and economic freedom working together came to their greatest fruition in the United States. Those ideas are still very much with us. We are all of us imbued with them. They are part of the very fabric of our being. But we have been straying from them. We have been forgetting the basic truth that the greatest threat to human freedom is the concentration of power, whether in the hands of government or anyone else. We have persuaded ourselves that it is safe to grant power, provided it is for good purposes.

Fortunately, we are waking up. . . .

Fortunately, also, we are as a people still free to choose which way we should go—whether to continue along the road we have been following to ever bigger government, or to call a halt and change direction.

76

DAVID WESSEL

From *Red Ink*

When David Wessel outlines the size of the national debt, he writes that "... taxpayers in the future will pick up the tab for government spending today." Those taxpayers are mostly you so read this excerpt carefully. Wessel discusses from whom the U.S. government borrows money. He explains the difference between the deficit and the debt. He traces their size, past and present. There are varying views on the impact of deficits and debt, offered by key players in the economic debate. Finally, Wessel introduces us to then-director of the Congressional Budget Office, Doug Elmendorf. Elmendorf sketches out some basic economic realities: the demographics of a graying nation, the limited impact of potential alterations in Social Security, Medicare, and Medicaid, and the effect of theoretical tax increases. Wessel has outlined the scope and depth of America's fiscal problems. There is no final answer available in the excerpt to solve this huge national problem. After a lot of explaining, hand-wringing, and blaming, that answer will be for you to find.

———

EXCEPT FOR FOUR UNUSUAL YEARS at the end of the 1990s and the beginning of the 2000s, the federal government has spent more than it took in every year for the past four decades. It borrows the difference, essentially promising that taxpayers in the future will pick up the tab for government spending today. The U.S. government is by far the world's biggest borrower even though the United States is by far the world's biggest and richest economy, a historical anomaly. By any yardstick, its borrowing in recent years has been huge. Part of this was automatic: when people are out of work, they pay less in taxes, and government spending on unemployment benefits and food stamps goes up because more people qualify. Part of this was deliberate policy: Congress increased spending and cut taxes.

The bottom line is that the U.S. government borrowed $3.6 billion a day in 2011, holidays and weekends included, or about $11,500 for every man, woman, and child in the country. About half of that borrowing *came from overseas*. The net interest tab on the government debt was about $230 billion last year, which exceeded the budgets of the departments of Commerce, Education, Energy, Homeland Security, Interior, Justice, and State, plus the federal courts, *combined*. As deficits persist and interest rates rise from recent very low levels, as they inevitably will, interest payments will claim an increasing slice of the federal budget, crowding out spending on other things. . . .

For all the dire rhetoric about the dangers of debt, all the scares about the United States becoming another (albeit far larger) Greece, big U.S. government deficits have not been an economic problem—at least not yet.

The deficits have been big. Measured against the value of all the goods and services produced in the United States, known as the gross domestic product (GDP), deficits in the Ronald Reagan years peaked at 6 percent. In the past three years, they came in at 10 percent of GDP in 2009 (the fiscal year that spans the end of the George W. Bush presidency and the beginning of Barack Obama's) and at 9 percent and 8.7 percent in the two subsequent years.

Running bigger deficits in a deep recession and sluggish recovery is still Economics 101—even if one can get a good debate going among serious people about how best to do that and how well the medicine works. Running *deficits* means the government has to borrow the difference between income and outgo. The sum of all that borrowing is the government *debt*. Borrowing by government, banks, business, and consumers soared so much during the 2000s that at the end of 2008 the U.S. economy as a whole owed twice as much as it did in 1975, measured against the size of the economy. Since then, private borrowing has come down, but government borrowing has gone up—a lot—in a deliberate effort to cushion the economy from the pain caused when so many lenders pull back and so many borrowers try to pay off loans or walk away from them.

Despite the anxiety about the capacity of a paralyzed political system to grapple with deficits projected for the future—and despite the headline-making move by ratings agency Standard & Poor's to strip the U.S. Treasury of the prized AAA credit rating that signifies the safest risks—savers, investors, and governments around the world still view U.S. Treasury bonds as the most secure place to put their money. For now. The only other big government bond markets—Europe and Japan—are in places that have big problems of their own, which makes the United States the world's tallest midget. What's more, the flood of money from all over the world has pushed down the interest rate that the U.S. Treasury pays to fifty-year lows. But this ability to borrow enormous sums at incredibly low interest rates cannot and will not last forever, even if no one can say exactly when the day of reckoning will arrive.

"A lot of us . . . didn't see this last crisis as it came upon us. This one is really easy to see," says Erskine Bowles, a former investment banker who was Bill Clinton's chief of staff, later cochairman of an Obama-appointed commission on the deficit, and now an unlikely itinerant preacher on the urgency of dealing with the deficit. "The fiscal path we are on today is simply not sustainable. These deficits that we are incurring on an annual basis are like a cancer, and they are truly going to destroy this country from within unless we have the common sense to do something about it.

"We face the most predictable economic crisis in history." . . .

At seventy-four years old, Leon Panetta [President Clinton's Director of the Office of Management and Budget and President Obama's Secretary of Defense] is one of the few American politicians who can give a truly emotional speech about the federal deficit. Maybe that's because he is one of a generation of thrifty Americans who elected politicians unwilling to fund many of the benefits they promised. Or maybe it's because he has spent so much of his adult life in the belly of government—from the House of Representatives to the White House to, now, the top job at the Pentagon. "This country cannot continue to run trillion-dollar deficits and expect that we can remain a powerful nation," Panetta has said, meshing a little old-time deficit religion with his current job. "When you run those size deficits . . . the borrowing we have to do around the world . . . makes us more dependent on those countries that are purchasing our securities. It deprives the country of the resources we need regardless of your priorities. Worst of all, it raises the most regressive tax of all: the tax on our children who have to ultimately pay the interest on that debt." . . .

The 2012 election campaign has produced a lot of talk about taxes, spending, and deficits, much of it less than useful in understanding the choices the country faces. Basically, there are three poles in the debate.

The first says: The deficit is a problem. But not now, especially when there is still so much unemployment. The poster boy: Paul Krugman, a Princeton University economist and *New York Times* columnist.

The second says: The deficit is a problem. And the solution is to shrink the government and cut taxes. The poster boy: Paul Ryan, the Republican congressman from Wisconsin and chairman of the House Budget Committee [and as of 2015, Speaker of the House of Representatives].

The third says: The deficit is a big problem. In fact, it is the "transcendent threat to our economic future." The poster boy: Peter G. Peterson, an octogenarian who is spending a large part of his considerable fortune to warn about the five-alarm fiscal fire ahead. . . .

Inside the White House, the banner for doing more, much more, to help the economy than Obama and Congress did was carried by Christina Romer, the Berkeley economist and chair of the Council of Economic Advisers. The CEA is an unusual cog in the economic-policy-making apparatus. Created by Congress in 1946, the three-member council of economists, usually drawn from academia, controls nothing. Its sole task is to give the president "objective economic advice and analysis." Its influence varies from administration to administration, and its fiscal advice over the years is a history of the evolution of economists' thinking about budgets. . . .

Romer and Ryan, Krugman and Peterson are full-throated advocates with clear and loudly stated views on what the government should and shouldn't do differently. In contrast, Doug Elmendorf, director of the CBO [Congressional Budget Office], is more of a national truth teller, trying to make the public and the politicians understand choices they cannot evade while at the same time not hurting his—and the CBO's—credibility by taking sides. The *Washington Examiner* once dubbed him "a geek with guts." At a time when almost every fact about the federal budget is the subject of fierce debate, Elmendorf's measured voice can be hard to hear, but some people do listen. When he called a press briefing on the agency's annual economic and budget outlook in January 2012, he drew ten television cameras to record his carefully calibrated words.

Slim and bespectacled, Elmendorf could play a college professor on TV. "A quiet man who thinks carefully about everything," the *New York Times* once said of him. Indeed, he deliberately chose a baseball game for one of his first dates with his future wife. "You want to be sure there's something going on to fill the lull in the conversation but not like a movie where you can't talk," he explained.

Elmendorf's academic pedigree is impeccable: Princeton, 1983; Harvard Ph.D., 1989. The advisers for his dissertation—"Fiscal Policy and Financial Markets"—were Martin Feldstein and Greg Mankiw, top economic advisers, respectively, to Reagan and George W. Bush, and Larry Summers, top economic adviser to Clinton and Obama. After five years helping to teach the big introductory economics course at Harvard, Elmendorf came to Washington in the mid-1990s to work at the CBO. "Starting about then," he said, "I thought being CBO director would be a very good job." But first he went to work on the staff of the Federal Reserve Board, with a couple of breaks to work on the staffs of the White House Council of Economic Advisers and the Clinton Treasury. Elmendorf left government in 2007 for the Brookings Institution think tank but came back in 2009 when the congressional leadership—then all Democrats—picked him to run the CBO, succeeding Peter Orszag, who went to the White House to be Obama's budget director.

At congressional hearings, Elmendorf is like the referee in a food fight. With calm dispassionate words and charts, he tries to give his bosses in Congress a reality check. Members of Congress cross-examine Elmendorf as if he were an expert witness in a murder trial, laboring to get him to support the questioner's point of view. (Senator Kent Conrad, a Democrat from North Dakota, at a February 2012 hearing: "Why wouldn't one conclude from what you've said here that the best policy in the short term would be to extend tax cuts, at least some significant part of the tax cuts, and defer some of the spending cuts . . . several years, but right now agree to a plan that will raise revenue and cut spending so that at the end of the 10 years we've dramatically reduced deficits and reduced the growth of debt?")

Elmendorf tries just as hard to be sure Congress understands the daunting dimensions of the deficit and the alternative ways to reduce it while avoiding taking sides in the partisan debate, particularly over taxes. ("I don't want to speak to a specific combination of policies that the Congress might choose to extend or let expire," he told Conrad. "But on your general point, I think agreement about how the country's budget will be put on a sustainable path would be a good thing for the economy in the short run because it would give people some confidence that they knew where policies were headed, which is very hard to have in the current environment.")

Elmendorf, in short, is a good guide to the fiscal landscape. His tour begins with a couple of observations.

One is a demographic fact. "We cannot go back to the tax and spending policies of the past because the number of people sixty-five or older will increase by one-third between 2012 and 2022," Elmendorf says. As more baby boomers cross the threshold for collecting Social Security or being covered by Medicare, spending on those programs will rise. And even hard-core spending cutters willing to talk about paring Social Security or Medicare or raising the eligibility age propose exempting those who have already turned fifty-five.

The other is a political fact that sums up the entire budget dilemma in a single sentence. "The country faces a fundamental disconnect between the services the people expect the government to provide, particularly in the form of benefits for older Americans, and the tax revenues that people are willing to send to the government to finance those services," he has said.

The CBO's traditional role is to take budget plans that the president and members of Congress devise and put numbers on them: what would the course of spending and taxes and deficits be if they were enacted. To that end, it also produces a Chinese menu of deficit-reducing options from which Congress can choose.

But none of that seemed to be penetrating the political debate. So Elmendorf tried a different tack. He started by projecting today's tax and spending policies ten years out, the baseline referred to earlier. That would put the budget deficit in 2022 above $1 trillion and rising. By then, the U.S. government would be borrowing so much that the national debt, as a percentage of the GDP, would be dangerously high (over 90 percent) and still rising.

Then he asked: What would have to happen to avoid that outcome, to bring the spending and revenue lines close enough together so that the national debt would at least stop climbing, as a percentage of GDP? His answer: spending cuts or tax increases or a combination of the two that add up to $750 billion a year by 2022. Even in Washington that's a big number.

What would it take to get to that goal? Remember, the starting point for the exercise is that Congress sticks to the caps it has set on annually appropriated defense and domestic spending. "The country," Elmendorf pointed out, "is [already] on track to substantially reduce the role of most federal activities, relative to the size of the economy." Perhaps Congress will squeeze more out of defense between now and 2022, depending on the state of the world. But it's a good bet that what it saves in defense, it'll end up spending on domestic programs—highways or job training or disaster relief or something.

So say Congress decided to get really serious about the deficit by looking at spending on the big benefit programs that today account for 40 percent of all federal outlays: Social Security and the growing Medicare and Medicaid budgets. Say it raised the age at which the elderly become eligible for Medicare to sixty-seven (from sixty-five) and the age at which they're eligible for full Social Security benefits to seventy (from sixty-seven). Say it shifted to a less generous formula for setting Social Security benefits and adjusting them for inflation. Say it boosted the premiums that the elderly on Medicare pay for their coverage and made them pay more of their health care bills out of pocket. And say it limited increases in federal spending for Medicaid, the joint state-federal health insurance program for the poor, so the tab rose no faster than the pace at which private sector wages rise.

Any one of those would be a very big deal. But if Congress did all that, it would be saving about $250 billion annually by 2022. That's a big number to be sure, but here's the rub: all those measures combined would save only a third of what's needed to reach Elmendorf's budget nirvana goal. If *all* the weight is put on the big entitlement programs—Social Security, Medicare, and Medicaid—they would need to be cut by 25 percent to put the budget on a sustainable course by 2022.

Which is why the conversation inevitably turns to raising taxes alongside cutting spending.

Elmendorf's starting point for the exercise is that all the tax cuts that Bush instigated and Obama continued are extended at the end of the year. Say Congress took Obama's advice and let income tax rates on the over-$250,000-a-year crowd rise to pre-Bush levels. That would bring in between $100 billion and $150 billion in 2020. Say it also eliminated the federal income tax deductions for mortgage interest and state and local taxes, changes that would raise taxes on many more people. That would yield another $180 billion. Both would be huge changes, and they, too, would get Congress only about one-third of the way toward the goal. If Social Security, Medicare, and Medicaid were shielded altogether, then taxes would have to be raised by about one-sixth. That's a big tax increase.

Put all the spending cuts and the tax increases on this shopping list into the deficit-reduction basket, and there still would not be enough money to bring the deficit to sustainable levels by 2022. Elmendorf's list of options is hardly exhaustive: if Congress let *all* the Bush tax cuts expire, raising the taxes of almost everyone who pays income taxes, it would, by CBO estimates, come close to hitting the target. But the point is clear: small changes will *not* suffice.

That's not to say that the nation's fiscal problem is unsolvable. The proliferation of reports by bipartisan commissions illustrates the mix of significant, but manageable, policies that could arrest the rise in the federal debt over the next decade. Most of them raise some taxes by eliminating deductions, credits, loopholes, and exemptions; cut the defense budget; restrain spending on health and other benefits; and spread the pain widely while trying to shield the poorest Americans. Yet the polarization of the American political system has left it, so far, unable to choose between Barack Obama's approach to reducing the deficit or Paul Ryan's. Neither side has enough votes to prevail, and neither is willing to compromise on some amalgam that might spread the pain and that both can live with. This is the crux of the issue: the deficit widens, the debt grows, the interest burden gets heavier, the voices grow even more shrill as the budget burden is passed to future generations, and nothing gets done.

"I used to tell the students that we are either governed by leadership or crisis," Leon Panetta said in a recent interview. "And I always thought that if leadership wasn't there, then ultimately you rely on crisis to drive decisions. In the last few years, my biggest concern is that crisis doesn't seem to drive decisions either. So there goes my theory."

77

MICHELE WUCKER

From *Lockout*

American history is the history of immigrants, but in the early twenty-first century, the debate over immigration is far from settled. Michele Wucker first offers some survey research data on the jobs that immigrants fill in the American economy. She finds that immigrants take both menial and highly technical positions; they could be uneducated laborers or they could be doctors. She finds that Americans' views toward recent immigrants reflect contradictory attitudes. Immigrants make important contributions but are simultaneously looked down on. Wucker then brings us to a New York town that's the scene of a confrontation between the Minutemen Civil Defense Corps, a group that has tried to guard the Mexican border, and pro-immigration demonstrators. A place for day laborer immigrants to gather was the immediate cause of the fray. Flags, digital cameras, banners, and chants all contributed to the tense confrontation, with news reporters finding themselves in the middle of the action. The author profiles one of the Minutemen whom she finds to be willing to exchange ideas in a friendly way. In fact, Wucker and her interviewee agree on a villain: employers who use immigrants' illegal status to cover up labor violations. Today, the issue of immigration remains a divisive one in American society, intertwined as it is with issues of the economy, of race, and of the nation's heritage.

———

DURING HIS TENURE AS FEDERAL RESERVE Board chairman, Alan Greenspan made the case often that the U.S. economy needs immigration of both skilled and unskilled workers. "As we are creating an ever more complex, sophisticated, accelerating economy, the necessity to have the ability to bring in resources and people from abroad to keep it functioning in the most effective manner increasingly strikes me as relevant policy," he testified to the U.S. Senate in 2000. During the 1990s, he frequently praised immigration for keeping inflation in check and thus enabling the Fed to keep interest rates low and in turn create the longest stretch of peacetime prosperity in memory. The low wages that kept inflation tame were, of course, a bane as well as a boon, since immigration of low-skilled workers was thought to hurt the job prospects of America's least educated and lowest-paid workers, and resentment soon grew over society's poorest members having to pay a heavy price for everyone else's prosperity.

There should be no doubt that immigration is a pillar of the U.S. economy as a whole. A 1995 survey polled a group of economists that included Nobel Prize winners, former members of the President's Council of Economic Advisers, and past presidents of the American Economic Association. When asked, "On balance, what effect has twentieth-century immigration had on the nation's economic growth?" an overwhelming 81 percent of respondents answered "favorable," with the remaining 19 percent replying "slightly favorable." Not a single one believed that immigration hurt America's economy.

Many Americans think of immigrants as doing "the jobs that Americans won't do"—the jobs that occupy most of the long-running U.S. argument over whether immigration is too high, too low, or at just about the right level. Certainly, these jobs—farming, construction, services—are so important to the day-to-day functioning of our economy that even Americans who believe that immigration is too high recognize that we depend on low-skilled immigrant workers. Immigrants make up a large percentage of employees in agriculture (37 percent), services (23 percent), and home maintenance work, such as landscaping and housecleaning (42 percent). Overall, however, this work is not representative of the jobs immigrants do.

Few Americans realize how much we depend on the immigrants at the other end of the socioeconomic spectrum: the engineers, scientists, entrepreneurs, and scholars who drive the knowledge economy. Immigrants make up only 20 percent of low-wage workers but represent 50 percent of research and development workers and 25 percent of doctors and nurses. About a quarter of foreign-born workers are managers and professionals; one-fifth are in technical, sales, and administrative support, and another fifth are in service occupations; 18 percent work as operators, fabricators, and laborers. Only 4 percent work in stereotypical fields like farming, forestry, and fishing.

Despite the stereotype of the immigrant as a low-skilled and poorly educated worker, the vast majority of foreign-born workers have completed high school, and 45 percent of foreign workers have attended or completed college—a rate higher than among American workers. To be sure, 30 percent of foreign-born workers here have not completed high school, compared with just 7 percent of those born in this country.

Although they are spread across occupations, immigrants nevertheless are overrepresented among low-skilled workers, underrepresented among those with high school and some college education, and overrepresented among the highest-skilled population. They represent only a small number relative to the total foreign-born population, yet the lowest-skilled immigrants are at the center of a growing controversy over how warm a welcome America should give immigrants. Although Americans are likely to agree that low-skilled immigrants, legal and illegal, make essential contributions to our economy, these immigrants are also the ones who attract the most profound resentment. They represent the other half of America's immigration mythology: the tired, the poor, the huddled masses yearning to breathe free. America's attitudes toward unskilled immigrants have come to define the national immigration debate and shape policies toward all the noncitizens on whom the U.S. economy depends—and thus the fate of the huddled masses will profoundly affect our future ability to attract the best and the brightest as well. . . .

On a clear late-summer day in the town of Babylon, a crowd gathered in front of American Legion Post 94 on an otherwise quiet Long Island street an hour's train ride from New York City. With pale yellow wood siding and white trim, the building could have come straight out of *Leave It to Beaver* had it not been for the graffiti freshly painted on it the night before. Several grim-faced men stood on the front steps, monitoring everyone who approached and letting in select groups, two or three at a time, of people whose main distinguishing feature was that they were so nondescript: the kind of typical white Americans you might see at the supermarket or the hardware store. They were members of the Minutemen Civil Defense Corps, the group that organized a month-long volunteer patrol of the U.S.-Mexico border in April 2005, and they had called this September meeting on Long Island to organize a similar vigil along the U.S.-Canada border in October 2005. The Minutemen had attracted attention not only for their border patrol efforts, but also for the white-supremacist groups that had embraced their work. The Minutemen tried to portray themselves as law-abiding concerned citizens, but it was hard to live down America's sad history of crimes committed when individuals have taken the law into their own hands. Nor did widely circulated photographs of Nazi flags being waved at a Minutemen rally help their cause. President George W. Bush and Secretary of State Condoleezza Rice had called the Minutemen vigilantes, a term that still rankled members of the group.

Long Island was far from the Canadian and Mexican borders, but it was nonetheless a major battleground in an intensifying war over illegal immigration. A few weeks earlier, Suffolk County Executive Steve Levy had ordered the expulsion of immigrants living in an overcrowded house, responding to residents' understandable complaints over building code violations but leaving the residents with no place at all to live. The new controversy stirred up emotions that were still raw from a fight that took

place after a brutal attack in 2000 on Mexican day laborers in Farmingville, a once bucolic town of 15,000. The attack, portrayed movingly in
the documentary film *Farmingville,* polarized residents, some of whom saw
illegal immigration as the main problem and deportation as the only solution, and others who felt that the blame fell on unscrupulous employers
and landlords. Residents fought tooth and nail over a proposal to provide
a central place where day laborers could seek work instead of congregating on streets and curbs. National pro- and anti-immigration groups had
adopted Farmingville as a cause, drawing the town into a high-stakes
struggle that was a proxy for national issues.

Eventually the Minutemen joined the fray. Not surprisingly, many of
the Long Islanders who had opposed the day laborer center were among
the forty or so people who showed up that September afternoon. The
Minutemen stationed on the American Legion hall steps warily eyed a
growing delegation of protesters on the sidewalk. Both sides were armed
with digital cameras and video recorders, photographing each other. As
the protesters marched back and forth on the sidewalk, a man who sym-
pathized with the Minutemen stood in their midst, audio-recording the
whole thing.

The protesters were a hodgepodge: families of liberal Jewish New
Yorkers; serious-faced Mexican and Central American men and women;
greasy-haired teenagers dressed in black with pierced noses and eyebrows;
and white middle-class Long Islanders. Holding a saucepan and a wooden
spoon, a frightened-looking boy who was about six years old walked beside his mother, caught between the shouting protesters and Minutemen.
A poster reading "Stop the Hate," clearly a veteran of many marches, waved
above the protesters' heads next to an anarchist flag and several prints of a
Native American chief declaring "Deport Illegal Immigrants"—clearly
suggesting that the immigrants whose presence the Minutemen were
protesting had as much right to be here as the white Minutemen who
held their own "Deport Illegal Immigrants" signs. "No Human Being Is
Illegal!" read another placard.

"Are you Native American?" one of the protesters screamed. "If you're
not, then you're an immigrant too. We're all immigrants." A wiry Minuteman with sun-leathered skin and a nervous, angry energy screamed back
at them, "Illegal means illegal! Do you know what the word illegal means?"
The protesters tried out various chants against Nazis, fascists, racists, and
homophobes. "Racists Go Home!" they yelled. A heavyset middle-aged
woman sitting on the steps hollered back, "I *am* home!" Both sides mirrored the increasingly polarized tone of a national debate. To the protesters, the Minutemen were Nazis, vigilantes, fascists, racists. Too many of the

Minutemen, for their part, had taken the stance that anyone who wasn't
with them was against them: if you didn't agree with their methods, then
you were against protecting America.

At the foot of the steps of the American Legion hall, an argument
broke out as several newspaper reporters—many of them from Hispanic
media—protested loudly that they were not being allowed in to what had
been billed as a public meeting. Reporters from two local television stations were allowed in, but no one else from the media (except for a Long
Island newspaper reporter who pretended not to be one). Later, when a
television reporter from Univision tried to get in, she was refused. "It's too
bad my wife isn't here," said the gatekeeper. "She's from Venezuela and
she's very upset by illegal immigration." The reporter stiffened at his con-
descension. "Sir, I was born in Puerto Rico and you should know that I
am an American citizen," she said. The gatekeeper told her he'd send
someone out to be interviewed, but after the reporter descended the steps,
he made no move to do so. If the Minutemen hoped to control damage
to their image by barring reporters from their meeting, they had succeeded in doing exactly the opposite through their unsubtle choices of
which media representatives to let in and through the question they left
in everyone's mind: If they were indeed the law-abiding citizens they
claimed to be, what did they have to hide?

During the course of the afternoon, it became clear that there was no
such thing as a typical Minuteman. There was, of course, Chris Simcox,
the group's thin, tense-lipped founder, wound up with nervous energy,
who had moved to Arizona from California and bought a local newspaper, which he used as a mouthpiece for his campaign. There were the
angry men dressed in varying combinations of red, white, and blue. There
were the Farmingville residents who complained about overcrowded
homes, public urination, the illegal status of day laborers, and the government's failure to do anything about illegal immigration.

A Minuteman in a cowboy hat and boots was a Pennsylvania native
who had made Arizona his home for more than a decade and become fed
up with rising petty crime and the complaints of ranchers whose land the
migrants were crossing indiscriminately. As I asked questions to try to
understand where he was coming from—and he asked questions of his
own to try to get a sense of how I might portray him—I was pleasantly
surprised that he seemed open to information that contradicted his assumptions. When I told him about a recent study suggesting that there
were many times more people who wanted to learn English in New York
than there were classroom spaces for, he said he was glad to hear that. We
disagreed, of course, on how to address the problem of illegal immigra-

tion. He was confident that it was possible to secure the Mexican bor-der—after all, the Minutemen had succeeded in closing down part of it in April, he said. But, I pointed out, that was only twenty miles. To secure more than 2,000 miles would require more than 50,000 people, not just for one month but for a very long time. And that wouldn't solve the problem of making sure that the American economy had the workers it needed.

We agreed to disagree on the border issue, but he agreed wholeheart-edly when I said I thought a big problem was the unscrupulous employers who used immigrants' illegal status to abuse them—some employers even call immigration authorities on themselves to clear out workers who complained about violations of labor and safety laws. It was that type of employer that dragged down wages and made American workers far less attractive than illegal immigrants to employers. Why hire someone at higher wages who was not afraid of being deported if he stood up for his rights? By making it impossible for honest businesses to find legal immi-grant workers, and by not imposing any meaningful financial or other kinds of penalties on abusive employers, our lawmakers had been making the problem worse.

The Minuteman in the cowboy hat nodded. "I feel for them. I really do," he said. "The illegal immigrants are caught in the middle, and so are the American people." Our conversation was interrupted as the group on the sidewalk degenerated into a series of catch-all slogans. As they in-veighed against President Bush and the war in Iraq, the Minuteman shook his head. "You know, I actually agree with those protesters on a lot of things." . . .

We Americans view ourselves as the most tolerant nation in the world, able to create *e pluribus unum,* one out of many. "The nature of this coun-try is one that is good-hearted and our people are compassionate," Presi-dent Bush declared in 2004 after he relaunched a plan to give guest work-er status to undocumented immigrants who have been working hard in American jobs. Most of us would agree. We cannot separate our identity and our future from the question of whom to welcome to America and how to welcome them. The fear is that losing control of who is American means losing control of America. But our demographics are only part of our destiny. What has made America great has been our ability to shape that destiny as one nation made of many peoples.

When I told a friend who heads research at a respected New York think tank that I was writing about the growing pressures to close the doors to immigrants, he raised an eyebrow. But America is one of the most open countries in the world, he said, noting the president's guest worker proposal, the size of the foreign-born population, and our open society.

He is right. After all, roughly a million immigrants come here each year, more by far than to any other country in the world; America hosts one out of five immigrants worldwide. One in eight people in this country were born elsewhere, the highest level in a century. About half a million newcomers take the Oath of Citizenship each year to become naturalized Americans. The stars of the 2004 Democratic and Republican national conventions both came with stories of the immigrant's American Dream: Arnold Schwarzenegger, the Austrian immigrant turned movie star and California governor, and Barack Obama, the son of an American mother and a Kenyan father who had emigrated to America. We like to be inspired by our apparent openness to immigrants. We are even talking about amending the Constitution to allow a foreign-born president—inspired, of course, by the ultimate American Dream success story of an Austrian bodybuilder who became a movie superstar, married into American political royalty, and won a landslide election to become governor of California.

"In my book, anyone who comes here and gives an honest day's work for an honest day's pay is not only putting himself closer to the American Dream, he's helping the rest of us get there too," the Australian-born media mogul, Rupert Murdoch, wrote in the *Wall Street Journal*. "Frankly it doesn't bother me in the least that millions of people are attracted to our shores. What we should worry about is the day they no longer find these shores attractive. In an era when too many of our pundits declare that the American Dream is a fraud, it is America's immigrants who remind us—by dint of their success—that the Dream is alive, and well within reach of anyone willing to work for it." . . .

America is at a tipping point in our attitudes not only toward immigration but toward our country's role in the world. Today's mix of global interdependence with the threat of global terrorism and economic and demographic change has created a maelstrom of fears. Encompassing concerns about our borders, our cultural and national identity, and our ability to maintain unity, immigrants represent all of the touch-points of our collective insecurity. Any change that comes too rapidly creates anxiety in even the most tolerant of societies. The contradictory and uniquely American tendency to both demonize and romanticize the immigrant has only confused matters. Politicians and interest groups cynically invoke both emotions, sending the country swinging wildly from one pole to the other and making it all the harder to see through the fog of rhetoric.

The terrorist attacks of September 11, carried out by foreigners who

had come here under various immigrant and nonimmigrant visa categories (some of which had lapsed, making their continued presence illegal),
merely catalyzed an immigration debate that had already been building
for many years. With roughly a million immigrants arriving in the United
States each year through the 1980s and 1990s, the foreign-born population was approaching 12 percent of the U.S. population, the highest
proportion in a century. The sheer mass of people had long since overwhelmed our immigration bureaucracy, and as a result more and more
immigrants—about one in three, by some estimates—have been coming
here illegally. Many of the new immigrants, legal and illegal, come from
Latin America and Asia and are not white, which adds a racial element to
the massive demographic change taking place.

The ending in the 1950s and 1960s of race-based immigration bars,
combined with growing diversity and racial acceptance, opened many
doors for immigrants who did not happen to be born white. This change
speaks worlds of Americans' ability to find common ground in differences,
yet it also exposes the lingering prejudices that we have not yet overcome.
Recessions and the loss of manufacturing jobs in recent decades have
made Americans feel that their economic future is insecure even as they
noticed that immigrants who looked different no longer occupy mainly
the stereotypical jobs at the bottom of the ladder, the work that "Americans didn't want to do," but instead are solidly embedded in the American
middle class. The racial and ethnic differences represented by recent immigration catalyze the volatility of the country's reaction to them.

78

STEVEN COHEN

From *Understanding Environmental Policy*

The subject of the environment does not belong to any one set of experts, author Steven Cohen explains. That's part of the problem. Political scientists, economists, scientists, and business owners each have a unique but incomplete perspective. Cohen offers a simple but not simplistic way to approach environmental issues. While citizens often view the environment in very large and extremely complex terms—cap-and-trade legislation, multination anti-pollution pledges, global warming and melting ice caps—Cohen observes that environmental issues also exist in much smaller, more local, less dramatic yet still highly complicated ways, such as New York City's solid waste disposal: that is, garbage. The author gives us the basics on the city's waste disposal history, strategies, and upcoming crises. Many elements in this case study are applicable to other environmental problems in other places. NIMBY (Not In My Backyard) is a controversy that surfaces in almost every environmental debate in each city and town in America. Cohen provides a detailed analysis of the New York City garbage problem, with special emphasis on the role of new technologies—both good and bad—in the decision-making process. Cohen concludes by noting that New York City is not the only city with solid waste disposal problems. Some solutions may come from other U.S. cities that have tried innovative ideas.

ENVIRONMENTAL POLICY IS A COMPLEX and multidimensional issue. As Harold Seidman observed in *Politics, Position, and Power: The Dynamics of Federal Organization,* "Where you stand depends on where you sit." Put another way, one's position in an organization influences one's stance and perspective on the issues encountered. Similarly, one's take on an environmental issue or the overall issue of environmental protection varies according to one's place in society and the nature of one's professional training.

For example, to a business manager, the environmental issue is a set of rules one needs to understand in order to stay out of trouble. For the most part, environmental policy is a nuisance or at least an impediment to profit. Perhaps someday business managers will see it as a set of conditions that facilitate rather than impede the accumulation of wealth. For now, most business practitioners see a conflict between environmental protection and economic development, although this view of a trade-off is false. To an engineer, the environmental problem is essentially physical and subject to solution through the application of technology. Engineers tend to focus on pollution control, pollution prevention (through changes in manufacturing processes or end-of-pipeline controls), and other technological fixes. Lawyers view the environment as an issue of property rights and contracts, and the regulations needed to protect them. Economists perceive the environment as a set of market failures resulting from problems of consumption or production. They search for market-driven alternatives to regulation. Political scientists view environmental policy as a political concern. To them, it is a problem generated by conflicting interests. Finally, for philosophers, the environment is an issue of values and differing worldviews.

The environment is subject to explanation and understanding through all these disciplines and approaches. It is, in fact, a composite of the elements identified by the various disciplines and societal positions, and likely has dimensions where the disciplines and social perspectives intersect. The difficulty is that each view tends to oversimplify environmental problems, contending with only one facet of the situation. . . .

For purposes of this analysis, an environmental problem is conceptualized as follows:

- *An issue of values.* What type of ecosphere do we wish to live in, and how does our lifestyle impact that ecosphere? To what extent do environmental problems and the policy approaches we take reflect the way that we value ecosystems and the worth we place on material consumption?

- *A political issue.* Which political processes can best maintain environmental quality, and what are the political dimensions of this environmental problem? How has the political system defined this problem and set the boundaries for its potential solution?

- *A technology and science issue.* Can science and technology solve environmental problems as quickly as they create them? Do we have the science in place to truly understand the causes and effects of this environmental problem? Does the technology exist to solve the environmental problem or mitigate its impacts?

- *A policy design and economic issue.* What public policies are needed to reduce environmentally damaging behaviors? How can corporate and private behavior be influenced? What mix of incentives and disincentives seem most effective? What economic factors have caused pollution and stimulated particular forms of environmental policy? Economic forces are a major influence on the development of environmental problems and the shape of environmental policy. In this framework we view these economic forces as part of the more general issue of policy design. While most of the causes and effects of policy are economic, some relate to other factors such as security and political power.

• *A management issue.* Which administrative and organizational arrangements have proven most effective at protecting the environment? Do we have the organizational capacity in place to solve the environmental problem?

This multifaceted framework is delineated as an explicit corrective to analysts who narrowly focus on only one or two dimensions of an environmental problem....

... We now turn to an application of that framework for understanding the problem of disposing New York City's garbage. Examining each dimension of the city's solid waste problem will provide a comprehensive explanation of the problem and its potential solution. The city's garbage problem will be examined as an issue of values, as a political issue, and as a problem for science and technology. Finally, we will address the policy design and management dimensions of the issue.

As noted, solid waste is not only an issue for New York City but is also a national problem. In 1960 Americans generated approximately 88.1 million tons of waste per year, which is equivalent to 2.7 pounds per person every day. By 1990 that number grew to 205.2 million tons per year and 4.5 pounds per person per day. During the next decade per capita waste remained stable at 4.5 pounds per day, but total waste rose to 232 tons in 2000. From 1960 to 2000 the total amount of waste generated grew from 88 to 232 tons per year....

New York City's eight million residents and millions of businesses, construction projects, and nonresident employees generate as much as 36,200 tons of municipal solid waste per day. The city's Department of Sanitation (DOS) handles nearly 13,000 tons per day of waste generated by residents, public agencies, and nonprofit corporations; private carting companies handle the remainder. During the twentieth century the DOS relied on a number of landfills for garbage disposal. Then, in December 2001, the city's last garbage dump, Fresh Kills Landfill in Staten Island, closed. In response, the City Council adopted a twenty-year plan for exporting DOS-managed waste. Export became the exclusive waste disposal option for New York City.

Throughout New York City's history it has had problems with solid waste management. In 1894, four years before the incorporation of the City of Greater New York, the city stopped its practice of dumping garbage into the ocean. Instead, it began a new program that included recycling and composting. Soon, however, a new administration took office, and ocean dumping resumed. A federal lawsuit filed by a group of New Jersey coastal cities forced New York City to end ocean dumping in 1935. With plans for new incinerators slowed, first by the Great Depression and then by World War II, the city found it more and more difficult to meet its waste disposal needs. In 1947 the Fresh Kills Landfill opened. Initially the Staten Island dump was going to be a "clean fill," and the city's new mayor promised that "raw" garbage would only be landfilled at Fresh Kills for three years, the time it would take to design, site, and build a large incinerator in every borough. By the 1960s, however, one-third of the city's trash was burned in more than seventeen thousand apartment building incinerators and twenty-two municipal incinerators. The remaining residential refuse was still sent to Fresh Kills as well as to the city's other landfills.

As we noted in an Earth Institute report: "As environmental awareness grew, public pressure began to mount against incineration and landfilling. Old landfills and incinerators were gradually shut down, with the last municipal incinerator closed in 1992." By the late 1990s only Fresh Kills remained as a waste disposal option for the residential and public waste managed by the DOS.

In May 1996 Mayor Rudolph Giuliani and Governor George Pataki announced that Fresh Kills would receive its last ton of garbage no later than January 1, 2002. With the exception of the remains of the World Trade Center, that landfill has been closed since the last day of 2001. In an effort to determine how the city should go about disposing nearly 13,000 tons of daily waste previously sent to the site, a Fresh Kills Closure Task Force was established by the city government. The principal goal of the task force was to develop a short-term plan for diverting the waste from Fresh Kills up to its full closure in 2001. The next step was to develop a longer-term solution. . . .

In the summer of 2002 the city began to take some steps to develop elements of a true long-term plan for managing waste. While the overall waste export strategy was still being pursued, Mayor Michael Bloomberg announced a plan to develop garbage transfer stations that would compact refuse and ship it by barge for disposal. These stations would be placed in waterfront locations in each of the five New York City boroughs and would replace a system of land-based waste transfer that currently uses thousands of diesel-fueled trucks daily to haul garbage through city streets to disposal sites in other states. In late 2003 the projected expense of building these transfer stations grew, putting the plan on hold.

The current system of waste export in 2005 still leaves the city vulnerable over the long run, as both restrictions on waste disposal and its costs are likely to escalate. . . .

Our discussion of New York City's solid waste problem begins with an analysis of the values intrinsic to the issue, beginning with those that shape the consumption patterns responsible for creating 13,000 tons of residential garbage each day. The use of large amounts of packaging material, and the relatively minimal level of recycling, reflect the community's collective values. The preference for exporting waste is based on a desire to avoid the potential environmental insult of treating garbage and on the values underlying the "not in my backyard" (NIMBY) syndrome. The consumption behaviors described show little sign of fundamental change from decade to decade. Although the growth in per capita waste disposal in New York City has begun to slow, mirroring national trends, New Yorkers clearly value the benefits of a throwaway society. The value system supporting this mode of consumption dominates and has kept waste reduction off the political agenda. The issue does not pertain only to New York City; although the size and density of that city's population intensify its solid waste problem. At the root of the problem are consumption patterns that currently prevail in all modern, developed economies. New Yorkers probably place a higher value on convenience and service than may be typical, but the difference is one of degree rather than kind.

A subtle choice of values is also reflected in the way the public and the governing elite try to avoid the waste issue. Perhaps that is partly because garbage is physically unpleasant and also because it is a reminder of the great wealth some of us enjoy in the face of poverty. We discard food and clothing that could provide sustenance to the world's poor. And then, too, garbage is ugly and foul-smelling; we prefer not to think about it or where it ends up. Coupled with this attitude is the historic tendency to process garbage as far away as possible from the middle and upper classes. This helps to propagate the fantasy that all those green plastic mounds of garbage bags on the street are placed in a garbage truck and magically transported to some mythical solid waste heaven.

This pairing of convenience-driven consumption with waste avoidance is the value underpinning the city's solid waste management crisis. In contrast, throughout the twentieth century, New York invested many billions of dollars in a water supply system that is arguably the best in the world. As this demonstrates, the city does have the capacity and resources to develop long-term plans for infrastructure investment to address environmental problems—just not for garbage. . . .

The value issues described . . . have created a climate of opinion for the politics of waste that makes it difficult for local decision makers to address the city's solid waste issues. At the core of this issue is the local politics around choosing the sites for waste disposal, transfer, and treatment facilities. Garbage is inherently undesirable, and obviously there is no positive spin that can be placed on being the host site for a community's waste. The political antipathy to waste in New York was demonstrated for more than two decades by the local politics of waste in Staten Island. The highest priority for most of Staten Island's elected officials during the 1990s was to close the Fresh Kills Landfill. In the late 1980s and early 1990s the borough engaged in an effort to secede from New York City, partly to end the use of Staten Island as the city's dump. As a sparsely populated and predominantly Republican borough in a Democratic city, Staten Island had little leverage until Republican Rudolph Giuliani was elected mayor in 1993.

Local politicians, with few exceptions, have caved in to the long-standing antipathy toward locating waste facilities in New York City. In the 1980s, highly conflicted but with enormous political courage, the then mayor Ed Koch obtained an agreement to site a waste incinerator in each borough. Mayor Koch's incinerator agreement collapsed during the Dinkins and Giuliani administrations, as each subsequent mayor decided that community opposition to the siting was too intense to override. Even environmentalists, while arguing against landfilling and long-distance waste transportation, are even more opposed to siting a garbage incinerator or a waste-to-energy plant within New York City's five boroughs. The politics of waste, particularly the community politics of siting, has been the principal constraint on policy options for managing the city's waste. . . .

New York City's extreme population density has necessitated a number of technological innovations including an extensive mass transit network, electricity and water systems, modern sewage treatment and removal, product packaging, food refrigeration, preservatives, and, of course, solid waste removal. The technology of waste incineration has advanced dramatically since the 1960s, when much of the city's waste was burned in apartment building and municipal incinerators. Today probably the most environmentally sound methods for disposing the daily waste generated by the city's eight million residents and four million workers or visitors are regional or local waste-to-energy plants or other new and advanced waste treatment technologies. The remaining smaller volume of waste would be exported via marine waste transfer stations or rail transfer through a train tunnel from New Jersey to Brooklyn. Marine or rail transfer of waste and modern incineration or waste treatment can significantly reduce the number of collection truck miles and also maximize the ability to collect and recycle toxic materials and heavy metals. The potential for waste leakage from landfills would also be reduced. But despite the existence of appropriate and effective waste disposal technology that is actually more affordable than the current waste system, the politics of siting continues to dominate the issue.

Experts in waste disposal are not trusted and the government lacks credibility, and so even though there is a scientific solution to the problem, politics disallows the use of the new technology. If science could reduce waste plant emissions to zero, and if experts credible to the public and interest groups could confirm the improved technology, scientific fact *might* influence the political dialogue. A non-incinerator-based technology in which garbage is treated by a closed-system chemical process and transformed into a more useful, non-waste product or lower-volume material might achieve greater public acceptance. But as demonstrated by the debate over the global climate change, the more complex the issue, the more likely that scientific uncertainty remains. Thus the NIMBY syndrome and the political self-interest of some local community-based organizations continue to take precedence over scientific progress. . . .

Another aspect of the solid waste dilemma as a policy issue is its regulatory dimension. Local, state, and federal governments in the United States regulate waste disposal. Individuals and apartment building staff must package and sort garbage in specified ways. If it is packaged or sorted incorrectly, fines or noncollection may result. The visibility of the issue and the immediacy of enforcement make the regulatory dimensions of this issue relatively straightforward.

One partial solution is a policy that encourages waste reduction. The tax system or command-and-control regulation can be used to reduce packaging or to encourage the development and use of biodegradable packaging. For several reasons, however, these kinds of policies would be difficult for a city government to implement. . . .

More than five thousand communities nationwide have implemented a Pay-As-You-Throw system, making it available to 20 percent of the population. This number includes many smaller municipalities but also urban centers such as San Francisco, Seattle, Fort Worth, Austin, Buffalo, New Orleans, and the second largest U.S. city, Los Angeles, with a population of 3.8 million. As noted above, these cities have a distinct advantage in implementing this type of program as they consist largely of single-family or small-unit apartments in contrast to the high-rise residential buildings of New York City.

Arguably, Chicago and San Francisco offer the greatest comparisons to New York because of their population density and prevalence of older, multi-family structures. Chicago, with a population of 2.85 million, offers residential solid waste pickup only to structures that have fewer than five housing units. Residential buildings with more than four units must contract with a private solid waste removal or recycling company. The City of Chicago, Department of Streets and Sanitation collects 1.1 million tons of residential garbage and 300,000 tons of recycling annually. All this was collected from approximately 750,000 residential structures. Thus the waste from more than 300,000 larger residential units and all commercial properties were managed by private firms.

San Francisco has a residential population of nearly 800,000. Its entire municipal waste system is contracted out to the private firm Norcal Waste Systems. Sixty percent of housing in the city is comprised of structures of five units or fewer. These smaller units participate in a Pay-As-You-Throw program through a privately contracted firm. The remaining 40 percent of the city's housing is six-units or more. The city has been in a state of flux for several years trying to implement appropriate volume/frequency rates that still provide an appropriate level of incentive for individual residents to reduce waste. To its credit, San Francisco has one of the most aggressive recycling campaigns in the United States. Recycling, which is also conducted by Norcal, is available to nearly 90 percent of the city's apartment houses. The city reports a diversion rate upward of 63 percent. San Francisco has set an ambitious goal to divert 75 percent of the garbage generated by city businesses, residents, and visitors from landfills by 2010. Clearly, other cities in the United States are more successful than New York in managing solid waste. Perhaps New York can learn from these other cities and will some day be able to take out its own garbage.

79

SASHA ABRAMSKY

From *The American Way of Poverty*

Sasha Abramsky updates the classic work of Michael Harrington whose The Other America *first brought poverty in the U.S. into the public's view in the early 1960s. Harrington termed the poor "invisible" and they still are, Abramsky believes. In the wake of the deep recession starting in 2008, many families lost the meager financial security they had counted on; they became poverty-stricken. We tour with Abramsky, starting with some young people in Pomona, California. The barren outskirts of Las Cruces, New Mexico is his next stop: no actual bathroom, even. Then, it's on to Detroit, Michigan. What was once a thriving working class city is now nearly abandoned. Some of the empty lots have become urban farms. He asks, "How will people live?" We then finish up in New Orleans, Louisiana, after Hurricane Katrina.*

————

FIFTY YEARS AFTER THE SOCIAL CRITIC Michael Harrington published his groundbreaking book *The Other America*, in which he chronicled the lives lived of those excluded from the Age of Affluence, poverty in America is back with a vengeance. It is made up both of the long-term, chronically poor and the newly impoverished, the victims of a broken economy and a collapsed housing market.

The saga of the timeless poor, of individuals immersed in poverty for decades, of communities mired in poverty for generations, is something of a dog-bites-man story: It's sad, but it's not new. The tale of the newly poor, however, is more akin to the man-bites-dog story: It is surprising and counterintuitive. It is the narrative of millions of Americans who had economic security, enjoyed something of the comforts of an affluent society, and then lost it. Not since the Great Depression have so many millions of people been so thoroughly beaten down by vast, destructive forces. Yet while the story of the more recent poor has more of a sensation factor to it, in reality the stories of the long-term poor and the newly destitute increasingly blend together, creating a common set of experiences that pummel the bodies and minds of those who live them; that corrode communities; and that, all too often, obliterate optimism.

As with the men and women Harrington wrote about in 1962, too frequently these poor Americans are invisible. "Here are the unskilled workers, the migrant farm workers, the aged, the minorities, and all the others who live in the economic underworld of American life," Harrington wrote in his opening chapter. "The other America, the America of poverty, is hidden today in a way that it never was before. Its millions are socially invisible to the rest of us. . . . The new poverty is constructed so as to destroy aspiration; it is a system designed to be impervious to hope."

Harrington was a Jesuit-educated political activist, born and raised in St. Louis during the years between the world wars. Over several decades he carved out a reputation for himself as a longtime chronicler of the American condition. In the run-up to his book's publication, he had spent years in poor communities as a volunteer with Catholic Worker and as a left-leaning political organizer—hardly the most fruitful of pursuits in the conservative, affluent era following the end of World War II. In fact, *The Other America* hit a raw nerve at least in part because so many Americans, living comfortably in suburbias miles from the epicenters of hardship, thought their country had already solved the poverty conundrum. With many having a mind-set of out of sight, out of mind, poverty simply wasn't a part of the national political discourse in the 1950s. Indeed, the Harvard Kennedy School of Government lecturer and author Richard Parker, in his biography of the progressive economist John Kenneth Galbraith, noted that when the Joint Economic Committee of Congress commissioned University of Wisconsin economist Robert Lampman to put together "a complete bibliography of postwar books and articles by economists on modern poverty, his typed list required only two pages." That the Gordian knot of poverty hadn't actually been unraveled, and that it could continue to exist alongside the Affluent Society, was a source of tremendous national embarrassment for many. In the wake of *The Other America*'s publication, a critical mass of policy makers doubled down, using Harrington's writings as a Virgil-like guide to America's hidden underbelly and laying the foundations for an all-out assault on the causes and conditions of poverty that would fundamentally impact American social policy for a generation.

Liberal America's belief during the 1960s that with one more great push the scourges associated with poverty could be forever eradicated from America's shores was naïve, possibly even disingenuous. After all, no society in human history has ever successfully banished poverty; and no polity with a modicum of respect for individual liberty has entirely negated the presence of inequality. But it did reflect a confidence in America's innate sense of possibility; in an era of space travel and antibiotics, computers and robots, poverty was just one more frontier to be con-

quered, one more communal obstacle to be pushed aside. When it turned
out to be an order of magnitude more complicated, Americans quickly
grew tired of the effort. In 1968, four years after the War on Poverty was
launched, Richard Nixon won election to the White House, in part by
stoking popular resentment against welfare recipients. Twelve years after
that, Ronald Reagan was elected president on a platform of rolling back
much of the Great Society. Today, after four decades during which tack-
ling economic hardship took a distant backseat to other priorities, one in
six Americans live below the poverty line, their lives as constricted and as
difficult as those of the men, women, and children who peopled the pages
of *The Other America* in the Kennedy era. And this is despite the fact that
the president, Barack Obama, is a onetime community organizer who
understands the impact of poverty on people's lives better than almost any
other of his predecessors.

Too poor to participate in the consumption rituals that define most
Americans' lives, too cash-strapped to go to malls, to visit cafés or movie
theaters, to buy food anywhere other than dollar stores, these men and
women live on America's edge. The poorest of the poor live under free-
way ramps and bridges in out-of-the-way neighborhoods such as the Al-
phabet district of northern Las Vegas or Los Angeles's Skid Row. Others
live in trailer parks far from central cities. Then there are those living in
apartment buildings and even suburban houses, who for a variety of reasons have lost their financial security; their deprivation remains hidden
behind closed doors. All of these people share an existential loneliness, a
sense of being shut out of the most basic rituals of society. . . .

Variations on the stories . . . could be encountered in cities and regions across America. After all, an economic free-fall of the kind that the
United States underwent after the housing market collapse and then
the broader financial meltdown leaves carnage in its wake. For those
born into poverty, the hardship is magnified. For millions of others who
thought of themselves as upwardly mobile, with middle-class aspirations
and middle-class spending patterns, the crisis flung them down the economic ladder, replacing a precarious fiscal stability with a continuous
struggle to survive.

In the working-class, immigrant community of Pomona, a few miles
east of downtown Los Angeles, in fall 2008 five eleventh-grade and ten
twelfth-grade students in Village Academy teacher Michael Steinman's
English classes began compiling their stories of poverty for a video project. "I was aware of the economy, but I wasn't personally affected too terribly," Steinman explained. "But when I asked my students how things
were going, in my AP class—we were studying *The Great Gatsby* at the

time—every single student had been affected. I wanted them to give testimony to what they had witnessed and they were going through. The
concept of the American Dream has either evaporated or gone away. Daily, I work with kids who are very much stressed. They hide it well; there's
a certain amount of shame that they carry about being poor or struggling.
But I do know they're going through circumstances that definitely impact
their studies and their ability to think about the future and be positive."
The video footage that they created and put up on YouTube went viral
in January 2009. Barack Obama's presidential transition team was shown
the video. A couple of months later when he visited Southern California,
the newly inaugurated president held a rally in a lot adjacent to the buildings that housed the experimental school—whose student body is overwhelmingly made up of young people from ethnic minority backgrounds,
and one ranked by *U.S. News & World Report* as one of California's best
educational establishments. Obama also invited Steinman and his students
to the White House.

Yet for all the hoopla around their project, nearly a full presidential
cycle later, conditions for many of the students at the Village Academy
high school remained appalling. Large numbers of the kids lived with
parents who had lost their jobs during the recession and either failed to
find new employment or were working long hours at jobs that paid only
minimum wage. Many had lost homes to foreclosure—either because of
variable-rate, subprime mortgages or because of unemployment—or, behind on mortgage or rent payments, lived in constant fear of losing their
homes to the banks or to landlords. Almost all of Steinman's students
qualified for free school breakfasts and lunches—and, for many of these
kids, these were the only hot meals they ate. Evenings and weekends, they
either went without or grabbed some dry cereal to stanch their hunger.
Several honors students at the high-performing school, who should have
been applying to college, were instead thinking of quitting education and
getting dead-end work just to help their families pay the bills.

"Sometimes I cry," Oliver Lopez explained as he described his family's
struggles—his mother out of work, his father working two part-time
minimum-wage jobs, he and his three younger brothers living from meal
to meal. "I see how hard my father works; and I'm 18 years old and just
come to school. I don't do nothing. Sometimes we don't even have food
to eat."

One of Oliver's classmates described how he, his mother, his two sisters, his grandmother, two uncles, an aunt, and her daughter all lived in a
one-bedroom apartment, most of them sleeping on the floor, until they

fell behind on their rent and were evicted in early 2010. The family had split up, with groups of two or three going off to stay with different relatives. The young man was living with his mother, who in a good week was earning $300 as a housecleaner, and his two younger sisters in a single room in a friend's house. During mealtimes, the mother would eat leftovers off of his and his sisters' barely filled plates. "I'm depressed. I spend most of my time crying alone. My mom tells me I should get a job. She gets mad at me. She works from 6 A.M. to 5 P.M. I'm actually out trying to find a job. But there's nothing."

In the tiny community of Anthony, just outside of Las Cruces, New Mexico, Lorenza and Jorge Caro lived on a piece of scrubby land in the harsh but beautiful high desert. Their living conditions were, to say the least, extraordinary. At the back end of a sandy, cluttered lot, the pastel blues of the New Mexican sky providing a backdrop, they lived in an uninsulated, windowless, cinder-block storage space with an unfinished concrete floor. One half was crammed floor to ceiling with pickings from street fairs and yard sales—they toured the region, buying goods on the cheap and then reselling them at a fraction above what they paid in the street markets of Las Cruces. The other half of the room, divided from the pile by a hung blue tarpaulin, contained a high bed, a propane-fueled stove, huge piles of clothes and bric-a-brac, and a plastic chair with a circular hole cut in its wicker seat. When in use, a chamber pot would be placed beneath the chair. This, said Lorenza in Spanish, her eyes lowered as she talked, was the device on which they performed their morning ablutions.

It was a strange scene, at once theatrical and also deeply depressing. The storage space was dank and chilly, an incubator of germs. Its occupants, wrapped up in heavy layers against the cold—she in lilac sweatpants and a thick white coat, he in workmen's boots, jeans, a wool-lined blue jean jacket, and a woolen hat—were edgy, kind yet skittish, nervous that they were being judged for how they lived.

The Caros lost their mobile home in 2010, when they fell behind on their payments after Jorge lost his job. Now, despite the fact that Jorge had managed to get another minimum-wage job as a cleaner at a local company, and that Lorenza brought in a few dollars from her flea market sales, they lived in the storage room on the land that used to host their home. "We meet our necessities, we don't have beyond our necessities, but we meet our necessities here," explained Lorenza in a soft voice. "It's very, very cold when I use the toilet seat. We have electricity, so we have little heaters right now. But when we run out of gas—the stove is propane and helps to keep the heat—it gets colder. Last January it was very bad for us. We had the freezer, didn't have any water. I had colds. When we need medical care we drink whatever herbs we can, [take] Tylenol."

During the toughest times, they had gotten food on credit from women at the flea market and made do on one or two meals a day. "In the morning we'd have a cup of coffee and a piece of bread; in the afternoon a burrito or gorditas—Mexican sandwiches. Nothing in the evening. Sometimes we had those little instant soup cups out here." On the rare instances they had spare money, they bought potatoes and beans in bulk and made them last for weeks.

The dreams the Caros had were impossibly modest. "I expect things to get better," said Lorenza. "Now that Jorge has a full-time job we hope things will get better. I want to live in a house with an indoor toilet. A nice, big toilet." She laughed, the nervous laugh of someone on the verge of tears. Jorge fiddled with a kettle of water on the propane stove. The sun was starting to go down, and already the mid-December evening was desperately cold. . . .

In Detroit . . . where hundreds of thousands of workers had once made good money working in auto manufacturing, so many people had departed the city in recent decades, and so many lots had been abandoned, that in large numbers of neighborhoods there were more vacant homes than occupied ones.

From the 1960s onward, plants started to shed jobs, as production processes increasingly became automated. In 1979, for example, General Motors was producing as many cars in Detroit as it had done twenty years earlier, but with half the number of workers. Finally, however, even those workers proved too costly, and companies shuttered their factories entirely, the jobs outsourced to nonunion sites in other states, or overseas. Once iconic factories, such as the enormous Packard complex that, at its mighty zenith, had employed 60,000 people, remained only as vast shells, the ground carpeted by broken glass, the entranceways to buildings that used to house state-of-the-art industrial machinery piled high with tires, bricks, and twisted metal piping. "Detroit had what appeared to be a curse," explained Shea Howell, a local university professor of communications and longtime community organizer, who had made something of a hobby of taking out-of-towners on tours of the Motor City's underside. "People left to follow a job. In the late '70s, there used to be a bumper sticker: 'Last one out of Michigan, turn out the lights.' It was so many people leaving so fast. They just walked out of the house, got in the car and left behind the house. You have magnificent one- and two-story brick homes built for the workers of the auto industry. And people walked out, couldn't afford them, couldn't afford the heat, couldn't pay the mortgages. It's overwhelming. Over 30 percent of the city is abandoned; over forty square miles. The abandoned land became a curse; it pulled the heart out of neighborhoods."

During the days, tourists, engaging in what locals termed "ruins porn" watching, would venture out to the Packard plant in their cars to take photographs of the ruins—as impressive in their own way as those of the pyramids of Egypt. At night, the ruins belonged to graffiti artists, the homeless, drug addicts, and scrap metal scavengers, who would load up stolen grocery store carts with their wares and cart them off to recycling plants. "Decay," one tagger had thoughtfully painted along one shattered interior wall, empty windows staring vacantly on either side. There was enough piping and other metal amidst the ruins to keep the scavengers occupied for decades.

From one neighborhood to the next, blight flourished, although the word itself didn't really do justice to the magnitude of the catastrophe. Jobs disappeared; factories ceased operations; supermarkets, banks and other basic business amenities closed up shop. And, in their hundreds of thousands, those residents who could left. Abandoned, their homes—once some of working-class America's loveliest housing—fell into disrepair, burned down, or crumbled to the ground. The lots became overgrown. At night, coyotes, possums, and other wildlife roamed free. For those who remained, two-thirds of them living at or near the poverty line, the poverty getting deeper and more entrenched by the year, converting the vacant lots to urban gardens became both a way to keep neighborhoods functioning and also a somewhat desperate pathway toward self-sufficiency in an environment increasingly hostile to the poor.

And thus the surreal sight, in the shadows of the Packard ruins barely a stone's throw from downtown, of small family farms dotting the landscape. Many of them were farmed by African American residents whose families had migrated from the rural Deep South decades earlier and who still retained knowledge of family farming methods from their youth. By 2012, there were perhaps as many as 2,600 such farms in the city, community organizers estimated. Some of them were just a few rows of vegetables; others, however, included rambling orchards, chicken runs, little plots on which resided sheep and goats; a few were even home to bulls and horses. One, run by a group of Capuchin friars, was experimenting with year-round growing techniques; others were using sophisticated organic methods to leach the myriad of pollutants from the topsoil. A minute or two's drive from the heart of what used to be one of America's largest and fastest cities, one could see locals, dressed in muddied jeans and shirts, straw hats atop their heads, pushing wheelbarrows filled with dirt down cracked sidewalks, and carefully hoeing their farms.

By necessity, said Howell, Detroit had become something of an incubator for a new kind of urban living, a kind of utopia carved out of despair and post-industrial desolation. "What will replace industrial society? How will people live? What creates work? How do we do that now? These are fundamental questions. Human beings are in a transition now that's as great as the transition from hunting and gathering to agriculture, or from agriculture to industry." . . .

How . . . would a post-war American optimist—even one with as keen an eye for the underbelly of America as Harrington—have interpreted Hurricane Katrina, and the destruction both of the physical infrastructure of much of New Orleans and also of a huge number of lives? How would he have reacted to the orgy of impotent finger-pointing that was indulged in by local, state, and federal officials both during the flooding itself, and then in the months and years following—as swaths of land were left to decay and the rotten wooden hulls of thousands of homes were simply left to pockmark the devastated city?

There's a loneliness to this landscape, a Mad Max edge. It looks like a world abandoned to its own devices, with street after street of destroyed, gutted houses, and acres of overgrown lots where once stood stores and homes, churches and schools. It is an utterly apocalyptic landscape; yet it is also a strangely invisible one—off the beaten path, away from the decadent, jazzy splendors of Bourbon Street, a place of national shame that, for those fortunate enough not to have lived in the area, is all too easy to forget exists.

It is, explained Darren McKinney, a middle-aged resident on disability and food stamps who had spent the years since the hurricane hit working with a nonprofit group to salvage some of the wooden homes of the Lower Ninth, "like a ghost town at nighttime."

Taking a break from working on one graffiti-covered skeleton of a building, on Caffin Avenue, in the last weeks of 2011, McKinney sat on a concrete slab that used to be the base of a house, and looked around. "That was a barber shop, that was a grocery store. That slab right there, it used to be a doctor's office. That place used to be an after-school place for kids. This here used to be a church right behind us," said Darren, pointing to the rear of the empty lot. "I stood, watched the water come up fifteen feet, fifteen to twenty feet in this area. St. Claude and Delaware, I watched it. I watched the little birds and fishes in the water, people yelling at night-time for help. I lost my step-mamma, a couple of my best friends in the storm." Surveying the damage, half a decade on from the storm, Darren struggled to put a positive spin on things. "Up in this area, you might have 30 percent of the people back. It's getting better—'cause every day I see a new person moving into the neighborhood, someone moving back in. The neighborhood coming back; but it's going to be another five to six years to get some action back into the neighborhood again. You just gotta think positive."

Of course, much of New Orleans's troubles, much of the texture of its poverty, predates Hurricane Katrina not just by decades but by centuries. It is a city long plagued by violence, by racial and economic divides as stark as any in America—fully half of the residents of Orleans Parish were low-income even prior to the hurricane—and by endemic levels of cor-ruption. Yet all of these were worsened by the calamitous events of the late summer of 2005. Disproportionately, it was African Americans who were left behind in the city as those with cars evacuated. Disproportion-ately, it was African American neighborhoods like the Lower Ninth Ward that suffered the most physical damage and then were least likely to be speedily rebuilt after the disaster. By contrast, more affluent areas, like the fabled French Quarter, which had grown up on high land over the years, suffered less damage during the flood and returned to relative normality within months of the waters draining out of the city. For tourists, in town to splurge on *les bons temps*—booze, food, and extraordinary music—the city presented a near-intact public visage within a remarkably short stretch of time. But, barely a couple of miles from Bourbon Street, entire city blocks were still obliterated years later, concrete foundation slabs rest-ing at odd angles amidst overgrown grass, graffiti-covered house shells still waiting to be torn down.

And, while the number of African Americans who died in the flood was roughly proportionate to the percentage of the New Orleans popula-tion who were African American, disproportionately it was the poor, and elderly, of all races who were the ones to die in the flood itself and its chaotic aftermath. In a city where the public health system had already suffered epic cutbacks—losing a majority of its public-sector hospital beds and in-patient mental health facilities in the years preceding Ka-trina—the disaster simply overwhelmed the first-responder system. It was one's economic status in New Orleans that was the best predictor of whether one would survive or succumb to the flood; and, after the flood, for the survivors it was one's economic status that generally determined one's access to housing, to healthcare, to all of the basics of life in a shattered community. Fully a quarter of local residents had no health insurance, and for African Americans that number was higher. As for work, a year before the disaster, the unemployment rate stood at 12 percent, roughly double the national average. Despite the construction boom generated by the hurricane, in the years immediately following Katrina, unemployment remained stubbornly high: More than one in ten workers in the shrunken city were unemployed in the first few years.

And, later, during the post-2008 recession, when the city's unemployment numbers actually dipped below the national average, demographers believed that at least in part this number was an illusion; it was based on the fact that so many former residents who lost everything during the flood—a large number of whom counted amongst the city's poorest and least employed residents—had yet to return to the city. Yes, the Big Easy's unemployment rate *had* gone down, but the total number of abandoned homes still hovered in the tens of thousands. In 2010, the *Los Angeles Times* reported that the advocacy organization UNITY estimated that the homeless population had doubled in the years following Katrina, and that 6,000 New Orleanians were living in these abandoned buildings.

As for child poverty—one of the key measures of societal health—in pre-Katrina New Orleans, U.S. Census Bureau data showed that about 40 percent of African American children under the age of 5 were living in poverty. That number was terrifyingly high—but not as high as the estimates six years later. Post-Katrina, the Census Bureau found that more than 65 percent of black children under the age of 5 in New Orleans, many of them still living in the blitzed landscape of the Lower Ninth and other devastated neighborhoods, were living at or below the poverty line.

Hurricane Katrina is where old poverty meets new, where the intergenerational poverty of the inner city becomes magnified by natural disaster and political ineptitude. It is where the plight of the poor is most clearly exposed—as an ongoing experience in vulnerability, as people thought of as being somehow disposable. . . .

PART FOURTEEN

America in a Changed World

80

SAMUEL HUNTINGTON

From *The Clash of Civilizations*

Renowned scholar Samuel Huntington's 1996 book has received much attention since the terrorist attacks against the United States in 2001. Writing several years earlier, Huntington anticipates the vastly changed landscape of world conflict after the collapse of Soviet communism and after the end of the U.S.-Soviet Cold War. "Power is shifting from the long predominant West to non-western civilizations," Huntington writes. He explores the reasons why he believes this is happening, emphasizing the renewal of religion as central to the changes in power. Religious conflicts, especially between Islam and Christianity, are inevitable, the author believes. Not all Americans will agree with Huntington's grim thesis, but his ideas are important reading for people who have been brought up in the United States. Modernism, reason, progress, and prosperity are key American values, but not necessarily those of much of the rest of the world.

IN THE POST-COLD WAR WORLD,* for the first time in history, global politics has become multipolar *and* multicivilizational. During most of human existence, contacts between civilizations were intermittent or nonexistent. Then, with the beginning of the modern era, about A.D. 1500, global politics assumed two dimensions. For over four hundred years, the nation states of the West—Britain, France, Spain, Austria, Prussia, Germany, the United States, and others—constituted a multipolar international system within Western civilization and interacted, competed, and fought wars with each other. At the same time, Western nations also expanded, conquered, colonized, or decisively influenced every other civilization. During the Cold War global politics became bipolar and the world was divided into three parts. A group of mostly wealthy and democratic societies, led by the United States, was engaged in a pervasive ideological, political, economic, and, at times, military competition with a group of

---

*The Cold War refers to the hostility that existed between the United States and the Soviet Union from the end of World War II until recent times. The Cold War involved many forms of hostility: democracy versus communism; America's NATO allies versus the Soviet Union's Warsaw Pact military partners; the threat of nuclear war; economic competition; the dividing of Third World nations into pro-U.S. and pro-Soviet camps. With the demise of communism in Eastern Europe and the disintegration of the Soviet Union, the Cold War era has ended.—EDS.

somewhat poorer communist societies associated with and led by the Soviet Union. Much of this conflict occurred in the Third World outside
these two camps, composed of countries which often were poor, lacked
political stability, were recently independent, and claimed to be non-
aligned.

In the late 1980s the communist world collapsed, and the Cold War
international system became history. In the post-Cold War world, the
most important distinctions among peoples are not ideological, political,
or economic. They are cultural. Peoples and nations are attempting to
answer the most basic question humans can face: Who are we? And they
are answering that question in the traditional way human beings have
answered it, by reference to the things that mean most to them. People
define themselves in terms of ancestry, religion, language, history, values,
customs, and institutions. They identify with cultural groups: tribes, ethnic
groups, religious communities, nations, and, at the broadest level, civilizations. People use politics not just to advance their interests but also to
define their identity. We know who we are only when we know who we
are not and often only when we know whom we are against.

Nation states remain the principal actors in world affairs. Their behavior is shaped as in the past by the pursuit of power and wealth, but it is
also shaped by cultural preferences, commonalities, and differences. The
most important groupings of states are no longer the three blocs of the
Cold War but rather the world's seven or eight major civilizations. Non-
Western societies, particularly in East Asia, are developing their economic
wealth and creating the basis for enhanced military power and political
influence. As their power and self-confidence increase, non-Western societies increasingly assert their own cultural values and reject those "imposed" on them by the West. The "international system of the twenty-first
century," Henry Kissinger has noted, " . . . will contain at least six major
powers—the United States, Europe, China, Japan, Russia, and probably
India—as well as a multiplicity of medium-sized and smaller countries."
Kissinger's six major powers belong to five very different civilizations, and
in addition there are important Islamic states whose strategic locations,
large populations, and/or oil resources make them influential in world
affairs. In this new world, local politics is the politics of ethnicity; global
politics is the politics of civilizations. The rivalry of the superpowers is
replaced by the clash of civilizations. . . .

The philosophical assumptions, underlying values, social relations,
customs, and overall outlooks on life differ significantly among civilizations. The revitalization of religion throughout much of the world is reinforcing these cultural differences. Cultures can change, and the nature of

their impact on politics and economics can vary from one period to another. Yet the major differences in political and economic development among civilizations are clearly rooted in their different cultures. East Asian economic success has its source in East Asian culture, as do the difficulties East Asian societies have had in achieving stable democratic political systems. Islamic culture explains in large part the failure of democracy to emerge in much of the Muslim world. Developments in the postcommunist societies of Eastern Europe and the former Soviet Union are shaped by their civilizational identities. Those with Western Christian heritages are making progress toward economic development and democratic politics; the prospects for economic and political development in the Orthodox countries are uncertain; the prospects in the Muslim republics are bleak.

The West is and will remain for years to come the most powerful civilization. Yet its power relative to that of other civilizations is declining. As the West attempts to assert its values and to protect its interests, non-Western societies confront a choice. Some attempt to emulate the West and to join or to "bandwagon" with the West. Other Confucian and Islamic societies attempt to expand their own economic and military power to resist and to "balance" against the West. A central axis of post-Cold War world politics is thus the interaction of Western power and culture with the power and culture of non-Western civilizations.

In sum, the post-Cold War world is a world of seven or eight major civilizations. Cultural commonalities and differences shape the interests, antagonisms, and associations of states. The most important countries in the world come overwhelmingly from different civilizations. The local conflicts most likely to escalate into broader wars are those between groups and states from different civilizations. The predominant patterns of political and economic development differ from civilization to civilization. The key issues on the international agenda involve differences among civilizations. Power is shifting from the long predominant West to non-Western civilizations. Global politics has become multipolar and multi-civilizational. . . .

The distribution of cultures in the world reflects the distribution of power. Trade may or may not follow the flag, but culture almost always follows power. Throughout history the expansion of the power of a civilization has usually occurred simultaneously with the flowering of its culture and has almost always involved its using that power to extend its values, practices, and institutions to other societies. A universal civilization requires universal power. Roman power created a near-universal civilization within the limited confines of the Classical world. Western power in the form of European colonialism in the nineteenth century and American hegemony in the twentieth century extended Western culture throughout much of the contemporary world. European colonialism is over; American hegemony is receding. The erosion of Western culture follows, as indigenous, historically rooted mores, languages, beliefs, and institutions reassert themselves. The growing power of non-Western societies produced by modernization is generating the revival of non-Western cultures throughout the world.

A distinction exists, Joseph Nye has argued, between "hard power," which is the power to command resting on economic and military strength, and "soft power," which is the ability of a state to get "other countries to *want* what it wants" through the appeal of its culture and ideology. As Nye recognizes, a broad diffusion of hard power is occurring in the world and the major nations "are less able to use their traditional power resources to achieve their purposes than in the past." Nye goes on to say that if a state's "culture and ideology are attractive, others will be more willing to follow" its leadership, and hence soft power is "just as important as hard command power." What, however, makes culture and ideology attractive? They become attractive when they are seen as rooted in material success and influence. Soft power is power only when it rests on a foundation of hard power. Increases in hard economic and military power produce enhanced self-confidence, arrogance, and belief in the superiority of one's own culture or soft power compared to those of other peoples and greatly increase its attractiveness to other peoples. Decreases in economic and military power lead to self-doubt, crises of identity, and efforts to find in other cultures the keys to economic, military, and political success. As non-Western societies enhance their economic, military, and political capacity, they increasingly trumpet the virtues of their own values, institutions, and culture.

Communist ideology appealed to people throughout the world in the 1950s and 1960s when it was associated with the economic success and military force of the Soviet Union. That appeal evaporated when the Soviet economy stagnated and was unable to maintain Soviet military strength. Western values and institutions have appealed to people from other cultures because they were seen as the source of Western power and wealth. This process has been going on for centuries. Between 1000 and 1300, as William McNeill points out, Christianity, Roman law, and other elements of Western culture were adopted by Hungarians, Poles, and Lithuanians, and this "acceptance of Western civilization was stimulated by mingled fear and admiration of the military prowess of Western princes." As Western power declines, the ability of the West to impose

Western concepts of human rights, liberalism, and democracy on other civilizations also declines and so does the attractiveness of those values to other civilizations.

It already has. For several centuries non-Western peoples envied the economic prosperity, technological sophistication, military power, and political cohesion of Western societies. They sought the secret of this success in Western values and institutions, and when they identified what they thought might be the key they attempted to apply it in their own societies. To become rich and powerful, they would have to become like the West. Now, however, these Kemalist attitudes have disappeared in East Asia. East Asians attribute their dramatic economic development not to their import of Western culture but rather to their adherence to their own culture. They are succeeding, they argue, because they are different from the West. Similarly, when non-Western societies felt weak in relation to the West, they invoked Western values of self-determination, liberalism, democracy, and independence to justify their opposition to Western domination. Now that they are no longer weak but increasingly powerful, they do not hesitate to attack those same values which they previously used to promote their interests. The revolt against the West was originally legitimated by asserting the universality of Western values; it is now legitimated by asserting the superiority of non-Western values.

The rise of these attitudes is a manifestation of what Ronald Dore has termed the "second-generation indigenization phenomenon." In both former Western colonies and independent countries like China and Japan, "The first 'modernizer' or 'post-independence' generation has often received its training in foreign (Western) universities in a Western cosmopolitan language. Partly because they first go abroad as impressionable teenagers, their absorption of Western values and life-styles may well be profound." Most of the much larger second generation, in contrast, gets its education at home in universities created by the first generation, and the local rather than the colonial language is increasingly used for instruction. These universities "provide a much more diluted contact with metropolitan world culture" and "knowledge is indigenized by means of translations—usually of limited range and of poor quality." The graduates of these universities resent the dominance of the earlier Western-trained generation and hence often "succumb to the appeals of nativist opposition movements." As Western influence recedes, young aspiring leaders cannot look to the West to provide them with power and wealth. They have to find the means of success within their own society, and hence they have to accommodate to the values and culture of that society. . . .

In the first half of the twentieth century intellectual elites generally assumed that economic and social modernization was leading to the withering away of religion as a significant element in human existence. This assumption was shared by both those who welcomed and those who deplored this trend. Modernizing secularists hailed the extent to which science, rationalism, and pragmatism were eliminating the superstitions, myths, irrationalities, and rituals that formed the core of existing religions. The emerging society would be tolerant, rational, pragmatic, progressive, humanistic, and secular. Worried conservatives, on the other hand, warned of the dire consequences of the disappearance of religious beliefs, religious institutions, and the moral guidance religion provided for individual and collective human behavior. The end result would be anarchy, depravity, the undermining of civilized life. "If you will not have God (and He is a jealous God)," T. S. Eliot said, "you should pay your respects to Hitler or Stalin."

The second half of the twentieth century proved these hopes and fears unfounded. Economic and social modernization became global in scope, and at the same time a global revival of religion occurred. This revival, *la revanche de Dieu*, Gilles Kepel termed it, has pervaded every continent, every civilization, and virtually every country. In the mid-1970s, as Kepel observes, the trend to secularization and toward the accommodation of religion with secularism "went into reverse. A new religious approach took shape, aimed no longer at adapting to secular values but at recovering a sacred foundation for the organization of society—by changing society if necessary. Expressed in a multitude of ways, this approach advocated moving on from a modernism that had failed, attributing its setbacks and dead ends to separation from God. The theme was no longer *aggiornamento* but a 'second evangelization of Europe,' the aim was no longer to modernize Islam but to 'Islamize modernity.'"

This religious revival has in part involved expansion by some religions, which gained new recruits in societies where they had previously not had them. To a much larger extent, however, the religious resurgence involved people returning to, reinvigorating, and giving new meaning to the traditional religions of their communities. Christianity, Islam, Judaism, Hinduism, Buddhism, Orthodoxy, all experienced new surges in commitment, relevance, and practice by erstwhile casual believers. In all of them fundamentalist movements arose committed to the militant purification of religious doctrines and institutions and the reshaping of personal, social, and public behavior in accordance with religious tenets. The fundamentalist movements are dramatic and can have significant political impact. They are, however, only the surface waves of the much broader and more fundamental religious tide that is giving a different cast to human

life at the end of the twentieth century. The renewal of religion throughout the world far transcends the activities of fundamentalist extremists. In
society after society it manifests itself in the daily lives and work of people
and the concerns and projects of governments. The cultural resurgence in
the secular Confucian culture takes the form of the affirmation of Asian
values but in the rest of the world manifests itself in the affirmation of
religious values. The "unsecularization of the world," as George Weigel
remarked "is one of the dominant social facts in the late twentieth century." . . .

How can this global religious resurgence be explained? Particular
causes obviously operated in individual countries and civilizations. Yet it is
too much to expect that a large number of different causes would have
produced simultaneous and similar developments in most parts of the
world. A global phenomenon demands a global explanation. However
much events in particular countries may have been influenced by unique
factors, some general causes must have been at work. What were they?

The most obvious, most salient, and most powerful cause of the global religious resurgence is precisely what was supposed to cause the death
of religion: the processes of social, economic, and cultural modernization
that swept across the world in the second half of the twentieth century.
Long-standing sources of identity and systems of authority are disrupted.
People move from the countryside into the city, become separated from
their roots, and take new jobs or no job. They interact with large numbers
of strangers and are exposed to new sets of relationships. They need new
sources of identity, new forms of stable community, and new sets of moral
precepts to provide them with a sense of meaning and purpose. Religion,
both mainstream and fundamentalist, meets these needs. As Lee Kuan Yew
explained for East Asia:

We are agricultural societies that have industrialized within one or two generations. What happened in the West over 200 years or more is happening here in
about 50 years or less. It is all crammed and crushed into a very tight time frame,
so there are bound to be dislocations and malfunctions. If you look at the fast-
growing countries—Korea, Thailand, Hong Kong, and Singapore—there's been
one remarkable phenomenon: the rise of religion. . . . The old customs and religions—ancestor worship, shamanism—no longer completely satisfy. There is a
quest for some higher explanations about man's purpose, about why we are here.
This is associated with periods of great stress in society.

People do not live by reason alone. They cannot calculate and act ra-
tionally in pursuit of their self-interest until they define their self. Interest
politics presupposes identity. In times of rapid social change established
identities dissolve, the self must be redefined, and new identities created.

For people facing the need to determine Who am I? Where do I belong? religion provides compelling answers, and religious groups provide small social communities to replace those lost through urbanization. All religions, as Hassan al-Turabi said, furnish "people with a sense of identity and a direction in life." In this process, people rediscover or create new historical identities. Whatever universalist goals they may have, religions give people identity by positing a basic distinction between believers and nonbelievers, between a superior in-group and a different and inferior out-group.

In the Muslim world, Bernard Lewis argues, there has been "a recurring tendency, in times of emergency, for Muslims to find their basic identity and loyalty in the religious community—that is to say, in an entity defined by Islam rather than by ethnic or territorial criteria." Gilles Kepel similarly highlights the centrality of the search for identity: "Re-Islamization 'from below' is first and foremost a way of rebuilding an identity in a world that has lost its meaning and become amorphous and alienating." In India, "a new Hindu identity is under construction" as a response to tensions and alienation generated by modernization. In Russia, the religious revival is the result "of a passionate desire for identity which only the Orthodox church, the sole unbroken link with the Russians' 1000-year past, can provide," while in the Islamic republics the revival similarly stems "from the Central Asians' most powerful aspiration: to assert the identities that Moscow suppressed for decades." Fundamentalist movements, in particular, are "a way of coping with the experience of chaos, the loss of identity, meaning and secure social structures created by the rapid introduction of modern social and political patterns, secularism, scientific culture and economic development." The fundamentalist "movements that matter," agrees William H. McNeill, " . . . are those that recruit from society at large and spread because they answer, or seem to answer, newly felt human needs. . . . It is no accident that these movements are all based in countries where population pressure on the land is making continuation of old village ways impossible for a majority of the population, and where urban-based mass communications, by penetrating the villages, have begun to erode an age-old framework of peasant life."

More broadly, the religious resurgence throughout the world is a reaction against secularism, moral relativism, and self-indulgence, and a reaffirmation of the values of order, discipline, work, mutual help, and human solidarity. Religious groups meet social needs left untended by state bureaucracies. These include the provision of medical and hospital services, kindergartens and schools, care for the elderly, prompt relief after natural and other catastrophes, and welfare and social support during periods of economic deprivation. The breakdown of order and of civil society creates vacuums which are filled by religious, often fundamentalist, groups. . . .

. . . "More than anything else," William McNeill observes, "reaffirmation of Islam, whatever its specific sectarian form, means the repudiation of European and American influence upon local society, politics, and morals." In this sense, the revival of non-Western religions is the most powerful manifestation of anti-Westernism in non-Western societies. That revival is not a rejection of modernity; it is a rejection of the West and of the secular, relativistic, degenerate culture associated with the West. It is a rejection of what has been termed the "Westoxification" of non-Western societies. It is a declaration of cultural independence from the West, a proud statement that: "We will be modern but we won't be you." . . .

Some Westerners, including [former] President Bill Clinton, have argued that the West does not have problems with Islam but only with violent Islamist extremists. Fourteen hundred years of history demonstrate otherwise. The relations between Islam and Christianity, both Orthodox and Western, have often been stormy. Each has been the other's Other. The twentieth-century conflict between liberal democracy and Marxist-Leninism is only a fleeting and superficial historical phenomenon compared to the continuing and deeply conflictual relation between Islam and Christianity. At times, peaceful coexistence has prevailed; more often the relation has been one of intense rivalry and of varying degrees of hot war. Their "historical dynamics," John Esposito comments, " . . . often found the two communities in competition, and locked at times in deadly combat, for power, land, and souls." Across the centuries the fortunes of the two religions have risen and fallen in a sequence of momentous surges, pauses, and countersurges. . . .

A . . . mix of factors has increased the conflict between Islam and the West in the late twentieth century. First, Muslim population growth has generated large numbers of unemployed and disaffected young people who become recruits to Islamist causes, exert pressure on neighboring societies, and migrate to the West. Second, the Islamic Resurgence has given Muslims renewed confidence in the distinctive character and worth of their civilization and values compared to those of the West. Third, the West's simultaneous efforts to universalize its values and institutions, to maintain its military and economic superiority, and to intervene in conflicts in the Muslim world generate intense resentment among Muslims. Fourth, the collapse of communism removed a common enemy of the West and Islam and left each the perceived major threat to the other. Fifth, the increasing contact between and intermingling of Muslims and Westerners stimulate in each a new sense of their own identity and how it differs from that of the other. Interaction and intermingling also exacerbate differences over the rights of the members of one civilization in a country dominated by members of the other civilization. Within both Muslim and Christian societies, tolerance for the other declined sharply in the 1980s and 1990s.

The causes of the renewed conflict between Islam and the West thus lie in fundamental questions of power and culture. *Kto? Kovo?* Who is to rule? Who is to be ruled? The central issue of politics defined by Lenin is the root of the contest between Islam and the West. There is, however, the additional conflict, which Lenin would have considered meaningless, between two different versions of what is right and what is wrong and, as a consequence, who is right and who is wrong. So long as Islam remains Islam (which it will) and the West remains the West (which is more dubious), this fundamental conflict between two great civilizations and ways of life will continue to define their relations in the future even as it has defined them for the past fourteen centuries. . . .

The underlying problem for the West is not Islamic fundamentalism. It is Islam, a different civilization whose people are convinced of the superiority of their culture and are obsessed with the inferiority of their power. The problem for Islam is not the CIA or the U.S. Department of Defense. It is the West, a different civilization whose people are convinced of the universality of their culture and believe that their superior, if declining, power imposes on them the obligation to extend that culture throughout the world. These are the basic ingredients that fuel conflict between Islam and the West.

In the 1950s Lester Pearson warned that humans were moving into "an age when different civilizations will have to learn to live side by side in peaceful interchange, learning from each other, studying each other's history and ideals and art and culture, mutually enriching each others' lives. The alternative, in this overcrowded little world, is misunderstanding, tension, clash, and catastrophe." The futures of both peace and Civilization depend upon understanding and cooperation among the political, spiritual, and intellectual leaders of the world's major civilizations. In the clash of civilizations, Europe and America will hang together or hang separately. In the greater clash, the global "*real* clash," between Civilization and barbarism, the world's great civilizations, with their rich accomplishments in religion, art, literature, philosophy, science, technology, morality, and compassion, will also hang together or hang separately. In the emerging era, clashes of civilizations are the greatest threat to world peace, and an international order based on civilizations is the surest safeguard against world war.

81

FAREED ZAKARIA

From *The Post-American World*

Dr. Fareed Zakaria is a scholar, writer, and TV host whose views on American foreign policy and international affairs are highly regarded by people of varying political ideologies. In this book, Zakaria addresses the changing nature of international politics and the United States' place within it. As the rest of the world—especially Asia—grows dramatically, the United States is no longer in the position of uncontested dominance that it had enjoyed over the past century. Zakaria is careful to distinguish between an "anti-American world" and a "post-American world." The latter, not the former, is the reality. The author sketches out a role for the United States in the world order that is developing: "global broker." More like a "chair of the board" than the single superpower, this role is not a familiar one for America, but one that promises great influence and power in the global community. Zakaria concludes his vision for the future with a plea for less fear about the rest of the world and more of the American generosity of spirit that he experienced first hand decades ago, as a young visiting college student.

THIS IS A BOOK not about the decline of America but rather about the rise of everyone else. It is about the great transformation taking place around the world, a transformation that, though often discussed, remains poorly understood. This is natural. Changes, even sea changes, take place gradually. Though we talk about a new era, the world seems to be one with which we are familiar. But in fact, it is very different.

There have been three tectonic power shifts over the last five hundred years, fundamental changes in the distribution of power that have reshaped international life—its politics, economics, and culture. The first was the rise of the Western world, a process that began in the fifteenth century and accelerated dramatically in the late eighteenth century. It produced modernity as we know it: science and technology, commerce and capitalism, the agricultural and industrial revolutions. It also produced the prolonged political dominance of the nations of the West.

The second shift, which took place in the closing years of the nineteenth century, was the rise of the United States. Soon after it industrialized, the United States became the most powerful nation since imperial Rome, and the only one that was stronger than any likely combination of

other nations. For most of the last century, the United States has dominated global economics, politics, science, and culture. For the last twenty
years, that dominance has been unrivaled, a phenomenon unprecedented
in modern history.

We are now living through the third great power shift of the modern
era. It could be called "the rise of the rest." Over the past few decades,
countries all over the world have been experiencing rates of economic
growth that were once unthinkable. While they have had booms and busts,
the overall trend has been unambiguously upward. This growth has been
most visible in Asia but is no longer confined to it. That is why to call this
shift "the rise of Asia" does not describe it accurately. In 2006 and 2007,
124 countries grew at a rate of 4 percent or more. That includes more
than 30 countries in Africa, two-thirds of the continent. Antoine van
Agtmael, the fund manager who coined the term "emerging markets," has
identified the 25 companies most likely to be the world's next great mul-
tinationals. His list includes four companies each from Brazil, Mexico,
South Korea, and Taiwan; three from India; two from China; and one each
from Argentina, Chile, Malaysia, and South Africa. . . .

. . . For the first time ever, we are witnessing genuinely global growth.
This is creating an international system in which countries in all parts of
the world are no longer objects or observers but players in their own
right. It is the birth of a truly global order.

A related aspect of this new era is the diffusion of power from states to
other actors. The "rest" that is rising includes many nonstate actors. Groups
and individuals have been empowered, and hierarchy, centralization, and
control are being undermined. Functions that were once controlled by
governments are now shared with international bodies like the World
Trade Organization and the European Union. Nongovernmental groups
are mushrooming every day on every issue in every country. Corporations and capital are moving from place to place, finding the best location
in which to do business, rewarding some governments while punishing
others. Terrorists like Al Qaeda, drug cartels, insurgents, and militias of all
kinds are finding space to operate within the nooks and crannies of the
international system. Power is shifting away from nation-states, up, down,
and sideways. In such an atmosphere, the traditional applications of national power, both economic and military, have become less effective.

The emerging international system is likely to be quite different from
those that have preceded it. One hundred years ago, there was a multipolar order run by a collection of European governments, with constantly
shifting alliances, rivalries, miscalculations, and wars. Then came the bipo-

lar duopoly of the Cold War,* more stable in many ways, but with the superpowers reacting and overreacting to each other's every move. Since 1991, we have lived under an American imperium, a unique, unipolar world in which the open global economy has expanded and accelerated dramatically. This expansion is now driving the next change in the nature of the international order.

At the politico-military level, we remain in a single-superpower world. But in every other dimension—industrial, financial, educational, social, cultural—the distribution of power is shifting, moving away from American dominance. That does not mean we are entering an anti-American world. But we are moving into a *post-American world,* one defined and directed from many places and by many people.

What kinds of opportunities and challenges do these changes present? What do they portend for the United States and its dominant position? What will this new era look like in terms of war and peace, economics and business, ideas and culture?

In short, what will it mean to live in a post-American world? . . .

Imagine that it is January 2000, and you ask a fortune-teller to predict the course of the global economy over the next several years. Let's say that you give him some clues, to help him gaze into his crystal ball. The United States will be hit by the worst terrorist attack in history, you explain, and will respond by launching two wars, one of which will go badly awry and keep Iraq—the country with the world's third-largest oil reserves—in chaos for years. Iran will gain strength in the Middle East and move to acquire a nuclear capability. North Korea will go further, becoming the world's eighth declared nuclear power. Russia will turn hostile and imperious in its dealings with its neighbors and the West. In Latin America, Hugo Chávez of Venezuela will launch the most spirited anti-Western campaign in a generation, winning many allies and fans. Israel and Hezbollah will fight a war in southern Lebanon, destabilizing Beirut's fragile government, drawing in Iran and Syria, and rattling the Israelis. Gaza will become a failed state ruled by Hamas, and peace talks between Israel and the Palestinians will go nowhere. "Given these events," you say to the sage, "how will the global economy fare over the next six years?"

*The Cold War refers to the hostility that existed between the United States and the Soviet Union from the end of World War II until the late 1980s. The Cold War involved many forms of hostility: Democracy versus communism; America's NATO allies versus the Soviet Union's Warsaw Pact military partners; the threat of nuclear war; economic competition; the dividing of Third World nations into pro-U.S. and pro-Soviet camps. With the demise of communism in Eastern Europe and the disintegration of the Soviet Union, the Cold War era has ended.—Eds.

This is not really a hypothetical. We have the forecasts of experts from those years. They were all wrong. The correct prediction would have been that, between 2000 and 2007, the world economy would grow at its fastest pace in nearly four decades. Income per person across the globe would rise at a faster rate (3.2 percent) than in any other period in history.

In the two decades since the end of the Cold War, we have lived through a paradox, one we experience every morning when reading the newspapers. The world's politics seems deeply troubled, with daily reports of bombings, terror plots, rogue states, and civil strife. And yet the global economy forges ahead, not without significant interruptions and crises, but still vigorously upward on the whole. Markets do panic but over economic not political news. The front page of the newspaper seems unconnected to the business section. . . .

What explains this mismatch between a politics that spirals downward and an economy that stays robust? First, it's worth looking more carefully at the cascade of bad news. It seems that we are living in crazily violent times. But don't believe everything you see on television. Our anecdotal impression turns out to be wrong. War and organized violence have declined dramatically over the last two decades. Ted Robert Gurr and a team of scholars at the University of Maryland's Center for International Development and Conflict Management tracked the data carefully and came to the following conclusion: "the general magnitude of global warfare has decreased by over sixty percent [since the mid-1980s], falling by the end of 2004 to its lowest level since the late 1950s." Violence increased steadily throughout the Cold War—increasing sixfold between the 1950s and early 1990s—but the trend peaked just before the collapse of the Soviet Union in 1991 and "the extent of warfare among and within states lessened by nearly half in the first decade after the Cold War." Harvard's polymath professor Steven Pinker argues "that today we are probably living in the most peaceful time in our species' existence."

One reason for the mismatch between reality and our sense of it might be that, over these same decades, we have experienced a revolution in information technology that now brings us news from around the world instantly, vividly, and continuously. The immediacy of the images and the intensity of the twenty-four-hour news cycle combine to produce constant hyperbole. Every weather disturbance is "the storm of the century." Every bomb that explodes is BREAKING NEWS. It is difficult to put this all in context because the information revolution is so new. We didn't get daily footage on the roughly two million who died in the killing fields of Cambodia in the 1970s or the million who perished in the sands of the Iran-Iraq war in the 1980s. We have not even seen much footage from the war in Congo in the 1990s, where millions died. But now, we see almost daily, live broadcasts of the effects of IEDs or car bombs or rockets—tragic events, to be sure, but often with death tolls under ten. The randomness of terrorist violence, the targeting of civilians, and the ease with which modern societies can be penetrated add to our disquiet. "That could have been me," people say after a terrorist attack.

It *feels* like a very dangerous world. But it isn't. Your chances of dying as a consequence of organized violence of any kind are low and getting lower. The data reveal a broad trend away from wars among major countries, the kind of conflict that produces massive casualties.

I don't believe that war has become obsolete or any such foolishness. Human nature remains what it is and international politics what it is. History has witnessed periods of calm that have been followed by extraordinary bloodshed. And numbers are not the only measure of evil. The nature of the killings in the former Yugoslavia in the early 1990s—premeditated, religiously motivated, systematic—makes that war, which had 200,000 casualties, a moral obscenity that should register very high on any scale. Al Qaeda's barbarism—cold-blooded beheadings, the deliberate targeting of innocents—is gruesome despite its relatively low number of casualties.

Still, if we are to understand the times we are living in, we must first accurately describe them. And they are, for now, in historical context, unusually calm. . . .

Islamic terror, which makes the headlines daily, is a large and persistent problem, but one involving small numbers of fanatics. It feeds on the dysfunctions of the Muslim world, the sense (real and imagined) of humiliation at the hands of the West, and easy access to technologies of violence. And yet, does it rank as a threat on the order of Germany's drive for world domination in the first half of the twentieth century? Or Soviet expansionism in the second half? Or Mao's efforts to foment war and revolution across the Third World in the 1950s and 1960s? These were all challenges backed by the power and purpose of major countries, often with serious allies, and by an ideology that was seen as a plausible alternative to liberal democracy. By comparison, consider the jihadist threat. Before 9/11, when groups like Al Qaeda operated under the radar, governments treated them as minor annoyances, and they roamed freely, built some strength, and hit symbolic, often military targets, killing Americans and other foreigners. Even so, the damage was fairly limited. Since 2001, governments everywhere have been aggressive in busting terrorists' networks, following their money, and tracking their recruits—with almost immediate results. In Indonesia, the largest Muslim nation in the world, the government captured both the chief and the military leader of Jemaah Islamiah, the country's deadliest jihadist group and the one that carried out the Bali bombings in 2002. With American help, the Filipino army battered the Qaeda-style terrorist outfit Abu Sayyaf. The group's leader was killed by Filipino troops in January 2007, and its membership has declined from as many as two thousand guerrillas six years ago to a few hundred today. In Egypt and Saudi Arabia—Al Qaeda's original bases and targets of attack—terrorist cells have been rounded up, and those still at large have been unable to launch any new attacks in three years. Finance ministries—especially the U.S. Department of the Treasury—have made life far more difficult for terrorists. Global organizations cannot thrive without being able to move money around, and so the more terrorists' funds are tracked and targeted, the more they have to resort to small-scale and hastily improvised operations. This struggle, between governments and terrorists, will persist, but it is the former who have the upper hand. . . .

Here is the bottom line. In the six years since 9/11, Al Qaeda Central—the group led by Osama bin Laden and Ayman Zawahiri—has been unable to launch a major attack anywhere. It was a terrorist organization; it has become a communications company, producing the occasional videotape rather than actual terrorism. Jihad continues, but the jihadists have had to scatter, make do with smaller targets, and operate on a local level— usually through groups with almost no connection to Al Qaeda Central. And this improvised strategy has a crippling weakness: it kills locals, thus alienating ordinary Muslims—a process that is well underway in countries as diverse as Indonesia, Iraq, and Saudi Arabia. Over the last six years, support for bin Laden and his goals has fallen steadily throughout the Muslim world. Between 2002 and 2007, approval of suicide bombing as a tactic—a figure that was always low—has dropped by over 50 percent in most Muslim countries that have been tracked. There have been more denunciations of violence and fatwas against bin Laden than ever before, including from prominent clerics in Saudi Arabia. Much more must happen to modernize the Muslim world, but the modernizers are no longer so scared. They have finally realized that, for all the rhetoric of the madrassas and mosques, few people want to live under the writ of Al Qaeda. Those who have, whether in Afghanistan or Iraq, have become its most dedicated opponents. In contrast to Soviet socialism or even fascism in the 1930s, no society looks with admiration and envy on the fundamentalist Islamic model. On an ideological level, it presents no competition to the Western-originated model of modernity that countries across the world are embracing.

A cottage industry of scaremongering has flourished in the West—especially in the United States—since 9/11. Experts extrapolate every trend they don't like, forgoing any serious study of the data. Many conservative commentators have written about the impending Islamization of Europe (Eurabia, they call it, to make you even more uncomfortable). Except that the best estimates, from U.S. intelligence agencies, indicate that Muslims constitute around 3 percent of Europe's population now and will rise to between 5 and 8 percent by 2025, after which they will probably plateau. The watchdogs note the musings of every crackpot Imam, search the archives for each reference to the end of days, and record and distribute the late-night TV musings of every nutcase who glorifies martyrdom. They erupt in fury when a Somali taxi driver somewhere refuses to load a case of liquor into his car, seeing it as the beginning of sharia in the West. But these episodes do not reflect the basic direction of the Muslim world. That world is also modernizing, though more slowly than the rest, and there are those who try to become leaders in rebellion against it. The reactionaries in the world of Islam are more numerous and extreme than those in other cultures—that world does have its dysfunctions. But they remain a tiny minority of the world's billion-plus Muslims. And neglecting the complicated context in which some of these pseudoreligious statements are made—such as an internal Iranian power struggle among clerics and nonclerics—leads to hair-raising but absurd predictions, like Bernard Lewis's confident claim that Iran's President Mahmoud Ahmadinejad planned to mark an auspicious date on the Islamic calendar (August 22, 2006) *by ending the world.* (Yes, he actually wrote that.)

The ideological watchdogs have spent so much time with the documents of jihad that they have lost sight of actual Muslim societies. Were they to step back, they would see a frustration with the fundamentalists, a desire for modernity (with some dignity and cultural pride for sure), and a search for practical solutions—not a mass quest for immortality through death. When Muslims travel, they flock by the millions to see the razzle-dazzle of Dubai, not the seminaries of Iran. The minority that wants jihad is real, but it operates within societies where such activities are increasingly unpopular and irrelevant. . . .

In some unspoken way, people have recognized that the best counterterrorism policy is resilience. Terrorism is unusual in that it is a military tactic defined by the response of the onlooker. If we are not terrorized, then it doesn't work. And, from New York and London to Mumbai and Jakarta, people are learning this fact through experience and getting on with life even amid the uncertainty. The most likely scenario—a series of backpack or truck bombings in the United States—would be a shock, but in a couple of weeks its effects would fade and the long-term consequences would likely be minimal. In vast, vigorous, and complex societies—the American economy is now $13 trillion—problems in a few places do not easily spill over. Modern civilization may be stronger than we suspect. . . .

The rise of the rest, while real, is a long, slow process. And it is one that ensures America a vital, though different, role. As China, India, Brazil, Russia, South Africa, and a host of smaller countries all do well in the years ahead, new points of tension will emerge among them. Many of these rising countries have historical animosities, border disputes, and contemporary quarrels with one another; in most cases, nationalism will grow along with economic and geopolitical stature. Being a distant power, America is often a convenient partner for many regional nations worried about the rise of a hegemon in their midst. In fact, as the scholar William Wohlforth notes, American influence is strengthened by the growth of a dominant regional power. These factors are often noted in discussions of Asia, but it is true of many other spots on the globe as well. The process will not be mechanical. As one of these countries rises (China), it will not produce a clockwork-like balancing dynamic where its neighbor (India) will seek a formal alliance with the United States. Today's world is more complicated than that. But these rivalries do give the United States an opportunity to play a large and constructive role at the center of the global order. It has the potential to be what Bismarck helped Germany become (briefly) in the late nineteenth-century—Europe's "honest broker," forging close relationships with each of the major countries, ties that were closer than the ones those countries had with one another. It was the hub of the European system. Being the global broker today would be a job involving not just the American government but its society, with all the strengths and perspectives that it will bring to the challenge. It is a role that the United States—with its global interests and presence, complete portfolio of power, and diverse immigrant communities—could learn to play with great skill.

This new role is quite different from the traditional superpower role. It involves consultation, cooperation, and even compromise. It derives its power by setting the agenda, defining the issues, and mobilizing coalitions. It is not a top-down hierarchy in which the United States makes its decisions and then informs a grateful (or silent) world. But it is a crucial role because, in a world with many players, setting the agenda and organizing coalitions become primary forms of power. The chair of the board who can gently guide a group of independent directors is still a very powerful person. . . .

Before it can implement any of these specific strategies, however, the United States must make a much broader adjustment. It needs to stop cowering in fear. It is fear that has created a climate of paranoia and panic in the United States and fear that has enabled our strategic missteps. Having spooked ourselves into believing that we have no option but to act fast and alone, preemptively and unilaterally, we have managed to destroy decades of international goodwill, alienate allies, and embolden enemies, while solving few of the major international problems we face. To recover its place in the world, America first has to recover its confidence.

By almost all objective measures, the United States is in a blessed position today. It faces problems, crises, and resistance, but compared with any of the massive threats of the past—Nazi Germany, Stalin's aggression, nuclear war—the circumstances are favorable, and the world is moving our way. In 1933, Franklin Delano Roosevelt diagnosed the real danger for the United States. "The only thing we have to fear is fear itself," he said. "Nameless, unreasoning, unjustified terror." And he was arguing against fear when America's economic and political system was near collapse, when a quarter of the workforce was unemployed, and when fascism was on the march around the world. Somehow we have managed to spook ourselves in a time of worldwide peace and prosperity. Keeping that front and center in our minds is crucial to ensure that we do not miscalculate, misjudge, and misunderstand.

America has become a nation consumed by anxiety, worried about terrorists and rogue nations, Muslims and Mexicans, foreign companies and free trade, immigrants and international organizations. The strongest nation in the history of the world now sees itself as besieged by forces beyond its control. While the Bush administration has contributed mightily to this state of affairs, it is a phenomenon that goes beyond one president. Too many Americans have been taken in by a rhetoric of fear. . . .

We will never be able to prevent a small group of misfits from planning some terrible act of terror. No matter how far-seeing and competent our intelligence and law-enforcement officials, people will always be able to slip through the cracks in a large, open, and diverse country. The real test of American leadership is not whether we can make 100 percent sure we prevent the attack, but rather how we respond to it. Stephen Flynn, a homeland-security expert at the Council on Foreign Relations, argues that our goal must be resilience—how quickly can we bounce back from a disruption? In the material sciences, resilience is the ability of a material to recover its original shape after a deformation. If one day bombs do go off, we must ensure that they cause as little disruption—economic, social, political—as possible. This would prevent the terrorist from achieving his main objective. If we are not terrorized, then in a crucial sense we have defeated terrorism. . . .

At the end of the day, openness is America's greatest strength. Many smart policy wonks have clever ideas that they believe will better American productivity, savings, and health care. More power to them all. But historically, America has succeeded not because of the ingenuity of its government programs but because of the vigor of its society. It has thrived because it has kept itself open to the world—to goods and services, to ideas and inventions, and, above all, to people and cultures. This openness has allowed us to respond quickly and flexibly to new economic times, to manage change and diversity with remarkable ease, and to push forward the boundaries of individual freedom and autonomy. It has allowed America to create the first universal nation, a place where people from all over the world can work, mingle, mix, and share in a common dream and a common destiny.

In the fall of 1982, I arrived here as an eighteen-year-old student from India, eight thousand miles away. . . .

. . . Everywhere I went, the atmosphere was warm and welcoming. It was a feeling I had never had before, a country wide open to the world, to the future, and to anyone who loved it. To a young visitor, it seemed to offer unlimited generosity and promise.

For America to thrive in this new and challenging era, for it to succeed amid the rise of the rest, it need fulfill only one test. It should be a place that is as inviting and exciting to the young student who enters the country today as it was for this awkward eighteen-year-old a generation ago.

82

CHALMERS JOHNSON

From *Blowback*

A scholar on American foreign affairs, Chalmers Johnson applies the CIA term "blowback" to the dilemma of this nation's military and diplomatic actions: many problems we grapple with currently are "unintended consequences of policies that were kept secret from the American people." Johnson discusses drug trafficking, terrorist acts, and economic retaliation as examples of other nations reacting to American policies, no matter how unintentional the negative results of those policies were. The country's actions may well produce more future blowback without citizens realizing what's ahead. Johnson's warning about American foreign policy is harsh: " . . . a nation reaps what it sows, even if it does not fully know or understand what it has sown."

———

NORTHERN ITALIAN COMMUNITIES HAD, for years, complained about low-flying American military aircraft. In February 1998, the inevitable happened. A Marine Corps EA-6B Prowler with a crew of four, one of scores of advanced American jet fighters and bombers stationed at places like Aviano, Cervia, Brindisi, and Sigonella, sliced through a ski-lift cable near the resort town of Cavalese and plunged twenty people riding in a single gondola to their deaths on the snowy slopes several hundred feet below. Although marine pilots are required to maintain an altitude of at least one thousand feet (two thousand, according to the Italian government), the plane had cut the cable at a height of 360 feet. It was traveling at 621 miles per hour when 517 miles per hour was considered the upper limit. The pilot had been performing low-level acrobatics while his co-pilot took pictures on videotape (which he later destroyed).

In response to outrage in Italy and calls for vigorous prosecution of those responsible, the marine pilots argued that their charts were inaccurate, that their altimeter had not worked, and that they had not consulted U.S. Air Force units permanently based in the area about local hazards. A court-martial held not in Italy but in Camp Lejeune, North Carolina, exonerated everyone involved, calling it a "training accident." Soon after, President Bill Clinton apologized and promised financial compensation to the victims, but on May 14, 1999, Congress dropped the provision for aid to the families because of opposition in the House of Representatives and from the Pentagon. . . .

I believe it is past time for such a discussion to begin, for Americans to consider why we have created an empire—a word from which we shy away—and what the consequences of our imperial stance may be for the rest of the world and for ourselves. Not so long ago, the way we garrisoned the world could be discussed far more openly and comfortably because the explanation seemed to lie at hand—in the very existence of the Soviet Union and of communism. Had the Italian disaster occurred two decades earlier, it would have seemed no less a tragedy, but many Americans would have argued that, given the Cold War, such incidents were an unavoidable cost of protecting democracies like Italy against the menace of Soviet totalitarianism. With the disappearance of any military threat faintly comparable to that posed by the former Soviet Union, such "costs" have become easily avoidable. American military forces could have been withdrawn from Italy, as well as from other foreign bases, long ago. That they were not and that Washington instead is doing everything in its considerable powers to perpetuate Cold War structures, even without the Cold War's justification, places such overseas deployments in a new light. They have become striking evidence, for those who care to look, of an imperial project that the Cold War obscured. The by-products of this project are likely to build up reservoirs of resentment against all Americans—tourists, students, and businessmen, as well as members of the armed forces—that can have lethal results.

For any empire, including an unacknowledged one, there is a kind of balance sheet that builds up over time. Military crimes, accidents, and atrocities make up only one category on the debit side of the balance sheet that the United States has been accumulating, especially since the Cold War ended. To take an example of quite a different kind of debit, consider South Korea, a longtime ally. On Christmas Eve 1997, it declared itself financially bankrupt and put its economy under the guidance of the International Monetary Fund, which is basically an institutional surrogate of the United States government. Most Americans were surprised by the economic disasters that overtook Thailand, South Korea, Malaysia, and Indonesia in 1997 and that then spread around the world, crippling the Russian and Brazilian economies. They could hardly imagine that the U.S. government might have had a hand in causing them, even though various American pundits and economists expressed open delight in these disasters, which threw millions of people, who had previously had hopes of achieving economic prosperity and security, into the most abysmal poverty. At worst, Americans took the economic meltdown of places like

Indonesia and Brazil to mean that beneficial American-supported policies of "globalization" were working—that we were effectively helping restructure various economies around the world so that they would look and work more like ours. . . .

If Washington is the headquarters of a global military-economic dominion, the answers will be very different than if we think of the United States as simply one among many sovereign nations. There is a logic to empire that differs from the logic of a nation, and acts committed in service to an empire but never acknowledged as such have a tendency to haunt the future.

The term "blowback," which officials of the Central Intelligence Agency first invented for their own internal use, is starting to circulate among students of international relations. It refers to the unintended consequences of policies that were kept secret from the American people. What the daily press reports as the malign acts of "terrorists" or "drug lords" or "rogue states" or "illegal arms merchants" often turn out to be blowback from earlier American operations.

It is now widely recognized, for example, that the 1988 bombing of Pan Am flight 103 over Lockerbie, Scotland, which resulted in the deaths of 259 passengers and 11 people on the ground, was retaliation for a 1986 Reagan administration aerial raid on Libya that killed President Muammar Khadaffi's stepdaughter. Some in the United States have suspected that other events can also be explained as blowback from imperial acts. For example, the epidemic of cocaine and heroin use that has afflicted American cities during the past two decades was probably fueled in part by Central and South American military officers or corrupt politicians whom the CIA or the Pentagon once trained or supported and then installed in key government positions. For example, in Nicaragua in the 1980s, the U.S. government organized a massive campaign against the socialist- oriented Sandinista government. American agents then looked the other way when the Contras, the military insurgents they had trained, made deals to sell cocaine in American cities in order to buy arms and supplies.

If drug blowback is hard to trace to its source, bomb attacks, whether on U.S. embassies in Africa, the World Trade Center in New York City, or an apartment complex in Saudi Arabia that housed U.S. servicemen, are another matter. One man's terrorist is, of course, another man's freedom fighter, and what U.S. officials denounce as unprovoked terrorist attacks on its innocent citizens are often meant as retaliation for previous American imperial actions. Terrorists attack innocent and undefended American targets precisely because American soldiers and sailors firing cruise mis-

siles from ships at sea or sitting in B-52 bombers at extremely high alti-
tudes or supporting brutal and repressive regimes from Washington seem
invulnerable. As members of the Defense Science Board wrote in a 1997
report to the undersecretary of defense for acquisition and technology,
"Historical data show a strong correlation between U.S. involvement in
international situations and an increase in terrorist attacks against the
United States. In addition, the military asymmetry that denies nation
states the ability to engage in overt attacks against the United States drives
the use of transnational actors [that is, terrorists from one country attacking in another]." . . .

Blowback itself can lead to more blowback, in a spiral of destructive
behavior. A good illustration of this lies in the government's reaction to
the August 7, 1998, bombings of American embassy buildings in Nairobi
and Dar es Salaam, with the loss of 12 American and 212 Kenyan and Tan-
zanian lives and some 4,500 injured. The U.S. government promptly
placed the blame on Osama bin Laden, a Saudi who had long denounced
his country's rulers and their American allies. On August 20, the United
States retaliated by firing nearly eighty cruise missiles (at a cost of $750,000
each) into a pharmaceutical plant in Khartoum, Sudan, and an old muja-
hideen camp site in Afghanistan. (One missile went four hundred miles
off course and landed in Pakistan.) Both missile targets had been identified by American intelligence as enterprises or training areas associated
with bin Laden or his followers. It was soon revealed, however, that the
intelligence on both places had been faulty and that neither target could
be connected with those who were suspected of attacking the embassies.
On September 2, 1998, the U.S. secretary of defense said that he had been
unaware that the plant in Khartoum made medicines, not nerve gas, when
he recommended that it be attacked. He also admitted that the plant's
connection to bin Laden was, at best, "indirect." Nonetheless, President
Clinton continued to insist that he had repelled an "imminent threat to
our national security," and Secretary of State Madeleine Albright called
Sudan a "viper's nest of terrorists."

Government spokesmen continue to justify these attacks as "deter-
ring" terrorism, even if the targets proved to be irrelevant to any damage
done to facilities of the United States. In this way, future blowback possibilities are seeded into the world. The same spokesmen ignore the fact
that the alleged mastermind of the embassy bombings, bin Laden, is a
former protégé of the United States. When America was organizing Afghan rebels against the USSR in the 1980s, he played an important role in
driving the Soviet Union from Afghanistan and only turned against the
United States in 1991 because he regarded the stationing of American

troops in his native Saudi Arabia during and after the Persian Gulf War as a violation of his religious beliefs. Thus, the attacks on our embassies in Africa, if they were indeed his work, are an instance of blowback rather than unprovoked terrorism. Instead of bombing sites in Sudan and Afghanistan in response, the United States might better have considered reducing or removing our large-scale and provocative military presence in Saudi Arabia. . . .

In a sense, blowback is simply another way of saying that a nation reaps what it sows. Although people usually know what they have sown, our national experience of blowback is seldom imagined in such terms because so much of what the managers of the American empire have sown has been kept secret. As a concept, blowback is obviously most easy to grasp in its most straightforward manifestation. The unintended consequences of American policies and acts in country X are a bomb at an American embassy in country Y or a dead American in country Z. Certainly any number of Americans have been killed in that fashion, from Catholic nuns in El Salvador to tourists in Uganda who just happened to wander into hidden imperial scenarios about which they knew nothing. But blowback, as demonstrated in this book, is hardly restricted to such reasonably straightforward examples. . . .

I do not believe that America's "vast array of strategical commitments" were made in past decades largely as the result of attempts to exploit other nations for economic gain or simply to dominate them politically and militarily. Although the United States has in the past engaged in imperialist exploitation of other nations, particularly in Latin America, it has also tried in various ways to liquidate many such commitments. The roots of American "imperial overstretch" today are not the same as those of past empires. Instead they more closely resemble those that brought down the Soviet Union.

Many Americans do not care to see their country's acts, policies, or situations compared with the Soviet Union's; some condemn such a comparison because it commits the alleged fallacy of "moral equivalence." They insist that America's values and institutions are vastly more humane than those of Stalin's Russia. I agree. Throughout the years of the Cold War, the United States remained a functioning democracy, with rights for its citizens unimaginable in the Soviet context (even if its more recent maintenance of the world's largest prison population suggests that it should be cautious in criticizing other nations' systems of criminal justice). Comparisons between the United States and the former Soviet Union are useful, however, because those two hegemons developed in tandem, challenging each other militarily, economically, and ideologically.

In the long run, it may turn out that, like two scorpions in a bottle, they succeeded in stinging each other to death. The roots of both modern empires lay in World War II and in their subsequent contest to control the forces that the war unleashed. A stress on the costs of the Cold War to the United States also draws attention to the legacies of that struggle. America's role as the planet's "lone superpower"—as leader of the peace-loving nations and patron of such institutions as the United Nations, the World Bank, and the World Trade Organization—is made much more difficult by the nature of the harvest we continue to reap for imprudent, often secret operations undertaken in the past. . . .

Terrorism by definition strikes at the innocent in order to draw attention to the sins of the invulnerable. The innocent of the twenty-first century are going to harvest unexpected blowback disasters from the imperialist escapades of recent decades. Although most Americans may be largely ignorant of what was, and still is, being done in their names, all are likely to pay a steep price—individually and collectively—for their nation's continued efforts to dominate the global scene. Before the damage of heedless triumphalist acts and the triumphalist rhetoric and propaganda that goes with them becomes irreversible, it is important to open a new discussion of our global role during and after the Cold War. . . .

The American military at the end of the century is becoming an autonomous system. We no longer have a draft army based on the obligation of citizens to serve their nation. When the Vietnam War exposed the inequities of the draft—for example, the ease with which college students could gain deferments—Congress decided to abolish conscription rather than enforce it in an equitable manner. Today, the military is an entirely mercenary force, made up of volunteers paid salaries by the Pentagon. Although the military still tries to invoke the public's support for a force made up of fellow citizens, this force is increasingly separated from civilian interests and devoted to military ones.

Equipped with the most advanced precision-guided munitions, high-performance aircraft, and intercontinental-range missiles, the American armed forces can unquestionably deliver death and destruction to any target on earth and expect little in the way of retaliation. Even so, these forces voraciously demand more and newer equipment, while the Pentagon now more or less sets its own agenda. Accustomed to life in a half-century-old, well-established empire, the corporate interests of the armed forces have begun to take precedence over the older idea that the military is only one of several means that a democratic government might employ to implement its policies. As their size and prominence grow over time, the armed forces of an empire tend to displace other instruments of foreign policy implementation. What also grows is militarism, "a vast array of customs, interests, prestige, actions, and thought associated with armies and wars and yet transcending true military purpose"—and certainly a reasonable description of the American military ethos today.

"Blowback" is shorthand for saying that a nation reaps what it sows, even if it does not fully know or understand what it has sown. Given its wealth and power, the United States will be a prime recipient in the foreseeable future of all of the more expectable forms of blowback, particularly terrorist attacks against Americans in and out of the armed forces anywhere on earth, including within the United States. But it is blowback in its larger aspect—the tangible costs of empire—that truly threatens it. Empires are costly operations, and they become more costly by the year. The hollowing out of American industry, for instance, is a form of blowback—an unintended negative consequence of American policy—even though it is seldom recognized as such. The growth of militarism in a once democratic society is another example of blowback. Empire is the problem. Even though the United States has a strong sense of invulnerability and substantial military and economic tools to make such a feeling credible, the fact of its imperial pretensions means that a crisis is inevitable. More imperialist projects simply generate more blowback. If we do not begin to solve problems in more prudent and modest ways, blowback will only become more intense.

83

JOSEPH NYE

From *Soft Power*

When the United States flexes its military or economic muscle, it is using "hard power," a long used and much relied upon strategy for a superpower. Foreign policy specialist Joseph Nye introduces us here to "soft power," a littler known but no less important source of international influence. "Soft power," Nye explains, "rests on the ability to shape the preferences of others." Culture, values, and the legitimacy of foreign policy all contribute to a nation's soft power. In this selection, Nye gives a brief introduction to some of the competing views of foreign policy, including the Realists, the Wilsonians, the Neoconservatives, and the New Unilateralists. Nye believes that the ultimate success of the United States in protecting its interests in today's world lies in learning how to better utilize soft power along with the hard power we so quickly embrace. Whether you fully agree or not, Nye raises interesting points about the importance of soft power, the power that brought the United States into such prominence after World War II and won the Cold War.

———

MORE THAN FOUR CENTURIES AGO, Niccolo Machiavelli advised princes in Italy that it was more important to be feared than to be loved. But in today's world, it is best to be both. Winning hearts and minds has always been important, but it is even more so in a global information age. Information is power, and modern information technology is spreading information more widely than ever before in history. Yet political leaders have spent little time thinking about how the nature of power has changed and, more specifically, about how to incorporate the soft dimensions into their strategies for wielding power. . . .

Everyone is familiar with hard power. We know that military and economic might often get others to change their position. Hard power can rest on inducements ("carrots") or threats ("sticks"). But sometimes you can get the outcomes you want without tangible threats or payoffs. The indirect way to get what you want has sometimes been called "the second face of power." A country may obtain the outcomes it wants in world politics because other countries—admiring its values, emulating its example, aspiring to its level of prosperity and openness—want to follow it. In this sense, it is also important to set the agenda and attract others in world politics, and not only to force them to change by threatening military force or economic sanctions. This soft power—getting others to want the outcomes that you want—co-opts people rather than coerces them.

Soft power rests on the ability to shape the preferences of others. At the personal level, we are all familiar with the power of attraction and seduction. In a relationship or a marriage, power does not necessarily reside with the larger partner, but in the mysterious chemistry of attraction. And in the business world, smart executives know that leadership is not just a matter of issuing commands, but also involves leading by example and attracting others to do what you want. It is difficult to run a large organization by commands alone. You also need to get others to buy in to your values. Similarly, contemporary practices of community-based policing rely on making the police sufficiently friendly and attractive that a community wants to help them achieve shared objectives.

Political leaders have long understood the power that comes from attraction. If I can get you to want to do what I want, then I do not have to use carrots or sticks to make you do it. Whereas leaders in authoritarian countries can use coercion and issue commands, politicians in democracies have to rely more on a combination of inducement and attraction. Soft power is a staple of daily democratic politics. The ability to establish preferences tends to be associated with intangible assets such as an attractive personality, culture, political values and institutions, and policies that are seen as legitimate or having moral authority. If a leader represents values that others want to follow, it will cost less to lead. . . .

The soft power of a country rests primarily on three resources: its culture (in places where it is attractive to others), its political values (when it lives up to them at home and abroad), and its foreign policies (when they are seen as legitimate and having moral authority.)

Let's start with culture. Culture is the set of values and practices that create meaning for a society. It has many manifestations. It is common to distinguish between high culture such as literature, art, and education, which appeals to elites, and popular culture, which focuses on mass entertainment.

When a country's culture includes universal values and its policies promote values and interests that others share, it increases the probability of obtaining its desired outcomes because of the relationships of attraction and duty that it creates. Narrow values and parochial cultures are less likely to produce soft power. The United States benefits from a universalistic culture. The German editor Josef Joffe once argued that America's soft power was even larger than its economic and military assets. "U.S. culture, low-brow or high, radiates outward with an intensity last seen in the days of the Roman Empire—but with a novel twist. Rome's and Soviet Russia's cultural sway stopped exactly at their military borders. America's soft power, though, rules over an empire on which the sun never sets."

Some analysts treat soft power simply as popular cultural power. They make the mistake of equating soft power behavior with the cultural resources that sometimes help produce it. They confuse the cultural resources with the behavior of attraction. For example, the historian Niall Ferguson describes soft power as "nontraditional forces such as cultural and commercial goods" and then dismisses it on the grounds "that it's, well, soft." Of course, Coke and Big Macs do not necessarily attract people in the Islamic world to love the United States. The North Korean dictator Kim Jong-il is alleged to like pizza and American videos, but that does not affect his nuclear programs. Excellent wines and cheeses do not guarantee attraction to France, nor does the popularity of Pokémon games assure that Japan will get the policy outcomes it wishes. . . .

The values a government champions in its behavior at home (for example, democracy), in international institutions (working with others), and in foreign policy (promoting peace and human rights) strongly affect the preferences of others. Governments can attract or repel others by the influence of their example. But soft power does not belong to the government in the same degree that hard power does. Some hard-power assets such as armed forces are strictly governmental; others are inherently national, such as oil and mineral reserves, and many can be transferred to collective control, such as the civilian air fleet that can be mobilized in an emergency. In contrast, many soft-power resources are separate from the American government and are only partly responsive to its purposes. In the Vietnam era, for example, American popular culture often worked at cross-purposes to official government policy. Today, Hollywood movies that show scantily clad women with libertine attitudes or fundamentalist Christian groups that castigate Islam as an evil religion are both (properly) outside the control of government in a liberal society, but they undercut government efforts to improve relations with Islamic nations. . . .

Hard and soft power sometimes reinforce and sometimes interfere with each other. A country that courts popularity may be loath to exercise its hard power when it should, but a country that throws its weight around without regard to the effects on its soft power may find others placing obstacles in the way of its hard power. No country likes to feel manipulated, even by soft power. . . .

. . . Moreover, as we saw earlier, hard power can sometimes have an attractive or soft side. As Osama bin Laden put it in one of his videos,

"When people see a strong horse and a weak horse, by nature, they will like the strong horse." And to deliberately mix the metaphor, people are more likely to be sympathetic to underdogs than to bet on them.

The 2003 Iraq War provides an interesting example of the interplay of the two forms of power. Some of the motives for war were based on the deterrent effect of hard power. Donald Rumsfeld is reported to have entered office believing that the United States "was seen around the world as a paper tiger, a weak giant that couldn't take a punch" and determined to reverse that reputation. America's military victory in the first Gulf War had helped to produce the Oslo process on Middle East peace, and its 2003 victory in Iraq might eventually have a similar effect. Moreover, states like Syria and Iran might be deterred in their future support of terrorists. These were all hard power reasons to go to war. But another set of motives related to soft power. The neoconservatives believed that American power could be used to export democracy to Iraq and transform the politics of the Middle East. If successful, the war would become self-legitimizing. As William Kristol and Lawrence Kaplan put it, "What is wrong with dominance in the service of sound principles and high ideals?" . . .

Foreign policies also produce soft power when they promote broadly shared values such as democracy and human rights. Americans have wrestled with how to integrate our values with other interests since the early days of the republic, and the main views cut across party lines. Realists like John Quincy Adams warned that the United States "goes not abroad in search of monsters to destroy," and we should not involve ourselves "beyond the power of extrication in all the wars of interest and intrigue." Others follow the tradition of Woodrow Wilson and emphasize democracy and human rights as foreign policy objectives. As we shall see . . . , today's neoconservatives are, in effect, right-wing Wilsonians, and they are interested in the soft power that can be generated by the promotion of democracy.

During the 2000 election campaign, when George W. Bush frequently expressed traditional realist warnings that the United States should not become overextended, leading neoconservatives urged him to make human rights, religious freedom, and democracy priorities for American foreign policy and "not to adopt a narrow view of U.S. national interests." After 9/11, Bush's policy changed and he spoke of the need to use American power to bring democracy to the Middle East. As Lawrence Kaplan and William Kristol put it, "When it comes to dealing with tyrannical regimes like Iraq, Iran and, yes, North Korea, the U.S. should seek transformation, not coexistence, as a primary aim of U.S. foreign policy. As such, it commits the U.S. to the task of maintaining and enforcing a decent world order."

The neoconservatives are correct that such a world order could be a global public good, but they are mistaken to assume that their vision will be shared by all those affected by it. Whether the neoconservative approach creates rather than consumes American soft power depends not only on the results but also on who is consulted and who decides. The neoconservatives pay less heed than traditional Wilsonians to consultation through international institutions. But because the currency of soft power is attraction, it is often easier to generate and wield in a multilateral context.

In recent years, other countries have increasingly complained about the unilateralism of American foreign policy. Of course such differences are a matter of degree, and there are few countries that are pure unilateralists or multilateralists. International concerns about unilateralism began well before George W. Bush became president, and involved Congress as well as the executive branch. The president has disclaimed the label but most observers describe his administration as divided between traditional pragmatists and a more ideological school that the columnist Charles Krauthammer celebrated as "the new unilateralism."

The "new unilateralists" advocate an assertive approach to promoting American values. They worry about a flagging of internal will and a reluctance to turn a unipolar moment into a unipolar era. American intentions are good, American hegemony is benevolent, and that should end the discussion. To them, multilateralism means "submerging American will in a mush of collective decision-making—you have sentenced yourself to reacting to events or passing the buck to multilingual committees with fancy acronyms." They deny that American "arrogance" is a problem. Rather, the problem is "the inescapable reality of American power in its many forms." Policy is legitimized by its origins in a democracy and by the outcome—whether it results in an advance of freedom and democracy. That post hoc legitimization will more than compensate for any loss of legitimacy through unilateralism.

Unfortunately, the approach of the new unilateralists is not very convincing to other countries whose citizens observe that Americans are not immune from hubris and self-interest. Americans do not always have all the answers. As one realist put it, "If we were truly acting in the interests of others as well as our own, we would presumably accord to others a substantive role and, by doing so, end up embracing some form of multilateralism. Others, after all, must be supposed to know their interests

better than we can know them." Since the currency of soft power is attraction based on shared values and the justness and duty of others to
contribute to policies consistent with those shared values, multilateral
consultations are more likely to generate soft power than mere unilateral
assertion of the values. . . .

Anti-Americanism has increased in the past few years. Thomas Pick-
ering, a seasoned diplomat, considered 2003 "as high a zenith of anti-
Americanism as we've seen for a long time." Polls show that our soft-
power losses can be traced largely to our foreign policy. "A widespread
and fashionable view is that the United States is a classically imperialist
power. . . . That mood has been expressed in different ways by different
people, from the hockey fans in Montreal who boo the American national anthem to the high school students in Switzerland who do not
want to go to the United States as exchange students." An Australian observer concluded that "the lesson of Iraq is that the US's soft power is in
decline. Bush went to war having failed to win a broader military coalition or UN authorization. This had two direct consequences: a rise in
anti-American sentiment, lifting terrorist recruitment; and a higher cost
to the US for the war and reconstruction effort." Pluralities in 15 out of
24 countries responding to a Gallup International poll said that American
foreign policies had a negative effect on their attitudes toward the United
States. . . .

Skeptics about soft power say not to worry. Popularity is ephemeral
and should not be a guide for foreign policy in any case. The United
States can act without the world's applause. We are so strong we can do as
we wish. We are the world's only superpower, and that fact is bound to
engender envy and resentment. Fouad Ajami has stated recently, "The
United States need not worry about hearts and minds in foreign lands."
Columnist Cal Thomas refers to "the fiction that our enemies can be
made less threatening by what America says and does." Moreover, the
United States has been unpopular in the past yet managed to recover. We
do not need permanent allies and institutions. We can always pick up a
coalition of the willing when we need to. Donald Rumsfeld is wont to
say that the issues should determine the coalitions, not vice versa.

But it would be a mistake to dismiss the recent decline in our attractiveness so lightly. It is true that the United States has recovered from
unpopular policies in the past, but that was against the backdrop of the
Cold War, in which other countries still feared the Soviet Union as the
greater evil. Moreover, . . . while the United States' size and association
with disruptive modernity is real and unavoidable, smart policies can soft-
en the sharp edges of that reality and reduce the resentments they engen-

der. That is what the U.S. did after World War II. We used our soft-power resources and co-opted others into a set of alliances and institutions that lasted for 60 years. We won the Cold War against the Soviet Union with a strategy of containment that used our soft power as well as our hard power.

It is true that the new threat of transnational terrorism increased American vulnerability, and some of our unilateralism after September 11 was driven by fear. But the United States cannot meet the new threat identified in the national security strategy without the cooperation of other countries. They will cooperate up to a point out of mere self-interest, but their degree of cooperation is also affected by the attractiveness of the United States. Take Pakistan for example. President Pervez Musharraf faces a complex game of cooperating with the United States in the war on terrorism while managing a large anti-American constituency at home. He winds up balancing concessions and retractions. If the United States were more attractive to the Pakistani populace, we would see more concessions in the mix.

It is not smart to discount soft power as just a question of image, public relations, and ephemeral popularity. As we argued earlier, it is a form of power—a means of obtaining desired outcomes. When we discount the importance of our attractiveness to other countries, we pay a price. Most important, if the United States is so unpopular in a country that being pro-American is a kiss of death in that country's domestic politics, political leaders are unlikely to make concessions to help us. Turkey, Mexico, and Chile were prime examples in the run-up to the Iraq War in March 2003. When American policies lose their legitimacy and credibility in the eyes of others, attitudes of distrust tend to fester and further reduce our leverage. For example, after 9/11 there was an outpouring of sympathy from Germans for the United States, and Germany joined a military campaign against the Al Qaeda network. But as the United States geared up for the unpopular Iraq War, Germans expressed widespread disbelief about the reasons the U.S. gave for going to war such as the alleged connection of Iraq to 9/11 and the imminence of the threat of weapons of mass destruction. German suspicions were reinforced by what they saw as biased American media coverage during the war, and by the failure to find weapons of mass destruction or prove the connection to 9/11 in the aftermath of the war. The combination fostered a climate in which conspiracy theories flourished. By July 2003, according to a Reuters poll, one-third of Germans under the age of 30 said that they thought the American government might even have staged the original September 11 attacks.

Absurd views feed upon each other, and paranoia can be contagious.

American attitudes toward foreigners harden, and we begin to believe that the rest of the world really does hate us. Some Americans begin to hold grudges, to mistrust all Muslims, to boycott French wines and rename French fries, to spread and believe false rumors. In turn, foreigners see Americans as uninformed and insensitive to anyone's interests but their own. They see our media wrapped in the American flag. Some Americans in turn succumb to residual strands of isolationism, and say that if others choose to see us that way, "To hell with 'em." If foreigners are going to be like that, who cares whether we are popular or not. But to the extent that Americans allow ourselves to become isolated, we embolden our enemies such as Al Qaeda. Such reactions undercut our soft power and are self-defeating in terms of the outcomes we want.

Some hard-line skeptics might say that whatever the merits of soft power, it has little role to play in the current war on terrorism. Osama bin Laden and his followers are repelled, not attracted, by American culture, values, and policies. Military power was essential in defeating the Taliban government in Afghanistan, and soft power will never convert fanatics. Charles Krauthammer, for example, argued soon after our swift military victory in Afghanistan that it proved that "the new unilateralism" worked. That is true up to a point, but the skeptics mistake half the answer for the whole solution.

Look again at Afghanistan. Precision bombing and Special Forces defeated the Taliban government, but U.S. forces in Afghanistan wrapped up less than a quarter of Al Qaeda, a transnational network with cells in 60 countries. The United States cannot bomb Al Qaeda cells in Hamburg, Kuala Lumpur, or Detroit. Success against them depends on close civilian cooperation, whether sharing intelligence, coordinating police work across borders, or tracing global financial flows. America's partners work with us partly out of self-interest, but the inherent attractiveness of U.S. policies can and does influence their degree of cooperation.

Equally important, the current struggle against Islamist terrorism is not a clash of civilizations but a contest whose outcome is closely tied to a civil war between moderates and extremists within Islamic civilization. The United States and other advanced democracies will win only if moderate Muslims win, and the ability to attract the moderates is critical to victory. We need to adopt policies that appeal to moderates, and to use public diplomacy more effectively to explain our common interests. We need a better strategy for wielding our soft power. We will have to learn better to combine hard and soft power if we wish to meet the new challenges. . . .

Americans are still working their way through the aftermath of September 11. We are groping for a path through the strange new landscape created by technology and globalization whose dark aspects were vividly illuminated on that traumatic occasion. The Bush administration has correctly identified the nature of the new challenges that the nation faces and has reoriented American strategy accordingly. But the administration, like the Congress and the public, has been torn between different approaches to the implementation of the new strategy. The result has been a mixture of successes and failures. We have been more successful in the domain of hard power, where we have invested more, trained more, and have a clearer idea of what we are doing. We have been less successful in the areas of soft power, where our public diplomacy has been woefully inadequate and our neglect of allies and institutions has created a sense of illegitimacy that has squandered our attractiveness.

Yet this is ironic, because the United States is the country that is at the forefront of the information revolution as well as the country that built some of the longest-lasting alliances and institutions that the modern world has seen. We should know how to adapt and work with such institutions since they have been central to our power for more than half a century. And the United States is a country with a vibrant social and cultural life that provides an almost infinite number of points of contact with other societies. What's more, during the Cold War, we demonstrated that we know how to use the soft-power resources that our society produces. . . .

. . . In short, America's success will depend upon our developing a deeper understanding of the role of soft power and developing a better balance of hard and soft power in our foreign policy. That will be smart power. We have done it before; we can do it again.

84

RICHARD HAASS

From *Foreign Policy Begins at Home*

Council on Foreign Relations President Richard Haass offers a formula for American policy abroad in a selection that might be appropriately placed in the Political Economy and Public Welfare section of this book of readings. His thesis is that the nation should first solve its key domestic problems, which would in turn help solve its international quandaries. We have made mistakes abroad, he feels, citing the Iraq War and the Afghan troop surge. And we have made mistakes at home, as we have run up a huge debt, neglected our infrastructure, allowed education to lag, and ignored the immigration dilemma. The U.S. economy has become stagnant without sufficient growth and dynamism. Haass grapples with charges of pessimism and isolationism, claiming he's advocating neither. He acknowledges the challenges that the rest of the world present to the U.S. But ultimately, these challenges can only be met by a nation that, as Haass writes, has "put its house in order."

THIS RELATIVELY SHORT BOOK is predicated on a consequential idea: The biggest threat to America's security and prosperity comes not from abroad but from within. The United States has jeopardized its ability to act effectively in the world because of runaway domestic spending, underinvestment in human and physical capital, an avoidable financial crisis, an unnecessarily slow recovery, a war in Iraq that was flawed from the outset and a war in Afghanistan that became flawed as its purpose evolved, recurring fiscal deficits, and deep political divisions. For the United States to continue to act successfully abroad, it must restore the domestic foundations of its power. Foreign policy needs to begin at home, now and for the foreseeable future.

Foreign Policy Begins at Home is a book that I never imagined writing. Sandpaper off the nuances and subtleties, and this is a book that argues for less foreign policy of the sort the United States has been conducting and greater emphasis on domestic investment and policy reform. For someone such as me, a card-carrying member of the foreign policy establishment for nearly four decades, this borders on heresy.

What got me to this point? More than anything else it began with the second Iraq war (begun in 2003) and the Afghan troop surge initiated in

2009. I mention both because my differences over the trajectory of American foreign policy are not with a single party. Many participants in the foreign policy debate in both parties appear to have forgotten the injunction of former president and secretary of state John Quincy Adams (that America "goes not abroad in search of monsters to destroy"), along with the lessons of Vietnam about the limits of military force and the tendency of local realities to prevail over global abstractions. As was the case with Vietnam, neither Iraq nor Afghanistan (as of 2009) was a war of necessity; more important, neither was a justifiable war of choice. In both cases, the interests at stake were decidedly less than vital. In both cases, alternative policies were available that promised outcomes of comparable benefit to this country at far less cost. And in both cases, history and even a cursory study of the societies in question suggested that ambitious attempts to refashion the workings and political cultures of these countries would founder. What is more, all this was predictable at the time. Now, with the advantage of hindsight, we can see that more than a decade of enormous sacrifice has hurt this country's reputation for judgment and competence and failed to produce results in any way commensurate with the human, military, and economic costs of the undertakings. Such an imbalance between means and ends makes no strategic sense at the best of times; it is even less defensible now, when the United States faces difficult challenges to its solvency. . . .

Where this book differs most from my previous books is in its focus on domestic policy, for remaking ourselves more than the world. There are, of course, external challenges, including but hardly limited to a rising China, a militarized North Korea, an Iran possibly moving to acquire nuclear weapons, an unstable Pakistan, violent terrorists, and a warming planet. These are real and justified concerns that warrant serious responses. But what makes the situation particularly worrisome are a large number of internal developments, including a burgeoning deficit and debt, crumbling infrastructure, second-class schools, an outdated immigration system, and the prospect for a prolonged period of low economic growth. Many of the foundations of this country's power are eroding; the effect, however, is not limited to a deteriorating transportation system or jobs that go unfilled or overseas owing to a lack of qualified American workers. To the contrary, shortcomings here at home directly threaten America's ability to project power and exert influence overseas, to compete in the global marketplace, to generate the resources needed to promote the full range of US interests abroad, and to set a compelling example that will influence the thinking and behavior of others. As a result, the ability of the United States to act and lead in the world is diminishing. I would prefer not to test the notion that this country requires a full-fledged crisis, be it in the form of a run on the dollar or some catastrophe brought about by terrorists or nature, to get its government to do what needs doing, in part because if it does, it will be that much more painful and expensive to address the shortcomings of America's economy, schools, immigration policy, infrastructure, and much more.

I write all this with the expectation I may well be caricatured on two fronts. One possibility is that I will be depicted as a defeatist, just another apostle of American decline. So let me be as clear as I can: I believe the United States enjoys great strengths and great potential. The US economy is the world's largest and is still growing; the best in American higher education is the best in the world; this society remains remarkably innovative and adaptive; its endowment of fresh water, energy, and arable land is nothing less than bountiful; and the population is relatively "balanced" in that it suffers from neither the bulges in young people nor old people that characterize so many other societies around the world. Recent breakthroughs in domestic oil and gas production thanks to new technologies and techniques are but the latest example of this country's ability to handle the significant challenges it faces.

But to say the United States is not in decline is something different from suggesting Americans ought to be sanguine with where they are and where they are heading. Given its considerable endowments and advantages, this country is clearly underperforming. Meanwhile, many other countries are performing better than they did in the past, and in some areas are doing better than the United States. The combination of these trends bodes poorly for the ability of the United States to compete economically and to shape international events.

I also anticipate being denounced as an isolationist. Isolationism is the willful turning away from the world even when a rigorous assessment of national interests argues for acting on their behalf. Isolationism makes absolutely no sense in the twenty-first century. Even if it wanted to, the United States could not wall itself off from global threats such as terrorism, nuclear proliferation, trade and investment protectionism, pandemic disease, climate change, or a loss of access to financial, energy, or mineral resources. Borders are not the same as barriers. The US government must be active in addressing these threats. There are also opportunities to be had, including the possibility of lifting hundreds of millions and potentially billions of people out of poverty, increasing the quality of life as well as life expectancy, expanding individual freedom, and settling disputes before they lead to armed conflict. Embracing isolationism would accelerate the emergence of a more disorderly and dangerous world, one that would be less safe, less free, and less prosperous. Isolationism would be folly.

At the same time, the United States must become significantly more discriminating in choosing what it does in the world and how it does it. Hard choices need to be made. It is not simply that it needs to recognize that the limits to its resources require it to be exacting in setting priorities; it must also recognize the limits to its influence. The United States needs to rethink what it seeks to accomplish abroad. Americans must distinguish between the desirable and the vital as well as between the feasible and the impossible. For the past two decades, American foreign policy, consumed with remaking large parts of the greater Middle East, has quite simply overreached. There is a strong case to be made that US attention and efforts should be better distributed around the world, with greater focus on the increasingly critical Asia-Pacific region and the Western Hemisphere and somewhat less on the Middle East; there is an even stronger case that US foreign policy should focus not so much on what other countries *are* within their borders and more on what they *do* outside their borders. This will be difficult at times, as situations will arise in which standing aside will appear to be immoral or strategically shortsighted or both; that said, the United States needs to balance its desire to do good with its ability to do good—as well as with the need to do many other things on behalf of its citizens at home and its interests abroad.

To mount an effective foreign policy the United States must first put its house in order. The most obvious reason is resources. National security does not come cheap. Money—lots of it—is required to field a capable modern military with a broad range of missions, to generate necessary intelligence against a broad range of threats, to protect the homeland against a broad range of contingencies, to carry out diplomacy and dispense assistance to promote a broad range of interests. The United States now spends close to $800 billion a year on these tasks—roughly one-fifth of all federal spending and some 5 percent of total GDP. The economy must grow at traditional rates (near or above 3 percent) and domestic spending that does not qualify as investment must be kept in check if this country is not to be forced to choose between national security and all else. Alas, the US economy is now growing at only half this rate, while domestic spending that has nothing to do with investment is rising.

The United States is far more likely to find itself threatened and attacked if it is perceived to be weak and vulnerable. A strong United States will discourage would-be competitors or adversaries from going down the path of confrontation. A strong United States would make others more likely to work with it than against it. And a strong United States would be better able to deal with any foe that miscalculated.

The United States must also put its house in order if it is to avoid placing itself in a position of high vulnerability to forces or actions beyond its control. Right now the US government requires an inflow of more than $1 billion a day to support a gross federal debt that stands at about $16 trillion and increases by more than $1 trillion a year. We can look to our own history to see what can happen when foreign governments obtain this kind of leverage. In 1956, the US government, furious over Great Britain's participation in the invasion of Egypt after Nasser's nationalization of the Suez Canal, blocked international loans the British needed to avert a collapse of their currency. The British government of the day was forced to back down. Now imagine what might happen were China to threaten a similar action against the United States amid a crisis over Taiwan or the South China Sea.

Another scenario is simply one in which money markets lose confidence in America's ability to manage its own finances and start to exact a higher price for their continued willingness to lend money. This would force the Federal Reserve to raise interest rates, not for the traditional purpose of cooling inflationary pressures, but rather to attract needed dollars that demand a higher return given concerns over American creditworthiness. This would spell disaster for an economy barely out of recession. This scenario might have come to pass already had it not been for the Eurozone crisis, which removed a viable alternative to the dollar. But Americans cannot count on Europeans to forever do the wrong thing, or on China's remaining unwilling to allow its currency to take on an international role.

Then there is the power of example. A successful American economy, one that is generating wealth and jobs and innovation, along with a successful American political system and society, one that is willing and able to take difficult but necessary decisions, presents not just the image but the reality of a country functioning at a high level, one with political freedom, a high and rising standard of living, and social mobility. This is a model other countries will want to emulate. The battle of ideas is far from over; indeed, it has grown more intense with the economic success of China and other authoritarian regimes, with the difficulties experienced by the mature democracies in 2008 and subsequently, and with the dramatic developments that have taken place across the Middle East starting in late 2010. Foreign policy is not just about what diplomats say and soldiers do: It is also about the example a country sets.

It is also true that a more effective foreign policy would redound to the benefit of Americans at home, with more resources to be spent on and in their society, be it by individuals or the federal, state, and local government to enhance the quality of life, standard of living, or security. A more peaceful and organized world would create conditions in which the American economy should thrive. And a thriving economy—one growing at relatively robust levels—will improve the lot of most Americans. This is important, as tolerance for income and wealth inequality tends to be greater if everyone's situation is improving. Absent such growth, social and economic mobility will atrophy and class frictions will increase, leaving the population focused inward.

It is not too late for the United States to put its house in order. It is not simply a case of necessity; currently it has an extraordinary opportunity to do so. The world is a relatively forgiving place now and for the foreseeable future. There is no twenty-first-century equivalent to what Germany was in the first half of the twentieth century and the Soviet Union was in the second. Of course, there are actual and potential threats to American interests and well-being, but none rises to the existential. China could in theory come to challenge the United States for primacy, but it is far from assured that it will have the means and the appetite to do so. In any event, and as will be discussed, any such challenge is neither inevitable nor imminent. The United States is fortunate to have something of a strategic respite; how long-lasting and extensive it will be will, of course, depend in part on the decisions and actions of others. But even more it will depend on how successful the United States proves to be at repairing the foundations of its power, how disciplined it can be at wielding that power, and how wise it is in providing others an incentive to share in the building and operating of the international order. . . .

The stakes are enormous. The world will not sort itself out absent US leadership. This is not a call for unilateralism, which in most instances is not a viable option. Nor is it a reflection of American arrogance. It is simple fact. No other country has the capacity, habits, and willingness to take on this responsibility. Without such a benign force, order never just emerges. No invisible hand is at work to sort out the geopolitical marketplace. The question is whether the visible hand of the United States will be up to the challenge. One sincerely hopes for this to be so, as nothing less than the future of this country and the character of the twenty-first century are in the balance.

PERMISSIONS ACKNOWLEDGMENTS

1. From *Democracy in America* by Alexis de Tocqueville, translated by Henry Reeve, published by Schoeken Books, 1961. Originally published in 1835.
2. From "Dinner with Democracy" by Cynthia Farrar in *Democratic Vistas: Reflections on the Life of American Democracy*, edited by Jedediah Purdy. Copyright © 2004 by Yale University. Reprinted by permission of the publisher, Yale University Press.
3. From "The Enduring Culture War" by James Davison Hunter in *Is There a Culture War?* by James Davison Hunter and Alan Wolfe. Copyright © 2006 by the Brookings Institution and Pew Research Center. Reprinted by permission of the Brookings Institution Press.
4. From *The Power Elite, New Edition* by C. Wright Mills. Copyright © 1956, 2000 by Oxford University Press, Inc. Used by permission of Oxford University Press, USA.
5. From Richard Zweigenhaft and G. William Domhoff, *Diversity in the Power Elite*. Copyright © 1998, 2006 by Rowman and Littlefield. Reprinted by permission of Rowman and Littlefield Publishers, Inc., a subsidiary of The Rowman and Littlefield Publishing Group, Inc.
6. From *Who Governs* by Robert Dahl. Copyright © 1961 by Yale University Press. Reprinted by permission of Yale University Press. From *A Preface to Democratic Theory* by Robert Dahl. Copyright © 1956 by The University of Chicago Press. Reprinted by permission of The University of Chicago Press.
7. From *Race Matters*, by Cornel West. Copyright © 1993, 2001 by Cornel West. Reprinted by permission of Beacon Press, Boston.
8. Excerpts from *People of Paradox* by Michael Kammen. Copyright © 1972 by Michael Kammen. Reprinted by permission of Alfred A. Knopf, an imprint of the Knopf Doubleday Publishing Group, a division of Penguin Random House LLC. All rights reserved.
9. From *Habits of the Heart: Individualism and Commitment in American Life* by Robert Bellah, et al. Copyright © 1985, 1996 The Regents of the University of California. Reprinted by permission of The University of California Press in the format Textbook *via* Copyright Clearance Center.
10. *The Federalist* 10 and 51, by James Madison, 1787.
11. Excerpts from *The American Political Tradition* by Richard Hofstadter. Copyright © 1948, 1973 by Alfred A. Knopf, a division of Penguin Random House LLC, and renewed 1976 by Beatrice Hofstadter. Reprinted by permission of

Alfred A. Knopf, an imprint of the Knopf Doubleday Publishing Group, a division of Penguin Random House LLC. All rights reserved.

12. From *Democracy in America* by Alexis de Tocqueville, translated by Henry Reeve, published by Schoeken Books, 1961. Originally published in 1835.

13. From David Brian Robertson, *The Constitution and America's Destiny*. Copyright © 2005 by David Brian Robertson. Reprinted by permission Cambridge University Press.

14. From *Executive Privilege: Presidential Power, Secrecy, and Accountability* by Mark J. Rozell. Copyright © 2010 by the University of Kansas. Reprinted by permission of the University of Kansas Press.

15. *The Federalist* 39 and 46, by James Madison, 1787.

16. From *Democratic Laboratories: Policy Diffusion among the American States* by Andrew Karch. Copyright © 2007 by the University of Michigan. Reprinted by permission of University of Michigan Press.

17. From *Federalism and the Tug of War Within* by Erin Ryan. Copyright © 2011 by Oxford University Press. Reprinted by permission of Oxford University Press, USA.

18. From *Renegade Cities, Public Policy, and the Dilemmas of Federalism* by Lori Riverstone-Newell. Copyright © 2013 by Lynne Rienner Publishers, Inc. Used by permission of the publisher.

19. From *Congress: The Electoral Connection* by David Mayhew, published by Yale University Press. Copyright © 1974 by Yale University Press. Reprinted by permission of Yale University Press.

20. Fenno, Richard F., *Home Style: House Members in Their Districts*, 1st Ed. Copyright © 1978. Reproduced by permission of Pearson Education Inc., New York, New York.

21. From *The Senate Syndrome: The Evolution of Procedural Warfare in the Modern U.S. Senate* by Steven S. Smith. Copyright © 2014 by the University of Oklahoma Press, Norman, Publishing Division of the University. Reprinted by permission of the University of Oklahoma Press.

22. From *Women in the Club: Gender and Policy Making in the Senate* by Michele L. Swers. Copyright © 2013 by the University of Chicago Press. Reprinted by permission of the University of Chicago Press.

23. "Pork: A Time-Honored Tradition Lives On" by Paul Starobin from *Congressional Quarterly Weekly Report*, Oct. 24, 1987. Copyright © 1987 by Congressional Quarterly, Inc. Reprinted by permission in the format Textbook *via* Copyright Clearance Center.

24. From "In Praise of Pork," by John Ellwood and Eric Patashnik, from *The Public Interest*, Number 110, Winter 1993, pp. 19–23, 31. © 1993 by National Affairs, Inc. Reprinted by permission National Affairs, Inc.

25. From Twitter, "Hey there! SenJohnMcCain is Using Twitter."

26. Chuck McCutcheon & David Mark. *Dog Whistles, Walk-Backs, and Washington Handshakes: Decoding the Jargon, Slang, and Bluster of American Political Speech.* Hanover, NH ForeEdge. © 2014 Chuck McCutcheon & David Mark. Reprinted with permission of the University Press of New England.

27. Reprinted with the permission of The Free Press, a Division of Simon & Schuster, Inc., from *Presidential Power and the Modern Presidents: The Politics of Leadership from Roosevelt to Reagan* by Richard E. Neustadt. Copyright © 1990 by Richard E. Neustadt. All rights reserved.